The Earth and Its Peoples

A GLOBAL HISTORY

D0025583

EDITION 6

The Earth and Its Peoples

A GLOBAL HISTORY

Volume C: Since 1750

Richard W. Bulliet
Columbia University

Pamela Kyle Crossley
Dartmouth College

Daniel R. Headrick
Roosevelt University

Steven W. Hirsch
Tufts University

Lyman L. Johnson
University of North Carolina—Charlotte

David Northrup
Boston College

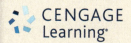
CENGAGE
Learning

Australia • Brazil • Japan • Korea • Mexico • Singapore • Spain • United Kingdom • United States

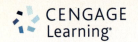
CENGAGE
Learning®

**The Earth and Its Peoples: A Global History,
Sixth Edition Volume C: Since 1750**
Richard W. Bulliet, Pamela Kyle Crossley,
Daniel R. Headrick, Steven W. Hirsch,
Lyman L. Johnson, David Northrup

Product Director: Suzanne Jeans

Product Manager: Brooke Barbier

Senior Content Developer: Tonya Lobato

Product Assistant: Katie Coaster

Media Developer: Kate MacLean

Marketing Development Manager:
   Kyle Zimmerman

Senior Content Project Manager:
   Carol Newman

Associate Art Director: Hannah Wellman

Manufacturing Planner: Sandee Milewski

Senior Rights Acquisition Specialist:
   Jennifer Meyer Dare

Production Service/Compositor:
   Lachina Publishing Services

Text Designer: Diane Beasley

Cover Designer: Wing Ngan, Ink Design, Inc.

Cover Image: Headdress of a mask with
   bird and a family. Baga people, Guinea.
   Polychrome wood, 60.5 x 23.5 x 37.0 cm.
   Inv.: 73.1963.153. Photo: Jean-Gilles
   Berizzi/Musee du Quai Branly, Paris,
   France/Image # ART150654/© RMN-Grand
   Palais/Art Resource, NY

© 2014, 2011, 2008 Cengage Learning

ALL RIGHTS RESERVED. No part of this work covered by the copyright herein may be reproduced, transmitted, stored, or used in any form or by any means graphic, electronic, or mechanical, including but not limited to photocopying, recording, scanning, digitizing, taping, Web distribution, information networks, or information storage and retrieval systems, except as permitted under Section 107 or 108 of the 1976 United States Copyright Act, without the prior written permission of the publisher.

For product information and technology assistance, contact us at
Cengage Learning Customer & Sales Support, 1-800-354-9706
For permission to use material from this text or product,
submit all requests online at **www.cengage.com/permissions**.
Further permissions questions can be emailed to
permissionrequest@cengage.com.

Library of Congress Control Number: 2013932724

Student Edition:

ISBN-13: 978-1-285-43701-9

ISBN-10: 1-285-43701-2

Cengage Learning
200 First Stamford Place, 4th Floor
Stamford, CT 06902
USA

Cengage Learning is a leading provider of customized learning solutions with office locations around the globe, including Singapore, the United Kingdom, Australia, Mexico, Brazil, and Japan. Locate your local office at **international.cengage.com/region**

Cengage Learning products are represented in Canada by Nelson Education, Ltd.

For your course and learning solutions, visit **www.cengage.com**.

Purchase any of our products at your local college store or at our preferred online store **www.cengagebrain.com**.

Instructors: Please visit **login.cengage.com** and log in to access instructor-specific resources.

Printed in the United States of America
1 2 3 4 5 6 7 17 16 15 14 13

Brief Contents

Contents

PART VI Revolutions Reshape the World, 1750–1870 — 546

Maps

Features

ENVIRONMENT + TECHNOLOGY

DIVERSITY + DOMINANCE

MATERIAL CULTURE

ISSUES IN WORLD HISTORY

Preface

In preparing the sixth edition of this book, we examined the flow of topics from chapter to chapter and decided that certain rearrangements within chapters and in the order of chapters would accommodate the needs of instructors and students better than the template they had followed since the first edition. The first change was reversing the order of the third and fourth chapters to have early Mediterranean and Middle Eastern history directly follow the discussion of the origins of civilization in the Nile Valley and Mesopotamia.

The second change addressed the problem of when and how to discuss the history of pre-Columbian America. The time span to be covered, ranging from roughly 1500 B.C.E. to 1500 C.E., was too long to fit easily into the book's division into eight parts. The new structure we have adopted relocates the long pre-Aztec and pre-Inka narrative from Part III, Growth and Interaction of Cultural Communities, to the end of Part II, The Formation of New Cultural Communities. This change puts the status of the earliest civilizations in the Western Hemisphere on the same footing as the civilizations of early Greece, China, and South and Southeast Asia. It has the added benefit of making the history of East Asia in the Tang and Song periods directly precede the history of the Mongol empire, which allows instructors to have an uninterrupted focus on East Asia. The histories of the Aztecs and Inkas have been shifted to the chapter on tropical history located in Part IV, Interregional Patterns of Culture and Contact. This allows for a discussion of the overall influence of tropical environments and places them in close proximity to our treatment of the coming of Europeans to the New World.

A third structural change has shortened the length of the book from 34 to 33 chapters. To lessen the impression that Europe's domination of the world should always be the primary focus of student attention between the eighteenth and mid-twentieth centuries we have combined the two separate chapters on European imperialism, Chapters 26 and 28 in previous editions, into one. We feel that this change provides a better balance between the saga of European imperialism, accounts of resistance to imperialism, and the rise of independence movements in different parts of the world.

In a related change, we have relocated the chapter dealing with the histories of India, Latin America, and Africa in the first half of the twentieth century from after World War II, the old Chapter 31, to a position between the world wars. The aim of this chapter, titled "Revolutions in Living," is to portray that period not only as a time of political change in parts of the world subjected to European imperialism, but also as one of transformation of daily lives of people in both the industrialized and nonindustrialized worlds. The added focus of the chapter fills a gap between discussion of the Industrial Revolution in the eighteenth and nineteenth centuries and the advent of major technological changes in the post-World War II era.

Finally in this new edition, contributor and East Asian specialist Michael Wert of Marquette University brought a fresh perspective to many of our chapters dealing with East Asia, helping ensure that our coverage is at the forefront of emerging scholarship.

The authors believe that these changes, along with myriad smaller changes detailed below, significantly enhance the overall goal of *The Earth and Its Peoples*, namely, to be a textbook that speaks not only for the past but also to today's student and teacher. Students and instructors alike should take away from this text a broad, and due to the changes, more flowing impression of human societies beginning as sparse and disconnected communities reacting creatively to local circumstances; experiencing ever more intensive stages of contact, interpenetration, and cultural expansion and amalgamation; and arriving at a twenty-first-century world in which people increasingly visualize a single global community.

Process, not progress, is the keynote of this book: a steady process of change over time, at first experienced differently in various regions, but eventually connecting peoples and traditions from all parts of the globe. Students should come away from this book with a sense that the problems and promises of their world are rooted in a past in which people of every sort, in every part of the world, confronted problems of a similar character and coped with them as best they could. We believe that our efforts will help students see where their world has come from and learn thereby something useful for their own lives.

CENTRAL THEMES AND GOALS

We subtitled *The Earth and Its Peoples* "A Global History" because the book explores the common challenges and experiences that unite the human past. Although the dispersal of early humans to every livable environment resulted in a myriad of different economic, social, political, and cultural systems, all societies displayed analogous patterns in meeting their needs and exploiting their environments. Our challenge was to select the particular data and episodes that would best illuminate these global patterns of human experience.

To meet this challenge, we adopted two themes for our history: "technology and the environment" and "diversity and dominance." The first theme represents the commonplace material bases of all human societies at all times. It grants no special favor to any cultural group even as it embraces subjects of the broadest topical, chronological, and geographical range. The second theme expresses the reality that every human society has constructed or inherited structures of domination. We examine practices and institutions of many sorts: military, economic, social, political, religious, and cultural, as well as those based on kinship, gender, and literacy. Simultaneously we recognize that alternative ways of life and visions of societal organization continually manifest themselves both within and in dialogue with every structure of domination.

With respect to the first theme, it is vital for students to understand that technology, in the broad sense of experience-based knowledge of the physical world, underlies all human activity. Writing is a technology, but so is oral transmission from generation to generation of lore about medicinal or poisonous plants. The magnetic compass is a navigational technology, but so is Polynesian mariners' hard-won knowledge of winds, currents, and tides that made possible the settlement of the Pacific islands.

All technological development has come about in interaction with environments, both physical and human, and has, in turn, affected those environments. The story of how humanity has changed the face of the globe is an integral part of our first theme. Yet technology and the environment do not explain or underlie all important episodes of human experience. The theme of "diversity and dominance" informs all our discussions of politics, culture, and society. Thus when narrating the histories of empires, we describe a range of human experiences within and beyond the imperial frontiers without assuming that imperial institutions are a more fit topic for discussion than the economic and social organization of pastoral nomads or the lives of peasant women. When religion and culture occupy our narrative, we focus not only on the dominant tradition but also on the diversity of alternative beliefs and practices.

ORGANIZATION

The *Earth and Its Peoples* uses eight broad chronological divisions to define its conceptual scheme of global historical development.

In **Part One: The Emergence of Human Communities, to 500 B.C.E.**, we examine important patterns of human communal organization primarily in the Eastern Hemisphere. Small, dispersed human communities living by foraging spread to most parts of the world over tens of thousands of years. They responded to enormously diverse environmental conditions, at different times in different ways, discovering how to cultivate plants and utilize the products of domestic animals. On the basis of these new modes of sustenance, population grew, permanent towns appeared, and political and religious authority, based on collection and control of agricultural surpluses, spread over extensive areas.

Part Two: The Formation of New Cultural Communities, 1000 B.C.E.–400 C.E., introduces the concept of a "cultural community," in the sense of a coherent pattern of activities and symbols pertaining to a specific human community. While all human communities develop distinctive cultures, including those discussed in Part One, historical development in this stage of global history prolonged and magnified the impact of some cultures more than others. In the geographically contiguous African-Eurasian landmass, as well as in the Western Hemisphere, the cultures that proved to have the most enduring influence traced their roots to the second and first millennia B.C.E.

Part Three: Growth and Interaction of Cultural Communities, 300 B.C.E.–1200 C.E., deals with early episodes of technological, social, and cultural exchange and interaction on a continental scale both within and beyond the framework of imperial expansion. These are so different from earlier interactions arising from more limited conquests or extensions of political boundaries that they constitute a distinct era in world history, an era that set the world on the path of increasing global interaction and interdependence that it has been following ever since.

In **Part Four: Interregional Patterns of Culture and Contact, 1200–1550**, we look at the world during the three and a half centuries that saw both intensified cultural and commercial contact and increasingly confident self-definition of cultural communities in Europe, Asia, Africa, and the Americas. The Mongol conquest of a vast empire extending from the Pacific Ocean to eastern Europe greatly stimulated trade and interaction. In the West, strengthened European kingdoms began maritime expansion in the Atlantic, forging direct ties with sub-Saharan Africa and entering into conflict with the civilizations of the Western Hemisphere.

Part Five: The Globe Encompassed, 1500–1750, treats a period dominated by the global effects of European expansion and continued economic growth. European ships took over, expanded, and extended the maritime trade of the Indian Ocean, coastal Africa, and the Asian rim of the Pacific Ocean. This maritime commercial enterprise had its counterpart in European colonial empires in the Americas and a new Atlantic trading system. The contrasting capacities and fortunes of traditional land empires and new maritime empires, along with the exchange of domestic plants and animals between the hemispheres, underline the technological and environmental dimensions of this first era of complete global interaction.

In **Part Six: Revolutions Reshape the World, 1750–1870**, the word *revolution* is used in several senses: in the political sense of governmental overthrow, as in France and the Americas; in the metaphorical sense of radical transformative change, as in the Industrial Revolution; and in the broadest sense of a perception of a profound change in circumstances and worldview. Technology and environment lie at the core of these developments. With the rapid ascendancy of the Western belief that science and technology could overcome all challenges—environmental or otherwise—technology became an instrument not only of transformation but also of domination, to the point of threatening the integrity and autonomy of cultural traditions in nonindustrial lands and provoking strong movements of resistance.

Part Seven: Global Diversity and Dominance, 1750–1945, examines the development of a world arena in which people conceived of events on a global scale. Imperialism, international economic connections, and world-encompassing ideological tendencies, such as nationalism and socialism, present the picture of a globe becoming increasingly involved with European political and ideological concerns. Two world wars arising from European rivalries provide a climax to these developments, and European exhaustion affords other parts of the world new opportunities for independence and self-expression.

For **Part Eight: Perils and Promises of a Global Community, 1945 to the Present**, we divide the period since World War II into three time periods: 1945–1975, 1975–2000, and 2000 to the present. The challenges of the Cold War and postcolonial nation building dominate much of the period and unleash global economic, technological, and political forces that become increasingly important in all aspects of human life. With the end of the Cold War, however, new forces come to the fore. Technology is a key topic in Part Eight because of its integral role in both the growth and the problems of a global community. However, its many benefits in improving the quality of life become clouded by negative impacts on the environment.

FEATURES AND NEW PEDAGOGICAL AIDS

As with previous editions, the sixth edition offers a number of valuable features and pedagogical aids designed to pique student interest in specific world history topics and help them process and retain key information. Historical essays for each of the eight parts called Issues in World History are specifically designed to alert students to broad and recurring conceptual issues that are of great interest to contemporary historians; this feature has proved to be an instructor and student favorite. Six in-chapter essays on Material Culture call particular attention to the many ways in which objects and processes of everyday life can play a role in understanding human history on a broad scale. Thus essays like "Bells, Gongs, and Drums" and "Lamps and Candles" are not only interesting in and of themselves but also suggestive of how today's world historians find meaning in the ordinary dimensions of human life. The Environment and Technology feature, which has been a valuable resource in all prior editions of *The Earth and Its Peoples*, serves to illuminate the major theme of the text by demonstrating the shared material bases of all human societies across time. Finally, Diversity and Dominance, also core to the theme of the text, is the primary source feature that brings a myriad of real historical voices to life in a common struggle for power and autonomy.

Pedagogical aids include the following:

- **Chapter Opening Focus Questions** These questions are keyed to every major subdivision of the chapter and serve to help students focus on the core chapter concepts.
- **Section Reviews** Short bullet-point reviews summarize each major section in every chapter and remind students of key information.
- **Chapter Conclusions** Every chapter ends with a comparative conclusion that helps students better synthesize chapter material and understand how it fits into the larger picture.
- **Marginal Key Term with Definitions** Students can handily find key term definitions on the same page where the term first appears.
- **Pronunciation Guide** Hard-to-pronounce words are spelled phonetically for students throughout the text.

CHANGES IN THIS EDITION

In addition to the pedagogical aids outlined above, numerous chapter-by-chapter changes have been made, including new illustrations, new maps, streamlining of the textual discussion, and updates to many of the boxed feature essays. Here are a few highlights:

- In Chapter 1 the feature on "Cave Art" has been expanded.
- Chapter 4 descriptions of early civilizations in the Western Hemisphere have been shifted to Chapter 8 in order to facilitate a more unified discussion of Pre-Columbian America.
- Chapter 4 also contains a substantial new section on pastoral nomadism in the Eurasian steppe. Chapter 6 has a new Diversity and Dominance feature, "Socioeconomic Mobility: Winners and Losers in Imperial Rome and Han China," and a new Environment and Technology feature, "Ancient Glass." A Material Culture essay, "Lamps and Candles," has also been added.
- Chapter 8 has been extensively revised. Discussion of the Olmec and Chavín have been moved from Chapter 3 and the discussion of the Toltec, Tiwanaku, Wari, and Chimú civilizations expanded. Discussion of the Aztec and Inka civilizations appears in Chapter 15.
- Chapter 9 includes discussion of early Egyptian archaeological site of Nabta Playa.
- Chapter 12 contains expanded coverage of Korea.
- Chapter 13 contains expanded coverage of Vietnam and Yunnan province in southwest China.
- Chapter 14 has expanded coverage of eastern Europe and the Ottoman empire.
- Chapter 15 bears a new title, "Southern Empires, Southern Seas," and includes treatment of the Aztec and Inka empires that were previously covered much earlier in the book.
- Chapter 16 reflects new research on South Asian and Polynesian maritime cultures.

- Chapter 17 includes a new feature devoted to the first joint stock company and foreign trade. Coverage of early capitalism is expanded to include a discussion of stock markets and speculative bubbles like the Tulip, South Sea, and Mississippi Company frenzies.
- Chapter 19 includes a new feature, "Hurricanes and the Caribbean Plantation Economy."
- Chapter 20 has expanded to include the history of Russia, hence a new opening that features a Russian popular hero and the change of title to "Territorial Empires Between Europe and China."
- Chapter 21 has a new discussion of Korean history and the Imjin War.
- Chapters 22–23 have been reversed in sequence to provide better continuity to discussions of revolutions in Europe and parallel changes in the Americas.
- Chapter 22 includes a new discussion of proto-industrialization as well as augmented discussions of the spread of industrialization to continental Europe and North America and the early career of Karl Marx. The section "Protest and Reform" has been broadly revised to include machine breaking in the textile sector and rural resistance to mechanization in the Captain Swing riots.
- Chapter 25 has a new feature: "Industrializing Sugar Agriculture in Cuba."
- Chapter 26 combines accounts of European imperialism that were previously contained in this chapter and in Chapter 28.
- Chapter 27 features a revised discussion of early Japanese industrialization as well as an expanded treatment of Marx and Marxism and a new discussion of Mikhail Bakunin and anarchism. The chapter also includes a new feature: "Giuseppe Mazzini on Revolutionary Nationalism."
- Chapter 29 combines in a new chapter a discussion of technology and lifestyle changes that occurred between 1900 and 1945 with accounts of political movements in India, Latin America, and Africa that were previously located in Chapter 31. Highlights include a Diversity and Dominance feature, "Gandhi and the Media," an Environment and Technology feature, "New Materials," and a Material Culture essay, "Bells, Gongs, and Drums."
- Chapter 30 includes a new Environment and Technology feature, "The Magnetophon."
- Chapter 31 includes an updated discussion about the Cold War confrontation between West and East plus a revised discussion of apartheid and South Africa's struggle for independence.
- Chapter 32 contains a thoroughly updated feature, "Connected" to include discussion and pictures of the latest technology. The best current data are included in the demographic tables and discussion.
- Chapter 33 updates world affairs through the first half of 2013 and incorporates new statistical information on maps.

FORMATS

To accommodate different academic calendars and approaches to the course, *The Earth and Its Peoples* is available in three formats. There is a one-volume hardcover version containing all 33 chapters, along with a two-volume paperback edition: Volume I: To 1550 (Chapters 1–16) and Volume II: Since 1500 (Chapters 16–33). For readers at institutions with the quarter system, we offer a three-volume paperback version: Volume A: To 1200 (Chapters 1–12), Volume B: From 1200 to 1870 (Chapters 12–25), and Volume C: Since 1750 (Chapters 22–33). Volume II includes an Introduction that surveys the main developments set out in Volume I and provides a groundwork for students studying only the period since 1500.

ANCILLARIES

A wide array of supplements accompany this text to assist students with different learning needs and to help instructors master today's various classroom challenges.

Instructor Resources

Aplia™ [ISBN: 9781285768113] is an online interactive learning solution that improves comprehension and outcomes by increasing student effort and engagement. Founded by a professor to enhance his own courses, Aplia provides automatically graded assignments with detailed, immediate explanations on every question. The interactive assignments have been developed to address the major concepts covered in *The Earth and Its Peoples* and are designed to promote critical thinking and engage students more fully in learning. Question types include questions built around animated maps, primary sources such as newspaper extracts, or imagined scenarios, like engaging in a conversation with a historical figure or finding a diary and being asked to fill in some blanks; more in-depth primary source question sets address a major topic with a number of related primary sources and questions that promote deeper analysis of historical evidence. Many of the questions incorporate images, video clips, or audio clips. Students get immediate feedback on their work (not only what they got right or wrong, but why), and they can choose to see another set of related questions if they want more practice. A searchable eBook is available inside the course as well so that students can easily reference it as they work. Map-reading and writing tutorials are also available to get students off to a good start.

Aplia's simple-to-use course management interface allows instructors to post announcements, upload course materials, host student discussions, e-mail students, and manage the gradebook; a knowledgeable and friendly support team offers assistance and personalized support in customizing assignments to the instructor's course schedule. To learn more and view a demo for this book, visit www.aplia.com.

MindTap Reader for *The Earth and Its Peoples* is an eBook specifically designed to address the ways students assimilate content and media assets. MindTap Reader combines thoughtful navigation ergonomics, advanced student annotation, note-taking, and search tools, and embedded media assets such as video and MP3 chapter summaries, primary source documents with critical thinking questions, and interactive (zoomable) maps. Students can use the eBook as their primary text or as a multimedia companion to their printed book. The MindTap Reader eBook is available within the MindTap and Aplia online offerings found at www.cengagebrain.com.

Online PowerLecture with Cognero® [ISBN: 9781285455013] This PowerLecture is an all-in-one online multimedia resource for class preparation, presentation, and testing. Accessible through Cengage.com/login with your faculty account, you will find available for download: book-specific Microsoft® PowerPoint® presentations; a Test Bank in both Microsoft® Word® and Cognero® formats; an Instructor Manual; Microsoft® PowerPoint® Image Slides; and a JPEG Image Library.

The **Test Bank**, offered in Microsoft® Word® and Cognero® formats, contains multiple-choice and essay questions for each chapter. Cognero® is a flexible, online system that allows you to author, edit, and manage test bank content for *The Earth and Its People*, sixth edition. Create multiple test versions instantly and deliver through your LMS from your classroom, or wherever you may be, with no special installs or downloads required.

The **Instructor's Manual** contains for each chapter: an outline and summary; critical thinking questions; in-class activities; lecture launching suggestions; a list of key terms with definitions; and suggested readings and Web resources. The *Microsoft® PowerPoint® presentations* are ready-to-use, visual outlines of each chapter. These presentations are easily customized for your lectures and offered along with chapter-specific Microsoft® PowerPoint® Image Slides and JPEG Image Libraries. Access your Online PowerLecture at **www.cengage.com/login**.

History CourseMate Cengage Learning's History CourseMate brings course concepts to life with interactive learning, study tools, and exam preparation tools that support the printed textbook. Use Engagement Tracker to monitor student engagement in the course and watch student comprehension soar as your class works with the printed textbook and the textbook-specific website. An interactive eBook allows students to take notes, highlight, search, and interact with embedded media (such as quizzes, flashcards, primary sources, and videos). Learn more at **www.cengage.com/coursemate**.

CourseReader CourseReader is an online collection of primary and secondary sources that lets you create a customized electronic reader in minutes. With an easy-to-use interface and assessment tool, you can choose exactly what your students will be assigned—simply search or browse Cengage Learning's extensive document database to preview and select your customized collection of readings. In addition to print sources of all types (letters, diary entries, speeches, newspaper accounts, etc.), their collection includes a growing number of images and video and audio clips.

Each primary source document includes a descriptive headnote that puts the reading into context and is further supported by both critical thinking and multiple-choice questions designed to reinforce key points. For more information visit **www.cengage.com/coursereader**.

Cengagebrain.com   Save your students time and money. Direct them to **www.cengagebrain.com** for choice in formats and savings and a better chance to succeed in your class. Cengagebrain.com, Cengage Learning's online store, is a single destination for more than 10,000 new textbooks, eTextbooks, eChapters, study tools, and audio supplements. Students have the freedom to purchase a-la-carte exactly what they need when they need it. Students can save 50% on the electronic textbook, and can pay as little as $1.99 for an individual eChapter.

Reader Program   Cengage Learning publishes a number of readers, some containing exclusively primary sources, others a combination of primary and secondary sources, and some designed to guide students through the process of historical inquiry. Visit Cengage.com/history for a complete list of readers.

Custom Options   Nobody knows your students like you, so why not give them a text that is tailor-fit to their needs? Cengage Learning offers custom solutions for your course—whether it's making a small modification to The Earth and Its Peoples to match your syllabus or combining multiple sources to create something truly unique. You can pick and choose chapters, include your own material, and add additional map exercises along with the Rand McNally Atlas to create a text that fits the way you teach. Ensure that your students get the most out of their textbook dollar by giving them exactly what they need. Contact your Cengage Learning representative to explore custom solutions for your course.

Student Resources

Writing for College History, **first edition [ISBN: 9780618306039]** Prepared by Robert M. Frakes, Clarion University. This brief handbook for survey courses in American history, Western Civilization/European history, and world civilization guides students through the various types of writing assignments they encounter in a history class. Providing examples of student writing and candid assessments of student work, this text focuses on the rules and conventions of writing for the college history course.

The History Handbook, **second edition [ISBN: 9780495906766]** Prepared by Carol Berkin of Baruch College, City University of New York and Betty Anderson of Boston University. This book teaches students both basic and history-specific study skills such as how to read primary sources, research historical topics, and correctly cite sources. Substantially less expensive than comparable skill-building texts, *The History Handbook* also offers tips for Internet research and evaluating online sources.

Doing History: Research and Writing in the Digital Age, **second edition [ISBN: 9781133587880]**   Prepared by Michael J. Galgano, J. Chris Arndt, and Raymond M. Hyser of James Madison University. Whether you're starting down the path as a history major, or simply looking for a straightforward and systematic guide to writing a successful paper, you'll find this text to be an indispensable handbook to historical research. This text's "soup to nuts" approach to researching and writing about history addresses every step of the process, from locating your sources and gathering information, to writing clearly and making proper use of various citation styles to avoid plagiarism. You'll also learn how to make the most of every tool available to you—especially the technology that helps you conduct the process efficiently and effectively.

The Modern Researcher, **sixth edition [ISBN: 9780495318705]** Prepared by Jacques Barzun and Henry F. Graff of Columbia University. This classic introduction to the techniques of research and the art of expression is used widely in history courses, but is also appropri-ate for writing and research methods courses in other departments. Barzun and Graff thoroughly cover every aspect of research, from the selection of a topic through the gathering, analysis, writing, revision, and publication of findings, presenting the process not as a set of rules but through actual cases that put the subtleties of research in a useful context. Part One covers the principles and methods of research; Part Two covers writing, speaking, and getting one's work published.

Rand McNally Historical Atlas of the World, **second edition [ISBN: 9780618841912]**   This valuable resource features over 70 maps that portray the rich panoply of the world's history from preliterate times to the present. They show how cultures and civilization were linked and how they interacted. The maps make it clear that history is not static. Rather, it is about change and movement across time. The maps show change by presenting the dynamics of expansion, cooperation, and conflict. This atlas includes maps that display the world from the beginning of civilization; the political development of all major areas of the world; expanded coverage of Africa, Latin America, and the Middle East; the current Islamic World; and the world population change in 1900 and 2000.

ACKNOWLEDGMENTS

In preparing the sixth edition, we benefited from the critical readings of many colleagues. Our sincere thanks go in particular to contributor Michael Wert of Marquette University who lent his fresh perspective to our coverage of East Asia. We thank Beatrice Manz of the History Department at Tufts University who provided guidance on the new Pastoral Nomads section in Part I. We are also indebted to the following instructors who lent their insight over various editions: Hedrick Alixopuilos, Santa Rosa Junior College; Hayden Bellenoit, U.S. Naval Academy; Dusty Bender, Central Baptist College; Cory Crawford, Ohio University; Adrian De Gifis, Loyola University New Orleans; Peter de Rosa, Bridgewater State University; Aaron Gulyas, Mott Community College; Darlene Hall, Lake Erie College; Vic Jagos, Scottsdale Community College; Adrien Ivan, Vernon College; Andrew Muldoon, Metropolitan State College of Denver; Percy Murray, Shaw University; Dave Price, Santa Fe College; Anthony Steinhoff, University of Tennessee-Chattanooga; Anara Tabyshalieva, Marshal University; Susan Autry, Central Piedmont Community College; Christopher Cameron, University of North Carolina at Charlotte; Anna Collins, Arkansas Tech University; William Connell, Christopher Newport University; Gregory Crider, Winthrop University; Shawn Dry, Oakland Community College; Nancy Fitch, California State University, Fullerton; Christine Haynes, University of North Carolina at Charlotte; Mark Herman, Edison College; Ellen J. Jenkins, Arkansas Tech University; Frank Karpiel, The Citadel; Ken Koons, Virginia Military Institute; David Longfellow, Baylor University; Heather Lucas, Georgia Perimeter College; Jeff Pardue, Gainesville State College; Craig Patton, Alabama A & M University; Amanda Pipkin, University of North Carolina at Charlotte; Linda Scherr, Mercer County Community College; Robert Sherwood, Georgia Military College; Brett Shufelt, Copiah-Lincoln Community College; Peter Thorsheim, University of North Carolina at Charlotte; Kristen Walton, Salisbury University; Christopher Ward, Clayton State University; William Wood, Point Loma Nazarene University.

When textbook authors set out on a project, they are inclined to believe that 90 percent of the effort will be theirs and 10 percent that of various editors and production specialists employed by their publisher. How very naïve. This book would never have seen the light of day had it not been for the unstinting labors of the great team of professionals who turned the authors' words into beautifully presented print. Our debt to the staff of Cengage Learning remains undiminished in the sixth edition. Brooke Barbier, product manager, has offered us firm but sympathetic guidance throughout the revision process. Tonya Lobato, senior content developer, offered astute and sympathetic assistance as the authors worked to incorporate many new ideas and subjects into the text. Carol Newman, senior content project manager, moved the work through the production stages to meet a challenging schedule. Abbey Stebing did an outstanding job of photo research.

We thank also the many students whose questions and concerns, expressed directly or through their instructors, shaped much of this revision. We continue to welcome all readers' suggestions, queries, and criticisms. Please contact us at our respective institutions.

About the Authors

RICHARD W. BULLIET Professor of Middle Eastern History at Columbia University, Richard W. Bulliet received his Ph.D. from Harvard University. He has written scholarly works on a number of topics: the social and economic history of medieval Iran (The Patricians of Nishapur and Cotton, Climate, and Camels in Early Islamic Iran), the history of human-animal relations (The Camel and the Wheel and Hunters, Herders, and Hamburgers), the process of conversion to Islam (Conversion to Islam in the Medieval Period), and the overall course of Islamic social history (Islam: The View from the Edge and The Case for Islamo-Christian Civilization). He is the editor of the Columbia History of the Twentieth Century. He has published four novels, coedited The Encyclopedia of the Modern Middle East, and hosted an educational television series on the Middle East. He was awarded a fellowship by the John Simon Guggenheim Memorial Foundation and was named a Carnegie Corporation Scholar.

PAMELA KYLE CROSSLEY Pamela Kyle Crossley received her Ph.D. in Modern Chinese History from Yale University. She is currently the Robert and Barbara Black Professor of History at Dartmouth College. Her books include The Wobbling Pivot: An Interpretive History of China Since 1800; What Is Global History?; A Translucent Mirror: History and Identity in Qing Imperial Ideology; The Manchus; Orphan Warriors: Three Manchu Generations and the End of the Qing World; and (with Lynn Hollen Lees and John W. Servos) Global Society: The World Since 1900.

DANIEL R. HEADRICK Daniel R. Headrick received his Ph.D. in History from Princeton University. Professor of History and Social Science, Emeritus, at Roosevelt University in Chicago, he is the author of several books on the history of technology, imperialism, and international relations, including The Tools of Empire: Technology and European Imperialism in the Nineteenth Century; The Tentacles of Progress: Technology Transfer in the Age of Imperialism; The Invisible Weapon: Telecommunications and International Politics; Technology: A World History; Power Over Peoples: Technology, Environments and Western Imperialism, 1400 to the Present; and When Information Came of Age: Technologies of Knowledge in the Age of Reason and Revolution, 1700–1850. His articles have appeared in the Journal of World History and the Journal of Modern History, and he has been awarded fellowships by the National Endowment for the Humanities, the John Simon Guggenheim Memorial Foundation, and the Alfred P. Sloan Foundation.

STEVEN W. HIRSCH Steven W. Hirsch holds a Ph.D. in Classics from Stanford University and is currently Associate Professor of Classics and History at Tufts University. He has received grants from the National Endowment for the Humanities and the Massachusetts Foundation for Humanities and Public Policy. His research and publications include The Friendship of the Barbarians: Xenophon and the Persian Empire, as well as articles and reviews in the Classical Journal, the American Journal of Philology, and the Journal of Interdisciplinary History. He is currently completing a comparative study of ancient Greco-Roman and Chinese civilizations.

LYMAN L. JOHNSON Professor Emeritus of History at the University of North Carolina at Charlotte, Lyman L. Johnson earned his Ph.D. in Latin American History from the University of Connecticut. A two-time Senior Fulbright-Hays Lecturer, he also has received fellowships from the Tinker Foundation, the Social Science Research Council, the National Endowment for the Humanities, and the American Philosophical Society. His recent books include Workshop of Revolution: Plebeian Buenos Aires and the Atlantic World, 1776-1810; Death, Dismemberment, and Memory; The Faces of Honor (with Sonya Lipsett-Rivera); Aftershocks: Earthquakes and Popular Politics in Latin America (with Jürgen Buchenau); Essays on the Price History of Eighteenth-Century Latin America (with Enrique Tandeter); and Colonial Latin America (with Mark A. Burkholder). He also has published in journals, including the Hispanic American Historical Review, the Journal of Latin American Studies, the International Review of Social History, Social History, and Desarrollo Económico. He has served as president of the Conference on Latin American History.

DAVID NORTHRUP David Northrup earned his Ph.D. in African and European History from the University of California, Los Angeles. He has published scholarly works on African, Atlantic, and world history. His most recent books are How English Became the Global Language, the third edition of Africa's Discovery of Europe, 1450-1850, and the Diary of Antera Duke, an Eighteenth-Century African Slave Trader. He taught at a rural secondary school on Nigeria, Tuskegee Institute in Alabama, Boston College, and Venice International University and is a past president of the World History Association.

Note on Spelling and Usage

Where necessary for clarity, dates are followed by the letters C.E. or B.C.E. The abbreviation C.E. stands for "Common Era" and is equivalent to A.D. (anno Domini, Latin for "in the year of the Lord"). The abbreviation B.C.E. stands for "before the Common Era" and means the same as B.C. ("before Christ"). In keeping with our goal of approaching world history without special concentration on one culture or another, we chose these neutral abbreviations as appropriate to our enterprise. Because many readers will be more familiar with English than with metric measurements, however, units of measure are generally given in the English system, with metric equivalents following in parentheses.

In general, Chinese has been Romanized according to the pinyin method. Exceptions include proper names well established in English (e.g., Canton, Chiang Kaishek) and a few English words borrowed from Chinese (e.g., kowtow). Spellings of Arabic, Ottoman Turkish, Persian, Mongolian, Manchu, Japanese, and Korean names and terms avoid special diacritical marks for letters that are pronounced only slightly differently in English. An apostrophe is used to indicate when two Chinese syllables are pronounced separately (e.g., Chang'an).

For words transliterated from languages that use the Arabic script—Arabic, Ottoman Turkish, Persian, Urdu—the apostrophe indicating separately pronounced syllables may represent either of two special consonants, the hamza or the ain. Because most English-speakers do not hear the distinction between these two, they have not been distinguished in transliteration and are not indicated when they occur at the beginning or end of a word. As with Chinese, some words and commonly used place-names from these languages are given familiar English spellings (e.g., Quran instead of Qur'an, Cairo instead of al-Qahira). Arabic romanization has normally been used for terms relating to Islam, even where the context justifies slightly different Turkish or Persian forms, again for ease of comprehension.

Before 1492 the inhabitants of the Western Hemisphere had no single name for themselves. They had neither a racial consciousness nor a racial identity. Identity was derived from kin groups, language, cultural practices, and political structures. There was no sense that physical similarities created a shared identity. America's original inhabitants had racial consciousness and racial identity imposed on them by conquest and the occupation of their lands by Europeans after 1492. All of the collective terms for these first American peoples are tainted by this history. Indians, Native Americans, Amerindians, First Peoples, and Indigenous Peoples are among the terms in common usage. In this book the names of individual cultures and states are used wherever possible. Amerindian and other terms that suggest transcultural identity and experience are used most commonly for the period after 1492.

There is an ongoing debate about how best to render Amerindian words in English. It has been common for authors writing in English to follow Mexican usage for Nahuatl and Yucatec Maya words and place-names. In this style, for example, the capital of the Aztec state is spelled Tenochtitlán, and the important late Maya city-state is spelled Chichén Itzá. Although these forms are still common even in the specialist literature, we have chosen to follow the scholarship that sees these accents as unnecessary. The exceptions are modern place-names, such as Mérida and Yucatán, which are accented. A similar problem exists for the spelling of Quechua and Aymara words from the Andean region of South America. Although there is significant disagreement among scholars, we follow the emerging consensus and use the spellings khipu (not quipu), Tiwanaku (not Tiahuanaco), and Wari (not Huari). In this edition we have introduced the now common spelling Inka (not Inca) but keep Cuzco for the capital city (not Cusco), since this spelling facilitates locating this still-important city on maps.

Library of Congress

South America 1820s   This map of South America from the 1820s records the comprehensive success of the independence movements. With the exception of the Guyanas, no colonial governments remain. As we examine this map, we are also reminded of the failure of two political experiments designed to hold together geographically and ethnically diverse regions in a single national government. In the northwest is Colombia (also called Gran Colombia), created by the era's greatest revolutionary leader, Simón Bolívar. It quickly broke apart to form the modern nations of Venezuela, Colombia, and Ecuador. The United Provinces of Río de la Plata, located in the southeast, also soon collapsed, giving birth to the nations of Argentina, Paraguay, and Uruguay.

Revolutions Reshape the World, 1750–1870

Between 1750 and 1870, nearly every part of the world experienced dramatic political, economic, and social change. The beginnings of industrialization and the American, French, and Haitian revolutions, as well as the revolutions for independence in Latin America, transformed political and economic life. European nations expanded into Africa, Asia, and the Middle East, while Russia and the United States acquired vast new territories.

The Industrial Revolution introduced new technologies and patterns of work that made these societies wealthier and militarily more powerful. Western intellectual life became more secular. The Atlantic slave trade and later slavery itself were abolished, and the first efforts to improve the status of women were initiated.

The Industrial Revolution also led to a new wave of imperialism. France conquered Algeria, and Great Britain expanded its colonial rule in India and established colonies in Australia and New Zealand. European political and economic influence also expanded in Africa and Asia. The Ottoman Empire and the Qing Empire met this challenge by implementing reform programs that preserved traditional structures while adopting elements of Western technology and organization. Though lagging behind western Europe in transforming its economy and political institutions, Russia attempted modernization efforts, including the abolition of serfdom.

The economic, political, and social revolutions that began in the mid-eighteenth century shook the foundations of European culture and led to the expansion of Western power around the globe. Some of the nations of Asia, Africa, and Latin America reformed and strengthened their own institutions and economies, while others pushed for more radical change. After 1870 Western imperialism became more aggressive, and few parts of the world were able to resist it.

Chapter Outline

Causes of the Industrial Revolution
➤ *What caused the Industrial Revolution?*

The Technological Revolution
➤ *What were the key innovations that increased productivity and drove industrialization?*

The Impact of the Early Industrial Revolution
➤ *What was the impact of these changes on the society and environment of the industrializing countries?*

New Economic and Political Ideas
➤ *How did the Industrial Revolution influence the rise of new economic and political ideas?*

The Limits of Industrialization Outside the West
➤ *How did the Industrial Revolution affect the relations between the industrialized and the nonindustrialized parts of the world?*

Conclusion

● **DIVERSITY + DOMINANCE**   Adam Smith and the Division of Labor

● **ENVIRONMENT + TECHNOLOGY**   Gas Lighting

Manchester from Kersal Moor, 1852 (w/c with bodycolour and gum arabic on paper), Wyld, William (1806-891)/The Royal Collection © 2011 Her Majesty Queen Elizabeth II/The Bridgeman Art Library

Manchester, the First Industrial City   The first cotton mills, built on the banks of the River Irwell in northern England, transformed Manchester from a country town into a booming industrial city. The use of chemicals to bleach and dye the cloth and the introduction of steam engines in the early nineteenth century to power the spinning and weaving machines made Manchester, for a time, the most polluted city on earth.

The Early Industrial Revolution, 1760–1851

Manchester was just a small town in northern England in the early eighteenth century. A hundred years later, it had turned into the fastest-growing city in history. To contemporaries, it was both a marvel and a horror. Prosperous cotton mills were interspersed with workers' housing, built as cheaply as possible. The economist Nassau Senior described these workers' quarters:

> But when I went through their habitations . . . my only wonder was that tolerable health could be maintained by the inmates of such houses. These towns . . . have been erected by small speculators with an utter disregard to everything except immediate profit. . . . In one place we saw a whole street following the course of a ditch, in order to have deeper cellars (cellars for people, not for lumber) without the expense of excavation. Not a house in this street escaped cholera. . . . the streets are unpaved, with a dunghill or a pond in the middle; the houses built back to back, without ventilation or drainage, and whole families occupy each a corner of a cellar or of a garret.[1]

Not everyone deplored the living conditions in the new industrial city. Friedrich Engels, both a factory owner and critic of capitalism, recounted a meeting with a well-to-do citizen:

> One day I walked with one of these middle-class gentlemen into Manchester. I spoke to him about the disgraceful unhealthy slums and drew his attention to the disgusting condition of that part of the town in which the factory workers lived. I declared that I had never seen so badly built a town in my life. He listened patiently and at the corner of the street at which we parted company, he remarked: "And yet there is a great deal of money made here. Good morning, Sir!"[2]

Manchester's rise as a large, industrial city was a result of what historians call the **Industrial Revolution**, the most profound transformation in human life since the beginnings of agriculture. This revolution involved dramatic innovations in manufacturing, mining, transportation, and communications and equally rapid changes in society and commerce, as new relationships between social groups created an environment that was conducive to technical innovation and economic growth. These changes allowed the industrializing countries—first Britain, then western Europe and the United States—to unleash massive increases in production and productivity, exploit the world's natural resources as never before, and transform the environment and human life in unprecedented ways.

Industrialization widened the gap between rich and poor. The people who owned and controlled industrial innovations amassed wealth and power over nature as well as over other people. While some lived in spectacular luxury, workers, including large

Industrial Revolution The transformation of the economy, the environment, and living conditions, occurring first in England in the eighteenth century, that resulted from the use of steam engines, the mechanization of manufacturing in factories, and innovations in transportation and communication.

---

[1]Nassau W. Senior, *Letters on the Factory Act, as it affects the cotton manufacture, addressed to the Right Honourable, the President of the Board of Trade*, 2d ed. (London: Fellows, 1844), 20.

[2]Friedrich Engels, *Condition of the Working Class in England*, trans. and ed. by W. O. Henderson and W. H. Chaloner (Oxford: Blackwell, 1958), 312.

numbers of children, worked long hours in dangerous factories and lived crowded together in unsanitary tenements. At the same time, the middle class of industrializing nations grew rapidly, exercising increased influence in politics and culture.

The effect of the Industrial Revolution around the world was also very uneven. The first countries to industrialize grew rich and powerful, facilitating a second great wave of European imperialism in the nineteenth century. In Egypt and India, the economic and military power of Europe stifled the tentative beginnings of industrialization. The disparity in wealth and power between the industrial and the developing countries that exists today has its origins in the early nineteenth century.

CAUSES OF THE INDUSTRIAL REVOLUTION

What caused the Industrial Revolution, and why did it develop so rapidly in England in the eighteenth century? These are two of the great questions of history. The basic preconditions of this momentous event seem to have been population growth that increased demand for goods, an agricultural revolution, the expansion of trade, and an openness to experimentation and innovation.

Population Growth

Population growth helped fuel the Industrial Revolution by increasing the demand for goods and by lowering labor costs. Between 1650 and 1850 Europe's population grew from 100 million to 266 million. Simultaneously, Europe became more urban, with the number of city dwellers more than doubling in this same period. This pattern was clearest in England and Wales, where population increased from about 6 million in 1700 to 9 million in 1800 and 18 million by 1850—increases never before experienced in European history. As the pace of manufacturing mounted in the eighteenth century, rural laborers and their families moved to cities in hope of higher earnings and better lives.

The growth of population resulted from more widespread resistance to disease and from more abundant and reliable food supplies, thanks to the new crops that originated in the Americas (see Chapter 18). Gradual improvements in income allowed Europeans to marry at earlier ages and have more children. As a result, roughly 40 percent of the population of Britain was under fifteen years of age in the nineteenth century. This high proportion of youths explains the vitality of the British people in that period as well as the widespread use of child labor. People also migrated at an unprecedented rate—not only from the countryside to the cities, but also from Ireland to England and, more generally, from Europe to the Americas. Thanks to immigration, the population of the United States rose from 4 million in 1791 to 9.6 million in 1820 and 31.5 million in 1860—faster than in any other part of the world at the time.

The Agricultural Revolution

agricultural revolution The transformation of farming in the eighteenth century that resulted from the spread of new crops, improvements in cultivation techniques and livestock breeding, and the consolidation of small holdings into large farms from which tenants and sharecroppers were forcibly expelled.

A revolution in farming provided an increased food supply to fast-growing urban populations and at the same time forced many peasants off the land. This **agricultural revolution** had begun long before the eighteenth century. One important aspect was the introduction of new crops like the potato, introduced from South America in the sixteenth century. In the cool and humid regions of Europe, potatoes yielded two or three times more calories per acre than did the wheat, rye, and oats they replaced. Maize (American corn) was also grown across Europe from northern Iberia to the Balkans, adding substantially to the food supply.

Prosperous landowners with secure titles to their land could afford to bear the risk of trying new methods and new crops. In Great Britain rich landowners "enclosed" the land—that is, consolidated their holdings—and got Parliament to give them title to the commons that in the past had been open to all. Once in control of the land, they could drain and improve the soil, breed better livestock, and introduce crop rotation. This "enclosure movement" further impoverished the rural poor by turning tenants and sharecroppers into landless farm laborers. Many of the displaced rural poor moved to the cities to seek work; others became vagrants; still others emigrated to Canada, Australia, and the United States.

CHRONOLOGY

	Technology	Economy, Society, and Politics
1750	1702–1712 Thomas Newcomen builds first steam engine 1759 Josiah Wedgwood opens pottery factory 1764 Spinning jenny 1769 Richard Arkwright's water frame; James Watt patents steam engine 1779 First iron bridge 1785 Samuel Crompton's mule 1793 Eli Whitney's cotton gin	1776 Adam Smith's *Wealth of Nations* 1776–1783 American Revolution 1789–1799 French Revolution 1792 Mary Wollstonecraft's *A Vindication of the Rights of Woman*
1800	1800 Alessandro Volta's battery 1807 Robert Fulton's *North River* 1820s Construction of Erie Canal 1829 *Rocket*, first prize-winning locomotive 1837 Wheatstone and Cooke's telegraph; Morse's code 1838 First ships steam across the Atlantic 1840 *Nemesis* sails to China 1843 Samuel Morse's Baltimore-to-Washington telegraph	1804–1815 Napoleonic Wars 1820s U.S. cotton industry begins 1833 Factory Act in Britain 1834 German Zollverein; Robert Owen's Grand National Consolidated Trade Union 1847–1848 Irish famine 1848 Collapse of Chartist movement; revolutions in Europe 1848 Publication of *Communist Manifesto*
1850	1851 Crystal Palace opens in London	1854 First cotton mill in India

Trade and Inventiveness

The Industrial Revolution was preceded by a long period of commercial expansion based on growing population and on a much deeper engagement with colonial possessions and with other foreign markets. The innovations of the industrial age came about in part as manufacturers sought to meet increased domestic and foreign demand for textiles and other products through improved efficiency and productivity.

Traditionally, European textiles were produced by skilled artisans organized in guilds using centuries-old technologies. In this system increasing production meant training more artisans, an expensive process that took years. Beginning in the seventeenth century, merchant investors began to relocate some basic textile production away from guild-dominated cities to benefit from lower-cost rural labor, especially during the period between harvesting and planting. Called proto-industrialization, merchant investors delivered raw materials and supplied simple machinery, like looms and spinning wheels, to the homes of farm families and to rural jobbers who organized groups of laborers. In this system the complex tasks associated with artisan production were subdivided into simple procedures that allowed rural workers to quickly gain competence and become productive. Unlike urban artisans, who typically earned daily wages, these proto-industrial workers were only paid for what they produced thus reducing labor costs. Skilled manufacturers then transformed the spun wool and rough cloth produced by rural laborers into finished goods for domestic and foreign consumers. While proto-industrialization increased cloth production and lowered labor costs, there were chronic problems with quality control and inefficiencies that resulted from the dispersal of production.

In the eighteenth century a dramatic expansion of European commerce with markets in the Americas, Africa, and Asia reinforced the economic effects of the fast-growing European population. Nearly all the European powers profited from plantation colonies in the Americas. As Europeans of even modest means consumed ever-growing quantities of sugar to sweeten their tea, coffee, cocoa, pastries, and candies, the demand for manufactures like porcelain cups and dinnerware increased as well. At the same time planters in the Caribbean imported a steeply rising volume of cotton textiles to clothe themselves and their slaves. Initially, these cotton textiles were imported from Asia, but increasing demand led to the creation of domestic cotton textile industries, the first truly modern mechanized industry.

European governments played a key role in this economic expansion. Governments across Europe sponsored improvements in road networks, but maintenance was often inadequate. In Britain local governments' neglect of the roads that served long-distance traffic led to the formation of private "turnpike trusts" that built numerous toll roads. As the volume of commerce increased, canal-building booms occurred in Britain, France, and the low countries in the late eighteenth century. Governments also directly invested in skills and new technologies by creating royal manufacturers that produced fine china, silks, and carpets. Authorities in England, France, Prussia, and Spain, among other European nations, recruited skilled artisans from rival nations, subsidized periodicals that disseminated new technologies, and expanded their navies to better protect foreign trade.

Beginning in the seventeenth century, educated people throughout Europe and the Americas were increasingly fascinated by technology and innovation (see Chapter 17). Across Europe inexpensive periodicals informed the general public of new technologies and scientific discoveries. But it was the *Encyclopédie*, published in France over a period of more than twenty years, that most influenced the dissemination of useful technologies by providing detailed diagrams of everything from printing and textile machinery to canal locks and foundry equipment. During the eighteenth century the French, Spanish, and British governments also sought to promote economic growth by sending expeditions around the world to collect plants that could profitably be grown domestically or in their colonies. They also offered prizes for scientific discoveries, like determining the longitude of a ship at sea and the accurate measurement of the earth's circumference. It was an era when innovators and scientists were celebrities.

Britain and Continental Europe

Industrialization did not take place everywhere at once. Great Britain took the lead in introducing new technologies and maintained its place as Europe's major industrial power to the end of the nineteenth century. It is useful to divide the British experience into two phases. In the eighteenth century inventors developed machines that multiplied the productive capacities of individual workers, especially in the textile industry. While production increased dramatically, British industry continued to rely on traditional sources of energy, particularly wind, water, and animal power. Then early in the nineteenth century the development of efficient steam engines allowed British entrepreneurs to apply this potent source of energy to industrial machinery.

The technologies associated with both stages of this revolution spread rapidly to continental Europe and the United States. British engineers and skilled machinists were the most active agents in the dissemination of the new technologies. European and American investors quickly recognized the advantages of the new technologies and provided high salaries and other inducements to skilled British workers willing to immigrate and introduce the newest technologies. Belgium had the earliest successes in imitating the British industrial model, becoming the continent's most industrialized economy by 1840. While slower to embrace the new technologies, Germany after 1850 became the continent's major producer of coal, iron, and steel. The United States was well established as a major industrial power by 1860, having quickly adopted textile and metallurgical technologies developed first in Great Britain.

Historians disagree about why Britain played such an important role in the introduction of industrial technologies in the eighteenth and nineteenth centuries. It is clear that Britain enjoyed a rising standard of living, thanks to good harvests and a booming overseas trade, and that this prosperity increased consumption and stimulated innovation in manufacturing. Britain was already the world's leading exporter of tools, guns, hardware, clocks, and other manufactured goods (see Map 22.1), and it had a strong craft tradition that trained a large number of skilled mechanics. At the same time, its mining and metal industries employed engineers with a tradition of experimentation and innovation. British commercial culture was also among Europe's most modern, having long enjoyed the benefits of strong banks, joint-stock companies, a stock market, and commercial insurance. In addition, its patent system offered inventors the hope of rich rewards by protecting their intellectual property rights. Growing public awareness of early innovators who became wealthy and respected for their inventions stimulated others to experiment.

At the dawn of the industrial age, Britain had one of the most fluid societies in Europe. The court was less ostentatious, its aristocracy was less powerful, and the lines separating the social classes were not as sharply drawn as elsewhere in Europe, with the exception of the Netherlands. Compared to France or Spain, the two most important continental powers, British political power was not as centralized or intrusive. There were fewer bureaucrats and officials and

MAP 22.1 The Industrial Revolution in Britain, ca. 1850 The first industries arose in northern and western England. These regions had abundant coal and iron-ore deposits for the iron industry, as well as moist climate and fast-flowing rivers, factors important for the cotton textile industry. © Cengage Learning

fewer obstacles to commerce and manufacturing than in most continental nations. As commoners grew wealthy in trade and manufacturing, society became less hierarchical and more fluid.

At a time when transportation by land was very costly, Great Britain had good water transportation thanks to its long coastline, navigable rivers, and growing network of canals. It also had a unified internal market with none of the duties and tolls that goods had to pay every few miles in France or Spain. This advantage facilitated a growing trade between regions. More important still, Britain had abundant supplies of coal and iron ore, two key ingredients in the Industrial Revolution.

In contrast to Britain, the economies of continental Europe were hampered by high transportation costs, misguided government regulations, and rigid social structures. As a result, attempts to import British techniques and organize factory production elsewhere often foundered for lack of markets or management skills. Nevertheless, British textile machinery was introduced in France and Spain before the French Revolution (see Chapter 23). From then until the end of the Napoleonic wars in 1815, Europe's economies were distorted by the effects of mass military mobilizations and warfare. Although war created opportunities for suppliers of weapons and uniforms, the interruption of trade between Britain and continental Europe slowed the diffusion of new technologies, and the insecurity of countries at war discouraged businessmen from investing in factories and machinery.

Once revolutions had swept away most of the restrictions of Europe's old regimes, both private investors and European governments acted to import new technologies and adapt them to local conditions. Acutely aware of Britain's head start and the need to stimulate their own industries, continental governments sponsored efforts to imitate or steal British industrial secrets. They recruited British engineers and artisans, created technical schools, and eliminated internal tariff barriers, tolls, and other hindrances to trade. By the 1820s there were several thousand Britons working on the continent, setting up machines, training workers in the new methods, and even starting their own businesses. European governments also encouraged the formation of joint-stock companies and banks to channel private savings into industrial investments. By 1830 the political climate in western Europe had become as favorable to business as Britain's had been a half century earlier. First Belgium and then, after 1850, Germany and France enjoyed industrial booms based on iron, cotton, steam engines, and railroads. Key to the success of Belgium and Germany was the existence of abundant coal and iron-ore deposits. Without abundant coal, France retained a more traditional manufacturing economy until the introduction of electricity late in the nineteenth century.

SECTION REVIEW

- The Industrial Revolution arose from population growth, an agricultural revolution, increased trade, and an interest in innovation.

- Britain industrialized first, thanks to its fluid political structures, transportation infrastructure, inventiveness, and society open to talented and enterprising people.

- Among educated Europeans, practical subjects like business, science, and technology became fashionable.

- On the European continent, the revolutions of 1789–1815 swept away the restrictions of the old aristocratic regimes and allowed for more industrial growth.

THE TECHNOLOGICAL REVOLUTION

Five innovations spurred industrialization: (1) mass production through the division of labor, (2) new machines and mechanization, (3) a great increase in the manufacture of iron, (4) the steam engine, and (5) the electric telegraph. While the full realization of these innovations occurred first in Great Britain and then spread to the United States and continental Europe in the nineteenth century, China had achieved the first three during the Song dynasty (960–1279). But China did not develop the steam engine or electricity, innovations that dramatically multiplied human productivity. The transformation of Western economies through industrialization depended on the full integration of these new forms of energy with the process of mechanical innovation.

Mass Production: Pottery

The pottery industry offers a good example of **mass production**, the making of many identical items by breaking the process into simple repetitive tasks. Before the mid-eighteenth century, only the wealthy could afford imported Chinese porcelain. Middle-class people used pewter tableware, and the poor ate from wooden or earthenware bowls. Royal manufacturers produced exquisite handmade products for the courts and aristocracy, but their products were much too expensive for mass consumption. As more and more Europeans acquired a taste for tea, cocoa, and coffee, they wanted porcelain that would not spoil the flavor of hot beverages. This demand created opportunities for inventive entrepreneurs.

Britain had many small pottery workshops where craftsmen made a few plates and cups at a time. Much of this activity took place in a part of the Midlands that possessed good clay, coal for firing, and lead for glazing. In 1759, **Josiah Wedgwood**, the son of a potter, started his own pottery business. Today the name *Wedgwood* is associated with expensive, highly decorated china. But Wedgwood's most important contribution lay in producing ordinary porcelain cheaply by means of the **division of labor** (see Diversity and Dominance: Adam Smith and the Division of Labor).

Wedgwood subdivided the work into simple repetitive tasks, such as unloading the clay, mixing it, pressing flat pieces, dipping the pieces in glaze, putting handles on cups, packing

mass production The manufacture of many identical products by the division of labor into many small repetitive tasks. This method was introduced into the manufacture of pottery by Josiah Wedgwood and into the spinning of cotton thread by Richard Arkwright.

Josiah Wedgwood English industrialist whose pottery works first produced fine-quality pottery by industrial methods.

division of labor A manufacturing technique that breaks down a craft into many simple and repetitive tasks that can be performed by unskilled workers. Pioneered in the pottery works of Josiah Wedgwood and in other eighteenth-century factories, it greatly increased the productivity of labor and lowered the cost of manufactured goods.

Wedgwood's Potteries
In Staffordshire, England, Josiah Wedgwood established a factory to mass-produce beautiful and inexpensive china. The bottle-shaped buildings are kilns in which thousands of pieces of china could be fired at one time. Kilns, factories, and housing were all mixed together in pottery towns, and smoke from burning coal filled the air.

Mary Evans Picture Library / Alamy

6.—THE BANK.

kilns, and carrying things from one part of his plant to another. To prevent interruptions, he instituted strict discipline among his workers. He substituted molds for the potter's wheel whenever possible, a change that not only saved labor but also created uniform plates and bowls that could be stacked. The end result was that while workers became more productive, they had fewer skills and were paid less.

Wedgwood's interest in applying technology to manufacturing was sparked by his membership in the Lunar Society, a group of businessmen, scientists, and craftsmen that met each month when the moon was full to discuss the practical application of knowledge. In 1782 the naturalist Erasmus Darwin encouraged him to purchase a steam engine from Boulton and Watt, a firm founded by two other members of the society. The engine that Wedgwood bought to mix clay and grind flint was one of the first to be installed in a factory. The division of labor and new steam-driven machinery allowed Wedgwood to lower the cost of his products while improving their quality, and to offer his wares for sale at lower prices.

Mechanization: The Cotton Industry

mechanization The application of machinery to manufacturing and other activities. Among the first processes to be mechanized were the spinning of cotton thread and the weaving of cloth in late-eighteenth- and early-nineteenth-century England.

The cotton industry, the largest industry in this period, illustrates the role of **mechanization**, the use of machines to do work previously done by hand. Cotton had long been grown in China,

Adam Smith and the Division of Labor

Adam Smith (1723–1790), a Scottish philosopher, is famous for his book An Inquiry into the Nature and Causes of the Wealth of Nations, *first published in 1776. It was the first work to explain the economy of a nation as a system. Smith criticized the notion, common in the eighteenth century, that a nation's wealth was synonymous with the amount of gold and silver in the government's coffers. Instead, he defined wealth as the amount of goods and services produced by a nation's people. By this definition, labor and its products are an essential element in a nation's prosperity.*

In the passage that follows, Smith contrasts two methods of making pins. In one a team of workers divided up the job of making pins and produced a great many every day; in the other pin workers "wrought separately and independently" and produced very few pins per day. It is clear that the division of labor produced more pins per worker per day. But who benefited? Left unsaid is that a pin factory had to be owned and operated by a manufacturer who hired workers and assigned a task to each one.

The illustration shows a pin-maker's workshop in late-eighteenth-century France. Each worker is performing a specific task on a few pins at once, and all the energy comes from human muscles. These are the characteristics of a proto-industrial workshop.

To take an example, therefore, from a very trifling manufacture—but one in which the division of labour has been very often taken notice of—the trade of the pin-maker: a workman not educated to this business (which the division of labour has rendered a distinct trade), nor acquainted with the use of machinery employed in it (to the invention of which the same division of labour has probably given occasion), could scarce, perhaps, with his utmost industry, make one pin in a day, and certainly could not make twenty. But in the way in which this business is now carried on, not only the whole work is a peculiar trade, but it is divided into a number of branches, of which the greater part are likewise peculiar trades. One man draws out the wire, another straights it, a third cuts it, a fourth points it, a fifth grinds it at the top for receiving the head; to make the head requires two or three distinct operations, to put it on, is a peculiar business, to whiten the pins is another; it is even a trade by itself to put them into the paper; and the important business of making a pin is, in this manner, divided into about eighteen distinct operations, which, in some manufactories, are all performed by distinct hands, though in others the same man will sometimes perform two or three of them. I have seen a small manufactory of this kind where ten men only were employed, and where some of them, consequently, performed two or three distinct operations. But though they were very poor, and therefore but indifferently accommodated with the necessary machinery, they could, when they exerted themselves, make among them about twelve pounds of pins in a day.

There are in a pound upwards of four thousand pins of a middling size. Those ten persons, therefore, could make among them upwards of forty-eight thousand pins in a day. Each person, therefore, making a tenth part of forty-eight thousand pins, might be considered as making four thousand eight hundred pins a day. But if they had all wrought separately and independently, and without any of them having been educated to this peculiar business, they certainly could not each of them have made twenty, perhaps not one pin in a day; that is, certainly, not the two hundred and fortieth, perhaps not the four thousand eight hundredth part of what they are at present

Richard Arkwright English inventor and entrepreneur who became the wealthiest and most successful textile manufacturer of the early Industrial Revolution. He invented the water frame, a machine that, with minimal human supervision, could spin many strong cotton threads at once.

India, and the Middle East, where it was spun and woven by hand. The cloth was so much cooler, softer, and cleaner than wool that wealthy Europeans developed a liking for the costly import. When the powerful English woolen industry persuaded Parliament to forbid the import of cotton cloth, that prohibition stimulated attempts to import cotton fiber and make the cloth domestically. Here was an opportunity for enterprising inventors to reduce costs with laborsaving machinery.

Beginning in the 1760s a series of inventions revolutionized the spinning of cotton thread. The first was the jenny, invented in 1764, which mechanically drew out the cotton fibers and twisted them into thread. The jenny was simple, cheap to build, and easy for one person to operate. Early models permitted a single worker to spin six or seven threads at once, later ones up to eighty. The thread, however, was soft and irregular and could be used only in combination with linen, a strong yarn derived from the flax plant.

In 1769 **Richard Arkwright** invented another spinning machine, the water frame, which produced thread strong enough to be used without linen. Arkwright was both a gifted inventor and a

A Pin-Maker's Workshop The man in the middle (Fig. 2) is pulling wire off a spindle (G) and through a series of posts. This ensures that the wire will be perfectly straight. The worker seated on the lower right (Fig. 3) takes the long pieces of straightened wire and cuts them into shorter lengths. The man in the lower left-hand corner (Fig. 5) sharpens twelve to fifteen wires at a time by holding them against a grindstone turned by the worker in Fig. 6. The men in Figs. 4 and 7 put the finishing touches on the points. Other operations—such as forming the wire to the proper thickness, cleaning and coating it with tin, and attaching the heads—are depicted in other engravings in the same encyclopedia. The Pin Factory, plate 2 from Volume IV of the Encyclopedia of Denis Diderot (1713-84) and Jean le Rond d'Alembert (1717-83), 1751-52 (engraving), French School, (18th century) / Private Collection/The Bridgeman Art Library

capable of performing, in consequence of a proper division and combination of their different operations.

QUESTIONS FOR ANALYSIS

1. Why does dividing the job of pin-making into ten or more operations result in the production of more pins per worker? How much more productive are these workers than if each one made complete pins from start to finish?

2. How closely does the picture of a pin-maker's workshop illustrate Smith's verbal description?

3. What disadvantage would there be to working in a pin factory where the job was divided as in Smith's example, compared to making entire pins from start to finish?

4. What other examples can you think of, from Adam Smith's day or from more recent times, of the advantages of the division of labor?

Source: Adam Smith, *An Inquiry into the Nature and Causes of the Wealth of Nations*, ed. Edward Gibbon Wakefield (London: Charles Knight and Co., 1843), 7–9.

successful businessman. His machine was larger and more complex than the jenny and required a source of power such as a water wheel, hence the name "water frame." To obtain the necessary energy, he installed dozens of machines in a building next to a fast-flowing river. The resemblance to a flour mill gave such enterprises the name *cotton mill*. Within a few decades of the introduction of the jenny and water frame, these technologies were imported and adapted to local conditions elsewhere. The skilled mechanics who built British machines served as vectors for this dissemination as they moved to France, Belgium, and the United States to seek higher wages.

In 1785 British inventor Samuel Crompton patented a machine that combined the best features of the jenny and the water frame. This device, called a mule, produced a strong thread that was thin enough to be used to make a high-quality cotton cloth called muslin. The mule could make a finer, more even thread than could any human being, and at a lower cost. At last British industry could undersell high-quality handmade cotton cloth from India. With these innovations in place, British cotton output increased tenfold between 1770 and 1790, despite the fact that these large-scale producers still depended on waterpower.

The boom in thread production and the soaring demand for cloth encouraged inventors to mechanize the rest of textile manufacturing. Power looms were perfected after 1815. Other inventions of the period included carding machines, chlorine bleach, and cylindrical presses to print designs on fabric. By the 1830s large textile mills powered by steam engines were performing all the steps necessary to turn raw cotton into printed cloth.

Mechanization offered two advantages: increased productivity for the manufacturer and lower prices for the consumer. Whereas in India it took five hundred hours to spin a pound of cotton, the mule of 1790 could do so in three person-hours, and the self-acting mule—an improved version introduced in 1830—required only eighty minutes. Cotton mills needed very few skilled workers, and managers often hired children to tend the spinning machines. The same was true of power looms, which gradually replaced handloom weaving: the number of power looms rose from 2,400 in 1813 to 500,000 by 1850. Meanwhile, the price of cloth fell by 90 percent between 1782 and 1812 and kept on dropping.

The industrialization of Britain made cotton America's most valuable crop (see Chapter 25). In the 1790s most of Britain's cotton came from India. But in 1793 the American Eli Whitney patented his cotton gin, a simple device that separated the bolls or seedpods from the fiber and made cotton growing economical. This invention permitted the spread of cotton farming into Georgia, then into Alabama, Mississippi, and Louisiana, and finally as far west as Texas. By the late 1850s the southern states were producing a million tons of cotton a year, five-sixths of the world's total.

With the help of British craftsmen who introduced jennies, mules, and power looms, Americans developed their own cotton industry in the 1820s. Immigrants from Great Britain played a key role in this process, as did the willingness of American investors to ignore the patent rights of British inventors. By 1840 the United States had twelve hundred cotton mills that served the booming domestic market, two-thirds of them in New England.

While the resistance of long-established artisan guilds to the introduction of new technologies slowed technological innovation in the wool textile industry in Britain and elsewhere, machinery adapted from cotton production quickly transformed the spinning of woolen thread by the 1830s. Steam-driven looms soon followed. In Belgium in 1810, only 5 of 144 woolen factories were mechanized, but they produced more than 50 percent of total production.

The Iron Industry

Iron making also was transformed during the Industrial Revolution. Throughout Eurasia and Africa, iron had long been used for tools, weapons, and household items. During the Song period, Chinese forges had produced cast iron in large quantities. Although production declined after the Song, iron continued to be common and inexpensive in China. Wherever iron was produced, however, deforestation eventually drove up the cost of charcoal (used for smelting) and restricted output. Furthermore, iron had to be repeatedly heated and hammered to drive out impurities, a difficult and costly process. Because of limited wood supplies and the high cost of skilled labor, iron was a rare and valuable metal outside China before the eighteenth century.

A first breakthrough occurred in 1709 when Abraham Darby discovered that coke (coal from which the impurities have been cooked out) could be used in place of charcoal. The resulting metal was of lower quality than charcoal-smelted iron but much cheaper to produce, for coal was plentiful. In 1784 British inventor Henry Cort found a way to remove some of the impurities in coke-iron by puddling—stirring the molten iron with long rods. Cort's process made it possible to turn coal into coke to produce wrought iron (a soft and malleable form of iron) very cheaply. By 1790 four-fifths of Britain's iron was made with coke, while other countries still used charcoal. Coke-iron allowed a great expansion in the size of individual blast furnaces. As a result, Britain's iron production rose fast, from 17,000 tons in 1740 to 3 million tons in 1844, as much as in the rest of the world put together. As in Britain, the existence of large supplies of coal and iron ore largely explains the fast pace of industrialization of Belgium and Germany after 1820.

In turn, there seemed no limit to the novel applications for this cheap and useful material. In 1779 Abraham Darby III (grandson of the first Abraham Darby) built a bridge of iron across the Severn River. In 1851 Londoners marveled at the **Crystal Palace**, a huge exhibition hall made entirely of iron and glass. The Great Exhibition showcased British industry and power but included exhibits from the colonies and from other nations.

Crystal Palace Building erected in Hyde Park, London, for the Great Exhibition of 1851. Made of iron and glass, like a gigantic greenhouse, it was a symbol of the industrial age.

Walker Art Gallery, National Museums Liverpool/The Bridgeman Art Library

Pit Head of a Coal Mine   This is a small coal mine. In the center of this picture stands a Newcomen engine used to pump water from the shaft. The work of hauling coal out of the mine was still done by horses and mules. The smoke coming out of the smokestack is a trademark of the early industrial era.

The availability of cheap iron made the mass production of objects such as guns, hardware, and tools appealing. However, fitting together the parts of these products required a great deal of labor. To reduce labor costs, manufacturers, like the Americans Eli Whitney (firearms) and Eli Terry (clocks), contributed to the development of standardized interchangeable parts. By the mid-nineteenth century, interchangeable-parts manufacturing had been widely adopted, including the manufacture of farm equipment and sewing machines. By the 1850s Europeans had begun to call this the "American system of manufactures."

The Steam Engine

steam engine A machine that turns the energy released by burning fuel into motion. Thomas Newcomen built the first crude but workable steam engine in 1712. James Watt vastly improved his device in the 1760s and 1770s. Steam power was later applied to moving machinery in factories and to powering ships and locomotives.

James Watt Scot who invented the condenser and other improvements that made the steam engine a practical source of power for industry and transportation. The watt, an electrical measurement, is named after him.

In the history of the world, there had been a number of periods of great technological inventiveness and economic growth. But in all previous cases, the dynamism eventually faltered. The Industrial Revolution, in contrast, has only accelerated. One reason has been increased interactions between scientists, technicians, and businesspeople. Another has been access to a source of cheap energy, namely fossil fuels. The first machine to transform fossil fuel into mechanical energy was the **steam engine**, a device that set the Industrial Revolution apart from all previous periods of growth and innovation.

Before the eighteenth century, deep mines filled with water faster than pumps powered by horses could lift it out. Then, between 1702 and 1712, Thomas Newcomen developed the first practical steam engine, a crude but effective device that could clear water from mines much faster than earlier pumps. The Newcomen engine's voracious appetite for fuel mattered little in coal mines, where fuel was cheap, but it made the engine too costly for other uses. In 1764 another Briton, **James Watt**, a maker of scientific instruments at Glasgow University in Scotland, was asked to repair the university's model Newcomen engine. Watt realized that the engine wasted fuel because the cylinder had to be alternately heated and cooled. He developed a separate condenser—a vessel into which the steam was allowed to escape, leaving the cylinder always hot and the condenser always cold. Watt patented his idea in 1769 and enlisted the help of the iron manufacturer Matthew Boulton to turn his invention into a commercial product. Their first engines were sold to pump water out of copper and tin mines, where fuel was too costly for Newcomen engines. In 1781 Watt invented the sun-and-planet gear, which turned the back-and-forth action of the piston into rotary motion. This allowed steam engines to power machinery

Science & Society Picture Library/Contributo/Getty Images

Transatlantic Steamship Race In 1838, two ships equipped with steam engines, the *Sirius* and the *Great Western*, steamed from England to New York. Although the *Sirius* left a few days earlier, the *Great Western*—shown here arriving in New York harbor—almost caught up with it, arriving just four hours after the *Sirius*. This race inaugurated regular transatlantic steamship service.

in flour and cotton mills, pottery manufactures, and other industries as well. Because there seemed almost no limit to the amount of coal in the ground, steam-generated energy appeared to be an inexhaustible source of power, and steam engines could be used where animal, wind, and water power were lacking. By the 1820s steam engines were powering textile machinery in Belgium and the United States as well as in Great Britain. In places where coal supplies were limited, like France, the application of steam power to manufacturing developed slowly.

Inspired by the success of Watt's engine, several inventors put steam engines on boats. The first commercially successful steamboat was Robert Fulton's *North River*, which sailed the Hudson River between New York City and Albany, New York, in 1807. Soon steamboats were launched on the Ohio and the Mississippi, gateways to the Midwest. By 1830 some three hundred steamboats plied the Mississippi and its tributaries. The United States was fast becoming a nation that moved by water.

Oceangoing steam-powered ships were much more difficult to build than river boats, for the first steam engines used so much coal that no ship could carry more than a few days' supply. The *Savannah*, which crossed the Atlantic in 1819, was a sailing ship with an auxiliary steam engine that was used for only ninety hours of its twenty-nine-day trip. Engineers soon developed more efficient engines, and in 1838 two steamers, the *Great Western* and the *Sirius*, crossed the Atlantic on steam power alone.

Railroads

After Watt's patent expired in 1800, inventors experimented with lighter, more powerful high-pressure engines—an idea Watt had rejected as too dangerous. In 1804 Richard Trevithick built

Bettmann/Corbis

The *De Witt Clinton* Locomotive, 1835–1840   The *De Witt Clinton* was the first steam locomotive built in the United States. The high smokestack let the hot cinders cool so they would not set fire to nearby trees, an important consideration at a time when eastern North America was still covered with forest. The three passenger cars are clearly horse carriages fitted with railroad wheels.

an engine that consumed only one-third the coal used by Watt's design and then created several steam-powered vehicles able to travel on roads or rails.

By the 1820s England had many railways on which horses pulled heavy wagons. In 1829, the owners of the Liverpool and Manchester Railway organized a contest between steam-powered locomotives and horse-drawn wagons. George Stephenson and his son Robert won the contest with their locomotive *Rocket*, which pulled a 20-ton train at up to 30 miles (48 kilometers) per hour. After that triumph, a railroad-building mania swept Britain. In the late 1830s, as passenger traffic soared, entrepreneurs built lines between the major cities and even to small towns. Railroads were far cheaper, faster, and more comfortable than stagecoaches, and millions of people got in the habit of traveling. By 1850 Great Britain had 6,087 miles (9,797 kilometers) of railroad line.

The introduction of railroads had their most transformative effects in the United States. By the 1840s, 6,000 miles (10,000 kilometers) of track radiated from Boston, New York, Philadelphia, and Baltimore. In the 1850s, 21,000 miles (34,000 kilometers) of additional track were laid, much of it westward across the Appalachians to Memphis, St. Louis, and Chicago. After 1856 the trip from New York to Chicago, which had once taken three weeks by boat and on horseback, could be made in forty-eight hours. This rapid expansion of railroads opened up the Midwest, dispersing the waves of immigrants, turning the vast prairie into farms to feed the industrial cities of the eastern United States, and creating a vast internal market for manufactures.

Railways also accelerated the industrialization of Europe (see Map 22.2). Belgium, independent since 1830, quickly copied the British railways. In France and Prussia, construction was delayed until the mid-1840s. When it began, however, it not only satisfied the long-standing need for transportation in those countries but also stimulated the iron, machinery, and construction industries. By 1850 Germany had built 3,639 miles (5,856 kilometers) of railroad line and France 1,811 miles (2,915 kilometers).

Communication over Wires

electric telegraph   A device for rapid, long-distance transmission of information over an electric wire. It was introduced in England and North America in the 1830s and 1840s and replaced telegraph systems that utilized visual signals such as semaphores.

After the Italian scientist Alessandro Volta invented the battery in 1800, making it possible to produce an electric current, many inventors tried to apply electricity to communication. The first practical **electric telegraph** systems were developed almost simultaneously in England and

America. In 1837 in England Charles Wheatstone and William Cooke introduced a five-wire telegraph, while the American Samuel Morse introduced a code of dots and dashes that could be transmitted with a single wire. Morse convinced the Congress to provide $30,000 (nearly $800,000 in 2012) to "wire" America in 1842 and built a telegraph line connecting Baltimore and Washington D.C. a year later.

The railroad companies allowed telegraph companies to string wires along the tracks in exchange for the right to send telegrams from station to station announcing the departure and arrival of trains. Such messages made railroads much safer as well as more efficient. By the late 1840s telegraph wires crisscrossed the eastern United States and western Europe. In 1851 the first submarine telegraph cable was laid across the English Channel from England to France (cutting the transmission of news from up to four days to minutes); it was the beginning of a network that eventually connected the entire globe. No longer were communications limited to the speed of a sailing ship, a galloping horse, or a fast-moving train. Together railroads and telegraphs had an enormous economic impact. While railroads could move bulk goods more rapidly and at lower cost than other forms of land transportation, telegraphs dramatically transformed market intelligence by making it possible for producers to keep track of distant consumer needs and prices, thus making markets more efficient and profits more dependable.

SECTION REVIEW

- A series of technological and organizational innovations transformed manufacturing, transportation, and communication.
- Mechanization, pioneered by Wedgwood, meant that work formerly done by skilled craftsmen was divided into many simple tasks assigned to workers in factories.
- New machines allowed the mass production of cotton yarn and cloth.
- The use of coke and new machines made iron cheap and abundant.
- Steam engines provided power for mines, factories, ships, and railroads.
- Electricity found its first practical application in telegraphy.

THE IMPACT OF THE EARLY INDUSTRIAL REVOLUTION

The Industrial Revolution led to profound changes in society, politics, and the economy. At first, the changes were local. Some people became wealthy and built mansions, while others lived in slums with polluted water and air. By the mid-nineteenth century, the worst local effects were being alleviated and cities had become cleaner and healthier. Industrial nations then faced more complex problems: business cycles, labor conflicts, and the degradation of entire regions by mining and industrial pollution. At the global level, industrialization empowered the nations of western Europe and North America to impose themselves on less developed nations.

The New Industrial Cities

The most dramatic environmental changes brought about by industrialization occurred in the towns. Towns had never before grown so fast. London, one of the largest cities in Europe in 1700 with 500,000 inhabitants, grew to 1,117,000 by 1800 and to 2,685,000 by 1850; it was then the largest city the world had ever known. Manchester, a small town of 20,000 in 1758, reached 303,000 a century later, a fifteenfold increase. New York City, already 100,000 strong in 1815, reached 600,000 (including Brooklyn) in 1850. In some areas, towns merged and formed megalopolises, such as Greater London, the English Midlands, central Belgium, and the Ruhr district of Germany.

A great deal of money went into the building of fine homes, churches, museums, and theaters in wealthy neighborhoods. Much of the beauty of London dates from the time of the Industrial Revolution. Yet, by all accounts, industrial cities grew much too fast, and much of the growth occurred in the poorest neighborhoods. As poor migrants streamed in from the countryside, developers built the cheap, shoddy row houses for them to rent that Nassau Senior described.

Sudden population growth caused serious urban environmental problems. Town dwellers recently arrived from the country brought country ways with them. People threw their sewage and trash out the windows to be washed down the gutters in the streets. The poor kept pigs and chickens; the rich kept horses; and pedestrians stepped into the street at their own risk. Air pollution from burning coal, a problem since the sixteenth century, got steadily worse. People drank water drawn from wells and rivers contaminated by sewage and industrial runoff. The River Irwell, which ran through Manchester, was, in the words of one visitor, "considerably less

MAP 22.2 **Industrialization in Europe, ca. 1850** In 1850 industrialization was in its early stages on the European continent. The first industrial regions were comparatively close to England and possessed rich coal deposits: Belgium and the Ruhr district of Germany. Politics determined the location of railroads. Notice the star-shaped French network of rail lines emanating from Paris and the lines linking the different parts of the German Confederation. © Cengage Learning

a river than a flood of liquid manure."[3] "Every day that I live," wrote an American visitor to Manchester, "I thank Heaven that I am not a poor man with a family in England."[4] At the same time, railroads invaded the towns, bringing noise and smoke into densely populated neighborhoods. On the outskirts of cities, railroad yards, sidings, and repair shops covered acres of land, surrounded by miles of warehouses and workers' housing.

Under these conditions, diseases proliferated. To the long list of preindustrial diseases, industrialization added new ailments. Rickets, a bone disease caused by lack of sunshine, became endemic in dark and smoky industrial cities. Steamships brought cholera from India, causing great epidemics that struck poor neighborhoods especially hard. Observers documented the horrors of slum life in vivid detail. Their shocking reports led to municipal reforms, such as garbage removal, water and sewage systems, and parks and schools. These measures began to alleviate the ills of urban life after the mid-nineteenth century.

---

[3]Quoted in Lewis Mumford, *The City in History* (New York: Harcourt Brace, 1961), 460.
[4]Quoted in F. Roy Willis, *Western Civilization: An Urban Perspective*, vol. II (Lexington, MA: D.C. Heath, 1973), 675.

Section of a Parisian building, illustration from 'Le Magasin Pittoresque', engraved by John Quartley (fl.1835–67) 1847 (engraving) (b/w photo), Girardet, Karl (1813-71) (after) / Bibliotheque des Arts Decoratifs, Paris, France / Archives Charmet / The Bridgeman Art Library

Paris Apartment at Night   This cutaway drawing in a French magazine shows the vertical segregation by social class that prevailed in the 1840s. The lower level is occupied by the concierge and her family. The first floor belongs to a wealthy family throwing a party for high-society friends. Middle-class people living on the next floor seem annoyed by the noise coming from below. Above them, a thief has entered an artist's studio. A poor seamstress and her child live in the garret under the roof. When elevators were introduced in the late nineteenth century, people of different income levels were more likely segregated by neighborhoods instead of by floors.

Rural Environments

Long before the Industrial Revolution began, practically no wilderness areas were left in Britain and very few in western Europe. Almost every piece of land was covered with fields, forests, or pastures shaped by human activity, or by towns; yet humans continued to alter the environment. As they had been doing for centuries, people cut timber to build ships and houses, to heat homes, and to manufacture bricks, iron, glass, beer, bread, and many other items.

North Americans transformed their environment on a vast scale. The Canadian and American governments seized land from the Indians and made it available at low cost to farmers and logging companies. Settlers viewed forests not as a valuable resource but as a hindrance to development. In their haste to "open up the wilderness," pioneers felled trees and burned them, built houses and abandoned them, and moved on. The cultivation of cotton in the South was especially harmful. Planters cut down forests, grew cotton for a few years until the soil was depleted, and then moved west, abandoning the land to scrub pines (see Chapter 25).

In industrializing Europe, raw materials once grown on the land—such as wood, hay, and wool—were replaced by materials found underground, like iron ore and coal, or obtained overseas, like cotton. Across Europe the expansion of coal and iron mining had dramatic effects on the environment. As the population increased and land grew scarcer, the cost of growing feed for horses rose, creating incentives to find new, less land-hungry means of transportation. Likewise, as iron became cheaper and wood more expensive, ships and many other objects formerly made of wood began to be made of iron.

Working Conditions

Industrialization offered new opportunities to the enterprising. Carpenters, metalworkers, and machinists were in great demand. Some workers became engineers or went into business for themselves. The boldest Britons moved to the European continent, the Americas, or India, using their skills to establish new industries.

The successful, however, were a minority. Most industrial jobs were unskilled, repetitive, and boring. Factory work did not vary with the seasons or the time of day but began and ended by the clock. Gas lighting expanded the working day past sunset (see Environment and Technology: Gas Lighting). Workdays were long, there were few breaks, and foremen watched constantly. Workers who performed one simple task over and over had little sense of achievement or connection to the final product. Industrial accidents were common and could ruin a family. Unlike the artisans they replaced, factory workers had no control over their tools, jobs, or working hours.

Industrial work had a major impact on women and family life. Women who could not afford servants had always worked, but mostly within the family: spinning and weaving, sewing hats and clothes, preparing food, washing, and doing a myriad other household chores. In rural areas, women also did farm work, especially caring for gardens and small animals.

Bibliotheque des Arts Decoratifs, Paris/Gianni Dagli Orti/The Art Archive

An Industrial Canal   In the late eighteenth and early nineteenth centuries, before railroads were introduced, many canals were constructed in England so that barges could transport heavy materials cheaply, such as coal for industrial works and steam engines, stone and bricks for buildings, clay for pottery works, and ores for metal foundries. Canals such as this one, which ran alongside a copper foundry, contributed greatly to Britain's industrial development.

In the early years of industrialization, even where factory work was available, it was never the main occupation of working women. Most young women who sought paid employment became domestic servants in spite of the low pay, drudgery, and risk of sexual abuse by male employers. Women with small children tried hard to find work they could do at home, such as laundry, sewing, embroidery, millinery, or taking in lodgers. Those who worked in factories were concentrated in textile mills, because textile work required less strength than metalworking, construction, or hauling. On average, women earned one-third to one-half as much as men. The economist Andrew Ure wrote in 1835: "It is in fact the constant aim and tendency of every improvement in machinery to supersede human labour altogether or to diminish its cost, by substituting the industry of women and children for that of men."[5] Young unmarried women worked to support themselves or to save for marriage. Married women took factory jobs when their husbands were unable to support the family. Mothers of infants faced a hard choice: whether to leave their babies with wet nurses at great expense or bring them to the factory and keep them drugged. Husbands and wives increasingly worked in different places.

As in preindustrial societies, parents thought children should contribute to their upkeep as soon as they were able to. The first generation of industrial workers brought children as young as five or six with them to the factories and mines, since there were no public schools or day-care centers. Employers preferred child workers because they were cheaper and more docile than adults and because they were better able to tie broken threads or crawl under machines to sweep

---

[5]Quoted in Joan W. Scott, "The Mechanization of Women's Work," *Scientific American* 247, no. 3 (September 1982): 171.

Gas Lighting

Before the nineteenth century, the night was a dangerous time to be out, and almost everyone went to bed at sundown and got up at dawn. For the managers of industrial establishments, daylight hours were too short, especially in the winter months. They knew that they could keep their factories running after sunset if they had light, but lanterns and candles were costly and dangerous. Wealthy people wanted to light up their homes, and businesses and government offices also needed light as well. While cities had sought to illuminate major thoroughfares since the eighteenth century, most city streets remained dark and dangerous. This situation inspired inventors to look for new ways to produce light.

The French engineer Philippe Lebon knew that heating wood to make charcoal produced a flammable gas. In the 1790s he channeled this gas through pipes to illuminate a home and garden. In Britain, the engineer William Murdock used the gas released in the process of making coke to light up a house. Moving from these experiments to commercial applications was a long and complicated process, however. Coal gas was smelly and explosive and full of impurities that gave off toxic fumes when it burned. Engineers had to learn ways to extract the gas efficiently, make strong pipes that did not leak, and market the product.

In 1806 Frederick Albert Winsor founded the National Light and Heat Company to produce and distribute gas in London. By 1816, London had 26 miles (42 kilometers) of gas mains bringing gas to several neighborhoods. That same year, Baltimore became the first American city to install gas mains and streetlamps. In the following decades, engineers developed ways of making gas safer and cleaner. They also invented meters to measure the amount of gas consumed and burners that produced a brighter light. As a result of these improvements, the cost of gas dropped to less than a third that of oil lamps of equivalent lighting power. From the 1840s until the early twentieth century, gaslights were installed in homes, businesses, and factories and along streets in the major cities of Europe and America.

The results were astonishing and delighted city dwellers. Mill and factory owners were able to extend the workday and increase production, while shops, restaurants, and other businesses were able to stay open late. Now people could now

walk the streets in greater safety. Evening illumination also contributed to the tremendous increase in adult education, as working people attended classes after work. Sales of books soared as increasing numbers of people stayed up late reading. Brightly lit cities attracted migrants from the still-dark countryside. Gas lighting had banished the terrors of the night.

Mary Evans Picture Library/The Image Works

Gas Lighting For city dwellers, one of the most dramatic improvements brought by industrialization was the introduction of gas lighting. The gas used, a byproduct of heating coal to make coke for the iron industry, was distributed in iron pipes throughout the wealthier neighborhoods of big cities. Every evening at dusk, lamplighters went around lighting the street lamps.

the dust. In Arkwright's cotton mills, for example, two-thirds of the workers were children. Mine operators used children to pull coal carts along the low passageways from the coal face to the mine shaft. Nearly all these children worked fourteen to sixteen hours a day and were beaten if they made mistakes or fell asleep. Some manufacturers tried to provide more humane environments. When Francis Cabot Lowell built a cotton mill in Massachusetts, he hired the unmarried daughters of New England farmers, promising them decent wages and housing in dormitories under careful moral supervision. Other manufacturers eager to combine profits with morality followed his example. But soon these early social experiments were overwhelmed by the profit motive, and manufacturers, especially in highly competitive industries, imposed longer hours, harsher working conditions, and lower wages. When young women in New England factories

From William Playfair, The Commercial and Political Atlas, 1801. Visual Connection Archive

"Love Conquers Fear" This is a sentimental Victorian drawing of children in a textile mill. Child labor was common in the first half of the nineteenth century, and workers were exposed to dangerous machines and moving belts, as well as to dust and dirt.

went on strike, the mill owners replaced them with impoverished Irish immigrants willing to accept lower pay and worse conditions.

The cotton boom enriched planters, merchants, and manufacturers and also reinforced and expanded the institution of slavery in the Americas. In the 1790s, there were 700,000 slaves of African descent in the United States. As the "Cotton Kingdom" expanded, the number of slaves increased, reaching 3.2 million by 1850, 60 percent located in the cotton region. While cotton profits soared, the lives of slaves grew more oppressive. Thousands of slave families were broken up by the internal slave trade that moved slaves from tobacco regions to the cotton frontier. At the same time, slave states also limited or outlawed manumissions, closing the door on slave families' hopes for freedom. Similarly, European demand for sugar prolonged plantation slavery in the West Indies and spread it to the coffee-growing regions of southern Brazil. Slavery was not, as white American southerners maintained, a "peculiar institution," a consequence of biological differences or biblical injunctions, but an integral part of both commercial capitalism and the Industrial Revolution.

Changes in Society

In his novel *Sybil*, or, *The Two Nations*, the British politician Benjamin Disraeli **(diz-RAY-lee)** (1804–1881) spoke of "two nations between whom there is no intercourse and no sympathy, who are as ignorant of each other's habits, thoughts, and feelings as if they were dwellers in different zones, or inhabitants of different planets . . . the rich and the poor."[6]

In Britain the worst-off were those who clung to an obsolete skill or craft. The high wages and low productivity of hand-loom weavers in the 1790s induced inventors to develop power looms. As a result, by 1811 handloom weavers' wages had fallen by a third; by 1832, by two-thirds. Even by working longer hours, they could not escape destitution. The standard of living of factory workers did not decline steadily like those of hand-loom weavers but fluctuated wildly.

During the war years of 1792 to 1815, the price of food, on which the poor spent most of their income, rose faster than wages, causing widespread hardship. Then, in the 1820s real wages and public health began to improve. Prices for food, housing, and clothing fell and wages rose. Even the poor could afford comfortable, washable cotton clothes and underwear. But hard times returned in the "hungry forties." In 1847–1848 the potato crop failed in Ireland. One-quarter of the Irish population died in the resulting famine, and another quarter emigrated to England and North America. As these desperate men and women entered the workforce, wages fell.

The real beneficiaries of the early Industrial Revolution were the middle class. In Britain landowning gentry and merchants had long shared wealth and influence. In the late eighteenth century a new group arose: entrepreneurs whose money came from manufacturing. Most, like Arkwright and Wedgwood, were the sons of middling shopkeepers, craftsmen, or farmers. Their enterprises were usually self-financed, for little capital was needed to start a cotton-spinning or machine-building business. A generation later, in the nineteenth century, some newly rich industrialists bought their way into high society. The same happened in western Europe and the United States after 1815.

Before the Industrial Revolution, wives of merchants had often participated in the family business, and widows occasionally managed sizable businesses on their own. With industrialization came a "cult of domesticity" to justify removing middle-class women from contact with

[6]J. P. T. Bury, *The New Cambridge Modern History*, vol. 10 (Cambridge: Cambridge University Press, 1967), 10.

SECTION REVIEW

- The Industrial Revolution changed people's lives and the environments in which they lived.

- Cities grew huge and, for most of their inhabitants, unsightly and unhealthy.

- Roads, canals, and railroads crisscrossed open land, changing rural environments.

- Middle-class women were consigned to caring for the home and children, while many working-class women had to earn their living in mines and factories.

- Serious social problems arose, such as unemployment, alcoholism, and the abandonment of children.

the business world. Instead, they became responsible for the home, the servants, the education of children, and the family's social life (see Chapter 27). Not all women accepted the change; in response Mary Wollstonecraft (1759–1797) wrote the first feminist manifesto, *Vindication of the Rights of Woman*, in 1792.

Middle-class people who attributed their success to their own efforts and virtues believed that if some people could succeed through hard work, thrift, and temperance, then those who did not succeed had no one but themselves to blame. Many workers, however, were newly arrived from rural districts and earned too little to save for the long stretches of unemployment they experienced. The moral position of the middle class mingled condemnation with concern, coupled with feelings of helplessness in the face of terrible social problems, such as drunkenness, prostitution, and child abandonment.

NEW ECONOMIC AND POLITICAL IDEAS

The profound changes unleashed by the Industrial Revolution triggered political ferment and ideological conflict. So many wars and revolutions took place during those years that we cannot neatly separate out the consequences of industrialization from the rest (see Chapter 23). But it is clear that by undermining social traditions and causing a growing gap between rich and poor, the Industrial Revolution strengthened the ideas of laissez faire **(LAY-say fair)** and socialism and sparked workers' protests.

Laissez Faire and Its Critics

laissez faire The idea that government should refrain from interfering in economic affairs. The classic exposition of laissez-faire principles is Adam Smith's *Wealth of Nations* (1776).

mercantilism European government policies of the sixteenth, seventeenth, and eighteenth centuries designed to promote overseas trade between a country and its colonies and accumulate precious metals by requiring colonies to trade only with their motherland country. The British system was defined by the Navigation Acts, the French system by laws known as the *Exclusif*.

The most celebrated exponent of **laissez faire** ("let them do") was Adam Smith (1723–1790), a Scottish economist. In *The Wealth of Nations* (1776) Smith argued that if individuals were allowed to seek personal gain, the effect, as though guided by an "invisible hand," would be to increase the general welfare. The government should refrain from interfering in business, except to protect private property; it should even allow duty-free trade with foreign countries. By advocating free-market capitalism, Smith was challenging the prevailing economic doctrine, **mercantilism**, which argued that governments should regulate trade in order to maximize their hoard of precious metals (Chapter 19).

Persuaded by Adam Smith's arguments, governments after 1815 dismantled many of their regulations, but no major power opened its economy to foreign competitors. Nonetheless, it was obvious that industrialization was causing widespread misery. Two other British thinkers, Thomas Malthus (1766–1834) and David Ricardo (1772–1832), attempted to explain the poverty they saw without challenging the basic premises of laissez faire. The cause of the workers' plight, they said, was the population boom, which outstripped the food supply and led to falling wages. The workers' poverty, they claimed, was as much a result of "natural law" as was the wealth of successful businessmen. For them the only way for the working class to avoid mass famine was to delay marriage and practice self-restraint and sexual abstinence.

Businesspeople in Britain eagerly adopted laissez-faire ideas that justified their activities and kept the government at bay. But not everyone accepted the grim conclusions of the "dismal science," as economics was then known. The British philosopher Jeremy Bentham (1748–1832) believed that it was possible to maximize "the greatest happiness of the greatest number," if only Parliament would study the social problems of the day and pass appropriate legislation. The German economist Friedrich List (1789–1846) rejected laissez faire and free trade as a British trick "to make the rest of the world, like the Hindus, its serfs in all industrial and commercial relations." To protect their "infant industries" from British competition, he argued, the German states had to erect high tariff barriers against imports from Britain. On the European continent, List's ideas helped lead to the formation of the Zollverein **(TSOLL-feh-rine)**, a customs union of most of the German states, in 1834.

positivism A philosophy developed by the French count of Saint-Simon. Positivists believed that social and economic problems could be solved by the application of the scientific method, leading to continuous progress. Their ideas became popular in France and Latin America in the nineteenth century.

French social thinkers, moved by sincere concern for the poor, offered a radically new vision of a just civilization. Espousing a philosophy called **positivism**, the count of Saint-Simon (1760–1825) and his disciple Auguste Comte (COMB-tuh) (1798–1857) argued that the scientific method could solve social as well as technical problems. They recommended that the poor, guided by scientists and artists, form workers' communities under the protection of benevolent business leaders. These ideas attracted the enthusiastic support of bankers and entrepreneurs, for whom positivism provided a rationale for investing in railroads, canals, and other symbols of modernity. Positivism was most influential in Latin America, where the political elites of Brazil and Mexico pursued a top-down program of economic development reinforced by harsh police controls and the manipulation of political institutions. Its chief tenets are emblazed on the Brazilian flag: Order and Progress.

As numerous protest organizations formed across Europe in the wake of the Industrial Revolution, a minority sought to overthrow the new industrial order. Groups calling themselves communists were the most prominent of these radical groups. Two German-born intellectuals, Karl Marx (1818–1883) and his long-time collaborator and benefactor Friedrich Engels (1820–1895), played key roles in formulating this movement's criticism of industrial capitalism. They argued that the concentration of wealth and power associated with industrialization had led to the unbearable oppression of industrial workers (what they called the **proletariat**) and justified revolution. While the monumental work *Das Kapital* (Capital) was Marx's major intellectual achievement, it was *The Communist Manifesto*, published in 1848 with Engels, that proved most influential in spreading his radical critique of capitalism and urging the mobilization of the working class. This short, powerful book argued that history was dominated by class struggle and that proletarians would inevitably come together to overthrow the bourgeoisie, the modern class that controlled industry. The book's final words were "Proletarians of all countries unite!"

proletariat The class of industrial wage earners who possess neither capital nor the tools of production. They, therefore, must earn their living by selling their labor.

Protests and Reforms

Workers benefited little from the ideas of these middle-class philosophers. Instead, they resisted harsh working conditions in their own ways. Periodically, they rioted or went on strike, especially when food prices were high or when downturns in the business cycle left many unemployed. In some places, craftsmen broke into factories and destroyed the machines that threatened their livelihoods. Such acts of resistance did little to change the nature of industrial work.

From the beginnings of the Industrial Revolution workers resisted the introduction of new technologies. They believed that mechanized production would diminish the value of their skills and force them into poverty. As early as 1767, disgruntled textile workers mobilized to destroy one of the first innovations, James Hargreaves' spinning jenny. Subsequent innovations in both the cotton and woolen industries were also attacked by angry crowds of workers. In 1779, for example, workers destroyed nearly every machine driven by waterpower in Blackburn, England. Then in 1811 angry workers in the lace and stocking industries began a campaign of systematic machine breaking. Calling themselves Luddites, they attacked more than one hundred businesses and destroyed nearly every machine in the district. Machine breaking in France was even more violent. As French entrepreneurs began introducing British industrial technologies in textiles and metallurgy in the late 1770s, workers organized protests against these "foreign" innovations, attacking British craftsmen and destroying the new machines. In the early stages of the French Revolution (see Chapter 23), popular revolutionary sentiment reinforced the resistance of workers to new machinery and undermined the ability of the government to protect factories. The result was that French artisans retained traditional control of production and France fell decades behind Britain in industrializing.

Mechanization was also resisted in rural areas. The effects of enclosure (described earlier in this chapter) and rural population growth combined to force many rural families in Great Britain into poverty. Thousands of tenants and small farmers lost their land, becoming seasonal labors or migrating to industrial cities. This impoverished class of rural workers rose up when wealthy farmers began to introduce reapers and other machines. Often called the "Captain Swing" riots, rural laborers organized against mechanization, setting fires, threatening landlords, demanding higher wages, and breaking machines. This popular movement culminated after 1830 when widespread rural riots forced the British government to mobilize troops and militia in defense of property. In the end, thousands of protestors were arrested and either imprisoned in Britain or transported to Australia as convict laborers.

These violent efforts to block innovation and protect long-established customs in manufacturing and agriculture were superseded by laboring class organizations focused on workplace

Captain Swing Riots When English landowners introduced reapers and other machines, rural laborers violently resisted by destroying the machines, setting fires, and sometimes attacking the owners and farm managers. The movement was finally repressed by county militias and troops.

reform, higher wages, and expanded political rights. Gradually, workers organized to demand universal male suffrage and shorter workdays. In 1834 Robert Owen founded the Grand National Consolidated Trade Union to lobby for an eight-hour workday; it quickly gained half a million members but collapsed a few months later in the face of government prosecution. A new movement called Chartism arose soon thereafter, led by William Lovett and Fergus O'Connor, that appealed to miners and industrial workers. It demanded universal male suffrage, the secret ballot, salaries for members of Parliament, and annual elections. Chartism collapsed in 1848, but it left a legacy of labor organizing (see Chapter 23). By 1850 the beginnings of the modern union movement were in place in Europe's most industrialized nations.

Eventually, mass movements persuaded the British Parliament to investigate conditions in factories and mines and initiate some reforms. The Factory Act of 1833 prohibited the employment of children younger than nine in textile mills. It also limited the working hours of children between the ages of nine and thirteen to eight hours a day and of fourteen- to eighteen-year-olds to twelve hours. The Mines Act of 1842 prohibited the employment of women and boys under age ten underground. Belgium and other European nations were slower to introduce workplace reforms. The British learned to seek reform through accommodation. On the European continent, in contrast, the revolutions of 1848 revealed widespread discontent with repressive governments but failed to soften the hardships of industrialization (see Chapter 27).

SECTION REVIEW

- Many people sought explanations and proposed solutions for the changes in society and the economy.

- Some economists defended the growing disparities between rich and poor in the name of laissez faire, the free-market idea proposed by Adam Smith that appealed to businesspeople.

- Positivists deplored the hardships caused by industrialization but asserted that they could be ameliorated by technological advances and wise policies.

- Agitation by workers led politicians to investigate the working conditions in mines and factories, especially the work of women and children.

THE LIMITS OF INDUSTRIALIZATION OUTSIDE THE WEST

Muhammad Ali Leader of Egyptian modernization in the early nineteenth century. He ruled Egypt as an Ottoman governor but had imperial ambitions. His descendants ruled Egypt until overthrown in 1952.

Egypt

The spread of the Industrial Revolution in the early nineteenth century transformed the relations of western Europe and North America with the rest of the world. Egypt, strongly influenced by European ideas since the French invasion of 1798, began to industrialize in the early nineteenth century. The driving force was its ruler, **Muhammad Ali** (1769–1849), a man who was to play a major role in the history of the Middle East and East Africa (see Chapters 24 and 26). Muhammad Ali wanted to build up the Egyptian economy and military in order to become less dependent on the Ottoman sultan, his nominal overlord. To do so, he imported advisers and technicians from Europe and built cotton mills, foundries, shipyards, weapons factories, and other industrial enterprises. To pay for all this, he made the peasants grow wheat and cotton, which the government bought at a low price and exported at a profit. He also imposed high tariffs on imported goods to force the pace of industrialization.

Muhammad Ali's efforts fell afoul of the British, who did not want a powerful country threatening to interrupt the flow of travelers and mail across Egypt, the shortest route between Europe and India. When Egypt went to war against the Ottoman Empire in 1839, Britain intervened and forced Muhammad Ali to eliminate all import duties in the name of free trade. Unprotected, Egypt's fledgling industries could not compete with the flood of cheap British products. Thereafter, Egypt exported raw cotton, imported manufactured goods, and became an economic dependency of Britain.

India

Until the late eighteenth century, India had been the world's largest producer and exporter of cotton textiles, handmade by skilled spinners and weavers. The British East India Company took over large parts of India just as the Industrial Revolution was beginning in Britain. It then allowed cheap British factory-made yarn and cloth to flood the Indian market duty-free, putting spinners and handloom weavers out of work. Unlike Britain, India had no factories to which displaced handicraft workers could turn for work and most of them became landless peasants, eking out a precarious living.

Like other tropical regions, India became an exporter of raw materials and an importer of British industrial goods. To hasten the process, British entrepreneurs and colonial officials introduced railroads into the subcontinent. The construction of India's railroad network began in the mid-1850s, along with coal mining to fuel the locomotives and the installation of telegraph lines to connect the major cities.

Some Indian entrepreneurs saw opportunities in the atmosphere of change that the British created. In 1854 the Bombay merchant Cowasjee Nanabhoy Davar imported an engineer, four skilled workers, and several textile machines from Britain and started India's first textile mill. This was the beginning of India's mechanized cotton industry. Despite many gifted entrepreneurs, however, India's industrialization proceeded at a snail's pace, for the government was in British hands and the British did nothing to encourage Indian industry.

China

In the eighteenth century the Chinese economy benefited from a long period of relative political stability and from population growth and commercial expansion. During the Qing dynasty,

A Railroad Bridge Across the Nile   In the second half of the nineteenth century, industrialized nations, especially Great Britain, sent engineers and equipment to build railroads in less industrialized parts of the world, such as India, South Africa, Latin America, and the Middle East. One such railway connected Cairo and Alexandria in Egypt. Here a railroad bridge crosses the Nile at Benha near the pyramids.   Corbis specialized market towns devoted to cotton textiles, silk, and staples developed in east-central China. At the same time, China developed markets in land and labor as well as rudimentary banking and credit mechanisms that facilitated long-distance trade. There were few direct threats to either Chinese borders or Chinese trade. This situation changed as European powers, first the Portuguese and Dutch and then the British and French, established highly militarized commercial presences in Asia. Nevertheless, even as European power grew, China continued to play a major role in the major markets of Asia, maintaining a favorable balance of trade with Europe that was financed by silver from European colonies.

China, however, remained an agrarian empire much less dependent on foreign trade than the major European powers, especially Great Britain. As a result, the Chinese government focused its attention and resources on the production and distribution of food, an effective guarantee of social peace, rather than on trade. While Britain and its European rivals viewed foreign trade as crucial to national well-being and as inherently competitive (see Chapter 17, Diversity and Dominance: Commercial Expansion and Risk), the Chinese government saw foreign trade as narrowly supplemental to the domestic economy.

With inexpensive and abundant labor, the absence of a true national market, and limited engagement in foreign markets, the Chinese government did not see a clear need to subsidize or promote technology transfers as new machine technologies rapidly transformed the European economy in the first half of the nineteenth century. This situation began to rapidly change when Great Britain, its military transformed by the Industrial Revolution, pressed to reverse the steep trade imbalance long enjoyed by China. Compelled now to recognize the economic and military transformations wrought by industrial innovation in Europe, China faced a succession of internal and foreign threats to stability before its own reforms could begin to take hold.

In January 1840 a shipyard in Britain launched a radically new ship. The *Nemesis* had an iron hull, a flat bottom that allowed it to navigate in shallow waters, and a steam engine to power it upriver and against the wind. In November it arrived off the coast of China, heavily armed. Though ships from Europe had been sailing to China for three hundred years, the *Nemesis* was the first steam-powered iron gunboat in Asian waters. It was soon joined by other steam-powered warships that collectively established European control of Chinese rivers, bombarding forts and cities and transporting troops and supplies far more quickly than Chinese soldiers could move on foot. With this new weapon, Britain, a small island nation half a world away, was able to defeat the largest and most populated country in the world (see Chapter 24). The cases of Egypt, India, and China show how the demands of Western nations and the military advantage they gained from industrialization led them to interfere in the internal affairs of nonindustrial societies. As we shall see in Chapter 27, this was the start of a new age of Western dominance.

SECTION REVIEW

- Industrialization gave the newly industrialized nations of the West the power to coerce non-Western societies.

- Britain snuffed out the incipient industrialization in Egypt and India and turned these countries intro producers of raw materials.

- China stagnated and was defeated by Britain and its steam-powered gunboats.

CONCLUSION

The Industrial Revolution was the most momentous transformation in history since the beginning of agriculture. The steam engine and other new machines greatly lowered the cost and increased the production of goods like cotton and iron, as well as increased the speed of transportation and communication.

The process caused social upheavals and environmental problems, however. Many entrepreneurs and businesspeople became very wealthy, while industrial workers—many of them children—worked under appalling conditions and lived in overcrowded tenements in badly polluted cities. Economists and philosophers proposed many theories and offered many solutions to the radical problems of industrial societies.

Industrialization had political consequences on a global scale. A small number of industrializing nations—first Great Britain, then those of western Europe and North America—grew more powerful. Other parts of the world were left behind to become political or economic dependencies of these powerful nations.

Eventually the industrial nations learned to alleviate their social problems, but the disparity between the rich and poor nations persisted for two centuries or more, and the environmental effects of industrialization have changed from local to global.

KEY TERMS

Industrial Revolution p. 549
agricultural revolution p. 550
mass production p. 554

Josiah Wedgwood p. 554
division of labor p. 554
mechanization p. 555
Richard Arkwright p. 556
Crystal Palace p. 558

steam engine p. 559
James Watt p. 559
electric telegraph p. 561
laissez faire p. 568
mercantilism p. 568

positivism p. 569
proletariat p. 569
Muhammad Ali p. 570

SUGGESTED READING

Allen, Robert C. *The British Industrial Revolution in Global Perspective*. 2009. Analysis of why the Industrial Revolution occurred first in Britain.

Goodman, J., and K. Honeyman. *Gainful Pursuits: The Making of Industrial Europe: 1600–1914*. 1988. Discusses industrialization outside of Britain.

Harris, J. R. *Industrial Espionage and Technology Transfer: Britain and France in the Eighteenth Century*. 1998. A very useful discussion of the ways that technology moved across political boundaries.

Henderson, W. O. *The Rise of German Industrial Power, 1834–1914*. 1976. An important discussion of the German case.

Horn, Jeff. *The Path Not Taken: French Industrialization in the Age of Revolution, 1750–1830*. 2006. A sensible and useful discussion of comparative industrialization.

Inkster, Ian. *Technology and Industrialization: Historical Case Studies and International Perspectives*. 1998. A global view of the Industrial Revolution.

Jeremy, David. *Artisans, Entrepreneurs, and Machines: Essays on the Early Anglo-American Textile Industry, 1770–1840*. 1998. Describes how American industry got started.

Landes, David. *The Unbound Prometheus: Technological Change and Industrial Development in Western Europe from 1750 to the Present*, 2d ed. 2003. A broad synthesis of modern industrial development.

McClellan, James, III, and Harold Dorn. *Science and Technology in World History*. 1999. Emphasizes the intersection of technology and science.

Meyer, David R. *The Roots of American Industrialization*. 2003. A valuable analysis of early American engagement with industrialization.

Mokyr, Joel. *The Gifts of Athena: Historical Origins of the Knowledge Economy*. 2002. Examines the role and institutional bases of knowledge in the growth of the modern industrial world.

Otter, Chris. *The Victorian Eye: A Political History of Light and Vision in Britain, 1800–1910*. 2008. An original and innovative examination of the intersection of technology and politics in the industrial age.

Pomeranz, Kenneth. *The Great Divergence: Europe, China, and the Making of the Modern World Economy*. 2000. An important work comparing China and Europe in the eighteenth century.

Stearns, Peter. *The Industrial Revolution in World History*, 3d ed. 2007. A broad discussion of industrialization as a global phenomenon.

Thorsheim, Peter. *Inventing Pollution: Coal, Smoke and Culture in Britain Since 1800*. 2006. A well-written and innovative discussion of the topic.

Wong, Roy Bin. *China Transformed: Historical Change and the Limits of European Experience*. 1997. An insightful and convincing examination of Chinese economic history.

Wrigley, E. A. *Energy and the English Industrial Revolution*. 2010. One of the most accessible and convincing discussions of the role of energy sources in the period.

CourseMate Go to the History CourseMate website for primary source links, study tools, and review materials for this chapter. www.cengagebrain.com

Chapter Outline

Prelude to Revolution: The Eighteenth-Century Crisis
➤ *How did the costs of imperial wars and the Enlightenment challenge the established authority of monarchs and religion in Europe and the American colonies?*

The American Revolution, 1775–1800
➤ *What were the direct causes of the American Revolution?*

The French Revolution, 1789–1815
➤ *What were the origins and accomplishments of the French Revolution?*

Revolution Spreads, Conservatives Respond, 1789–1850
➤ *How did revolution in one country help incite revolution elsewhere?*

Conclusion

- **ENVIRONMENT + TECHNOLOGY** The Guillotine
- **DIVERSITY + DOMINANCE** Robespierre and Wollstonecraft Defend and Explain the Terror

Burning of the town of Cap-Francais, Saint-Domingue (Haiti), 1795 (colour engraving), French School, (18th century)/Private Collection/ Archives Charmet/The Bridgeman Art Library

Burning of Cap Français, Saint Domingue, in 1793 In 1791, the slaves of Saint Domingue, France's richest colony, began a rebellion that, after years of struggle, ended slavery and created the Western Hemisphere's second independent nation, Haiti.

Revolutionary Changes in the Atlantic World, 1750–1850

In August 1791 slaves and free blacks began an insurrection in the plantation district of northern Saint Domingue (san doe-MANG) (present-day Haiti). During the following decade and a half, Haitian revolutionaries abolished slavery; defeated military forces from Britain and France; and achieved independence.

News and rumors about revolutionary events in France had helped move the island's slave community to rebel. These same events had divided the island's white population into royalists (supporters of France's King Louis XVI) and republicans (who sought an end to monarchy). The large free mixed-race population had secured some political rights from the French Assembly but was forced into rebellion by the violent resistance of the slave-owning elite to these reforms.

A black freedman, François Dominique Toussaint, led the insurrection. Taking the name Toussaint L'Ouverture (too-SAN loo-ver-CHORE), he became one of the most remarkable representatives of the revolutionary era. He organized the rebels militarily, negotiated with the island's competing factions and with representatives of Britain and France, and wrote his nation's first constitution. Commonly portrayed as a fiend by slave owners, Toussaint became a towering symbol of resistance to oppression to slaves everywhere.

The Haitian slave rebellion was an important event in the political and cultural transformation of the Western world. Profound changes to the economy, politics, and intellectual life occurred as well. The Industrial Revolution (see Chapter 22) increased manufacturing productivity and led to greater global interdependence, new patterns of consumerism, and altered social structures. At the same time, intellectuals questioned the traditional place of monarchy and religion in Western society. Enriched by the economic dynamism of this period, merchants, professionals, and manufacturers provided an audience for the new intellectual currents as they pressed for a larger political role.

This revolutionary era turned the Western world "upside down." The *ancien régime* (ahn-see-EN ray-ZHEEM), the French term for Europe's old order, rested on medieval principles: politics dominated by powerful monarchs, intellectual and cultural life dominated by religion, and economics dominated by hereditary agricultural elites. In the West's new order, commoners entered political life; science took the place of religion in intellectual life; and economies opened to competition.

This radical transformation did not take place without false starts or setbacks. Imperial powers resisted the loss of colonies; monarchs and nobles struggled to retain their ancient privileges; and church authorities fought against the claims of science. While the liberal and nationalist ideals of the eighteenth-century revolutionary movements were sometimes thwarted in Europe and the Americas, belief in national self-determination and universal suffrage and a passion for social justice continued to animate reformers into the twentieth century.

PRELUDE TO REVOLUTION: THE EIGHTEENTH-CENTURY CRISIS

The cost of wars fought among Europe's major powers over colonies and trade helped precipitate the revolutionary era that began in 1775 with the American Revolution. Britain, France, and Spain were the central actors in these global struggles, but other imperial powers participated as well. While these nations had previously fought unpopular and costly wars and paid for them with new taxes, changes in Western intellectual and political environments now produced a much more critical response. Any effort to extend monarchical power or impose new taxes now raised questions about the rights of individuals and the legitimacy of political institutions.

Colonial Wars and Fiscal Crises

In the seventeenth century competition among European powers became global in character. The newly independent Netherlands attacked the trade routes that linked Spain and Portugal to their American and Asian colonies, even seizing parts of Portugal's colonial empire in Brazil and Angola. Europe's other emerging sea power, Great Britain, also attacked Spanish fleets and seaports in the Americas. These rivalries made the defense of trade routes and distant colonies more expensive and difficult.

The eighteenth century further tested the ability of European powers to pay for their imperial ambitions. As Dutch power ebbed, Britain and France began a long struggle for political preeminence in western Europe and for territory and trade outlets in the Americas and Asia as the older empires of Spain and Portugal struggled to hang on. Nearly all of Europe's great powers participated in the War of the Spanish Succession (1701–1714). A few decades later war between Britain and Spain over smuggling broadened into a generalized European conflict, the War of Austrian Succession (1740–1748). Less than two decades later a frontier conflict between French and British forces and their Amerindian allies then led to a wider struggle, the Seven Years' War (1756–1763). With peace Britain emerged with undisputed control of North America east of the Mississippi River while France had been forced to surrender Canada and its holdings in India.

The enormous cost of these conflicts distinguished them from earlier wars. Traditional taxes collected in traditional ways no longer covered the obligations of governments. While Britain's total budget before the Seven Years' War had averaged only £8 million, in 1763 its war debt had reached £137 million and interest payments alone exceeded £5 million. Even as European economies expanded, fiscal crises overtook one European government after another. In an intellectual environment transformed by the Enlightenment, the need for new revenues provoked debate and confrontation within a vastly expanded and more critical public.

The Enlightenment and the Old Order

Enlightenment A philosophical movement in eighteenth-century Europe that fostered the belief that one could reform society by discovering rational laws that governed social behavior and were just as scientific as the laws of physics.

The complex and diverse intellectual movement called the **Enlightenment** applied the methods and questions of the Scientific Revolution of the seventeenth century to the study of human society as well as to the natural world (see Chapter 17). Some European intellectuals sought to systematize knowledge and organize reference materials. For example, the Swedish botanist Carolus Linnaeus (kar-ROLL-uhs lin-NEE-uhs) sought to categorize all living organisms, and Samuel Johnson published a comprehensive English dictionary. In France Denis Diderot (duh-nee DEE-duh-roe) worked with other thinkers to create a compendium of human knowledge, the thirty-five-volume *Encyclopédie*.

Other thinkers pursued lines of inquiry that more directly challenged long-established religious and political institutions. Some argued that if scientists could understand the laws of nature, then surely similar forms of disciplined investigation might reveal laws of human nature. The most radical wondered whether society and government could be better regulated and more productive if guided by science rather than by hereditary rulers and the church. These new perspectives and the intellectual optimism that fed them helped guide the revolutionary movements of the late eighteenth century.

The English political philosopher John Locke (1632–1704) argued in 1690 that governments were created to protect life, liberty, and property and that the people had a right to rebel when a monarch violated these natural rights. Locke's closely reasoned theory began with the assumption that individual rights were the foundation of civil government. In *The Social Contract*,

CHRONOLOGY

	The Americas	Europe
1750	1754–1763 French and Indian War 1770 Boston Massacre	1756–1763 Seven Years' War
1775	1776 American Declaration of Independence 1778 United States alliance with France 1781 British surrender at Yorktown 1783 Treaty of Paris ends American Revolution 1791 Slaves revolt in Saint Domingue (Haiti) 1798 Toussaint L'Ouverture defeats British in Haiti	1778 Death of Voltaire and Rousseau 1789 Storming of Bastille begins French Revolution; Declaration of the Rights of Man and the Citizen in France 1793–1794 Reign of Terror in France 1795–1799 The Directory rules France 1799 Napoleon overthrows the Directory
1800	1804 Haitians defeat French invasion and declare independence	1804 Napoleon crowns himself emperor 1814 Napoleon abdicates; Congress of Vienna opens 1815 Napoleon defeated at Waterloo 1830 Greece gains independence; revolution in France overthrows Charles X 1848 Revolutions in France, Austria, Germany, Hungary, and Italy

published in 1762, the French-Swiss intellectual Jean-Jacques Rousseau (zhan-zhock roo-SOE) (1712–1778) asserted that the will of the people was sacred and that the legitimacy of monarchs depended on the consent of the people. Although both men believed that government rested on the will of the people, Locke emphasized the importance of individual rights secured institutionally while Rousseau, much more distrustful of society and government, envisioned the people acting collectively as a result of their shared historical experience.

All Enlightenment thinkers were not radicals like Rousseau. There was never a uniform program for political and social reform, and the era's intellectuals often disagreed about principles and objectives. While the Enlightenment is commonly associated with hostility toward religion and monarchy, few intellectuals openly expressed republican or atheist sentiments. Even Voltaire, one of the Enlightenment's most critical intellects and great celebrities, believed that Europe's monarchs were likely agents of political and economic reform.

Indeed, sympathetic members of the nobility and reforming European monarchs such as Charles III of Spain (r. 1759–1788), Catherine the Great of Russia (r. 1762–1796), and Frederick the Great of Prussia (r. 1740–1786) actively sponsored and promoted the dissemination of new ideas, providing patronage for many intellectuals. They recognized that elements of the Enlightenment buttressed their own efforts to expand royal authority at the expense of religious institutions, the nobility, and regional autonomy. Goals such as the development of national bureaucracies staffed by civil servants selected on merit, the creation of national legal systems, and the modernization of tax systems united many of Europe's monarchs and intellectuals. Monarchs also understood that the era's passion for science and technology held the potential of fattening national treasuries and improving economic performance.

Though willing to embrace reform proposals when they served royal interests, Europe's monarchs moved quickly to suppress or ban radical ideas that promoted republicanism or directly attacked religion. However, too many channels of communication were open to permit a thoroughgoing suppression of ideas. In fact, censorship tended to enhance intellectual reputations, and persecuted intellectuals generally found patronage in the courts of foreign rivals.

Many of the major intellectuals of the Enlightenment corresponded with each other as well as with political leaders. This communication led to numerous firsthand contacts among the intellectuals of different nations and helped create a more coherent assault on what they saw as ignorance—beliefs and values associated with the ancien régime. Rousseau met the Scottish philosopher David Hume in Paris. Later, when Rousseau feared arrest, Hume helped him seek refuge in Britain. Similarly, Voltaire sought patronage and protection in England and later in Prussia when facing threats in France.

Women were instrumental in the dissemination of these new ideas. In England large numbers of educated middle-class women purchased and discussed books and pamphlets. Some, like Mary Wollstonecraft (see Diversity and Dominance: Robespierre and Wollstonecraft Defend and Explain the Terror), were important contributors to intellectual life as writers and commentators, raising by example and in argument the issue of the rights of women. In Paris wealthy women made their homes centers of debate, intellectual speculation, and free inquiry. Their salons brought together philosophers, social critics, artists, members of the aristocracy, and the commercial elite.

The intellectual ferment of the era deeply influenced the expanding middle class in Europe and the Western Hemisphere. Members of this class were eager consumers of books and inexpensive newspapers and journals, which were widely available. This broadening of the intellectual audience overwhelmed traditional institutions of censorship. New public venues like the thousands of coffeehouses and teashops of cities and market towns also became locations to discuss scientific discoveries, new technologies, and controversial works on human nature and politics, expanding the Enlightenment's influence beyond the literate minority.

Many European intellectuals were interested in the Americas. Some continued to dismiss the region as barbaric and inferior, but others used idealized accounts of the New World to support their critiques of European society. Many looked to Britain's North American colonies for confirmation of their belief that human nature unconstrained by the corrupted practices of Europe's old order would quickly produce material abundance and social justice. More than any other American, the writer and inventor **Benjamin Franklin** came to symbolize the vast potential of America to Europe's intellectuals.

Benjamin Franklin American intellectual, inventor, and politician who helped negotiate French support for the American Revolution.

Born in Boston in 1706, the young Franklin trained as a printer. In Philadelphia he succeeded in business and became famous for his *Poor Richard's Almanac*. At forty-two he retired to pursue writing, science, and public affairs. Franklin was instrumental in the creation of the Philadelphia Free Library, the American Philosophical Society, and the University of Pennsylvania. His contributions were both practical and theoretical. The inventor of bifocal glasses, the lightning rod, and an efficient wood-burning stove, he also contributed to scientific knowledge with publications like his 1751 paper, *Experiments and Observations on Electricity*, which won him acclaim from European intellectuals.

Franklin was also an important political figure. He served in many capacities in the colonies and was selected as a delegate to the Continental Congress that issued the Declaration of Independence in 1776. He later became ambassador to Paris, where his achievements, witty conversation, and careful self-promotion made him the symbol of the era. His life seemed to confirm the Enlightenment's most radical objective, the freeing of human potential from the effects of inherited privilege.

As Franklin demonstrates, the Western Hemisphere shared in Europe's intellectual ferment. As the Enlightenment penetrated the New World, intellectuals actively debated the legitimacy of colonialism itself. European efforts to reform colonial policies by unilaterally altering colonial institutions and overturning long-established political practices further radicalized colonial intellectuals. Among peoples compelled to accept the dependence and inferiority explicit in colonial rule, the idea that government authority rested on the consent of the governed proved explosive.

Many intellectuals resisted the Enlightenment, seeing it as a dangerous assault on the authority of the church and monarchy. This Counter Enlightenment was most influential in France and other Catholic nations. Its adherents emphasized the importance of faith to human happiness and social well-being. They also emphasized duty and obligation to the community of believers in opposition to the concern for individual rights and individual fulfillment common in the works of the Enlightenment. Most importantly for the politics of the era, they rejected their enemies' enthusiasm for change and utopianism, reminding their readers of human fallibility and the importance of history and tradition. While the central ideas of the Enlightenment gained strength across the nineteenth century, the Counter Enlightenment provided ideological support for the era's conservatism and later popular antidemocratic movements.

Folk Cultures and Popular Protest

While intellectuals and the reforming royal courts of Europe debated the rational and secular enthusiasms of the Enlightenment, most people in Western society remained loyal to competing cultural values grounded in the preindustrial past. Regional folk cultures were rooted in the memory of shared experience and nourished by religious practices that encouraged emotional release. These cultural traditions included coherent expressions of the rights and obligations

Beer Street (1751)   William Hogarth's engraving shows an idealized London street scene where beer drinking is associated with manly strength, good humor, and prosperity. The self-satisfied corpulent figure in the left foreground reads a copy of the king's speech to Parliament. We can imagine him offering a running commentary to his drinking companions as he reads.

The Art Archive

that connected people with their rulers. Authorities who violated these understandings were likely to face violent opposition.

In the eighteenth century, European monarchs sought to increase their authority and to centralize power by reforming tax collection, judicial practice, and public administration. Although monarchs viewed these changes as reforms, common people often saw them as violations of sacred customs and responded with bread riots, tax protests, and attacks on royal officials. These violent actions sought to preserve custom and precedent rather than overturn traditional authority. In Spain and the Spanish colonies, protesting mobs often expressed love for their monarch while at the same time assaulting his officials and preventing the implementation of reforms, shouting "Long Live the King! Death to Bad Government!"

Enlightenment-era reformers sought to bring order and discipline to the citizenry by banning or altering numerous popular traditions—such as harvest festivals, religious holidays, and country fairs—that enlivened the drudgery of everyday life. These events were popular celebrations of sexuality and individuality as well as opportunities for masked and costumed celebrants to mock the greed, pretension, and foolishness of government officials,

SECTION REVIEW

- Wars fought to protect colonies and trade routes overwhelmed the fiscal resources of European powers.

- European intellectuals applied the methods of scientific inquiry to political and cultural issues in the Enlightenment.

- In the Counter Enlightenment some intellectuals rejected attacks on tradition and religion.

- The effort to create uniform and rational administration provoked popular protest in defense of folk culture and tradition.

the wealthy, and the clergy. Hard drinking, gambling, and blood sports like cockfighting and bearbaiting were popular in preindustrial mass culture, but reformers viewed them as corrupt and decadent. As reforming governments undertook to substitute civic rituals, patriotic anniversaries, and institutions of self-improvement for older customs, they often provoked protests and riots.

The efforts of ordinary men and women to resist the growth of government power and the imposition of new cultural forms provide an important political undercurrent to much of the revolutionary agitation and conflict between 1750 and 1850. Spontaneous popular uprisings and protests punctuated nearly every effort at reform in the eighteenth century. But popular protest gained revolutionary potential only when it coincided with ideological division and conflict within the governing class.

THE AMERICAN REVOLUTION, 1775–1800

In British North America, clumsy efforts to increase colonial taxes to cover rising defense expenditures and to diminish the power of elected colonial legislatures outraged a populace accustomed to local autonomy. Once begun, the American Revolution ushered in a century-long process of political and cultural transformation in Europe and the Americas. By the end of this revolutionary century, constitutions had limited or overturned the authority of monarchs, and religion had lost its dominance of Western intellectual life. At the same time revolutionary changes in manufacturing and commerce replaced the long-established social order determined by birth with a new social ideal emphasizing competition and social mobility.

Frontiers and Taxes

After defeating the French in 1763, the British government faced two related problems in its North American colonies. As settlers pushed west into Amerindian lands, Britain feared the likelihood of renewed conflict and rising military expenses. Already burdened with heavy debts, Britain tried to limit settler pressure on Amerindian lands and get colonists to shoulder more of the costs of colonial defense and administration.

In the Great Lakes region the British tried to contain costs by reducing fur prices and by refusing to continue the French practice of giving gifts and paying rent for frontier forts to Amerindian peoples. But lower fur prices forced native peoples to hunt more aggressively, putting pressure on the environment and endangering some species. The situation got worse as settlers and white trappers pushed across the Appalachians to compete directly with native hunters. The predictable result was renewed violence along the frontier led by Pontiac, an Ottawa chief. His broad alliance of native peoples forged in 1763 drove the British military from some western outposts but was unable to take Fort Detroit. Failure led to disaffection among the Amerindian allies and finally to a peace treaty in 1766.

With the outbreak of this conflict the British government reacted by publishing the Proclamation of 1763. This policy established a western limit for settlement, thus undermining the claims of thousands of established farmers without effectively protecting Amerindian land. No one was satisfied. In 1774 Britain tried again to slow the movement of settlers onto Amerindian lands by annexing western territories to the province of Quebec. Like the 1763 proclamation, this action provoked bitter resentment in the colonies.

In comparison with the French, Spanish, and Portuguese colonies of the Americas, the settlers of the British colonies enjoyed substantial political autonomy, exercising effective local control through elected legislatures and courts. Even as slavery expanded in the southern colonies, free settlers prospered. One measure of this mounting, broadly distributed wealth was the rising tide of imported British consumer goods. While enriching metropolitan producers and merchants, colonial consumption of British cloth, porcelains, tea, and other imports also played a key role in forging a unified colonial culture that transcended regional economic, social, and even religious differences.

When the British government sought to assert greater political control and force the colonies to pay a much larger share of the costs of defense and governance in the wake of the French and Indian War, colonial settlers would use consumer boycotts to great effect. While frontier policies imposed following Pontiac's rebellion led to colonial hostility and suspicion, they did not lead to a breach. British fiscal reforms and new taxes, however, sparked a series of political confrontations that led to political mobilizations and popular protests across the colonies and, ultimately, to rebellion. For example, British regulations imposed in 1764 threatened New England's profitable trade with Spanish and French Caribbean sugar colonies and more effectively policed colonial smuggling. More disruptive still was Britain's outlawing of colonial issues of paper money, a custom made necessary by the colonies' chronic balance-of-payments deficits. Each of these measures met with the protests of colonial legislatures and popular assemblies.

The Stamp Act of 1765—a tax on all legal documents, newspapers, pamphlets, and nearly all printed material—caused especially deep resentment. Propertied colonists, including holders of high office and members of the colonial elite, assumed leading roles in protests and used fiery political language, identifying Britain's rulers as "parricides" and "tyrants" and suggesting that a dependence on British imports threatened traditional liberties. Women from prominent colonial families played a crucial role in organizing boycotts of British goods. For them and for poorer women as well, producing and wearing homespun textiles was increasingly seen as a patriotic obligation. Organizations such as the Sons of Liberty were more confrontational, holding public meetings, intimidating royal officials, and organizing committees to enforce the boycotts. Although this combination of protest and boycott forced the repeal of the Stamp Act, Britain imposed new taxes and duties in 1767. Parliament also sent British troops to quell colonial riots. While the boycotts against the Stamp Act were mostly confined to cities, these new taxes ignited protests across the colonies. Legislatures, town governments, and *ad hoc* committees mobilized the colonists to boycott British goods. One indignant woman expressed her anger to a British officer:

> [T]he most ignorant peasant knows . . . that no man has the right to take their money without their consent. The supposition is ridiculous and absurd, as none but highwaymen and robbers attempt it. Can you, my friend, reconcile it with your own good sense, that a body of men in Great Britain, who have little intercourse with America . . . shall invest themselves with a power to command our lives and properties [?][1]

British authorities reacted to boycotts and attacks on royal officials by threatening colonial liberties. They dissolved the colonial legislature of Massachusetts and sent two regiments of soldiers to re-establish control of Boston's streets. Popular support for a complete break with Britain grew after March 5, 1770, when British soldiers fired at an angry Boston crowd, killing five civilians. The "Boston Massacre" exposed the naked force on which colonial rule rested and radicalized public opinion throughout the colonies.

Parliament attempted to calm colonial opinion by repealing some taxes and duties, but it stumbled into another crisis when it granted the East India Company a monopoly to import tea to the colonies. This decision raised again the constitutional issue of Parliament's right to tax the colonies. It also provided the perfect target for colonial dissidents seeking to organize protest on a broad scale. Since tea was consumed by nearly everyone, its boycott would potentially unite nearly every class and region. In the heated language of protest, buying and drinking tea was acquiescing to British tyranny. The crisis came to a head when protesters dumped tea worth £10,000 (about £1.3 million or $1.9 million in 2012) into Boston harbor. As news of this act spread, tea was surrendered or, in some cases, seized and burned in innumerable towns and villages across the colonies. Britain responded by appointing a military man, Thomas Gage, as governor of Massachusetts and by closing the port of Boston. British troops now enforced public order in Boston, and public administration was in the hands of a general. This militarization of colonial government undermined Britain's constitutional authority and made rebellion inevitable.

The Course of Revolution, 1775–1783

In 1775 representatives from the colonies met in Philadelphia to discuss the situation. Most of the representatives elected to this Continental Congress had been active in the boycotts and protests of the previous decade, and they again used nonimportation as a political weapon. But events were moving quickly toward armed confrontation and revolution. Patriot militias had already fought British troops at Lexington and Concord, Massachusetts (see Map 23.1), and few thought compromise possible. The Congress now assumed the powers of government, created a currency, and organized an army led by **George Washington** (1732-1799), a Virginia planter who had served in the French and Indian War.

George Washington Military commander of the American Revolution. He was the first elected president of the United States (1789–1799).

---

[1]Quoted in Ray Raphael, *A People's History of the American Revolution* (New York: Perennial, 2001), 141.

The Tarring and Feathering of a British Official, 1774 British periodicals responded to the rising tide of colonial protest by focusing on mob violence and the breakdown of public order. This illustration portrayed the brutal treatment given John Malcomb, commissioner of customs at Boston. For many in Britain, colonial demands for liberty were little more than an excuse for mob violence.

Joseph Brant Mohawk leader who supported the British during the American Revolution.

The angry rhetoric of thousands of street-corner speakers and the inflammatory pamphlet *Common Sense*, written by Thomas Paine, a recent immigrant from England, propelled popular support for independence. On July 4, 1776, Congress approved the Declaration of Independence, the document that proved to be the most enduring statement of the revolutionary era's ideology:

> *We hold these truths to be self evident: That all men are created equal; that they are endowed by their creator with certain unalienable rights; that among these are life, liberty and the pursuit of happiness; that, to secure these rights, governments are instituted among men, deriving their just powers from the consent of the governed.*

The Declaration's affirmation of popular sovereignty and individual rights would influence the language of revolution and popular protest around the world.

Great Britain reacted by sending additional military forces to pacify the colonies. By 1778 Britain had 50,000 British troops and 30,000 German mercenaries in the colonies. Despite the existence of a large loyalist community, the British army found it difficult to control the countryside. Although British forces won most of the battles, Washington slowly built a competent Continental army as well as civilian support networks that provided supplies and financial resources.

The British government also tried to find a political compromise that would satisfy colonial grievances. Half-hearted efforts to resolve the conflict over taxes failed, and an offer to roll back the clock and re-establish the administrative arrangements of 1763 made little headway. Overconfidence in its military and poor leadership kept the British from finding a political solution before revolutionary institutions were in place and the armies engaged. By allowing confrontation to occur, the British government lost the opportunity to mobilize and give direction to the large numbers of loyalists and pacifists in the colonies.

Along the Canadian border, both sides solicited Amerindians as allies and feared them as potential enemies. For over a hundred years, members of the powerful Iroquois Confederacy—Mohawk, Oneida, Onondaga, Cayuga, Seneca, and (after 1722) Tuscarora—had protected their traditional lands with a combination of diplomacy and warfare. Just as the American Revolution forced settler families to join the rebels or remain loyal, it divided the Iroquois, who fought on both sides.

The Mohawk proved to be valuable British allies. Their loyalist leader **Joseph Brant** (Thayendanegea [ta-YEHN-dah-NEY-geh-ah]) organized Britain's most potent fighting force along the Canadian border. His raids along the northern frontier earned him the title "Monster" Brant, but he was actually a man who moved easily between European and Amerindian cultures. Educated by missionaries, he was fluent in English and helped translate Protestant religious tracts into Mohawk. He was friendly with many loyalist families and British officials and had traveled to London for an audience with George III (r. 1760–1820).

The defeat in late 1777 of Britain's general John Burgoyne by General Horatio Gates at Saratoga, New York, put the future of the Mohawk at risk. American forces followed this victory with destructive attacks on Iroquois villages that reduced their political and military power. After Britain's defeat, Brant and the Mohawk joined the loyalist exodus to Canada.

The British defeat at Saratoga also convinced France to enter the war as an ally of the United States in 1778. French military help proved crucial, supplying American forces and forcing the British to defend their colonies in the Caribbean. The French contribution was most clear in the final battle, fought at Yorktown, Virginia, in 1781 (see Map 23.1). With the American army

Fotosearch/Archive Photos/Getty Images

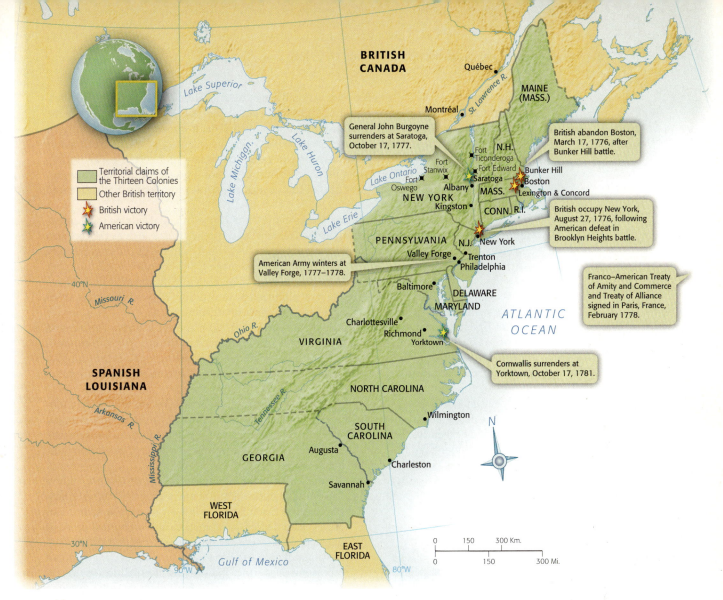

MAP 23.1 **The American Revolutionary War** The British army won most of the major battles, and British troops held most of the major cities. Even so, the American revolutionaries eventually won a comprehensive military and political victory. © Cengage Learning

supported by French soldiers and a French fleet, General Charles Cornwallis surrendered to Washington as the British military band played "The World Turned Upside-Down."

This victory effectively ended the war, and the Continental Congress sent representatives to the peace conference with instructions to work in tandem with the French. Believing that France was more concerned with containing British power than with guaranteeing a strong United States, America's peace delegation chose to negotiate directly with Britain and gained a generous settlement. The Treaty of Paris (1783) granted unconditional independence and established generous boundaries for the former colonies. In return the United States promised to repay prewar debts due to British merchants and to allow loyalists to recover property confiscated by patriot forces. In the end, loyalists were badly treated, and thousands left for Canada.

The Construction of Republican Institutions, to 1800

Even before the Declaration of Independence, many colonies had created new governments and summoned constitutional conventions to draft formal charters. Europeans were fascinated by the drafting of written constitutions and by their ratification by popular vote. Many early state constitutions were translated and published in Europe. Remembering colonial conflicts with royal governors, state constitutions placed severe limits on executive authority and granted broad powers to legislatures. Many also included bills of rights to provide further protection against tyranny.

It proved more difficult to frame a national constitution. The Second Continental Congress sent the Articles of Confederation—the first constitution of the United States—to the states for approval in 1777, but it was not accepted until 1781. It created a one-house legislature in which each state had a single vote. While a simple majority of the thirteen states was sufficient to pass minor legislation, nine votes were necessary for declaring war, imposing taxes, and coining or borrowing money. A committee, not a president, exercised executive power. Given the intended weakness of this government, it is remarkable that it defeated Great Britain.

Many of the most powerful political figures in the United States recognized that the Confederation was unable to enforce unpopular requirements of the peace treaty such as the recognition of loyalist property claims, the payment of prewar debts, and even the payment of military salaries and pensions due veterans. As a result, in September 1786 Virginia invited the other states to discuss the government's failure to deal with trade issues. This assembly called for a new convention to meet in Philadelphia. A rebellion led by Revolutionary War veterans in western Massachusetts gave the assembling delegates a sense of urgency.

Constitutional Convention
Meeting in 1787 of the elected representatives of the thirteen original states to write the Constitution of the United States.

The **Constitutional Convention**, which met in May 1787, achieved a nonviolent second American Revolution. The delegates pushed aside the announced purpose of the convention—"to render the constitution of the federal government adequate to the exigencies of the union"—and secretly undertook to write a new constitution with George Washington serving as presiding officer.

Debate focused on representation, electoral procedures, executive powers, and the relationship between the federal government and the states. The final compromise distributed political power among executive, legislative, and judicial branches and divided authority between the federal government and the states. The chief executive—the president—was to be elected indirectly by "electors" selected by ballot in the states.

Although this constitution created the most democratic government of the era, only a minority of the adult population had full political rights. While some northern states were hostile to slavery, southern leaders protected the institution. Slaves were denied participation in the political process, but slave states were permitted to count three-fifths of the slave population to allocate the number of congressional representatives, thus multiplying the political power of the slave-owning class. Southern delegates also gained a twenty-year continuation of the slave trade to 1808 and a fugitive slave clause that required all states to return runaway slaves to masters.

During the war, women had led prewar boycotts and organized relief and charitable organizations. Some had also served in the military as nurses, and a smaller number had joined the ranks disguised as men. Nevertheless, women were denied political rights in the new republic. Only New Jersey granted the vote to women and African Americans who met property requirements, and in 1807 state lawmakers eliminated this right.

SECTION REVIEW

- Britain tried to prevent new settlements on Amerindian lands and to limit the expense of frontier defense.

- New colonial tax and commercial policies provoked colonial protests and boycotts in North America.

- Armed conflict between British troops and colonists led to the calling of the Continental Congress and the Declaration of Independence.

- French support for the American Revolution proved crucial.

- The American states supported the creation of a new constitution that divided the powers of government.

THE FRENCH REVOLUTION, 1789–1815

The French Revolution undermined traditional monarchy and hereditary aristocracy as well as the power of the Catholic Church but, unlike the American Revolution, did not create enduring representative institutions. The colonial revolution in North America, however, did not confront so directly the entrenched privileges of an established church, monarchy, and aristocracy. Among its achievements, the French Revolution expanded mass participation in political life and radicalized the democratic tradition inherited from the English and American experiences. The political passions unleashed by revolutionary events in France also ultimately led to rule by popular demagogues and the dictatorship of Napoleon.

French Society and Fiscal Crisis

French society was divided in three estates. The clergy, called the First Estate, numbered about 130,000 in a nation of 28 million. The Catholic clergy was organized hierarchically, and priests from noble families held almost all top positions in the church. The church owned about 10 percent of the nation's land and extracted substantial amounts of wealth from the economy in the form of tithes and ecclesiastical fees, but it paid few taxes.

The 300,000 members of the nobility, the Second Estate, controlled about 30 percent of the land and retained ancient rights on much of the rest. Nobles held most high administrative, judicial, military, and church positions. Though barred from some types of commercial activity, nobles were important participants in wholesale trade, banking, manufacturing, and mining. Like the clergy, this estate was hierarchical: important differences in wealth, power, and outlook separated the higher from the lower nobility. In the eighteenth century many wealthy commoners who purchased administrative and judicial offices claimed noble status.

The Third Estate included everyone else, from wealthy financiers to beggars. The number of propertied and successful commoners grew rapidly in the eighteenth century. Commerce, finance, and manufacturing accounted for much of the wealth of the Third Estate. Wealthy commoners also owned nearly a third of the nation's land. This literate and socially ambitious group supported an expanding publishing industry, subsidized the fine arts, and purchased many of the extravagant new homes built in Paris and other cities.

Parisian Stocking Mender The poor lived very difficult lives. This woman uses a discarded wine barrel as a shop where she mends socks.

Artisans, shopkeepers, and small landowners owned property and lived decently when crops were good and prices stable, but by 1780 poor harvests had increased their cost of living and led to a decline in consumer demand for their products. They were rich enough to fear the loss of their property and status and well educated enough to be aware of the growing criticism of the king, but they lacked the means to influence policy.

Poverty was common. Among peasants, who accounted for 80 percent of the French population, family poverty and vulnerability forced young children to seek seasonal work and led many to crime and beggary. In Paris and other French cities the vile living conditions and unhealthy diet of the urban poor were startling to visitors from other European nations. City streets swarmed with beggars and prostitutes. The problem of child abandonment suggests the wretchedness of the French poor: on the eve of the French Revolution French parents gave up at least 40,000 children per year. Their belief that these children would be adopted was no more than a convenient fiction; in reality the majority died of neglect.

Unable to afford decent housing, obtain steady employment, or protect their children, the poor periodically erupted in violent protest and rage. In the countryside the decisions of the nobility or clergy to increase taxes and other burdens often led to violence. In towns and cities any increase in the price of bread could spark a riot, since bread prices determined the quality of life of the poor. These explosive episodes, however, were not revolutionary in character; rioters sought immediate relief rather than structural change. That was to change when the Crown tried to solve its fiscal crisis.

The cost of the War of the Austrian Succession (1740-1748) began the crisis. When Louis XV (r. 1715-1774) tried to impose new taxes on the nobility and other privileged groups, widespread protests erupted. New debt from the Seven Years' War deepened the crisis and compelled the king to impose emergency fiscal measures, but the Parlement of Paris, an appeal court, resisted these measures. Frustrated by these actions, French authorities exiled members of the Parlement and pushed through a series of unpopular fiscal measures.

When the twenty-two-year-old Louis XVI assumed the throne in 1774, he faced a desperate fiscal situation compounded by the growing opposition of French courts to new taxes. In 1774 his chief financial adviser warned that the government could barely afford to operate; as he put it, "the first gunshot [act of war] will drive the state to bankruptcy." Despite this warning, the king decided to support the American Revolution, delaying financial collapse by borrowing enormous sums and disguising the growing debt in misleading fiscal accounts. By the end of the war, more than half of France's national budget was required to pay the interest on its debt.

In 1787 the desperate king called an Assembly of Notables to approve a radical and comprehensive reform of economic and fiscal policy. Despite the fact that the king's advisers selected this assembly from the high nobility, the judiciary, and the clergy, these representatives of privilege proved unwilling to support the proposed reforms and new taxes.

Protest Turns to Revolution, 1789–1792

In frustration, the king dismissed the Notables and attempted to implement reforms on his own, but his effort was met by an increasingly hostile judiciary and by popular demonstrations. The refusal of the elite to grant needed tax concessions forced the king to call the **Estates General**, a customary consultative body representing the three estates that had not met since 1614. The narrow self-interest and greed of the rich—who would not tolerate an increase in their own taxes—rather than the grinding poverty of the common people had created the conditions for revolution.

In late 1788 and early 1789 members of the three estates came together throughout the nation to discuss grievances and elect representatives to meet at Versailles **(vuhr-SIGH)**. The Third Estate's representatives were mostly men of substantial property, but some were angry with the king's ministers and inclined to move France toward constitutional monarchy with an elected legislature. Many nobles and members of the clergy sympathized with the reform agenda of the Third Estate, but deep internal divisions over procedural and policy issues limited the power of the First and the Second Estates. Nevertheless, some clergy, and eventually nobles, joined the debates of the Third Estate, beginning a transition toward an assembly that could claim to represent the nation.

After six weeks of deadlock, the Third Estate, with allies from the other estates, signaled its ambitions by calling itself the National Assembly. Fearful of the growing assertiveness of these representatives, the king locked them out of their meeting place. They then moved to an indoor tennis court and pledged to write a constitution. The ascendant ideas of the era, that the people are sovereign and the legitimacy of rulers depends on their fulfilling the people's will, now swept away the king's narrow desire to solve the nation's fiscal crisis. Louis prepared for a confrontation with the National Assembly by moving military forces to Versailles. Before he could act, the people of Paris intervened.

A succession of bad harvests beginning in 1785 had propelled bread prices upward throughout France and provoked an economic depression as demand for nonessential goods collapsed. By the time the Estates General met, nearly a third of the Parisian workforce was unemployed. Hunger and anger marched hand in hand through working-class neighborhoods.

When the people of Paris heard that the king was massing troops in Versailles to arrest the representatives, crowds of common people began to seize arms and mobilize. On July 14, 1789, a crowd attacked the Bastille **(bass-TEEL)**, a medieval fortress used as a prison. The futile defense of the Bastille cost ninety-eight lives before its garrison surrendered. Enraged, the attackers hacked the commander to death and then paraded through the city with his head and that of Paris's chief magistrate stuck on pikes.

These events coincided with uprisings by peasants in the country. Peasants sacked manor houses and destroyed documents that recorded their traditional labor and tax obligations. They then refused to pay taxes and dues to landowners and seized common lands. Forced to recognize the fury raging through rural areas, the National Assembly voted to end traditional obligations and the privileges of the nobility and church, essentially ending the feudal system. Having won this victory, peasants ceased their revolt.

Estates General France's traditional national assembly with representatives of the three estates, or classes, in French society: the clergy, nobility, and commoners. The calling of the Estates General in 1789 led to the French Revolution.

Declaration of the Rights of Man and the Citizen Statement of fundamental political rights adopted by the French National Assembly at the beginning of the French Revolution.

These popular uprisings strengthened the hand of the National Assembly in its dealings with the king and led to passage of the **Declaration of the Rights of Man and the Citizen**, which stated the principles for a future constitution. Similarities between the language of this declaration and the U.S. Declaration of Independence resulted in part from the limited participation of Thomas Jefferson, author of the American document, who was U.S. ambassador to Paris. The French declaration, however, was more sweeping in its language. Among the enumerated natural rights were "liberty, property, security, and resistance to oppression." The Declaration of the Rights of Man and the Citizen also guaranteed free expression of ideas, equality before the law, and representative government.

While delegates debated political issues in Versailles, the economic crisis worsened in Paris. Women employed in the garment industry and small shopkeepers were particularly hard hit. Because the working women of Paris faced high food prices every day as they struggled to feed their families, their anger had a hard edge. Public markets became political arenas where the urban poor met daily in angry assembly. Here the revolutionary link between the material deprivation of the French poor and the political aspirations of the French bourgeoisie was forged.

On October 5, thousands of market women marched the 12 miles (19 kilometers) to Versailles and forced their way into the National Assembly, shouting "the point is that we want bread." The crowd then entered the royal apartments, killed some of the king's guards, and searched for Queen Marie Antoinette **(ann-twah-NET)**, whom they hated as a symbol of extravagance. They then forced the royal family to relocate to Paris.

With the king's ability to resist democratic change overcome by the Paris crowd, the National Assembly achieved a radically restructured French society in the next two years. A new constitution dramatically limited monarchial power and abolished the nobility as a hereditary class. Economic reforms swept away monopolies and trade barriers within France. Renamed the Legislative Assembly, legislators took on the church, seizing its lands to use as collateral for a new paper currency; they also mandated the election of priests and placed them on the public payroll. When the Assembly forced priests to take a loyalty oath, however, many Catholics joined a growing counterrevolutionary movement.

At first, many European monarchs welcomed the weakening of the French king, but by 1791 Austria and Prussia threatened to intervene in support of the monarchy. The Legislative Assembly responded by declaring war. Although the war went badly at first for French forces, people across France responded patriotically to foreign invasions, forming huge new volunteer armies and mobilizing national resources to meet the challenge.

Parisians Storm the Bastille An eyewitness to the storming of the Bastille on July 14, 1789, painted this representation of this epochal event, still celebrated by the French as a national holiday.

The Siege of the Bastille, 1789 (gouache on card), Cholat, Claude (18th-19th century) / Musee de Paris, Musee Carnavalet, Paris, France / Giraudon / The Bridgeman Art Library

The Terror, 1793–1794

In this period of national crisis and foreign threat, the French Revolution entered its most radical phase. A failed effort by the king and queen to escape from Paris cost the king his remaining popular support. On August 10, 1792, a crowd invaded his palace in Paris, forcing the king to seek protection in the Legislative Assembly, which suspended his authority and ordered his imprisonment. These actions helped lead to the formation of a new legislative and executive body, the National Convention. They also created a political environment where competing political factions used rumors of plots and conspiracies to justify the use of violence against their enemies.

Rumors of counterrevolutionary plots also kept working-class neighborhoods in an uproar, and in September a mob surged through the city's prisons, killing nearly half the prisoners. Swept along by popular passion and fear of conspiracy, the newly elected National Convention convicted Louis XVI of treason, sentenced him to death, and proclaimed France a republic. The guillotine ended the king's life in January 1793 (see Environment and Technology: The Guillotine). These events precipitated a wider war with nearly all of Europe's powers allied against France.

The National Convention—the new legislature of the French Republic—convened in September. Almost all its members were from the middle class, and nearly all were **Jacobins (JAK-uh-bin)**—the most uncompromising democrats. Deep political differences, however, separated moderate Jacobins—called "Girondists **(juh-RON-dist)**," after a region in southern France—and radicals known as "the Mountain." Members of the Mountain—so named because their seats were on the highest level in the assembly hall—were more sympathetic than the Girondists to the demands of the Parisian working class and less patient with parliamentary procedure. **Maximilien Robespierre (ROBES-pee-air)**, a young, little-known lawyer influenced by Rousseau's ideas, dominated the Mountain.

With the French economy in crisis and Paris suffering from inflation, high unemployment, and scarcity, Robespierre used the popular press and political clubs to forge an alliance with the volatile Parisian working class. His growing strength in the streets allowed him to purge and execute many of his enemies in the National Convention and to restructure the government. He placed executive power in the hands of the newly formed Committee of Public Safety, which created special courts to seek out and punish enemies of the Revolution.

Among the groups that lost influence were the active feminists of the Parisian middle class and the working-class women who had sought the right to bear arms in defense of the Revolution. These women had provided decisive leadership at crucial times, helping propel the Revolution toward widened suffrage and a more democratic structure. Armed women had actively participated in every confrontation with conservative forces. It is ironic that the National Convention—the revolutionary era's most radical legislative body—chose to repress the militant feminist forces that had prepared the ground for its creation.

Faced with rebellion in the provinces and foreign invasion, Robespierre and his allies unleashed a period of repression called the Reign of Terror (1793–1794) (see Diversity and Dominance: Robespierre and Wollstonecraft Defend and Explain the Terror). During the Terror, executions and deaths in prison claimed 40,000 lives while another 300,000 suffered imprisonment. In the Vendée region as many as 170,000 died as the government in Paris asserted control. One general stated, "I crushed the children under the feet of the horses, massacred the women who, at least for these, will not give birth to any more brigands. I do not have a prisoner to reproach me. I have exterminated all."[2]

The revolutionary government also took new actions against the clergy as well, including the provocative measure of forcing priests to marry. Even time was subject to revolutionary change. A new republican calendar created twelve 30-day months divided into 10-day weeks. Sunday, with its Christian meanings, was removed from this revolutionary calendar.

By spring 1794 the Revolution was secure from foreign and domestic enemies, but repression continued. Among the victims were some of Robespierre's closest political collaborators during the Terror. The execution of these former allies prepared the way for Robespierre's own fall by undermining the sense of invulnerability that had secured the loyalty of his remaining partisans. After French victories eliminated the immediate foreign threat in 1794, conservatives in the Convention voted to arrest Robespierre and then ordered his execution along with that of nearly a hundred of his allies in July.

Jacobins Radical republicans during the French Revolution. They were led by Maximilien Robespierre from 1793 to 1794.

Maximilien Robespierre Young provincial lawyer who led the most radical phases of the French Revolution. His execution ended the Reign of Terror.

---

[2]Quoted in David A. Bell, *The First Total War: Napoleon's Europe and the Birth of Warfare as We Know It* (Boston: Houghton Mifflin, 2007), 173.

mandate; the traitors who sell them; the mercenary pamphleteers hired to dishonor the people's cause, to kill public virtue, to stir up the fire of civil discord, and to prepare political counterrevolution by moral counterrevolution—are all those men less guilty or less dangerous than the tyrants whom they serve?

Mary Wollstonecraft, "An Historical and Moral View of the Origin and Progress of the French Revolution"

Weeping scarcely conscious that I weep, O France! Over the vestiges of thy former oppression, which, separating man from man with a fence of iron, sophisticated [complicated] all, and made many completely wretched; I tremble, lest I should meet some unfortunate being, fleeing from the despotism of licentious freedom, hearing the snap of the guillotine at his heels, merely because he was once noble, or has afforded an asylum to those whose only crime is their name—and, if my pen almost bound with eagerness to record the day that leveled the Bastille [an abbey used as a prison before the Revolution] with the dust, making the towers of despair tremble to their base, the recollection that still the abbey is appropriated to hold the victims of revenge and suspicion [she means that the Bastille remained a prison for those awaiting revolutionary justice]. . . .

Excuse for the Ferocity of the Parisians

The deprivation of natural, equal, civil, and political rights reduced the most cunning of the lower orders to practice fraud, and the rest to habits of stealing, audacious robberies, and murders. And why? Because the rich and poor were separated into bands of tyrants and slaves, and the retaliation of slaves is always terrible. In short, every sacred feeling, moral and divine, has been obliterated, and the dignity of man sullied, by a system of policy and jurisprudence as repugnant to reason as at variance with humanity.

The only excuse that can be made for the ferocity of the Parisians is then simply to observe that they had not any confidence in the laws, which they had always found to be merely cobwebs to catch small flies [the poor]. Accustomed to be punished themselves for every trifle, and often for only being in the way of the rich, or their parasites, when, in fact, had the Parisians

seen the execution of a noble, or priest, though convicted of crimes beyond the daring of vulgar minds? When justice, or the law, is so partial, the day of retribution will come with the red sky of vengeance, to confound the innocent with the guilty. The mob were barbarous beyond the tiger's cruelty. . . .

Let us cast our eyes over the history of man, and we shall scarcely find a page that is not tarnished by some foul deed or bloody transaction. Let us examine the catalogue of the vices of men in a savage state, and contrast them with those of men civilized; we shall find that a barbarian, considered as a moral being, is an angel, compared with the refined villain of artificial life. Let us investigate the causes which have produced this degeneracy, and we shall discover that they are those unjust plans of government which have been formed by peculiar circumstances in every part of the globe.

Then let us coolly and impartially contemplate the improvements which are gaining ground in the formation of principles of policy; and I flatter myself it will be allowed by every humane and considerate being that a political system more simple than has hitherto existed would effectually check those aspiring follies, which, by imitation, leading to vice, have banished from governments the very shadow of justice and magnanimity.

Thus had France grown up and sickened on the corruption of a state diseased . . . . it is only the philosophical eye, which looks into the nature and weighs the consequences of human actions, that will be able to discern the cause, which has produced so many dreadful effects.

QUESTIONS FOR ANALYSIS

1. Why does Robespierre believe that revolution cannot tolerate diversity of opinion? Are his reasons convincing?

2. How does Robespierre distinguish the terror of despots from the terror of liberty?

3. How does Wollstonecraft explain the "ferocity" of the Parisians?

4. What does Wollstonecraft believe will come from this period of violence?

Sources: Maximilien Robespierre, "On the Moral and Political Principles of Domestic Policy," February 5, 1794, *Modern History Sourcebook: Robespierre: Terror and Virtue*, 1794, http://www.fordham.edu/halsall/mod/robespierre-terror.html; Mary Wollstonecraft, "An Historical and Moral View of the Origin and Progress of the French Revolution," *A Mary Wollstonecraft Reader*, ed. Barbara H. Solomon and Paula S. Berggren (New York: New American Library, 1983), 374–375, 382–383.

the start of the modern democratic tradition, the military intervention that brought Napoleon to power in 1799 marked the advent of another modern form of government: popular authoritarianism.

The American and French Revolutions resulted in part from conflicts over representation. If the people were sovereign, what institutions best expressed popular will? In the United States the answer was the expansion of the right to vote and creation of representative institutions. The French Revolution took a different direction with the Reign of Terror. Interventions on the floor of the National Convention by market women and soldiers, the presence of common people at revolutionary tribunals and at public executions, and the expansion of military service were all forms of political communication that temporarily satisfied the French people's desire to influence their government. Napoleon tamed these forms of political expression to organize Europe's first popular dictatorship. He succeeded because his military reputation promised order to a society exhausted by a decade of crisis, turmoil, and bloodshed.

Napoleon sought to realize France's dream of dominating Europe while providing effective protection for persons and property at home. Negotiations with the Catholic Church led to the Concordat of 1801. This agreement gave French Catholics the right to freely practice their religion, but it also recognized the French government's authority to nominate bishops and retain priests on the state payroll. In his comprehensive rewriting of French law, the Civil Code of 1804, Napoleon won the support of the peasantry and the middle class by asserting two basic principles inherited from the moderate first stage of the French Revolution: equality in law and protection of property. Some members of the nobility were won over when Napoleon declared himself emperor and France an empire in 1804. Despite his willingness to make dramatic changes, however, Napoleon continued the denial of political rights for women begun during the Terror. The Civil Code denied women basic political rights and only allowed them to participate in the economy with the guidance and supervision of fathers and husbands.

While it re-established order, the Napoleonic system denied or restricted many individual rights. Free speech was limited. Criticism of the government, viewed as subversive, was proscribed, and most opposition newspapers disappeared. Spies and informers directed by the minister of police enforced these draconian policies.

Ultimately, the Napoleonic system depended on the success of French arms (see Map 23.2). From Napoleon's assumption of power until his fall, no single European state could defeat the French military. Austria and Prussia suffered humiliating defeats and became allies of France. Only Britain, protected by its powerful navy, remained able to thwart Napoleon's plans to dominate Europe.

Desiring to again extend French power to the Americas, Napoleon invaded Portugal in 1807 and Spain in 1808. Despite early French victories, Spanish and Portuguese patriots supported by Great Britain eventually tied French armies down in a costly conflict. Frustrated by events on the Iberian Peninsula and faced with a faltering economy, Napoleon made the fateful decision to invade Russia. In June 1812 he began his campaign with the largest army ever assembled in Europe, approximately 600,000 men. His army took Moscow but after five weeks abandoned the city. During the retreat, the brutal Russian winter and attacks by Russian forces destroyed Napoleon's army. A broken and battered remnant of 30,000 men made it back to France.

After the debacle in Russia, Austria and Prussia deserted Napoleon and entered an alliance with England and Russia against France. Unable to defend Paris, Napoleon abdicated the throne in April 1814 and was exiled to the island of Elba off the coast of Italy. The victorious allies then restored the French monarchy. The following year Napoleon escaped from Elba and returned to France, but an allied army defeated his forces in 1815 at Waterloo, in Belgium. His final exile was on the distant island of St. Helena in the South Atlantic, where he died in 1821.

SECTION REVIEW

- The heavy burden of debt, caused in part by support of the American Revolution, forced Louis XVI to call the Estates General.

- When some members of the nobility and clergy joined the rebellious Third Estate they formed the National Assembly.

- The hungry Parisian masses radicalized the movement for reform by storming the Bastille and forcing the king to move to Paris.

- The Legislative Assembly, led by Robespierre, executed the king and initiated the Terror.

- Exhausted by the violence of the Terror and threatened by foreign enemies, France turned to Napoleon Bonaparte, who dominated Europe until he was defeated in 1814.

REVOLUTION SPREADS, CONSERVATIVES RESPOND, 1789–1850

Even as the dictatorship of Napoleon tamed the democratic legacy of the French Revolution, revolutionary ideology was spreading and taking hold in Europe and the Americas. In Europe the French Revolution promoted nationalism and republicanism. In the Americas the legacies of the American and French Revolutions led to a new round of struggles for independence. News of revolutionary events in France destabilized the colonial regime in Saint Domingue (present-day

Haiti), a small French colony on the western half of the island of Hispaniola, and helped initiate the first successful slave rebellion. In Europe, however, the spread of revolutionary fervor was met by the concerted reaction of an alliance of conservative monarchs committed to extinguishing further revolutionary outbreaks.

The Haitian Revolution, 1789–1804

In 1789 the French colony of Saint Domingue was among the richest colonies in the Americas. Its production of sugar, cotton, indigo, and coffee accounted for two-thirds of France's tropical imports and generated nearly one-third of all French foreign trade. This wealth depended on a brutal slave regime. The harsh punishments and poor living conditions experienced by Saint Domingue's slaves were notorious throughout the Caribbean. The resulting high mortality and low fertility rates created an insatiable demand for African slaves. As a result, in 1790 the majority of the colony's 500,000 slaves were African-born.

When news of the meeting of the Estates General arrived on the island in 1789, wealthy planters sent a delegation to Paris to seek more home rule and greater economic freedom for Saint Domingue. The free mixed-race population, the *gens de couleur* (zhahn deh koo-LUHR), also sent representatives. Representing a large class of free black planters and urban merchants who owned slaves, they sought political rights and a limit to race discrimination, not an end to slavery. As the French Revolution became more radical, the gens de couleur forged an alliance with sympathetic French radicals, who saw the colony's wealthy planters as royalists and aristocrats.

The political turmoil in France weakened the authority of colonial administrators in Saint Domingue. In the vacuum that resulted, rich planters, poor whites, and the gens de couleur all pursued their narrow interests, engendering an increasingly bitter and confrontational struggle. Given the slaves' hatred of the brutal regime that oppressed them and the accumulated grievances of the free people of color, there was no way to limit the violence once the control of the slave owners slipped. When Vincent Ogé (oh-ZHAY), a leader of the gens de couleur mission to France, returned to Saint Domingue in 1790, the planters captured him and ordered his torture and execution. The free black and slave populations soon repaid this cruelty in kind.

By 1791 whites, led by the planter elite, and the gens de couleur were engaged in open warfare. This conflict was transformed when a slave rebellion began on the plantations of the north (see Map 23.3). Rebelling slaves destroyed plantations, killed masters and overseers, and

gens de couleur Free men and women of color in Haiti. They sought greater political rights and later supported the Haitian Revolution.

Haiti's Former Slaves Defend Their Freedom In this representation, a veteran army sent by Napoleon to reassert French control in Haiti battles with Haitian forces in a tropical forest. The combination of Haitian resistance and yellow fever defeated the French invasion.

Bettmann/Corbis

MAP 23.2 **Napoleon's Europe, 1810** By 1810 Great Britain was the only remaining European power at war with Napoleon. Because of the loss of the French fleet at the Battle of Trafalgar in 1805, Napoleon was unable to threaten Britain with invasion, and Britain was able to actively assist the resistance movements in Spain and Portugal, thereby helping weaken French power. © Cengage Learning

Legend

- French empire
- Dependent states
- Allied with Napoleon
- At war with Napoleon
- ⭐ Major battle

Scale
400 Mi.
400 Km.

GREAT BRITAIN
London

ATLANTIC OCEAN

North Sea

KINGDOM OF NORWAY AND DENMARK
Copenhagen

KINGDOM OF SWEDEN
Stockholm
St. Petersburg

Baltic Sea
SWEDISH POMERANIA

RUSSIAN EMPIRE
Moscow
Borodino 1812
Smolensk
Kiev

Tilsit
Friedland 1807
Königsberg
Danzig

PRUSSIA
Berlin

GRAND DUCHY OF WARSAW

SAXONY

WESTPHALIA
Hamburg
Bremen
Lübeck
Elbe R.
Rhine R.
Neman R.

Jena 1806
Auerstädt 1806

CONFEDERATION OF THE RHINE

BAVARIA
WÜRTTEMBERG
BADEN
Zurich
SWITZERLAND

Austerlitz 1805
Wagram 1804
Vienna
Pressburg
Buda
Pest
Danube R.

AUSTRIAN EMPIRE

ILLYRIAN PROVINCES

OTTOMAN EMPIRE
Constantinople

Black Sea

Athens

Ionian Is. (Gr. Br.)

Brussels
Waterloo 1815
Paris
Lunéville
Amiens

FRANCE

Marseilles

Milan
Marengo 1800
Genoa

KINGDOM OF ITALY

Corsica
Elba
Sardinia

Rome
Naples

KINGDOM OF NAPLES

Palermo
KINGDOM OF SICILY

Malta (Gr. Br.)

Mediterranean Sea

SPAIN
Madrid

PORTUGAL
Lisbon

Trafalgar 1805

GIBRALTAR (Gr. Br.)

MAP 23.3 **The Haitian Revolution** On their way to achieving an end to slavery and gaining national independence, the Haitian revolutionaries were forced to defeat British and French military interventions as well as the local authority of the slave masters. © Cengage Learning

François Dominique Toussaint L'Ouverture Leader of the Haitian Revolution. He freed the slaves and gained effective independence for Haiti despite military interventions by the British and French.

burned crops. A leadership emerged among the rebellious slaves that relied on elements of African political practice and revolutionary ideology from France to mobilize and direct their supporters. With the colony in flames, the French Assembly finally granted political rights to the gens de couleur in April 1792.

The rebellious slaves gained the upper hand under the command of **François Dominique Toussaint L'Ouverture**, a former domestic slave, who created a disciplined military force. While some French radicals had attacked the institution of slavery from the early days of the Revolution, the radical National Convention in Paris only abolished slavery in all French possessions in 1794. This was not narrowly the triumph of idealism over greed. With France at war with Britain and other European powers and Saint Domingue threatened by a British military force, the French government realized that its control of its colony could only be salvaged by acknowledging Toussaint's political and military dominance. Legitimized by the French government's decision, Toussaint swept aside his local rivals, defeated the British expeditionary force in 1798, and then led an invasion of the neighboring Spanish colony of Santo Domingo, freeing slaves there. While Toussaint asserted his loyalty to France, he gave the French government no effective role in local affairs.

As reaction overtook revolution in France, both the abolition of slavery and Toussaint's political position were threatened. When the Directory contemplated the re-establishment of slavery, Toussaint protested:

> *Do they think that men who have been able to enjoy the blessing of liberty will calmly see it snatched away? They supported their chains only so long as they did not know any condition of life more happy than slavery. But today when they have left it, if they had a thousand lives they would sacrifice them all rather than be forced into slavery again.*[3]

---

[3]Quoted in C. L. R. James, *The Black Jacobins*, 2d ed. (New York: Vintage Books, 1963), 196.

In 1802 Napoleon sent a large military force to re-establish both French colonial authority and slavery in Saint Domingue (see Map 23.3), as well as in Guadeloupe. At first French forces were successful, capturing Toussaint and sending him to France, where he died in prison. Eventually, however, the loss of thousands of lives to yellow fever and the resistance of the revolutionaries turned the tide. In 1804 Toussaint's successors declared independence, and the free republic of Haiti joined the United States as the second independent nation in the Western Hemisphere.

The Congress of Vienna and Conservative Retrenchment, 1815–1820

Congress of Vienna Meeting of representatives of European monarchs called to re-establish the old order after the defeat of Napoleon I.

In 1814–1815 representatives of Britain, Russia, Austria, Prussia, and other European nations met as the **Congress of Vienna** to re-establish political order in Europe. The French Revolution and Napoleon's imperial ambitions had threatened the survival of Europe's old order. The very existence of the nobility and church had seemed at risk at the height of the revolutionary era. Ancient monarchies had been overturned and dynasties had been replaced with interlopers, often relatives of Napoleon. International borders were redrawn or ignored, while long-established political institutions were threatened or overturned. Responding to more than two decades of revolution and war, the Austrian foreign minister, Prince Klemens von Metternich **(MET-uhr-nik)** (1773–1859), provided key leadership as the victorious allies sought to create a comprehensive peace settlement that would safeguard the conservative order.

The central objective of the Congress of Vienna was to create a strong and stable France as the best guarantee of future peace. To this end it re-established the French monarchy and recognized France's 1792 borders, although most of the allies received some territorial gains. Metternich believed that a strong and stable France had to be offset by a balance of power. Austria, Russia, and Prussia therefore formed a separate alliance to repress revolutionary and nationalist movements that sought to imitate the French Revolution. In 1820 this "Holy Alliance" used military force to defeat liberal revolutions in Spain and Italy. The Holy Alliance also attempted to blunt the force of revolutionary ideas by repressing republican and nationalist ideas in universities and the press.

Nationalism, Reform, and Revolution, 1821–1850

While Metternich's program of conservative retrenchment succeeded in the short term, the powerful ideas associated with liberalism and nationalism remained a vital part of European political life throughout the nineteenth century. Despite the power of the conservative monarchs, popular support for national self-determination and democratic reform grew throughout Europe.

Greece had been under Ottoman control since the fifteenth century. In 1821 Greek patriots launched an independence movement. While Metternich and other conservatives opposed Greek independence, European artists and writers enamored with the cultural legacy of ancient Greece rallied political support for intervention. After years of struggle, Russia, France, and Great Britain forced the Ottoman Empire to recognize Greek independence in 1830.

In 1814 the victorious allies placed Louis XVIII, brother of the executed Louis XVI, on the throne of France. Unlike his ancestors, he ruled as a constitutional monarch until his death in 1824, when his brother, the conservative Charles X, inherited the throne. In 1830 Charles decided to repudiate the constitution, provoking a mass uprising in Paris that forced him to abdicate. The crown then went to the king's cousin, Louis Philippe **(loo-EE fee-LEEP)** (r. 1830–1848), who agreed to accept the constitution and extended voting privileges.

Revolutionary violence in France made the British aristocracy and the conservative Tory Party fearful of democracy and mass movements of any kind. In 1815 the British government passed the Corn Laws, which limited the importation of foreign grains. The laws favored the profits of wealthy landowners who produced grain, rather than the poor who would now be forced to pay more for their bread. When poor consumers organized to overturn these laws, the government outlawed public meetings and used troops to crush protest in Manchester. Reacting against these policies, English reformers increased the power of the House of Commons, redistributed votes from agricultural to industrial districts, and increased the number of voters by nearly 50 percent. Although the most radical demands of reformers, called Chartists, were defeated, new labor and economic reforms addressing the grievances of workers were put in place (see Chapter 22).

Revolutions of 1848 Democratic and nationalist revolutions that swept across Europe. The monarchy in France was overthrown. In Germany, Austria, Italy, and Hungary the revolutions failed.

Despite the achievement of Greek independence and limited political reform in France and Great Britain, conservatives continued to hold the upper hand. In 1848 the desire for democratic reform and national self-determination led to upheavals across Europe. The **Revolutions of 1848** began in Paris, where members of the middle class and workers united to overthrow the regime of Louis Philippe and create the Second French Republic. Reformers gave adult men voting rights, abolished slavery in French colonies, ended the death penalty, and legislated the ten-hour workday. But Parisian workers' demands for programs to reduce unemployment and prices provoked conflicts with the middle class, which wanted to protect property rights. When workers rose up against the government, French troops crushed them. Desiring the re-establishment of order, the French elected Louis Napoleon, nephew of the former emperor, president in December 1848. Three years later, he overturned the constitution and, after ruling briefly as dictator, proclaimed himself Emperor Napoleon III.

In 1848 reformers in Hungary, Italy, Bohemia, and elsewhere pressed for greater national self-determination from the Austro-Hungarian Empire. When the monarchy did not meet their demands, students and workers in Vienna took to the streets to force political reforms similar to those sought in Paris. With revolution spreading throughout the empire, Metternich, the symbol of reaction, fled Vienna in disguise. Little lasting change occurred, however, because the new Austrian emperor, Franz Joseph (r. 1848–1916), used Russian military assistance and loyal Austrian troops to re-establish his authority.

Similarly, middle-class reformers and workers in Berlin joined forces to force the Prussian king to accept a liberal constitution and seek German unification. But the Constituent Assembly called to write a constitution and negotiate national integration was diverted to deal with diplomatic conflicts with Austria and Denmark. As a result, Frederick William IV (r. 1840–1861) reasserted his authority and thwarted constitutional reform and unification.

SECTION REVIEW

- The slaves of Saint Domingue, led by Toussaint L'Ouverture, overthrew slavery and gained independence.

- The Congress of Vienna and the Holy Alliance attempted to prevent new revolutionary outbreaks in Europe.

- Nationalism and the desire for democracy led to revolutions in 1830 and 1848, but most failed.

Despite their heroism on the barricades of Paris, Vienna, Rome, and Berlin, the revolutionaries of 1848 failed to gain their nationalist and republican objectives. Monarchs retained the support not only of aristocrats but also of professional militaries, largely recruited from among peasants who had little sympathy for urban workers. Revolutionary coalitions, in contrast, proved fragile, as when workers' demands for higher wages and labor reform drove their middle-class allies into the arms of the reactionaries.

The Revolution of 1830 in Belgium After the 1830 uprising that overturned the restored monarchy in France, Belgians rose up to declare their independence from Holland. In Poland and Italy, similar uprisings combining nationalism and a desire for self-governance failed. This painting by Baron Gustaf Wappers romantically illustrates the popular nature of the Belgian uprising by bringing to the barricades men, women, and children drawn from both the middle and the working classes.

Clément Philippe/Arterra Picture Library/Alamy

CONCLUSION

The last decades of the eighteenth century began a long period of revolutionary upheaval in the Atlantic world. Costly wars in Europe and along Europe's colonial frontiers in the Americas and Asia helped to provoke change, forcing European monarchs to impose new and unpopular taxes. The American Revolution initiated these transformations. Having defeated Britain, the citizens of this new American republic created the most democratic government of the time. While full rights were limited and slavery persisted, many Europeans saw this experiment as demonstrating the efficacy of the Enlightenment's most revolutionary political ideas. In the end, however, the compromises over slavery that had made a new Constitution possible in 1787 failed, and, as discussed in Chapter 25, the new nation nearly disintegrated after 1860.

The French Revolution led temporarily to a more radical formulation of representative democracy, but it also led to the Terror, which cost tens of thousands of lives, the militarization of western Europe, and a destructive cycle of wars. Yet, despite these terrible costs, the French Revolution propelled the idea of democracy and the ideal of equality far beyond the boundaries established by the American Revolution. The Haitian Revolution, set in motion by events in France, not only created the second independent nation of the Western Hemisphere but also delivered a powerful blow to the institution of slavery. In Europe the excesses of the French Revolution and the wars that followed in its wake promoted the political ascent of Napoleon Bonaparte and democracy's modern nemesis, popular authoritarianism.

Each revolution had its own character. The revolutions in France and Haiti proved to be more violent and destructive than the American Revolution. American revolutionaries defeated Great Britain and established independence without overturning a colonial social and political order that depended on slavery in most of the southern colonies. Revolutionaries in France and Haiti faced more strongly entrenched and more powerful oppositions as well as greater social inequalities than American revolutionaries. The resistance of entrenched and privileged elites led inexorably to greater violence. Both French and Haitian revolutionaries also faced powerful foreign interventions that intensified the bloodshed and destructiveness of these revolutions.

The conservative retrenchment that followed the defeat of Napoleon succeeded in the short term. Monarchy, multinational empires, and the established church retained the loyalty of millions of Europeans and could count on the support of many of Europe's wealthiest and most powerful individuals. But liberalism and nationalism continued to stir revolutionary sentiment. The contest between adherents of the old order and partisans of change was to continue well into the nineteenth century. In the end, the nation-state, the Enlightenment legacy of rational inquiry, broadened political participation, and secular intellectual culture prevailed. This outcome was determined in large measure by the old order's inability to satisfy the demands of new social classes tied to an emerging industrial economy. The narrow confines of a hereditary social system could not contain the material transformations generated by industrial capitalism, and the doctrines of traditional religion could not contain the rapid expansion of scientific learning.

These revolutions began the transformation of Western society, but they did not complete it. Only a minority gained full political rights. Women did not achieve full political rights until the twentieth century. Democratic institutions, as in revolutionary France, often failed. Moreover, as Chapter 25 discusses, slavery endured in the Americas past the mid-1800s, despite the revolutionary era's enthusiasm for individual liberty.

KEY TERMS

Enlightenment p. 576
Benjamin Franklin p. 578
George Washington
  p. 581
Joseph Brant p. 582

Constitutional
  Convention p. 584
Estates General p. 586
Declaration of the Rights of
  Man and the Citizen p. 587

Jacobins p. 588
Maximilien
  Robespierre p. 588
Napoleon Bonaparte p. 590
gens de couleur p. 593

François Dominique
  Toussaint
  L'Ouverture p. 595
Congress of Vienna p. 596
Revolutions of 1848 p. 597

SUGGESTED READING

Andress, David. *The Terror: The Merciless War for Freedom in Revolutionary France.* 2006. A recent summary of this era.

Bell, David A. *The Cult of the Nation in France: Inventing Nationalism, 1680—1800.* 2001. Traces prerevolutionary roots of modern nationalism in France.

_____. *The First Total War: Napoleon's Europe and the Birth of Warfare as We Know It.* 2008. Explores the Enlightenment-era intellectual origins of revolutionary total war.

Craveri, Benedetta. *The Age of Conversation.* 2005. Illuminates the culture of the French aristocracy prior to the French Revolution.

Damrosch, Leo. *Jean-Jacques Rousseau.* 2005. The best biography of Rousseau.

Dubois, Laurent. *A Colony of Citizens.* 2004. Connects the revolutions in France and Haiti to create a single struggle for liberty and citizenship.

Dwyer, Phillip. *Napoleon: The Path to Power.* 2008. A reliable and convincing modern biography.

Fenton, William N. *The Great Law and the Long-house: A Political History of the Iroquois Confederacy.* 1998. An essential study of this powerful indigenous alliance.

Fitzsimmons, Michael. *The Night the Old Regime Ended: August 14, 1789, and the French Revolution.* 1998.

Geggus, David. *Haitian Revolutionary Studies.* 2002. A collection of essays by the revolution's key historian.

_____, ed. *The World of the Haitian Revolution (Blacks in the Diaspora).* 2009. A collection of essays on the revolution and its influence in the Americas.

Godineau, Dominique. *The Women of Paris and Their French Revolution.* 1998. An essential introduction to this topic.

Goldstone, Lawrence. *Dark Bargain: Slavery, Profits and the Struggle for the Constitution.* 2005.

Hesse, Carla. *The Other Enlightenment: How French Women Became Modern.* 2001. Demonstrates that women intellectuals were not marginalized after 1790.

Holtman, Robert B. *The Napoleonic Revolution.* 1967. Provides a reliable summary of the period.

Hunt, Lynn. *The Family Romance of the French Revolution.* 1992. Examines the gender content of revolutionary politics.

Israel, Jonathon. *A Revolution of the Mind: Radical Enlightenment and the Intellectual Origins of Modern Democracy.* 2009. Key synthesis of the Enlightenment's role in the development of the West.

James, C. L. R. *The Black Jacobins,* 2d ed. 1963. The classic study of the Haitian Revolution.

Lefebvre, Georges. *The Coming of the French Revolution.* Trans. R. R. Palmer. 1947. A classic class-based analysis.

McMahon, Darrin M. *Enemies of the Enlightenment, The French Counter-Enlightenment and the Making of Modernity.* 2001. A helpful discussion of the Counter Enlightenment.

Norton, Mary Beth. *Liberty's Daughters: The Revolutionary Experience of American Women, 1750–1800.* 1980. Studies the role of women in the revolutionary era.

Rudé, George. *The Crowd in History: Popular Disturbances in France and England.* 1981. The best introduction to the role of mass protest in the revolutionary period.

Stearns, Peter, and Herrick Chapman. *European Society in Upheaval.* 1991. A valuable summary of events.

Taylor, Alan. *The Divided Ground. Indians, Settlers, and the Northern Borderland of the American Revolution.* 2006. The best analysis of the topic.

Taylor, Barbara. *Eve and the New Jerusalem: Socialism and Feminism in the Nineteenth Century.* 1983. Analyzes connections between workers' and women's rights issues in England.

Te Brake, Wayne. *Shaping History: Ordinary People in European Politics, 1500–1700.* 1998. Discusses the "underside" of this era and the importance of "folk culture."

Will, Gary. *Inventing America, Jefferson's Declaration of Independence.* 1978. An essential inquiry into this pivotal moment.

Wood, Gordon S. *Revolutionary Characters. What Made the Founders Different.* 2006. A convincing exploration of this crucial generation.

CourseMate Go to the History CourseMate website for primary source links, study tools, and review materials for this chapter. www.cengagebrain.com

Chapter Outline

The Ottoman Empire
➤ *What were the benefits and the drawbacks to the Ottoman Empire of the reforms adopted during the Tanzimat period?*

The Russian Empire
➤ *How did the Russian Empire maintain its status as both a European power and a great Asian land empire?*

The Qing Empire
➤ *How did the impact of European imperialism on China differ from its impact on Russia and the Ottoman Empire?*

Conclusion

● **ENVIRONMENT + TECHNOLOGY** The Web of War

● **DIVERSITY + DOMINANCE** Chinese Responses to Imperialism

Trade Warehouse in Guangzhou   A European merchant enters in the background while Chinese workers pack tea and porcelain.

Peabody Essex Museum, Salem, Massachusetts/The Bridgeman Art Library

Land Empires in the Age of Imperialism, 1800–1870

During the late 1860s, a little-known warlord named Yaqub Beg unified several Muslim uprisings in Central Asia against a foreign occupier, the Qing Empire. Only a hundred years earlier, in 1759, Qing armies had successfully conquered a vast region of Central Asia and called it Xinjiang, meaning "new territory." Despite attempts to work with local leaders, tensions between locals and Chinese never eased, and the natives rebelled.

Yaqub took full diplomatic advantage of the empires surrounding him. To his south lay India, under control of an expanding British Empire. To his north was the Russian Empire, Britain's rival in the quest to gain territory in Central Asia. Yaqub sent emissaries to both empires in 1868 and signed commercial treaties in 1872 in exchange for their recognition of his rule over Xinjiang. He even received military support from the distant Ottoman Empire, whose ruler bestowed upon him the title *Commander of the Faithful*. For a time it seemed that the Qing might not try to retake Xinjiang. It would be an expensive venture for a government that was looking to spend money modernizing its army and navy. But fears that Russia might take over neighboring Mongolia drove the Chinese back into Xinjiang, and Yaqub's regime collapsed in 1877.

Yaqub's story illustrates the challenges facing Eurasian empires as they overextended themselves. The largest problem, common to all the land-based empires of Eurasia, was the old and inefficient ways of governing that put states at risk. While the international climate was increasingly dominated by industrializing European economies drawing on the wealth of their overseas colonies, during the early 1800s rapid population growth and slow agricultural growth affected much of Eurasia. In addition, earlier military expansion had stretched the resources of imperial treasuries (see Chapter 21), leaving the land-based empires vulnerable to European military pressure. Responses to this pressure varied, with reform and adaptation gaining headway in some lands and tradition being reasserted in others. In the long run, attempts to meet western Europe's economic and political demands produced financial indebtedness to France, Britain, and other Western powers.

This chapter contrasts the experiences of the Qing Empire with those of the Russian and Ottoman Empires. Whereas the Qing opted for resistance, the others made varying attempts to adapt and reform. Russia eventually became part of Europe and shared in many aspects of European culture, while the Ottomans and the Qing became subject to ever-greater imperialist pressure. These different responses raise the question of the role of culture in shaping western Europe's relations with the rest of the world in the nineteenth century.

THE OTTOMAN EMPIRE

During the eighteenth century the central government of the Ottoman Empire lost much of its power to provincial governors, military commanders, ethnic leaders, and bandit chiefs. In several parts of the empire local officials and large landholders tried to increase their independence and divert imperial funds into their own coffers.

A kingdom in Arabia led by the Saud family, following the puritanical and fundamentalist religious views of an eighteenth-century leader named Muhammad ibn Abd al-Wahhab (moo-HAH-muhd ib-uhn ab-dahl-wa-HAHB), took control of the holy cities of Mecca and Medina and deprived the sultan of the honor of organizing the annual pilgrimage. Meanwhile, in Egypt factions of mamluk slave-soldiers purchased as boys in Georgia and nearby parts of the Caucasus and educated for war reasserted their influence. Such soldiers had ruled Egypt between 1260 and 1517, when they were defeated by the Ottomans. Now Ottoman weakness allowed mamluk factions based on a revival of the slave-soldier tradition to re-emerge as local military forces.

For the sultans, the outlook was bleak. At the end of the eighteenth century, the inefficient Janissary corps used the political power it enjoyed in Istanbul to force Sultan Selim III to abandon efforts to train a modern, European-style army. This situation unexpectedly changed when France invaded Egypt.

Egypt and the Napoleonic Example

Napoleon Bonaparte and an invasion force of 36,000 men and four hundred ships invaded Egypt in May 1798. The French quickly defeated the mamluk forces that for several decades had dominated the country under the loose jurisdiction of the Ottoman sultan in Istanbul. Fifteen months later, after being stopped by Ottoman land and British naval forces in an attempted invasion of Syria, Napoleon secretly left Cairo and returned to France. Three months later he seized power and made himself emperor.

Back in Egypt, his generals tried to administer a country that they only poorly understood. Cut off from France by British ships in the Mediterranean, they had little hope of remaining in power and agreed to withdraw in 1801. For the second time in three years, a collapse of military power produced a power vacuum in Egypt. The winner of the ensuing contest was **Muhammad Ali** (moo-HAM-mad AH-lee), the commander of a contingent of Albanian soldiers sent by the sultan to restore imperial control. By 1805 he had taken the place of the official Ottoman governor, and by 1811 he had dispossessed the mamluks of their lands and privileges.

Muhammad Ali's rise to power coincided with the meteoric career of Emperor Napoleon I. It is not surprising, therefore, that he adopted many French practices in rebuilding the Egyptian state. Militarily, he established special schools for training artillery and cavalry officers, army surgeons, military bandmasters, and others. The curricula of these schools featured European skills and sciences, and Muhammad Ali began to send promising officer trainees to France for education. In 1824 he started a gazette devoted to official affairs, the first newspaper in the Islamic world.

As discussed in Chapter 22, Muhammad Ali built all sorts of factories to outfit his new army. These did not prove efficient enough to survive, but they showed a determination to achieve independence and parity with the European powers.

In the 1830s Muhammad Ali's son Ibrahim invaded Syria and instituted some of the changes already under way in Egypt. The improved quality of the new Egyptian army had been proven during the Greek war of independence (see below), when Ibrahim had commanded an expeditionary force to help the sultan. In response, the sultan embarked on building his own new army in 1826. The two armies met when Ibrahim attacked northward into Anatolia in 1839 and defeated the army of his suzerain, the Ottoman sultan. The road to Istanbul seemed open until the European powers intervened and forced a withdrawal to the present-day border between Egypt and Israel.

Muhammad Ali remained Egypt's ruler, under the suzerainty of the sultan, until his death in 1849; and his family continued to rule the country until 1952. But his dream of making Egypt a mighty country capable of standing up to Europe faded. What survived was the example he had set for the sultans in Istanbul.

Muhammad Ali Leader of Egyptian modernization in the early nineteenth century. He ruled Egypt as an Ottoman governor but had imperial ambitions. His descendants ruled Egypt until overthrown in 1952.

CHRONOLOGY

	Ottoman Empire	Russian Empire	Qing Empire
1800			1794–1804 White Lotus Rebellion
	1805–1849 Muhammad Ali governs Egypt	1801–1825 Reign of Alexander I	
	1808–1839 Rule of Mahmud II		
		1812 Napoleon's retreat from Moscow	
		1825 Decembrist revolt	
		1825–1855 Reign of Nicholas I	
	1826 Janissary corps dissolved		
	1830 Greek independence		
	1839 Abdul Mejid begins Tanzimat reforms		1839–1842 Opium War
1850			1850–1864 Taiping Rebellion
	1853–1856 Crimean War	1853–1856 Crimean War	
		1855–1881 Reign of Alexander II	1856–1860 Arrow War
		1861 Emancipation of the serfs	
	1876 First constitution by an Islamic government		1877 Collapse of Yaqub Beg's revolt in Xinjiang

Ottoman Reform and the European Model, 1807–1853

At the end of the eighteenth century Sultan Selim (seh-LEEM) III (r. 1789–1807), a forward-looking ruler who stayed abreast of events in Europe, introduced reforms to create European-style military units, bring provincial governors under central government control, and standardize taxation. The rise in government expenditures to implement the reforms was supposed to be offset by taxes on selected items, primarily tobacco and coffee.

The reforms failed for political more than economic reasons. The most violent and persistent opposition came from the **Janissary** (JAN-nih-say-ree) military corps (see Chapter 20). In the eighteenth century the Janissaries became a significant political force in Istanbul and in provincial capitals like Damascus and Aleppo. Their interest in preserving special economic privileges made them resist the creation of new military units.

At times, Janissary power produced military uprisings. In the Ottoman territory of **Serbia**, local residents intensely resented the control exercised by Janissary governors. The Orthodox Christians claimed that the Janissaries abused them. In response, Selim threatened to reassign the Janissaries to Istanbul. Suspecting that the sultan wanted to curb their political power, in 1805 the Janissaries revolted and massacred Christians in Serbia. Unable to re-establish central Ottoman rule over Serbia, the sultan had to rely on the ruler of Bosnia, another Balkan province, who joined his troops with the peasants of Serbia to suppress the Janissary uprising. The threat of Russian intervention prevented the Ottomans from disarming the victorious Serbians, so Serbia became effectively independent.

Other opponents of reform included ulama, or Muslim religious scholars, who distrusted the secularization of law and taxation that Selim proposed. In the face of widespread rejection of his reforms, Selim suspended his program in 1806. Nevertheless, a massive military uprising occurred at Istanbul, and the sultan was deposed and imprisoned. Reform forces recaptured the capital, but not before Selim had been executed. Selim's cousin, Sultan Mahmud (mah-MOOD) II (r. 1808–1839), cautiously revived Selim's program, but he realized that reforms needed to be more systematic and imposed more forcefully. The effectiveness of radical reform in Muhammad Ali's Egypt drove this lesson home, as did the insurrection in Greece, during which the Egyptian military performed much better than the main Ottoman army.

Greek independence in 1830 had dramatic international significance. A combination of Greek nationalist organizations and interlopers from Albania formed the independence movement. Europe's interest in the classical age of Greece and Rome led many Europeans to consider the Greeks' struggle for independence a campaign to recapture their classical glory from Muslim oppression. Some—including the "mad, bad and dangerous to know" English poet Lord Byron, who lost his life in the war—went to Greece to fight as volunteers. When the combined squadrons of the British, French, and Russian fleets, under orders to observe but not intervene

Janissaries Infantry, originally of slave origin, armed with firearms and constituting the elite of the Ottoman army from the fifteenth century until the corps was abolished in 1826.

Serbia The Ottoman province in the Balkans that rose up against Janissary control in the early 1800s. After World War II the central province of Yugoslavia. Serb leaders struggled to maintain dominance as the Yugoslav federation dissolved in the 1990s.

MAP 24.1 **The Ottoman and Russian Empires, 1829–1914** At its height the Ottoman Empire controlled most of the perimeter of the Mediterranean Sea. But in the 1800s Ottoman territory shrank as many countries gained their independence. The Black Sea, where the Turkish coast was vulnerable to assault, became a weak spot as Russian naval power grew. Russian challenges to the Ottomans at the eastern end of the Black Sea and to the Persians east and west of the Caspian aroused fears in Europe that Russia was trying to reach the Indian Ocean. © Cengage Learning

**Legend (map):**

The Ottoman Empire
- Territory lost, 1829–1877
- Territory lost, 1878–1913
- Ottoman Empire in 1914

The Russian Empire
- Russia in 1802
- Territory gained, by 1914

- Persia

in the war, made an unauthorized attack that sank the Ottoman fleet at the Battle of Navarino, Greek victory was assured (see Map 24.1).

Mahmud II concurred with the pro-Greek Europeans in viewing Ottoman military reversals in Greece as a sign of profound weakness. With popular outrage over the military setbacks strong, the sultan made his move in 1826. First he announced the creation of a new artillery unit, which he had secretly been training. When the Janissaries rose in revolt, he ordered the new unit to bombard the Janissary barracks. The Janissary corps was officially dissolved.

Like Muhammad Ali, Mahmud felt he could not implement major changes without reducing the political power of the religious elite. He visualized restructuring the bureaucracy and the educational and legal systems, where ulama power was strongest. Before such strong measures could be undertaken, however, Ibrahim attacked from Syria in 1839. Battlefield defeat, the decision of the rebuilt Ottoman navy to switch sides and support Egypt, and the death of Mahmud, all in the same year, left the empire completely dependent on the European powers for survival.

Mahmud's reforming ideas received their widest expression in the **Tanzimat** (TAHNZ-ee-MAT) ("reorganization"), a series of reforms announced by his sixteen-year-old son and successor, Abdul Mejid (ab-dul meh-JEED), in 1839 and strongly endorsed by the European ambassadors. One proclamation called for public trials and equal protection under the law for all, whether Muslim, Christian, or Jew. It also guaranteed some rights of privacy, equalized the eligibility of men for conscription into the army (a practice copied from Egypt), and provided for a new, formalized method of tax collection that legally ended tax farming in the Ottoman Empire. It took many years and strenuous efforts by reforming bureaucrats, known as the "men of the Tanzimat," to give substance to these reforms.

Tanzimat Restructuring reforms by the nineteenth-century Ottoman rulers, intended to move civil law away from the control of religious elites and make the military and the bureaucracy more efficient.

Over time, one legal code after another—commercial, criminal, civil procedure—was introduced to take the place of the corresponding areas of religious legal jurisdiction. All the codes were modeled closely on those of Europe. The Shari'a, or Islamic law, gradually became restricted to matters of family law such as marriage and inheritance. As the Shari'a was displaced, job opportunities for the ulama shrank.

European observers praised the reforms for their noble principles and rejection of religious influence. Ottoman citizens were more divided; the Christians and Jews, for whom the Europeans showed the greatest concern, were generally more enthusiastic than the Muslims. Many historians see the Tanzimat as the dawn of modern thought and enlightened government in the Middle East. Others point out that removing the religious elite from influence in government also removed the one remaining check on authoritarian rule.

Like Muhammad Ali, Sultan Mahmud sent military cadets to France and the German states for training. In the 1830s an Ottoman imperial school of military sciences, later to become Istanbul University, was established in which instructors from western Europe taught chemistry, engineering, mathematics, and physics in addition to military history. Military education became the model for more general educational reforms. In 1838 the first medical school was established to train army doctors and surgeons. Later, a national system of preparatory schools was created to feed graduates into the military schools. The subjects that were taught and many of the teachers were foreign, raising the issue of whether Turkish should be a language of instruction. Because it was easier to import and use foreign textbooks than to write new ones in Turkish, French became the preferred language in all advanced professional and scientific training. In numerical terms, however, the great majority of students still learned to read and write in Quran schools down to the twentieth century.

In the capital city of Istanbul, the reforms stimulated the growth of a small but cosmopolitan milieu embracing European language and culture. The first Turkish newspaper, a government gazette modeled on that of Muhammad Ali, appeared in 1831. Other newspapers followed, many written in French. Travel to Europe—particularly to England and France—became popular among wealthy Turks. Interest in importing European military, industrial, and communications technology remained strong through the 1800s.

Changes in military practice had unforeseen cultural and social effects. Accepting the European notion that modern weapons and drill required modern military dress, beards were deemed unhygienic and, in artillery units, a fire hazard. Military headgear also became controversial. European military caps, which had leather bills on the front to protect against the glare of the sun,

Modernized Ottoman Troops This photograph of a contingent of Imperial Guards in the late nineteenth century shows them equipped and uniformed much like any other European army of the time. The only distinctive feature is the fez, a brimless hat adopted earlier in the century as a symbol of reform. Comparison with the soldiers in the funeral procession of Suleiman the Magnificent (page 498) shows the degree of change from the traditional military uniforms that were still being worn in the eighteenth century.

From one of the original photographic albums of Sultan Abdul Hamid II, 1842–1918/Library of Congress

were not acceptable because they interfered with Muslim soldiers' touching their foreheads to the ground in prayer. The compromise was the brimless cap now called the *fez*, which was adopted by the military and then by Ottoman civil officials in the early years of Mahmud II's reign.

The empire's new orientation spread beyond the military. Government ministries that normally recruited from traditional bureaucratic families and relied on on-the-job training were gradually transformed into formal civil services hiring men educated in the new schools. Among self-consciously progressive men, particularly those in government service, European dress became the fashion in the Ottoman cities of the later 1800s, while traditional dress became a symbol of the religious, the rural, and the parochial.

Secularization of the legal code particularly affected non-Muslim Ottoman subjects. Islamic law had required non-Muslims to pay a special head tax that was sometimes explained as a substitute for military service. Under the Tanzimat, the tax was abolished and non-Muslims became liable for military service—unless they bought their way out by paying a new military exemption tax. The new law codes gave all male subjects equal access to the civil courts, while the operations of the Islamic law courts shrank. What enhanced the status of non-Muslims most, however, was the strong concern for their welfare consistently expressed by the European powers. The Ottoman Empire became a rich field of operation for Christian missionaries and European supporters of Jewish community life in the Muslim world.

The public rights and political participation granted during the Tanzimat applied specifically to men. Private life, including everything connected to marriage and divorce, remained within the sphere of religious law, and at no time was there a question of political participation or reformed education for women. Indeed, the reforms may have decreased the influence of women. The political changes ran parallel to economic changes that also narrowed women's opportunities.

After silver from the Americas began to flood the empire in the 1600s, workers were increasingly paid in cash rather than in goods, and businesses associated with banking and finance developed. But women were barred from the early industrial labor and the professions, and traditional "woman's work" such as weaving was increasingly mechanized and done by men.

From Ignatius Mouradgea d'Ohsson, *Tableau General de l'Empire Ottoman*, large folio edition, Paris, 1787–1820, pl. 178, following p. 340

Interior of the Ottoman Financial Bureau This engraving from the eighteenth century depicts the governing style of the Ottoman Empire before the era of westernizing reforms. By the end of the Tanzimat period in 1876, government offices and the costumes of officials looked much more like those in contemporary European capitals.

From Edward William Lane, *The Manners and Customs of the Modern Egyptians* (London: J. M. D & Co. 1860)

Street Scene in Cairo This engraving from Edward William Lane's influential travel book, *Account of the Manners and Customs of the Modern Egyptians Written in Egypt During the Years 1833–1835* conveys the image of narrow lanes and small stores that became stock features of European thinking about Middle Eastern cities.

Crimean War Conflict between the Russian and Ottoman Empires fought primarily in the Crimean Peninsula. To prevent Russian expansion, Britain and France sent troops to support the Ottomans.

Nevertheless, in the early 1800s women retained considerable power in the management and disposal of their own property, gained mostly through fixed shares of inheritance. After marriage a woman was often pressured to convert her landholdings to cash in order to transfer her personal wealth to her husband's family, with whom she and her husband would reside. However, this was not a requirement, since men were legally obligated to support their families single-handedly. Until the 1820s many wealthy women retained their say in the distribution of property through the creation of charitable trusts for their offspring. Because these trusts were set up in the religious courts, they could be designed to conform to the wishes of family members. Then, in the 1820s and 1830s the secularizing reforms of Mahmud II, which did not always produce happy results, transferred jurisdiction over the charitable trusts from religious courts to the state and ended women's control over this form of property.

The Crimean War and Its Aftermath

Since the reign of Peter the Great (r. 1689–1725), the Russian Empire had been attempting to expand southward at the Ottomans' expense (see the section on Russia and Asia). His successor, Catherine the Great (r. 1762–1796), had captured control of the north shore of the Black Sea by 1783, and by 1815 Russia had pried the Georgian region of the Caucasus away from the Ottomans. Moreover, the threat of Russian intervention had prevented the Ottomans from crushing Serbian independence. When Muhammad Ali's Egyptian army invaded Syria in 1833, Russia signed a treaty in support of the Ottomans. In return, the sultan recognized Russia's claim to being the protector of all of the empire's Orthodox subjects. This set the stage for an obscure dispute that resulted in war.

Bowing to British and French pressure, the sultan named France Protector of the Holy Sepulchre in Jerusalem in 1852. Russia protested, but the sultan held firm. So Russia invaded Ottoman territories in what is today Romania, and Britain and France went to war as allies of the sultan. The real causes of the war went beyond church quarrels in Jerusalem and involved diplomatic maneuvering among European powers over whether the Ottoman Empire should continue to exist and, if not, who should take over its territory. The *Eastern Question* was the simple name given to this complex issue. Though the powers, including Russia, had agreed to save the empire in 1839, Britain subsequently became suspicious of Russian ambitions. Prominent anti-Russian politicians in Britain feared that Russia would threaten the British hold on India.

Between 1853 and 1856 the **Crimean (cry-ME-uhn) War** raged in Romania, on the Black Sea, and on the Crimean peninsula. Britain, France, and the Italian kingdom of Sardinia-Piedmont sided with the Ottomans. Britain and France trapped the Russian fleet in the Black Sea, where its commanders decided to sink the ships to protect the approaches to Sevastopol, their main base in Crimea. However, an army largely made up of British and French troops landed and laid siege to the city. Official corruption and lack of railways hampered the Russians' attempts to supply their forces. On the Romanian front, the Ottomans resisted effectively. At Sevastopol, the Russians were outmatched militarily and suffered badly from disease. Tsar Nicholas died as defeat loomed, leaving his successor, Alexander II (r. 1855–1881), to sue for peace when Sevastopol finally fell three months later.

The Crimean War brought significant changes to all the combatants. The tsar and his government, already beset by demands for the reform of serfdom, education, and the military (discussed later), were further discredited. In Britain and France, the conflict was accompanied by massive propaganda campaigns. For the first time newspapers effectively mobilized public support for a war. British press accounts so glamorized British participation that the false impression has lingered that Ottoman troops played a negligible role in the conflict. At the time, however, British and French commanders noted the massive losses among Turkish troops in particular. The French press, dominant in Istanbul, promoted a sense of unity between Turkish and French society that continued to influence many aspects of Turkish urban culture.

The larger significance of the Crimean War was that it marked the transition from traditional to modern warfare (see Environment and Technology: The Web of War). All the combatants had previously prided themselves on the use of highly trained cavalry to smash through the front lines of infantry. Cavalry coexisted with firearms until the early 1800s, primarily because early rifles were awkward to load and not very accurate. Cavalry could attack during the intervals between volleys. Then in the 1830s and 1840s percussion caps that did away with pouring gunpowder into the barrel of a musket came into use. In Crimean War battles many cavalry units were destroyed by the rapid fire of rifles that loaded at the breech rather than down the barrel. That was the fate of the famed British Light Brigade, which was sent to relieve an Ottoman unit surrounded by Russian troops.

After the Crimean War, the Ottoman Empire increased its involvement with European commerce. The Ottoman imperial bank was founded in 1840, and a few years later currency reform pegged the value of Ottoman gold coins to the British pound. Sweeping changes in the 1850s expedited the creation of banks, insurance companies, and legal firms throughout the empire. Bustling trade also encouraged a migration from country to city between about 1850 and 1880. Many of the major cities of the empire—Istanbul, Damascus, Beirut, Alexandria, Cairo—expanded. A small but influential urban professional class emerged, as did a considerable class of wage laborers. Other demographic shifts involved refugees from Poland and Hungary, where rivalry between the European powers and the Russian Empire caused political tension and sporadic warfare, and from Georgia and other parts of the Caucasus, where Russian expansion forced many Muslims to emigrate (discussed later).

However, commercial vigor and urbanization could not make up for declining revenues and the chronic insolvency and corruption of the imperial government. From the conclusion of the Crimean War in 1856 on, the Ottoman government became heavily dependent on foreign loans. In return it lowered tariffs to favor European imports and allowed European banks to open in Ottoman cities. Europeans living in Istanbul and other commercial centers enjoyed **extraterritoriality**, the right to be subject to their own laws and exempt from Ottoman jurisdiction.

As the result of these measures, imported goods multiplied, but—apart from tobacco and the Turkish opium that American traders took to China to compete against British opium from India—Anatolia produced few exports. As foreign debt grew, so did inflationary trends that left urban populations in a precarious position. By contrast, Egyptian cotton exports soared during the American Civil War, when American cotton exports plummeted; but the profits benefited Muhammad Ali's descendants, who had become the hereditary governors of Egypt, rather than the Ottoman government. The Suez Canal, which was partly financed by cotton profits, opened in 1869, and Cairo was redesigned and beautified. Eventually overexpenditure on such projects plunged Egypt into the same debt crisis that plagued the empire as a whole.

The decline of Ottoman power and prosperity had a strong impact on a group of well-educated young urban men who aspired to wealth and influence. They doubted that the empire's rulers and the Tanzimat officials who worked for them would ever stand up to European domination. Though lacking a sophisticated organization, these Young Ottomans (sometimes called Young Turks, though that term properly applies to a later movement) promoted a mixture of liberal ideas derived from Europe, national pride in Ottoman independence, and modernist views of Islam. Prominent Young Ottomans helped draft a constitution that was promulgated in 1876 by a new and as yet untried sultan, Abdul Hamid II. This apparent triumph of liberal reform was short-lived. With war against Russia again threatening in the Balkans in 1877, Abdul Hamid suspended the constitution and the parliament that had been elected that year. Though he ruthlessly opposed further political reforms, the Tanzimat programs of extending modern schooling, utilizing European military practices and advisers, and making the government bureaucracy more orderly continued during his reign.

extraterritoriality The right of foreign residents in a country to live under the laws of their native country and disregard the laws of the host country. In the nineteenth and early twentieth centuries, European and American nationals living in certain areas of Chinese and Ottoman cities were granted this right.

SECTION REVIEW

- After French withdrawal from Egypt, Muhammad Ali seized control and began a French-influenced modernization program.

- His successors continued the program and attacked the Ottoman Empire, but they were thwarted by the European powers.

- The Greek insurrection, European intervention, and Egyptian attack drove the westernizing reform efforts of Mahmud II and his successors.

- The most comprehensive reform initiative was Abdul Mejid's Tanzimat program.

- The Crimean War marked the transition from traditional to modern warfare and drew the Ottoman Empire into greater involvement with European commerce.

- Declining power and prosperity led to the rise of the Young Ottomans.

The Web of War

The lethal military technologies of the mid-nineteenth century that were used on battlefields in the United States, Russia, India, and China were rapidly transmitted from one conflict to the next. This dissemination was due not only to the rapid development of communications but also to the existence of a new international network of soldiers who moved from one trouble spot to another, bringing expertise in the use of new techniques.

General Charles Gordon (1833–1885), for instance, who was commissioned in the British army in 1852, served in the Crimean War after Britain entered on the side of the Ottomans. In 1860 he was dispatched to China, where he served with British forces during the Arrow War and took part in the sack of Beijing. Afterward, he stayed in China and was assigned to the Qing imperial government until the suppression of the Taipings in 1864, earning himself the nickname "Chinese" Gordon. Gordon later served the Ottoman rulers of Egypt as governor of territory along the Nile. He was killed in Sudan in 1885 while leading his Egyptian troops in defense of the city of Khartoum against an uprising by the Sudanese religious leader, the Mahdi.

Journalism played an important part in the developing web of telegraph communications that sped orders to and from the battlefields. Readers in London could learn details of the drama occurring in the Crimea or in China within a week—or in some cases days—after they occurred. Print and, later, photographic journalism created new "stars" from these war experiences. Charles Gordon was one. Florence Nightingale was another.

In the great wars of the 1800s, the vast majority of deaths resulted from infection or excessive bleeding, not from the wounds themselves. Florence Nightingale (1820–1910), while still a young woman, became interested in hospital management and nursing and went to Prussia and France to study advanced techniques. Before the outbreak of the Crimean War she was credited with bringing about marked improvement in British health care. When the public reacted to news reports of the suffering in the Crimea, the British government sent Nightingale to the region. Within a year of her arrival the death rate in the military hospitals there dropped from 45 percent to under 5 percent. Her techniques for preventing septicemia and dysentery, essentially sanitary measures like washing bed linens after a death and emptying toilet buckets outside, were quickly adopted by those working for and with her. On her return to London, Nightingale established institutes for nursing that soon were recognized as leaders around the world. She herself was lionized by the British public and received the Order of Merit in 1907, three years before her death.

The importance of Nightingale's innovations in public hygiene is underscored by the life of her contemporary, Mary Seacole (1805–1881). A Jamaican woman who volunteered to nurse British troops in the Crimean War, Seacole was repeatedly excluded from nursing service by British authorities. She eventually went to Crimea and used her own funds to run a hospital there, bankrupting herself in the process. The drama of the Crimean War moved the British public to support Seacole after her sacrifices were publicized. She was awarded medals by the British, French, and Turkish governments and today is recognized with her contemporary Florence Nightingale as an innovative field nurse and a champion of public hygiene in peacetime.

Florence Nightingale During Crimean War This 1856 lithograph shows Florence Nightingale supervising nursing care in a hospital in Scutari (Üsküdar) across the Bosphorus strait from Istanbul. Though the artist may have exaggerated the neatness and cleanliness of the ward, sanitary measures proved the key to Nightingale's raising of the survival rate of sick and wounded soldiers.

Private Collection/The Stapleton Collection/The Bridgeman Art Library

THE RUSSIAN EMPIRE

In 1812, when Napoleon's march on Moscow ended in a disastrous retreat brought on more by what a later tsar called "Generals January and February" than by Russian military action, the European image of Russia changed. Just as Napoleon's withdrawal from Egypt led to Muhammad Ali briefly becoming a political power, so his withdrawal from Russia conferred status on Tsar Alexander I (r. 1801–1825). Conservative Europeans still saw Russia as alien, backward, and oppressive, but they acknowledged its immensity and potential and included the tsar in efforts to suppress revolutionary tendencies throughout Europe.

In several important respects Russia resembled the Ottoman Empire more than the conservative kingdoms of Europe whose autocratic practices it so staunchly supported. Socially dominated by nobles whose country estates were worked by unfree serfs, Russia had almost no middle class. Industry was still at the threshold of development by the standards of the rapidly industrializing European powers, though it was somewhat more dynamic than Ottoman industry. Like Egypt and the Ottoman Empire, Russia engaged in reforms from the top down under Alexander I, but when his conservative brother Nicholas I (r. 1825–1855) succeeded to the throne, iron discipline and suspicion of modern ideas took priority over reform.

Russia and Europe

In 1700 only three Russians out of a hundred lived in cities, two-thirds of them in Moscow alone. By the mid-1800s the town population had grown tenfold, though it still accounted for only 6 percent of the total because the territories of the tsars had grown greatly through wars and colonization (see Chapter 21). These figures demonstrate that, like the Ottoman Empire, Russia was an overwhelmingly agricultural land. However, it had poorer transportation than the Ottoman Empire, since many Ottoman cities were seaports. Both empires encompassed peoples speaking many different languages.

Well-engineered roads did not begin to appear until 1817, and steam navigation commenced on the Volga in 1843. Tsar Nicholas I built the first railroad from St. Petersburg, the Russian capital, to his summer palace in 1837. A few years later his commitment to strict discipline led him to insist that the trunk line from St. Petersburg to Moscow run in a perfectly straight line. American engineers, among them the father of the painter James McNeill Whistler, who learned to paint in St. Petersburg, oversaw the laying of track and built locomotive workshops. Industrialization projects depended heavily on foreign expertise. British engineers set up the textile mills that gave woolens and cottons a prominent place among Russia's industries.

Until the late nineteenth century the Russian government's interest in industry was limited. An industrial revolution required educated and independent-minded artisans and entrepreneurs, but Nicholas feared the spread of literacy and modern education—especially anything smacking of liberalism, socialism, or revolution—beyond the minimum needed to train the officer corps and the bureaucracy. He preferred serfs to factory workers, and he paid for imported industrial goods with exports of grain and timber.

Like Egypt and the Ottoman Empire, Russia aspired to Western-style economic development. But when France and Britain entered the Crimean War, they faced a Russian army equipped with obsolete weapons and bogged down by lack of transportation. At a time when European engineers were making major breakthroughs in loading cannon through an opening at the breech end, muzzle-loading artillery remained the Russian standard.

Yet in some ways Russia bore a closer resemblance to other European countries than the Ottoman Empire did. From the point of view of the French and the British, the Cyrillic alphabet and the Russian Orthodox form of Christianity seemed foreign, but they were not nearly as foreign as the Arabic alphabet and the Muslim faith. Britain and France feared Russia as a rival for power in the east, but they increasingly accepted Tsar Nicholas's view of the Ottoman Empire as "the sick man of Europe," capable of surviving only so long as the European powers permitted.

From the Russian point of view, kinship with western Europe was of questionable value. Westernizers, like the men of the Tanzimat in the Ottoman Empire, put their trust in technical advances and governmental reform. Opposing them were intellectuals known as **Slavophiles**, who considered the Orthodox faith, the solidity of peasant life, and the tsar's absolute rule to be the proper bases of Russian civilization. After Russia's humiliation in the Crimea, the Slavophile

Slavophiles Russian intellectuals in the early nineteenth century who favored resisting western European influences and taking pride in the traditional peasant values and institutions of the Slavic people.

Pan-Slavism Movement among Russian intellectuals in the second half of the nineteenth century to identify culturally and politically with the Slavic peoples of eastern Europe.

tendency gave rise to **Pan-Slavism**, a militant political doctrine advocating unity of all the Slavic peoples, including those living under Austrian and Ottoman rule.

On the diplomatic front, the tsar's inclusion as a major European ruler contrasted sharply with the sultan's exclusion. However, this did not prevent a powerful sense of Russophobia from developing in the West. Britain in particular saw Russia as a threat to India and despised the subjection of the serfs, who gained their freedom from Tsar Alexander II only in 1861, twenty-seven years after the British had abolished slavery. In addition, the passions generated by the Crimean War and its outcome affected the relations of Russia, Europe, and the Ottoman Empire for the remainder of the nineteenth century.

Russia and Asia

The Russian drive to the east in the eighteenth century brought the tsar's empire to the Pacific Ocean and the frontiers of China (see Map 21.1) by century's end. In the nineteenth century Russian expansionism focused on the south. There the backwardness of the Russian military did not matter since the peoples they faced were even less industrialized and technologically advanced. In 1860 Russia established a military outpost on the Pacific coast that would eventually grow into the great naval port of Vladivostok, today Russia's most southerly city. In Central Asia the steppe lands of the Kazakh nomads came under Russian control early in the century, setting the stage for a confrontation with three Uzbek states farther south. They succumbed one by one, beginning in 1865, giving rise to the new province of Turkestan, with its capital at Tashkent in present-day Uzbekistan.

In the region of the Caucasus Mountains, the third area of southward expansion, Russia first took over Christian Georgia (1786), Muslim Azerbaijan (ah-zer-by-JAHN) (1801), and Christian Armenia (1813) before gobbling up the many small principalities in the heart of the mountains. Between 1829 and 1864 Dagestan, Chechnya (CHECH-nee-yah), Abkhazia (ab-KAH-zee-yah), and other regions that would one day gain political prominence after the breakup of the Soviet Union became parts of the Russian Empire.

The drive to the south intensified political friction with Russia's new neighbors: Qing China and Japan in the east, Iran on the Central Asian and Caucasus frontiers, and the Ottoman Empire at the eastern end of the Black Sea. In the latter two instances, Muslim refugees from the territories newly absorbed by Russia spread anti-Russian feelings, though some of them brought with them modern skills and ideas gained from exposure to Russian administration and education.

The Russian drive to the south added a new element to the Eastern Question. Many British statesmen and strategists reckoned that a warlike Russia would press on until it had conquered all the lands separating it from British India, a prospect that made them shudder, given India's enormous contribution to Britain's prosperity. The competition that ensued over which power would control southern Central Asia resulted in a standoff in Afghanistan, which became a buffer zone under the control of neither. In Iran, the standoff between the powers helped preserve the weak Qajar dynasty of shahs.

Cultural Trends

Unlike Egypt and the Ottoman Empire, which began to send students to Europe for training only in the nineteenth century, Russia had been in cultural contact with western Europe since the time of Peter the Great (r. 1689–1725). Members of the Russian court knew Western languages, and the tsars employed officials and advisers from Western countries. Peter had also enlisted the well-educated Ukrainian clerics who headed the Russian Orthodox Church to help spread a Western spirit of education. As a result, Alexander I's reforms met a more positive reception than those of Muhammad Ali and Mahmud II. However, his reforms promised more on paper than they brought about in practice. It took many years to develop a sufficient pool of trained bureaucrats to make the reforms effective.

Ironically, much of the opposition to Alexander's reforms came from well-established families that were not at all unfriendly to Western ideas. Their fear was that the new government bureaucrats, who often came from humbler social origins, would act as agents of imperial tyranny. This fear was realized during the conservative reign of Nicholas I in the same way that the Tanzimat-inspired bureaucracy of the Ottoman Empire served the despotic purposes of Sultan Abdul Hamid II after 1877. Individuals favoring more liberal reforms, including military officers

Visual Connection Archive

Raising of the Alexander Monument in St. Petersburg   The death of Alexander I in 1825 brought to power his conservative brother Nicholas I. Yet Alexander remained a heroic figure for his resistance to Napoleon. This monument in Winter Palace Square was erected in 1829.

who had served in western Europe, intellectuals who read Western political tracts, and members of Masonic lodges who exchanged views with Freemasons in the West, formed secret societies of opposition. Some placed their highest priority on freeing the serfs; others advocated a constitution and a republican form of government. When Alexander I died in December 1825, confusion over who was to succeed him encouraged a group of reform-minded army officers to try to take over the government and provoke an uprising. This so-called **Decembrist revolt** failed, and many of the participants were severely punished. These events ensured that the new tsar, Nicholas I, would pay little heed to calls for reform over the next thirty years.

The great powers meeting in Paris to settle the Crimean War in 1856 forced Russia to return land to the Ottomans in both Europe and Asia. This humiliation spurred Nicholas's son and successor, Alexander II (r. 1855–1881), to institute major new reforms to reinvigorate the country. The greatest of his reforms was the emancipation of the serfs in 1861. He also authorized new joint-stock companies, projected a railroad network to tie the country together, and modernized the legal and administrative arms of government.

Decembrist revolt Abortive attempt by army officers to take control of the Russian government upon the death of Tsar Alexander I in 1825.

Earlier intellectual and cultural trends flourished under Alexander II. More and more people became involved in intellectual, artistic, and professional life. Most prominent intellectuals received some amount of instruction at Moscow University or some German university. Universities also appeared in provincial cities like Kharkov in Ukraine and Kazan on the Volga River. Student clubs, along with Masonic lodges, became places for discussing new ideas. As Russian scholars and scientists began to achieve recognition for their contributions to European thought, scholarly careers attracted young men from clerical families, who in turn helped stimulate reforms in religious education.

Just as the Tanzimat reforms of the Ottoman Empire preceded the emergence of the Young Ottomans as a new and assertive political and intellectual force in the second half of the nineteenth century, so the initially ineffective reforms of Alexander I set in motion cultural currents that would make Russia a dynamic center of intellectual, artistic, and political life under his nephew Alexander II. Thus Russia belonged to two different spheres of development. It entered the nineteenth century a recognized force in European politics, but in other ways it resembled

SECTION REVIEW

- Russian society resembled Ottoman society, but Alexander I undertook top-down westernizing reforms.

- Nicholas I's suspicion of Western ideas stalled reform and slowed industrial development.

- Slavophiles opposed westernizers and, after the Crimean War, embraced Pan-Slavism, contributing to Russophobia in the West.

- Russian expansion southward and eastward added vast territories to the empire and caused friction with China, Japan, Iran, and the Ottoman Empire.

- Resistance to Alexander I's bureaucratic reforms sparked the Decembrist revolt, which stiffened Nicholas I's hostility to Western ideas.

- The humiliation of the Crimean War drove Alexander II's reforms, including emancipation of the serfs.

the Ottoman Empire. Rulers in both empires instituted reforms, overcame opposition, and increased the power of their governments. These activities stimulated intellectual and political trends that would ultimately work against the absolute rule of tsar and sultan. Yet Russia would eventually develop much closer relations with western Europe and become an arena for every sort of European intellectual, artistic, and political tendency, while the Ottoman Empire would ultimately succumb to European imperialism.

THE QING EMPIRE

In 1800 the Qing Empire faced many problems, but no reform movement of the kind initiated by Sultan Selim III emerged in China. The reasons are not difficult to understand. The Qing emperors had skillfully countered Russian strategic and diplomatic moves in the 1600s. Instead of having a Napoleon threatening them with invasion, they enjoyed the admiration of Jesuit priests, who likened them to enlightened philosopher-kings. In 1793, however, a British attempt to establish diplomatic and trade relations—the Macartney mission—turned European opinion against China (see Chapter 21).

China's most serious crises were domestic, not foreign: rebellions by displaced indigenous peoples and the poor, and protests against the injustice of the local magistrates. The Qing dealt with these problems by suppressing rebels and dismissing incompetent or untrustworthy officials. They also brushed aside the complaints from European merchants who chafed against the restrictions of the "Canton system" by which the Qing limited and controlled foreign trade.

Economic and Social Disorder

Early Qing successes and territorial expansion sowed the seeds of the domestic and political chaos of the later period. The early emperors encouraged the recovery of farmland, the opening of previously uncultivated areas, and the restoration and expansion of the road and canal systems. These measures expanded the agricultural base and supported a doubling of the population between about 1650 and 1800. Enormous numbers of farmers, merchants, and day laborers migrated in search of less crowded conditions, and a permanent floating population of the unemployed and homeless emerged. By 1800 population strain had caused serious environmental damage in some parts of central and western China.

While farmers tried to cope with agricultural deterioration, other groups vented grievances against the government: minority peoples in central and southwestern China complained about being driven off their lands during the boom of the 1700s; Mongols resented appropriation of their grazing lands and the displacement of their traditional elites. In some regions, village vigilante organizations took over policing and governing functions from Qing officials who had lost control. Growing numbers of people mistrusted the government, suspecting that all officials were corrupt. The increasing presence of foreign merchants and missionaries in Canton and in the Portuguese colony of Macao aggravated discontent in neighboring districts.

In some parts of China the Qing were hated as foreign conquerors and were suspected of sympathy with the Europeans. In 1794 the White Lotus Rebellion—partly inspired by a messianic ideology that predicted the restoration of the Chinese Ming dynasty and the coming of the Buddha—raged across central China and was not suppressed until 1804. It initiated a series of internal conflicts that continued through the 1800s (see discussion of Yaqub Beg's revolt at the beginning of this chapter). Ignited by deepening social instabilities, these movements were sometimes intensified by local ethnic conflicts and by unapproved religions. The ability of some village militias to defend themselves and attack others intensified the conflicts, though the same techniques proved useful to southern coastal populations attempting to fend off British invasion.

The Opium War and Its Aftermath, 1839–1850

Unlike the Ottomans, the Qing knew little about the enormous fortunes being made in the early 1800s by European and American merchants smuggling opium into China. They did not know that silver gained in this illegal trade was helping finance the industrial transformation of England and the United States. Only slowly did Qing officials become aware of British colonies in

India that grew and exported opium, and of the major naval base at Singapore through which British opium reached East Asia.

In 1729 the first Qing law banning opium imports was promulgated. By 1800, however, opium smuggling had swelled the annual import level to as many as four thousand chests. Though British merchants had pioneered this profitable trade, Chinese merchants likewise profited from distributing the drugs. A price war in the early 1820s stemming from competition between British and American importers raised demand so sharply that as many as thirty thousand chests were being imported by the 1830s. Addiction spread to people at all levels of Qing society, including high-ranking officials. The Qing emperor and his officials debated whether to legalize and tax opium or to enforce the existing ban more strictly. Having decided to root out the use and importation of opium, in 1839 they sent a high official to Canton to deal with the matter.

Britain considered the ban on opium importation an intolerable limitation on trade, a direct threat to Britain's economic health, and a cause for war. British naval and marine forces arrived on the south China coast in late 1839. The **Opium War** (1839–1842) broke out when negotiations between the Qing official and British representatives reached a stalemate. The war exposed the fact that the traditional, hereditary soldiers of the Qing Empire—the **Bannermen**—were, like the Janissaries of the Ottoman Empire, hopelessly obsolete. As in the Crimean War, the British excelled at sea, where they deployed superior technology. British ships landed marines who pillaged coastal cities and then sailed to new destinations (see Map 24.2). The Qing lacked a navy powerful enough to deal with the British. Thus until they were able to engage the British in prolonged fighting on land, they were unable to defend themselves against British attacks. Even in the land engagements, Qing resources proved woefully inadequate. The British could quickly transport their forces by sea along the coast, whereas Qing troops moved primarily on foot. Moving Qing reinforcements from central to eastern China took more than three months; and when the defense forces arrived, they were exhausted and basically without weapons.

The Bannermen used the few muskets the Qing had imported during the 1700s. The weapons were matchlocks, which required the soldiers to ignite the load of gunpowder in them by hand. Firing the weapons was dangerous, and the canisters of gunpowder that each musketeer carried on his belt were likely to explode if a fire broke out nearby—a frequent occurrence in encounters with British artillery. Most of the Bannermen, however, had no guns at all and fought with swords, knives, spears, and clubs. They were greatly outmatched by the soldiers under British command—many of them Indians—who carried percussion-cap rifles, which were far quicker, safer, and more accurate than the matchlocks. In addition, the long-range British artillery could be moved from place to place and proved deadly in the cities and villages of eastern China.

Qing commanders thought that British gunboats rode so low in the water that they could not sail up the Chinese rivers. So they evacuated the coastal areas to counter the British threat. But the British deployed new gunboats for shallow waters and moved without difficulty up the Yangzi River (see Chapter 22).

When the invaders approached Nanjing, the former Ming capital, the Qing decided to negotiate. In 1842 the terms of the **Treaty of Nanking** (the British name for Nanjing) dismantled the old Canton system. The number of **treaty ports**—cities opened to foreign residents—increased from one (Canton) to five (Canton, Xiamen, Fuzhou, Ningbo, and Shanghai [shahng-hie]). The island of Hong Kong became a British colony, and British residents in China gained extraterritorial rights. The Qing government agreed to set a low tariff of 5 percent on imports and to pay Britain an indemnity of 21 million ounces of silver as a penalty for having started the war. A supplementary treaty the following year guaranteed **most-favored-nation status** to Britain: any privileges that China granted to another country would be automatically extended to Britain as well. This provision effectively prevented the colonization of China, because giving land to one country would have necessitated giving it to all.

With each round of treaties came a new round of privileges for foreigners. In 1860 a new treaty legalized their right to import opium. Later, French treaties established the rights of foreign missionaries to travel in the Chinese countryside and preach their religion. The number of treaty ports grew, too; by 1900 they numbered more than ninety.

The treaty system and the principle of extraterritoriality resulted in the colonization of small pockets of Qing territory, where foreign merchants lived at ease. Greater territorial losses resulted when outlying regions gained independence or were ceded to neighboring countries.

Opium War War between Britain and the Qing Empire that was, in the British view, occasioned by the Qing government's refusal to permit the importation of opium into its territories. The victorious British imposed the one-sided Treaty of Nanking on China.

Bannermen Hereditary military servants of the Qing Empire, in large part descendants of peoples of various origins who had fought for the founders of the empire.

Treaty of Nanking The treaty that concluded the Opium War. It awarded Britain a large indemnity from the Qing Empire, denied the Qing government tariff control over some of its own borders, opened additional ports of residence to Britons, and ceded the island of Hong Kong to Britain.

treaty ports Cities opened to foreign residents as a result of the forced treaties between the Qing Empire and foreign signatories. In the treaty ports, foreigners enjoyed extraterritoriality.

most-favored-nation status A clause in a commercial treaty that awards to any later signatories all the privileges previously granted to the original signatories.

Districts north and south of the Amur River in the northeast fell to Russia by treaty in 1858 and 1860; parts of modern Kazakhstan and Kyrgyzstan in the northwest met the same fate in 1864. From 1865 onward the British gradually gained control of territories on China's Indian frontier. In the late 1800s France forced the court of Vietnam to end its tribute relationship to the Qing, while Britain encouraged Tibetan independence.

In Canton, Shanghai, and other coastal cities, Europeans and Americans maintained offices and factories that employed local Chinese as menial laborers. The foreigners built comfortable housing in zones where Chinese were not permitted to live, and they entertained themselves in exclusive restaurants and bars. Around the foreign establishments, gambling and prostitution offered employment to part of the local urban population.

MAP 24.2 **Conflicts in the Qing Empire, 1839–1870** In both the Opium War of 1839–1842 and the Arrow War of 1856–1860, the seacoasts saw most of the action. Since the Qing had a weak navy, the well-armed British ships encountered little resistance as they shelled the southern coasts. In inland conflicts, such as the Taiping Rebellion, the opposing armies were massive and slow moving. Battles on land were often prolonged attempts by one side to starve out the other side before making a major assault. © Cengage Learning

Whether in town or in the countryside, Christian missionaries whose congregations sponsored hospitals, shelters, and soup kitchens or gave stipends to Chinese who attended church enjoyed a good reputation. But just as often the missionaries themselves were regarded as another evil. They seemed to subvert Confucian beliefs by condemning ancestor worship, pressuring poor families to put their children into orphanages, or fulminating against footbinding. The growing numbers of foreigners, and their growing privileges, became targets of resentment for a deeply dissatisfied, daily more impoverished, and increasingly militarized society.

The Taiping Rebellion, 1850–1864

Taiping Rebellion A Christian-inspired rural rebellion that threatened to topple the Qing Empire.

The inflammatory mixture of social unhappiness and foreign intrusion exploded in the great civil war usually called the **Taiping (tie-PING) Rebellion**. In Guangxi, where the Taiping movement originated, entrenched social problems had been generating disorders for half a century. Agriculture in the region was unstable, and many people made their living from arduous and despised trades such as disposing of human waste, making charcoal, and mining. Ethnic divisions complicated economic distress. The lowliest trades frequently involved a minority group, the Hakkas, and tensions between them and the majority were rising. Problems may have been intensified by sharp fluctuations in the opium trade and reactions to the cultural and economic impact of the Europeans and Americans in Canton.

Hong Xiuquan **(hoong shee-OH-chew-an)**, the founder of the Taiping movement, experienced all of these influences. Hong came from a humble Hakka background. After years of study, he competed in the provincial Confucian examinations, hoping for a post in government. He failed the examinations repeatedly, and it appears that he suffered a nervous breakdown in his late thirties. Afterward he spent some time in Canton, where he met both Chinese and American Protestant missionaries, who inspired him with their teachings. Hong had his own interpretation of the Christian message. He saw himself as the younger brother of Jesus, commissioned by God to found a new kingdom on earth and drive the Manchu conquerors, the Qing, out of China. The result would be universal peace. Hong called his new religious movement the "Heavenly Kingdom of Great Peace."

Hong quickly attracted a community of believers, primarily Hakkas like himself. They believed in the prophecy of dreams and claimed they could walk on air. Hong and his rivals for leadership in the movement went in and out of ecstatic trances. They denounced the Manchus as creatures of Satan. News of the sect reached the government, and Qing troops arrived to arrest the Taiping leaders. But the Taipings soundly repelled the imperial troops. Local loyalty to the Taipings spread quickly; their numbers multiplied; and they began to enlarge their domain.

The Taipings relied at first on Hakka sympathy and the charismatic appeal of their religious doctrine to attract followers. But as their numbers and power grew, they altered their methods of preaching and governing, replacing the anti-Chinese appeals used to enlist Hakkas with anti-Manchu rhetoric designed to enlist Chinese. They forced captured villages to join their movement. Once people were absorbed, the Taipings strictly monitored their activities. They also segregated men and women and organized them into work and military teams. Women were forbidden to bind their feet (the Hakkas had never practiced footbinding) and participated fully in farming and labor. Brigades of women soldiers took to the field against Qing forces.

As the movement grew, it began to move toward eastern and northern China (see Map 24.2). Panic preceded the Taipings. Villagers feared being forced into Taiping units, and Confucian elites recoiled in horror from the bizarre ideology of foreign gods, totalitarian rule, and walking, working, warring women. But the huge numbers the Taipings were able to muster overwhelmed attempts at local defense. The tremendous growth in the number of Taiping followers required the movement to establish a permanent base. When the rebel army conquered Nanjing in 1853, the Taiping leaders decided to settle there and make it the capital of the new "Heavenly Kingdom of Great Peace."

Qing forces attempting to defend north China became more successful as problems of organization and growing numbers slowed Taiping momentum. Increasing Qing military success resulted mainly from the flexibility of the imperial military commanders in the face of an unprecedented challenge. In addition, the military commanders received strong backing from a group of civilian provincial governors who had studied the techniques developed by local militia forces for self-defense. Certain provincial governors combined their knowledge of civilian self-defense and local terrain with more efficient organization and the use of modern weaponry. The result was the formation of new military units, in which many of the Bannermen voluntarily served under civilian governors. The Qing court agreed to special taxes to fund the new armies and acknowledged the new combined leadership.

Nanjing Encircled For a decade the Taipings held the city of Nanjing as their capital. For years Qing and international troops attempted to break the Taiping hold. By the summer of 1864, Qing forces had built tunnels leading to the foundations of Nanjing's city walls and had planted explosives. The detonation of the explosives signaled the final Qing assault on the rebel capital. As shown here, the common people of the city, along with their starving livestock, were caught in the crossfire. Many of the Taiping leaders escaped the debacle at Nanjing, but nearly all were hunted down and executed.

When the Taipings settled into Nanjing, the new Qing armies surrounded the city, hoping to starve out the rebels. The Taipings, however, had provisioned and fortified themselves well. They also had the services of several brilliant young military commanders, who mobilized enormous campaigns in nearby parts of eastern China, scavenging supplies and attempting to break the encirclement of Nanjing. For more than a decade the Taiping leadership remained ensconced at Nanjing, and the "Heavenly Kingdom" endured.

In 1856 Britain and France, freed from their preoccupation with the Crimean War, turned their attention to China. European and American missionaries had visited Nanjing, curious to see what their fellow Christians were up to. Their reports were discouraging. Hong Xiuquan and the other leaders appeared to lead lives of indulgence and abandon, and more than one missionary accused them of homosexual practices. Relieved of the possible accusation of quashing a pious Christian movement, the British and French surveyed the situation. Though the Taipings were not going to topple the Qing, rebellious Nian ("Bands") in northern China added a new threat in the 1850s. A series of simultaneous large insurrections might indeed destroy the empire. Moreover, since the Qing had not observed all the provisions of the treaties signed after the Opium War, Britain and France were now considering renewing war on the Qing themselves.

In 1856 the British and French launched a series of swift, brutal coastal attacks—a second opium war, called the Arrow War (1856–1860)—that culminated in a British and French invasion of Beijing and the sacking of the Summer Palace in 1860. A new round of treaties punished the Qing for not enacting all the provisions of the Treaty of Nanking. Having secured their principal objective, the British and French forces then joined the Qing campaign against the Taipings.

Street Scene in Guangzhou This photograph taken in the 1860s by an Englishman shows a comparatively wide market street with signs advertising drugs, cushions, seals, ink, etc. The engraving of a Cairo street scene (page 607) shows a much more exotic stereotype of the orient, complete with young girl displaying her body while covering her face.

Photo by John Thomson/George Eastman House/Getty Images

Attempts to coordinate the international forces were sometimes riotous and sometimes tragic, but the injection of European weaponry and money helped quell both the Taiping and the Nian rebellions during the 1860s.

The Taiping Rebellion ranks as the world's bloodiest civil war and the greatest armed conflict before the twentieth century. Estimates of deaths range from 20 million to 30 million. The loss of life came primarily from starvation and disease, for most engagements consisted of surrounding fortified cities and waiting until the enemy forces died, surrendered, or were so weakened that they could be easily defeated. Many sieges continued for months. Reports of people eating grass, leather, hemp, and human flesh were widespread. The dead were rarely buried properly, and epidemic disease was common.

The area of early Taiping fighting was close to the regions of southwest China in which bubonic plague had been lingering for centuries. When the rebellion was suppressed, many Taiping followers sought safety in the highlands of Laos and Vietnam, which soon showed infestation by plague. Within a few years the disease reached Hong Kong. From there it spread to Singapore, San Francisco, Calcutta, and London. In the late 1800s there was intense apprehension over the possibility of a worldwide outbreak, and Chinese immigrants were regarded as likely carriers. This fear became a contributing factor in the passage of discriminatory immigration bans on Chinese in the United States in 1882.

The Taiping Rebellion devastated the agricultural centers of China. Many of the most intensely cultivated regions of central and eastern China were depopulated. Some were still uninhabited decades later, and major portions of the country did not recover until the twentieth century.

Cities, too, were hard hit. Shanghai, a treaty port of modest size before the rebellion, saw its population multiplied many times by the arrival of refugees from war-blasted neighboring provinces. The city then endured months of siege by the Taipings. Major cultural centers in eastern

Cixi's Allies In the 1860s and 1870s, Cixi was a supporter of reform (see page 622). In later years she was widely regarded as corrupt and self-centered and as an obstacle to reform. Her greatest allies were the court eunuchs. Introduced to palace life in early China as managers of the imperial harems, eunuchs became powerful political parties at court. The first Qing emperors refused to allow the eunuchs any political influence, but by Cixi's time the eunuchs once again were a political factor. Tz'u Hsi

(1835-1908) Empress Dowager of China, 1903 (b/w photo), French Photographer, (20th century)/Private Collection/The Bridgeman Art Library

China lost masterpieces of art and architecture; imperial libraries were burned or their collections exposed to the weather; and the printing blocks used to make books were destroyed. While the empire faced the mountainous challenge of dealing with the material and cultural destruction of the war, it also was burdened by a major ecological disaster in the north. The Yellow River changed course in 1855, destroying the southern part of impoverished Shandong province with flood and initiating decades of drought along the former riverbed in northern Shandong.

Decentralization at the End of the Qing Empire, 1864–1875

The Qing government emerged from the 1850s with no hope of achieving solvency. The corruption of the 1700s, attempts in the very early 1800s to restore waterworks and roads, and declining yields from land taxes had bankrupted the treasury. By 1850, before the Taiping Rebellion, Qing government expenditures were ten times revenues. The indemnities demanded by Europeans

Chinese Responses to Imperialism

The Opium War, followed by the Taiping Rebellion, revealed China's weakness for all to see, but there was no agreement on what should be done to restore its strength. A few provincial officials were able to take effective action, but the competing ideas that were heard at the imperial court tended to cancel each other out.

Feng Guifen, an official and a scholar, came into contact with Westerners defending Shanghai when he took refuge there from the Taipings. The following is from a book of essays he published in 1861.

According to a general geography compiled by an Englishman, the territory of China is eight times that of Russia, ten times that of the United States, one hundred times that of France, and two hundred times that of Great Britain.... Yet we are shamefully humiliated by the four nations, not because our climate, soil, or resources are inferior to theirs, but because our people are inferior.... Now, our inferiority is not due to our allotment from Heaven [i.e., our inherent nature], but is rather due to ourselves....

Why are the Western nations small and yet strong? Why are we large and yet weak? We must search for the means to become their equal, and that depends solely upon human effort....

We have only one thing to learn from the barbarians, and that is strong ships and effective guns.... Funds should be allotted to establish a shipyard and arsenal in each trading port. A few barbarians should be employed, and Chinese who are good in using their minds should be selected to receive instruction so that in turn they may teach many craftsmen. When a piece of work is finished and is as good as that made by the barbarians, the makers should be rewarded with an official *juren* degree and be permitted to participate in the metropolitan examinations on the same basis as other

scholars. Those whose products are of superior quality should be rewarded with the *jinshi* degree [ordinarily conferred in the metropolitan examinations] and be permitted to participate in the palace examinations like others. The workers should be paid double so that they will not quit their jobs.

Our nation's emphasis on civil service examinations has sunk deep into people's minds for a long time. Intelligent and brilliant scholars have exhausted their time and energy in such useless things as the stereotyped examination essays, examination papers, and formal calligraphy.... We should now order one-half of them to apply themselves to the manufacturing of instruments and weapons and to the promotion of physical studies.... The intelligence and ingenuity of the Chinese are certainly superior to those of the various barbarians; it is only that hitherto we have not made use of them. When the government above takes delight in something, the people below will pursue it further: their response will be like an echo carried by the wind. There ought to be some people of extraordinary intelligence who can have new ideas and improve on Western methods. At first they may take the foreigners as their teachers and models; then they may come to the same level and be their equals; finally they may move ahead and surpass them. Herein lies the way to self-strengthening.

In 1867 the debate over how to resist foreign military pressure surged through the imperial court. Woren, a Mongol who held the rank of grand secretary, spoke for the conservatives.

Mathematics, one of the six arts, should indeed be learned by scholars as indicated in the imperial decree, and it should not be considered an unworthy subject. But according to the viewpoint of your servant, astronomy and mathematics are of very little use. If these subjects are going to be taught by Westerners as regular studies, the damage will be great.... Your

after the Opium and Arrow Wars compounded the problem. Vast stretches of formerly productive rice land were devastated, and the population was dispersed. Refugees pleaded for relief, and the imperial, volunteer, foreign, and mercenary troops that had suppressed the Taipings demanded unpaid wages.

Britain and France became active participants in the period of recovery that followed the rebellion (see Diversity and Dominance: Chinese Responses to Imperialism). To ensure repayment of the debt to Britain, Robert Hart was installed as inspector-general of a newly created Imperial Maritime Customs Service. Britain and the Qing split the revenues he collected. Britons and Americans worked for the Qing government as advisers and ambassadors, attempting to smooth communications between the Qing, Europe, and the United States.

The real work of the recovery, however, was managed by provincial governors who had come to the forefront in the struggle against the Taipings. To prosecute the war, they had won the right to levy their own taxes, raise their own troops, and run their own bureaucracies. These special powers were not entirely canceled when the war ended. Chief among these governors servant has learned that the way to establish a nation is to lay emphasis on rites and rightness, not on power and plotting. The fundamental effort lies in the minds of people, not in techniques. Now, if we seek trifling arts and respect barbarians as teachers . . . all that can be accomplished is the training of mathematicians. From ancient down to modern times, your servant has never heard of anyone who could use mathematics to raise the nation from a state of decline or to strengthen it in time of weakness. . . .

Since the conclusion of the peace, Christianity has been prevalent, and half of our ignorant people have been fooled by it. The only thing we can rely on is that our scholars should clearly explain to the people the Confucian tenets, which may be able to sustain the minds of the ignorant populace. Now if these brilliant and talented scholars, who have been trained by the nation and reserved for great future usefulness, have to change from their regular course of study to follow the barbarians, then the correct spirit will not be developed, and accordingly the evil spirit will become stronger. After several years it will end in nothing less than driving the multitudes of the Chinese people into allegiance to the barbarians.

The opposing group of ministers who backed the idea of "self-strengthening" responded.

Your ministers have examined the memorial of Woren: the principles he presents are very lofty and the opinion he maintains is very orthodox. Your ministers' point of view was also like that before they began to manage foreign affairs; and yet today they do not presume to insist on such ideas, because of actual difficulties that they cannot help. . . .

From the beginning of foreign relations to the present there have been twenty or thirty years. At first the officials inside and outside the capital did not grasp the crux of the matter, and whether they negotiated peace or discussed war, generally these were empty words without effect. . . . Therefore your ministers have pondered a long-term policy and discussed the situation thoroughly with all the provincial officials. Proposals to learn the written and spoken languages of foreign countries, the various methods of making machines, the training of troops with foreign guns, the dispatching of officials to travel in all countries, the investigation of their local customs and social conditions . . . all these painstaking and special decisions represent nothing other than a struggle for self-strengthening. . . .

We too are afraid that the people who are learning these things will have no power of discrimination and are likely to be led astray by foreigners, as Woren fears. Therefore we have deliberated and decided that those who participate in these examinations must be persons from regular scholastic channels. It is indeed those students who have read widely and who understand right principles and have their minds set upon upright and grand purposes—and the present situation is just what causes the scholars and officials to feel pain in heart and head—who would certainly be able to lie on faggots and taste gall [i.e., nurse vengeance] in order to encourage each other vigorously to seek the actual achievement of self-strengthening. They are different from those who have vague, easygoing, or indifferent ideas.

QUESTIONS FOR ANALYSIS

1. **How do the views of the writers reflect their own backgrounds as officials who achieved their offices through the traditional examination system?**

2. **In what ways do these passages indicate a deep or a shallow understanding of the West?**

3. **How do the ideas expressed here compare with the attitudes toward reform in the Ottoman and Russian Empires as discussed elsewhere in this chapter?**

Source: Essays of Feng Tuifen published in 1861 in Jiaobinlu kangyi (Personal Protests from the Study of Jiaobin). English translations from Chester Tan, published in Wm. Theodore de Bary and Richard Lafrano, *Sources of Chinese Tradition*, vol. 2, 2d ed. pp. 235–236, 238–239. Copyright © 2000 Columbia University Press. Reprinted with permission of the publisher.

was Zeng Guofan **(zung gwoh-FAN)**, who oversaw programs to restore agriculture, communications, education, and publishing, as well as efforts to reform the military and industrialize armaments manufacture.

Like many provincial governors, Zeng preferred to look to the United States rather than to Britain for models and aid. He therefore hired American advisers to run his weapons factories, shipyards, and military academies. He also sponsored a daring program in which promising Chinese boys were sent to Hartford, Connecticut, a center of missionary activity, to learn English, science, mathematics, engineering, and history. They returned to China to assume some of the positions previously held by foreign advisers. Though Zeng was never an advocate of participation in public life by women, his Confucian convictions taught him that educated mothers were more than ever a necessity. He not only encouraged but also partly oversaw the advanced classical education of his own daughters. Zeng's death in 1872 deprived the empire of a major force for reform.

The period of recovery marked a fundamental structural change in the Qing Empire. Although the emperors after 1850 were ineffective rulers, a coalition of aristocrats supported

SECTION REVIEW

- Social unrest grew in Qing China through a combination of discontent among the poor and displaced indigenous peoples and resentment of growing European influence.

- Qing attempts to ban opium imports provoked the Opium War with Britain, which exposed Qing military inferiority.

- The Treaty of Nanking gave extraterritoriality and other privileges to Britain and led to further losses to other Western powers.

- Social resentment and foreign intrusion ignited the Taiping Rebellion, which, after the Arrow War, the Qing quelled with British and French aid.

- The rebellion encouraged epidemics, devastated agriculture, produced overcrowded cities filled with refugees, and coincided with environmental disasters.

- The rebellion and China's recovery afterward resulted in a process of decentralization led by reformist aristocrats.

the reform and recovery programs. Without their legitimization of the new powers of provincial governors like Zeng Guofan, the empire might have evaporated within a generation. A crucial member of this alliance was Cixi (TSUH-shee), who was known as the "Empress Dowager" after the 1880s. Later observers, both Chinese and foreign, reviled her as a monster of corruption and arrogance. But in the 1860s and 1870s Cixi supported the provincial governors, some of whom became so powerful that they were managing Qing foreign policy as well as domestic affairs.

No longer a conquest regime dominated by a Manchu military caste and its Chinese civilian appointees, the empire came under the control of a group of reformist aristocrats and military men, independently powerful civilian governors, and a small number of foreign advisers. The Qing lacked strong, central, unified leadership and could not recover their powers of taxation, legislation, and military command once these had been granted to the provincial governors. From the 1860s forward, the Qing Empire disintegrated into a number of large power zones in which provincial governors handed over leadership to their protégés in a pattern that the Qing court eventually could only ritually legitimate.

CONCLUSION

The Ottoman, Qing, and Russian Empires shared several characteristics both in their early successes and late-stage challenges. All three maintained a flexible approach when incorporating a diverse group of peoples and cultures into their growing empires. Around the mid-eighteenth century, however, the need to maintain order and increase tax revenues pushed rulers to differentiate groups of people and create stricter hierarchies within each empire, leading to conflict between the minority rulers and the ruled. In addition, population growth that began in the sixteenth century throughout Eurasia, which had been sustainable and beneficial in the expanding territories of Russia and the Qing, eventually became unsupportable. By the nineteenth century, even the Qing Empire, the largest and most advanced Eurasian empire in terms of commercial economy and efficient bureaucratic structures, could no longer effectively deal with the increasing demographic pressures, regional conflict, and political dysfunctions.

Most of the subjects of the Ottoman, Russian, and Qing rulers did not think of European pressure or competition as determining factors in their lives during the first half of the nineteenth century. They continued to live according to the social and economic institutions they inherited from previous generations. By the 1870s, however, the challenge of Europe had become widely realized. The Crimean War, where European allies achieved a hollow victory for the Ottomans and then pressured the sultan for more reforms, confirmed both Ottoman and Russian military weakness. The Opium War did the same for China. But China, unlike the other empires, was also stricken by rampaging civil war and regional uprisings.

In analyzing the crises of the three empires, historians today stress European economic pressures and observe that all three empires ultimately became insolvent and saw the overthrow of their ruling dynasties. However, at the time what most impressed the Ottomans, Russians, and Chinese was European military superiority, as demonstrated in the Greek war of independence, the Crimean War, and the Opium War. Thus for all three empires, dealing with military emergency took priority over deeper reforms throughout most of the time period of this chapter.

KEY TERMS

Muhammad Ali p. 602	**Crimean War** p. 607	**Decembrist revolt** p. 612	**treaty ports** p. 614
Janissaries p. 603	**extraterritoriality** p. 608	**Opium War** p. 614	**most-favored-nation**
Serbia p. 603	**Slavophiles** p. 610	**Bannermen** p. 614	**status** p. 614
Tanzimat p. 604	**Pan-Slavism** p. 611	**Treaty of Nanking** p. 614	**Taiping Rebellion** p. 616

SUGGESTED READING

Bassin, Mark. *Imperial Visions: Nationalist Imagination and Geographical Expansion in the Russian Far East, 1840–1865.* 1999. Addresses Russia's little-studied eastward expansion.

Blackwell, W. L. *The Beginnings of Russian Industrialization, 1800–1860.* 1968. A standard introduction.

Crossley, Pamela Kyle. *Orphan Warriors: Three Manchu Generations and the End of the Qing World.* 1990. Presents a Manchu perspective on the late Qing.

Deringil, Selim. *The Well-Protected Domains: Ideology and the Legitimation of Power in the Ottoman Empire, 1876–1909.* 1998. A revisionist view of the reign of Abdul Hamid II.

Field, Daniel. *The End of Serfdom: Nobility and Bureaucracy in Russia, 1855–1861.* 1976. Studies the primary problem besetting Russian society during this period.

Kappeler, Andreas. *The Russian Multi-Ethnic Empire.* 2001. Puts an emphasis on ethnic diversity.

Lewis, Bernard. *The Emergence of Modern Turkey,* 3d ed. 2001. A treatment of late Ottoman history based on Europeanization as a sign of progress.

Mardin, Serif. *The Genesis of Young Ottoman Thought: A Study in the Modernization of Turkish Political Ideas.* Reprint, 2000. Classic study of intellectual developments.

Pamuk, Sevket. *The Ottoman Empire and European Capitalism, 1820–1913: Trade, Investment, and Production.* 1987. An economic analysis of the Ottoman Empire.

Polachek, James M. *The Inner Opium War.* 1992. Details a major event in Chinese-Western confrontation.

Quataert, Donald. *The Ottoman Empire, 1700–1922,* 2d ed. 2005. A survey of late Ottoman history.

Raeff, Marc. *Understanding Imperial Russia.* 1984. Sets nineteenth-century Russian developments in a broad context and challenges many standard ideas.

Spence, Jonathan D. *God's Chinese Son: The Taiping Heavenly Kingdom of Hong Xiuquan.* 1996. A highly readable account of the Taiping movement that focuses on religious leadership.

Walicki, Andrzej. *The Slavophile Controversy.* 1975. A study in intellectual history.

Zelin, Madeleine. *The Merchants of Zigong: Industrial Entrepreneurship in Early Modern China.* 2005. A revealing study of indigenous economic development.

CourseMate Go to the History CourseMate website for primary source links, study tools, and review materials for this chapter. www.cengagebrain.com

Chapter Outline

Independence in Latin America, 1800–1830
➤ *What were the causes of the revolutions for independence in Latin America?*

The Problem of Order, 1825–1890
➤ *What major political challenges did Western Hemisphere nations face in the nineteenth century?*

The Challenge of Social and Economic Change
➤ *How did economic modernization and the effects of abolition, immigration, and women's rights change the nations of the Western Hemisphere?*

Conclusion

● **DIVERSITY + DOMINANCE** The Afro-Brazilian Experience, 1828
● **ENVIRONMENT + TECHNOLOGY** Industrializing Sugar Agriculture in Cuba

Station at Orizaba, 1878 (colour litho), Castro, Casimir (fl.1878)/Private Collection/The Stapleton Collection/The Bridgeman Art Library

The Train Station in Orizaba, Mexico, 1877 In the last decades of the nineteenth century Mexico's political leaders actively promoted economic development. The railroad became the symbol of this ideal.

Nation Building and Economic Transformation in the Americas, 1800–1890

During the nineteenth century the newly independent nations of the Western Hemisphere sought to emulate the rapid economic progress of Europe under the influence of the Industrial Revolution. No technology seemed to represent that progress better than railroads. Everywhere from Argentina to Canada, governments sponsored railroad development. By 1850 there were 9,000 miles (14,480 kilometers) of track in the United States, as much as in the rest of the world. Latin American nations committed to this technology later than the United States, but railroads there also soon proved important to exports, to new industries, and to political and cultural integration.

Mexico granted the first concession for railroad construction in 1837, but the first significant rail line was completed in 1873. Few new projects were begun until the presidency of Porfirio Díaz (1876–1880 and 1884–1911), who promoted railroad construction. By the time revolutionaries forced him from office, Mexico had 12,000 miles (19,300 kilometers) of track. Although railroads proved crucial to Mexican economic growth, there was a downside. Foreign investment helped pay for new railroads, but this dependence on foreign capital led to political protests and economic nationalism. Railroad development also had a powerful effect on native peoples, who still controlled large areas of rural Mexico. Because railroads made their lands more valuable, powerful landed families used their political influence to strip this land from indigenous subsistence farmers and use it to produce export crops. As Amerindian villagers lost their traditional lands, the number of rural uprisings increased.

In the nineteenth century the Western Hemisphere witnessed radical political and social changes in addition to technological innovations and economic expansion. Brazil and nearly all of Spain's American colonies achieved independence by 1825. As was true in the earlier American and French Revolutions (see Chapter 23), rising nationalism and the ideal of political freedom promoted these changes. Despite the achievement of independence, however, Mexico and other nations in the hemisphere faced foreign interventions and other threats to sovereignty, including regionalism and civil war.

The new nations of the Western Hemisphere faced difficult questions. If colonies could reject submission to imperial powers, could not regions with distinct cultures, social structures, and economies refuse to accept the political authority of newly formed national governments? How could nations born in revolution accept the political strictures of written constitutions—even those they wrote themselves? How could the ideals of liberty and freedom expressed in those constitutions be reconciled with the denial of rights to Amerindians, slaves, recent immigrants, and women?

While trying to resolve these political questions, the new nations also attempted to promote economic growth. They imported new technologies like railroads, opened new areas to settlement, and promoted immigration. But the legacy of colonial economic development, with its emphasis on agricultural and mining exports, inhibited efforts to promote diversification and industrialization, just as the legacy of class and racial division thwarted the realization of political ideals.

INDEPENDENCE IN LATIN AMERICA, 1800–1830

As the eighteenth century drew to a close, Spain and Portugal held vast colonial possessions in the Western Hemisphere, although their power had declined relative to that of their British and French rivals. Both Iberian empires had reformed their colonial administration and strengthened their military forces in the eighteenth century (see Chapter 18). Despite these efforts, the same economic and political forces that had undermined Britain's rule in its colonies were present in Spanish America and Brazil.

Roots of Revolution, to 1810

The great works of the Enlightenment as well as revolutionary documents like the American Declaration of Independence and the French Declaration of the Rights of Man and the Citizen circulated widely in Latin America, but few colonial residents wanted revolutionary change. While colonial elites and middle classes were frustrated by imperial policies, it was events in Europe that propelled the colonies toward independence. Napoleon's decision to invade Portugal (1807) and Spain (1808), not revolutionary ideas, created a crisis of legitimacy that undermined the authority of colonial officials and ignited Latin America's struggle for independence.

As a French army neared Lisbon in 1808, the Portuguese royal family fled to Brazil. Once arrived, King John VI would maintain his court there for over a decade. Soon Napoleon forced King Ferdinand VII of Spain to abdicate and placed his own brother, Joseph Bonaparte, on the throne. Spanish patriots fighting against the French created a new political body, the Junta **(HUN-tah)** Central, to administer the areas they controlled. The junta claimed authority over Spain's colonies, inviting the election of colonial deputies to help write the nation's first written constitution.

Most residents of colonial Spanish America favored obedience to the Junta Central and many colonies elected deputies, but a vocal minority, including some members of the elite, objected. These dissenters argued that they were subjects of the king, not dependents of the Spanish nation. They wanted to create local juntas and govern their own affairs until Ferdinand regained the throne. Spanish loyalists resisted this assertion of local autonomy, provoking armed uprisings. In late 1808 and 1809 popular movements overthrew Spanish colonial officials in Venezuela, Mexico, and Alto Peru (modern Bolivia) and created local juntas. In each case, Spanish officials quickly reasserted control and punished the leaders. This harsh repression, however, further polarized public opinion in the colonies and gave rise to a greater sense of a separate American nationality. By 1810 Spanish colonial authorities were facing a new round of revolutions now focused on independence.

Spanish South America, 1810–1825

In Caracas (the capital city of modern Venezuela) a revolutionary junta led by creoles (colonial-born whites) declared independence in 1811. Although this group espoused representative democracy, its leaders were landowners who defended slavery and opposed full citizenship for the black and mixed-race majority. Their aim was to expand their own privileges by eliminating Spaniards from the upper levels of government and the church. The junta's narrow agenda spurred Spanish loyalists to rally thousands of free blacks and slaves to defend the Spanish Empire. Faced with this determined resistance, the revolutionary movement placed overwhelming political authority in the hands of its military leader **Simón Bolívar (see-MOAN bow-LEE-varh)** (1783–1830), who would become the preeminent leader of the independence movement.

The son of wealthy Venezuelan planters, Bolívar had traveled in Europe and studied the works of the Enlightenment. He was a charismatic personality who effectively mobilized

Simón Bolívar The most important military leader in the struggle for independence in South America. Born in Venezuela, he led military forces there and in Colombia, Ecuador, Peru, and Bolivia.

CHRONOLOGY

	United States and Canada	Mexico and Central America	South America
1800	1789 U.S. Constitution ratified 1803 Louisiana Purchase		
	1812–1815 War of 1812	1810–1821 Mexican movement for independence	1808 Portuguese royal family arrives in Brazil 1808–1809 Revolutions for independence begin in Spanish South America
1825	1836 Texas gains independence from Mexico 1845 Texas admitted as a state 1848 Women's Rights Convention in Seneca Falls, New York	1846–1848 War between Mexico and the United States 1847–1870 Caste War	1822 Brazil gains independence 1831 Brazil signs treaty with Great Britain to end slave trade. Illegal trade continues.
1850	1861–1865 Civil War 1867 Creation of Dominion of Canada	1857 Mexico's new constitution limits power of Catholic Church and military 1862–1867 French invade Mexico 1867 Emperor Maximilian executed	1850 Brazilian illegal slave trade suppressed 1865–1870 Argentina, Uruguay, and Brazil wage war against Paraguay
1875	1876 Sioux and allies defeat U.S. Army in Battle of Little Bighorn 1890 "Jim Crow" laws enforce segregation in South 1890s United States becomes world's leading steel producer		1870s Governments of Argentina and Chile begin final campaigns against indigenous peoples 1879–1883 Chile wages war against Peru and Bolivia; telegraph, refrigeration, and barbed wire introduced in Argentina 1888 Abolition of slavery in Brazil

political support and held the loyalty of his troops. Defeated on many occasions, Bolívar successfully adapted his objectives and policies to attract new allies and build coalitions. Although initially opposed to the abolition of slavery, for example, he agreed to support emancipation in order to draw slaves and freemen to his cause and to gain military supplies from Haiti. Bolívar was also capable of using harsh methods to ensure victory, proclaiming in 1813 that "any Spaniard who does not . . . work against tyranny in behalf of this just cause will be considered an enemy and punished; as a traitor to the nation, he will inevitably be shot by a firing squad."[1]

Military advantage shifted back and forth between the patriots and loyalists until Bolívar enlisted demobilized English and French veterans of the Napoleonic Wars. Spanish resolve was then fatally weakened by a military revolt in Spain in 1820. The European veterans, hardened by combat, improved the battlefield performance of Bolívar's army, while the revolt in Spain in 1820 forced Ferdinand VII—restored to power in 1814—to accept a constitution that limited the powers of both the monarch and the church. Colonial loyalists who for a decade had fought to maintain the authority of monarch and church viewed these reforms as unacceptably liberal.

With the king's supporters now divided, momentum swung to the patriots. After liberating present-day Venezuela, Colombia, and Ecuador, Bolívar's army entered Peru and Bolivia and defeated the last Spanish armies in 1824. Bolívar and his supporters then attempted to create a

[1]Quoted in Lyman L. Johnson, "Spanish American Independence and Its Consequences," in *Problems in Modern Latin American History: A Reader*, ed. John Charles Chasteen and Joseph S. Tulchin (Wilmington, DE: Scholarly Resources, 1994), 21.

confederation of the former Spanish colonies. The first steps were the creation of Gran Colombia (now Venezuela, Colombia, and Ecuador) and the unification of Peru and Bolivia, but these initiatives had failed by 1830 (see Map 25.1).

Buenos Aires (the capital city of modern Argentina) was the second important center of revolutionary activity in Spanish South America. In Buenos Aires news of French victories in Spain led to the creation of a junta organized by militia commanders, merchants, and ranchers, which overthrew the viceroy in 1810. To deflect the opposition of Spanish loyalists, the junta claimed loyalty to the imprisoned king. Two years after Ferdinand regained the Spanish throne in 1814, junta leaders declared independence as the United Provinces of the Río de la Plata.

Patriot leaders in Buenos Aires at first sought to retain control over the territory of the Viceroyalty of Río de la Plata, but Spanish loyalists in Uruguay and Bolivia and a separatist movement in Paraguay defeated these ambitions. Even within the territory of Argentina, the government in Buenos Aires was unable to control regional rivalries and political differences. As a result, the region rapidly descended into political chaos.

A weak succession of juntas, collective presidencies, and dictators lost control over much of the interior of Argentina. But the government in Buenos Aires did manage to support a mixed force of Chileans and Argentines led by José de San Martín (hoe-SAY deh san mar-TEEN) (1778–1850), who crossed the Andes Mountains to attack Spanish forces in Chile and Peru. During this campaign San Martín's most effective troops were former slaves, who had gained their freedom by enlisting in the army. After gaining victory in Chile, San Martín pushed on to Peru in 1820, but he failed to gain a clear victory there. Unable to make progress, San Martín surrendered command of patriot forces in Peru to Simón Bolívar, who overcame final Spanish resistance in 1824.

Mexico, 1810–1823

In 1810 Mexico was Spain's wealthiest and most populous colony. Its silver mines were the richest in the world, and the colony's capital, Mexico City, was larger than any city in Spain. Mexico also had the largest population of Spanish immigrants among the colonies. When news of Napoleon's invasion of Spain reached Mexico, conservative Spaniards in Mexico City overthrew the local viceroy, thinking him too sympathetic to the creoles. This action by Spanish loyalists underlined the new reality: with the king removed from his throne by the French, colonial authority now rested on brute force.

The first stage of the revolution against Spain occurred in central Mexico, where ranchers and farmers had aggressively forced Amerindian communities from their traditional agricultural lands. Crop failures and epidemics afflicted the region's rural poor, while miners and the urban poor faced higher food prices and rising unemployment as well. With the power of colonial authorities weakened by events in Spain, anger and fear spread through towns and villages in central Mexico.

Miguel Hidalgo y Costilla Mexican priest who led the first stage of the Mexican independence war in 1810. He was captured and executed in 1811.

On September 16, 1810, the parish priest of the small town of Dolores, **Miguel Hidalgo y Costilla (mee-GEHL ee-DAHL-go ee cos-TEA-ah)**, rang the church bells and attracted a crowd. In a fiery speech he urged the crowd to rise up against the oppression of Spanish officials. Tens of thousands of the rural and urban poor soon joined his movement. While they lacked military discipline and weapons, they knew who their oppressors were, the Spanish and colonial-born whites who owned the ranches and mines. Recognizing the threat posed by the angry masses following Hidalgo, most wealthy Mexicans supported the Spanish authorities. The military tide quickly turned, and Spanish forces captured and executed Hidalgo in 1811.

José María Morelos Mexican priest and former student of Miguel Hidalgo y Costilla, he led the forces fighting for Mexican independence until he was captured and executed in 1815.

The revolution continued under the leadership of another priest, **José María Morelos (hoe-SAY mah-REE-ah moh-RAY-los)**, a former student of Hidalgo's. A more adept military and political leader than his mentor, Morelos created a formidable fighting force and, in 1813, convened a congress that declared independence and drafted a constitution. Despite these achievements, loyalist forces defeated and executed Morelos in 1815. Although small numbers of insurgents continued to fight Spanish forces, colonial rule seemed secure in 1820, but news of the military revolt in Spain unsettled the conservative groups who had opposed Hidalgo and Morelos. In 1821 Colonel Agustín de Iturbide (ah-goos-TEEN deh ee-tur-BEE-deh) and other loyalist commanders forged an alliance with insurgents to declare Mexico's independence. The conservative origins of Mexico's independence were made clear by the decision to create a monarchial government and crown Iturbide emperor. In early 1823, however, the army overthrew Iturbide and Mexico became a republic. When Iturbide returned to Mexico from exile in 1824, he was captured and, like Hidalgo and Morelos, was executed by a firing squad.

OREGON
COUNTRY
(Joint U.S.-British
occupation)

BRITISH NORTH AMERICA
(CANADA)
(Gr. Br.)

Mississippi R.

UNITED STATES

New York
Philadelphia
Washington, D.C.

MEXICO
1821

Colorado R.

Rio Grande

San
Antonio

New Orleans

Charleston

N

ATLANTIC
OCEAN

Gulf of Mexico

Mexico City

Veracruz

BAHAMA IS.
(Gr. Br.)

Havana

HAITI 1804

CUBA
(Spain)

PUERTO RICO (Spain)

20°N

BRITISH
HONDURAS (Gr. Br.)

JAMAICA
(Gr. Br.)

GUATEMALA
Guatemala City

Caribbean Sea

UNITED PROVINCES OF
CENTRAL AMERICA
1823–1839

Panama

TRINIDAD (Gr. Br.)

Caracas

BR. GUIANA (Gr. Br.)

VENEZUELA

Magdalena R.

Orinoco R.

DUTCH GUIANA (Neth.)

FRENCH GUIANA (France)

Socorro
Bogotá

GRAN COLOMBIA
1819–1830

Equator   0°

Quito

ECUADOR

*Galápagos
Islands*

Amazon R.

EMPIRE OF BRAZIL
1822

PACIFIC

OCEAN

Lima

PERU
1824

Salvador

BOLIVIA
1825

La Paz

Sucre

Paraná R.

20°S

PARAGUAY
1811

Rio de Janeiro

São Paulo

CHILE
1817

UNITED
PROVINCES OF
THE RIO DE
LA PLATA
1816

URUGUAY
1828

Valparaíso

Santiago

ARGENTINA

Montevideo

Buenos Aires

Bahía
Blanca

PATAGONIA
(Disputed between
Argentina and Chile)

*Islas Malvinas
(Falkland Islands)*

80°W   60°W

0   500   1000 Km.

0   500   1000 Mi.

1811 Year independence gained

Colony

40°W

40°N

MAP 25.1 **Latin America by 1830** By 1830 patriot forces had overturned the Spanish and Portuguese Empires of the Western Hemisphere. Regional conflicts, local wars, and foreign interventions challenged the survival of many of these new nations following independence. © Cengage Learning

Schaalkwijk/Art Resource, NY

Miguel Hidalgo y Costilla   Padre Miguel Hidalgo y Costilla led the first stage of Mexico's revolution for independence by rallying the rural masses. His defeat, trial, and execution made him one of Mexico's most important political martyrs.

Brazil, to 1831

The arrival of the Portuguese royal family in Brazil in 1808 helped maintain the loyalty of the colonial elite. With Napoleon's defeat, the Portuguese government called for King John VI to return to Portugal. At first he resisted, but a liberal revolt in Portugal forced the king to return to Portugal in 1821 to protect his throne. He left his son Pedro in Brazil as regent.

By this date the Spanish colonies along Brazil's borders had experienced ten years of revolution and civil war, and some, like Argentina and Paraguay, had gained independence. Unable to ignore these struggles, some Brazilians began to reevaluate Brazil's relationship with Portugal. Many resented their homeland's economic subordination to Portugal, while the arrogance of Portuguese soldiers and bureaucrats led others to talk openly of independence.

Unwilling to return to Portugal and committed to maintaining his family's hold on Brazil, Pedro aligned himself with rising separatist sentiment, and in 1822 declared Brazilian independence. Pedro's decision launched Brazil on a unique political trajectory. Unlike its neighbors, which became constitutional republics, Brazil gained independence as a constitutional monarchy with Pedro I, son of the king of Portugal, as emperor.

Pedro I was committed to both monarchy and to liberal principles. The constitution of 1824 provided for an elected assembly and granted rights to the political opposition, but Pedro made enemies by protecting the Portuguese who remained in Brazil from arrest and seizure of property. Pedro I also opposed slavery, even though the slave-owning class dominated Brazil. In 1823 he anonymously published an article that characterized slavery as a "cancer eating away at Brazil" (see Diversity and Dominance: The Afro-Brazilian Experience, 1828). His decision in 1831 to ratify a treaty with Great Britain ending Brazilian participation in the slave trade provoked opposition, as did his use of military force to control neighboring Uruguay. As military losses and costs rose, the Brazilian public grew impatient. A vocal minority that sought the creation of a democracy used these issues to rally public opinion against the emperor. Confronted by street demonstrations, Pedro I abdicated the throne in 1831 in favor of his five-year-old son Pedro II. After a nine-year regency, Pedro II assumed full powers as emperor of Brazil and reigned until overthrown by republicans in 1889.

SECTION REVIEW

- The French invasion of Portugal and Spain created a political crisis in their American colonies that in turn led to independence movements.

- Under the leadership of Simón Bolívar, several South American countries gained independence.

- Mexico gained independence after a long and destructive war.

- Led by the son of the Portuguese king, Brazil gained independence as a monarchy.

THE PROBLEM OF ORDER, 1825–1890

All the newly independent nations of the Western Hemisphere encountered difficulties establishing stable political institutions. Popular sovereignty found broad support across the hemisphere as all the new nations sought to establish constitutions and elected assemblies. However, this widespread support for constitutional order and for representative government failed to prevent bitter factional conflict, regionalism, and the threats posed by charismatic political leaders and military uprisings.

Constitutional Experiments

In reaction to what they saw as arbitrary and tyrannical rule by colonial authorities, revolutionary leaders in the United States and Latin America espoused constitutionalism. They believed that the careful description of political powers in written constitutions offered the best protection for individual rights and liberties. In practice, however, many new constitutions proved unworkable. In the United States, George Washington, James Madison, and other leaders became dissatisfied with the first constitution, the Articles of Confederation, and helped write a new constitution. In Latin America few constitutions survived the rough-and-tumble of national politics. For example, Venezuela and Chile ratified and then rejected a combined total of nine constitutions between 1811 and 1833.

Important differences in colonial political experience influenced later political developments in the Americas. The ratification of a new constitution in the United States was the culmination of a long historical process that had begun with the development of English constitutional law and continued under colonial charters. The British colonies provided many opportunities for holding elective offices, and, by the time of independence, citizens had grown accustomed to elections, political parties, and factions. In contrast, neither Brazil nor Spanish America had significant experience with elections and representative institutions prior to independence.

Democratic passions and the desire for effective self-rule led to significant political reform in the Americas, even in regions that remained colonies. British Canada included a number of separate colonies and territories, each with a discrete government. A provincial governor and appointed advisory council drawn from the local elite dominated political life in each colony, while elected assemblies exercised limited power. The desire to make government responsive to the will of the assemblies led to armed rebellion in 1837. Britain responded by establishing limited self-rule in each of the Canadian provinces. By the 1860s regional political leaders realized that economic development required a government with a "national" character. Negotiations between Canadian leaders and the British government led to a union of Canadian provinces, the **Confederation of 1867**, and to the creation of the Dominion of Canada with a central government in Ottawa (see Map 25.2 on page 634).

The path to effective constitutional government was rockier to the south. Because neither Spain nor Portugal had permitted anything like the elected legislatures and municipal governments of colonial British America, the drafters of Latin American constitutions were less constrained by practical political experience. As a result, many of the new Latin American nations experimented with untested political institutions.

Latin American nations found it particularly difficult to define the role of the Catholic Church after independence. In the colonial period the Catholic Church was a religious monopoly that controlled all levels of education and dominated intellectual life. Many early constitutions aimed to reduce this power by making education secular and by permitting other religions. The church reacted by organizing and financing conservative movements. Conflicts between liberals who sought the separation of church and state and conservatives who supported the church's traditional powers dominated political life in the nineteenth century.

Limiting the power of the military was another obstacle to the creation of constitutional governments in Latin America. The wars for independence elevated the prestige of military leaders, and, when the wars were over, military commanders seldom proved willing to subordinate themselves to civilian authorities. Frustrated by the chaotic workings of democracy, many citizens saw dictatorships led by the heroes of independence as better protection for their lives and property.

Personalist Leaders

Patriot leaders in both the United States and Latin America gained mass followings during the wars for independence, and some used these followings to gain political power. George Washington's ability to dominate early republican politics in the United States anticipated the later political ascendancy of revolutionary heroes such as Iturbide in Mexico and Bolívar in Gran Colombia. In each case, military reputation provided the foundation for personal political power. Washington was distinguished from most other military leaders by his willingness to surrender power at the end of a term determined by a constitution. More commonly, **personalist leaders** relied on their mass followings rather than on constitutions and laws to govern. In Latin America, a personalist leader who gained and held political power without constitutional sanction was called a *caudillo* (kouh-DEE-yoh).

Confederation of 1867 Negotiated union of the formerly separate colonial governments of Ontario, Quebec, New Brunswick, and Nova Scotia. This new Dominion of Canada with a central government in Ottawa is seen as the beginning of the Canadian nation.

personalist leaders Political leaders who rely on charisma and their ability to mobilize and direct the masses of citizens outside the authority of constitutions and laws. Nineteenth-century examples include José Antonio Páez of Venezuela and Andrew Jackson of the United States. Twentieth-century examples include Getulio Vargas of Brazil and Juan Perón of Argentina.

The Afro-Brazilian Experience, 1828

Brazil was the most important destination for the Atlantic slave trade. From the sixteenth century to the 1850s it imported more than 2 million African slaves. Beginning in the 1820s, Great Britain, Brazil's main trading partner, began to press for an end to the slave trade. British visitors to Brazil became an important source of critical information for those who sought to end the trade.

A British clergyman, Robert Walsh, who traveled widely in Brazil in 1828 and 1829 left an account of the complex and unexpected ways that slaves and black freedmen were integrated into Brazilian society.

[At the Alfandega, or custom house,] . . . for the first time I saw the Negro population under circumstances so striking to a stranger. The whole labour of bearing and moving burdens is performed by these people, and the state in which they appear is revolting to humanity. Here were a number of beings entirely naked, with the exception of a covering of dirty rags tied about their waists. Their skins, from constant exposure to the weather, had become hard, crusty, and seamed, resembling the coarse black covering of some beast, or like that of an elephant, a wrinkled hide scattered with scanty hairs. On contemplating their persons, you saw them with a physical organization resembling beings of a grade below the rank of man. . . . Some of these beings were yoked to drays, on which they dragged heavy burdens. Some were chained by the necks and legs, and moved with loads thus encumbered. Some followed each other in ranks, with heavy weights on their heads, chattering the most inarticulate and dismal cadence as they moved along. Some were munching young sugar-canes, like beasts of burden eating green provender [animal feed], and some were seen near water, lying on the bare ground among filth and offal, coiled up like dogs, and seeming to expect or require no more comfort or accommodation, exhibiting a state and conformation so un-human, that they not only seemed, but actually were, far below the inferior animals around them. Horses and mules were not employed in this way; they were used only for pleasure, and not for labour. They were seen in the same streets, pampered, spirited, and richly caparisoned, enjoying a state far superior to the negroes, and appearing to look down on the fettered and burdened wretches they were passing, as on beings of an inferior rank in the creation to themselves. . . .

The first impression of all this on my mind, was to shake the conviction I had always felt, of the wrong and hardship inflicted on our black fellow creatures, and that they were only in that state which God and nature had assigned them; that they were the lowest grade of human existence, and the link that connected it with the brute, and that the gradation was so insensible, and their natures so intermingled, that it was impossible to tell where one had terminated and the other commenced; and that it was not surprising that people who contemplated them every day, so formed, so employed, and so degraded, should forget their claims to that rank in the scale of beings in which modern philanthropists are so anxious to place them. I did not at the moment myself recollect, that the white man, made a slave on the coast of Africa, suffers not only a similar mental but physical deterioration from hardships and emaciation, and becomes in time the dull and deformed beast I now saw yoked to a burden.

A few hours only were necessary to correct my first impressions of the negro population, by seeing them under a different aspect. We were attracted by the sound of military music, and found it proceeded from a regiment drawn up in one of the streets. Their colonel had just died, and they attended to form a procession to celebrate his obsequies. They were all of different shades of black, but the majority were negroes. Their equipment was excellent; they wore dark jackets, white pantaloons, and black leather caps and belts, all which, with their arms, were in high order. Their band produced sweet and agreeable music, of the leader's own composition, and the men went through some evolutions with regularity and dexterity. They were only a militia regiment, yet were as well appointed and disciplined as one of our regiments of the line. Here then was the first step in that gradation by which the black population of this country ascend in the scale of humanity; he advances from the state below that of a beast of burden into a military rank, and he shows himself as capable of discipline and improvement as a human being of any other colour.

Our attention was next attracted by negro men and women bearing about a variety of articles for sale; some in baskets, some on boards and cases carried on their heads. They

---

Andrew Jackson First president of the United States to be born in humble circumstances. He was popular among frontier residents, urban workers, and small farmers. He had a successful political career as judge, general, congressman, senator, and president. After being denied the presidency in 1824 in a controversial election, he won in 1828 and was reelected in 1832.

Powerful personal followings allowed **Andrew Jackson** of the United States and **José Antonio Páez** (hoe-SAY an-TOE-nee-oh PAH-ays) of Venezuela to challenge constitutional limits to their authority. During the independence wars in Venezuela and Colombia, Páez (1790–1873) was one of Bolívar's most successful generals. Like most of his followers, Páez was uneducated and poor, but his physical strength, courage, and guile made him a natural guerrilla leader and helped him build a powerful political base. Páez described his authority in the following manner: "[The soldiers] resolved to confer on me the supreme command and blindly to obey my will, confident . . . that I was the only one who could save them."[2] Able to count on the personal loyalty of his followers, Páez was seldom willing to accept the constitutional authority of a distant president.

---

[2]José Antonio Páez, *Autobiografía del General José Antonio Páez*, vol. 1 (New York: Hallety Breen, 1869), 83.

belonged to a class of small shopkeepers, many of whom vend their wares at home, but the greater number send them about in this way, as in itinerant shops. A few of these people were still in a state of bondage, and brought a certain sum every evening to their owners, as the produce of their daily labour. But a large proportion, I was informed, were free, and exercised this little calling on their own account. They were all very neat and clean in their persons, and had a decorum and sense of respectability about them, superior to whites of the same class and calling. All their articles were good in their kind, and neatly kept, and they sold them with simplicity and confidence, neither wishing to take advantage of others, nor suspecting that it would be taken of themselves. I bought some confectionary from one of the females, and I was struck with the modesty and propriety of her manner; she was a young mother, and had with her a neatly dressed child, of which she seemed very fond. I gave it a little comfit [candy covered nut], and it turned up its dusky countenance to her and then to me, taking my sweetmeat, and at the same time kissing my hand. As yet unacquainted with the coin of the country, I had none that was current about me, and was leaving the articles; but the poor young woman pressed them on me with a ready confidence, repeating in broken Portuguese, *outo tempo*. [sic.], I am sorry to say, the "other time" never came, for I could not recognize her person afterwards to discharge her little debt, though I went to the same place for the purpose.

It soon began to grow dark, and I was attracted by a number of persons bearing large lighted wax tapers, like torches, gathering before a house. As I passed by, one was put into my hand by a man who seemed in some authority, and I was requested to fall into a procession that was forming. It was the preparation for a funeral, and on such occasions, I learned that they always request the attendance of a passing stranger, and feel hurt if they are refused. I joined the party, and proceeded with them to a neighbouring church. When we entered we arranged ourselves on each side of a platform which stood near the choir, on which was laid an open coffin, covered with pink silk and gold borders. The funeral service was chanted by a choir of priests, one of whom was a negro, a large comely man, whose jet black visage formed a strong and striking contrast to his white vestments. He seemed to perform his part with a decorum and sense of solemnity, which I did not observe in his brethren. After scattering flowers on the coffin, and fumigating it with incense, they retired, the procession dispersed, and

we returned on board. I had been but a few hours on shore, for the first time, and I saw an African negro under four aspects of society; and it appeared to me, that in every one his character depended on the state in which he was placed, and the estimation in which he was held. As a despised slave, he was far lower than other animals of burthen that surrounded him; more miserable in his look, more revolting in his nakedness, more distorted in his person, and apparently more deficient in intellect than the horses and mules that passed him by. Advanced to the grade of a soldier, he was clean and neat in his person, amenable to discipline, expert at his exercises, and showed the port [sic.] and being of a white man similarly placed. As a citizen, he was remarkable for the respectability of his appearance, and the decorum of his manners in the rank assigned him; and as a priest, standing in the house of God, appointed to instruct society on their most important interests, and in a grade in which moral and intellectual fitness is required, and a certain degree of superiority is expected, he seemed even more devout in his impressions, and more correct in his manners, than his white associates. I came, therefore, to the irresistible conclusion in my mind, that colour was an accident affecting the surface of a man, and having no more to do with his qualities than his clothes—that God had equally created an African in the image of his person, and equally given him an immortal soul; and that an European had no pretext but his own cupidity, for impiously thrusting his fellow man from that rank in the creation which the Almighty had assigned him, and degrading him below the lot of the brute beasts that perish.

QUESTIONS FOR ANALYSIS

1. What is the author's first impression of the Brazilian slave population?

2. What does the author later observe that changes this opinion?

3. How did slavery dehumanize slaves?

4. What circumstances or opportunities permitted Brazil's free blacks to improve their lives?

Source: Robert Walsh, *Notices of Brazil in 1828 and 1829*, 2 vols. (London: Frederick Westley and A. H. Davis, 1830), I, 134-141.

José Antonio Páez Venezuelan soldier who led Simón Bolívar's cavalry force. He became a successful general in the war and built a powerful political base. Unwilling to accept the constitutional authority of Bolívar's government in distant Bogotá, he declared Venezuela's independence from Gran Colombia in 1829.

After defeating the Spanish, Bolívar pursued his dream of forging a union of former Spanish colonies modeled on the United States. But he underestimated the strength of nationalist sentiment unleashed by the independence wars. Páez and other Venezuelan leaders resisted the surrender of their hard-won power to Bolívar's Gran Colombian government in distant Bogotá. When political opponents challenged Bolívar in 1829, Páez declared Venezuela's independence. Merciless to his enemies and indulgent with his followers, Páez ruled the country as president or dictator for the next eighteen years. Despite implementing an economic program favorable to the elite, Páez remained popular with the masses. Even as his personal wealth grew, he took care to present himself as a common man.

Andrew Jackson (1767–1845) was the first U.S. president born in humble circumstances. A self-made man who eventually acquired substantial property and owned over a hundred slaves, Jackson was extremely popular among frontier residents, urban workers, and small farmers.

MAP 25.2 **Dominion of Canada, 1873** Although independence was not yet achieved and settlement remained concentrated along the U.S. border, Canada had established effective political and economic control over its western territories by 1873. © Cengage Learning

Although he was notorious for his untidy personal life as well as for dueling, his courage, individualism, and willingness to challenge authority helped him attain political success as judge, general, congressman, senator, and president.

During his military career, Jackson proved to be impatient with civilian authorities. Widely known because of his victories over the Creek and Seminole peoples, he was elevated to the pinnacle of American politics by his celebrated defeat of the British at the Battle of New Orleans in 1815 and by his seizure of Florida from the Spanish in 1818. In 1824 he received a plurality of the popular votes for president but failed to win a majority of electoral votes. His followers were embittered when the House of Representatives chose John Quincy Adams as president.

Jackson's followers viewed his landslide election victory in 1828 and reelection in 1832 as the triumph of democracy over entrenched aristocracy. In office Jackson challenged constitutional limits on his authority, increasing presidential power at the expense of Congress and the Supreme Court. Like Páez, Jackson was able to dominate national politics by blending a populist political style that celebrated the virtues and cultural enthusiasms of common people with support for policies that promoted the economic interests of powerful propertied groups.

Personalist leaders were common in both Latin America and the United States, but Latin America's weaker constitutional tradition, more limited protection of property rights, lower literacy levels, and less-developed communications systems facilitated the ambitions of popular politicians. Latin America's personalist leaders often ignored constitutional restraints on their authority, and election results seldom determined access to presidential power. As a result, by 1900 every independent Latin American nation had experienced periods of dictatorship.

The Threat of Regionalism

After independence, national governments were generally weaker than the colonial governments they replaced. Debates over tariffs, tax and monetary policies, and, in many nations, slavery and the slave trade led regional elites to attempt secession. Some of the hemisphere's newly independent nations did not survive these struggles, while others lost territories to aggressive neighbors.

In Spanish America all efforts to forge large multistate federations after independence failed. The Viceroyalty of New Spain had included Central America and Mexico, but after independence this union failed when in 1823 local elites broke with Mexico to form the Republic of Central America. A new round of regional disputes and civil wars led to the creation of five separate nations during the 1820s and 1830s. In South America, Bolívar attempted to maintain the colonial unity of Venezuela, Colombia, and Ecuador by creating Gran Colombia with its capital in Bogotá. But even before his death in 1830, Venezuela and Ecuador had become independent states. In the colonial era Argentina, Uruguay, Paraguay, and Bolivia were organized as a single viceroyalty with its capital in Buenos Aires. After the defeat of Spain, the leaders in Paraguay, Uruguay, and Bolivia declared their independence from Argentina.

Regionalism threatened the United States as well. The defense of state and regional interests played an important role in the framing of the U.S. Constitution. Many important constitutional provisions represented compromises forged among competing state and regional leaders. Yet, despite these constitutional compromises, regional rivalries still threatened the nation.

Slavery divided the nation into two separate and competitive societies. A rising tide of immigration to the northern states in the 1830s and 1840s began to move the center of political power away from the South. Southern leaders sought to protect slavery by expanding into new territories. They supported the Louisiana Purchase in 1803 (see Map 25.3), which transferred to

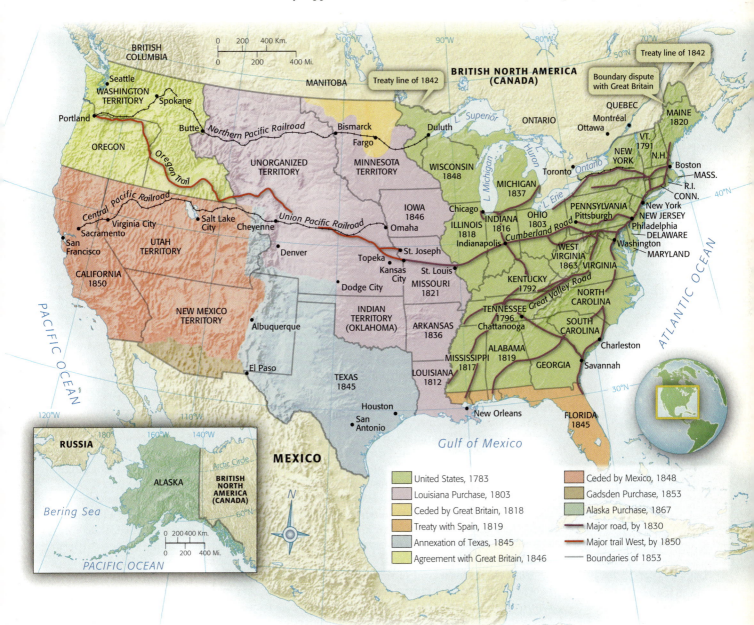

MAP 25.3 **Territorial Growth of the United States, 1783–1853** The rapid western expansion of the United States resulted from aggressive diplomacy and warfare against Mexico and Amerindian peoples. Railroad development helped integrate the trans-Mississippi west and promote economic expansion. © Cengage Learning

the United States a vast French territory extending from the Gulf of Mexico to Canada, and the Mexican-American War in 1846, which added nearly half of Mexico to the United States. However, this territorial expansion forced a national debate about slavery that contributed to the election of Abraham Lincoln as president in 1860.

Lincoln was committed to checking the spread of slavery, and his election provoked the southern planter elite to choose the dangerous course of secession from the Union. The seceding states formed a new government, the Confederate States of America, known as the Confederacy. Lincoln preserved the Union but at an enormous cost. The U.S. Civil War (1861–1865) was the most destructive conflict in the history of the Western Hemisphere. Up to 750,000 lives were lost before the Confederacy surrendered in 1865. The Union victory led to the abolition of slavery and also transferred national political power to a northern elite committed to industrial expansion and federal support for the construction of railroads and other internal improvements.

The Confederate States of America was better prepared politically and economically for independence than were the successful secessionist movements that broke up Gran Colombia and other Spanish American federations. Nevertheless, the Confederacy failed, in part because of poor timing. The new nations of the Western Hemisphere were most vulnerable to secessionist movements in the early years of their existence; indeed, all the successful secessions occurred shortly after independence. In the case of the United States, an experienced national government legitimated and strengthened by more than seven decades of relative stability and reinforced by dramatic economic and population growth defeated secession only with enormous effort.

Foreign Interventions and Regional Wars

Wars often determined national borders, access to natural resources, and control of markets in the Western Hemisphere. Even after the achievement of independence, Mexico and other Western Hemisphere nations were forced to defend themselves against Europe's great powers. Contested national borders and regional rivalries also led to wars between Western Hemisphere nations. By the end of the nineteenth century the United States, Brazil, Argentina, and Chile had all successfully waged wars against their neighbors and established themselves as regional powers.

Within thirty years of independence, the United States fought a second war with England—the War of 1812. The burning of the White House and Capitol by British troops in 1814 symbolized the weakness of the new republic. By the end of the nineteenth century, however, the United States was the hemisphere's greatest military power. Its war against Spain in 1898–1899 created an American empire that reached from the Philippines in the Pacific Ocean to Puerto Rico in the Caribbean (see Chapter 26).

European powers challenged the sovereignty of Latin American nations as well. Following independence Argentina faced British and French naval blockades, and British naval forces systematically violated Brazil's territorial waters to stop the importation of slaves. Mexico faced the most serious threats to sovereignty, defeating a weak Spanish invasion in 1829, a French assault on the city of Veracruz in 1838, and a large-scale French invasion in 1862.

Mexico also faced a grave threat from the United States. In the 1820s Mexico had encouraged Americans to immigrate to its northern province of Texas. By the early 1830s Americans outnumbered Mexican nationals in Texas and were aggressively challenging Mexican laws such as the prohibition of slavery. An alliance of Mexican liberals and American settlers rebelled in 1835 and gained independence for Texas in 1836. In 1845 the United States made Texas a state, provoking war with Mexico a year later. The surrender of Mexico City in 1848 to American forces compelled Mexico to accept a harsh treaty that forced it to cede vast territories to the United States, including present-day New Mexico, Arizona, and California. In return Mexico received $15 million. When gold was discovered in California in 1848, the magnitude of Mexico's loss became clear.

Benito Juárez President of Mexico (1858–1872). Born in poverty in Mexico, he was educated as a lawyer and rose to become chief justice of the Mexican supreme court and then president. He led Mexico's resistance to a French invasion in 1862 and the installation of Maximilian as emperor.

With the very survival of the nation at stake, Mexico's liberals took power and imposed sweeping reforms, including a new constitution in 1857 that limited the power of the Catholic Church and military. This provoked a civil war with conservatives (1858–1861). **Benito Juárez (beh-NEE-toh WAH-rez)** assumed the presidency and defeated the conservatives, who then turned to Napoleon III of France for assistance. In 1862, French forces invaded Mexico, forced Juárez to flee Mexico City, and installed the Austrian Habsburg Maximilian as emperor of Mexico. After years of warfare, Juárez drove the French army out of Mexico in 1867, aided by U.S. diplomatic pressure. After capturing Maximilian, Juárez ordered his execution.

Execution of Emperor Maximilian of Mexico
This painting by Edouard Manet shows the 1867 execution by firing squad of Maximilian and two of his Mexican generals. The defeat of the French intervention was a great triumph for Mexican patriots led by Benito Juárez.

Erich Lessing/Art Resource, NY

This victory over a powerful foreign enemy redeemed a nation humiliated two decades earlier by the United States. But the creation of democracy proved more elusive than the protection of Mexican sovereignty. Despite the Mexican constitution's prohibition of presidential reelection, Juárez would serve as president until his death in 1872.

As was clear in the Mexican-American War, wars between Western Hemisphere nations could lead to dramatic territorial changes. Chile established itself as the leading military and economic power on the west coast of South America when it fought two successful wars against an alliance of Peru and Bolivia (1836–1839 and 1879–1883). The second contest, the War of the Pacific, forced Bolivia to cede its only outlet to the sea and Peru to yield rich mining districts.

Argentina and Brazil fought for control of Uruguay in the 1820s, but a military stalemate eventually forced them to recognize Uruguayan independence. Then, in 1865, Argentina and Uruguay joined Brazil to wage war against Paraguay (War of the Triple Alliance). After five years of warfare, the Paraguayan dictator Francisco Solano López **(fran-CEES-co so-LAN-oh LOH-pehz)** and more than 20 percent of the nation's population had died. Paraguay then experienced military occupation, loss of territory, and economic penalties.

Native Peoples and the Nation-State

Both diplomacy and war shaped relations between the Western Hemisphere's new nation-states and indigenous peoples. During late colonial times, Spanish, Portuguese, and British colonial governments attempted to restrict the expansion of settlements into territories occupied by Amerindians. With independence, the colonial powers' role as mediator and protector ended.

Still-independent Amerindian peoples posed a significant military challenge to many Western Hemisphere republics. Weakened by civil wars and constitutional crises, new nations were less able to maintain frontier peace than the colonial governments they replaced. After independence Amerindian peoples in Argentina, the United States, Chile, and Mexico succeeded in pushing back frontier settlements. But despite early victories, native military resistance was overcome in most of the hemisphere by 1890.

After the American Revolution, tens of thousands of settlers entered territories previously guaranteed to Amerindians by treaties with Britain. Indigenous leaders responded by forging military alliances with British officials in Canada and with other native peoples. In the Ohio

Tecumseh Shawnee leader who attempted to organize an Amerindian confederacy to prevent the loss of additional territory to American settlers. He became an ally of the British in War of 1812 and died in battle.

River Valley two Shawnee brothers, **Tecumseh (teh-CUM-sah)** and the Prophet (Tenskwatawa), created a broad, well-organized alliance among Amerindian peoples that gained British support. During the War of 1812, American military forces defeated the alliance. Tecumseh died in battle fighting alongside his British allies.

Throughout the 1820s native peoples lost lands to settlers across the Midwest and Southeast. The 1828 presidential election of Andrew Jackson, a veteran of earlier wars against native peoples, brought matters to a head. The Indian Removal Act of 1830 forced the resettlement of Cherokee, Creek, Choctaw, and other eastern peoples to land west of the Mississippi River. Nearly half these forced migrants died on this journey, known as the Trail of Tears.

The native peoples of the Great Plains offered formidable resistance to the expansion of white settlement. By the time substantial numbers of white buffalo hunters, cattlemen, and settlers reached the American west, indigenous peoples were skilled in the use of horses and firearms. These technologies allowed the Sioux, Comanche, Pawnee, Kiowa, and other plains peoples to hunt more efficiently and develop potent military capacities.

After the Civil War, however, a new wave of settlers pushed onto the plains. Buffalo herds were hunted to near extinction and native lands were appropriated by farmers and ranchers. Amerindian resistance to these assaults on their way of life led to four decades of armed conflict with the United States Army. The U.S. government forced the Comanche, who had long dominated the southern plains, to cede their traditional lands in Texas in 1865. The Sioux and their allies held out longer, overwhelming General George Armstrong Custer and the Seventh Cavalry in the Battle of Little Bighorn in 1876, but they were also soon forced to accept reservation life. Military campaigns in the 1870s and 1880s then broke the resistance of the Apache.

The indigenous peoples of Argentina and Chile experienced a similar trajectory of adaptation, resistance, and defeat. Herds of wild cattle provided these peoples with a limitless food supply, and their mastery of the horse increased their military capacities. For a while the natives of Argentina and Chile were able to check the southern expansion of agriculture and ranching. Unable to defeat these resourceful enemies, the governments of Argentina and Chile relied on an elaborate system of gift giving and prisoner exchanges to maintain peace on the frontier.

By the 1860s, however, population increase, political stability, and military modernization allowed Argentina and Chile to take the offensive. In the 1870s the government of Argentina used a large military force armed with modern weapons to crush native resistance on the pampas. In the 1850s, civil war and an economic depression weakened the Chilean government, and the Mapuches **(mah-POO-chez)** (also called "Araucanians") pushed back frontier settlements, but by the 1870s Chilean forces had overwhelmed Amerindian resistance.

In Chile, Argentina, and the United States, national governments justified military campaigns by demonizing native peoples. Newspaper editorials and the speeches of politicians

Navajo Leaders Gathered in Washington to Negotiate As settlers pushed west in the nineteenth century, Amerindian peoples were forced to negotiate territorial concessions with the U.S. government. This photo shows Navajo leaders and their Anglo translators in Washington, D.C., in 1874.

National Anthropological Archives, Smithsonian Institution, SPC BAE 4420 Vol 6 01007800

SECTION REVIEW

- The new nations of the Western Hemisphere, including the United States, found it difficult to establish constitutional governments.

- Charismatic military leaders with large followings, like Andrew Jackson and José Antonio Páez, often took power and challenged constitutional limits on presidential power.

- Secessionist movements and civil wars threatened the survival of many Latin American nations and the United States.

- Wars with foreign powers and neighboring states endangered the independence and national borders of many Western Hemisphere nations.

- Native peoples throughout the hemisphere tried to defend their territories, but by the end of the nineteenth century, national governments had overcome native resistance.

portrayed Amerindians as brutal and cruel and as obstacles to progress. In April 1859 a Chilean newspaper commented:

> The necessity, not only to punish the Araucanian [Mapuche] race, but also to make it impotent to harm us, is well recognized . . . as the only way to rid the country of a million evils. It is well understood that they are odious and prejudicial guests in Chile . . . conciliatory measures have accomplished nothing with this stupid race—the infamy and disgrace of the Chilean nation.[3]

The author of this racist pronouncement apparently felt no obligation to explain how his nation's original inhabitants had become "guests."

Political divisions and civil wars within the new nations also provided opportunities for some long-pacified native peoples to rebel. In the Yucatán region of Mexico, large landowners forced many Maya **(MY-ah)** communities from traditional agricultural lands, reducing thousands to peonage. Weakened by internal rebellions and by the American invasion, the Mexican government faced a

Caste War A rebellion of the Maya people against the government of Mexico in 1847 that nearly returned the Yucatán to Maya rule. Some Maya rebels retreated to unoccupied territories, where they held out until 1901.

mass rebellion by the Maya in 1847. This well-organized and popular uprising, known as the **Caste War**, nearly returned the Yucatán to native control. Grievances accumulated over more than three hundred years led to great violence and property destruction. The end of the war with the United States allowed the government of Mexico to regain control of major towns. Even then, some Maya rebels retreated to unoccupied territories and created an independent state, which they called the "Empire of the Cross." Organized around a mix of traditional beliefs and Christian symbols, this indigenous state resisted Mexican forces until 1870. A few Maya strongholds survived until 1901.

THE CHALLENGE OF SOCIAL AND ECONOMIC CHANGE

During the nineteenth century the newly independent nations of the Western Hemisphere struggled to realize the Enlightenment ideals of freedom and individual liberty that had helped ignite the revolutions for independence. The persistence of slavery and other oppressive colonial-era institutions slowed this process. Nevertheless, by century's end reform movements had ended the slave trade, abolished slavery, expanded voting rights, and assimilated immigrants from Asia and Europe.

Industrialization and integration in the world economy sometimes challenged political stability and social arrangements. While a small number of Western Hemisphere nations embraced industrialization, most were dependent on the export of agricultural and mining production. By the end of the century it was clear that the industrializing nations had grown richer than the nations that remained exporters of raw materials. All the region's economies, regardless of development path, had become more vulnerable and volatile as a result of greater dependence on foreign markets. Like contemporary movements for social reform, efforts to assert economic sovereignty produced powerful new political forces.

The Abolition of Slavery

abolitionists Men and women who agitated for a complete end to slavery. Abolitionist pressure ended the British transatlantic slave trade in 1808 and slavery in British colonies in 1834. In the United States the activities of abolitionists were one factor leading to the Civil War (1861–1865).

Leaders of the independence movements of the United States and Latin America asserted ideals of universal freedom and citizenship that contrasted sharply with the reality of slavery. Those who sought to end the institution were called **abolitionists**. Despite their efforts, slavery survived in most of the hemisphere until the 1850s. It proved especially difficult to eradicate in regions where the export of plantation products was most important—such as the United States, Brazil, and Cuba.

---

[3]Quoted in Brian Loveman, *Chile: The Legacy of Hispanic Capitalism* (New York: Oxford University Press, 1979), 170.

Slavery in the United States was weakened first by the abolition of slavery in some northern states and by the end of the African slave trade in 1808. But the profitable expansion of cotton agriculture after the War of 1812 stalled further progress. In Spanish America tens of thousands of slaves gained freedom by joining revolutionary armies during the wars for independence (see Chapter 23). After independence, most Spanish American republics prohibited the slave trade, but growing international demand for sugar and coffee slowed the achievement of abolition. As prices rose for plantation products, Brazil and Cuba increased their imports of slaves.

During the long struggle to end slavery in the United States, American abolitionists argued that slavery offended Christian morality and the universal rights asserted in the Declaration of Independence. Abolitionist Theodore Weld articulated the religious objection to slavery in 1834:

> *No condition of birth, no shade of color, no mere misfortune of circumstance, can annul the birth-right charter, which God has bequeathed to every being upon whom he has stamped his own image, by making him a free* moral agent *[emphasis in original], and that he who robs his fellow man of this tramples upon right, subverts justice, outrages humanity . . . and sacrilegiously assumes the prerogative of God.*[4]

Two groups denied full rights under the Constitution, women and free African Americans, played important roles in the abolition of slavery. Women were among the leaders of the American Anti-Slavery Society and produced effective propaganda against slavery. Eventually, thousands of women joined the abolitionist cause. Social conservatives attacked their highly visible public role, leading many women to become public advocates of female suffrage as well. Frederick Douglass, a former slave, was one of the most visible and effective leaders of the abolitionist movement. Some black leaders, believing that peaceful means would fail, pushed the abolitionist movement to accept the inevitability of violence. In 1843 Henry Highland Garnet stirred the National Colored Convention when he demanded, "Brethren, arise, arise, arise! . . . Let every slave in the land do this and the days of slavery are numbered."[5]

In the 1850s the electoral strength of the newly formed Republican Party forced a confrontation between slave and free states. Following the election of Abraham Lincoln in 1860, eleven southern states seceded from the Union. During the Civil War pressure for emancipation rose as tens of thousands of black freemen and escaped slaves joined the Union army. In 1863, in the midst of the Civil War and two years after the abolition of serfdom in Russia (see Chapter 27), Lincoln issued the Emancipation Proclamation, ending slavery in rebel states not occupied by the Union army. In 1865 the Thirteenth Amendment to the Constitution abolished slavery completely, but most African Americans continued to live in harsh conditions. By the end of the century southern states had instituted "Jim Crow" laws that segregated blacks in public transportation, jobs, and schools. The implementation of these laws coincided with increased racial violence that saw an average of fifty African Americans lynched each year.

In Brazil slavery survived for more than two decades after abolition in the United States. Britain, Brazil's major trading partner, pressed for an end to the slave trade after prohibiting this trade to its own colonies. Despite agreeing to end the trade in 1830, Brazil imported another half-million African slaves before the British navy forced compliance in the 1850s. The Brazilian emperor, Pedro II, and many liberals worked to abolish slavery, but their effort to find a form of gradual emancipation acceptable to slave owners failed.

During Brazil's war with Paraguay (1865–1870), large numbers of slaves joined the Brazilian army in exchange for freedom. Their patriotism and heroism convinced many Brazilians of the injustice of slavery. Educated Brazilians had also come to view slavery as an obstacle to economic development and as an impediment to democratic reform. As political support for slavery weakened in the 1880s, growing numbers of slaves fled their masters and army officers resisted demands to capture and return the runaways. Brazil finally abolished slavery in 1888. A year later a rebellion ended the Brazilian monarchy.

The Caribbean received almost 40 percent of all African slaves shipped to the New World. Throughout the region, tiny white minorities lived surrounded by slave and free colored majorities. In the eighteenth century the slave rebellion in Saint Domingue (see Chapter 23) spread terror among slave owners across the Caribbean, convincing slave owners that any effort to overthrow colonial rule would unleash new insurrections. As a result, there was little local support

---

[4]Quoted in Bernard Bailyn, David Brion Davis, David Herbert Donald, John L. Thomas, Robert H. Wiebe, and Gordon S. Wood, *The Great Republic: A History of the American People* (Lexington, MA: D. C. Heath, 1981), 398.

[5]Quoted in Mary Beth Norton et al., *A People and a Nation: A History of the United States*, 6th ed. (Boston: Houghton Mifflin, 2001), 284.

Courtesy, Fundacao Biblioteca Nacional, Brazil

A Former Brazilian Slave Returns from Military Service
The heroic actions of black freemen and slaves in the Paraguayan War (1865–1870) led many Brazilians to condemn slavery. The original caption for this drawing reads: "On his return from the war in Paraguay: Full of glory, covered with laurels, after having spilled his blood in defense of the fatherland and to free a people from slavery, the volunteer sees his own mother bound and whipped! Awful reality!"

for abolition in the Caribbean. In these colonies abolition would result from decisions made in Europe by imperial governments.

In the Caribbean, as in Brazil and other plantation economies, slaves helped to force abolition by rebelling, running away, and resisting in more subtle ways. Although slave rebellions in Jamaica and Cuba and other Caribbean colonies failed to achieve the success of the Haitian Revolution (1791–1804), they made clear that slaves would never accept their condition.

After 1800, when the profitability of sugar plantations in the British West Indian colonies declined, a coalition of British labor unions, Protestant ministers, and free traders pushed for the abolition of slavery. Britain, the major participant in the eighteenth-century expansion of slavery in the Americas, ended its participation in the slave trade in 1807. It then negotiated treaties with Spain, Brazil, and other importers of slaves to eliminate the slave trade and used its naval forces to force compliance.

Abolition in British colonies occurred in 1834, but "freed" slaves were compelled to remain with former masters as "apprentices." Abuses by planters and resistance to apprenticeship by former slaves led to complete abolition in 1838. A decade later, France abolished slavery in its Caribbean colonies. The decision to abolish slavery in the Dutch Empire in 1863 freed 33,000 slaves in Surinam and 12,000 in the Antilles.

In the Caribbean, slavery lasted longest in Spain's remaining colonies of Cuba and Puerto Rico. Britain used diplomatic pressure and naval force to undermine the slave trade after 1820, but local support for abolition appeared as well. Both Cuba and Puerto Rico had larger white and free colored populations than did the Caribbean colonies of Britain and France, and there was little fear that abolition would lead to the political ascendancy of former slaves. In Puerto Rico, where slaves numbered approximately 30,000, local reformers secured the abolition of slavery in 1873. In Cuba, where slavery was much more important because of a booming sugar industry, forces supporting independence helped propel the Spanish colonial government toward abolition (see Environment and Technology: Industrializing Sugar Agriculture in Cuba). Beginning in the 1870s, Spain passed a series of laws promoting gradual abolition but requiring long periods of service to former masters. Spain finally abolished slavery in 1886.

Immigration

During the colonial period free Europeans were a minority among immigrants to the Western Hemisphere. From 1500 to 1760 imported African slaves outnumbered European immigrants in the Western Hemisphere by nearly two to one. Another 4 million African slaves were then imported before the end of the slave trade in the 1850s. After the African slave trade came to an end, millions of Europeans and Asians arrived in the Western Hemisphere as immigrants. This new flood of immigrants in the nineteenth century helped foster the rapid economic growth and territorial occupation of frontier regions in the United States, Canada, Argentina, Chile, and Brazil. By century's end nearly all of the hemisphere's fastest-growing cities (Buenos Aires, Chicago, New York, and São Paulo, for example) had large immigrant populations. In general, European immigrants avoided regions that had depended on slavery with their traditions of oppressive labor conditions and low wages. At the same time, tens of thousands of immigrants from China and India arrived with indenture contracts that directed them to plantation zones in the Caribbean region.

Europe provided the majority of immigrants to the Western Hemisphere in the nineteenth century. Initially, most came from western Europe, but after 1870 most immigrants were southern or eastern Europeans. The United States received approximately 600,000 European immigrants in the 1830s, 1.5 million in the 1840s, and then 2.5 million per decade until 1880. In the 1890s an astonishing total of 5.2 million immigrants arrived. Immigration helped push the national population from 39 million in 1871 to 63 million in 1891. Most of these immigrants settled in cities. Chicago, for example, grew from 444,000 in 1870 to 1.7 million in 1900.

Chinese Funeral in Vancouver, Canada In the 1890s Vancouver was an important destination for Chinese immigrants. This photo shows how an important element of traditional Chinese culture thrived among the storefronts and streetcar lines of the late-Victorian Canadian city.

Vancouver Public Library, Special Collections, VPL #17064

European immigration to Latin America also increased dramatically. Combined immigration to Argentina and Brazil rose from under 130,000 in the 1860s to 1.7 million in the 1890s. By 1910, 30 percent of the Argentine population was foreign-born, more than twice the proportion in the U.S. population. Argentina was an extremely attractive destination for European immigrants, receiving more than twice as many immigrants as Canada between 1870 and 1930. Even so, immigration to Canada increased tenfold during this period.

Asian immigration to the Western Hemisphere also increased after 1850. Between 1849 and 1875, approximately 100,000 Chinese immigrants arrived in Peru and another 120,000 entered Cuba. Canada attracted about 50,000 Chinese immigrants in the second half of the century, and the United States received 300,000 Chinese immigrants between 1854 and 1882. India also contributed to the social transformation of the Western Hemisphere, sending more than a half-million immigrants to the Caribbean region. British Guiana alone received 238,000 immigrants, mostly indentured laborers, from the Asian subcontinent.

Despite the obvious economic benefits that accompanied this inflow of people, hostility to immigration mounted in many nations. Nativist political movements argued that it was impossible to integrate large numbers of foreigners into national political cultures. By the end of the century, fear and prejudice led many governments in the Western Hemisphere to limit immigration or to distinguish between "desirable" and "undesirable" immigrants, commonly favoring Europeans over Asians.

Asians faced more obstacles than did Europeans and were more often victims of violence and discrimination. In the 1870s and 1880s anti-Chinese riots erupted in many western cities in the United States. Congress responded to this wave of racism by passing the Chinese Exclusion Act in 1882, which eliminated most Chinese immigration. In 1886 popular fears that "inferior races" threatened Canada led that government to impose a head tax, making immigration more difficult for Chinese families. During this same period strong anti-Chinese prejudice surfaced in Peru, Mexico, and Cuba. Japanese immigrants in Brazil and East Indians in the English-speaking Caribbean faced similar prejudice.

European immigrants faced prejudice and discrimination as well. Popular opinion portrayed Italians as criminals or anarchists. In Argentina and the United States, some social

Arrest of Labor Activist in Buenos Aires   The labor movement in Buenos Aires grew in numbers and became more radical with the arrival of tens of thousands of Italian and Spanish immigrants. Fearful of socialist and anarchist unions, the government of Argentina used an expanded police force to break strikes.

Archivo General de la Nación, Buenos Aires

scientists argued that Italian immigrants were more violent and less honest than the native-born population. Immigrants from Spain were widely stereotyped in Argentina as miserly and dishonest. Eastern European Jews seeking to escape pogroms and discrimination at home found themselves barred from many educational institutions and professional careers in both the United States and Latin America. Irish, German, Swedish, Polish, and Middle Eastern immigrants were branded with negative stereotypes as well. The justifications for these prejudices were remarkably similar from Canada to Argentina. Immigrants, critics claimed, threatened the well-being of native-born workers by accepting low wages and threatened national culture by resisting assimilation.

Many intellectuals and political leaders wondered if the evolving mix of culturally diverse populations could sustain a common citizenship. This concern led to efforts to compel immigrants to assimilate. Schools became cultural battlegrounds where language, cultural values, and patriotic attitudes were transmitted to the children of immigrants. Ignoring Canada's large French-speaking population, an English-speaking Canadian reformer commented on recent immigration: "If Canada is to become in a real sense a nation, if our people are to become one people, we must have one language."[6] These fears and prejudices promoted the singing of patriotic songs, the veneration of national flags and other symbols, and the writing of national histories that emphasized patriotism and civic virtue.

American Cultures

Despite discrimination, immigrants continued to stream into the Western Hemisphere, where they introduced new languages, living arrangements, technologies, and customs. Immigrants also altered politics in many of the hemisphere's nations as they sought to influence government policies and gain access to power. To compensate for their isolation from home, language, and culture, most immigrant groups created ethnically based mutual aid societies, sports and leisure clubs, and neighborhoods. These organizations provided valuable social and economic support for recent arrivals while sometimes worsening the fears of the native-born that immigration posed a threat to national culture. At the same time, shared experiences in their adopted nations as workers, neighbors, or soldiers changed immigrants individually and collectively. The modification of language, customs, values, and behaviors as a result of contact with people from another culture is called **acculturation**.

acculturation The adoption of the language, customs, values, and behaviors of host nations by immigrants.

[6]J. S. Woodsworth in 1909, quoted in R. Douglas Francis, Richard Jones, and Donald B. Smith, *Destinies: Canadian History Since Confederation*, 2d ed. (Toronto: Holt, Rinehart and Winston, 1992), 141.

Immigrants and their children, in turn, made their mark on the cultures of their adopted nations. They learned the language spoken in their adopted countries as fast as possible in order to improve their earning capacity, while words and phrases from their languages entered the vocabularies of their adoptive nations. Languages as diverse as Yiddish and Italian strongly influenced American English, Argentine Spanish, and Brazilian Portuguese. Dietary practices introduced from Europe and Asia altered the cuisine of nearly every American nation. In popular music, the Argentine tango, based on African rhythms, was transformed by new instrumentation and orchestral arrangements brought by Italian immigrants. Mexican ballads blended with English folk music in the U.S. Southwest, and Italian operas played to packed houses in Buenos Aires.

Union movements and electoral politics in the hemisphere also felt the influence of new arrivals who aggressively sought to influence politics and improve working conditions. The anarchist and socialist beliefs of European immigrants influenced the labor movements of Mexico, Argentina, and the United States. Immigrants also helped form new political movements. Their mutual benevolent societies and less formal ethnic associations pooled resources to help immigrants open businesses, aid the immigration of relatives, or bury family members.

Women's Rights and the Struggle for Social Justice

Women's Rights Convention
An 1848 gathering of women angered by their exclusion from an international antislavery meeting. They met at Seneca Falls, New York, to discuss women's rights.

In 1848 a group of women angered by their exclusion from an international antislavery meeting issued a call for a conference to discuss women's rights. The resulting **Women's Rights Convention** at Seneca Falls, New York, issued a statement that said, in part, "We hold these truths to be self-evident: that all men and women are equal." While moderates focused on the issues of economic independence and legal rights, increasing numbers of women demanded the right to vote. Others lobbied to provide better conditions for women working outside the home, especially in textile factories. Sarah Grimké responded to criticism of women's activism:

> This has been the language of man since he laid aside the whip as a means to keep woman in subjection. He spares her body, but the war he has waged against her mind, her heart, and her soul, has been no less destructive to her as a moral being. How monstrous is the doctrine that woman is to be dependent on man![7]

Progress toward equality between men and women was equally slow in Canada and in Latin America. Canada's first women doctors received their training in the United States because women could not receive medical degrees until 1895. Argentina and Uruguay were among the first Latin American nations to provide public education for women, introducing coeducation in the 1870s. Chilean women gained access to some careers in medicine and law in the 1870s, while in Brazil the first women graduated in medicine in 1882. In Argentina the first woman doctor graduated from medical school in 1899.

Throughout the hemisphere more rapid progress occurred in lower-status careers that threatened male economic power less directly, and, by the end of the century, women dominated elementary school teaching. From Canada to Argentina and Chile, the majority of working-class women, although having no direct involvement in reform movements, succeeded in transforming gender relations in their daily lives. By the end of the nineteenth century, large numbers of poor women worked outside the home on farms, in markets, and, increasingly, in factories. Many bore full responsibility for providing for their children. Whether men thought women should remain in the home or not, by the end of the century women were unambiguously present in the economy (see also Chapter 27).

There was little progress toward eliminating racial discrimination in the nineteenth century. Blacks were denied the vote throughout the southern United States and were subjected to the indignity of segregation—consigned to separate schools, hotels, restaurants, seats in public transportation, and even water fountains. Racial discrimination against men and women of African descent was also common in Latin America. Unlike the southern states of the United States, however, Latin American nations did not insist on formal racial segregation or permit lynching. Nor did they enforce a strict color line. Many men and women of mixed background were able to enter the skilled working class or middle class, and some rose to political prominence. Latin Americans tended to view racial identity across a continuum of physical characteristics rather than in the narrow terms of black and white that defined race relations in the United States.

---

[7]Sarah Grimké, "Reply to the Massachusetts Clergy," in *Early American Women: A Documentary History, 1600–1900*, ed. Nancy Woloch (Belmont, CA: Wadsworth, 1992), 343.

The abolition of slavery in Latin America did not end discrimination. Some leaders of the abolition struggles later organized to promote racial integration. They demanded access to education, the right to vote, and greater economic opportunity, pointing out the economic and political costs of denying full rights to all citizens. Their success depended on effective political organization and on forging alliances with sympathetic white politicians. Black intellectuals also struggled to overturn racist stereotypes. In Brazil, Argentina, and Cuba, as in the United States, political and literary magazines celebrating black cultural achievement became powerful weapons in the struggle against racial discrimination. While men and women of African descent continued to experience prejudice and discrimination everywhere in the Americas, successful men and women of mixed descent in Latin America confronted fewer obstacles to advancement than did similar groups in the United States.

Development and Underdevelopment

While the Atlantic economy experienced three periods of severe economic contraction during the nineteenth century, nearly all the nations of the Western Hemisphere were richer in 1900 than in 1800. The effects of the Industrial Revolution, worldwide population growth, and an increasingly integrated world market combined to stimulate economic expansion (see Environment and Technology: Industrializing Sugar Agriculture in Cuba). Wheat, corn, wool, meats, and nonprecious minerals joined the region's earlier exports of silver, sugar, dyes, coffee, and cotton. The United States was the only Western Hemisphere nation to industrialize, but nearly every government promoted new industries and technologies. Governments invested in roads, railroads, canals, and telegraph systems to better serve distant markets, while adopting tariff and monetary policies to foster economic diversification and growth. Despite these efforts, by 1900 only three Western Hemisphere nations—the United States, Canada, and Argentina—achieved individual income levels similar to those of western Europe. All three nations had open land, temperate climates, diverse resources, and large inflows of immigrants.

New demands for copper, zinc, lead, coal, and tin unleashed by the Industrial Revolution led to mining booms in the western United States, Mexico, and Chile. The mining companies of the late nineteenth century were heavily capitalized international corporations that could bully governments and buy political favors. By 1900 European and North American corporations owned nearly all the largest mining enterprises in Latin America. Petroleum development, which occurred at the end of the century in Mexico and elsewhere, followed this pattern as well (see the discussion of the Mexican economy during the Díaz dictatorship in Chapter 26).

New technology accelerated economic integration, but the high cost of this technology often increased dependence on foreign capital. Many governments promoted railroads by granting tax benefits, free land, and monopoly rights to both domestic and foreign investors. As a result, by 1890 vast areas of the Great Plains in the United States, the Canadian prairie, the Argentine pampas, and parts of northern Mexico were producing grain and livestock for foreign markets opened by the development of railroads. Steamships also lowered the cost of transportation to distant markets, and the telegraph stimulated expansion by speeding information about the demand for and availability of products.

The simultaneous acquisition of several new technologies could have a dramatic effect on a nation's economy. In Argentina, for example, the railroad, the telegraph, barbed wire, and refrigeration were all introduced in the 1870s and 1880s. Although Argentina had

Courtesy, Hack Hoffenburg

Excavation of Port of Buenos Aires, Argentina   Relying on foreign capital and engineering, the government of Argentina improved the port to facilitate the nation's rapidly expanding export economy.

Industrializing Sugar Agriculture in Cuba

Sugar played a key role in the development of the Western Hemisphere, with the profits of sugar plantations rivaling the vast wealth in silver and gold extracted from Spain's colonial empire. The expansion of sugar agriculture from Brazil to the Caribbean was the major driving force in the African slave trade until its effective end in the 1850s. The fact that 70 percent of all African slaves brought to the Americas were distributed to sugar-producing regions is one measure of sugar's influence in the hemisphere. When most of Haiti's sugar plantations were destroyed by revolutionary violence, world sugar prices shot upward in the early nineteenth century. Cuban planters jumped into the vacuum, importing tens of thousands of slaves and opening new lands to sugar production. Within two decades, Cuba had become the world's largest sugar producer.

Cuba's sugar industry soon confronted two challenges to its ascendency. Having already ended the slave trade to its own sugar islands in 1807, Great Britain pushed Spain to end the slave trade to Cuba, ultimately using its navy to reduce imports to a trickle. Almost simultaneously, new technologies were introduced in Europe that permitted the profitable extraction of sugar from beets. As a result, labor became more expensive for Cuban planters at the same time that sugar prices fell internationally. To remain profitable, the Cuban sugar industry embraced technological innovations that had earlier revolutionized manufacturing.

Planters with the largest estates and the largest numbers of slaves had always enjoyed a competitive advantage over smaller producers because they could afford the most efficient crushing and refining technologies, benefiting from what economists call economies of scale (see Chapter 19). With beet sugar production driving prices lower, Cuba's large-scale producers displaced their less efficient competitors while at the same opening virgin land to sugar production. Between 1878 and 1900 alone, more than 1.4 million acres of forest were lost to the expanding sugar plantations. As lower prices increased competition and as the volume of sugar production soared in Cuba, the number of sugar producers steadily decreased, a pattern that neither political violence nor the abolition of slavery (1886) could alter.

Concentration was also promoted by the high cost of mechanization. The most heavily capitalized producers imported steam engines to replace the animal traction and water power previously used to crush cane and then introduced new, more efficient refining technologies. As crushing and refining capacities expanded in the modern mills, called *centrales* in Spanish, small-scale producers closed their expensive and inefficient mills to concentrate on growing sugar cane. Railroad construction multiplied the effects of these innovations, tying distant sugar growers to the mechanized refiners, many of them foreign owned. As had happened in English textile manufacturing during the Industrial Revolution (see Chapter 22), technological innovation in Cuba's sugar industry had concentrated the control of production and wealth in the hands of a new elite. The centrales were truly factories in the fields. As Cuba neared independence in the 1890s, the island's modernized sugar sector consisted of a relatively small number of industrialized refiners and a mass of increasingly vulnerable and dependent cane farmers.

Cuban sugar refinery showing mix of traditional and modern technologies Sugar cane was delivered to the crushing mill by both ox carts and railroad lines. In the background, steam-driven machinery moves cane to a crusher.

Library of Congress Prints and Photographs Division [LC-D4-9223]

MAP 25.4 **The Expansion of the United States, 1850–1920** The settlement of western territories and their admission as states depended on migration, the exploitation of natural resources, and important new technologies like railroads and telegraphs that facilitated economic and political integration. © Cengage Learning

development In the nineteenth and twentieth centuries, the economic process that led to industrialization, urbanization, the rise of a large and prosperous middle class, and heavy investment in education.

underdevelopment The condition experienced by economies that depend on colonial forms of production such as the export of raw materials and plantation crops with low wages and low investment in education.

had abundant livestock herds since the colonial period, the distance from Europe's markets prevented Argentine cattle raisers from exporting fresh meat or live animals. Technology overcame these obstacles. The combination of railroads and the telegraph lowered freight costs and improved information about markets, steamships shortened the time needed for transatlantic crossings, and refrigerated ships made it possible to sell meat in distant markets. As land values rose and livestock breeding improved, ranchers protected new investments with barbed wire, the first inexpensive fencing available on the nearly treeless plains.

Growing interdependence and increased competition produced deep structural differences among Western Hemisphere economies by 1900. Two distinct economic tracks became visible. One led to industrialization and prosperity: **development**. The other continued colonial dependence on exporting raw materials and on low-wage industries: **underdevelopment**. By 1900 prosperity was greater and economic development more diversified in English-speaking North America than in the nations of Latin America. With a temperate climate, vast fertile prairies, and an influx of European immigrants, Argentina was the only Latin American nation to approach the prosperity of the United States and Canada in 1900.

Changes in the performance of international markets helped determine the trajectory of Western Hemisphere economies as new nations promoted economic development. When the United States gained independence, the world economy enjoyed rapid growth. With a large merchant fleet, a diversified economy that included some manufacturing, and adequate banking and insurance services, the United States benefited from this expansion. Rapid population growth due in large measure to immigration, high levels of individual wealth, widespread landownership, and relatively high literacy rates also fostered rapid economic development. By 1865 the United States had already established the world's largest railroad network, but by 1915 railroad mileage had multiplied elevenfold (see Map 25.4). Steel production grew rapidly as well, with the United States overtaking world leaders Britain and Germany in the 1890s.

Canada's achievement of greater political autonomy, the Confederation of 1867, coincided with a second period of global economic expansion. Canada also benefited from a special trading relationship with Britain, the world's preeminent industrial nation, and from a rising tide of immigrants after 1850. Nevertheless, some regions within each of these prosperous North American nations—Canada's Maritime Provinces and the southern part of the United States—demonstrated the same patterns of underdevelopment found in Latin America.

Most Latin American nations gained independence in the 1820s when the global economy contracted. In the colonial period, Spain and Portugal had promoted the production of agricultural and mining exports in their colonies. After independence these exports faced increased competition. Although these sectors experienced periods of great prosperity in the nineteenth century, they also faced stiff competition and falling prices as new regions began production or competing products captured markets.

The history of the Latin American economies, subject to periodic problems of oversupply and low prices, was one of boom and bust. Many Latin American governments sought to promote exports in the face of increased competition and falling prices by resisting union activity and demands for higher wages and by opening domestic markets to foreign manufactures. The resulting low wages and an abundance of foreign manufactured goods, in turn, undermined efforts to promote industrialization in Latin America.

Weak governments, political instability, and, in some cases, civil war also slowed Latin American economic development. Because Latin America was also dependent on importing foreign capital and technology, Great Britain and, by the end of the century, the United States often imposed unfavorable trade conditions or even intervened militarily to protect their investments. The combined impact of these domestic and international impediments to development became clear when Mexico, Chile, and Argentina failed to achieve high levels of domestic investment in manufacturing late in the nineteenth century, despite a rapid accumulation of wealth derived from traditional exports.

Altered Environments

Population growth, economic expansion, new technologies, and the introduction of foreign plants and animals dramatically altered American environments in the nineteenth century. Cuba's planters cut down the island's forests in the early nineteenth century to expand sugar production. Growing demand for meat led ranchers to expand livestock-raising into fragile environments in Argentina, Uruguay, southern Brazil, and the southwestern United States. Other forms of commercial agriculture also threatened the environment. Farmers in South Carolina and Georgia gained a short-term increase in cotton production by abandoning crop rotation after 1870, but this practice quickly led to soil exhaustion and erosion. Similarly, coffee planters in Brazil exhausted fertility with a destructive cycle of overplanting followed by expansion onto forest reserves cleared by cutting and burning. The transfers of land from public to private ownership in order to promote livestock-raising and agriculture also altered landscapes. Finally, new technologies had environmental effects. For example, the use of steel plows on North American prairies and Argentine pampas eliminated many native grasses and increased the threat of soil erosion.

Rapid urbanization also imposed environmental costs. New York, Chicago, Rio de Janeiro, Buenos Aires, and Mexico City were among the world's fastest-growing cities in the nineteenth century, and governments strained to provide sewers, clean water, and garbage disposal. Timber companies clear-cut large areas of Michigan, Wisconsin, and the Appalachian Mountains in the United States

SECTION REVIEW

- Following independence, American nations eventually abolished the slave trade and slavery.

- After the abolition of slavery, a rush of immigrants from Europe and Asia diversified American nations, though most immigrants faced prejudice.

- The long struggle to achieve women's rights and end racial and ethnic discrimination altered the Western Hemisphere's political culture.

- Although most Western Hemisphere nations were richer in 1900 than in 1800, only Argentina could match the levels of average wealth found in the United States and Canada; nations and regions dependent on exporting raw materials remained underdeveloped.

- Increased logging, grazing, and mining ruined vast areas of the hemisphere, but minor conservation efforts were under way by the end of the nineteenth century.

to provide lumber for railroad ties and housing, pulp for paper, and fuel for locomotives and foundries. At the same time, the forest industries of British Honduras (now Belize), Nicaragua, and Guatemala grew rapidly in response to demand in Europe and North America for tropical hardwoods like mahogany. As forests throughout the hemisphere were cleared, animal habitats and native plant species disappeared.

The scale of mining in Nevada, Montana, and California accelerated erosion and pollution. Similar results occurred in other mining areas as well. Nitrate mining and open-pit copper mining in Chile scarred and polluted the environment. The state of Minas Gerais (ME-nas JER-aize) in Brazil experienced a series of mining booms that began with gold in the late seventeenth century and continued with iron ore in the nineteenth. By the end of the nineteenth century, its red soil had been ripped open, its forests were depleted, and erosion was uncontrolled. Similar devastation afflicted parts of Bolivia and Mexico.

By the end of the nineteenth century, small-scale conservation efforts were under way in many nations, and the first national parks and nature reserves were created. In the United States large areas remained undeveloped. In 1872 Yellowstone in Wyoming became the first national park. President Theodore Roosevelt (1901–1909) and the naturalist John Muir played major roles in preserving large areas of the western states. Canada created its first national park in Banff in 1885 and expanded it from 10 to 260 square miles (26 to 673 square kilometers) two years later. When confronted with a choice between economic growth and environmental protection, however, the hemisphere's nations embraced growth.

CONCLUSION

While the new nations of the Western Hemisphere faced similar challenges in the nineteenth century, they had developed from different colonial traditions. The effort to establish stable constitutional systems proved difficult nearly everywhere. While the constitution of the United States endured, conflict over slavery led to a civil war that threatened the nation's survival. Elsewhere most new constitutions failed within a generation. In Argentina, for example, fifty years passed before a stable national government was in place. Personalist political leaders with large followings, like José Antonio Páez and Andrew Jackson, resisted the constraints of constitutions. Regionalism, ideological confrontations, racial divisions, and conflict with native peoples all threatened stability as well.

New nations also faced foreign interventions and local wars with regional powers. By 1850 Mexico had lost 50 percent of its territory to the United States and then faced a French invasion in 1862. Bolivia and Peru lost territory to an expansive Chile, while Paraguay lost a disastrous war to an alliance of Argentina, Brazil, and Uruguay. American nations also fought numerous wars with indigenous peoples, crushing resistance by the 1890s.

The nations of the hemisphere also experienced a series of dramatic social and economic changes in this period. The slave trade and slavery persisted long after independence (see Chapter 19), but after a century of protest and political mobilization, the hemisphere's last slave state, Brazil, freed its slaves in 1888. Slavery left a legacy of racism and discrimination across the Americas. In places where the institution was most important—the plantation regions of Brazil, the Caribbean, and the American South—racial prejudice, discrimination, and persistent low levels of investment in education and internal improvements slowed economic growth and weakened democracy. By 1890 many of the hemisphere's poorest nations or poorest regions within nations were those that had depended on slavery.

Amerindian populations experienced centuries of exploitation, forced integration in market economies, and compulsory removal to marginal lands. In most of Latin America, Amerindians had been subjected to exploitation for centuries when the Spanish and Portuguese empires finally fell. Once in place, forced labor and other abuses persisted into the twentieth century in nations like Guatemala and Bolivia. With independence, new national governments undertook the pacification of the hemisphere's remaining independent native peoples. By the 1890s nearly all were reduced to reservations or forced onto marginal lands. As a result, Amerindians were among the poorest peoples in the hemisphere, suffering oppression, poverty, and disenfranchisement.

Immigration transformed many Western Hemisphere nations. As a general rule, the millions of European immigrants that entered the Western Hemisphere in the nineteenth century avoided regions where slavery dominated or where indigenous populations were compelled to labor. Argentina, Brazil, Canada, and the United States were the most popular destinations, and immigrants to Brazil and the United States avoided the former plantation zones. Instead, hundreds of thousands of Chinese and East Indians, migrating as indentured laborers, were directed to plantation regions, especially in the Caribbean, where they faced racism and discrimination.

Industrialization had a transforming effect on the hemisphere. Wealth, political power, and population were increasingly concentrated in urban areas, and bankers and manufacturers, rather than farmers and plantation owners, increasingly directed national destinies. Industrialization altered the natural environment in dramatic ways. Modern factories consumed huge amounts of raw materials and energy. Copper mines in Chile and Mexico, Cuban sugar plantations, Brazilian coffee plantations, and Canadian lumber companies all left their mark on the natural environment, and all had ties to markets in the United States.

In 1900 nearly every American nation was wealthier, better educated, more democratic, and more populous than at independence. But most of these new nations were also more vulnerable to distant economic forces and more profoundly split between haves and have-nots. The hemisphere was also more clearly divided into a rich north and a poorer south. A small number of nations located in the temperate regions—Canada, the United States, Argentina, and Chile—had become prosperous regional powers relative to their neighbors. While most of the hemisphere's growth continued to depend on the export of agricultural goods and raw materials—sugar, cotton, grains, minerals, and livestock products—the United States had become one of the world's richest industrial nations by 1890.

KEY TERMS

Simón Bolívar p. 626
Miguel Hidalgo y Costilla p. 628
José María Morelos p. 628

Confederation of 1867 p. 631
personalist leaders p. 631
Andrew Jackson p. 632
José Antonio Páez p. 633

Benito Juárez p. 636
Tecumseh p. 638
Caste War p. 639
abolitionists p. 639
acculturation p. 643

Women's Rights Convention p. 644
development p. 647
underdevelopment p. 647

SUGGESTED READING

Anderson, Wanni W. and Robert Lee, eds., *Displacements and Diasporas: Asians in the Americas*. 2005. The essays provide a broad introduction to Asian immigration to the Western Hemisphere.

Andrews, George Reid. *Afro-Latin America, 1800–2000*. 2004. An excellent synthesis of the Latin American experience.

Barth, Gunther. *Bitter Strength: A History of Chinese in the United States, 1850–1870*. 1964. A reliable introduction to this topic.

Brands, H. W. *Andrew Jackson, His Life and Times*. 2005. A reliable exploration of the Jacksonian era.

Creighton, Donald. *The Road to Confederation. The Emergence of Canada, 1863–1867*. Reissued 2012. Still a reliable guide to Canada's unique path to independence.

Cronon, William. *Nature's Metropolis: Chicago and the Great West*. 1991. An excellent discussion of the environment during nineteenth-century development.

Crosby, Alfred. *Ecological Imperialism: The Biological Expansion of Europe, 900–1900*. 1986. A seminal study of environment.

Dean, Warren. *With Broadax and Firebrand: The Destruction of the Brazilian Atlantic Forest*. 1995.

Funes Monzote, Reinaldo. *From Rainforest to Cane Field in Cuba. An Environmental History Since 1492*. 2008. The environmental history of the nineteenth century's preeminent plantation society.

Ginzberg, Lori D. *Women and the Work of Benevolence: Morality, Politics, and Class in the Nineteenth-Century United States*. 1990. Still a valuable survey of this important topic.

Graden, Dale T. *From Slavery to Freedom in Brazil: Bahia, 1835–1900*. 2006.

Howe, Daniel Walker. *What God Hath Wrought. The Transformation of America, 1815–1848*. A masterful work of synthesis.

Kinsbruner, Jay. *Independence in Spanish America*, 2d ed. 2000. The best short analysis of the independence period.

Krech III, Shepard. *The Ecological Indian*. 1999.

Lock Lai, Walton. *Indentured Labor, Caribbean Sugar. Chinese and Indian Migrants to the British West Indies, 1838–1918*. 2004. The best introduction to this topic.

Mar, Lisa Rose. *Brokering Belonging: Chinese in Canada's Exclusion Era, 1885–1945*. 2010. A useful summary of the Canadian experience.

Martin, Ged, ed. *The Causes of Canadian Confederation*. 1990.

McMillen, Sally. *Seneca Falls and the Origins of the Women's Rights Movements in American History*. 2009. A useful discussion of a crucial period in the American reform tradition.

McNeil, J. R. *Mosquito Empires: Ecology and War in the Greater Caribbean, 1620–1914*. 2010. A broadly framed argument about the role of the environment in regional development.

Miller, Francesca. *Latin American Women and the Search for Social Justice*. 1991.

Miller, Shawn William. *An Environmental History of Latin America*. 2007. The best synthesis of this topic.

Nugent, Walter. *Crossing: The Great Transatlantic Migrations, 1870–1914*. 1992.

Remini, Robert V. *Andrew Jackson and His Indian Wars*. 2001. Still the best exploration of this topic.

Rodriguez O., Jaime. *The Origins of Mexican National Politics*. 1997.

Scott, Rebecca. *Slave Emancipation in Cuba: The Transition to Free Labor, 1860–1899*. 1985.

Thomas, Victor Bulmer. *The Economic History of Latin America Since Independence*. 2003.

Worster, Donald. *Rivers of Empire: Water, Aridity, and the Growth of the American West*. 1985.

CourseMate Go to the History CourseMate website for primary source links, study tools, and review materials for this chapter. www.cengagebrain.com

State Power, the Census, and the Question of Identity

Between the American Revolution and the last decades of the nineteenth century, Europe and the Americas were transformed. The ancient power of kings and the authority of religion were eclipsed by muscular new ways of organizing political, economic, and intellectual life. The Western world was vastly different in 1870 than it had been a century earlier. One of the less heralded but enduringly significant changes was the huge expansion of government statistical services.

The rise of the nation-state was associated with the development of modern bureaucratic departments that depended on reliable statistics to measure the nation's achievements and discover its failures. The nation-state, whether democratic or not, mobilized resources on a previously unimaginable scale. Modern states were more powerful and wealthier, and they were also more ambitious and more intrusive. The growth of their power can be seen in the modernization of militaries, the commitment to internal improvements such as railroads, and the growth in state revenues. In recent years historians have begun to examine a less visible but equally important manifestation of growing state power: census taking.

Governments and religious authorities have counted people since early times. Our best estimates of the Amerindian population of the Western Hemisphere in 1500 rest almost entirely on what were little more than missionaries' guesses about the numbers of people they baptized. Spanish and Portuguese kings were eager to count native populations, since "indios" (adult male Amerindians) were subject to special labor obligations and tribute payments. So, from the mid-sixteenth century onward, imperial officials conducted regular censuses of Amerindians, adapting practices already in place in Europe.

The effort to measure and categorize populations was transformed in the last decades of the eighteenth century when the nature of European governments began to change. The Enlightenment belief that the scientific method could be applied to human society proved to be attractive both to political radicals, like the French revolutionaries, and to reforming monarchs like Maria Theresa of Austria. Enlightenment philosophers had argued that a science of government could remove the inefficiencies and irrationalities that had long subverted the human potential for prosperity and happiness. The French intellectual Condorcet wrote in 1782:

Those sciences, created almost in our own days, the object of which is man himself, the direct goal of which is the happiness of man, will enjoy a progress no less sure than that of the physical sciences. . . . In meditating on the nature of the moral sciences [what we now call the social sciences], one cannot help seeing that, as they are based like the physical sciences on the observation of fact, they must follow the method, acquire a language equally exact and precise, attaining the same degree of certainty.[1]

As confidence in this new "science" grew, the term previously used to describe the collection of numbers about society, *political arithmetic*, was abandoned by governments and practitioners in favor of *statistics*, a term that clearly suggests its close ties to the "state." In the nineteenth century the new objectives set out by Condorcet and others led to both the formal university training of statisticians and the creation of government statistical services.

The ambitions of governments in this new era were great. Nation-states self-consciously sought to transform society, sponsoring economic development, education, and improvements in health and welfare. They depended on statistics to measure the effectiveness of their policies and, as a result, were interested in nearly everything. They counted taverns, urban buildings, births and deaths, and arrests and convictions. They also counted their populations with a thoroughness never before seen. As statistical reporting became more uniform across Europe and the Americas, governments could measure not only their own progress but also that of their neighbors and rivals.

The revolutionary governments of France modernized the census practices of the overthrown monarchy. They spent much more money, hired many more census takers, and devoted much more energy to training the staff that designed censuses and analyzed results. Great Britain set up an official census in 1801, but it established a special administrative structure only in the 1830s. In the Western Hemisphere nearly every independent nation provided for "scientific" censuses. In the United States the federal constitution required that a census be taken every ten years. Latin American nations, often torn by civil war in the nineteenth century, took censuses less regularly, but even the poorest nations took censuses when they could. It was as if the census itself confirmed the existence of the government, demonstrating its modernity and seriousness.

Until recently, historians who relied on these documents in their research on economic performance, issues of race and ethnicity, family life, and fertility and mortality asked few questions about the politics of census design. What could be more objective than rows of numbers? But the advocates of statistics who managed census taking were uninhibited in advertising the usefulness of reliable numbers to the governments that employed them. At the 1860 International Statistical Congress held in London, one speaker said, "I think the true meaning to be attached to 'statistics' is not every collection of figures, but figures collected with the sole purpose of applying the principles deduced from them to questions of importance to the state."[2] The desire to be useful meant that statistics could not be fully objective.

Subjectivity was an unavoidable problem with censuses. Censuses identified citizens and foreign residents by place of residence, sex, age, and family relationships within households as well as profession and literacy. These determinations were sometimes subjective. Modern scholars have demonstrated that census takers also routinely undercounted the poor and those living in rural areas.

Because census takers, as agents of nation-states, were determined to be useful, they were necessarily concerned with issues of nationality and, in the Americas, with race because these characteristics commonly determined political rights and citizenship. The assessment and recording of nationality and race would prove to be among the most politically dubious objectives of the new social sciences.

Nationality had not been a central question for traditional monarchies. For the emerging nation-state, however, nationality was central. A nation's strength was assumed to depend in large measure on the growth of its population, a standard that, once articulated, suggested that the growth of minority populations was dangerous. Who was French? Who was Austrian or Hungarian? European statisticians relied on both *language of use* and *mother tongue* as proxies for *nationality*, the first term being flexible enough to recognize the assimilation of minorities, the second suggesting a more permanent identity based on a person's original language. Both terms forced bilingual populations to simplify their more complex identities. Ethnic minorities, once identified, were sometimes subject to discrimination such as exclusion from military careers or from universities. In parts of Spanish America, *language* was used as a proxy for *race*. Those who spoke Spanish were citizens in the full sense, even if they were indistinguishable from Amerindians in appearance. Those who spoke indigenous languages were "indios" and therefore subject to special taxes and labor obligations and effectively denied the right to vote.

Beyond providing a justification for continuing discrimination, census categories compressed and distorted the complexity and variety of human society to fit the preconceptions of bureaucrats and politicians. Large percentages of the residents of Mexico, Peru, and Bolivia, among other parts of the Americas, were descended from both Europeans and Amerindians and, in the Caribbean region, from Europeans and Africans. Census categories never adequately captured the complexities of these biological and cultural mixtures. We now know that the poor were often identified as "indios" or "blacks" and the better-off were often called something else—"Americanos," "criollos" (creoles), or even whites. Since this process flattened and streamlined the complexities of identity, censuses on their own are not reliable guides to the distribution of ethnicity and race in a population.

In Europe the issue of nationality proved similarly perplexing for census takers and similarly dangerous to those identified as minorities. Linguistic and ethnic minorities had always lived among the politically dominant majorities: Jewish and Polish minorities in areas controlled by German speakers, German speakers among the French, and Serbo-Croatian speakers among Hungarians, for example. The frontiers between these minority populations and their neighbors were always porous. Sexual unions and marriages were common, and two or more generations of a family often lived together in the same household, with the elder members speaking one language and the younger members another. Who was what? In a very real sense, nationality, like race in the Americas, was ultimately fixed by the census process, as the nation-state forced a limited array of politically utilitarian categories onto the rich diversity of ethnicity and culture.

NOTES

1. Quoted in James C. Scott, *Seeing like a State. How Certain Schemes to Improve the Human Condition Have Failed* (New Haven: Yale University Press, 1998), 91.
2. This discussion relies heavily on Eliza Johnson (now Ablovatski), "Counting and Categorizing: The Hungarian Gypsy Census of 1893" (M.A. Thesis, Columbia University, 1996), especially Chapter III. She quotes from the *Proceedings of the Sixth International Statistical Congress Held in London, 1860*, 379.

PART

VII

V&A Images, London/Art Resource, NY

Highways of the Empire   In the late nineteenth century, Europeans believed the world revolved around their subcontinent. World maps printed in Great Britain showed the British Empire in red, with informal dependencies and protectorates in pink. This map, a polar projection with Britain in the exact center, shows the major shipping routes and submarine telegraph cable lines that made London the center of global commerce and finance and ensured the supremacy of the Royal Navy around the world.

Global Diversity and Dominance, 1750–1945

During the century that preceded 1830, European imperialism gained new footholds, sometimes against intense resistance, in parts of Africa and Asia. Most expansion continued earlier patterns in which European trading companies rather than governments took the initiative.

From roughly 1830 onward, formal colonies governed by state-appointed administrators and supported by European armies came to the fore in a scramble for territory in Africa and the Pacific region. By World War I Europe, the United States, and Japan collectively dominated much of the world and tried to convert other peoples to their own cultures and ways of life.

In Europe, mounting tensions led to the Great War of 1914–1918. Russia and China erupted in revolution. Soon after, the heartland of the Ottoman Empire became modern Turkey, while its Arab provinces were taken over by France and Britain.

Amidst a worldwide transformation of lifestyles brought on by new technologies, the political and economic system the European powers crafted after the war fell apart in the 1930s. While the capitalist nations fell into a depression, the Soviet Union industrialized at breakneck speed. In Germany and Japan, extremists sought to solve their countries' grievances by military conquest.

As World War II loomed, nationalists in India yearned for independence while nationalists in Latin America sought an end to foreign military interventions, increasing global economic and political tensions.

The war caused the death of millions of people and the destruction of countless cities. It also weakened Europe's overseas empires. India gained its independence in 1947. Two years later, Mao Zedong led the Chinese communists to victory. Latin American leaders embraced nationalist economic and social policies that challenged the traditional role of foreign investors. Of all the once great powers, only the United States and the Soviet Union remained to compete for global dominance.

Chapter Outline

Changes and Exchanges in Africa
➤ *How did different African leaders and peoples interact with each other, and how did European nations' relationship to African peoples change during this period?*

India Under British Rule
➤ *How did Britain secure its hold on India, and what colonial policies led to the beginnings of Indian nationalism?*

Southeast Asia and the Pacific
➤ *What were the social and cultural effects of imperialism in Asia and the Pacific?*

Imperialism in Latin America
➤ *What were the economic motives behind imperialism in Latin America?*

The World Economy and the Global Environment
➤ *How did imperialism contribute to the growth and globalization of the world economy?*

Conclusion

● **DIVERSITY + DOMINANCE**   Two Africans Recall the Arrival of the Europeans
● **ENVIRONMENT + TECHNOLOGY**   Imperialism and Tropical Ecology

An Indian Railway Station, 1854 (engraving) (b/w photo), English School, (19th century)/The Illustrated London News Picture Library, London, UK/The Bridgeman Art Library

Indian Railroad Station, 1866   British India built the largest network of railroads in Asia. People of every social class traveled by train.

Varieties of Imperialism in Africa, India, Southeast Asia, and Latin America, 1750–1914

Like many regions that looked to be coherent countries on the maps drawn by imperialism, Algeria was not a unified realm in 1830 when France landed 35,000 troops outside of Algiers. Five days later, at a cost of 6,000 dead and wounded Frenchmen, the *dey* (ruler) of Algiers, an autonomous governor ruling under Ottoman suzerainty, surrendered the city. French nationalists called the invasion a defense of French honor because three years earlier the dey had struck a French diplomat with a fly whisk during an argument over debts lingering from the Napoleonic wars, which had ended more than a decade earlier. Actually the invasion plan had been drawn up by Napoleon himself in 1808 in response to commercial interests in southern France that sought to acquire new land in North Africa.

Control of Algiers, however, did not prevent the king of Morocco from pressing a claim to rule Algeria's western region, nor did it fit the political interests of the country's five major Sufi brotherhoods, which had earlier staged revolts against Ottoman imperialism. The brotherhood that would prove the hardest for the French to defeat was the Qadiriya, which waged a sixteen-year *jihad* (holy war) that only ended in 1847 with the surrender of its leader Abd al-Qadir.

Abd al-Qadir **(AHB-dahl-KAH-deer)** was only twenty-five when he took over from his father as head of the brotherhood, but he had spent three years traveling in the Middle East, making the pilgrimage to Mecca, getting to know other Qadiriya leaders, and studying at famous institutions of learning in Tunis and Cairo. He had also observed the efforts of Muhammad Ali in Egypt to build a modern army and state.

The key to Abd al-Qadir's success was a network of religious centers (*zawiyas*) that trained judges and administrators and disseminated his vision of an egalitarian society that would observe Islamic law and be dominated by neither Ottoman officials nor French generals. Other Sufi brotherhoods fought separately against the French, but not as successfully.

Though Abd al-Qadir was allowed to settle in Damascus after his defeat and there pursued an eminent career as a leader of the Muslim community, his historical image is primarily one of resistance to imperialism. Like most movements elsewhere opposing imperialist aggression, Abd al-Qadir's Sufi followers could not prevail against European firepower. In the long run, however, such histories of resistance laid the ideological, if sometimes semilegendary, groundwork for anticolonial movements that would gain momentum after World War II.

Defenders of imperialism often cite the benefits of European rule in terms of railroad construction, orderly governance, integration of local production with currents of international trade, and similar economic and administrative factors. But the reputations or legends of leaders like Abd al-Qadir would eventually eclipse the memory of some of the generals and administrators who oversaw a massive increase in European imperialism starting in the late eighteenth century.

CHANGES AND EXCHANGES IN AFRICA

Zulu A people of modern South Africa whom King Shaka united in 1818.

Afrikaners South Africans descended from Dutch and French settlers of the seventeenth century. Their Great Trek founded new settler colonies in the nineteenth century. Though a minority among South Africans, they held political power after 1910, imposing a system of racial segregation called apartheid after 1949.

In the century before 1870, Africa underwent dynamic political changes and a great expansion of foreign trade. While a few indigenous African leaders held out against European imperialism, maps of Africa became increasingly tinted with pink and green, the conventional colors of British and French colonies, respectively. On the economic plane, however, as the slave trade died under British pressure, trade in other goods grew sharply. Africans consumed large quantities of machine-made textiles, and those rulers who retained a measure of independence purchased European firearms.

Southern Africa

For many centuries the Nguni (ng-GOO-nee) peoples had farmed and raised cattle in the fertile coast-lands of southeastern Africa. When drought hit the region at the beginning of the nineteenth century, an upstart military leader named Shaka (r. 1818–1828) created the **Zulu** kingdom. Strict military drill and close-combat tactics featuring ox-hide shields and lethal stabbing spears made the Zulu the most powerful and most feared fighters in southern Africa.

Shaka expanded his kingdom by raiding his African neighbors, seizing their cattle, and capturing their women and children. Breakaway military bands spread this system of warfare and state building inland to the high plateau country as far north as Lake Victoria (see Map 26.1). As the power and population of these new kingdoms increased, so too did the number of displaced and demoralized refugees around them.

To protect themselves from the Zulu, some neighboring Africans created their own states. The Swazi kingdom consolidated north of the Zulu, and the kingdom of Lesotho (luh-SOO-too) grew by attracting refugees to strongholds in southern Africa's highest mountains. Both Lesotho and Swaziland survive as independent states to this day.

Although Shaka ruled for little more than a decade, he left behind a mythic identity as well as a new kingdom. These were destined to conflict, however, with southern Africa's attractiveness to European settlers. The Cape Colony, first a Dutch possession but definitively under British rule after 1806, flourished because of Cape Town's strategic importance as a supply station for ships making the long voyages between Europe and India. With the port city came some twenty thousand descendants of Dutch and French settlers who occupied farms and ranches in its hinterland. Despite their European origins, these people thought of themselves as permanent residents of Africa and were beginning to refer to themselves as **Afrikaners (af-rih-KAHN-uhr)**. British governors prohibited any expansion of the white settler frontier because such expansion invariably led to wars with indigenous Africans. This decision, along with the imposition of laws protecting African rights within Cape Colony (including the emancipation of slaves in 1834), alienated many Afrikaners.

Between 1836 and 1839 parties of Afrikaners embarked on a "Great Trek," leaving British-ruled Cape

Eileen Tweedy/The Art Archive/Art Resource, NY

Zulu in Battle Dress, 1838 Elaborate costumes helped impress opponents with the Zulus' strength. Shown here are long-handled spears and thick leather shields.

CHRONOLOGY

	Slavery	Africa	India and Southeast Asia	Latin America
1750			1756 Black Hole of Calcutta 1765 East India Company (EIC) rule of Bengal begins	
1800	1807 Britain outlaws slave trade 1834 Britain frees slaves in its colonies. Indentured labor migrations begin 1848 France abolishes slaves in its colonies	1808 Britain takes over Sierra Leone 1809 Sokoto Caliphate founded 1818 Shaka founds Zulu kingdom 1821 Foundation of Liberia 1831–1847 Algerians resist French takeover 1836–1839 Afrikaners' Great Trek 1840 Omani sultan moves capital to Zanzibar	1818 EIC creates Bombay Presidency 1826 EIC annexes Assam and northern Burma 1828 Brahmo Samaj founded	
1850	1867 End of Atlantic slave trade	1869 Jaja founds Opobo	1857–1858 Sepoy Rebellion leads to end of EIC rule and Mughal rule 1877 Queen Victoria becomes Empress of India 1885 Indian National Congress formed 1898 Spanish-American War. U.S. takes over Philippines	1876–1910 Porfirio Díaz, dictator of Mexico 1898 Spanish-American War. U.S. takes over Cuba
1900		1899–1902 Boer War 1900s Railroads connect ports to the interior		1910 Mexican Revolution begins 1917 New constitution proclaimed in Mexico

Colony for the fertile high *veld* (plateau) to the north that two decades of Zulu wars had depopulated. The Great Trek laid the foundation of three new settler colonies in southern Africa: the Afrikaners' Orange Free State and Transvaal on the high veld and the British colony of Natal on the Indian Ocean coast. Although firearms enabled the settlers to win some important battles against the Zulu and other Africans, they were still a tiny minority surrounded by the populous and powerful independent African kingdoms.

Phenomenal deposits of diamonds, gold, and copper, as well as coal and iron ore, soon added to the appeal of good pasture and farmland. The discovery of diamonds at Kimberley in 1868 lured thousands of European prospectors as well as Africans looking for work. Great Britain annexed the diamond area in 1871, angering the Afrikaners. Once in the interior, the British defeated the Xhosa (KOH-sah) people in 1877 and 1878. Then in 1879 they confronted the Zulu, militarily the most powerful of the African peoples in the region.

The Zulu, led by their king Cetshwayo (set-SHWAH-yo), resented their encirclement by Afrikaners and British, and their proud military tradition led them into a war with the British in 1879. They defeated the British at Isandhlwana (ee-sawn-dull-WAH-nuh), but a few months later they were in turn defeated. Cetshwayo was captured and sent into exile, and the Zulu lands were given to white ranchers.

Relations between the British and the Afrikaners, already tense as a result of British encroachment, took a turn for the worse when gold was discovered in the Afrikaner republic of Transvaal (trans-VAHL) in 1886. In the gold rush that ensued, the British soon outnumbered the Afrikaners.

MAP 26.1 **Africa in the Nineteenth Century** Expanding trade drew much of Africa into global networks, but foreign colonies in 1870 were largely confined to Algeria and southern Africa. Growing trade, Islamic reform movements, and other internal forces created important new states throughout the continent. © Cengage Learning

Cecil Rhodes British entrepreneur and politician involved in the expansion of the British Empire from South Africa into Central Africa. The colonies of Southern Rhodesia (now Zimbabwe) and Northern Rhodesia (now Zambia) were named after him.

Britain's invasion of southern Africa was driven in part by the ambition of **Cecil Rhodes** (1853–1902), who once declared that he would "annex the stars" if he could. Rhodes made his fortune in the Kimberley diamond fields, founding De Beers Consolidated, a company that has dominated the world's diamond trade ever since. He then turned to politics. He encouraged a concession company, the British South Africa Company, to push north into Central Africa, where he named two new colonies after himself: Southern Rhodesia (now Zimbabwe) and Northern Rhodesia (now Zambia). The Ndebele **(en-duh-BELL-ay)** and Shona peoples, who inhabited the region, resisted this invasion, but the machine guns of the British finally defeated them (see Diversity and Dominance: Two Africans Recall the Arrival of the Europeans).

The inflow of English-speaking whites into the gold- and diamond-mining areas and British attempts to annex the two Afrikaner, also called Boer, republics, Transvaal and Orange Free State, led to the South African or Boer War, which lasted from 1899 to 1902. At first the Afrikaners had the upper hand, for they were highly motivated, possessed modern rifles, and knew the land. In 1901, however, Great Britain brought in 450,000 troops and crushed the Afrikaner armies. Ironically, the Afrikaners' defeat in 1902 led to their ultimate victory. Wary of costly commitments overseas, the British government expected European settlers in Africa to manage their own affairs, as they were doing in Canada, Australia, and New Zealand. Thus, in 1910 the European settlers created the Union of South Africa, in which the Afrikaners eventually emerged as the ruling element.

Unlike Canada, Australia, and New Zealand, South Africa had a majority of indigenous inhabitants and substantial numbers of Indians and "Cape Coloureds" (people of mixed ancestry). Yet the Europeans were both numerous enough to demand self-rule and powerful enough to deny the vote and other civil rights to the majority. In 1913 the South African parliament passed the Natives Land Act, assigning Africans to reservations and forbidding them to own land elsewhere. This and other racial policies turned South Africa into a land of segregation and oppression.

West and Equatorial Africa

Simultaneous with the formation of Shaka's Zulu kingdom, Islamic reform movements were creating another cluster of powerful states in the savannas of West Africa. Islam had long been a force in the politics and cities of this region, but most Muslim rulers had found it prudent to tolerate the older religious practices of their subjects. In the 1770s, however, Muslim scholars began preaching the need to reform Islamic practices. They condemned the accommodations Muslim rulers had made with older traditions and called for a forcible conquest of rural "pagans." Their jihad added new lands where governments enforced Islamic laws and promoted the religion's spread.

South African Diamond Mine   When diamonds were found in Kimberley, South Africa, in 1868, the discovery precipitated a rush of prospectors from Europe and America. As soon as surface deposits were exhausted, their claims were bought by large companies that could afford the heavy equipment needed to mine deep underground. By the early twentieth century, diamonds came from major industrial mines like the Premier Mine shown here.

Gardiner F. Williams/NGS Image Collection

The largest of the new Muslim reform movements occurred in the Hausa **(HOW-suh)** states (in northern Nigeria) under the leadership of Usuman dan Fodio **(OO-soo-mahn dahn FOH-dee-oh)** (1745–1817). He charged that the Hausa kings, despite their official profession of Islam, were "undoubtedly unbelievers ... because they practice polytheistic rituals and turn people away from the path of God." Muslims unhappy with their social or religious position spread the movement to other Hausa states. The successful armies united the conquered Hausa states and neighboring areas under a caliph who ruled from the city of Sokoto.

These new Muslim states became centers of Islamic learning and reform. Schools for training boys in Quranic subjects spread rapidly, and the great library at Sokoto attracted many scholars. Officials permitted non-Muslims within the empire to follow their religions in exchange for paying a special tax, but they suppressed dances and ceremonies associated with traditional religions. The **Sokoto Caliphate** (1809–1906) was the largest state in West Africa since the sixteenth century.

Sokoto Caliphate   A large Muslim state founded in 1809 in what is now northern Nigeria.

In coastal West Africa, however, the French, who had maintained a foothold in Senegal for centuries, envisioned building a railroad from the upper Senegal River to the upper Niger in order to open the interior to French merchants. This in turn led the French military to undertake the conquest of the interior. Sokoto remained independent, but after 1890 it was embattled both

Two Africans Recall the Arrival of the Europeans

We know a great deal about the arrival of the Europeans into the interior of Africa from the perspective of the conquerors, but very little about how the events were experienced by Africans. Here are two accounts by African women, one from northern Nigeria whose land was occupied by the British, the other from the Congo Free State, a colony of King Leopold II of Belgium. They show not only how Africans experienced European colonial dominance but also how diverse these African experiences were.

Baba of Karo, a Nigerian Woman, Remembers Her Childhood

When I was a maiden the Europeans first arrived. Ever since we were quite small the *malams* had been saying that the Europeans would come with a thing called a train, they would come with a thing called a motor-car, in them you would go and come back in a trice. They would stop wars, they would repair the world, they would stop oppression and lawlessness, we should live at peace with them. We used to go and sit quietly and listen to the prophecies.

I remember when a European came to Karo on a horse, and some of his foot soldiers went into the town. Everyone came out to look at them, but in Zerewa they didn't see the European. Everyone at Karo ran away—"There's a European, there's a European!"

At that time Yusufu was the king of Karo. He did not like the Europeans, he did not wish them, he would not sign their treaty. Then he say that perforce he would have to agree, so he did. We Habe wanted them to come, it was the Fulani who did not like it. When the Europeans came the Habe saw that if you worked for them they paid you for it, they didn't say, like the Fulani, "Commoner, give me this! Commoner, bring me that!" Yes, the Habe wanted them; they saw no harm in them.

The Europeans said that there were to be no more slaves; if someone said "Slave!" you could complain to the *alkali* who would punish the master who said it, the judge said, "That

is what the Europeans have decreed." The first order said that any slave, if he was younger than you, was your younger brother, if he was older than you was your elder brother—they were all brothers of their master's family. No one used the word "slave" any more. When slavery was stopped, nothing much happened at our *rinji* except that some slaves whom we had bought in the market ran away. Our own father went to his farm and worked, he and his son took up their large hoes; they loaned out their spare farms. Tsoho our father and Kadiri my brother with whom I live now and Babambo worked, they farmed guineacorn and millet and groundnuts and everything; before this they had supervised the slaves' work—now they did their own.

In the old days if the chief liked the look of your daughter he would take her and put her in his house; you could do nothing about it. Now they don't do that.

Ilanga, a Congolese Woman, Recounts Her Capture by Agents of the Congo Free State

. . . we were all busy in the fields hoeing our plantations, for it was the rainy season, and the weeds sprang quickly up, when a runner came to the village saying that a large band of men was coming, that they all wore red caps and blue cloth, and carried guns and long knives, and that many white men were with them, the chief of whom was *Kibalanga* (Michaux). Niendo at once called all the chief men to his house, while the drums were beaten to summon the people to the village. A long consultation was held, and finally we were all told to go quietly to the fields and bring in ground-nuts, plantains, and cassava for the warriors who were coming, and goats and fowl for the white men. The women all went with baskets and filled them, and put them in the road, which was blocked up, so many were there. Niendo then commanded everyone to go and sit quietly in the houses until he gave other orders. This we did, everyone

King Leopold II King of Belgium (r. 1865–1909). He was active in encouraging the exploration of Central Africa and became the ruler of the Congo Free State (to 1908).

Henry Morton Stanley British-American explorer of Africa, famous for his expeditions in search of Dr. David Livingstone. Stanley helped King Leopold II establish the Congo Free State.

by neighboring rulers and European encroachment. In 1906 the empire came to an end with France, Britain, and Germany gobbling up various portions.

Farther south, **King Leopold II** of Belgium, following the advice of an American journalist and explorer, **Henry Morton Stanley**, invested his personal fortune in "opening up"—that is, occupying—the Congo Basin, an enormous forested region in the heart of equatorial Africa. With Leopold's money, Stanley returned to Africa from 1879 to 1884 to establish trading posts along the southern bank of the Congo River. At the same time, **Savorgnan de Brazza**, an Italian officer serving in the French army, obtained from an African ruler living on the opposite bank a treaty that placed the area under the "protection" of France.

The Berlin Conference

These events sparked a flurry of diplomatic activity. German chancellor Bismarck called the **Berlin Conference** on Africa of 1884 and 1885. There the major powers agreed that henceforth remaining quietly seated while Niendo went up the road with the head men to meet the white chief. We did not know what to think, for most of us feared that so many armed men coming boded evil; but Niendo thought that, by giving presents of much food, he would induce the strangers to pass on without harming us. And so it proved, for the soldiers took the baskets, and were then ordered by the white men to move off through the village. Many of the soldiers looked into the houses and shouted at us words we did not understand. We were glad when they were all gone, for we were much in fear of the white men and the strange warriors, who are known to all the people as being great fighters, bringing war wherever they go. . . .

When the white men and their warriors had gone, we went again to our work, and were hoping that they would not return; but this they did in a very short time. As before, we brought in great heaps of food; but this time *Kibalanga* did not move away directly, but camped near our village, and his soldiers came and stole all our fowl and goats and tore up our cassava; but we did not mind as long as they did not harm us. The next morning it was reported that the white men were going away; but soon after the sun rose over the hill, a large band of soldiers came into the village, and we all went into the houses and sat down. We were not long seated when the soldiers came rushing in shouting, and threatening Niendo with their guns. They rushed into the houses and dragged the people out. Three or four came to our house and caught hold of me, also my husband Oleka and my sister Katinga. We were dragged into the road, and were tied together with cords about our necks, so that we could not escape. We were all crying, for now we knew that we were to be taken away to be slaves. The soldiers beat us with the iron sticks from their guns, and compelled us to march to the camp of *Kibalanga*, who ordered the women to be tied up separately, ten to each cord, and the men in the same way. When we were all collected—and there were many from other villages whom we now saw, and many from Waniendo—the soldiers brought baskets of food for us to carry, in some of which was smoked human flesh (*niama na nitu*).

We then set off marching very quickly. My sister Katinga had her baby in her arms, and was not compelled to carry a basket; but my husband Oleka was made to carry a goat. We marched until the afternoon, when we camped near a stream, where we were glad to drink, for we were much athirst. We had nothing to eat, for the soldiers would give us nothing, so we lay upon the ground, and at night went to sleep. The next day we continued the march, and when we camped at noon were given some maize and plantains, which were gathered near a village from which the people had run away. So it continued each day until the fifth day, when the soldiers took my sister's baby and threw it in the grass, leaving it to die, and made her carry some cooking pots which they found in the deserted village. On the sixth day we became very weak from lack of food and from constant marching and sleeping in the damp grass, and my husband, who marched behind us with the goat, could not stand up longer, and so he sat down beside the path and refused to walk more. The soldiers beat him, but still he refused to move. Then one of them struck him on the head with the end of his gun, and he fell upon the ground. One of the soldiers caught the goat, while two or three others stuck the long knives they put on the ends of their guns into my husband. I saw the blood spurt out, and then saw him no more, for we passed over the brow of a hill and he was out of sight. Many of the young men were killed the same way, and many babies thrown into the grass to die. A few escaped; but we were so well guarded that it was almost impossible.

QUESTIONS FOR ANALYSIS

1. How do Baba and Ilanga recall their existence before the Europeans came?

2. What did they expect when they first heard of the arrival of Europeans? Instead, what happened to them, their relatives, and their towns?

3. How do you explain the difference between these two accounts?

Sources: From M. F. Smith, ed., *Baba of Karo: A Woman of the Muslim Hausa* (New York: Philosophical Library, 1955), 66–68. Edgar Canisius, *A Campaign Amongst Cannibals* (London: R. A. Everett & Co., 1903), 250–256.

Savorgnan de Brazza Franco-Italian explorer sent by the French government to claim part of equatorial Africa for France. Founded Brazzaville, capital of the French Congo, in 1880.

Berlin Conference Conference that German chancellor Otto von Bismarck called to set rules for the partition of Africa. It led to the creation of the Congo Free State under King Leopold II of Belgium.

"effective occupation" would replace the former trading relations between Africans and Europeans. Every country with colonial ambitions had to send troops into Africa and participate in the division of the spoils. As a reward for triggering the "scramble" for Africa, Leopold II acquired a personal domain under the name *Congo Free State*, while France and Portugal took most of the rest of equatorial Africa. In this manner, the European powers and King Leopold managed to divide Africa among themselves, at least on paper.

Except in Kenya, Northern Rhodesia, and South Africa, where Europeans found the land and climate to their liking and forced Africans to become squatters, sharecroppers, or ranch hands on land they had farmed for generations, the colonial rulers declared any land that was not farmed to be "vacant" and gave it to private concession companies. In the Gold Coast (now Ghana), British trading companies bought the cocoa grown by African farmers at low prices and resold it for large profits. The interior of French West Africa lagged behind. Although the region could produce cotton, peanuts, and other crops, the difficulties of transportation limited its development before 1914.

Compared to West Africa, equatorial Africa had few inhabitants and little trade. Rather than try to govern these vast territories directly, authorities in the Congo Free State, the French Congo, and the Portuguese colonies of Angola and Mozambique farmed out huge pieces of land to private concession companies, offering them monopolies on the natural resources and trade of their territories and the right to employ soldiers and tax the inhabitants. Freed from outside supervision, the companies forced the African inhabitants at gunpoint to produce cash crops and carry them, on their heads or backs, to the nearest railroad or navigable river. The worst abuses took place in the Congo Free State, where a rubber boom made it profitable for private companies to brutalize Africans collecting latex from vines that grew in the forests. After 1906 the British press began publicizing the horrors. The public outcry that followed, coinciding with the end of the rubber boom, convinced the Belgian government to take over Leopold's private empire in 1908.

Modernization in Egypt and Ethiopia

modernization The process of reforming political, military, economic, social, and cultural traditions in imitation of the early success of Western societies, often without regard for accommodating local traditions in non-Western societies.

Suez Canal Ship canal dug across the isthmus of Suez in Egypt, designed by Ferdinand de Lesseps. It opened to shipping in 1869 and shortened the sea voyage between Europe and Asia. Its strategic importance led to the British occupation of Egypt in 1882.

While colonial states were arising elsewhere, in northeastern Africa Egypt and Ethiopia retained their independence and experimented with **modernization**. Muhammad Ali, who ruled Egypt from 1805 to 1849, began a series of reforms aimed at creating a modern Egypt (see Chapter 24). European pressure sharply curtailed these efforts after 1839, but by the end of his reign Egypt's population had nearly doubled; trade with Europe had expanded by almost 600 percent; and a new class of educated Egyptians was beginning to wield some influence.

Muhammad Ali's grandson Ismail **(is-mah-EEL)** (r. 1863–1879) focused on westernizing Egypt rather than confronting Europe militarily. "My country is no longer in Africa," Ismail declared, "it is in Europe."[1] His efforts increased the number of European advisers in Egypt, as well as Egypt's debts to French and British banks. In the first decade of his reign, revenues increased thirtyfold and exports doubled (largely because of a huge increase in cotton exports during the American Civil War). By 1870 Egypt had a network of new irrigation canals, 800 miles (1,300 kilometers) of railroads, a postal service, and a few dazzling modernization projects in the capital city of Cairo. It also had the **Suez Canal**, which opened in 1969 and immediately affected communications between Europe and Asia.

Ambitions like the canal and Ismail's dream of an Egyptian empire extending south into Sudan and Ethiopia cost vast sums of money, which the khedives borrowed from European creditors at high interest rates. When the market for Egyptian cotton collapsed after the American Civil War, these debts became a problem. By 1876 foreign debt had risen to £100 million sterling, and the interest payments alone consumed one-third of Egypt's foreign export earnings. To avoid bankruptcy the Egyptian government sold its shares in the Suez Canal to Great Britain and accepted four foreign "commissioners of the debt" to oversee its finances. French and British bankers, still not satisfied, lobbied their governments to secure the loans by stronger measures. In 1878 the two governments obliged Ismail to appoint a Frenchman as minister of public works and a Briton as minister of finance. When high taxes caused hardship and popular discontent, the French and British persuaded the Ottoman sultan to depose Ismail. This foreign intervention provoked a military uprising under Egyptian army colonel Arabi Pasha, which threatened the Suez Canal.

Fearing for their investments, the British sent an army into Egypt in 1882. So important was the Suez Canal to Britain's maritime supremacy that they stayed for seventy years. During those years the British ruled Egypt "indirectly"—that is, they maintained the Egyptian government and the fiction of Egyptian sovereignty but retained real power in their own hands.

Eager to develop Egyptian cotton production, the British brought in engineers and contractors to build the first dam across the Nile, at Aswan in Upper Egypt. When completed in 1902, it captured the annual Nile flood and released its waters throughout the year, allowing farmers to grow two, sometimes three, crops a year. The economic development of Egypt by the British enriched a small elite of landowners and merchants, many of them foreigners. Egyptian peasants got little relief from the heavy taxes collected to pay for their country's crushing foreign debt and the expenses of the British army of occupation. Most Egyptians found British rule more onerous than that of the Ottomans. By the 1890s Egyptian politicians and intellectuals were demanding that the British leave.

State building and reform were also under way in Christian Ethiopia. Beginning in the 1840s, Ethiopian rulers purchased modern weapons from European sources and created strong

---

[1]Quoted in P. J. Vatikiotis, *The History of Modern Egypt: From Muhammad Ali to Mubarak*, 4th ed. (Baltimore: Johns Hopkins University Press, 1991), 74.

armies loyal to the ruler. Emperor Téwodros (tay-WOH-druhs) II (r. 1833–1868) also encouraged the manufacture of weapons locally. However, his efforts to coerce more technical aid by holding some British officials captive backfired when the British invaded instead. As the British forces advanced, Téwodros committed suicide to avoid being taken prisoner. Satisfied that their honor was avenged, the British withdrew. Téwodros's successor Yohannes (yoh-HAHN-nehs) IV (r. 1872–1889) continued to bring most highland regions under imperial rule. The only large part of ancient Ethiopia that remained outside Emperor Yohannes's rule was the independent Shoa kingdom, ruled by **Menelik II** (MEN-uh-lik) from 1865.

In 1889 Menelik II became emperor of Ethiopia, at a time when his country was threatened by Sudanese Muslims to the west and by France and Italy, which controlled the coast of the Red Sea to the east. As already stated, Ethiopia had been purchasing European and American weapons for many years. When Italians attempted to establish a protectorate over Ethiopia, they found the Ethiopians armed with thousands of rifles and even machine guns and artillery pieces. Although Italy sent twenty thousand troops to attack Ethiopia, in 1896 they were defeated at Adowa (AH-do-ah) by a larger and better-trained Ethiopian army.

Menelik II Emperor of Ethiopia (r. 1889–1911). He enlarged Ethiopia to its present dimensions and defeated an Italian invasion at Adowa (1896).

Transition from the Slave Trade

The successful slave revolt in Saint Domingue in the 1790s (see Chapter 23) ended slavery in the largest plantation colony in the West Indies. Elsewhere in the Americas, however, slave revolts were brutally repressed. As news of the slave revolts and their repression spread, humanitarians and religious reformers called for an end to the trade. Support for abolition of the trade was found even among Americans wanting to preserve slavery. In 1807 both Great Britain and the United States made importing slaves from Africa illegal for their citizens. Most other Western countries followed suit by 1850, but few enforced abolition with the vigor of the British.

"legitimate" trade Exports from Africa in the nineteenth century that did not include the newly outlawed slave trade.

Once the world's greatest slave traders, the British became the most aggressive abolitionists. Britain sent a naval patrol to enforce the ban along the African coast and negotiated treaties allowing the patrol to search other nations' vessels suspected of carrying slaves. Although British patrols captured 1,635 slave ships and liberated over 160,000 enslaved Africans, the trade proved difficult to stop. Cuba and Brazil continued to import huge numbers of slaves, which drove prices up and persuaded some African rulers and merchants to continue to sell slaves and to help foreign slavers evade the British patrols. Because the slave trade moved to other parts of Africa, the transatlantic slave trade did not end until 1867.

In exchange for slaves, Africans purchased cloth, metals, and other goods. To continue those imports, Africans expanded their **"legitimate" trade** (exports other than slaves). As the Atlantic slave trade was shut down, they revived old exports or developed new ones. The most successful of the new exports from West Africa was palm oil, used by British manufacturers for soap, candles, and lubricants. Though still a major source of slaves until the mid-1830s, the trading states of the Niger Delta emerged as the premier exporters of palm oil. Coastal African traders bought the palm oil at inland markets and delivered it to European ships at the coast.

The dramatic increase in palm-oil exports—from a few hundred tons at the beginning of the century to tens of thousands of tons by midcentury—altered the social structure of the coastal trading communities. Coastal traders used their wealth to buy slaves to paddle the giant dugout canoes that transported palm oil from inland markets

Hulton Archive/Getty Images

King Jaja of Opobo This talented man rose from slavery in the Niger Delta port of Bonny to head one of the town's major palm-oil trading firms, the Anna Pepple House, in 1863. Six years later, Jaja founded and ruled his own trading port of Opobo.

along the narrow delta creeks to the trading ports. Niger Delta slavery could be as harsh and brutal as slavery on New World plantations, but it offered some slaves a chance to gain wealth and power. Male slaves who supervised canoe fleets were well compensated, and a few even became wealthy enough to take over the leadership of coastal "canoe houses" (companies). The most famous, known as "Jaja" (ca. 1821–1891), rose from canoe slave to become the head of a major canoe house. In 1869, to escape discrimination by free-born Africans, he founded the new port of Opobo, which he ruled as king. In the 1870s Jaja of Opobo was the greatest palm-oil trader in the Niger Delta.

Another effect of the suppression of the slave trade was the spread of Western cultural influences in West Africa. To serve as a base for their anti-slave-trade naval squadron, the British had taken over the small colony of Sierra Leone **(see-AIR-uh lee-OWN)** in 1808. Over the next several years, 130,000 men, women, and children taken from "captured" vessels were liberated in Sierra Leone. Christian missionaries helped settle these **recaptives** in and around Freetown, the capital. Mission churches and schools made many converts among such men and women.

recaptives Africans rescued by Britain's Royal Navy from the illegal slave trade of the nineteenth century and restored to free status.

Sierra Leone's schools also produced a number of distinguished graduates. Samuel Adjai Crowther (1808–1891), freed from a slave ship in 1821, became the first Anglican bishop in West Africa in 1864, administering a pioneering diocese along the lower Niger River. James Africanus Horton (1835–1882), the son of slaves liberated in Sierra Leone, became a doctor and the author of many studies of West Africa.

Other Western cultural influences came from people of African birth or descent returning to their ancestral homeland. In 1821, free black Americans founded a settlement that grew into the Republic of Liberia, a place of liberty at a time when slavery was legal and flourishing in the United States. After their emancipation in 1865 other African Americans moved to Liberia. Emma White, a literate black woman from Kentucky, moved from Liberia to Opobo in 1875, where King Jaja employed her to write his commercial correspondence and run a school for his children. Edward Wilmot Blyden (1832–1912), born in the West Indies and proud of his West African parentage, emigrated to Liberia in 1851 and became a professor of Greek, Latin, and Arabic at the fledgling Liberia College.

Secondary Empire in Eastern Africa

When British patrols hampered the slave trade in West Africa, slavers moved to eastern Africa. There the Atlantic slave trade joined an existing trade in slaves to the Islamic world that also was expanding. Two-thirds of the 1.2 million slaves exported from eastern Africa in the nineteenth century went to markets in North Africa and the Middle East; the other third went to plantations in the Americas and to European-controlled Indian Ocean islands.

Slavery also became more prominent within eastern Africa itself. Between 1800 and 1873 Arab and Swahili **(swah-HEE-lee)** owners of clove plantations along the coast purchased some 700,000 slaves to do the hard work of harvesting this spice. The plantations were on Zanzibar Island and in neighboring territories belonging to the Sultanate of Oman, an Arabian kingdom on the Persian Gulf that had been expanding its control over the East African coast since 1698. The sultan had even moved his court to Zanzibar in 1840 to take advantage of the burgeoning trade in cloves. Zanzibar also was an important center of ivory and slaves until British pressure induced the sultan to ban the export of slaves in 1857 and their import in 1873.

SECTION REVIEW

- In the south, Shaka established an expansive Zulu kingdom that eventually came in conflict with European settlers.

- Differences between the British and Dutch-descended Afrikaners led to the Boer War, ultimately leaving the defeated Afrikaners in control of a segregated country.

- In the west, Usuman dan Fodio conquered the former Hausa states and formed the Sokoto Caliphate.

- Because the Suez Canal conferred new economic and political importance on Egypt, it came under British control; only Ethiopia defeated its European aggressors.

- The abolition of slavery had political consequences and increased the trade of goods like palm oil.

INDIA UNDER BRITISH RULE

The might of the Mughal Empire did not long outlast the reign of Aurangzeb, who died in 1707 (see Chapter 20). In 1739 Iranian invaders sacked Delhi and carried off vast amounts of booty. Indian states also took advantage of Mughal weakness to assert their independence. By

nawab A Muslim prince allied to British India; technically, a semi-autonomous deputy of the Mughal emperor.

sepoy An indigenous soldier in South Asia, especially in the service of the British.

midcentury, the Maratha (muh-RAH-tuh) Confederation, a coalition of states in central India, controlled more land than the Mughals did. Several **nawabs** (NAH-wab), a term used for Muslim princes who were nominally deputies of the Mughal emperor, carved out powerful states of their own.

Ambitious young "company men" employed by British, French, and Dutch trading companies used hard bargaining, and hard fighting when necessary, to persuade Indian rulers to allow them to establish coastal trading posts protected by Indian troops known as **sepoys** (SEE-poy). In divided India these private armies came to hold the balance of power.

East India Company

In 1691 Great Britain's East India Company (EIC) had persuaded the nawab of Bengal in northeast India to allow a company trading post at the fishing port of Calcutta. In 1756 a new nawab overran the post and imprisoned a group of EIC men in a cell so small that many died of suffocation. To avenge their deaths in this "Black Hole of Calcutta," a large EIC force from Madras, led by Robert Clive, overthrew the nawab. The weak Mughal emperor was persuaded to acknowledge the East India Company's right to rule Bengal in 1765. By 1788 Calcutta had grown into a city of 250,000.

Bombay was the third major center of British power in India. There, in 1818, the East India Company annexed large territories to form the core of what was called the "Bombay Presidency." This gave the East India Company an empire more populous than western Europe and with fifty times the population of the colonies the British had lost in North America. One goal of the **British raj** (regime) was to remake India on a British model through administrative and social reform, economic development, and the introduction of new technology. Yet the company men—like the Mughals before them—had to temper their interference with Indian social and religious customs lest they provoke rebellion or lose the support of their Indian princely allies.

British raj The rule over much of South Asia between 1765 and 1947 by the East India Company and then by a British government.

Another British policy was to substitute private property for India's complex and overlapping patterns of landholding. In Bengal this reform worked to the advantage of large landowners, but in Mysore the peasantry gained. Private ownership made it easier for the state to collect the taxes that were needed to pay for administration, the army, and economic reform.

Such policies of "westernization, Anglicization, and modernization," as they have been called, were only one side of British rule. The other side was the bolstering of "traditions"—both real and newly invented. In the name of tradition the Indian princes who ruled nearly half of British India were frequently endowed by their British overlords with greater power and splendor and longer tenure than their predecessors had ever had. Likewise, Hindu and Muslim holy men were able to expand their "traditional" power over property and people far beyond what had been the case in earlier times. At the same time, princes, holy men, and other Indians frequently used claims of tradition to resist British rule as well as to turn it to their advantage. The British rulers themselves invented many "traditions"—including elaborate parades and displays—half borrowed from European royal pomp, half from Mughal ceremonies.

The British and Indian elites worked sometimes in close partnership, sometimes in opposition, but always at the expense of the ordinary people of India. Women of every status, members of subordinate Hindu castes, the "untouchables" and "tribals" outside the caste system, and the poor experienced few benefits from the British reforms and much new oppression from the taxes and "traditions" that exalted their superiors' status.

The transformation of British India's economy was also doubled-edged. On the one hand, the raj created many new jobs as a result of the growth of trade and expanded crop production, such as opium in Bengal, largely for export to China (see Chapter 24); coffee in Ceylon; and tea in Assam in northeastern India. On the other hand, competition from cheap cotton goods produced in Britain's industrial mills drove many Indians out of the handicraft textile industry. In the eighteenth century India had been the world's greatest exporter of cotton textiles; in the nineteenth century India increasingly shipped raw cotton fiber to Britain.

During the first half of the nineteenth century, British rulers readily handled these isolated local rebellions, but they were more concerned about the loyalty of their Indian sepoys. The EIC employed 200,000 sepoys in 1857, along with 38,000 British troops. Armed with modern rifles and disciplined in fighting methods, the sepoys had a potential for successful rebellion that other groups lacked.

In the early decades of EIC rule, most sepoys came from Bengal. The Bengali sepoys resented the active recruitment of other ethnic groups into the army after 1848, such as Sikhs (sick) from

Punjab and Gurkhas from Nepal. In addition, many high-caste Hindus objected to a new law in 1856 requiring new recruits to be available for service overseas in the growing British empire, for their religion prohibited ocean travel. Finally, the replacement of the standard military musket by the more accurate Enfield rifle in 1857 required soldiers to use their teeth to tear open the ammunition cartridges, which were greased with animal fat. Hindus were offended by this order if the fat came from cattle, which they considered sacred. Muslims were offended if the fat came from pigs, which they considered unclean.

Although the cartridge-opening procedure was quickly changed, the initial discontent grew into rebellion by Hindu sepoys in May 1857. British troubles mushroomed when Muslim sepoys, peasants, and discontented elites joined in. The rebellion was put down ten months later, but it shook this empire to its core.

Historians have attached different names and meanings to the events of 1857 and 1858. Nineteenth-century British historians labeled it the "**Sepoy Rebellion**" or "Mutiny." Seeing in these events the beginnings of the later movement for independence, some modern Indian historians have termed it the "Revolution of 1857."

Sepoy Rebellion The revolt of Indian soldiers in 1857 against certain practices that violated religious customs; also known as the Sepoy Mutiny.

Political Reform and Industrial Impact

Regardless of label, the events of 1857–1858 marked a turning point in the history of modern India. In their wake Indians gained a new centralized government, entered a period of rapid economic growth, and began to develop a new national consciousness.

In 1858 Britain eliminated the last traces of Mughal and Company rule. In their place, a new secretary of state for India in London oversaw Indian policy, and a new governor-general in Delhi acted as the British monarch's viceroy. In November 1858 Queen Victoria guaranteed all Indians equal protection of the law and the freedom to practice their religions and social customs; she also assured Indian princes that so long as they were loyal to the queen British India would respect their control of territories and "their rights, dignity and honour."[2]

British rule continued to emphasize both tradition and reform after 1857. At the top, the British viceroys lived in enormous palaces amid hundreds of servants and gaudy displays of luxury meant to convince Indians that the British viceroys were legitimate successors to the Mughal emperors. They treated the quasi-independent Indian princes with elaborate ceremonial courtesy and maintained them in splendor. When Queen Victoria was proclaimed "Empress of India" in 1877 and periodically thereafter, the viceroys put on great pageants known as **durbars**. At the durbar in Delhi in 1902–1903 to celebrate the coronation of King Edward VII, Viceroy Lord Curzon honored himself with a 101-gun salute and a parade of 34,000 troops in front of 50 princes and 173,000 visitors.

durbar An elaborate display of political power and wealth in British India in the nineteenth century, ostensibly in imitation of the pageantry of the Mughal Empire.

Indian Civil Service The elite professional class of officials who administered the government of British India. Originally composed exclusively of well-educated British men, it gradually added qualified Indians.

Meanwhile, a powerful and efficient bureaucracy controlled India. Members of the elite **Indian Civil Service** (ICS) held the senior administrative and judicial posts. Numbering only a thousand at the end of the nineteenth century, these men visited the villages in their districts, heard lawsuits and complaints, and passed judgments.

Recruitment into the ICS was by open examinations. In theory any British subject could take these exams; since they were given in England, however, in practice the system worked to exclude Indians. In 1870 only one Indian was a member of the ICS. Subsequent reforms led to fifty-seven Indian appointments by 1887, but there the process stalled. Working under the ICS were thousands of lesser Indian officials.

The reason qualified Indians were denied entry into the upper administration of their country was the racist contempt most British officials felt for the people they ruled. When he became commander-in-chief of the Indian army in 1892, Lord Kitchener declared:

It is this consciousness of the inherent superiority of the European which had won for us India. However well educated and clever a native may be, and however brave he may have proved himself, I believe that no rank we can bestow on him would cause him to be considered an equal of the British officer.[3]

After 1857 the government invested millions of pounds sterling in harbors, cities, irrigation canals, and other public works. Forests were felled to make way for tea plantations. Indian

---

[2]Quoted by Bernard S. Cohn, "Representing Authority in Victorian India," in *The Invention of Tradition*, ed. Eric Hobsbawm and Terence Ranger (Cambridge, England: Cambridge University Press, 1983), 165.
[3]James Truslow, *Empire of the Seven Seas: The British Empire 1784–1939* (New York: Charles Scribners Sons, 2007), 268.

Topham/The Image Works

Delhi Durbar, January 1, 1903   The parade of Indian princes on ornately decorated elephants and accompanied by retainers fostered their sense of belonging to the vast empire of India that British rule had created.

farmers were persuaded to grow cotton and jute for export. Engineers built great irrigation systems to alleviate the famines that periodically decimated whole provinces. As a result, India's trade expanded rapidly.

Most of the exports were agricultural commodities: cotton fiber, opium, tea, silk, and sugar. In return India imported manufactured goods from Britain, including machine-made cotton textiles that undercut Indian hand-loom weavers. Some women found jobs at very low pay on plantations or in the growing cities, where prostitution flourished. Everywhere in India poverty remained the norm.

The Indian government also promoted the introduction of new technologies into India. Earlier in the century there were steamboats on the rivers and a massive program of canal building for irrigation. Beginning in the 1840s a railroad boom gave India its first national transportation network, followed by telegraph lines, and by 1870 India had the fifth largest rail network in the world. Originally designed to serve British commerce, the railroads were owned by British companies, constructed with British rails and equipment, and paid dividends to British investors. Ninety-nine percent of the railroad employees were Indians, but Europeans occupied all the top positions—"like a thin film of oil on top of a glass of water, resting upon but hardly mixing with [those] below," as one official report put it.

Although some Indians opposed the railroads at first because the trains mixed people of different castes, faiths, and sexes, the Indian people took to rail travel with great enthusiasm. Indians rode trains on business, on pilgrimage, and in search of work. In 1870 over 18 million passengers traveled along the network's 4,775 miles (7,685 kilometers) of track, and more than half a million messages were sent up and down the 14,000 miles (22,500 kilometers) of telegraph wires.

But the freer movement of Indian pilgrims and the flood of poor Indians into the cities also promoted the spread of cholera **(KAHL-uhr-uh)**, a disease transmitted through water contaminated by human feces. Cholera deaths rose rapidly during the nineteenth century, and eventually the disease spread to Europe. In many Indian minds *kala mari* ("the black death") was a divine punishment for failing to prevent the British takeover. This chastisement also fell heavily on British residents, who died in large numbers. In 1867 officials demonstrated the close connection between cholera and pilgrims who bathed in and drank from sacred pools and rivers. The installation of a new sewerage system and a filtered water supply (1869) in Calcutta dramatically reduced cholera deaths there. Similar measures in Bombay and Madras also led to great reductions, but most Indians lived in small villages where famine and lack of sanitation kept cholera deaths high.

Indian Nationalism

After the failure of the rebellion of 1857 to overthrow British rule, some Indians argued that the only way for Indians to regain control of their destiny was to reduce their country's social and ethnic divisions and promote Pan-Indian nationalism.

Individuals such as Rammohun Roy (1772–1833) had promoted development along these lines a generation earlier. A Western-educated Bengali from a Brahmin family, Roy was a successful administrator for the East India Company and a student of comparative religion. His Brahmo Samaj **(BRAH-moh suh-MAHJ)** (Divine Society), founded in 1828, attracted Indians who sought to reconcile the values of the West with the religious traditions of India. They advocated reforming some Hindu customs, such as the caste system and child marriage, and urged a return to the founding principles of the *Upanishads*, ancient sacred writings of Hinduism. They also backed British efforts to ban practices they found repugnant. Widow burning (*sati* **[suh-TEE]**) was outlawed in 1829 and slavery in 1843. Reformers sought to correct other abuses of women: prohibitions against widows remarrying were revoked in 1856, and female infanticide was made a crime in 1870.

Although Brahmo Samaj remained influential after the rebellion of 1857, many Indian intellectuals turned to Western secular values and nationalism as the way to reclaim India. In this process the spread of Western education played an important role, a process aided by European and American missionaries. Roy had studied both Indian and Western subjects and helped found the Hindu College in Calcutta in 1816. Other Western-curriculum schools quickly followed, including Bethune College in Calcutta, the first secular school for Indian women, in 1849. India's three universities were established in 1857. In 1870 there were over 24,000 elementary and secondary schools, whose graduates articulated a new Pan-Indian nationalism that transcended regional and religious differences.

Many of the new nationalists came from the Indian middle class, which had prospered from the increase of trade and manufacturing. Educated people were angered by the obstacles that British rules and prejudices put in the way of their advancement. Hoping to increase their influence and improve their employment opportunities in the Indian government, they convened the first **Indian National Congress** in 1885. The members sought a larger role for Indians in the Civil Service. They also called for reductions in military expenditures, which consumed 40 percent of the government's budget, so that more could be spent on alleviating the poverty of the Indian masses. But although the Indian National Congress promoted unity among the country's many religions and social groups, most early members were upper-caste Western-educated Hindus and Parsis. Until it attracted the support of the masses, it could not hope to challenge British rule.

Indian National Congress A movement and political party founded in 1885 to demand greater Indian participation in government. Its membership was middle class, and its demands were modest until World War I. Led after 1920 by Mohandas K. Gandhi, it appealed increasingly to the poor, and it organized mass protests demanding self-government and independence.

SECTION REVIEW

- Between 1757 and 1857, Britain gained nearly complete control of India.

- The British exploited local traditions and rulers and instituted a colonial government that conferred benefits on those Indians who governed on its behalf while most of the population lived in worsening conditions.

- The Sepoy Rebellion of 1857–1858 prompted reforms and substantial investments in railroads and other public works.

- In response to modernization, Indian nationalism arose in the educated middle class.

SOUTHEAST ASIA AND THE PACIFIC

Different parts of Southeast Asia and the Pacific region had differing histories, yet all came under intense imperialist pressure during the nineteenth century. Thomas Stamford Raffles had governed Java from 1811 to 1814, when the politics of Napoleon's wars in Europe allowed the

English to displace the Dutch. After a peace treaty in Europe dictated Java's return to the Dutch, Raffles helped establish, in 1824, a new free port at Singapore on the site of a small Malay fishing village with a superb harbor (see Map 26.2). British merchants and Chinese businessmen and laborers soon made Singapore the paramount center of trade and shipping between the Indian Ocean and China. Along with Malacca and other possessions on the strait, Singapore formed the "Straits Settlements," which British India administered until 1867.

British expansion came more quickly in neighboring Burma, which had emerged as a powerful kingdom by 1750. In 1785 Burma tried to annex neighboring territories of Siam (now Thailand) to the east, but a coalition of Thai leaders thwarted Burmese advances by 1802. Burma next attacked Assam to the west, but this provoked a war with British India. After a two-year war, India annexed Assam in 1826 and occupied two coastal provinces of northern Burma. As the rice and timber trade from these provinces grew important, the occupation became permanent, and in 1852 British India annexed the rest of coastal Burma. The last piece of the country was annexed in 1885, but Thailand remained an independent kingdom.

Indochina fell under French control piece by piece until it was finally subdued in 1895. Similarly, Malaya (now Malaysia) came under British rule in stages during the 1870s and 1880s. In northern Sumatra, however, a region that supplied half the world's production of black pepper, the Dutch fought a ferocious war between 1873 and 1913 against the rulers of Acheh. The Achehnese warriors were inspired, in part, by the mystique of an Islamic jihad, thus creating a tradition of resistance that would continue to resonate throughout the twentieth century.

Australia

In the once-remote South Pacific, British settlers displaced the indigenous populations of Australia and New Zealand, just as they had done in North America. Portuguese mariners had sighted Australia in the early seventeenth century, but it was too remote to be of much interest to Europeans. However, after the English captain James Cook explored New Zealand and the eastern coast of Australia between 1769 and 1778, expanding shipping networks brought in growing numbers of visitors and settlers.

At the time of Cook's visits, Australia was the home of about 650,000 hunting-and-gathering people, whose Melanesian (mel-uh-NEE-zhuhn) ancestors had settled there some forty thousand years earlier. New Zealand was inhabited by about 250,000 Maori (MOW-ree [ow as in cow]), who practiced hunting, fishing, and simple forms of agriculture, which their Polynesian ancestors had introduced around 1200. Because of their long isolation from the rest of humanity, the populations of Australia and New Zealand were as vulnerable as the Amerindians had been to unfamiliar diseases introduced by new overseas contacts. By the 1890s, only 93,000 aboriginal Australians and 42,000 Maori survived, and British settler populations outnumbered and dominated the indigenous peoples.

The first permanent British settlers in Australia were 736 convicts, of whom 188 were women, sent into exile in 1788. Over the next few decades, Australian penal colonies grew slowly and had only slight contact with the indigenous population, whom the British called "Aborigines." However, the discovery of gold in 1851 brought a flood of free European settlers (and some Chinese) and hastened the end of the penal colonies. When the gold rush subsided, government subsidies enabled tens of thousands of British settlers to settle "down under." Though it still took more than three months to reach Australia from Britain, by 1860 Australia had a million immigrants, and the settler population doubled during the next fifteen years.

New Zealand

British settlers were drawn more slowly to New Zealand. Some of the first were temporary residents along the coast who slaughtered seals and exported pelts to Western countries to be made into men's felt hats. A single ship in 1806 took away sixty thousand sealskins. By the early 1820s overhunting had nearly exterminated the seal population. Special ships also hunted sperm whales extensively near New Zealand for their oil, used for lubrication, soap, and lamps; ambergris (AM-ber-grees), an ingredient in perfume; and whalebone (actually baleen, feeding bristles made like fingernails of keratin), used as stays in women's corsets. A brief gold rush and faster ships and subsidized passages attracted more British immigrants after 1860. The colony especially courted women immigrants to offset the preponderance of single men. By the early 1880s this most distant frontier of the British Empire had a settler population of 500,000. Britain encouraged the

MAP 26.2 **Asia in 1914** By 1914, much of Asia was claimed by colonial powers. The southern rim, from the Persian Gulf to the Pacific, was occupied by Great Britain, France, the Netherlands, and the United States. Central Asia had been incorporated into the Russian Empire. © Cengage Learning

Territories held by
Western powers

- Great Britain
- France
- Netherlands
- United States
- Russian Empire

- Japan and its territories
- Independent Asian states
- Ottoman Empire
- Major railroads

Bettmann/CORBIS

Emilio Aguinaldo In 1896, a revolt led by Emilio Aguinaldo attempted to expel Spaniards from the Philippines. When the United States purchased the Philippines from Spain two years later, the Filipino people were not consulted. Aguinaldo continued his campaign, this time against the American occupation forces, until his capture in 1901. In this picture, he appears on horseback, surrounded by some of his troops.

settlers in Australia and New Zealand to become self-governing, following the 1867 model that had formed the Dominion of Canada out of the diverse and thinly settled colonies of British North America. By gradually turning over governing power to the colonies' inhabitants, Britain satisfied the settlers' desire for greater control over their own territories, muted demands for independence, and made the colonial governments responsible for most of their own expenses.

North American patterns also shaped the indigenous peoples' fate. Aborigines lacked the rights of Australian citizens. The requirement that voters had to be able to read and write English kept Maori from voting in early New Zealand elections, but four seats in the lower house of the legislature were reserved for Maori from 1867 on.

Hawaii and the Philippines, 1878–1902

The United States was a latecomer in the race for colonial territories. However, by the 1890s it had a fast-growing population and industries that produced more manufactured goods than they could sell at home. This growth contributed to economic depressions in 1893 and 1896 and led merchants and bankers to look to China as a new export market. Guam, Hawaii, and the Philippines being naval stations on the route to China, the new expansionism looked in that direction. China was in the minds of those who agreed with the naval strategist Alfred T. Mahan **(mah-HAHN)**: "Whether they will or no, Americans must now begin to look outward. The growing production of the country requires it."

This was not the beginning of American interest in the Pacific. In 1878 the United States obtained the harbor of Pago Pago in Samoa as a coaling and naval station, and in 1887 it secured the use of Pearl Harbor in Hawaii for the same purpose. By 1898 the United States under President William McKinley (1897–1901) had become openly imperialistic and annexed Hawaii as a steppingstone to Asia. As the United States became ever more involved in Asian affairs, Hawaii's strategic location brought an inflow of U.S. military personnel, and its fertile land caused planters to import laborers from Japan, China, and the Philippines. These immigrants soon outnumbered the native Hawaiians.

While large parts of Asia were falling under colonial domination, the people of the Philippines were chafing under their Spanish rulers. **Emilio Aguinaldo**, leader of a secret society, rose in revolt and proclaimed a republic in 1899. The revolutionaries had a good chance of winning independence, for Spain had its hands full with a revolution in Cuba. Unfortunately for Aguinaldo and his followers, the United States declared war against Spain in April 1898 and quickly

Emilio Aguinaldo Leader of the Filipino independence movement against Spain (1895–1898). He proclaimed the independence of the Philippines in 1899, but his movement was crushed and he was captured by the United States Army in 1901.

overcame Spanish forces in the Philippines and Cuba. After the Spanish defeat, President McKinley realized that a weakened Spain might lose the islands to another imperialist power. Japan, having recently defeated China in the Sino-Japanese War (1894–1895) and annexed Taiwan (see Chapter 27), was eager to expand its empire. So was Germany, which had taken over parts of New Guinea and Samoa and several Pacific archipelagoes during the 1880s. To forestall them, McKinley purchased the Philippines from Spain for $20 million.

The Filipinos were not eager to trade one master for another. For a while, Aguinaldo cooperated with the Americans in the hope of achieving full independence. When his plan was rejected, he rose up again in 1899 and proclaimed the independence of his country. In spite of protests by anti-imperialists in the United States, the U.S. government decided that its global interests outweighed the interests of the Filipino people. In rebel areas, a U.S. army of occupation tortured prisoners, burned villages and crops, and forced the inhabitants into "reconcentration camps." By the end of the insurrection in 1902, the war had cost the lives of 5,000 Americans and 200,000 Filipinos.

After the insurrection ended, the United States attempted to soften its rule with public works and economic development projects. New buildings went up in the city of Manila; roads, harbors, and railroads were built; and the Philippine economy was tied ever more closely to that of the United States. In 1907 Filipinos were allowed to elect representatives to a legislative assembly, but ultimate authority remained in the hands of a governor appointed by the president of the United States. In 1916 the Philippines were the first U.S. colony to be promised independence, a promise fulfilled only thirty years later.

SECTION REVIEW

- Britain, France, and the Netherlands gained economic and political colonial control of Southeast Asia.

- Australia and New Zealand attracted British settlers, whose diseases decimated the native aboriginal and Maori populations.

- The growing economy of the United States led it to pursue economic interests in the Pacific, including Hawaii.

- After a brutal struggle, the Philippines became an American colony.

IMPERIALISM IN LATIN AMERICA

The United States played a lesser role than Britain and other European countries in the economic dominance that characterized imperialism in Latin America, and business played a more important role than military intervention. But America's clash with Spain over control of the Philippines carried over into Spanish possessions closer to home.

American Expansionism and the Spanish-American War, 1898

The United States had long had interests in Cuba, the closest and richest of the Caribbean islands and a Spanish colony. American businesses had invested great sums of money in Cuba's sugar and tobacco industries, and thousands of Cubans had migrated to the United States. In 1895 the Cuban nationalist José Martí started a revolution against Spanish rule. American newspapers thrilled readers with lurid stories of Spanish atrocities; businessmen worried about their investments; and politicians demanded that the U.S. government help liberate Cuba.

On February 15, 1898, the U.S. battleship *Maine* accidentally blew up in Havana harbor, killing 266 American sailors. The U.S. government immediately blamed Spain and issued an ultimatum that the Spanish evacuate Cuba. Spain agreed to the ultimatum, but the American press and Congress were eager for war, and President McKinley did not restrain them.

Spanish-American War War fought in 1898 to expand American imperial possessions. Treaty of Paris ending the conflict confirmed U.S. control of Guam, Puerto Rico, and the Philippines.

The **Spanish-American War** was over quickly. On May 1, 1898, U.S. warships destroyed the Spanish fleet at Manila in the Philippines. Two months later the United States Navy sank the Spanish Atlantic fleet off Santiago, Cuba. By mid-August Spain was suing for peace. U.S. Secretary of State John Hay called it "a splendid little war." The United States purchased the Philippines from Spain but took over Puerto Rico and Guam as war booty. The two islands remain American possessions to this day. Cuba became an independent republic, subject to interference by the United States.

Economic Imperialism

Latin America achieved independence from Spain and Portugal in the nineteenth century but did not industrialize. Most Latin American republics, suffering from ideological divisions,

Topical Press Agency/Getty Images

Francisco "Pancho" Villa   Francisco "Pancho" Villa led an army of cowboys and ranch hands in northern Mexico during the revolution. He became very popular by confiscating large haciendas and dividing them among the poor. In March 1916 he entered the United States with 500 soldiers and attacked the town of Columbus, New Mexico, provoking an American invasion of Mexico. He was assassinated in 1923.

Francisco "Pancho" Villa A popular leader during the Mexican Revolution. An outlaw in his youth, when the revolution started, he formed a cavalry army in the north of Mexico and fought for the rights of the landless in collaboration with Emiliano Zapata. He was assassinated in 1923.

Francisco "Pancho" Villa (1877–1923), a former ranch hand, mule driver, and bandit, organized an army of three thousand men, most of them cowboys, and divided large haciendas into family ranches. After a failed and unexplained attack on the town of Columbus, New Mexico, the U.S. Army sent General John Pershing on a nine-month mission to hunt Villa down. The mission was cut short by American entry into World War I, but, like the occupation of Veracruz, it demonstrated increasing American concern for protecting land and business interests in Mexico.

Zapata and Villa enjoyed tremendous popular support but could never rise above their regional and peasant origins and lead a national revolution. The Constitutionalists had fewer soldiers than Zapata and Villa, but they held the major cities and used the proceeds of oil sales to buy modern weapons. Gradually the Constitutionalists took over most of Mexico. In 1919 they defeated and killed Zapata; Villa was given a large estate to retire to but was assassinated in 1923 after resuming political activity. An estimated 2 million people lost their lives in the civil war, and much of Mexico lay in ruins.

During their struggle to win support against Zapata and Villa, the Constitutionalists adopted many of their rivals' agrarian reforms, such as restoring communal lands to the Indians of Morelos. They also proposed social programs designed to appeal to workers and the middle class. The Constitution of 1917 set out first principles: a one-term limit on presidential power; economic nationalism (recapturing subsoil rights from foreigners, land reform, and the right of labor to organize); and severe constraints on the church. However, powerful Mexican forces and the United States sought to prevent full implementation of the constitution. By 1928 the Mexican government had made more progress against the church than in the implementation of either political or economic reform.

By the early 1920s a decade of violence had drained the country without resolving the question of who would rule. Carranza, elected president in 1917, did not wish Obregón to succeed him. In response, Obregón allied with two other ambitious leaders and marched on Mexico City. Carranza was killed as he fled. Following the constitution, Obregón served one four-year term as president. He then managed the election of Plutarco Elías Calles (KAH-yace), his colleague in the anti-Carranza plot, who served one term with the understanding that Obregón would return to the presidency in 1928. A Catholic militant put a stop to this arrangement by assassinating Obregón before he could take office.

American Intervention in the Caribbean and Central America, 1901–1914

American intervention in the Western Hemisphere was not limited to Mexico. The nations of the Caribbean and Central America were small and poor, and their governments were corrupt, unstable, and often bankrupt. They seemed to offer an open invitation to foreign interference. A government would borrow money to pay for railroads, harbors, electric power, and other symbols of modernity. When it could not repay the loan, the lending banks in Europe or the United States would ask for assistance from their home governments, which sometimes threatened to intervene. To ward off European intervention, the United States sent in the marines on more than one occasion.

Presidents Theodore Roosevelt (1901–1909), William Taft (1909–1913), and Woodrow Wilson (1913–1921) felt impelled to intervene in the region, though they differed sharply on the proper policy the United States should follow toward the small nations to the south. Roosevelt encouraged regimes friendly to the United States; Taft sought to influence them through loans from American banks; and the moralist Wilson tried to impose clean governments by military means.

Having "liberated" Cuba from Spain, in 1901 the United States forced the Cuban government to accept the Platt Amendment, which gave the United States the "right to intervene" to maintain order on the island. The United States used this excuse to occupy Cuba militarily from 1906 to 1909, in 1912, and again from 1917 to 1922. In all but name Cuba became an American protectorate. U.S. troops also occupied the Dominican Republic from 1904 to 1907 and again in 1916, Nicaragua and Honduras in 1912, and Haiti in 1915. They brought sanitation and material progress but no political improvements.

The United States was especially forceful in Panama, which was a province of Colombia. Here the issue was not corruption or debts but a more vital interest. When the United States acquired Hawaii and the Philippines, it recognized the need for a canal that would allow warships to move quickly between the Atlantic and Pacific Oceans. The main obstacle was Colombia, which refused to give the United States a piece of its territory. In 1903 the U.S. government supported a Panamanian rebellion against Colombia and quickly recognized the independence of Panama. In exchange, it obtained the right to build a canal and to occupy a zone 5 miles (8 kilometers) wide on either side of it. Work began in 1904, and the **Panama Canal** opened on August 15, 1914.

Panama Canal Ship canal cut across the isthmus of Panama by United States Army engineers; it opened in 1914. The canal greatly shortened the sea voyage between the east and west coasts of North America. The United States turned the canal over to Panama on January 1, 2000.

SECTION REVIEW

- The Spanish-American war made Cuba an unofficial American protectorate.

- Britain and the United States invested in railroads and other industrial enterprises throughout Latin America.

- Strong economic and social divisions in Mexico contributed to a revolution involving diverse players.

- After a decade of violence Mexico gained a new constitution.

- Repeated American interventions in the region peaked with the building of the Panama Canal.

THE WORLD ECONOMY AND THE GLOBAL ENVIRONMENT

The nineteenth-century imperialists were not traditional conquerors or empire builders like the Spanish conquistadors. They expressed their belief in progress and their good intentions in the clichés of the time: "the conquest of nature," "the annihilation of time and space," "the taming of the wilderness," and "our civilizing mission."

Expansion of the World Economy

For centuries Europe had been a ready market for spices, sugar, silk, and other imported products. The Industrial Revolution expanded this demand, especially for stimulants such as tea, coffee, and chocolate. The trade in industrial raw materials grew even faster, as well as trade in agricultural products like cotton, jute for bags, palm oil for soap and lubricants, and minerals like diamonds, gold, and copper. Some wild forest products eventually came to be cultivated: timber for buildings and railroad ties, cinchona bark, rubber for rainwear and tires, and gutta-percha **(gut-tah-PER-cha)** (the sap of a Southeast Asian tree) to insulate electric cables.

Economic botany and agricultural science were applied to every promising plant species. European botanists had long collected and classified exotic plants from around the world. In the nineteenth century they founded botanical gardens in Java, India, Mauritius **(maw-REE-shuss)**, Ceylon, Jamaica, and other tropical colonies. These gardens not only collected local plants but also transferred commercially valuable plant species from one tropical region to another. Cinchona **(sin-CHO-nah)** (the source of the antimalarial drug quinine), tobacco, sugar, coffee, tea, and other crops were introduced, improved, and vastly expanded in the colonies of Southeast Asia and Indonesia (see Environment and Technology: Imperialism and Tropical Ecology). Cacao and coffee growing spread over large areas of Brazil and Africa; oil-palm plantations were established in Nigeria and the Congo Basin. After 1910, rubber, used to make waterproof garments and bicycle tires, came from plantations in Southeast Asia.

Throughout the tropics, land once covered with forests or devoted to slash-and-burn agriculture was transformed into permanent farms and plantations. In Java and India farmers felled trees to obtain arable land and firewood, terraced hillsides, drained swamps, and dug wells. Colonial rule also fostered population growth. Even in areas not developed to export crops, growing populations put pressure on the land. For example, the population of Java, an island the size of Pennsylvania, doubled from 16 million in 1870 to over 30 million in 1914.

Mary Evans Picture Library/The Image Works

A Rubber Plantation   As bicycles and automobiles proliferated in the early twentieth century, the demand for rubber outstripped the supply available from wild rubber trees in the Amazon forest. Rubber grown on plantations in Southeast Asia came on the market from 1910 on. The rubber trees had to be tapped very carefully and on a regular schedule to obtain the latex or sap from which rubber was extracted. In this picture a woman and a boy perform this operation on a plantation in British Malaya.

Free Trade

By 1870 Britain had added several dozen colonies to the twenty-six colonies it had in 1792. The underlying goal of most British imperial expansion during these decades was trade rather than territory. Most of the new colonies were meant to serve as ports in the growing network of shipping that encircled the globe or as centers of production and distribution for those networks.

This new commercial expansion was closely tied to the needs of Britain's growing industrial economy and reflected a new philosophy of overseas trade. Rather than rebuilding the closed mercantilist network of trade with its colonies, Britain sought to trade freely with all parts of the world. Free trade was also a wise policy in light of the independence of so many former colonies in the Americas (see Chapter 23).

Whether colonized or not, more and more lands were being drawn into the commercial networks created by British expansion and industrialization. Uncolonized parts of West Africa became major exporters to Britain of vegetable oils and forest products, while areas of eastern

Imperialism and Tropical Ecology

Despite European enthusiasm for botanical research, introducing productive new crops into colonial economies was not always easy. Vanilla, for example, comes from a species of orchid that is native to central Mexico and had been known in Europe since the time of the Spanish conquistador Hernán Cortés. When transplanted into experimental gardens in other tropical regions, the orchid grew readily. But it produced no beans, and hence no vanilla flavoring.

For three hundred years Europeans who fancied the taste of vanilla had to rely on Mexican production. Then in 1837 a Belgian botanist named Charles François Antoine Morren discovered that a bee species particular to Mexico played an essential role in pollinating the plants. However, the bees could not survive when introduced to other lands. Morren devised a way of pollinating the vanilla plants by hand, but it proved slow and clumsy in practice and was never commercially adopted.

Four years later, Edmond Albius, a twelve-year-old African slave born and raised on the island of Réunion, a French colony in the Indian Ocean, invented a new method of hand pollination that was quick and efficient. A European scientist sought credit for the discovery, but Albius's master and adoptive father, Ferreol Bellier-Beaumont, defended the boy's claim. Réunion soon became the center of a new industry exporting a tropical commodity that was much in demand, but in time the larger island of Madagascar became the leading non-Mexican producer of vanilla.

As for Albius, after being freed when France outlawed slavery in 1848, he worked as a kitchen servant and then was sentenced to ten years in prison for stealing jewelry. After five years the governor of the colony granted him clemency in recognition of his role in creating the vanilla industry.

The story of Edmond Albius highlights the fact that credit for the development of new or transplanted industrial crops in Europe's tropical colonies belongs not just to European botanists and planters, but also to local farmers who learned to adapt their skills to the new plants. Most of the improvements originating with these non-European workers will never be known, but without their talents and ideas the transformation in the global trade in tropical crops that characterized the nineteenth century could scarcely have taken place.

amanaimages/Corbis

Painting of Vanilla Plant The European passion for creating botanical gardens for transplanting trees and flowers from colonial regions was matched by the production of albums of paintings of exotic flora. The long tubular shape of the vanilla blossom shows why it was difficult to pollinate by hand.

Africa free of European control exported ivory that ended up as piano keys and decorations in the homes of the middle and upper classes.

In return for the foodstuffs and industrial raw materials that flowed toward Europe and the United States, the factories of the industrialized nations supplied manufactured goods at very attractive prices. By the mid-nineteenth century a major part of their textile production was destined for overseas markets. Sales of cotton cloth to Africa increased 950 percent from the 1820s to the 1860s. British trade to India grew 350 percent between 1841 and 1870, while India's exports increased 400 percent. Trade with other regions also expanded rapidly. In most cases such trade benefited both sides, but there is no question that the industrial nations were the dominant partners.

New Labor Migrations

Between 1834 and 1870 many thousands of Indians, Chinese, and Africans went overseas to work, especially on sugar plantations. In the half century after 1870, tens of thousands of Asians and Pacific islanders made similar voyages.

In part these migrations were linked to the end of slavery. After their emancipation in British colonies in 1834, many slaves left the plantations. To compete with sugar plantations in Cuba, Brazil, and the French Caribbean that were still using slave labor, British colonies had to recruit new laborers.

India's impoverished people seemed one obvious alternative. After planters on Mauritius successfully introduced Indian laborers, the Indian labor trade moved to the British Caribbean in 1838. In 1841 the British government also allowed Caribbean planters to recruit Africans whom British patrols had rescued from slave ships and liberated in Sierra Leone and elsewhere. By 1870 nearly 40,000 Africans had settled in British colonies, along with over a half-million Indians and over 18,000 Chinese. After the French and Dutch abolished slavery in 1848, their colonies also recruited new laborers from Asia and Africa.

Slavery was not abolished in Cuba until 1886, but the rising cost of slaves led the burgeoning sugar plantations to recruit 138,000 new laborers from China between 1847 and 1873. Indentured labor recruits also became the mainstay of new sugar plantations in places that had never known slave labor. After 1850 American planters in Hawaii recruited labor from China and Japan; British planters in Natal (in South Africa) recruited from India; and those in Queensland (in northeastern Australia) relied on laborers from neighboring South Pacific islands.

Larger, faster ships (see Chapter 27) made transporting laborers halfway around the world affordable, though voyages from Asia to the Caribbean still took an average of three months. Despite close regulation and supervision of shipboard conditions, the crowded accommodations encouraged the spread of cholera and other contagious diseases that took many migrants' lives.

All of these laborers served under **contracts of indenture**, which bound them to work for a specified period (usually from five to seven years) in return for free passage to their overseas destination. They were paid a small salary and were provided with housing, clothing, and medical care. Indian indentured laborers also received the right to a free passage home if they worked a second five-year contract. British Caribbean colonies required forty women to be recruited for every hundred men as a way to promote family life. So many Indians chose to stay in Mauritius, Trinidad, British Guiana, and Fiji that they constituted a third or more of the total population of these colonies by the early twentieth century.

The indentured labor trade reflected the unequal commercial and industrial power of the West, but it was not an entirely one-sided creation. The men and women who signed indentured contracts were trying to improve their lives by emigrating, and many succeeded. Whether for good or ill, more and more of the world's peoples saw their lives being influenced by the existence of Western colonies, Western ships, and Western markets.

contract of indenture A voluntary agreement binding a person to work for a specified period of years in return for free passage to an overseas destination. Before 1800 most indentured servants were Europeans; after 1800 most indentured laborers were Asians.

SECTION REVIEW

- Industrialization increased demand for food imports and raw materials in Europe, which was met by its worldwide colonies.

- Free trade replaced the earlier focus on complete control of colonial production.

- As slavery ended, laborers were sent from heavily populated countries like India and China to work in European colonies.

- Contracts of indenture provided a framework for this labor migration.

CONCLUSION

What is the global significance of these complex political and economic changes in southern Asia, Africa, the South Pacific, and Latin America? One perspective stresses the continuing and growing imperialist exploitation of non-Europeans. From another perspective what was most important about this period was not the political and military strength of the Europeans but their growing domination of the world's commerce, especially investment in plantations, railroads, mines, and long-distance ocean shipping. Motives differed somewhat from region to region. Imperialists were drawn to Africa and Southeast Asia by a desire for tropical foodstuffs and industrial raw materials. Land for settlement was the attraction in Australia, New Zealand, and South Africa, as it earlier had been for European settlers in the New World. India and Latin America, having more prosperous middle classes, provided markets for European and American manufactures.

The growing exchanges could be mutually beneficial. As in Europe itself, overseas consumers found industrially produced goods far cheaper and sometimes better than the handicrafts they replaced. Industrialization also created new markets for African and Asian goods, as in the case of palm oil from West Africa or rubber from Malaya. There were also negative impacts, as in the case of weavers thrown out of work in India and the beginnings of deforestation in Southeast Asia.

Imperialist military and commercial strength did not reduce Africa, Asia, Latin America, and the Pacific to mere appendages of Europe. While the balance of power shifted in the Europeans' favor between 1750 and 1914, other cultures were still vibrant and local initiatives often dominant. Islamic reform movements, the rise of the Zulu nation, and the Mexican revolution had greater significance for their respective regions than did Western forces. Despite European power, Latin Americans and Southeast Asians were still largely in control of their own destinies. Even in India, most people's lives and beliefs maintained continuity with the past.

KEY TERMS

Zulu p. 658
Afrikaners p. 658
Cecil Rhodes p. 660
Sokoto Caliphate p. 661
King Leopold II p. 662
Henry Morton Stanley
p. 662
Savorgnan de Brazza
p. 663

Berlin Conference p. 663
modernization p. 664
Suez Canal p. 664
Menelik II p. 665
"legitimate" trade p. 665
recaptives p. 666
nawab p. 667
sepoy p. 667
British raj p. 667

Sepoy Rebellion p. 668
durbar p. 668
Indian Civil Service p. 668
Indian National
Congress p. 670
Emilio Aguinaldo p. 673
Spanish-American War
p. 674

Mexican Revolution
p. 676
Emiliano Zapata p. 676
Francisco "Pancho"
Villa p. 677
Panama Canal p. 678
contract of indenture
p. 681

SUGGESTED READING

Bayly, C. A. *Indian Society and the Making of the British Empire.* 1987. How Indians adapted to, and resisted, British rule.

Bose, Sugata. *A Hundred Horizons: The Indian Ocean in the Age of Global Empire.* 2006. Discusses British dominance in South Asia and the Indian Ocean.

Cook, Scott B. *Colonial Encounters in the Age of High Imperialism.* 1996. A brief, well-written account of the imperialism of this era.

Headrick, Daniel R. *The Tools of Empire: Technology and European Imperialism in the Nineteenth Century,* 1981; and *The Tentacles of Progress: Technology Transfer in the Age of Imperialism, 1850–1940,* 1988. Two books emphasizing the importance of technology in the conquests and the colonial era.

Karnow, Stanley. *In Our Image: America's Empire in the Philippines.* 1989. How the United States conquered and ruled the Philippines.

Krauze, Enrique. *Mexico: Biography of Power: A History of Modern Mexico, 1810–1996.* 1997. The political history of a nation in turmoil.

MacKenzie, John. *Imperialism and the Natural World.* 1990. The impact of economic development and agriculture on colonial environments.

Morris, Donald R. *The Washing of the Spears.* 1965. A very readable account of the rise and fall of Shaka's Zulu kingdom.

Northrup, David. *Indentured Labor in the Age of Imperialism, 1834–1922.* 1995. Summarizes recent scholarship on the indentured labor trade.

SarDesai, D. R. *Southeast Asia: Past and Present,* 5th ed. 2004. A good introduction to the complexities of Southeast Asian history.

Vandervort, Bruce. *Wars of Imperial Conquest in Africa, 1830–1914.* 1998. A brief account of the conflicts between Europeans and Africans.

Woodruff, William. *Impact of Western Man: A Study of Europe's Role in the World Economy, 1750–1960.* 1982. A general overview of the period covered in this chapter.

CourseMate Go to the History CourseMate website for primary source links, study tools, and review materials for this chapter. www.cengagebrain.com

Chapter Outline

Arrivals from the East   In 1853, Commodore Matthew Perry's fleet sailed into Edo (now Tokyo) Bay. The first steam-powered warships to appear in Japanese waters caused a sensation among the Japanese. In this print done after the Meiji Restoration, the traditionally dressed local samurai go out to confront the mysterious "black ships."

Courtesy of the Trustees of the British Museum/The Art Archive

The New Power Balance, 1850–1900

On July 8, 1853, four American warships, two of them steam-powered, appeared in Edo Bay, close to the capital of Japan. The commander of the fleet, **Commodore Matthew Perry**, delivered a letter from the president of the United States, demanding that Japan open its ports to foreign trade. Japan had had contact with Europe since the sixteenth century, when Portuguese mariners and Jesuit missionaries arrived. The Dutch followed in the seventeenth century. Worried by the disruptive effects of this Western presence, Japan suppressed Christian conversion efforts and then "excluded" European merchants in 1639, although limited contact was permitted at the port of Nagasaki.

While Japan had rejected a similar request delivered by a smaller U.S. naval force in 1845, Perry's modern, well-armed fleet and a series of threatening military maneuvers made clear the dangers associated with refusing his demand to open Japanese markets. When he returned the following year, the Japanese agreed to end the exclusion policies that had kept the nation isolated for two and a half centuries. If his display of military force had compelled change, Perry's visit also served to introduce a compelling array of the Industrial Revolution's technological and scientific triumphs to Japan, including a miniature railroad, a short telegraph line, and other marvels. For the next twenty years, Japanese society was torn between those who wanted to retreat into isolation and those who wished to embrace the foreign ways and acquire modern machines. For it was now clear that only by industrializing could Japan escape the fate of weaker nations then being taken over by Europe and the United States.

In the late nineteenth century a very small number of states, known as "great powers," dominated the world. Great Britain and France had been recognized as great powers long before the industrial age. Russia achieved that status as an ally against Napoleon and began industrializing in the late nineteenth century, as did Germany, the United States, and Japan. At the dawn of the twentieth century the economic and military capacities of these rapidly industrializing powers had dramatically altered long-standing political and cultural arrangements globally. Each had extended its territorial reach by establishing new colonies and also by creating informal empires where weak local authorities were compelled to grant preferable trade concessions. While rivalries among these powers could lead to conflict and competition, they collectively exercised a world-wide ascendancy never previously witnessed.

Commodore Matthew Perry
A navy commander who, on July 8, 1853, became the first foreigner to break through the barriers that had kept Japan isolated from the rest of the world for 250 years.

NEW TECHNOLOGIES AND THE WORLD ECONOMY

The Industrial Revolution marked the beginning of a massive transformation of the world. In the nineteenth century the technologies discussed in Chapter 22—textile mills, railroads, steamships, the telegraph, and others—spread from Britain to other parts of the world. By 1890 Germany and the United States had surpassed Great Britain as the world's leading industrial powers. Industrialization also introduced entirely new technologies, notably electricity and the steel and chemical industries, which revolutionized everyday life and transformed the world economy. The motive force behind this second phase of industrialization consisted of potent combinations of business, engineering, and science. By the mid-nineteenth century this combination was institutionalized in engineering schools and research laboratories, first in Germany and then in the United States.

Railroads

railroads Networks of iron (later steel) rails on which steam (later electric or diesel) locomotives pulled long trains at high speeds. The first railroads were built in England in the 1830s. Their success caused a railroad-building boom throughout the world that lasted well into the twentieth century.

By the mid-nineteenth century, steam engines had become the prime mover of industry and commerce. Nowhere was this more evident than in the spread of **railroads**. By 1850 the first railroads had proved so successful that every industrializing country, and many that aspired to become industrial, began to build lines. The next fifty years saw a tremendous expansion of the world's rail networks. After a rapid spurt of building new lines, British railroad mileage leveled off in the 1870s at around 20,000 miles (over 32,000 kilometers). France and Germany ultimately built networks larger than Britain's, as did Canada and Russia. The nation with the largest railroad network in 1865, the United States, then increased its mileage eleven times by 1917.

Railroads were not confined to the industrialized nations; they could be constructed almost anywhere they would be of value to business or government. That included regions with abundant raw materials or agricultural products, like South Africa, Mexico, and Argentina, or densely populated countries like Egypt. Great Britain built the fourth largest rail network in the world in its largest colony, India, to reinforce political control and develop new trade opportunities.

With the exception of Japan, European or American engineers built the railroads of Africa, Asia, and Latin America with equipment imported from the West. In 1855, barely a year after Commodore Perry's visit, the Japanese instrument maker Tanaka Hisashige built a model steam train that he demonstrated to an admiring audience. In the 1870s the Japanese government hired British engineers to build the first line from Tokyo to Yokohama and then sent them home in the 1880s once they had trained Japanese engineers. Within a few years, Japan began manufacturing its own railroad equipment.

Railroads consumed huge amounts of land. Many old cities doubled in size to accommodate railroad stations, sidings, tracks, warehouses, and repair shops. In the countryside, railroads required bridges, tunnels, and embankments. They also consumed vast quantities of timber, initially for fuel and then for ties to support the rails and for bridges. As railroads pushed across the landscape, they often left miles of deforested land on either side of their tracks. At the same time, railroads opened new land to agriculture, mining, and other human exploitation of natural resources wherever they were built, becoming major engines of global economic development.

Steamships and Telegraph Cables

In the mid-nineteenth century, a series of developments radically transformed ocean shipping. First iron, then steel, replaced the wood that had been used for hulls since shipbuilding began. Paddle wheels replaced sails and then were replaced by propellers as engineers built more powerful and fuel-efficient engines. The average size of freighters also increased, growing from an average of 200 tons in 1850 to 7,500 tons in 1900. As both the size of ships and the number of ships grew, coaling stations and ports able to handle large ships were built around the world. For example, the Suez Canal, constructed in 1869, shortened the distance between Europe and Asia and triggered a massive switch from sail power to steam (see Chapter 26).

These modern shipping lines offered fast, punctual, and reliable service on a fixed schedule for passengers, mail, and perishable freight as the world's fleet of merchant ships grew from 9 million tons in 1850 to 35 million tons in 1910. The result was falling freight costs and greater commercial integration, changes that benefited not only the exporters of industrial products in

CHRONOLOGY

	Political Events	Social, Cultural, and Technological Events
1850	1853–1854 Commodore Matthew Perry visits Japan	1851 Majority of British population living in cities 1856 Bessemer converter; first synthetic dye
1860	1860–1870 Unification of Italy 1861–1865 American Civil War 1862–1908 Rule of Empress Dowager Cixi (China) 1868 Meiji Restoration begins modernization drive in Japan	1859 Charles Darwin, *On the Origin of Species* 1861 Emancipation of serfs (Russia) 1866 Alfred Nobel develops dynamite 1867 Karl Marx, *Das Kapital* 1866 Transatlantic cable laid 1868–1894 Japan undergoes Western-style industrialization and societal changes
1870	1870–1871 Franco-Prussian War 1871 Unification of Germany	
1880		1879 Thomas Edison develops incandescent lamp
1890	1894 Sino-Japanese War	
1900	1900 Boxer Uprising (China) 1904–1905 Russo-Japanese War 1905 Revolution in Russia 1910 Japan annexes Korea	

Europe and North America but also the Asian, African, and Latin American exporters of agricultural and mining products.

At the same time, shipping companies and commercial firms were able to use a new medium of communication, **submarine telegraph cables**, to respond to changing conditions in distant markets. The early development of this technology depended on the financial support of the French and British governments, which sought to improve communication with distant colonies. European businesses were more interested in laying a cable across the Atlantic to further develop commercial linkages. The initial efforts of the 1850s failed, but an improved transatlantic cable was successfully laid in 1866. By the turn of the century, cables connected every country and almost every inhabited island. As they became the indispensable tools of modern shipping and business, the public and the press extolled this "annihilation of time and space."

submarine telegraph cables Insulated copper cables laid along the bottom of a sea or ocean for telegraphic communication. The first short cable was laid across the English Channel in 1851; the first successful transatlantic cable was laid in 1866.

The Steel and Chemical Industries

steel A form of iron that is both durable and flexible. It was first mass-produced in the 1860s and quickly became the most widely used metal in construction, machinery, and railroad equipment.

Until the nineteenth century **steel** could be made only by skilled blacksmiths in very small quantities and was reserved for swords, knives, axes, and watch springs. Then came a series of inventions that made it the cheapest and most versatile metal ever known. In the 1850s the American William Kelly and the Englishman Henry Bessemer discovered that air forced through molten pig iron by powerful pumps turned it into steel without additional fuel. Other new processes permitted steel to be made from scrap iron, an increasingly important raw material, and from the phosphoric iron ores common in western Europe. Following these discoveries, steel became cheap and abundant enough to make rails, bridges, ships, and even "tin" cans meant to be used once and thrown away.

The chemical industry followed a similar pattern of innovation. In 1856 the Englishman William Perkin created the first synthetic dye, aniline purple, from coal tar; the next few years were known in Europe as the "mauve decade" from the color of fashionable women's clothes. Industry began mass-producing other organic chemicals—compounds containing carbon atoms. Toward the end of the century German chemists synthesized red, violet, blue, brown, and black dyes as well. These bright, long-lasting colors were cheaper to manufacture and could be produced in much greater quantities and at much lower prices than natural dyes. They delighted consumers but ruined the indigo plantations of India and Latin America. Chemistry also made important advances in the manufacture of explosives. The first of these, nitroglycerin, was so dangerous that it exploded when shaken. In 1866 the Swedish scientist Alfred Nobel found a way to turn nitroglycerin into a stable solid—dynamite. This and other new explosives were useful in mining and were critical in the construction of railroads and canals. They also enabled the armies and navies of the great powers to arm themselves with increasingly accurate and powerful rifles and cannon.

The growing complexity of industrial chemistry made it one of the first fields where science and technology interacted on a daily basis. This development gave a great advantage to Germany, which had the most advanced engineering schools and scientific institutes of the time and whose government funded research and encouraged cooperation between universities and industries. By the end of the nineteenth century, Germany was the world's leading producer of dyes, drugs, synthetic fertilizers, ammonia, and nitrates used in making explosives.

Environmental Problems

Industrialization and rapid urbanization powerfully affected entire regions such as the English Midlands, the German Ruhr, parts of Pennsylvania in the United States, and the regions around Tokyo and Osaka in Japan. The new steel mills took up as much space as whole towns, belched smoke and particulates, and left behind huge hills of slag and other waste products. Coal-burning steam engines powered the new machine age and, along with mounting domestic coal consumption for cooking and heating, also filled the skies of Manchester, England, and the world's other manufacturing centers with dense smog.

Rapidly growing urban populations in industrializing European and American cities overwhelmed primitive sanitation systems until the last decades of the nineteenth century. When a drought lowered water levels in Britain's Thames River in 1858, Londoners experienced what they called the Big Stink caused by the vast quantities of untreated human and industrial waste long dumped into the river. More threatening still were pollution-related diseases like typhoid and cholera.

The coal smoke of railroad locomotives and other steam engines contributed to air pollution as well. The chemical industries also produced tons of toxic effluents that were dumped into rivers. Thus while industrialization brought vast amounts of wealth, without environmental regulations it also caused considerable damage to nature and to the health of nearby human populations.

Electricity

electricity A form of energy used in telegraphy from the 1840s on and for lighting, industrial motors, and railroads beginning in the 1880s.

No innovation of the late nineteenth century changed people's lives as radically as **electricity**. As an energy source, electricity was more flexible and much easier to use than water power or stationary steam engines. At first, producing electric current was so costly that it was used only for electroplating and telegraphy. Then in 1831 the Englishman Michael Faraday showed that the motion of a copper wire through a magnetic field induced an electric current in the wire. Based on this discovery, inventors in the 1870s devised generators that turned mechanical energy into electric current.

Thomas Edison American inventor best known for inventing the electric light bulb, acoustic recording on wax cylinders, and motion pictures.

Electricity now had a host of new applications. Initially, arc lamps lit up public squares, theaters, and stores, while homes continued to rely on gas lamps, which produced a softer light. Then in 1879 in the United States **Thomas Edison** developed an incandescent lamp well suited to lighting small rooms. In 1882 Edison created the world's first electrical distribution network in New York City. By the turn of the century electric lighting was rapidly replacing gas lamps in the cities of Europe and North America.

Other uses of electricity quickly appeared. Electric streetcars and subways transported people throughout the cities of Europe and North America. Electric motors replaced steam engines and power belts, increasing productivity and improving workers' safety. Commonly dependent on coal-fired generators, electric energy production contributed to air pollution as well. As demand for electricity grew, engineers built hydroelectric plants. The plant at Niagara Falls, on the border between Ontario, Canada, and New York State, produced an incredible 11,000 horsepower when it opened in 1895. At the newly created Imperial College of Engineering in Japan, an Englishman, William Ayrton, became the first professor of electrical engineering anywhere in the world; his students later went on to found major corporations and government research institutes.

Paris Lit Up by Electricity, 1900   The electric light bulb was invented in the United States and Britain, but Paris made such extensive use of the new technology that it was nick-named "city of lights." To mark the Paris Exposition of 1900, the Eiffel Tower and all the surrounding buildings were illuminated with strings of light bulbs while powerful spotlights swept the sky.

akg-images/Newscom

World Trade and Finance

Improvements in transportation and communication, along with rising world population, led to a tenfold increase in international trade between 1850 and 1913. Europe imported wheat from Canada, the United States, and India, wool from Australia, and beef from Argentina, while it exported coal, railroad equipment, textiles, and machinery to Asia, Africa, and the Americas. Because steamships were much more efficient and faster than sailing ships, the cost of freight dropped dramatically, intensifying long-distance commercial links.

The growth of world trade transformed different parts of the world in different ways. The economies of western Europe and North America, the first to industrialize and the prime beneficiaries, grew more diversified and prosperous. Industries mass-produced consumer goods for a growing number of middle-class and even working-class customers: soap, canned and packaged foods, ready-made clothes, household items, and small luxuries like cosmetics and engravings. This revolution in consumption occurred at a much slower pace in the developing world and the benefits were more narrowly limited to elites and the middleclass. These privileged sectors often paid for imported novelties by imposing harsh conditions on the masses who labored in plantations and mines.

Even growing capitalist economies were prey to sudden swings in the business cycle—booms followed by deep depressions, or busts, in which workers lost their jobs and investors their fortunes. Because of the close connections among the industrial economies, the collapse of a bank in Austria in 1873 triggered a depression that spread to the United States, causing mass unemployment. Destabilizing worldwide recessions also occurred in the mid-1880s and mid-1890s. Many contemporaries feared that industrial production was growing faster than the capacity of traditional markets to consume goods, leading to falling prices and recession. The perceived solution, to expand markets and gain protected access to raw materials, helped propel the United States and the European powers to undertake a new wave of imperialist adventures in Asia, Africa, and Latin America (see Chapter 26). Tariffs could not insulate countries from the business cycle, for money continued to flow almost unhindered around the world. One of the main causes of the growing interdependence of the global economy was the financial power of Great Britain, which dominated the flow of trade, finance, and information. In 1900 two-thirds of the world's submarine cables were British owned or passed through Britain, and over half of the world's shipping was British owned. Britain invested one-fourth of its national

SECTION REVIEW

- Industrialization spread throughout the world through trade and new technologies.

- Railroads, almost always financed by Western nations, spread to all continents, changing and enlarging cities and facilitating economic growth.

- Steamships and telegraph cables connected continents and encouraged trade.

- In three new industries—steel, chemicals, and electricity— the United States and Germany surpassed Great Britain.

- World trade boomed in an age of globalization.

wealth overseas, much of it in India, the United States, and Argentina. British money financed many of the railroads, harbors, mines, and other big projects outside Europe. While other currencies fluctuated, the pound sterling was as good as gold, and nine-tenths of international transactions used sterling.

Nonindustrial areas also were tied to the world economy as never before. Because many of them produced raw materials that could be replaced by synthetic substitutes (like dyestuffs) or alternative sources of supply, they were more vulnerable to changes in price and demand than were the industrialized nations. Developing regions that produced sugar, cotton, and dyes all experienced these upsets in the nineteenth century. Nevertheless, until 1913 the value of exports from the tropical countries generally kept up with the growth of their populations.

SOCIAL CHANGES

As fast-growing populations swelled Europe's cities to unprecedented size, millions of other Europeans emigrated to the Americas. At the same time, strained relations between industrial employers and workers spawned labor movements and new forms of radical politics. Women as well found their lives dramatically altered by economic and technological change, both in the home and in the public sphere.

Population and Migrations

The population of Europe grew faster from 1850 to 1914 than ever before or since, almost doubling from 265 million to 468 million. In non-European countries with predominantly white populations—the United States, Canada, Australia, New Zealand, and Argentina—the increase was even greater because of the inflow of European immigrants. There were many reasons for the mass migrations of this period: the Irish famine of 1847–1848; the persecution of Jews in Russia; poverty and population growth in Italy, Spain, Poland, and Scandinavia; and the cultural ties between Great Britain and English-speaking countries overseas. Equally important was the attraction of enhanced opportunities in places like Argentina, Australia, Canada, and the United States. The availability to travelers of cheap and rapid steamship and railroad transportation at both ends of immigration pathways also contributed to the scale of this massive population transfer (see Environment and Technology: Railroads and Immigration).

Between 1850 and 1900, on average, over 1 million Europeans migrated overseas every year; then, between 1900 and 1914, the flood rose to over 3 million a year. Over this same fifty-year period the population of the United States and Canada rose from 25 million to 98 million, and the proportion of people of European ancestry in the world's population rose from one-fifth to one-third. Great Britain was the most important source of immigrants by far, but very large numbers of Germans, Italians, and Spaniards joined the swelling ranks.

Why did the number of Europeans and their descendants overseas jump so dramatically? Much of the increase came from a drop in mortality, as epidemics and starvation became less common. The Irish famine of the 1840s was the last peacetime famine in European history. As farmers plowed up the plains of North America and planted wheat, much of which was shipped to Europe, food supplies increased faster than population. New technologies like canning and refrigeration also made food more abundant year-round, facilitating the export of Argentine beef and mutton to Europe. The diet of Europeans and North Americans also improved as meat, fruit, vegetables, and oils became part of the daily fare of city dwellers in winter as well as in summer.

During this period Asians also migrated in large numbers as indentured laborers who were recruited to work on distant plantations, in mines, and on railroads (see Chapter 26). Indians went to Africa, Southeast Asia, and other tropical colonies of Great Britain. Along with Chinese, Indians also emigrated to the East Indies and the Caribbean to work on sugar plantations. At the same time, Japanese migrated in large numbers to Brazil and other parts of Latin America. Many Japanese, as well as Chinese and Filipinos, also went to work in agriculture and menial trade in Hawaii and California, where they encountered growing hostility from European-Americans.

Urbanization and Urban Environments

In 1851 Britain became the first nation with a majority of its population living in towns and cities. By 1914, 80 percent of Britain's population was urban, as were 60 percent of the German population and 45 percent of the French. Cities grew to unprecedented size. London grew from 2.7 million in 1850 to 6.6 million in 1900. New York, a small town of 64,000 people in 1800, reached 3.4 million by 1900, more than a fiftyfold increase. In 1800 New York had covered only the southernmost quarter of Manhattan Island, some 3 square miles (nearly 8 square kilometers); by 1900 it covered 150 square miles (390 square kilometers). In the English Midlands, in the German Ruhr, and around Tokyo Bay, fast-growing towns fused into one another, filling in the fields and woods that had once separated them.

As cities grew, they changed in character. Newly built railroads not only brought goods into the cities on a predictable schedule but also allowed people to live farther apart. At first, only the well-to-do could afford to commute by train; by the end of the century, electric streetcars and subways allowed working-class people to live miles from their workplaces.

In preindustrial and early industrial cities, the poor crowded together in tenements; sanitation was bad; water was often contaminated with sewage; and darkness made life dangerous. New urban technologies and the growing powers and responsibilities of governments transformed city life for all but the poorest residents. The most important change was the installation of pipes to bring in clean water and to carry away sewage. At the same time, gas lighting and then electric lighting made cities safer at night. By the turn of the twentieth century municipal governments in Europe and North America provided police and fire protection, sanitation and garbage removal, building and health inspection, schools, parks, and other amenities unheard of a century earlier.

As sanitation improved, epidemics became rare. For the first time, urban death rates fell below birthrates. The decline in infant mortality was an especially significant indicator of improved hygiene and medical care. Confident that their children would survive infancy, couples began to limit the number of children they had, and ancient scourges like infanticide and child abandonment became less frequent.

To accommodate the growing population, builders created new neighborhoods, from crowded tenements for the poor to opulent mansions for the newly rich. In the United States urban planners laid out new cities, such as Chicago, on rectangular grids, and middle-class families moved to new developments on the edges of cities, the suburbs. In Paris older neighborhoods with narrow crooked streets and rickety tenements were torn down to make room for broad boulevards and modern apartment buildings. Brilliantly lit by gas and electricity, Paris became the "city of lights," a model for city planners from New Delhi to Buenos Aires. The rich continued to live in inner cities that contained the monuments, churches, and palaces of preindustrial times, while workers often moved to the outskirts.

Lower population densities and better transportation divided cities into industrial, commercial, and residential zones occupied by different social classes. Improvements such as water and sewerage, electricity, and streetcars always benefited the wealthy first, then the middle class, and finally the working class. In the complex of urban life, businesses of all kinds arose, and the professions—engineering, accounting, research, journalism, and the law, among others—took on increased importance. The new middle class exhibited its wealth in fine houses with servants and in elegant entertainment.

While urban environments improved in many ways, air quality worsened. Coal, burned to power steam engines and heat buildings, polluted the air, creating unpleasant and sometimes dangerous "pea-soup" fog and coating everything with a film of grimy dust. The thousands of horses that pulled carts and carriages covered the streets with their wastes, causing a terrible stench. The introduction of electricity helped alleviate some of these environmental problems.

Railroads and Immigration

Why did so many Europeans emigrate to North America in the late nineteenth and early twentieth centuries? The quick answer is that millions of people longed to escape the poverty or tyranny of their home countries and start new lives in a land of freedom and opportunity. Personal desire alone, however, does not account for the migrations. After all, poverty and tyranny existed long before the late nineteenth century. Two other factors helped determine when and where people migrated: whether they were allowed to migrate, and whether they were able to.

In the nineteenth century Asians were recruited to build railroads and work on farms. But from the 1890s on, the United States and Canada closed their doors to non-Europeans, so regardless of what they wanted, they could not move to North America. In contrast, emigrants from Europe were admitted almost without restriction until after the First World War.

The ability to travel was a result of improvements in transportation. Until the 1890s most immigrants came from Ireland, England, or Germany—countries with good rail transportation to their own harbors and low steamship fares to North America. As rail lines were extended into eastern and southern Europe, more and more immigrants came from Italy, Austria-Hungary, and Russia.

Similarly, until the 1870s most European immigrants to North America settled on the east coast. Then, as the railroads pushed west, more of them settled on farms in the central and western parts of the continent. The power of railroads moved people as much as their desires did.

Emigrant Waiting Room The opening of the western region of the United States attracted settlers from the east coast and from Europe. These migrants are waiting for a train to take them to the Black Hills of Dakota during one of the gold rushes of the late nineteenth century.

Electric motors and lamps did not pollute the air, and coal-burning power plants were built at a distance from cities. As electric trains and streetcars began replacing horse-drawn trolleys and coal-burning locomotives, cities became cleaner and healthier. However, most of the environmental benefits of electricity were to come in the twentieth century.

Middle-Class Women's "Separate Sphere"

Victorian Age The reign of Queen Victoria of Great Britain (r. 1837–1901). The term is also used to describe late-nineteenth-century society, with its rigid moral standards and sharply differentiated roles for men and women and for middle-class and working-class people.

"separate spheres" Nineteenth-century idea in Western societies that men and women, especially of the middle class, should have clearly differentiated roles in society: women as wives, mothers, and homemakers; men as breadwinners and participants in business and politics.

In English-speaking countries the period from about 1850 to 1901 is known as the **Victorian Age**. The expression refers not only to the reign of Queen Victoria of England (r. 1837–1901) but also to rules of behavior and to an ideology surrounding the family and the relations between men and women. The Victorians contrasted the masculine ideals of strength and courage with the feminine virtues of beauty and kindness, and they idealized the home as a peaceful and loving refuge from the dog-eat-dog world of competitive capitalism.

Victorian morality claimed to be universal, yet it best fit upper- and middle-class European families. Men and women were thought to belong in **"separate spheres."** Successful businessmen spent their time at work or relaxing in men's clubs. They put their wives in charge of rearing the children, running the household, and spending the family money to enhance the family's social status. The majority of women from the less privileged classes, however, lived constantly with financial pressures. Many worked outside the home for wages. Others took in laundry or did low-wage piecework, like sewing for garment companies to supplement household income.

Before electric appliances, maintaining a middle-class home involved enormous amounts of work. Not only were families larger, but middle-class couples entertained often and lavishly. Carrying out these tasks required servants. A family's status and the activities and lifestyle of the "mistress of the house" depended on the availability of servants to help with household tasks. Only families that employed at least one full-time servant were considered middle class.

Toward the turn of the century modern technology began to transform middle-class homes. Plumbing eliminated the pump and the outhouse. Central heating replaced fireplaces, stoves, trips to the basement for coal, and endless dusting. Gas and electricity lit houses and cooked food without soot, smoke, and ashes. In the early twentieth century wealthy families acquired the first vacuum cleaners and washing machines. However, these technological advances did not mean less housework for women. As families acquired new household appliances, they raised their standards of cleanliness, thus demanding just as much labor as before.

The most important duty of middle-class women was raising children. Victorian mothers nursed their own babies and showered their children with love and attention. Even those who could afford governesses remained personally involved in their children's education. Girls' education was very different from that of boys. While boys were being prepared for the business world or the professions, girls were taught embroidery, drawing, and music, skills that enhanced their social graces and marriage prospects.

Young middle-class women could work until they got married, but only in genteel places like stores and offices, never in factories. When the typewriter and telephone were introduced into the business world in the 1880s, businessmen found that they could get better work at lower

Separate Spheres in Great Britain   In the Victorian Age, men and women of the middle and upper classes led largely separate lives. In *Aunt Emily's Visit* (1845), we see women and children at home, tended by a servant. *The Royal Exchange*, meanwhile, was a place for men to transact business.

wages from educated young women than from men, and operating these machines was stereotyped as women's work.

Most professional careers were closed to women, and few universities granted women degrees. In the United States higher education was available to women only at elite colleges in the East and teachers' colleges in the Midwest. European women had fewer opportunities. Before 1914 very few women became doctors, lawyers, or professional musicians. Instead, women were considered well suited to teaching young children and girls—an extension of the duties of Victorian mothers—but only until marriage. A married woman was expected to become pregnant right away and to stay home taking care of her own children rather than other people's.

A home life, no matter how busy, did not satisfy all middle-class women. Some became volunteer nurses or social workers, receiving little or no pay. Others organized to fight prostitution, alcohol, and child labor. By the turn of the century a few challenged male domination of politics and the law. Suffragists, led in Britain by Emmeline Pankhurst and in the United States by Elizabeth Cady Stanton and Susan B. Anthony, demanded the right to vote. By 1914 U.S. women had won the right to vote in twelve states. British women did not gain the right to vote until 1918.

Working-Class Women

In the new industrial cities, men and women no longer worked together at home or in the fields, a separation of work and home that affected women even more than men. While working-class women formed a majority of the workers in the textile industries and in domestic service, they also needed to keep homes and raise children. As a result, they led lives of toil and pain. Parents expected girls as young as ten to contribute to the household. In Japan, as in Ireland and New England, tenant farmers, squeezed by rising taxes and rents, were forced to send their daughters to work in textile mills. Others became domestic servants, commonly working sixteen or more hours a day, six and a half days a week, for little more than room and board, usually in attics or basements. Without appliances, much of their work was physically hard: hauling coal and water up stairs, washing laundry by hand.

Young women often preferred factory work to domestic service. Men worked in construction, iron and steel, heavy machinery, or on railroads; women worked in textiles and the clothing trades, extensions of traditional women's household work (see Material Culture: Cotton Clothing).

Emmeline Pankhurst Under Arrest The leader of the British women's suffrage movement frequently called attention to her cause by breaking the law to protest discrimination against women. Here she is being arrested and carried off to jail by the police.

Jimmy Sime/Hulton Archive/Getty Images

Cotton Clothing

Of all the things that bring us comfort, nothing compares to cotton. For clothes, sheets, and towels, it is the world's favorite textile. And no wonder: cotton is cool next to the skin, can be dyed in bright colors, absorbs moisture, and, unlike other fabrics such as wool, can be washed easily.

The use of cotton for clothing has a long history dating back to 3000 B.C.E., when it was grown in the Indus River Valley. Originally, the cotton plant was grown and the cloth woven only in India, Mexico, Peru, and a few other places in the tropics. The Maya wove fine textiles from cotton and traded them with other parts of Mesoamerica. Indian cottons were particularly fine and exported as luxury items to China and Rome. Cotton replaced hemp clothing in China in the time of the Mongols and was used extensively for turbans, pants, and other items of clothing. The Arabs spread cotton growing and weaving to the Middle East and Spain. By the tenth century, it was a major crop in Iran and elsewhere in the region. Many of our names for particular kinds of cotton fabric come from cities in India, like *calico* (from Calicut) or *madras*, or in the Middle East, like *damask* (from Damascus) or *muslin* (from Mosul in Iraq).

Around 800 C.E., Arab merchants brought cotton cloth to Europe, where it became as precious as silk. Five centuries later Italy developed its own cotton industry. With the invention of machines like the spinning jenny and the water frame in the eighteenth century (see Chapter 22), cotton became less precious and more available. Cotton yarn and cloth were the first items to be mass-produced in the Industrial Revolution, with important consequences for India, the American South, and other countries.

Mass production means mass consumption. In the nineteenth century, for the first time, the poor could afford to wear bright, colorful clothes and—even more important—to wash them. Wealthy European families hired seamstresses and tailors who came to the house, took measurements, and returned a few days later with finished clothes. Poorer women sewed clothes for themselves and their families.

Sewing by hand was time-consuming and increasingly costly compared to the declining price of cloth. By the mid-nineteenth century, prosperity and a faster pace of life in Europe and America provided an incentive for inventors to devise a machine that could sew. In 1850, Isaac Singer manufactured the first practical machine for commercial use. A few years later, he designed the "Singer Family Sewing Machine" with an iron stand and a foot-treadle for home use. By 1891 Singer alone had manufactured 10 million machines in the United States and Europe. Some were industrial machines sold to makers of ready-to-wear clothes in the new garment districts. Others were home models, some inexpensive enough for the working class. There were even portable models that seamstresses could take with them to their clients' homes.

The combination of cotton cloth and sewing machines revolutionized clothing. A shirt that took fourteen and a half hours to sew by hand could be made in an hour and a quarter on a machine; an apron could be made in nine minutes instead of an hour and a half. This greater efficiency meant lower prices. Now the poor could afford to own several shirts, skirts, or pants, even underwear. Better-off homemakers subscribed to fashion magazines, bought patterns, and made blouses and dresses, even complicated items like crinolines and hoopskirts, which would once have been too tedious to sew by hand.

Today, the world uses more cotton than any other fiber. China is the largest producer (and consumer) of cotton, followed by the United States, India, and Pakistan. Almost all of the cotton clothing now sold is produced on powerful computerized machines in the developing countries of Asia and Latin America.

Image copyright © The Metropolitan Museum of Art. Image source: Art Resource, NY

The Sewing Machine The Japanese imported many innovations from the West after the Meiji Restoration of 1868. Among the most popular were Western-style clothing and sewing machines.

Appalled by the abuses of women and children in the early years of industrialization, most industrial countries eventually passed protective legislation limiting hours worked or forbidding the employment of women in the hardest and most dangerous occupations, such as mining and foundry work. While the stated intention was to protect women, such legislation reinforced gender divisions in industry, keeping women in low-paid, subordinate positions. Even where women worked alongside men, in factories, for example, they earned between one-third and two-thirds of the wages paid men.

Married women with children were expected to stay home, even if their husbands did not make enough to support the family. Yet they had to contribute to the family's income. Families who had room to spare, even a bed or a corner in the kitchen, took in boarders. Many women did piecework such as sewing dresses, making hats or gloves, or weaving baskets at home. The hardest and worst-paid work was washing other people's clothes. Overall, many poor women worked at home ten to twelve hours a day and enlisted the help of their small children, perpetuating practices long outlawed in factories. Without electric lighting and indoor plumbing, even ordinary household duties like cooking and washing remained heavy burdens.

SECTION REVIEW

- As European population grew, millions migrated to other continents.

- Cities grew to enormous size, changing in character and posing difficult housing, sanitation, and environmental problems.

- Middle-class women inhabited a "separate sphere" from men and devoted their lives to their homes and families, but a few fought for equal rights.

- Working-class women, who had to keep a home while earning a living, led hard lives.

SOCIALISM AND LABOR MOVEMENTS

socialism A political ideology that originated in Europe in the 1830s. Socialists advocated government protection of workers from exploitation by property owners and government ownership of industries. This ideology led to the founding of socialist or labor parties throughout Europe in the second half of the nineteenth century.

labor union An organization of workers in a particular industry or trade, created to defend the interests of members through strikes or negotiations with employers.

Karl Marx German journalist and philosopher, founder of the Marxist branch of socialism. He is known for two books: *Manifesto of the Communist Party* (1848) and *Das Kapital* (Vols. I–III, 1867–1894).

The experience of industrialization combined with the revolutionary ideas of the late eighteenth century to produce two kinds of movements that demanded economic and political reforms: socialism and labor unions. **Socialism** was an ideology developed by radical thinkers who questioned the sanctity of private property and argued in support of industrial workers against their employers. **Labor unions** were organizations formed by industrial workers to defend their interests in negotiations with employers. The socialist and labor movements were never identical. Most of the time they were allies; occasionally they competed for the support of workers.

Revolutionary Alternatives

The growing wealth and power of new industrial elites and the harsh living and working conditions experienced by industrial workers led to the formation of labor unions, the creation of the first social welfare policies, demands for voting rights, and, for some, the dream of revolutionary transformation. Those seeking a revolution were divided among numerous parties and factions. Within the diverse and contentious world of left-leaning politics (see Chapter 22), **Karl Marx** was a formidable theorist of revolution as well as a major contestant for power. Marx shared the Enlightenment's enthusiasm for reason and logic and identified his revolutionary ideal as "scientific socialism." His adherents generally referred to themselves as communists or Marxists. Marx believed that the relentless competition inherent in industrial capitalism would lead ultimately to a social order divided between a wealthy powerful few and a mass of exploited and impoverished workers. This division, once in place, would inevitably lead in Marx's view to revolutions that would end capitalism and create a dictatorship of the proletariat (industrial workers). Once accomplished, this revolution by workers would distribute the material benefits and scientific progress achieved by the Industrial Revolution to society in general. With private property abolished, Marx asserted, the resources of government and industry could be harnessed to end poverty and injustice.

Many of those committed to revolutionary change rejected Marx's insistence that revolutionary action, violent resistance to the status quo, wait for the full development of industrial capitalism and the appearance of the proletariat. Although in broad agreement with Marx's critique of capitalism, they believed that the levels of injustice and inequality already present in society justified revolutionary violence immediately. Some of the revolutionaries rejected Marx's belief that his proposed dictatorship of the proletariat, or, indeed, any form of government, could avoid recreating the inequality and injustice that already oppressed the poor. The

Bettmann/Corbis

Mikhail Bakunin   Anarchist, intellectual, and political rival of Karl Marx.

Russian intellectual Mikhail Bakunin (1814–1876) argued forcibly that peasants, displaced and unemployed artisans, and other exploited groups also had revolutionary potential and, consequently, that many unindustrialized regions of Europe were ready for revolution. He also dismissed Marx's faith in a future worker's government as naive.

Bakunin exercised a powerful influence over the development of anarchism, the chief revolutionary alternative to communism. Anarchists believed that revolution could be achieved through direct action by individuals and small groups, what they called "propaganda of the deed." The result of this movement's development was a series of assassinations and bombings that shook the political structures of Europe and the Americas. These attacks included the bombings of the opera (1893) and Corpus Christi celebration (1896) in Spain and the Haymarket bombing in Chicago (1896). They also included the assassinations of President Carnot of France (1894), Prime Minister Cánovas del Castillo of Spain (1897), Empress Elizabeth of Austria (1898), King Umberto of Italy (1900), and President McKinley of the United States (1901).

The conflict between Marx and Bakunin culminated in 1872 when Bakunin and his adherents were expelled from the revolutionary umbrella organization, the International Workingman's Association. While the followers of Marx forced Bakunin from the center of revolutionary activity, his followers remained a potent source of political violence and working-class mobilization in Italy, Spain, and Argentina well into the twentieth century.

Labor Unions and Movements

Since the beginning of the nineteenth century, workers had united to create "friendly societies" for mutual assistance in times of illness, unemployment, or disability. Laws that forbade workers to strike were abolished in Britain in the 1850s and in the rest of Europe soon thereafter. Labor unions sought not only better wages but also improved working conditions and insurance against illness, accidents, disability, and old age. They grew slowly because they required a permanent staff as well as a great deal of money to sustain their members during strikes. Nevertheless, by the end of the century, British labor unions counted 2 million members, and German and American unions had 1 million members each. Once organized, unions became a political force in all democratic countries, advocating for improved wages and working conditions.

Just as labor unions strove to share in the benefits of a capitalist economy, so did electoral politics persuade workers to become part of the existing political system. The nineteenth century saw a gradual extension of the right to vote throughout Europe and North America. Universal male suffrage became law in the United States in 1870, in France and Germany in 1871, in Britain in 1885, and in the rest of Europe soon thereafter. With so many newly enfranchised workers, many socialist politicians hoped to capture seats in their nations' parliaments. Rather than seize power through revolution, these democratic socialists expected to obtain concessions from government and eventually even to form a government.

Working-class women, burdened with both job and family responsibilities, found little time for politics and were not welcome in the male-dominated trade unions or radical political parties. A few radicals such as the German socialist Rosa Luxemburg and the American **anarchist** Emma Goldman became famous but did not have a large following. It was never easy to reconcile the demands of male workers with those of women. In 1889 the German socialist Clara Zetkin wrote: "Just as the male worker is subjected by the capitalist, so is the woman by the man, and she will always remain in subjugation until she is economically independent. Work is the indispensable condition for economic independence." Six years later, she recognized that the liberation of women would have to await a change in the position of the working class as a whole: "The

anarchists Revolutionaries who wanted to abolish all private property and governments, usually by violence, and replace them with free associations of groups.

SECTION REVIEW

- Karl Marx and Mikhail Bakunin expected a workers' revolution, but later socialists hoped to gain influence through elections.

- Labor movements and unions worked to improve workers' pay and working conditions.

proletarian woman cannot attain her highest ideal through a movement for the equality of the female sex, she attains salvation only through the fight for the emancipation of labor."[1]

NATIONALISM AND THE RISE OF ITALY, GERMANY, AND JAPAN

nationalism A political ideology that stresses people's membership in a nation—a community defined by a common culture and history as well as by territory. In the late eighteenth and early nineteenth centuries, nationalism was a force for unity in western Europe. In the late nineteenth century it hastened the disintegration of the Austro-Hungarian and Ottoman Empires. In the twentieth century it provided the ideological foundation for scores of independent countries emerging from colonialism.

The most influential idea of the nineteenth century was **nationalism**. Whereas people had previously been considered the subjects of a sovereign, French revolutionaries defined people as the citizens of a *nation*—a concept identified with a territory, the state that ruled it, and the culture of its people.

Language and National Identity in Europe Before 1871

Language was usually the crucial element in creating a feeling of national unity. It was important both as a way to unite the people of a nation and as the means of persuasion by which political leaders could inspire their followers. Language was the tool of the new generation of political activists, most of them lawyers, teachers, students, and journalists. Yet language and citizenship seldom coincided perfectly.

The fit between France and the French language was closer than in most large countries, though some French-speakers lived outside of France and some French people spoke other languages. Italian- and German-speaking people, however, were divided among many small states. Living in the Austrian Empire were peoples who spoke German, Czech, Slovak, Hungarian, Polish, and other languages. Even where people spoke a common language, they could be divided by religion or institutions. The Irish, though English-speaking, were mostly Catholic, whereas the English were primarily Protestant.

The idea of redrawing the boundaries of states to accommodate linguistic, religious, or cultural differences was revolutionary. In Italy and Germany it led to the forging of large new states out of many small ones in 1871. In central and eastern Europe, nationalism threatened to break up large states into smaller ones.

liberalism A political ideology that emphasizes the civil rights of citizens, representative government, and the protection of private property. This ideology, derived from the Enlightenment, was especially popular among the property-owning middle classes of Europe and North America.

Until the 1860s nationalism was associated with **liberalism**, the revolutionary middle-class ideology that emerged from the French Revolution, asserted the sovereignty of the people, and demanded constitutional government, a national parliament, and freedom of expression (see Chapter 23). The most famous nationalist of the early nineteenth century was the Italian liberal Giuseppe Mazzini (jew-SEP-pay mots-EE-nee) (1805–1872), the leader of the failed revolution of 1848 in Italy. Mazzini sought to unify the Italian peninsula into one nation and associated with revolutionaries elsewhere to bring nationhood and liberty to all peoples oppressed by tyrants and foreigners (see Diversity and Dominance: Giuseppe Mazzini on Revolutionary Nationalism). The governments of Russia, Prussia, and Austria censored the new ideas but could not quash them.

The revolutions of 1848 convinced conservatives that governments could not forever keep their citizens out of politics and that mass politics, if properly managed, could strengthen rather than weaken the state (see Chapter 23). A new generation of conservative political leaders learned how to preserve the status quo through public education, universal military service, and colonial conquests, all of which built a sense of national unity.

The Unification of Italy, 1860–1870

By midcentury, popular sentiment was building throughout Italy for unification. Opposing it were Pope Pius IX, who abhorred everything modern, and Austria, which controlled two Italian provinces, Lombardy and Venetia (see Map 27.1). The prime minister of Piedmont-Sardinia, Count Camillo Benso di Cavour, saw the rivalry between France and Austria as an opportunity to unify Italy. He secretly formed an alliance with France and then instigated a war with Austria in 1858. The war was followed by uprisings throughout northern and central Italy in favor of joining Piedmont-Sardinia, a moderate constitutional monarchy under King Victor Emmanuel.

---

[1]Quoted in Bonnie S. Anderson and Judith P. Zinsser, *A History of Their Own: Women in Europe from Prehistory to the Present*, vol. 2 (New York: Harper & Row, 1988), 372, 387.

MAP 27.1 **Unification of Italy, 1860–1870** The unification of Italy was achieved by the expansion of the kingdom of Piedmont-Sardinia, with the help of France.   © Cengage Learning

Giuseppe Garibaldi Italian nationalist and revolutionary who conquered Sicily and Naples and added them to a unified Italy in 1860.

If Cavour's conservative, top-down approach to unification prevailed in the north, a more radical approach was still possible in the south. In 1860 the fiery revolutionary **Giuseppe Garibaldi (jew-SEP-pay gary-BAHL-dee)** and a small band of followers landed in Sicily and then in southern Italy, overthrew the Kingdom of the Two Sicilies, and prepared to found a democratic republic. The royalist Cavour, however, took advantage of the unsettled situation to sideline Garibaldi and transform Piedmont-Sardinia into a new Kingdom of Italy. Unification was completed with the addition of Venetia in 1866 and the Papal States in 1870.

The process of Italian unification illustrates the shift of nationalism from a radical democratic idea to a conservative method of building popular support for a strong centralized government, even an aristocratic and monarchical one.

The Unification of Germany, 1866–1871

The unification of most German-speaking people into a single state in 1871 had momentous consequences for the world. Until the 1860s the region of central Europe where people spoke German consisted of Prussia, the western half of the Austrian Empire, and numerous smaller states (see Map 27.2). Some German nationalists wanted to unite all Germans under the Austrian throne. Others wanted to exclude Austria with its many non-Germanic peoples and unite all other German-speaking areas under Prussia. The divisions were also religious: Austria and southwestern Germany were Catholic; Prussia and the northeast were Lutheran. The Prussian state had two advantages: (1) the newly developed industries of the Rhineland, and (2) the first European army to make use of railroads, telegraphs, breechloading rifles, steel artillery, and other products of modern industry.

During the reign of King Wilhelm I (r. 1861–1888), Prussia was ruled by a brilliant and authoritarian aristocrat, Chancellor **Otto von Bismarck** (UTT-oh von BIS-mark) (1815–1898). Bismarck was determined to use Prussian industry and German nationalism to make his state the dominant power in Germany. In 1866 Prussia attacked and defeated Austria. To everyone's surprise, Prussia took no Austrian territory. Instead, Prussia and some smaller states formed the North German Confederation, the nucleus of a future Germany. Then in 1870 Bismarck attacked France. Prussian armies, joined by troops from other German states, used their superior firepower and tactics to achieve a quick victory. "Blood and iron" were the foundation of the new German Empire.

The spoils of victory included a large indemnity and two provinces of France bordering on Germany: Alsace and Lorraine. The French paid the indemnity easily enough but resented the loss of their provinces. To the Germans, this region was German because a majority of its inhabitants spoke German. To the French, it was French because most of its inhabitants considered themselves French. These two conflicting definitions of nationalism kept enmity between France and Germany smoldering for decades. In this case, nationalism turned out to be a divisive rather than a unifying force.

Otto von Bismarck Chancellor (prime minister) of Prussia from 1862 until 1871, when he became chancellor of Germany. A conservative nationalist, he led Prussia to victory against Austria (1866) and France (1870) and was responsible for the creation of the German Empire in 1871.

The West Challenges Japan

In Japan the emperor was revered but had no power. Instead, Japan was governed by the Tokugawa Shogunate—a secular government under a military leader, or *shogun*, that had come to power in 1600 (see Chapter 21). Local lords, called *daimyos*, were permitted to control their lands and populations with very little interference from the shogunate.

When threatened from outside, this system showed many weaknesses. For one thing, it did not permit the coordination of resources necessary to resist major political or military challenges. Attempting to minimize exposure to Christianity and other threats to traditional culture, the shoguns prohibited foreigners from entering Japan and Japanese from going abroad in the early 1600s. They did permit the Dutch to retain a small commercial outpost at Nagasaki. While the penalty for breaking these laws was death, many Japanese ignored them. The most flagrant violators were powerful lords in southern Japan who ran large and very successful pirate or black-market operations and benefited from the decentralization of the shogunal political system in their entrepreneurial activities. But when a genuine foreign threat was suggested— as when, in 1792, Russian and British ships were spotted off the Japanese coast—the local lords realized that Japan was too weak and decentralized to resist a foreign invasion. As a result, a few of the regional lords began to develop their own reformed armies, arsenals, and shipyards. At the same time a small number of Japanese intellectuals engaged European culture, what they called Dutch learning.

By the 1800s Satsuma (SAT-soo-mah) and Choshu (CHOE-shoo), two large domains in southern Japan, had become wealthy and ambitious, enjoying high rates of revenue and population growth. Their remoteness from the capital Edo (now Tokyo) and their economic vigor also fostered a strong sense of local self-reliance.

When Commodore Matthew C. Perry, backed by a powerful fleet, demanded that Japan open its ports to trade and allow American ships to refuel and take on supplies during their voyages between China and California in 1853, he precipitated a political crisis. After consultation with the provincial daimyos, the shogun's advisers advocated capitulation to Perry, pointing to China's humiliating defeats in the Opium and Arrow Wars. As a result, when Perry returned in 1854, representatives of the shogun indicated their willingness to sign the Treaty of Kanagawa (KAH-nah-GAH-wah), modeled on the unequal treaties between China and the Western powers. Angry and disappointed, some provincial governors began to encourage an underground

MAP 27.2 **Unification of Germany, 1866–1871** Germany was united after a series of short, successful wars by the kingdom of Prussia against Austria in 1866 and against France in 1871. © Cengage Learning

Map legend

- Prussia before 1866
- Conquered by Prussia in Austro-Prussian War, 1866
- Austrian territories excluded from North German Confederation, 1867
- Joined with Prussia to form North German Confederation, 1867
- South German states joining with Prussia to form German Empire, 1871
- Won by Prussia in Franco-Prussian War, 1871
- ★ Major battle
- German Confederation boundary, 1815–1866
- Bismarck's German Empire, 1871

movement calling for the destruction of the Tokugawa regime and the banning of foreigners from Japan.

Tensions between the shogunate and some provincial leaders, particularly in Choshu and Satsuma, increased in the early 1860s. Young, ambitious, educated men who faced mediocre prospects under the rigid Tokugawa class system emerged as provincial leaders. When British and French ships shelled the southwestern coasts in 1864 to protest the treatment of foreigners, the action enraged the provincial samurai who rejected the Treaty of Kanagawa and resented the shogunate's inability to protect the country. In 1867 the Choshu leaders Yamagata Aritomo and Ito Hirobumi finally realized that they should stop warring with their rival province, Satsuma, and join forces to lead a rebellion against the shogunate.

Giuseppe Mazzini on Revolutionary Nationalism

One of the most potent intellectual and political forces in nine-teenth-century Europe and the Americas was nationalism. At its most basic it was a shared pride in the history and accomplishments of one's native land. It was also often an emotional belief in national destiny and a determination to pursue national glory. Wherever peoples shared language, history, and culture but were divided politically and subject to different political institutions and laws, as in Italy and Germany, for example, popular movements supported unification. These desires to create nations organized around shared ethnicity directly threatened many of the long-standing political arrangements that had been created over centuries by the ruling dynasties of Europe.

In the 1830s many young Italians regarded the political divisions imposed on their native land by the Austrian crown, local monarchies, and the pope as intolerable. One of the most important advocates of Italian unification was Giuseppe Mazzini (1805–1872), whose revolutionary activities led to his imprisonment and exile in 1831. While in exile he created the patriot organization Young Italy and continued to urge insurrection. He then returned to Italy from England during the continent-wide revolutionary upheavals of 1848 (see Chapter 23). Although these events seemed to promise the realization of his dreams, a combination of Austrian and French military actions and deep divisions among Italian political leaders led to disappointment. Italy's unification came after 1860 through a military alliance between France and the king of Sardinia, disappointing Mazzini, who was a supporter of democracy and social justice as well as a patriot. While he continued to work for the full emancipation of Italy and for democracy, he refused a seat in the Italian Chamber of Deputies.

Every revolution is the work of a principle that has been accepted as a basis of faith. Whether it invoke nationality, liberty, equality, or religion, it always fulfills itself in the name of a principle, that is to say, of a great truth, which being recognized and approved by the majority of the inhabitants of a country, constitutes a common belief, and sets before the masses a new aim, while authority misrepresents or rejects it. A revolution, violent or peaceful, includes a negation and an affirmation: the negation of an existing order of things, the affirmation of a new order to be substituted for it. A revolution proclaims that the state is rotten; that its machinery no longer meets the needs of the greatest number of the citizens; that its institutions are powerless to direct the general movement; that popular and social thought has passed beyond the vital principle of those institutions; that the new phase in the development of the national faculties finds neither expression nor representation in the official constitution of the country, and that it must therefore create one for itself. This revolution does create. Since its task is to increase, and not diminish the nation's patrimony, it violates neither the truths that the majority possess, nor the rights they hold sacred; but it reorganizes everything on a new basis; it gathers and harmonizes round the new principle all the elements and forces of the country; it gives a unity of direction toward the new aim, to all those tendencies which before were scattered in the pursuit of different aims. Then the revolution has done its work.

We recognize no other meaning in revolution. If a revolution did not imply a general reorganization by virtue of a social principle; if it did not remove a discord in the elements of a state, and place harmony in its stead; if it did not secure a moral unity; so far from declaring ourselves revolutionists, we should believe it our duty to oppose the revolutionary movement with all our power.

Without the purpose hinted at above, there may be riots, and at times victorious insurrections, but no revolutions. You will have changes of men and administration; one caste succeeding to another; one dynastic branch ousting the other. This necessitates retreat; a slow reconstruction of the past, which the insurrection had suddenly destroyed; the gradual re-establishment, under new names, of the old order of things, which the people had risen to destroy. Societies have such

The Meiji Restoration and the Modernization of Japan, 1868–1894

Meiji Restoration The political program that followed the destruction of the Tokugawa Shogunate in 1868, in which a collection of young leaders set Japan on the path of centralization, industrialization, and imperialism.

The civil war was intense but brief. In 1868 provincial rebels overthrew the Tokugawa Shogunate and declared young emperor Mutsuhito (moo-tsoo-HEE-toe) (r. 1868–1912) "restored." The new leaders called their regime the "**Meiji (MAY-gee) Restoration**" after Mutsuhito's reign name (*Meiji* means "enlightened rule"). The "Meiji oligarchs," as the new rulers were known, were extraordinarily talented and far-sighted. Determined to protect their country from Western imperialism, they encouraged its transformation into "a rich country with a strong army" with world-class industries. Though imposed from above, the Meiji Restoration marked as profound a change as the French Revolution (see Map 27.3).

The oligarchs were under no illusion that they could fend off the Westerners without changing their institutions and their society. In the Charter Oath issued in 1868, the young emperor included a prophetic phrase: "Knowledge shall be sought throughout the world and thus shall be strengthened the foundation of the imperial polity." It was to be the motto of a new Japan, which embraced all foreign ideas, institutions, and techniques that could strengthen the nation. The literacy rate in Japan was the highest in Asia at the time, and the oligarchs shrewdly exploited it need of unity that if they miss it in insurrection they turn back to a restoration. Then there is a new discontent, a new struggle, a new explosion.

. . .

Wherever, in fact, individual rights are exercised without the influence of some great thought that is common to all; where every individual's interests are armonized by some organization that is directed by a positive ruling principle, and by the consciousness of a common aim, there must be a tendency for some to usurp others' rights. In a society like ours, where a division into classes, call them what you will, still exists in full strength, every right is bound to clash with another right, envious and mistrustful of it; every interest naturally conflicts with an opposing interest: the landlord's with the peasant's; the manufacturer's or capitalist's with the workman's. All through Europe—since equality, however accepted in theory, has been rejected in practice, and the sum of social wealth has accumulated in the hands of a small number of men, while the masses gain but a mere pittance by their relentless toil; it is a cruel irony, it gives inequality a new lease of life, if you establish unrestricted liberty, and tell men they are free, and bid them use their rights.

A social sphere must have its center; a center to the individualists that jostle with each other inside it; a center to all the scattered rays that diffuse and waste their light and heat. The theory that bases the social structure on individual interests cannot supply this center. The absence of a center, or the selection among opposing interests of that which has the most vigorous life, means either anarchy or privilege—that is, either barren strife or the germ of aristocracy, under whatever name it disguises itself, this is the parting of the ways, which it is impossible to avoid.

Is this what we want when we invoke a revolution, since a revolution is indispensable to reorganize our nationality?

. . . We are therefore driven to the sphere of principles. We must revive belief in them, we must fulfill a work of faith. The logic of things demands it. Principles alone are constructive. Ideals are never translated into facts without the general recognition of some strong belief. Great things are never done except by the rejection of individualism and a constant sacrifice of self to the common progress. Self-sacrifice is the sense of duty in action. . . . The individual is sacred; his interests, his rights are inviolable. But to make them the only foundation of the political structure, and tell each individual to win his future with his own unaided strength, is to surrender society and progress to the accidents of chance nature, his social instinct; to plant egotism in the soul; and in the long run impose the dominion of the strong over the weak, of those who have over those who have not. The many futile attempts of the past forty years prove this. . . . If by dint of example you can root in a nation's heart the principle that the French Revolution proclaimed but never carried out, that the State owes every member the means of existence or the chance to work for it, and add a fair definition of existence, you have prepared the triumph of right over privilege; the end of the monopoly of one class over another, and the end of pauperism; for which at present there are only palliatives . . . Christian charity, or cold and brutal maxims like those of the English school of political economists.

When you have raised men's minds to believe in the other principle that society is an association of laborers—and can, thanks to that belief, deduce both in theory and practice all its consequences; you will have no more castes, no more aristocracies, or civil wars, or crisis. You will have a People.

QUESTIONS FOR ANALYSIS

1. What does Mazzini mean when he says that a revolution begins with a "negation" and an "affirmation"?

2. According to Mazzini, how does the existence of "a division into classes" inhibit the achievement of revolutionary objectives?

3. What "principle" of the French Revolution does Mazzini say is key to the "triumph of right over privilege"?

Source: *The Literature of Italy, 1265-1907*, VI, edited by Rossiter Johnson and Dora K. Ranous, The National Alumni, New York, 1907, 296-300, 303, 305, translated by Thomas Okey.

in their introduction of new educational systems, a conscript army, and new communications. The government was able to establish heavy industry, thanks to decades of industrial development and financing in the provinces in the earlier 1800s. With a conscript army and a revamped educational system, the oligarchs attempted to create a new citizenry that was literate and competent but also loyal and obedient.

The Meiji leaders copied the government structure of imperial Germany and modeled the new Japanese navy on the British and the army on the Prussian. They also introduced Western-style postal and telegraph services, railroads and harbors, banking, clocks, and calendars. To learn the secrets of Western strength, they sent hundreds of students to Britain, Germany, and the United States. Western-style clothing and hairstyles and garden parties as well as formal dances became popular.

The government was especially interested in Western technology. It opened vocational, technical, and agricultural schools, founded four imperial universities, and brought in foreign experts to advise on medicine, science, and engineering. To encourage industrialization, the government set up state-owned enterprises to manufacture cloth and inexpensive consumer goods for sale abroad. The first Japanese industries exploited their workers ruthlessly, just as the first industries in Europe and America had done. In 1881 the government sold these enterprises

MAP 27.3 **Expansion and Modernization of Japan, 1868–1918** As Japan acquired modern industry, it followed the example of the European powers in seeking overseas colonies. Its colonial empire grew at the expense of its neighbors: Taiwan was taken from China in 1895; Karafutu (Sakhalin) was taken from Russia in 1905; and all of Korea became a colony in 1910. © Cengage Learning

to private investors, mainly large *zaibatsu* (zye-BOT-soo), or conglomerates, and also encouraged individual technological innovation. Thus the carpenter Toyoda Sakichi founded the Toyoda Loom Works (now Toyota Motor Company) in 1906; ten years later he patented the world's most advanced automatic loom.

Nationalism and Social Darwinism

The Franco-Prussian War of 1870–1871 changed the political climate of Europe, making France more liberal. Germany, Austria-Hungary (as the Austrian Empire had renamed itself in 1867), and Russia remained conservative and used nationalism to maintain the status quo. The kingdom of Italy completed the unification of the peninsula begun decades earlier.

Nationalism and parliamentary elections made politicians of all parties appeal to public opinion. They were greatly aided by the press, especially cheap daily newspapers that sought to increase circulation by publishing sensational articles about overseas conquests and foreign threats. As governments increasingly came to recognize the advantages of an educated population in the competition between states, they opened public schools in every town and admitted

Japan's New Army   After the Meiji Restoration in 1868, the leaders of the new government set out to make Japan "a rich country with a strong army." They modeled the new army on the European armies of the time, with Western-style uniforms, rifles, cannon, and musical instruments.

The Granger Collection, NYC

women into public-service jobs for the first time. Politicians and journalists appealed to the emotions of the poor, diverting their anger from their employers to foreigners and their votes from socialist to nationalist parties.

In many countries the dominant group used nationalism to impose its language, religion, or customs on minority populations. The Russian Empire attempted to "Russify" its diverse ethnic populations. The Spanish government made Spanish compulsory in the schools, newspapers, and courts of its Basque- and Catalan-speaking provinces. Similarly, immigrants to the United States were expected to learn English.

Western culture in the late nineteenth century exalted the powerful over the weak, men over women, rich over poor, Europeans over other races, and humans over nature. Some people attempted to use science to justify the harsh inequalities of gender, ethnicity, and class that were common across Europe and the Americas. One of the most influential scientists of the century, and the one whose ideas were most widely appropriated and misinterpreted, was the English biologist Charles Darwin (1809–1882).

In his 1859 book *On the Origin of the Species*, Darwin challenged common assumptions derived from religious beliefs by arguing that the earth was much older than previously believed. Based on years of research of the fossil record and careful observation of nature, he proposed that all forms of life had either evolved in the struggle for survival or become extinct over the course of hundreds of thousands of years. While controversial initially, Darwin's discoveries led to a revolution in the life sciences.

The philosopher Herbert Spencer (1820–1903) and others took up Darwin's ideas of "natural selection" and "survival of the fittest" and applied them to human society. These Social Darwinists developed elaborate pseudo-scientific theories of racial and ethnic differences, claiming that they were the result not of history but of biology. They saw social and racial differences as resulting from natural processes and opposed state intervention to alleviate inequities. Although not based on any research, these ideas gave a scientific-sounding justification for the power of the privileged and for imperialism.

SECTION REVIEW

- Nationalism, the most powerful new ideology of the nineteenth century, defined nations primarily on the basis of language.

- Garibaldi helped unify Italy between 1860 and 1870, and Bismarck unified Germany from 1866 to 1871.

- In response to Western intrusion, provincial Japanese lords launched the Meiji Restoration and quickly transformed Japan into a modern industrial nation.

- During this era, Charles Darwin's theory of evolution was often misinterpreted to justify the power of the privileged few.

THE GREAT POWERS OF EUROPE, 1871–1900

After the middle of the century, politicians and journalists discovered that minor incidents involving foreigners could be used to stir up popular indignation against neighboring countries. Military officers, impressed by the awesome power of the weapons that modern industry provided, began to think that the weapons were invincible. As a result, rivalries over colonial territories, ideological differences, and even minor border incidents or trade disagreements contributed to growing international tensions and, ultimately, to war.

Germany at the Center of Europe

International relations revolved around Germany because it was located in the center of Europe and had the most powerful army on the European continent. After creating a unified Germany in 1871, Bismarck declared that his country had no further territorial ambitions, and he put his efforts into maintaining the peace in Europe. To isolate France, he forged a loose coalition with Austria-Hungary and Russia, the other two conservative monarchical powers. Despite their competing ambitions in the Balkans, he was able to keep his coalition together for twenty years.

Bismarck proved equally adept at strengthening German unity at home. To weaken the influence of middle-class liberals, he extended the vote to all adult men, thereby allowing Socialists to win seats in the *Reichstag* or parliament. By imposing high tariffs on manufactured goods and wheat, he gained the support of both the wealthy industrialists of the Rhineland and the great landowners of eastern Germany, traditional rivals for power. His government supported public and technical education as a means to stimulate industrial expansion. Bismarck also introduced path-breaking social legislation—medical, unemployment, and disability insurance as well as old age pensions—long before other industrial countries. Under his leadership, the German people developed a strong sense of national unity and pride in their industrial and military power.

In 1888 Wilhelm I was succeeded by his grandson Wilhelm II (r. 1888–1918), an insecure and arrogant man who tried to gain respect by making belligerent speeches. Within two years he had dismissed Chancellor Bismarck and surrounded himself with yes men. He talked about his "global policy" and demanded the creation of a colonial empire. Ruler of the nation with the mightiest army and the largest industrial economy in Europe, he felt that Germany deserved "a place in the sun."

The Liberal Powers: France and Great Britain

France, once the dominant nation in Europe, had difficulty reconciling itself to being in second place. Though a prosperous country with flourishing agriculture and a large colonial empire, the French republic had some serious weaknesses. France trailed Great Britain and Germany in the development of modern heavy industry. Also troubling was the fact that France's population was scarcely growing; in 1911 France had only 39 million people compared to Germany's 64 million. In an age when the power of nations was roughly proportional to the size of their armies, France could field an army only two-thirds the size of Germany's.

The French people were also deeply divided over the very nature of the state: some were monarchists and Catholic, but a growing number held republican and anticlerical views. Yet if French political life seemed fragile and frequently in crisis, a long tradition of popular participation in politics and a strong sense of nationhood, reinforced by a fine system of public education, gave the French people a deeper cohesion than appeared on the surface.

Great Britain had a long experience with parliamentary elections and competing parties. The British government alternated smoothly between the Liberal and Conservative Parties, and the income gap between rich and poor gradually narrowed. Nevertheless, Britain had problems that grew more apparent as time went on. One was Irish resentment of English rule. Nationalism had strengthened the allegiance of the English, Scots, and Welsh to the British state. But the Irish, excluded from meaningful participation in government because they were Catholic and predominantly poor, saw the British as a foreign occupying force.

Another problem was the British economy. By the last decades of the nineteenth century, Great Britain had fallen behind the United States and Germany in such important industries as

The Doss House, 1889 (oil on canvas), Makovsky, Vladimir Egorovic (1846–1920)/State Russian Museum, St. Petersburg, Russia/The Bridge-man Art Library

The Doss House   Late-nineteenth-century cities showed more physical than social improvements. This painting by Makovsky of a street in St. Petersburg contrasts the broad avenue and impressive new buildings with the poverty of the crowd.

steel, chemicals, electricity, and textiles. Even in shipbuilding and shipping, Britain's traditional specialty, Germany was catching up.

Britain was also preoccupied with its enormous and fast-growing empire. A source of wealth for investors and the envy of other imperialist nations, the empire was a constant drain on Britain's finances, for it required Britain to maintain costly fleets of warships throughout the world.

For most of the nineteenth century Britain pursued a policy of "splendid isolation." Britain's preoccupation with India led British statesmen to exaggerate the Russian threat to the Ottoman Empire and to the Central Asian approaches to India. Periodic "Russian scares" and Britain's age-old rivalry with France for overseas colonies diverted the attention of British politicians from the potent threat posed by the rise of Germany.

The Conservative Powers: Russia and Austria-Hungary

The forces of nationalism weakened rather than strengthened Russia and Austria-Hungary. Their populations were far more divided, socially and ethnically, than were the German, French, or British peoples.

Nationalism was most divisive in south-central Europe, where many different language groups lived in close proximity. In 1867 the Austrian Empire renamed itself the Austro-Hungarian Empire to appease its Hungarian critics. Although its attempts to promote the cultures of its Slavic-speaking minorities failed to gain their political allegiance, it still thought of itself as a great power and attempted to dominate the Balkans. This strategy irritated Russia, which thought of itself as the protector of Slavic peoples everywhere.

Ethnic diversity also contributed to the instability of imperial Russia. The Polish people rebelled in 1830 and again in 1863–1864. The tsarist empire also included Finland, Estonia, Latvia, Lithuania, and Ukraine; the Caucasus; and the Muslim population of Central Asia conquered between 1865 and 1881. Furthermore, Russia had the largest Jewish population in Europe, and the harshness of its anti-Semitic laws and periodic *pogroms* (massacres) prompted many Jews to flee to America. Given this ethnic complexity, the state's attempts to impose the Russian language on its subjects were divisive instead of unifying.

In 1861 the moderate conservative Tsar Alexander II (r. 1855–1881) emancipated the peasants from serfdom. He did so partly out of a genuine desire to strengthen the bonds between the monarchy and the Russian people, and partly to promote industrialization by enlarging the labor pool. That half-hearted measure, however, only turned serfs into farm workers with few skills and little capital. Though "emancipated," the great majority of Russians had little education, few legal rights, and no say in the government. After Alexander's assassination in 1881, his successors Alexander III (r. 1881–1894) and Nicholas II (r. 1894–1917) reluctantly permitted limited attempts at social change. The Russian commercial middle class was small and had little influence. Industrialization consisted largely of state-sponsored projects, such as railroads, iron foundries, and armament factories, and led to social unrest among urban workers. Wealthy landowning aristocrats continued to dominate the Russian court and administration and blocked most reforms.

The weaknesses in Russia's society and government became glaringly obvious during a war with the rapidly industrializing Japan in 1904 and 1905. The fighting took place in Manchuria, a province in northern China far from European Russia and both armies suffered large losses. Ultimately, the Russian army, which received all its supplies by means of the inefficient Trans-Siberian Railway, was defeated by the better-trained and better-equipped Japanese. When the Russian navy finally arrived in Asian waters in 1905 after its long voyage around Eurasia and Africa, it was destroyed by the Japanese fleet at Tsushima Strait, validating the Meiji commitment to military modernization.

The shock of defeat caused a revolution in 1905 that forced Tsar Nicholas II to grant a constitution and permit an elected Duma (parliament). But as soon as he was able to rebuild the army and the police, he reverted to the traditional despotism of his forefathers. In response, small groups of radical intellectuals, angered by the contrast between the wealth of the elite and the poverty of the common people, began plotting the violent overthrow of the tsarist autocracy.

SECTION REVIEW

- A united Germany, the most powerful state in Europe, became a threat to peace under Wilhelm II.

- France and Great Britain, though liberal democracies, faced difficulties at home and overseas.

- Russia and Austria-Hungary, two conservative empires, failed to adapt their politics to the modernization of their societies.

CHINA, JAPAN, AND THE WESTERN POWERS

After 1850 China and Japan—the two largest countries in East Asia—felt the influence of the Western powers as never before, but their responses were completely opposite. China resisted Western influence and became weaker, while Japan transformed itself into a major industrial and military power. One reason for this difference was the Western powers' already deep involvement in China and the distance to Japan, the nation most remote from Europe by ship. More important was the difference between the Chinese and Japanese elites' attitudes toward foreign cultures.

China in Turmoil

Empress Dowager Cixi
Empress of China and mother of Emperor Guangxi. She put her son under house arrest, supported antiforeign movements, and resisted reforms of the Chinese government and armed forces.

China had been devastated by the Taiping (tie-PING) Rebellion that raged from 1850 to 1864 (see Chapter 24). The French and British took advantage of China's weakness to demand the establishment of treaty ports where they could trade at will. In addition, the British took over China's customs enforcement and allowed the free import of opium until 1917. In response a Chinese "self-strengthening movement" tried in vain to bring about significant reforms by reducing government expenditures and eliminating corruption. While Meiji reformers in Japan sought foreign technologies to defend against imperialist aggressions, the **Empress Dowager Cixi (TSUH-shee)** (r. 1862–1908) of China opposed railways and other foreign technologies that could carry foreign influences to the interior. Government officials, who did not dare resist the Westerners outright, secretly encouraged crowds to attack and destroy the intrusive devices.

Les Événements de Chine
MORT AUX ÉTRANGERS !

Yamagata Aritomo One of the leaders of the Meiji Restoration.

The Boxer Uprising   In 1900 a Chinese secret society, the Righteous Fists, rose up with the encouragement of the Empress Dowager Cixi and attacked foreigners and their establishments. In the Western press they were known as "Boxers." These men are putting up a poster that reads "Death to Foreigners!"

They were thus able to slow the foreign intrusion, but in doing so, they denied themselves the best means of defense against foreign pressure.

Japan Confronts China

The late nineteenth century marked the high point of European power and arrogance, as the nations of Europe, in a frenzy known as the "New Imperialism," rushed to gobble up the last remaining unclaimed pieces of the world. Yet at that very moment two nations outside Europe were becoming great powers. One of them, the United States, was inhabited mainly by people of European origin. Its rise to great-power status had been predicted early in the nineteenth century by astute observers like the French statesman Alexis de Tocqueville. The other one, Japan, seemed so distant and exotic in 1850 that no European guessed that it would join the ranks of the great powers.

The motive for the transformation of Japan was to protect the nation from the Western powers, but the methods that strengthened Japan against the imperial ambitions of others could also be used to carry out its own conquests. Japan's path to imperialism was laid out by **Yamagata Aritomo**, a leader of the Meiji oligarchs. He believed that to be independent Japan had to define a "sphere of influence" that included Korea, Manchuria, and part of China (see Map 27.3). If other countries controlled this sphere, Japan would be at risk. To protect this sphere of influence, Yamagata insisted, Japan must sustain a vigorous program of military industrialization, culminating in the building of battleships.

As Japan grew stronger, China was growing weaker. In 1894 the two nations went to war over Korea. The Sino-Japanese War lasted less than six months, and it forced China to evacuate Korea, cede Taiwan and the Liaodong (li-AH-oh-dong) Peninsula, and pay a heavy indemnity. France, Germany, Britain, Russia, and the United States, upset at seeing a newcomer join the ranks of the imperialists, made Japan give up Liaodong in the name of the "territorial integrity" of China. In exchange for their "protection," the Western powers then made China grant them additional territorial and trade concessions, including ninety treaty ports.

In 1900 Chinese officials around the Empress Dowager Cixi encouraged a series of antiforeign riots known as the Boxer Uprising. Military forces from the European powers, Japan, and the United States put down the riots and occupied Beijing. Emboldened by China's obvious weakness, Japan and Russia competed for possession of the mineral-rich Chinese province of Manchuria.

Japan's participation in the suppression of the Boxer Uprising demonstrated its military power in East Asia. Then in 1905 Japan surprised the world by defeating Russia in the Russo-Japanese War. By the Treaty of Portsmouth that ended the war, Japan established a protectorate over Korea. In spite of Western attempts to restrict it to the role of junior partner, Japan continued to increase its influence. It gained control of southern Manchuria, with its industries and railroads, and in 1910 it finally annexed Korea, joining the ranks of the world's colonial powers.

SECTION REVIEW

- China was weakened by the Taiping Rebellion, a reactionary government under Empress Dowager Cixi, and the demands of the West.

- Japan, in contrast, built up its military and industrial strength and became another imperial power, taking advantage of China's weakness to seize Korea, Taiwan, and southern Manchuria.

Mary Evans Picture Library/The Image Works

CONCLUSION

After World War I broke out in 1914, many people, especially in Europe, looked back on the period from 1850 to 1914 as a golden age. For some, and in certain ways, it was. Industrialization was a powerful torrent changing Europe, North America, and East Asia. While shipping and railroads increased their global reach, new technologies—electricity, the steel and chemical industries, and the global telegraph network—contributed to the enrichment and empowerment of the industrial nations.

With these new technologies, memories of the great scourges—famines, wars, and epidemics—faded. Clean water, electric lights, and railways began to improve the lives of city dwellers, even the poor. Municipal services made city life less dangerous and chaotic. Goods from distant lands, even travel to other continents, came within the reach of millions. Middle-class women continued to focus on domestic pursuits and lived in a "separate sphere" from men, but access to education and professional careers initiated a long cycle of change. Many working-class women took jobs in the textile industry, yet their work outside the home paid less that similar jobs held by men and their traditional domestic and child-rearing responsibilities continued.

Though Karl Marx predicted a class struggle between workers and employers, socialism became more an intellectual current than a revolutionary movement. Workers achieved improvements in wages, job security, and workplace safety through labor unions, not revolutions. By the turn of the century, liberal political reforms had taken hold in western Europe. Universal male suffrage became law in the United States in 1870 and in various parts of Europe by the 1880s. At the same time women mobilized in large numbers to demand political rights, an objective not attained in Europe or North America until the twentieth century.

The framework for all these changes was the nation-state. Until the 1860s nationalism was associated with liberalism, but later generations of conservatives used public education, military service, and colonial conquests to build a sense of national unity. By 1871 both Italy and Germany had become unified states. In Japan, the Meiji Restoration restored power to the emperor and ushered in a period of Western influences and rapid economic growth.

The world economy, international politics, and even cultural and social issues revolved around a handful of countries—the great powers—that believed they controlled the destiny of the world. These included the most powerful European nations of the previous century, as well as three newcomers—Germany, the United States, and Japan.

KEY TERMS

Commodore Matthew Perry p. 685
railroads p. 686
submarine telegraph cables p. 687
steel p. 687

electricity p. 688
Thomas Edison p. 688
Victorian Age p. 693
"separate spheres" p. 693
socialism p. 696
labor union p. 696

Karl Marx p. 696
anarchists p. 697
nationalism p. 698
liberalism p. 698
Giuseppe Garibaldi p. 699
Otto von Bismarck p. 700

Meiji Restoration p. 702
Empress Dowager Cixi p. 708
Yamagata Aritomo p. 709

SUGGESTED READING

Anderson, Benedict. *Imagined Communities: Reflections on the Origin and Spread of Nationalism*, rev. ed. 2006. Describes how nationalism spread beyond Europe.

Beales, Derek. *The Risorgimento and the Unification of Italy*, 2d ed. 2003. A fine introduction to the topic that includes some useful documents.

Belchem, John. *Popular Radicalism in Nineteenth-Century Britain.* 1996. Examines efforts to expand the franchise and to challenge the new industrial order.

Fairbank, John King. *The Great Chinese Revolution, 1800–1985.* 1987. The classic synthesis of China's decline and recovery.

Griffin, Ben. *The Politics of Gender in Victorian Britain: Masculinity, Political Culture and the Struggle for Women's Rights.* 2012. An excellent examination of politics, reform, and the women's rights movement.

Headrick, Daniel R. *The Tools of Empire: Technology and European Imperialism in the Nineteenth Century.* 1981. An illuminating examination of economic change and imperial expansion.

Hobsbawm, E. J. *Nation and Nationalism Since 1780.* 1992. Deals mainly with Europe.

Keene, Donald. *Emperor of Japan: Meiji and His World, 1852–1912.* 2005. A well-told biography of this important figure.

Kitchen, Martin. *A History of Modern Germany: 1800 to the Present.* 2011. A good introduction to German history.

Landes, David. *The Unbound Prometheus: Technological Change and Industrial Development in Western Europe from 1750 to the Present*, 2d ed. 2003. A broadly framed narrative of this complex story.

Moore, Barrington. *The Social Origins of Dictatorship and Democracy.* 1966. A classic essay on European society.

Pflanze, Otto. *Bismarck and the Development of Germany.* 1990. The best biography of Bismarck.

Read, Donald. *The Age of Urban Democracy: England, 1868–1914.* 1994. An excellent social history.

Silbey, David J. *The Boxer Rebellion and the Great Game in China.* 2012. A reliable discussion of China's political crisis and the imperial ambitions of Western powers.

Sked, Alan. *The Decline and Fall of the Habsburg Empire, 1815–1918.* 1989. Discusses how nationalism destroyed the Austrian state.

Spence, Jonathan D. *The Search for Modern China*, 2d ed. 1999. A monumental account of a complex society.

Stearns, Peter. *The Industrial Revolution in World History*, 3d ed. 2007. An updated and improved global history of industrialization.

Tilly, Louise, and Joan Scott. *Women, Work, and Family.* 1987. A wide-ranging history of Western women.

Waldron, Peter. *Governing Tsarist Russia.* 2007. A useful discussion of Russia in this period of political challenge.

CourseMate Go to the History CourseMate website for primary source links, study tools, and review materials for this chapter. www.cengagebrain.com

Chapter Outline

The Western Front in World War I   In a landscape ravaged by artillery fire, two soldiers dash for cover amid shell holes and the charred remains of a forest.

Imperial War Museum/The Art Archive

The Crisis of the Imperial Order, 1900–1929

On June 28, 1914, Archduke Franz Ferdinand, heir to the throne of Austria-Hungary, was riding in an open carriage through Sarajevo, a city Austria had annexed six years earlier. When the carriage stopped momentarily, Gavrilo Princip, member of a pro-Serbian conspiracy, fired his pistol twice, killing the archduke and his wife.

Those shots ignited a global conflict. All previous wars had caused death and destruction, but they were also marked by heroism and glory. In this new war, four years of bitter fighting produced no victories, no gains, and no glory, only death for millions of soldiers. The war became global as the Ottoman Empire fought against Britain and Japan attacked German positions in China. France and Britain involved their empires in the war and brought Africans, Indians, Australians, and Canadians to Europe to fight and labor on the front lines. Finally, in 1917, the United States entered the fray.

In this chapter, we will look at the causes of war between the great powers, the consequences of that conflict in Europe, the Middle East, and Russia, and the upheavals in China and Japan. We will also look at the more indirect impact of the war on noncombatant states in Latin America.

ORIGINS OF THE CRISIS IN EUROPE AND THE MIDDLE EAST

When the twentieth century opened, the world seemed firmly under the control of the great powers (see Chapter 27). The first decade of the twentieth century was a period of relative peace and economic growth in most of the world. Several new technologies—airplanes, automobiles, radio, and cinema—aroused much excitement (see Chapter 29). The great powers consolidated their colonial conquests of the previous decades, and their alliances were evenly matched. The only international war of the period, the Russo-Japanese War (1904–1905), ended quickly with a decisive Japanese victory.

However, two major changes undermined the apparent stability. In Europe, tensions mounted as Germany, with its growing industrial and military might, challenged Britain at sea and France in Morocco. And the Ottoman Empire grew weaker, leaving a dangerous power vacuum. The resulting chaos in the Balkans gradually drew the European powers into a web of hostilities.

The Ottoman Empire and the Balkans

From the fifteenth to the nineteenth centuries the Ottoman Empire was one of the most powerful states. By the late nineteenth century, however, it had fallen behind economically, technologically, and militarily. Europeans referred to it as the "sick man of Europe."

As the Ottoman Empire weakened, it began losing European provinces: Macedonia in 1902–1903, Bosnia in 1908, Crete in 1909, Albania in 1910. In 1912 Italy conquered Libya, the

Ottomans' last foothold in Africa. In 1912–1913 Serbia, Bulgaria, Romania, and Greece chased the Ottomans out of Europe, except for a small enclave around Constantinople.

In reaction, the Turks began to assert themselves against rebellious minorities and meddling foreigners. Many officers in the army, the most Europeanized segment of Turkish society, blamed Sultan Abdul Hamid II (r. 1876–1909) for the decline of the empire. A group known as "Young Turks" plotted to force the sultan to reinstate a stillborn constitution that he had suspended in 1876 before it could have an impact. They alienated other anti-Ottoman groups by advocating centralized rule and the Turkification of ethnic minorities.

In 1909 the parliament, dominated by Young Turks, overthrew Abdul Hamid. The new regime reinvigorated the Tanzimat reform movement (see Chapter 24) that had begun in the early nineteenth century. At the same time, it cracked down on Greek and Armenian minorities. Galvanized by their defeat in the Balkan Wars, the Turks hired a German general to modernize their armed forces. The dangerous mixture of modern armies and nationalism was not limited to the Ottoman Empire, however.

Nationalism, Alliances, and Military Strategy

The assassination of Franz Ferdinand triggered a chain of events over which military and political leaders lost control. The escalation from assassination to global war had causes that went back many years. One was nationalism, which bound citizens to their ethnic group and led them, when called upon, to kill people they viewed as enemies. Another was the system of alliances and military plans that the great powers had devised to protect themselves from their rivals. A third was Germany's yearning to dominate Europe.

Nationalism united the citizens of France, Britain, and Germany behind their respective governments and gave them tremendous cohesion and strength of purpose. Only the most powerful feelings could inspire millions of men to march into battle and sustain civilian populations through years of hardship.

Nationalism could also be a dividing force. The Russian, Austro-Hungarian, and Ottoman Empires, large but fragile, contained numerous ethnic and religious minorities. Having repressed some minorities for centuries, the governments could never count on their full support. The very existence of an independent Serbia threatened Austria-Hungary by stirring up the hopes and resentments of its Slavic populations.

Imbued with nationalism, most people viewed war as a crusade for liberty or as long-overdue revenge for past injustices. During the nineteenth century, as memories of the misery and carnage caused by the Napoleonic Wars faded, revulsion against war gradually weakened. The Crimean War of 1853–1856 and the Franco-Prussian War of 1871 had caused few casualties or long-term consequences. And in the imperialist wars in Africa and Asia (see Chapter 26), Europeans almost always had been victorious at a small cost in money and manpower.

What turned an incident in the Balkans into a conflict involving all the great powers was the system of alliances. At the center of Europe stood Germany, the most heavily industrialized country in Europe. Its army was the best trained and equipped, and it challenged Great Britain's naval supremacy by building "dreadnoughts"—heavily armed battleships. In 1882 it joined Austria-Hungary and Italy in the Triple Alliance, while France allied itself with Russia. In 1904 Britain and France reached an Entente **(on-TONT)** ("understanding"), joined by Russia in 1907. Europe was thus divided into two blocs of roughly equal power (see Map 28.1).

The alliance system was cursed by inflexible military planning. In 1914 western and central Europe had highly developed railroad networks but very few motor vehicles, and European armies had grown to include millions of soldiers and reservists. To mobilize these forces and transport them to battle would require thousands of trains running on precise schedules. Once under way, a country's mobilization could not be canceled or postponed without causing chaos.

In the years before World War I, military planners in France and Germany had worked out elaborate railroad timetables to mobilize their respective armies in a few days. Russia, a large country with an underdeveloped rail system, needed several weeks to mobilize its forces. Britain, with a tiny volunteer army, had no mobilization plans, and German planners believed that the British would stay out of a war on the European continent. So that Germany could avoid having to fight France and Russia at the same time, German war planners expected to defeat France in a matter of days, then transport the entire army across Germany to the Russian border by train before Russia could fully mobilize.

CHRONOLOGY

	Europe and North America	Middle East	East Asia
1900	1904 British-French Entente 1907 British-Russian Entente	1909 Young Turks overthrow Sultan Abdul Hamid	1900 Boxer uprising in China 1904–1905 Russo-Japanese War
1910	1912–1913 Balkan Wars 1914 Assassination of Archduke Franz Ferdinand sparks World War I 1916 Battles of Verdun and the Somme 1917 Russian Revolutions; United States enters the war 1918 Armistice ends World War I 1918–1921 Civil war in Russia 1919 Treaty of Versailles	1912 Italy conquers Libya, last Ottoman territory in Africa 1915 British defeat at Gallipoli 1916 Arab Revolt in Arabia 1917 Balfour Declaration 1919–1922 War between Turkey and Greece	1911 Chinese revolutionaries led by Sun Yat-sen overthrow Qing dynasty 1915 Japan presents Twenty-One Demands to China 1919 May Fourth Movement in China
1920	1923–1928 New Economic Policy in Russia	1922 Egypt nominally independent 1923 Mustafa Kemal proclaims Turkey a republic	1927 Guomindang forces occupy Shanghai and expel Communists

---

SECTION REVIEW

- As the Ottoman Empire declined, nationalists calling themselves Young Turks tried to create a new Turkish nation.

- Nationalism, competing alliances, and inflexible military plans based on railroads turned an assassination into a cause for war.

On July 28, Austria-Hungary declared war on Serbia. The declaration of war triggered the general mobilization plans of Russia, France, and Germany. On July 29 the Russian government ordered general mobilization to force Austria to back down. On August 1 France ordered general mobilization. Minutes later Germany did likewise. Because of the rigid railroad timetables, war was now automatic.

The German plan was to wheel around through neutral Belgium and into northwestern France. The German General Staff expected France to capitulate before the British could get involved. But on August 3, when German troops entered Belgium, Britain demanded their withdrawal. When Germany refused, Britain declared war on Germany.

THE "GREAT WAR" AND THE RUSSIAN REVOLUTIONS, 1914–1918

Throughout Europe, people greeted the outbreak of war with parades and flags, expecting a quick victory. German troops marched off to the front shouting "To Paris!" Spectators in France encouraged marching French troops with shouts of "Send me the Kaiser's moustache!" The German sociologist Max Weber wrote: "This war, with all its ghastliness, is nevertheless grand and wonderful. It is worth experiencing."[1] When the war began, very few imagined that their side might not win. No one foresaw that everyone would lose.

Stalemate, 1914–1917

The war that erupted in 1914 was known as the "Great War" until the 1940s, when a far greater one overshadowed it. Its form came as a surprise to all belligerents, from the generals on down. In the classic battles that every officer studied, the advantage always went to the fastest-moving army led by the boldest general. In 1914 the generals' carefully drawn plans went awry from the

---

[1]Frank B. Tipton, *A History of Modern Germany since 1815* (Berkeley: University of California Press, 2003), 295.

MAP 28.1 **Europe in 1913** On the eve of World War I, Europe was divided between two great alliance systems—the Triple Alliance (Germany, Austria-Hungary, and Italy) and the Entente (France, Great Britain, and Russia)—and their respective colonial empires. These alliances were not stable. When war broke out, the Triple Alliance lost Italy but gained the Ottoman Empire. © Cengage Learning

start. Believing that a spirited attack would always prevail, French generals hurled their troops, dressed in bright blue-and-red uniforms, against the well-defended German border and suffered a crushing defeat. In battle after battle the much larger German armies defeated the French and the British. By early September the Germans held Belgium and northern France and were fast approaching Paris.

German victory seemed assured. But German troops, who had marched and fought for a month, were exhausted, and their generals wavered. A gap opened between two German armies along the Marne River, into which General Joseph Joffre moved France's last reserves. At the Battle of the Marne (September 5–12, 1914), the Germans were thrown back several miles.

During the next month, both sides spread out until they formed an unbroken line extending over 300 miles (some 500 kilometers) from the North Sea to the border of Switzerland. All along

Western Front A line of trenches and fortifications in World War I that stretched without a break from Switzerland to the North Sea. Scene of most of the fighting between Germany, on the one hand, and France and Britain, on the other.

this **Western Front**, the opposing troops prepared their defenses. Their most potent weapons were machine guns, which provided an almost impenetrable defense against advancing infantry but were useless for the offensive because they were too heavy for one man to carry and took too much time to set up.

To escape the deadly streams of bullets, soldiers dug holes in the ground, connected the holes to form shallow trenches, then dug communications trenches to the rear. Within weeks, the battlefields were scarred by lines of trenches several feet deep, their tops protected by sandbags and their floors covered with planks. Trenches were nothing new. What was extraordinary was that the trenches along the entire Western Front were connected, leaving no gaps through which armies could advance (see Map 28.2). How, then, could either side ever hope to win?

For four years, generals on each side again and again ordered their troops to attack. In battle after battle, thousands of young men on one side climbed out of their trenches, raced across the open fields, and were mowed down by enemy machine-gun fire. Hoping to destroy the machine guns, the attacking force would saturate the entrenched enemy lines with artillery barrages. But this tactic alerted the defenders to an impending attack and allowed them to rush in reinforcements and set up new machine guns.

The year 1916 saw the bloodiest and most futile battles of the war. The Germans attacked French forts at Verdun, losing 281,000 men and causing 315,000 French casualties. In retaliation, the British attacked the Germans at the Somme River and suffered 420,000 casualties—60,000 on the first day alone—while the Germans lost 450,000 and the French 200,000.

Warfare had never been waged this way before. It was mass slaughter in a moonscape of mud, steel, and flesh. Both sides attacked and defended, but neither side could win, for the armies were stalemated by trenches and machine guns. During four years of the bloodiest fighting the world had ever seen, the Western Front moved no more than a few miles one way or another.

At sea, the war was just as inconclusive. As soon as war broke out, the British cut the German overseas telegraph cables, blockaded the coasts of Germany and Austria-Hungary, and set out to capture or sink all enemy ships still at sea. The German High Seas Fleet, built at enormous cost but mostly coal-fueled, seldom left port. Only once, in May 1916, did it confront the oil-fueled and thus more efficient British Grand Fleet (see Environment and Technology: Oil and War). At the Battle of Jutland, off the coast of Denmark, the two fleets lost roughly equal numbers of ships, and the Germans escaped back to their harbors.

In early 1915, in retaliation for the British naval blockade, Germany announced a blockade of Britain by submarines. German submarines attacked every vessel they could. One of their victims was the British ocean liner *Lusitania*. The death toll from that attack was 1,198 people, 139 of them Americans. When the United States protested, Germany ceased its submarine campaign, hoping to keep America neutral.

Airplanes were used for reconnaissance and engaged in spectacular but inconsequential dogfights above the trenches. Poison gas, introduced on the Western Front in 1915, killed and wounded attacking soldiers as well as their intended victims, adding to the horror of battle. Primitive tanks aided, but did not cause, the collapse of the German army in the last weeks of the war. Although these weapons were of limited effectiveness in World War I, they offered an insight into the future of warfare.

ON HER THEIR LIVES DEPEND

WOMEN MUNITION WORKERS

Enrol at once

Eileen Tweedy/The Art Archive

Women in World War I Women played a more important role in World War I than in previous wars. As the armies drafted millions of men, employers hired women for essential war work. This poster extolls the importance of women workers in supplying munitions.

The Home Front and the War Economy

Trench-bound armies demanded ever more weapons, ammunition, and food, so civilians had to work harder, eat less, and pay higher taxes. Textiles, coal, meat, fats, and imported products such as tea and sugar were strictly rationed. Governments gradually imposed stringent controls over all aspects of their economies.

Main map labels:

ATLANTIC OCEAN

RUSSIA

Treaty of Brest-Litovsk, March 1918

Armistice line, December 1917

Moscow
Don R.
Dnieper R.
Black Sea
OTTOMAN EMPIRE
Constantinople
Cyprus
Dardanelles
Gallipoli 1915
Crete
Mediterranean Sea

Petrograd (St. Petersburg)
Kiev
UKRAINE
Helsinki
FINLAND
Estonia
LATVIA
Riga
COURLAND
LITHUANIA
Wilno (Vilnius)
BELARUS
Brest-Litovsk
Masurian Lakes
Tannenberg 1914
E. PRUSSIA
Warsaw
KINGDOM OF POLAND (Russia)
GALICIA
Dniester R.
MAY 1915
TRANSYLVANIA
ROMANIA
Bucharest
Danube R.
BULGARIA
SERBIA
1916
1915
1917–1918
GREECE
ALBANIA
MONTENEGRO
Sarajevo
Balkan front

Farthest Russian advance, 1914

Jutland 1916
DENMARK
Kiel
Elbe R.
GERMANY
Berlin
AUSTRIA-HUNGARY
Vienna
Budapest
Caporetto 1917
AUG. 1917
MAR. 1918
Italian front
ITALY
Rome
Po R.
Adriatic Sea
Sardinia
Corsica
Elba
Malta
Sicily

SWEDEN
NORWAY
Baltic Sea

British blockade line
North Sea
NETHERLANDS
BELGIUM
Louvain
LUXEMBOURG
ALSACE-LORRAINE
SWITZERLAND
Western front
Paris
FRANCE
Seine R.
Rhone R.
Bordeaux
Loire R.
Garonne R.
Ebro R.
SPAIN
Balearic Is.

GREAT BRITAIN
London
IRELAND

Tunis
TUNISIA (France)

N

Scale: 0 200 400 Mi.
0 200 400 km.

Legend:
- Triple Entente and its Allies
- Central Powers
- Neutral nations
- Greatest extent of territory gained by Germany-Austria
- Battle line

Inset map labels:

NETHERLANDS
Antwerp
Brussels
BELGIUM
Ostend
FLANDERS
Ghent
Scheldt R.
Liège
Meuse R.
ARDENNES
LUXEMBOURG
Sedan
St. Quentin
Aisne R.
Reims
Arras
Somme
Amiens
Somme R.
Compiègne
Belleau Wood
Marne
Marne I
Marne II Château-Thierry
Chalons-sur-Marne
Verdun
ARGONNE FOREST
Nancy
St. Mihiel
LORRAINE
Moselle R.
Saar R.
Strasbourg
ALSACE
Mulhouse
Basel
Epinal
GERMANY
Cologne
Coblenz
Ruhr R.
Rhine R.
Paris
FRANCE
Seine R.
Calais
Dover
English Channel

Scale: 0 25 50 km.
0 25 50 Mi.

Inset legend:
- Germany, 1914
- German offensive, 1915
- Greatest extent of territory gained by Germany, Sept. 1914
- German offensive, Summer 1918
- Armistice line, November 1918
- Major battle
- Front at beginning of 1915

MAP 28.2 **The First World War in Europe** After an initial surge through Belgium into northern France, the German offensive bogged down for four years along the Western Front. To the East, the German armies conquered a large part of Russia during 1917 and early 1918. Despite spectacular victories in the east, Germany lost the war because its armies collapsed along the strategically important Western Front.   © Cengage Learning

The war economy transformed civilian life. In France and Britain food rations were allocated according to need, improving nutrition among the poor. Unemployment vanished. Thousands of Africans, Indians, and Chinese were recruited for heavy labor in Europe. Employers hired women to fill jobs vacated by men off to war. Some women became streetcar drivers, mail carriers, and police officers. Others found work in the burgeoning government bureaucracies. Many joined auxiliary military services as doctors, nurses, mechanics, and ambulance drivers; after 1917, as the war took its toll of young men, the British government established women's auxiliary units for the army, navy, and air force. These positions gave thousands of women a sense of participation in the war effort and a taste of personal and financial independence.

German civilians paid an especially high price for the war, for the British naval blockade severed their overseas trade. Wheat flour disappeared, replaced first by rye, then by potatoes and turnips, then by acorns and chestnuts, and finally by sawdust. After the failure of the potato crop in 1916 came the "turnip winter," when people had to survive on 1,000 calories per day, half the normal amount that an active adult needed. Women, children, and the elderly were especially hard hit. Soldiers at the front raided enemy lines to scavenge food.

The war also brought hardships to Europe's African colonies. When the war began, the British and French overran German Togo on the West African coast. The much larger German colonies of Southwest Africa and German Cameroon were conquered in 1915. In German East Africa, the Germans remained undefeated until the end of the war. The Europeans requisitioned foodstuffs, imposed heavy taxes, and forced Africans to grow export crops and sell them at low prices. As Europeans stationed in Africa joined the war, the combination of increased demands on Africans and fewer European officials led to uprisings that lasted for several years. Over a million Africans served in the various armies, and perhaps three times that number were drafted as porters to carry army equipment. Faced with a shortage of young Frenchmen, France drafted Africans into its army, where many fought side by side with Europeans.

One country grew rich during the war: the United States. For two and a half years the United States stayed technically neutral but did a roaring business supplying France and Britain. When the United States entered the war in 1917, businesses engaging in war production made spectacular profits. Civilians were exhorted to help the war effort by investing their savings in war bonds and growing food in backyard "victory gardens." Employment opportunities created by the war played a major role in the migration of African Americans from the rural South to the cities of the North.

The Ottoman Empire at War

On August 2, 1914, the Turks signed a secret alliance with Germany. In November they joined the fighting, hoping to gain land at Russia's expense. During the campaign in the Caucasus the Turks expelled the Armenians, whom they suspected of being pro-Russian, from their homelands in eastern Anatolia. Hunger and exposure killed hundreds of thousands during the forced march to Syria across the mountains in the winter. Many others were killed by regular and irregular Ottoman military forces.

The Turks also closed the Dardanelles, the strait between the Mediterranean and Black Seas (see Map 28.2). Seeing little hope of victory on the Western Front, Britain tried to open the Dardanelles by landing troops on the nearby Gallipoli Peninsula in 1915. Turkish troops pushed the invaders back into the sea. The British then promised the emir (hereditary governor) of Mecca, Hussein ibn Ali, a kingdom of his own if he would lead an Arab revolt against the Turks. In 1916 Hussein rose up and was proclaimed king of Hejaz **(heh-JAHZ)** (western Arabia). His son **Faisal (FIE-sahl)** then led an Arab army in support of the British advance from Egypt into Palestine and Syria. The Arab Revolt of 1916 did not affect the struggle in Europe, but it did contribute to the defeat of the Ottoman Empire.

The British made promises to Jews as well as Arabs. For centuries, Jewish minorities in eastern and central Europe had developed a thriving culture despite frequent persecutions. By the early twentieth century a nationalist movement called Zionism, led by **Theodore Herzl**, arose among those who wanted to return to their ancestral homeland in Palestine. The concept of a Jewish homeland appealed to many Europeans as a humanitarian solution to the problem of anti-Semitism.

By 1917 Chaim Weizmann **(hi-um VITES-mun)**, leader of the British Zionists, had persuaded several British politicians that a Jewish homeland in Palestine should be carved out of the Ottoman Empire and placed under British protection, thereby strengthening the Allied cause. In

Faisal Arab prince, leader of the Arab Revolt in World War I. The British made him king of Iraq in 1921, and he reigned under British protection until 1933.

Theodore Herzl Austrian journalist and founder of the Zionist movement urging the creation of a Jewish national homeland in Palestine.

November, as British armies were advancing on Jerusalem, Foreign Secretary Sir Arthur Balfour wrote:

> *His Majesty's Government view with favor the establishment in Palestine of a national home for the Jewish people and will use their best endeavours to facilitate the achievement of that object, it being clearly understood that nothing shall be done which may prejudice the civil and religious rights of existing non-Jewish communities in Palestine.*[2]

Balfour Declaration Statement issued by Britain's foreign secretary Arthur Balfour in 1917 favoring the establishment of a Jewish national homeland in Palestine.

The British did not foresee that this statement, known as the **Balfour Declaration**, would lead to conflicts between Arabs living in Palestine and Jewish settlers.

Double Revolution in Russia

At the beginning of the war Russia had the largest army in the world, but its generals were incompetent, supplies were lacking, and soldiers were poorly trained and equipped. In August 1914 two Russian armies invaded eastern Germany but were thrown back.

In 1916, after a string of defeats, the Russian army ran out of ammunition and other essential supplies. Soldiers were ordered into battle unarmed and told to pick up the rifles of fallen comrades. Railroads broke down for lack of fuel and parts, and crops rotted in the fields. Civilians faced shortages and widespread hunger, and food and fuel became scarce in the cities. During the bitterly cold winter of 1916–1917, factory workers and housewives had to line up in front of grocery stores before dawn to get food. The court of Tsar Nicholas II, however, remained as extravagant and corrupt as ever.

Bolsheviks Radical Marxist political party founded by Vladimir Lenin in 1903. Under Lenin's leadership, the Bolsheviks seized power in November 1917 during the Russian Revolution.

In early March 1917 (February by the old Russian calendar), food ran out in Petrograd (St. Petersburg), the capital. Women staged mass demonstrations, and soldiers mutinied and joined striking workers to form soviets (councils) to take over factories and barracks. A few days later the tsar abdicated, and leaders of the parliamentary parties, led by Alexander Kerensky, formed a Provisional Government. Thus began what Russians called the "February Revolution."

Vladimir Lenin Leader of the Bolshevik (later Communist) Party. He lived in exile in Switzerland until 1917, then returned to Russia to lead the Bolsheviks to victory during the Russian Revolution and the civil war that followed.

Revolutionaries formerly hunted by the tsar's police came out of hiding. Most numerous were the Social Revolutionaries, who advocated the redistribution of land to the peasants. The Mensheviks advocated electoral politics and reform in the tradition of European socialists and had a large following among intellectuals and factory workers. The **Bolsheviks**, their rivals, were a small but tightly disciplined group of radicals obedient to the will of their leader, **Vladimir Lenin** (1870–1924).

Lenin, the son of a government official, became a revolutionary in his teens when his older brother was executed for plotting to kill the tsar. He spent years in exile, first in Siberia and later in Switzerland, where he devoted his full attention to organizing his followers. His goal was to create a party that would lead the revolution rather than wait for it. He explained: "The will of a class is sometimes fulfilled by a dictator. . . . Soviet socialist democracy is not in the least incompatible with individual rule and dictatorship."[3]

In early April 1917 the German government, hoping to destabilize Russia, allowed Lenin to travel from Switzerland to Russia in a sealed railway car. As soon as he arrived in Petrograd, he announced his program: immediate peace, all power to the soviets, and transfers of land to the peasants and factories to the workers. This plan proved immensely popular among soldiers and workers exhausted by the war.

The next few months witnessed a tug-of-war between the Provisional Government and the various revolutionary factions in Petrograd. When Kerensky ordered another offensive against the Germans, Russian soldiers began to

SECTION REVIEW

- Europeans greeted the outbreak of war with joy.
- After a month-long German advance into Belgium and France, armies stalemated in a line of trenches along the Western Front, suffering huge casualties but no victory.
- On the home fronts, civilians suffered severe shortages and women entered the workforce, while the United States grew rich on profits from war production.
- The entry of the Ottoman Empire into the war did not tip the balance.
- In the Balfour Declaration, Great Britain promised Jews a "national homeland" in Palestine.
- As Russia weakened, Lenin's Bolsheviks seized power in November 1917.
- Goaded by German submarine warfare, in 1917 the United States entered the war on the Allied side, and Germany began to retreat.
- The war ended on November 11, 1918, with the defeat of Germany.

[2]Walter Z. Laqueur and Barry Rubin, eds., *The Arab-Israeli Reader: A Documentary History of the Middle East Conflict*, 4th ed. (New York: Penguin Books, 1984), 18.

[3]David Shub, *Lenin: A Biography* (Garden City, NY: Doubleday, 1948), 257.

desert by the hundreds of thousands, throwing away their rifles and walking back to their villages. As the Germans advanced, the government lost the little support it had.

Meanwhile, the Bolsheviks were gaining support among the workers of Petrograd and the soldiers and sailors stationed there. On November 6, 1917 (October 24 in the Russian calendar), they rose up and took over the city, calling their action the "October Revolution." Their sudden move surprised rival revolutionary groups that believed that a "socialist" revolution could happen only after many years of "bourgeois" rule. Lenin, more interested in power than in the fine points of Marxist doctrine, overthrew the Provisional Government and arrested Mensheviks, Social Revolutionaries, and other rivals.

Seizing Petrograd was only the first step, for the rest of Russia was in chaos. The Bolsheviks nationalized all private land and ordered the peasants to hand over their crops without compensation. The peasants, having seized their landlords' estates, resisted. In the cities the Bolsheviks took over the factories and drafted the workers into compulsory labor brigades. To enforce his rule Lenin created the Cheka, a secret police force with powers to arrest and execute opponents.

The Bolsheviks also sued for peace with Germany and Austria-Hungary. By the Treaty of Brest-Litovsk, signed on March 3, 1918, Russia lost territories containing a third of its population and wealth. Poland, Finland, and the Baltic states (Estonia, Latvia, and Lithuania) became independent republics. Russian colonies in Central Asia and the Caucasus broke away temporarily.

The End of the War in Western Europe, 1917–1918

Like many Americans, President **Woodrow Wilson** wanted to stay out of the European conflict. For nearly three years he kept the United States neutral and tried to persuade the belligerents to compromise. But in late 1916 German leaders decided to starve the British into submission by using submarines to sink ships carrying food supplies to Great Britain. The Germans knew that unrestricted submarine warfare was likely to bring the United States into the war, but they were willing to gamble that Britain and France would collapse before the United States could send enough troops to help them.

The submarine campaign resumed on February 1, 1917, and the German gamble failed. The British organized their merchant ships into convoys protected by destroyers, and on April 6 President Wilson asked the United States Congress to declare war on Germany.

In January 1918, President Wilson presented his **Fourteen Points**, a peace plan that called for the German evacuation of occupied lands, the settling of territorial disputes by the decisions of the local populations, and the formation of an association of nations to guarantee the independence and territorial integrity of all states. In response, General Erich von Ludendorff launched a series of surprise attacks that pushed to within 40 miles (64 kilometers) of Paris, but victory eluded him. Meanwhile, every month brought another 250,000 American troops to the front. In August the Allies counterattacked, and the Germans began a retreat that could not be halted.

In late October Ludendorff resigned, and sailors in the German fleet mutinied. Two weeks later, a new German government signed an armistice. At 11 A.M. on November 11, the guns on the Western Front went silent.

PEACE AND DISLOCATION IN EUROPE, 1919–1929

The Great War lasted four years. Millions of people had died or been disabled; political tensions and resentments lingered; and national economies remained depressed until the mid-1920s. In the late 1920s peace and prosperity finally seemed assured, but this hope proved to be illusory.

The Impact of the War

Between 9 million and 10 million soldiers died in the war, almost all of them young men. Among the dead were about 2 million Germans, 1.7 million Russians, and 1.7 million Frenchmen. Austria-Hungary lost 1.5 million, the British Empire a million, the Ottoman Empire half a million, Italy 460,000, and the United States 115,000. Perhaps twice that many returned home wounded, gassed, or shell-shocked, many of them injured for life.

War and revolution forced almost 2 million Russians, 750,000 Germans, and 400,000 Hungarians to flee their homes. Postwar conflicts also led to the expulsion of hundreds of thousands

Woodrow Wilson President of the United States (1913–1921) and the leading figure at the Paris Peace Conference of 1919. He was unable to persuade the U.S. Congress to ratify the Treaty of Versailles or join the League of Nations.

Fourteen Points A peace program presented to the U.S. Congress by President Woodrow Wilson in January 1918. It called for the evacuation of German-occupied lands, the drawing of borders and the settling of territorial disputes by the self-determination of the affected populations, and the founding of an association of nations to preserve the peace and guarantee their territorial integrity. It was rejected by Germany, but it made Wilson the moral leader of the Allies in the last year of World War I.

of Greeks from Anatolia and Muslims from Greece. Many refugees found shelter in France, which welcomed 1.5 million people to bolster its declining population. About 800,000 immigrants reached the United States before immigration laws passed in 1921 and 1924 closed the door to eastern and southern Europeans. Canada, Australia, and New Zealand adopted similar restrictions on immigration. The Latin American republics welcomed European refugees, but their poverty discouraged potential immigrants.

One unexpected byproduct of the war was the great influenza epidemic of 1918–1919, which started among soldiers heading for the Western Front. This virulent strain infected almost everyone on earth and killed one person in every forty. Half a million Americans perished in the epidemic—five times as many as died in the war. Worldwide, some 20 million people died.

The war also caused serious damage to the environment. No place was ever so completely devastated as the scar across France and Belgium known as the Western Front. The fighting ravaged forests and demolished towns. The earth was gouged by trenches, pitted with craters, and littered with ammunition, broken weapons, chunks of concrete, and the bones of countless soldiers. After the war, it took a decade to clear away the debris, rebuild the towns, and create dozens of military cemeteries with neat rows of crosses stretching for miles.

The Peace Treaties

In early 1919 delegates of the victorious powers met in Paris. The defeated powers were kept out until the treaties were ready for signing. Russia was not invited.

From the start, three men dominated the Paris Peace Conference: U.S. president Wilson, British prime minister David Lloyd George, and French premier Georges Clemenceau (zhorzh cluh-mon-SO). They ignored the Italians, who had joined the Allies in 1915, and paid even less attention to the delegates of smaller European nations. They rejected the Japanese proposal that all races be treated equally. They ignored the Pan-African Congress organized by the African American W. E. B. Du Bois to call attention to the concerns of African peoples around the world. They also ignored the ten thousand other delegates of various nationalities that did not represent sovereign states—the Arab leader Faisal, the Zionist Chaim Weizmann, and several Armenian delegations—but came to Paris to lobby for their causes. They were, in the words of Britain's Foreign Secretary Balfour, "three all-powerful, all-ignorant men, sitting there and carving up continents"[4] (see Map 28.3).

Wilson, a high-minded idealist, wanted to apply the principle of self-determination to European affairs, by which he meant creating nations that reflected ethnic or linguistic divisions. He proposed a **League of Nations**, a world organization to safeguard the peace and foster international cooperation. His idealism clashed with the more hardheaded and self-serving nationalism of the Europeans. Lloyd George insisted that Germany pay a heavy indemnity, while Clemenceau wanted Germany to return Alsace and Lorraine, provinces France had lost in the Franco-Prussian War of 1870–1871.

The result was a series of compromises that satisfied no one. The European powers formed a League of Nations, but the U.S. Congress refused to let the United States join. France recovered Alsace and Lorraine but had to content itself with vague promises of British and American protection if Germany ever rebuilt its army. Britain acquired new territories in Africa and the Middle East but was greatly weakened by human losses and the disruption of its trade.

On June 28, 1919, the German delegates reluctantly signed the **Treaty of Versailles (vuhr-SIGH)**. Germany was forbidden to have an air force and was permitted only a token army and navy. It also gave up large parts of its eastern territory to a newly reconstituted Poland. The Allies made Germany promise to pay reparations to compensate the victors for their losses, but they did not set a figure or a period of time for payment. A "guilt clause," which was to rankle for years to come, obliged the Germans to accept "responsibility for causing all the loss and damage" of the war. The treaty left Germany humiliated but largely intact. Establishing a peace neither of punishment nor of reconciliation, it was one of the great failures in history.

Meanwhile, the Austro-Hungarian Empire fell apart. New countries appeared in the lands lost by Russia, Germany, and Austria-Hungary: Poland, resurrected after over a century; Czechoslovakia, created from the northern third of Austria-Hungary; and Yugoslavia, combining Serbia and the former south Slav provinces of Austria-Hungary. The new boundaries coincided with the major linguistic groups of eastern Europe, but they all contained disaffected minorities. These small nations were safe only as long as Germany and Russia lay defeated and prostrate.

League of Nations International organization founded in 1919 to promote world peace and cooperation but greatly weakened by the refusal of the United States to join. It proved ineffectual in stopping aggression by Italy, Japan, and Germany in the 1930s, and it was superseded by the United Nations in 1945.

Treaty of Versailles The treaty imposed on Germany by France, Great Britain, the United States, and other Allied Powers after World War I. It demanded that Germany dismantle its military and give up some lands to Poland. It was resented by many Germans.

---

[4]David Vital, *A People Apart: The Jews of Europe, 1789–1939* (Oxford: Oxford University Press, 1999), 756.

MAP 28.3 **Territorial Changes in Europe After World War I** Although the heaviest fighting took place in western Europe, the territorial changes there were relatively minor. In eastern Europe, in contrast, the changes were enormous. The disintegration of the Austro-Hungarian Empire and the defeat of Russia allowed a belt of new countries to arise, stretching from Finland in the north to Yugoslavia in the south. © Cengage Learning

Russian Civil War and the New Economic Policy

In December 1918, civil war broke out in Russia. The Communists—as the Bolsheviks called themselves after March 1918—held central Russia, but all the surrounding provinces rose up against them. Counter-revolutionary armies led by former tsarist officers obtained weapons and supplies from the Allies. For three years the two sides burned farms and confiscated crops, causing a famine that claimed 3 million victims, more than had died in Russia in seven years of fighting. By 1921 the Communists had defeated most of their enemies.

Finland, the Baltic states, and Poland remained independent, but the Red Army reconquered other parts of the tsar's empire one by one. In 1922, Ukraine merged with Russia to create the Union of Soviet Socialist Republics (USSR), or Soviet Union. In 1920–1921 the Red Army reconquered the Caucasus and replaced the indigenous leaders with Russians. In 1922 the new Soviet republics of Georgia, Armenia, and Azerbaijan joined the USSR. In this way the Bolsheviks retained control over lands and peoples that had been part of the tsar's empire.

New Economic Policy Policy proclaimed by Vladimir Lenin in 1923 to encourage the revival of the Soviet economy by allowing small private enterprises. Joseph Stalin ended the NEP in 1928 and replaced it with a series of Five-Year Plans.

Years of warfare, revolution, and mismanagement had ruined the Russian economy. Factories and railroads had shut down for lack of fuel, raw materials, and parts. Farmland had been devastated and livestock killed, causing hunger in the cities. Finding himself master of a country in ruin, Lenin announced the **New Economic Policy** (NEP) in 1923. It allowed peasants to own land and sell their crops, private merchants to trade, and private workshops to produce goods and sell them on the free market. Only the biggest businesses, such as banks, railroads, and factories, remained under government ownership.

The relaxation of controls had an immediate effect. Production began to climb, and food and other goods became available. But the NEP reflected no change in the ultimate goals of the Communist Party. It merely provided breathing space, what Lenin called "two steps back to advance one step forward." The Communists had every intention of creating a modern industrial economy without private property. This meant investing in heavy industry and electrification and moving farmers to the cities to work in the new industries. It also meant providing food for the urban workers without spending scarce resources to purchase it from the peasants. In other words, it meant making the peasants, the great majority of the Soviet people, pay for the industrialization of Russia. This policy turned them into bitter enemies of the Communists.

When Lenin died in January 1924, his associates jockeyed for power. The leading contenders were Leon Trotsky, commander of the Red Army, and Joseph Stalin, general secretary of the Communist Party. Trotsky had the support of many "Old Bolsheviks" who had joined the party before the revolution. Having spent years in exile, he saw the revolution as a spark that would ignite a world revolution of the working class. Stalin, the only leading Communist who had never lived abroad, insisted that socialism could survive "in one country."

Stalin filled the party bureaucracy with individuals loyal to himself. In 1926–1927 he had Trotsky expelled for "deviation from the party line," and in January 1929 he forced Trotsky to flee the country. Then, as absolute master of the party, he prepared to industrialize the Soviet Union at breakneck speed.

An Ephemeral Peace

After the enormous sacrifices made during the war, the survivors developed hugely unrealistic expectations and were soon disillusioned. Conservatives in Britain and France longed for a return to the stability of the prewar era—the hierarchy of social classes, prosperous world trade, and European dominance over the rest of the world. All over the rest of the world, people's hopes had been raised by the rhetoric of the war, then dashed by its outcome. In Europe, Germans felt cheated out of a victory that had seemed within their grasp, and Italians were disappointed that their sacrifices had not been rewarded with large territorial gains. Arabs and Indians longed for independence; the Chinese looked for social justice and a lessening of foreign intrusion; and the Japanese hoped to expand their influence in China. In Russia, the Communists were eager to consolidate their power and export their revolution to the rest of the world.

In 1923 Germany suspended reparations payments. In retaliation for the French occupation of the Ruhr, the German government began printing money recklessly, causing the most severe inflation the world had ever seen. Soon German money was worth so little that it took a wheel-barrow full of it to buy a loaf of bread. As Germany teetered on the brink of civil war, radical nationalists tried to overthrow the government. Finally, the German government issued a new currency and promised to resume reparations payments, and the French agreed to withdraw their troops from the Ruhr.

Beginning in 1924 the world enjoyed a few years of calm and prosperity. After the end of the German crisis of 1923, the western European nations became less confrontational, and Germany joined the League of Nations. The vexed issue of reparations also seemed to vanish, as

SECTION REVIEW

- The war caused millions of deaths and injuries and millions of refugees.

- France, Britain, and the United States dominated the Paris Peace Conference, refusing to listen to other voices.

- The United States refused to join the League of Nations, thereby weakening it.

- The Treaty of Versailles humiliated Germany but did not weaken it, thus becoming one of the big failures in history.

- When Austria-Hungary and Russia fell apart, several smaller nations arose in Europe, creating another source of potential conflict.

- After the Bolshevik victory in the Civil War, the Russian economy was in ruins, and Stalin took power.

- After the German hyperinflation of 1923 was resolved, the world economy began to prosper in 1924.

Lenin the Orator The leader of the Bolshevik revolutionaries was a spellbinding orator. Here Lenin is addressing Red Army soldiers in Sverdlov Square, Moscow, in 1920.

Germany borrowed money from New York banks to make its payments to France and Britain, which used the money to repay their wartime loans from the United States. This triangular flow of money, based on credit, stimulated the rapid recovery of the European economies. France began rebuilding its war-torn northern zone; Germany recovered from its hyperinflation; and a boom began in the United States that was to last for five years.

While their economies flourished, governments grew more cautious and businesslike. Even the Communists, after Lenin's death, seemed to give up their attempts to spread revolution abroad. Yet neither Germany nor the Soviet Union accepted its borders with the small nations that had arisen between them. In 1922 they signed a secret pact allowing the German army to conduct maneuvers in Russia (in violation of the Versailles treaty) in exchange for German help in building up Russian industry and military potential.

The League of Nations proved adept at resolving numerous technical issues pertaining to health, labor relations, and postal and telegraph communications. Without U.S. participation, however, sanctions against states that violated League rules carried little weight.

CHINA AND JAPAN: CONTRASTING DESTINIES

China and Japan were both subject to Western pressures, but their modern histories have been strikingly opposite. China clung much longer than Japan to a traditional social structure and economy, then collapsed into chaos and revolution. Japan experienced reform from above (see Chapter 27), acquiring industry and a powerful military, which it used to take advantage of China's weakness. Their different reactions to the pressures of the West put these two great nations on a collision course.

Social and Economic Change

China's population—about 400 million in 1900—was the largest of any country in the world and growing fast. In 1900 peasant plots averaged between 1 and 4 acres (less than 2 hectares) apiece, half as large as they had been two generations earlier. Farming methods had not changed in centuries, and landlords and tax collectors took more than half of the harvest. Most Chinese worked incessantly, survived on a diet of grain and vegetables, and spent their lives in fear of floods, bandits, and tax collectors.

The Bund in Shanghai
On the Bund, the most important street in Shanghai, banks, corporate headquarters, and luxury hotels faced the waterfront where ships from around the world docked. Although Shanghai was China's industrial and commercial center, many of its workers loaded and unloaded ships by hand or pulled wealthy customers in rickshaws.

Bettmann/Corbis

Above the peasantry, Chinese society was divided into many groups and strata. Landowners lived off the rents of their tenants. Officials, chosen through an elaborate examination system, enriched themselves from taxes and the government's monopolies on salt, iron, and other products. Shanghai, China's financial and commercial center, was famous for its wealthy foreigners and its opium addicts, prostitutes, and gangsters.

Although foreign trade represented only a small part of China's economy, contact with the outside world had a tremendous impact on Chinese politics. Young men living in the treaty ports saw no chance for advancement in the old system of examinations and official positions. Some learned foreign ideas in Christian mission schools or abroad. The contrast between the squalor in which most urban residents lived and the luxury of the foreigners' enclaves in the treaty ports sharpened the resentment of educated Chinese.

Japan had few natural resources and very little arable land on which to grow food for its rising population. Typhoons regularly hit its southern regions, and earthquakes periodically shook the country, which lies on the great ring of tectonic fault lines that surround the Pacific Ocean. The Kanto earthquake of 1923 destroyed all of Yokohama and half of Tokyo and killed some 200,000 people.

Japan's population reached 60 million in 1925 and was increasing by a million a year. The crash program of industrialization begun in 1868 by the Meiji oligarchs (see Chapter 27) accelerated during the First World War, when Japan's economy grew four times as fast as western Europe's and eight times faster than China's.

Economic growth aggravated social tensions. The *narikin* ("new rich") affected Western ways and lifestyles that clashed with the austerity of earlier times. In the big cities *mobos* (modern boys) and *mogas* (modern girls) shocked traditionalists with their foreign ways: dancing together, wearing short skirts and tight pants, and behaving like Americans. Students who flirted with dangerous thoughts were called "Marx boys."

The main beneficiaries of prosperity were the *zaibatsu* **(zie-BOT-soo)**, or conglomerates, four of which—Mitsubishi, Sumitomo, Yasuda, and Mitsui—controlled most of Japan's industry and commerce. Farmers, who constituted half of the population, remained poor; in desperation some sold their daughters to textile mills or into domestic service. Labor unions were weak and repressed by the police.

Japanese prosperity depended on foreign trade. The country exported silk and light manufactures and imported almost all its fuel, raw materials, and machine tools, and even some of its food. Though less at the mercy of the weather than China, Japan was much more vulnerable to swings in the world economy.

Revolution and War, 1900–1918

In 1900 China's Empress Dowager Cixi **(TSUH-shee)**, who had seized power in a palace coup two years earlier, encouraged a secret society, the Righteous Fists, or Boxers, to rise up and expel all the foreigners from China. When the Boxers threatened the foreign legation in Beijing, an international force from the Western powers and Japan captured the city and forced China to pay a huge indemnity. Shocked by these events, many Chinese students became convinced that China needed a revolution to get rid of the Qing dynasty and modernize their country.

When Cixi died in 1908, the Revolutionary Alliance led by **Sun Yat-sen (soon yot-SEN)** (1866–1925) prepared to take over. Sun had spent much of his life in Japan, England, and the United States, plotting the overthrow of the Qing dynasty. His ideas were a mixture of nationalism, socialism, and Confucian philosophy. His patriotism, his powerful ambition, and his tenacious spirit attracted a large following.

The military thwarted Sun's plans. After China's defeat in the war with Japan in 1895, the government had agreed to equip the army with modern rifles and machine guns. This, combined with the fact that local armies were beholden to warlords rather than to the central government, created a threatening situation for the Qing. When a regional army mutinied in October 1911, **Yuan Shikai (you-AHN she-KIE)**, the most powerful of the regional generals, refused to defend the Qing. A revolutionary assembly at Nanjing elected Sun Yat-sen president of China in December 1911, but he had no military forces at his command. To avoid a clash with the army, he resigned after a few weeks, and a new national assembly elected Yuan president of the new Chinese republic.

Yuan was an able military leader, but he had no political program. When Sun reorganized his followers into a political party called the **Guomindang (gwo-min-dong)** (National People's Party), Yuan quashed every attempt at creating a Western-style government and harassed Sun's followers. Victory in the first round of the struggle to create a new China went to the military.

Meanwhile, the Japanese were quick to join the Allied side in World War I, since they saw the war as an opportunity to advance their interests while the Europeans were occupied elsewhere. They quickly conquered the German colonies in the northern Pacific and on the coast of China, then turned their attention to the rest of China. In 1915 Japan presented China with Twenty-One Demands, which would have turned it into a virtual protectorate. Britain and the United States persuaded Japan to soften the demands but could not prevent it from keeping the German coastal enclaves and extracting railroad and mining concessions at China's expense. In protest, anti-Japanese riots and boycotts broke out throughout China. Thus began a bitter struggle between the two countries that was to last for thirty years.

Chinese Warlords and the Guomindang, 1919–1929

At the Paris Peace Conference, the great powers accepted Japan's seizure of the German enclaves in China. To many Chinese, this decision was a cruel insult. On May 4, 1919, students demonstrated in front of the Forbidden City of Beijing. Despite a government ban, the May Fourth Movement spread to other parts of China. A new generation was growing up to challenge the old officials, the regional generals, and the foreigners.

Sun Yat-sen tried to make a comeback in Guangzhou (Canton) in the early 1920s. Though not a Communist, he was impressed with the efficiency of Lenin's revolutionary tactics and let a Soviet adviser reorganize the Guomindang along Leninist lines. He also welcomed members of the newly created Chinese Communist Party into the Guomindang.

When Sun died in 1925, the leadership of his party passed to Jiang Jieshi, known in the West as **Chiang Kai-shek (chang kie-shek)** (1887–1975). An officer and director of the military

Sun Yat-sen Chinese nationalist revolutionary, founder and leader of the Guomindang until his death. He attempted to create a liberal democratic political movement in China but was thwarted by military leaders.

Yuan Shikai Chinese general and first president of the Chinese Republic (1912–1916). He stood in the way of the democratic movement led by Sun Yat-sen.

Guomindang Nationalist political party founded on democratic principles by Sun Yat-sen in 1912. After 1925, the party was headed by Chiang Kai-shek, who turned it into an increasingly authoritarian movement.

Chiang Kai-shek Chinese military and political leader. Succeeded Sun Yat-sen as head of the Guomindang in 1925; headed the Chinese government from 1928 to 1949; fought against the Chinese Communists and Japanese invaders. After 1949 he headed the Chinese nationalist government in Taiwan.

academy, Chiang trained several hundred young officers who remained loyal to him thereafter. In 1927 he determined to defeat the regional warlords. As his army moved north from its base in Canton, he briefly formed an alliance with the Communists. Once his troops occupied Shanghai, however, he crushed the labor unions and decimated the Communists, whom he considered a threat. He then defeated or co-opted most of the other warlords and established a dictatorship.

Chiang's government issued ambitious plans to build railroads, develop agriculture and industry, and modernize China from the top down. However, his followers were neither competent administrators nor ruthless modernizers. Instead, his government attracted thousands of opportunists whose goals were to "become officials and get rich" by taxing and plundering businesses. In the countryside tax collectors and landowners squeezed the peasants ever harder, even in times of natural disasters. What little money reached the government's coffers went to the military. Thus for twenty years after the fall of the Qing, China remained mired in poverty, subject to corrupt officials and the whims of nature.

> ### SECTION REVIEW
>
> - Japan prospered during the war and quickly modernized; it also began preying on China.
>
> - When the Qing dynasty ended in 1911, the regional general Yuan Shikai took over China and repressed Sun Yat-sen's party, the Guomindang.
>
> - After Sun Yat-sen's death, Chiang Kai-shek established a corrupt military dictatorship.

THE NEW MIDDLE EAST

After the war, the Arab peoples expected to have a say in the outcome of the Great War. But the victorious French and British planned to treat the Middle East like a territory open to colonial rule. The result was a legacy of instability that has persisted to this day.

The Mandate System

At the Paris Peace Conference, France, Britain, Italy, and Japan proposed to divide the former German colonies and the territories of the Ottoman Empire among themselves, but their ambitions clashed with President Wilson's ideal of national self-determination. Eventually, the victors arrived at a compromise solution called the **mandate system**: colonial rulers would administer the territories but would be accountable to the League of Nations for "the material and moral well-being and the social progress of the inhabitants."

Class C Mandates—those with the smallest populations—were treated as colonies by their conquerors. South Africa replaced Germany in Southwest Africa (now Namibia); Britain, Australia, New Zealand, and Japan took over the German islands in the Pacific. Class B Mandates, larger than Class C but still underdeveloped, were to be ruled for the benefit of their inhabitants under League of Nations supervision. Most of Germany's African colonies, including Tanganyika, Cameroon, and Togo, fell into this category.

The Arab-speaking territories of the old Ottoman Empire were Class A Mandates. The League of Nations declared that they had "reached a state of development where their existence as independent nations can be provisionally recognized subject to the rendering of administrative advice and assistance by a Mandatory, until such time as they are able to stand alone." While Arabs interpreted this ambiguous wording as a promise of independence, Britain and France sent troops into the region "for the benefit of its inhabitants." Palestine (divided now into Israel in the west, Jordan in the east, and the Occupied West Bank in between) and Iraq (formerly Mesopotamia) became British mandates; France claimed Syria and Lebanon (see Map 28.4 on page 732). (See Diversity and Dominance: The Middle East After World War I.)

mandate system Allocation of former German colonies and Ottoman possessions to the victorious powers after World War I, to be administered under League of Nations supervision.

The Rise of Modern Turkey

At the end of the war, as the Ottoman Empire teetered on the brink of collapse, France, Britain, and Italy saw an opportunity to expand their empires, and Greece eyed those parts of Anatolia inhabited by Greeks. In 1919 French, British, Italian, and Greek forces occupied Constantinople and parts of Anatolia. By the Treaty of Sèvres (1920) the Allies made the sultan give up most of his lands.

absolutely unmolested opportunity of autonomous development. . . .

When the war ended, the victorious Allies assembled in Paris to determine, among other things, the fate of the former Arab provinces of the Ottoman Empire. Arab leaders had reason to doubt the intentions of the great powers, especially Britain and France. When the Allies decided to create mandates in the Arab territories on the grounds that the Arab peoples were not ready for independence, Arab leaders expressed their misgivings, as in the following statement:

Memorandum of the General Syrian Congress, July 2, 1919

We the undersigned members of the General Syrian Congress, meeting in Damascus on Wednesday, July 2nd, 1919, made up of representatives from the three Zones, viz., The Southern, Eastern, and Western, provided with credentials and authorizations by the inhabitants of our various districts, Moslems, Christians, and Jews, have agreed upon the following statement of the desires of the people of the country who have elected us. . . .

1. We ask absolutely complete political independence for Syria. . . .
3. Considering the fact that the Arabs inhabiting the Syrian area are not naturally less gifted than other more advanced races and that they are by no means less developed than the Bulgarians, Serbians, Greeks, and Roumanians at the beginning of their independence, we protest against Article 22 of the Covenant of the League of Nations, placing us among the nations in their middle stage of development which stand in need of a mandatory power.
4. . . . relying on the declarations of President Wilson that his object in waging war was to put an end to the ambition of conquest and colonization, . . . and believing that the American Nation is furthest from any thought of colonization and has no political ambition in our country, we will seek the technical and economic assistance from the United States of America, provided that such assistance does not exceed 20 years.

5. In the event of America not finding herself in a position to accept our desire for assistance, we will seek this assistance from Great Britain, also provided that such does not prejudice our complete independence and unity of our country and that the duration of such assistance does not exceed that mentioned in the previous article.
6. We do not acknowledge any right claimed by the French Government in any part whatever of our Syrian country and refuse that she should assist us or have a hand in our country under any circumstances and in any place.
7. We opposed the pretensions of the Zionists to create a Jewish commonwealth in the southern part of Syria, known as Palestine, and oppose Zionist migration to any part of our country; for we do not acknowledge their title but consider them a grave peril to our people from the national, economical, and political points of view. Our Jewish compatriots shall enjoy our common rights and assume our common responsibilities.

QUESTIONS FOR ANALYSIS

1. Was there a contradiction between Balfour's proposal to establish "a national home for the Jewish people" and the promise "that nothing shall be done which may prejudice the civil and religious rights of existing non-Jewish communities in Palestine"? If so, why did he make two contradictory promises?

2. How would Woodrow Wilson's statements about "an absolutely unmolested opportunity of autonomous development" apply to Palestine?

3. Why did the delegates to the General Syrian Congress object to the plan to create mandates in the former Ottoman provinces? What alternatives did they offer?

4. Why did the delegates object to the creation of a Jewish commonwealth?

Sources: The Balfour Declaration, *The Times* (London), November 9, 1917. Memorandum of the General Syrian Congress, *Foreign Relations of the United States: Paris Peace Conference*, vol. 12 (Washington, DC: Government Printing Office, 1919), 780–781.

women became schoolteachers or nurses. Secular educational opportunities varied widely from Lebanon, where French influence was strong; to Iran, whose first university was established in 1933; to Saudi Arabia, which strongly resisted Western influences.

The region in closest contact with Europe was the Maghrib—Algeria, Tunisia, and Morocco—which the French army considered its private domain. Alongside the old native quarters, the French built modern neighborhoods inhabited mainly by Europeans. France had occupied Algeria since 1830 and had encouraged European immigration. The settlers owned the best lands and monopolized government jobs and businesses, while Arabs and Berbers remained poor and suffered intense discrimination.

MAP 28.4 **Territorial Changes in the Middle East After World War I** The defeat and dismemberment of the Ottoman Empire at the end of World War I resulted in an entirely new political map of the region. The Turkish Republic inherited Anatolia and a small piece of the Europe, while the Ottoman Empire's Arab provinces were divided between France and Great Britain. Only Iran and Egypt did not change. © Cengage Learning

The British attempted to control the Middle East with a mixture of bribery and intimidation. They made Faisal, leader of the Arab Revolt, king of Iraq and used aerial bombing of rebellious nomads to enforce their will. In 1931 they reached an agreement with King Faisal's government: official independence for Iraq in exchange for the right to keep two air bases, a military alliance, and an assured flow of petroleum. France, meanwhile, sent thousands of troops to Syria and Lebanon to crush nationalist uprisings.

Hulton Archive/Getty Images

The Jewish Settlement of Palestine Thousands of Jews fleeing persecution and discrimination in Europe settled on the land and founded *kibbutzim*, or collective farms. In this picture taken in 1912, an eighty-four-year-old immigrant from Russia learns to plow the land.

In Egypt, as in Iraq, the British substituted a phony independence for official colonialism. They declared Egypt independent in 1922 but reserved the right to station troops along the Suez Canal to secure their link with India in the event of war. Most galling to the Wafd (Nationalist) Party was the British attempt to remove Egyptian troops from Sudan, a land many Egyptians considered a colony of Egypt. Britain was successful in keeping Egypt in limbo—neither independent nor a colony—thanks to an alliance with King Fuad and conservative Egyptian politicians who feared both secular and religious radicalism.

Before the war, a Jewish minority lived in Palestine, as in other Arab countries. Small numbers of Jews had immigrated to Palestine following their expulsion from Spain in 1492, and a trickle continued into the nineteenth century. As soon as Palestine became a British mandate in 1920, however, many more came from Europe, encouraged by the Balfour Declaration of 1917. Those supporting a socialist version of Zionism established *kibbutzim*, or communal farms, while nonsocialists belonging to the Revisionist wing of the Zionist movement preferred to settle in the cities. But purchases of land by Jewish agencies angered the indigenous Arabs, especially tenant farmers who were evicted to make room for settlers, and in 1920–1921 riots erupted between Jews and Arabs. When far more Jewish immigrants arrived than they had anticipated, the British tried to limit immigration, thereby alienating the Jews without mollifying the Arabs. Increasingly, Jews arrived without papers, smuggled in by militant Zionist organizations. In the 1930s the country was torn by strikes and guerrilla warfare that the British could not control. In the process, Britain earned the hatred of both sides.

SECTION REVIEW

- Former Arab provinces of the Ottoman Empire became "mandates" under French or British control.

- Mustafa Kemal Atatürk expelled the Greek minority from Anatolia and founded the Turkish Republic, then pushed it toward secular reform.

- As Middle Eastern society modernized, the Arabs became more politically active but had to endure the mandate system.

- Jewish immigration to Palestine caused growing tensions between Jews, Arabs, and the British.

Oil and War

New motorized weapons such as tanks and airplanes not only proved their worth in World War I, but also pointed to the future. Nevertheless, even though cavalry units became obsolete in the face of machine-gun fire, millions of horses were used to pull field artillery and transport supplies. Britain alone lost almost half a million horses in the fighting.

Horses were still the mainstay of artillery and logistics transportation during World War II. Germany used 2.75 million and the Soviet Union 3.5 million. But gasoline engines had by then become so important for fighting machines that whole campaigns were fought to acquire petroleum reserves.

At sea, horses were not an alternative. Steamships fueled by oil, which was better for that purpose than coal, were in use by 1894. Several European navies showed an interest, and by 1904 the destroyer fleet of Great Britain's Royal Navy, the world's paramount maritime power, was oil-fired. Cruisers and battleships built after 1912 were all designed to burn oil.

This created a problem. Britain had abundant coal resources but no oil, not even in its colonies. Britain's oil came primarily from John D. Rockefeller's Standard Oil Company or from the Royal-Dutch Shell Company, which operated wells in the Dutch East Indies. Winston Churchill, then First Lord of the Admiralty, did not care for this dependency, even though the "Shell" part of the latter's name reflected Britain's 40 percent share in the company.

When a British firm operating on a concession granted in 1901 to a British mining tycoon named William Knox D'Arcy struck oil in Iran in 1908, Churchill purchased for the government a controlling interest in the company that was created to exploit it: APOC, the Anglo-Persian Oil Company (later the Anglo-Iranian Oil Company). In 1912 APOC also acquired a controlling interest in what became the Iraq Petroleum Company after a major find around Kirkuk in northern Iraq.

The Royal Navy was now set to continue its rule of the seas undaunted by supply problems, but Britain's strategic security had become dependent on control of Iran, a nominally independent country, and of Iraq, a part of the Ottoman Empire. Oil supplies had become an essential feature of world military calculation, and with the accelerating spread of motorized land transport after World War I, the civilian economies of the industrialized world became equally dependent.

This dependency lies behind a myriad military and political decisions made over the subsequent decades, making the division between producing countries with surplus oil to sell and consuming countries reliant on a steady supply of imported fuel a crucial factor in world affairs.

British Warship Maneuvering This camouflage-painted, smoke-spouting vessel symbolizes the supremacy of Britain's navy in the World War I era. The British shift from coal to oil as a naval fuel triggered a change in petroleum supply-and-demand patterns that would strongly affect world politics in the following decades.

Hulton Archive/Getty Images

CONCLUSION

In the late 1920s it seemed as though the victors in the Great War might reestablish the prewar prosperity and European dominance of the globe. But the spirit of the 1920s was not real peace; instead it was the eye of a hurricane. The Great Depression and World War II were in the offing.

The Great War caused a major realignment among the nations of the world. France and Britain, the two leading colonial powers, emerged economically weakened despite their victory. The war brought defeat and humiliation to Germany but did not reduce its military or industrial potential. It destroyed the old regime of Russia, leading to civil war and revolution from which the victorious powers sought to isolate themselves. Two other old empires—the Austro-Hungarian and the Ottoman—were divided into many smaller and weaker nations.

Japan took advantage of the European conflict to develop its industries and press its demands on a China weakened by domestic turmoil and social unrest. The United States emerged as the most prosperous and potentially most powerful nation, restrained only by the isolationist sentiments of many Americans.

In the Middle East, the fall of the Ottoman Empire awakened aspirations of nationhood among the Turkish, Arab, Armenian, and Kurdish inhabitants and Jewish immigrants. These aspirations were thwarted when France and Great Britain succeeded in imposing their rule upon the former Ottoman lands, giving rise to conflicts and bitter enmities.

KEY TERMS

Western Front p. 717
Faisal p. 719
Theodore Herzl p. 719
Balfour Declaration p. 720
Bolsheviks p. 720

Vladimir Lenin p. 720
Woodrow Wilson p. 721
Fourteen Points p. 721
League of Nations p. 722
Treaty of Versailles p. 722

New Economic Policy p. 724
Sun Yat-sen p. 727
Yuan Shikai p. 727
Guomindang p. 727

Chiang Kai-shek p. 727
mandate system p. 728
Atatürk p. 729

SUGGESTED READING

Bianco, Lucien. *Origins of the Chinese Revolution, 1915–1949.* 1971. A succinct account of the rise of communism in China.

Figes, Orlando. *A People's Tragedy: The Russian Revolution, 1891–1924.* 1996. A well-written overview of the Russian Revolution.

Fromkin, David. *A Peace to End All Peace.* 1989. An excellent introduction of twentieth-century Middle Eastern history.

Higonnet, Margaret, et al., eds. *Behind the Lines: Gender and the Two World Wars.* 1987. Describes the contributions of women during wartime.

Hughes, H. Stuart. *Consciousness and Society: The Reorientation of European Social Thought, 1890–1930.* 1958. An intellectual and cultural history of early-twentieth-century Europe.

Keegan, John. *The First World War.* 1999. A short account of the war by an eminent military historian.

Remarque, Erich Maria. *All Quiet on the Western Front.* 1928. The classic novel about war from the soldiers' viewpoint.

Roberts, A. D., ed. *Cambridge History of Africa,* vol. 7, *1905–1940.* 1986. A complete but readable analysis of early-twentieth-century African history.

Sontag, Raymond. *A Broken World, 1919–1939.* 1971. Describes how the problems left by the First World War led to the Second World War.

Tuchman, Barbara. *The Guns of August.* 1962. A classic and very readable account of the first month of the Great War.

Go to the History CourseMate website for primary source links, study tools, and review materials for this chapter. CourseMate www.cengagebrain.com

Chapter Outline

Rickshaw Traffic   Invented in 1869, the rickshaw transformed urban life in East Asia and the lands bordering on the Indian Ocean.

Revolutions in Living, 1900–1950

In 1869 three Japanese businessmen—an entrepreneurial former cook, a green-grocer, and a wagon builder—responded to government concerns about urban congestion and applied for a license to build a *jinriksha* ("man-power-vehicle"). They described it as "a little seat in the Western style, mounted on wheels so that it can be pulled about. It does not shake as much as the usual cart, and it is easy to turn round. It will not hinder other traffic, and since it can be pulled by one person, it is very cheap."[1] Their first vehicles, which quickly came to be called rickshaws, appeared a year later. A year after that, in 1871, Japan enacted its first patent law, and the three applied for exclusive manufacturing rights. However, so many workshops were by then turning out rickshaws that their application was denied.

An alternative claim of invention arose when an irascible American Baptist missionary named Jonathan Goble petitioned the Tokyo Metropolitan Government to grant him a share of the tax levied on the thirty thousand rickshaws then officially registered. He claimed to be the inventor, and a number of Westerners living in Japan supported him, some stating that Goble had built the first rickshaw for his ailing wife, and others that he had designed it at the request of a Japanese officer for use in the "imperial pleasure gardens."

The Japanese version of the story, which was reinforced in 1900 by government cash awards to the three businessmen, is highly credible since two-wheeled carts with a similar arrangement of shafts for pulling were in use on Japanese farms and for transporting loads well before European carriages came to be known through the "opening of Japan" in the 1850s (see Chapter 27). Moreover, Japan became the export source for rickshaws throughout Asia and the Indian Ocean region. The Goble story, however, made better sense to Westerners, who had a hard time crediting non-Europeans with inventiveness.

People today often look back and marvel at the incredible material changes their parents and grandparents lived through in the twentieth century. Movies, radio, television, telephones, automobiles, and airplanes all developed during the first half of the century. Norms of daily life rooted in the nineteenth century gave way to new assumptions about many aspects of human life.

Yet many of these assumptions applied more to the industrialized countries of Europe and North America than to those parts of the world that before World War II consisted mostly of imperial possessions or, in the case of Latin America, politically independent countries whose economies were dominated by European or American businesses and investors. Automobiles may have changed dating habits in the United States, but not in China or India, where few private individuals owned cars. Telephones may have put people in easy contact with family and friends in Europe, but not in Africa, where imperialist economic interests saw no profit in stringing copper wire throughout the land.

---

[1]F. Calvin Parker, *Jonathan Goble of Japan: Marine, Missionary, Maverick* (Lanham, MD: University Press of America, 1990), 222.

Changes in the way people lived in the West between 1900 and 1950 will be discussed later in this chapter. First we will consider how other parts of the world experienced change in more limited ways, often incorporating local cultural traditions that took their societies in distinctive directions (see Material Culture: Bells, Gongs, and Drums).

NEW TECHNOLOGY OUTSIDE THE INDUSTRIALIZED WORLD

Urbanization

According to one estimate, Constantinople, the capital of the Byzantine Empire, had a population of 200,000 in 1000 C.E. and was the only European city to be ranked among the world's ten largest cities. By 1500 Paris had joined Constantinople on the list, and by 1800 so had London. Beijing, the most populous city, then had over 1 million inhabitants, about twice as many as the largest city in 1000.

Industrialization deeply affected population distribution in the course of the nineteenth century. By 1900 all of the world's top ten cities were European or American except for Tokyo. The largest, London, had 6.4 million inhabitants. European dominance waned in the first half of the twentieth century. In 1950 Shanghai, Buenos Aires, Tokyo, and Calcutta (now Kolkata) were on the list, and 12.4 million people resided in the largest city, New York. Today, two European cities, Moscow and Istanbul (formerly Constantinople), make the top ten. Of the rest, four are in China and two in South Asia. Tehran (Iran) and Sao Paulo (Brazil) round out the list. New York is nineteenth. The largest city, Shanghai, has a population of 17.8 million.

In Asia and the Indian Ocean basin, the rickshaw (see chapter opening) contributed to this transformation of urban life just as streetcars had earlier done in Europe and America. Before 1850, Japanese civilians either walked or were carried in plain (*kago*) or fancy (*norimono*) palanquins, small seats or cabins suspended from poles carried on the shoulders of bearers. A palanquin required a minimum of two men, or more if the trip was long or the rider wanted to display his or her wealth. The rickshaw cut the expense of personal transport in half and doubled its speed because a rickshaw puller, unlike palanquin bearers, usually ran rather than walked. Rickshaw transport effectively enlarged the area of cities that had previously been scaled for pedestrian access, just as public transport made it possible for Bostonians and Londoners to live away from the city center. Rickshaws also avoided the plague of Western cities: horse manure.

The technical specifications of the first rickshaws have not survived, but the claim that "it does not shake as much as the usual cart" suggests that what made the vehicle a sensational success from the very start was the provision of leaf springs (arced steel strips bound at the ends to form an ellipse). The first leaf spring design had been patented in England in 1804 and was probably in use on carriages imported into Japan in the 1850s. Early drawings and photographs of rickshaws consistently show them with leaf springs.

Japanese-made rickshaws stimulated the growth of big Asian cities like Shanghai, Beijing, Singapore, Calcutta, and Bombay and reached across the Indian Ocean to Madagascar and South Africa. Tens of thousands of unskilled workers flocked to these cities to become rickshaw pullers in the way that European villagers entered the urban economy by way of unskilled manufacturing jobs. Like European mill-hands, rickshaw pullers endured miserable living conditions and occasionally banded together in strikes, particularly in opposition to streetcar companies that threatened their livelihoods. However, streetcars could not deliver passengers directly to their homes or take children safely to school, so the rickshaws survived and evolved into the pedicabs and auto-rickshaws that are still common today.

The rickshaw provides a rare example of an Asian invention transforming urban life in ways unfamiliar to Europeans and Americans. The more frequently told stories focus on Western inventions like railroads and automobiles transforming the non-Western world. Yet even there, the innovations of the Industrial Revolution (see Chapter 22) that imperialist governments and businesses exported to their colonies affected the non-Western world differently than later innovations that spread worldwide in the first half of the twentieth century. Whereas railroads and automobiles required steel mills and factories, other new inventions were comparatively inexpensive and adaptable to local customs.

CHRONOLOGY

	Technology	India	Africa	Latin America
	1869 Rickshaw invented in Japan			
1900	1903 Wright brothers fly first airplane 1907 Bakelite, first plastic, invented 1912 first feature-length movie in India 1913 Henry Ford introduces assembly-line production 1915–1920 Women gain vote in Norway, Russia, Canada, Germany, Britain, and United States	1905 Viceroy Curzon splits Bengal; mass demonstrations 1906 Muslims found All-India Muslim League 1911 British transfer capital from Calcutta to Delhi	1900s Railroads connect ports to the interior 1912 African National Congress founded	
1920	1920 Commercial radio begins in United States 1923 Margaret Sanger opens first birth control clinic 1925 Commercial radio begins in Japan	1919 Amritsar Massacre 1929 Gandhi leads Walk to the Sea	1920s J. E. Casely Hayford organizes political movement in British West Africa	1928 Plutarco Elías Calles founds Mexico's National Revolutionary Party
1930	1932 Empire State Building opens 1936 Olympic games in Berlin	1930s Gandhi calls for independence; he is repeatedly arrested 1939 British bring India into World War II	1939–1945 A million Africans serve in World War II	1930–1945 Getulio Vargas, dictator of Brazil 1934–1940 Lázaro Cárdenas, president of Mexico 1938 Cárdenas nationalizes Mexican oil industry; Vargas proclaims Estado Novo in Brazil
1940		1940 Muhammad Ali Jinnah demands a separate nation for Muslims 1947 Partition and independence of India and Pakistan		1943 Juan Perón leads military coup in Argentina 1946 Perón elected president of Argentina

Electricity

Electricity, produced in industrial quantities since the 1890s (see Chapter 27), transformed home life in Europe and North America by attracting private customers. Middle-class home-owners wanted to replace their gas lamps with tungsten filament incandescent bulbs, which improved greatly in brightness and durability between 1904 and World War I. Household items like electric irons, fans, washing machines, and hot plates followed.

Outside of Europe and North America, however, the small size of the middle class made private subscription a poor business model. Electrical generators might be acquired to run factories or light a ruler's palace, but an appliance-oriented lifestyle was slow to develop. Consequently the foot-operated sewing machine, which had undergone a long development in America and Europe in the nineteenth century, had a wider global spread before World War II than any other appliance. The enormous Japanese electronics company Brother Industries, Ltd. began in 1908 as the Yasui Sewing Machine Company.

Bells, Gongs, and Drums

Thunder, the roar of surf, the gusting of wind—these were the loudest sounds normally heard in prehistoric communities. Other natural sounds were quieter: birdsong, insect whines, the occasional animal bark, grunt, or snuffle. The loudest sounds humans made for themselves were probably shouts, cries, and the pounding of wood and stone. Some loud sounds, such as thunderclaps or the braying of donkeys and the crowing of roosters, gave rise to strong feelings. Thunder seemed to be of supernatural origin, the cockcrow was associated with dawn, and the braying of donkeys, at least in the imaginations of ancient peoples in Egypt and western Asia, was a token of death and the underworld.

When humans devised their own ways of producing loud sounds, they often used them in religious rituals or as symbols of high social rank. Drums were undoubtedly the first man-made devices for making loud sounds. Though the date of 6000 B.C.E. is often given for the first drums, the generally poor preservation of wood and skin in archaeological sites makes it likely that they were in use much earlier but left no identifiable remains. Drumming retained its great ceremonial and political importance in sub-Saharan Africa and pre-Columbian America down to the modern era.

Bells and gongs, the latter either flat metal disks or upward-opening bowls, come much later. Bronze made from copper and tin, the preferred metal for these instruments, does not appear in western Asian archaeological sites before 3000 B.C.E. Bronze in China is almost as early, and it shows up somewhat later in tin-rich Southeast Asia.

Magnificent bronze drums were made and exported from Vietnam after 1000 B.C.E. But bells were more important than drums in early Chinese culture. By the late first millennium B.C.E., court ceremonies and musical performers utilized sets of tuned bells covering five octaves. Some could produce two separate notes, depending on where they were struck. Gongs appeared in China around 500 C.E. and spread from there to Southeast Asia, where they still play a central role in Indonesian percussion orchestras. Centuries later, when Buddhism spread in East Asia, bells became an essential part of Buddhist worship.

Though tin bronze may have originated in western Asia, large bells were not greatly used in ancient Egypt and Mesopotamia or in Greco-Roman antiquity. Following Jewish precedent, early Christian communities in Egypt and Syria summoned their congregations with trumpets. Around the sixth century C.E., rhythmic pounding with a mallet on a long piece of wood or metal called a "semantron" superseded trumpet calls in Eastern Orthodox churches. This device is still used in some Russian Orthodox monasteries.

Christian churches may have used bells as early as 500 C.E., but evidence of bell use becomes strong only a century later, mostly in connection with Irish churches. The Latin word *clocca*, from which English *clock* derives, comes from the Irish word *clog*, meaning "bell." More than sixty early Irish bells still survive, the earliest made of iron, with bronze becoming the preferred metal by 900 C.E.

Early Protestant claims that Catholic ceremonies for blessing bells were superstitious may reflect the fact that many rural communities did attribute supernatural powers to bells. As late as the eighteenth century many French villagers believed that they could ward off crop-damaging hail by ringing their church bell. At the end of the century, such beliefs contributed to villages defying the demand of the secular French Republic that all bells be melted down and the metal recast as cannon. Well into the nineteenth century, France witnessed many struggles between secular and religious officials—mayors and priests—for control of the village bell.

Some bells have gained symbolic importance more recently. In 1871 the New York Stock Exchange adopted a Chinese gong to signal its daily opening and closing in place of the traditional gavel. In 1903 a bell replaced the gong, but the "opening bell" became a media event only in 1995, when guests ranging from corporate executives and foreign dignitaries to basketball star LeBron James, actress Sarah Jessica Parker, and scourge of the universe Darth Vader were invited to mount the podium and perform the ceremony.

QUESTIONS FOR ANALYSIS

1. What comparison can you make between the sound environment of a modern city and that of the preindustrial countryside?
2. What makes the sound of a bell, gong, or drum more impressive than an equally loud automobile alarm or steam whistle?
3. Do drums have a greater or smaller emotional impact than bells and gongs?

Vanni/Art Resource, NY

Bell Pavilion in Nara, Japan   The Bell Pavilion at the Todai-ji Temple in Nara houses the biggest bell in Japan, cast in 752. Like all wooden buildings in Japan, the pavilion itself has been rebuilt several times, most recently in 1966–1967.

New Media

Auguste and Louis Lumière
French inventors of motion pictures whose equipment demonstrations abroad stimulated the growth of cinema around the world.

Auguste and Louis Lumière projected the first motion pictures in Paris in 1895. The following year the brothers held demonstrations in Bombay, London, Montreal, New York, and Buenos Aires. Other exhibitors soon showed off the new medium in Johannesburg, Alexandria, and Tokyo. Unlike expensive innovations like automobiles and airplanes, motion pictures could be made cheaply using fairly inexpensive equipment. The idea of moving images appealed just as much to non-European audiences as it did to Europeans.

The Art Archive/Musée Français de la Photographie Bievres/Gianni Dagli Orti

Lumière Brothers Camera   In this simple and lightweight early model turning the crank caused the chain drive to pull the film in front of the lens from a roll suspended above the device. The larger the roll of film (not shown), the longer the resulting movie.

The first experiments with film in India appeared two years after the Lumières' visit. The first full-length feature, screening in 1912, told the story of a legendary Indian king from the classical Sanskrit epics. Movies also caught on quickly in Japan, which had a tradition of magic lantern displays. Local theatrical traditions like *kabuki* and *bunraku* influenced the style and content of the earliest films just as early European film makers concentrated on reproducing stage plays. Japanese films of the silent era were usually accompanied by spoken narration, as were the films the Japanese exported to Formosa (now Taiwan), a Chinese-speaking island that came under Japanese control in 1895.

American and European silent films found ready markets around the world, but non-Western film making flourished in some countries. Moreover, the impact of film was not limited to entertainment. Documentary films and especially newsreels became major sources of information. Filmed news coverage of key political figures like Mahatma Gandhi in India played a major role in their success (see Diversity and Dominance: Gandhi and the New Media), especially after the advent of sound in the late 1920s.

Practical photography began in Europe in 1839, and forty years later an efficient way was developed for printing photographs in newspapers. Photographic images soon became common throughout the world, often as picture postcards. European photographers, however, tended to look upon Asians and Africans, particularly seminude women, as exotic subjects and thereby catered to common European assumptions about racial superiority.

Non-European photographers rarely became known outside their home countries. Nevertheless, they produced thousands of images that are now used to reconstruct history. Chinese newspapers and magazines usually published images without naming the photographers. A dozen early photographers became famous in Japan, however, possibly because popular woodblock prints had created an audience for artistic images of everyday scenes. In Iran, the most avid photographer was the ruler Naser al-Din Shah (r. 1848–1896). Despite Muslim clerical disapproval of making images of human beings, the shah shot some forty-eight thousand pictures, including members of his own family and even nudes and prisoners.

Photography enabled newspapers, magazines, and advertisements to inform even illiterate people about what their country and their fellow citizens looked like, who was ruling them, and how traditional elites and prosperous Europeanized families lived. Thus photography contributed to feelings of national identity and common experience even in lands that were internally divided by language and ethnicity.

Radio had served ships and the military during the Great War as a means of point-to-point telecommunication. After the war, amateurs used surplus radio equipment to talk to one another. The first commercial station began broadcasting in Pittsburgh in 1920. By 1924 six hundred stations were broadcasting news, sports, soap operas, and advertising to homes throughout North America. By 1930, 12 million families owned radio receivers. In Europe radio spread more slowly because governments reserved the airwaves for cultural and official programs and taxed radio owners to pay for the service.

SECTION REVIEW

- Urbanization expanded rapidly in East and South Asia.

- Rickshaws transformed the transportation systems of cities in East Asia, South Asia, and the Indian Ocean littoral.

- Cinema spread rapidly outside Europe and incorporated local performance traditions.

- Photography also spread, both for artistic expression and for newspaper and magazine articles and advertisements.

- Radio developed commercially in Japan, as it did in the United States; but in most European colonies it was controlled by the government.

Rural Japan Before World War I This village scene from Japan reflects the taste for landscapes and ordinary life typical of the earliest photographers in Japan, both European and Japanese. The popularity of such scenes in earlier colored woodcuts may have influenced the choice of such subjects.

SSPL/Getty Images

Japan followed the North American model of commercial radio. The first AM station began broadcasting in 1925, and by 1941 there were almost fifty stations organized in two networks covering both the home islands and imperial possessions in Formosa (Taiwan), Korea, and Manchuria. Programming increasingly reflected the militarist tendencies of the government, but it also included Japanese and classical Western music, English lessons, exercise programs, and tips for urban gardeners.

Radio development in Shanghai was also robust, with 100,000 receivers in use by 1936. Most were imported, but small local manufacturers contributed to the new fad. British authorities in India and Africa, on the other hand, established central control of radio transmissions and programming. French colonial administrations did likewise.

NEW WAYS OF LIVING IN THE INDUSTRIALIZED WORLD

World War I left a deep imprint on European society and culture. After the war, class and gender distinctions began to fade. Many European aristocrats had died on the battlefields, and with them went their class's long domination of the army, the diplomatic corps, and other elite sectors of society. The United States and Canada had never had as rigidly defined a class structure as European societies or as elaborate a set of traditions and manners. On both sides of the Atlantic, engineers, businessmen, lawyers, and other professionals rose to prominence while department stores, banks, insurance companies, and other businesses increased their white-collar workforce. At the same time government administrative jobs expanded in the areas of housing, transportation, schools, public health, and other services. The ambitions and tastes of the rapidly expanding middle class became increasingly evident in the postwar period, while the role of the working class remained about the same.

Identity

As the centuries-old European distinction between aristocrats and commoners faded in significance, standardized forms of identity became more common. An American passport issued in 1905 was a single 12- by 17-inch piece of paper bearing the seal of the State Department, the secretary of state's signature in facsimile, and in lieu of a photograph, one- or two-word descriptions of the holder's forehead, eyes, nose, mouth, chin, complexion, and facial shape. A Chinese passport of the same period was entirely in Chinese. Crossing international borders became a more complicated process during World War I, and in 1920 the League of Nations held the first of several conferences that standardized the now familiar photograph-and-booklet design.

Prussia in 1910 was the first country to require every automobile operator to have a driver's license, and the practice spread rapidly. In 1913 New Jersey was the first American state to institute such a requirement. These documents eventually became standard proofs of identity in countries that did not issue identity cards to their citizens. Social Security cards began to be issued in the United States in the 1930s, and they too acquired some of the functions of identity cards. In other countries, such as Germany, Great Britain, and Japan, national health system documents took on similar roles.

Hereditary titles and listings of noble lineages in reference books like *Burke's Peerage* continued in use among the nobility. However, the idea increasingly spread that a person's identity was tied to his or her name (without title), a photograph, and one or more official numbers issued by government agencies. This idea spread much more slowly outside of Europe and North America.

An additional form of personal identification came forth in 1897 when the world's first fingerprint bureau opened under British auspices in Calcutta (Kolkata). Two Indians, Azizul Haque and Hem Chandra Bose, devised the system of determining every human being's unique identity, but it became known as the Henry System from the name of their British supervisor. Scotland Yard adopted the system in 1901, and the New York Police Department did so in 1906.

Women's Lives

Women's lives changed more rapidly in the 1920s than ever before. Although the end of the war saw the end of wartime job opportunities, some women remained in the workforce. The young and wealthy enjoyed more personal freedoms than their mothers had before the war; they drove cars, played sports, traveled alone, and smoked in public. For others, the upheavals of war brought more suffering than liberation. Millions of women had lost their male kin in the war or in the great influenza epidemic. After the war many single women led lives of loneliness and destitution.

In Europe and North America advocates of women's rights had been demanding the vote for women since the 1890s. New Zealand was the only nation to grant women the vote before the twentieth century. Women in Norway were the first to obtain it in Europe, in 1915. Russian women followed in 1917, and Canadians and Germans in 1918. Britain gave women over age thirty the vote in 1918 and later extended it to younger women. The Nineteenth Amendment to the U.S. Constitution granted suffrage to American women in 1920. Women in Turkey began voting in 1934. Everywhere, their influence on politics was less radical than feminists had hoped and conservatives had feared. Even when it did not transform politics and government, however, the right to vote was a potent symbol.

Women were active in many other areas besides the suffrage movement. On both sides of the Atlantic women participated in social reform movements to prevent mistreatment of women and children and of industrial workers. In the United States such reforms were championed by Progressives like Jane Addams (1860–1935), who founded a settlement house in a poor neighborhood and received the Nobel Peace Prize in 1931. In Europe reformers were generally aligned with Socialist or Labour Parties.

Margaret Sanger American nurse and author; pioneer in the movement for family planning; organized conferences and established birth control clinics.

Among the most controversial, and eventually most effective, of the reformers were those who advocated contraception, such as the American **Margaret Sanger** (1883–1966). Her campaign brought her into conflict with many authorities, who equated birth control with pornography. Finally, in 1923 she was able to found a birth control clinic in New York. In France, the government prohibited contraception and abortion in 1920 in an effort to increase the birthrate and make up for the loss of so many young men in the war.

Revolution in the Sciences: The New Physics

The word *progress*, as much associated with extending "modern civilization" to the non-Western world as with technological developments such as railroads and undersea cables, had been a hallmark of most nineteenth-century Euro-American ideologies. After 1900 the word *science* increasingly took its place as a signifier of Western self-esteem. At the end of the nineteenth

Max Planck German physicist who developed quantum theory and was awarded the Nobel Prize for physics in 1918.

Albert Einstein German physicist who developed the theory of relativity, which states that time, space, and mass are relative to each other and not fixed.

Sigmund Freud Austrian psychiatrist, founder of psychoanalysis. He argued that psychological problems were caused by traumas, especially sexual experiences in early childhood, that were repressed in later life. His ideas caused considerable controversy among psychologists and in the general public. Although his views on repressed sexuality are no longer widely accepted, his psychoanalytic methods are still very influential.

Pablo Picasso Key figure in the movement of modern art away from realistic representation; a founder of cubism and surrealism.

Igor Stravinsky Influential modernist composer known for his experimentation and pulsing rhythms.

Dada Nihilistic movement in poetry and art that began during World War I in reaction to the vast and horrifying loss of life that seemed to make art meaningless.

century, a revolution in physics undermined the old certainties about nature that had already been shaken by Darwinism. Physicists discovered that atoms, the building blocks of matter, are not indivisible, but consist of far smaller subatomic particles. In 1900 the German physicist **Max Planck** (1858-1947) found that atoms emit or absorb energy in discrete amounts called *quanta.*

Few people understood these findings at the time, much less **Albert Einstein's** (1879-1955) pronouncement in 1916 that time, space, energy, and mass are not fixed but are relative to one another. But scientific discovery, punctuated by prestigious Nobel prizes that began to be awarded in 1901, excited pride and wonder in nations that contributed to such advances.

The New Social Sciences

The new social sciences were more understandable, and thus more unsettling, than the new physics, for they challenged Victorian morality and middle-class values. **Sigmund Freud** (1856-1939), a Viennese physician, developed the technique of psychoanalysis to probe the minds of his patients. His technique uncovered hidden layers of emotion and desire repressed by social restraints. "It is during this [childhood] period of . . . latency that the psychic forces develop which later act as inhibitions on the sexual life, and narrow its direction like dams. These psychic forces are loathing, shame, and moral and esthetic ideal demands,"[2] he declared. Meanwhile, sociologists and anthropologists had begun the empirical study of societies, both Western and non-Western. Before the war the French sociologist Emile Durkheim (1858-1917) had come to the then shocking conclusion that "there are no religions that are false. All are true after their own fashion."[3]

If the words *primitive* and *savage* applied to Europeans as well as to other peoples, and if religions were all equally "true," then what remained of the superiority of Western civilization? Cultural relativism, as the new approach to human societies was called, could be as unnerving as relativity in physics; but for many it stimulated a tenacious desire to cling to the old truths.

The arts became a battlefield for confronting traditional values with new images and rhythms. Cubism, an approach to painting and sculpture that sought to go beyond realism and depict many aspects of an image simultaneously, aroused lively debates in the 1910s. A painter like the Spaniard **Pablo Picasso** (1881-1973) changed his nonrealistic style of painting time and again over his long career. Paralleling his audacity in the field of music, the Russian composer **Igor Stravinsky** (1882-1971) incorporated so-called primitive rhythms in his ballet *The Rite of Spring*, which debuted in 1913.

The incredible human losses experienced during the Great War shook many artists' and intellectuals' faith in reason and progress. Some poets and artists joined the **Dada** movement, which abandoned rationality and relied instead on intuition, randomness, and nonsense—*dada* stood for the use of meaningless syllables in poetry. Others became Surrealists and produced dreamlike images incorporating what they considered to be symbols of the unconscious mind. Some people accepted the new ideas with enthusiasm. Others condemned and rejected them, particularly in the United States, and clung to the sense of order and faith in progress that had energized Western culture before the war.

New Technologies and Activities

Some people viewed the sciences with mixed feelings, but new technologies aroused almost universal excitement. In North America even working-class people could afford some of the new products of inventors' ingenuity (see Environment and Technology: New Materials). Mass consumption in Europe lagged behind the United States, but science and technology were just as advanced, and public fascination with the latest inventions—the cult of the modern—was just as strong.

Of all the innovations of the time, none attracted public interest more than airplanes. In 1903 two young American mechanics, **Wilbur and Orville Wright**, built the first aircraft that was heavier than air and could be maneuvered in flight. From that moment on, airplanes fascinated people. In 1911 a French pilot flew 6,500 letters from one city in British India to another 8.1 miles (13 kilometers) away, thus inaugurating the first important use of air transport. Military observation and aerial warfare came second. During the Great War the exploits of air aces relieved the tedium of news from the front.

Wilbur and Orville Wright American bicycle mechanics; the first to build and fly an airplane, at Kitty Hawk, North Carolina, December 7, 1903.

---

[2]Sigmund Freud, *Three Contributions to the Theory of Sex*, tr. A. A. Brill, 2 ed. (Washington: Nervous and Mental Health Disease Publishing Company, 1920), 40.

[3]Emile Durkheim, *The Elementary Forms of Religious Life*, trans. by Karen Elise Fields (New York: Free Press, 1995), 2.

First Aluminum Airplane
From the Wright Brothers' first aircraft in 1903 down to the air battles of World War I, wood, cloth, and wire made up the wings and bodies of airplanes. Metals were too heavy for anything but engines and weapons until the German manufacturer Hugo Junkers designed the first aluminum flying machine, shown here, in 1917.

Museum of Flight/Corbis

KLM Royal Dutch Airlines
Oldest major airline, operating since 1920 in Europe and connecting to the Dutch East Indies in 1929.

Marie Curie Polish-born pioneer in the study of radiation and winner of Nobel Prizes for physics (1903) and chemistry (1911); first female professor at the Sorbonne.

Baron Pierre de Coubertin
Founder of the modern Olympic movement, which held its first games in Athens in 1896.

The first flight of **KLM Royal Dutch Airlines**, the oldest continuously operating airline, took off in 1920. That year it carried 440 passengers and 22 tons of cargo. Scheduled service to a number of northern European cities soon followed. Its most important service, as an air link to the Dutch East Indies (now Indonesia), began in 1929. Every country with imperial possessions saw international air service as a political necessity. Two of the oldest airlines, however, Qantas in Australia and the German-owned precursor of Avianca in Colombia, functioned entirely outside of Europe.

Health and hygiene were part of the cult of modernity. Advances in medicine—some learned on the battlefield—saved many lives. Wounds were regularly disinfected, and **Marie Curie** (1867–1934), the French discoverer of x-rays, organized radiology vans to help army doctors diagnose fractures during the Great War. Cities built costly water supply and sewage treatment systems. By the 1920s indoor plumbing and flush toilets were becoming common even in working-class neighborhoods.

Interest in cleanliness entered private life. Doctors and home economists bombarded women with warnings and advice on how to banish germs. Soap and appliance manufacturers filled women's magazines with advertisements for products to help keep homes and clothing spotless and meals fresh and wholesome. The decline in infant mortality and improvements in general health and life expectancy in this period owe as much to the cult of cleanliness as to advances in medicine.

Organized baseball leagues arose in America after the Civil War. Football found favor as a college sport around the same time, while basketball originated in 1891 as a YMCA activity. In Britain soccer (football) and rugby leagues formed in the 1880s. All of these sports flourished as spectator activities in the early twentieth century and gave rise to lively press coverage in newspapers. Soccer and rugby, along with the much older sport of cricket, spread readily into Europe's colonies, while baseball found limited favor overseas, primarily in Japan, Cuba, and the Dominican Republic.

Internationally, the upsurge in the role of sports and spectating was closely tied to the revival of the Olympic Games. The ancient Greek games had been discontinued in 393 c.e.. The inspiration to create a modern form came from **Baron Pierre de Coubertin** (1863–1937), a French educator who was impressed by the sports played at English private schools like Eton and Rugby. He concluded that "organised sport can create moral and social strength."

Coubertin's aristocratic vision of purely amateur international competition came to fruition in Athens in 1896 when fourteen countries, all of them European except Australia and Chile, sent athletes to compete in nonteam sports like tennis, fencing, shooting, cycling, and gymnastics. Women were not included, nor did Coubertin realize his idea that medals should also be given for sports-themed art and architecture. The male-only rule was dropped starting with the Paris Olympics of 1900, where women competed in tennis and golf. The role of women increased steadily after that, though the arts medals were only given seven times between Stockholm in 1912 and London in 1948.

Individual excellence was the touchstone of Olympic competition, but nationalistic pride increasingly marked the quadrennial events. The Berlin Olympics of 1936 thus became a showcase for Nazi ideology and spectacle.

Technology and the Environment

Two new technologies—the skyscraper and the automobile—transformed the urban environment even more radically than the railroad had done. At the end of the nineteenth century architects had begun to design ever-higher buildings using load-bearing steel frames and elevators. Major corporations in Chicago and New York competed to build the most daring buildings in the world, such as New York's fifty-five-story Woolworth Building (1912). A building boom in the late 1920s produced dozens of skyscrapers, culminating with the eighty-six-story Empire State Building in New York in 1932.

Le Corbusier Professional name of architect Charles-Éduard Jeanneret, who led a modernist movement away from surface decoration and toward form following function.

European cities restricted the height of buildings to protect their architectural heritage; Paris forbade buildings over 56 feet (17 meters) high. In the 1920s the Swiss architect Charles Edouard Jeanneret (1887–1965), known as **Le Corbusier (luh cor-booz-YEH)**, outlined a new approach to architecture that featured simplicity of form, absence of surface ornamentation, easy manufacture, and inexpensive materials such as concrete and glass. Other architects—including the Finn Eero Saarinen, the Germans Ludwig Mies van der Rohe **(LOOD-vig MEES fon der ROW-uh)** and Walter Gropius, and the American Frank Lloyd Wright—also contributed to what became known as the International Style.

Meanwhile, outlying areas were spreading far into the countryside, thanks to the automobile. The assembly line pioneered by Henry Ford mass-produced vehicles in ever-greater volume and at falling prices. By 1929 the United States had one car for every five people, five-sixths of the world's automobiles. Automobiles were praised as the solution to urban pollution; as they replaced carts and carriages, horses disappeared from city streets, as did tons of manure.

The most important environmental effect of automobiles was suburban sprawl. Middle-class families could now live in single-family homes too far apart to be served by public transportation. As middle- and working-class families bought cars, cities acquired rings of automobile suburbs. Los Angeles, the first true automobile city, consisted of suburbs spread over hundreds of square miles and linked together by broad avenues. Many Americans saw Los Angeles as the portent of a glorious future in which everyone would have a car.

European cities that had inherited narrow streets from the premodern past adapted less easily to passenger automobiles. In the countryside, however, high-speed, limited-access expressways, called *autostrada* in Italy and *autobahn* in Germany, became sources of national pride for the regimes of Benito Mussolini and Adolf Hitler. Yet compared with the United States, private automobile ownership remained uncommon.

Technological advances also transformed rural economies. In 1915 Ford introduced a gasoline-powered tractor, and by the mid-1920s these versatile machines began replacing horses. Larger farms profited most from this innovation, while small farmers sold their land and moved to the cities. Tractors and other expensive equipment hastened the transformation of agriculture from family enterprises to larger businesses, or in the USSR to collective farms with state-owned tractor stations (see Chapter 30).

SECTION REVIEW

- Government bureaucracies and the middle class grew after the war, but not the working class.

- In many countries, women gained the right to vote and led reform movements.

- Max Planck and Albert Einstein led a revolution in physics.

- Social scientists like Sigmund Freud undermined the old certainties of European culture by revealing a dark side to human nature.

- After the Wright brothers' first flight, mail delivery and connection with colonies prompted the organization of airlines.

- The cult of cleanliness and spread of sporting activities improved health, with the latter providing new types of spectator entertainment.

- American cities were transformed by skyscrapers, and the automobile led to the creation of suburbs.

New Materials

Nineteenth-century commerce brought many raw materials from European colonies and other faraway places into industrial use. Examples include rubber, a Southeast Asian tree sap called gutta-percha used for electrical insulation, Central Asian camel's hair used for transmission belts, and whale oil for lighting. These exotic materials were valuable, but they did not change the age-old pattern of almost every useful item being manufactured from natural substances.

The first half of the twentieth century saw a revolutionary change in this pattern. Metallurgists and chemists led the way in creating new materials that wrought permanent changes in the look and feel of everyday life. Materials science would go on to become one of the most important areas of technical innovation in later decades.

Though aluminum follows oxygen and silicon as the third most abundant element, it combines so readily with other elements that it was not discovered until 1827. Initially as precious as silver, a 2.4-kilogram piece was installed as the capstone of the Washington Monument in 1884. Four years later, however, almost simultaneously in the United States and France, an inexpensive electrolytic method of extracting the metal from bauxite ore was discovered. The lightweight, noncorrosive metal now became available for all manner of uses, from airplanes, beginning with a design by the German Hugo Junkers in 1917, to aluminum foil, which was invented in 1910.

Stainless steel, made by combining noncorrosive chromium with steel, was invented in 1912, and its many uses accustomed people to thinking of metal products as shiny. Electroplating with chromium came into use in 1924 in Germany and two years later in the United States. The shiny, rust-free metal, which could be deposited as a thin film on either a metallic or plastic base, found numerous uses from musical instruments to automobiles.

Plastics were invented at about the same time. Alexander Parkes invented celluloid, a stable form of explosive guncotton—itself made by soaking fine cotton in sulfuric and nitric acids—and exhibited it at London's Great Exhibition in 1862. The first thermoplastic, it could be molded above a certain temperature but became solid when it cooled. It was used for detachable men's shirt collars, ping-pong balls, and photographic film, but it was both fragile and flammable.

Belgian-born Leo Hendrik Baekeland invented Bakelite, a more durable plastic that was also attractive enough to be used for jewelry in 1907. Five years later the Swiss chemist Jacques E. Brandenberger, trying to discover a way of waterproofing cloth, experimented with a cellulose-based coating that failed to stick to the cloth and instead peeled off in a clear sheet. Thus was cellophane invented. In the 1930s an American, Richard Drew, coated cellophane with adhesive and Scotch tape was born.

And there were others. Silklike rayon, 1904; isoprene synthetic rubber, 1909; vinyl, 1926; neoprene synthetic rubber, 1931; plexiglass, 1933; nylon, 1935; Lucite, 1936; fiberglass, 1938—the list goes on, with even more new materials being developed in the later decades of the century.

QUESTIONS FOR ANALYSIS

1. Why do we take for granted a material environment constructed from manufactured substances that did not even exist before 1900?

2. What are the objects we use every day made of?

3. Why did new materials find such broad acceptance?

Bakelite Jewelry   This pioneering plastic was so attractive that it was made into jewelry. However, its ease of manufacture, hardness, and resistance to electricity, heat, and chemicals suited it to thousands of other uses from clarinets to wire insulation to kitchenware. During World War II it was even considered as a replacement for the copper penny.

imagebroker/Alamy

In India, Australia, and the western United States, engineers built dams and canals to irrigate dry lands. Dams offered the added advantage of producing electricity, for which there was a booming demand. The immediate benefits of water control—irrigated land, prevention of floods, and generation of electricity—far outweighed such distant negative consequences as salt deposits on irrigated fields and harm to wildlife.

A NEW INDIA, 1905–1947

Some parts of the world, such as India, became much more involved in the emerging technologically oriented culture than others, such as sub-Saharan Africa (see below). The consequences of this inequality of access to "modern" developments are still felt today.

Under British rule India acquired railroads, harbors, modern cities, and cotton and steel mills, as well as an active and worldly middle class. The economic transformation of the region awakened in this educated middle class a sense of national dignity that demanded political fulfillment. In response, the British gradually granted India a limited amount of political autonomy while maintaining overall control. Religious and communal tensions among the Indian peoples were carefully papered over, and when the British, exhausted by World War II (see Chapter 30), withdrew in 1947, violent conflicts tore India apart (see Map 29.1).

The Land and the People

Much of India is fertile land, but it is vulnerable to droughts caused by the periodic failure of the monsoons. When the rains failed from 1896 to 1900, 2 million people died of starvation.

MAP 29.1 **The Partition of India, 1947** Before the British, India was divided among many states, ethnic groups, and religions. When the British left in 1947, the subcontinent split along religious lines. The predominantly Muslim regions in the northwest and East Bengal in the east formed the new nation of Pakistan. The predominantly Hindu center became the Republic of India. Jammu and Kashmir remained disputed territories and poisoned relations between the two new countries. © Cengage Learning

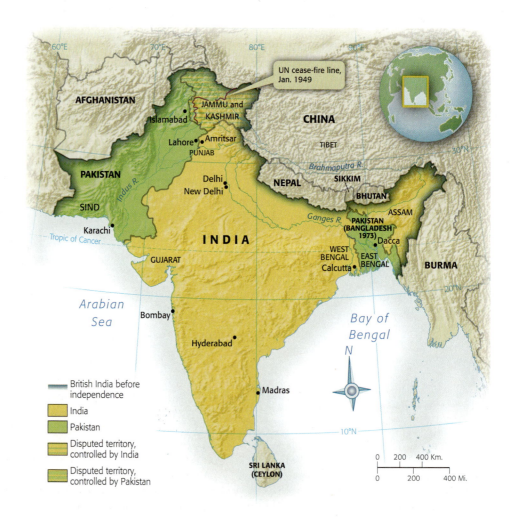

Despite periodic famines, the Indian population grew from 250 million in 1900 to 319 million in 1921 and 389 million in 1941. This growth created pressures in many areas. Landless young men converged on the cities, exceeding the number of jobs available in the slowly expanding industries. Many of them entered the urban economy as rickshaw pullers. To produce timber for construction and railroad ties and to clear land for tea and rubber plantations, foresters cut down most of the tropical hardwood forests that had covered the subcontinent in the nineteenth century. But in spite of deforestation and extensive irrigation, the amount of land available to peasant families shrank with each successive generation. Economic development hardly touched the average Indian.

Indians were divided into many classes. Peasants, always the great majority, paid rents to landowners, interest to village moneylenders, and taxes to the government and had little left to improve their land or raise their standard of living. The government protected property owners, from village moneylenders all the way up to the maharajahs (mah-huh-RAH-juh) or ruling princes, who owned huge tracts of land. The cities were crowded with craftsmen, traders, and workers of all sorts, most very poor. Although the British had banned the burning of widows on their husbands' funeral pyres, in other respects women's lives changed little under British rule.

Indians also spoke many different languages. As a result of British rule, increasing trade and travel, and newspapers like *The Times of India*, established under that name in 1861, English became the common medium of communication for the Western-educated middle class. This new class of English-speaking bureaucrats, professionals, and merchants was to play a leading role in the independence movement.

The majority of Indians who practiced Hinduism were subdivided into hundreds of castes (*jati*), each affiliated with a particular occupation or kinship group. Hinduism discouraged intermarriage and other social interactions among the castes and with non-Hindus. Until displaced by the British in the eighteenth century, Muslim rulers had dominated northern and central India, and Muslims now constituted one-quarter of the Indian population while forming a majority in the northwest and in eastern Bengal. They felt discriminated against by both British and Hindus.

British Rule and Indian Nationalism

Colonial India was ruled by a viceroy appointed by the British government and administered by a few thousand members of the Indian Civil Service. These men, drawn mostly from the English gentry, believed it was their duty to protect the Indian people from the dangers of industrialization and to defend their own positions from Indian nationalists.

As Europeans they admired modern technology. They encouraged railroads, harbors, telegraphs, and other communications technologies, as well as irrigation and plantations, because these increased India's foreign trade and strengthened British control. Yet, they discouraged the cotton and steel industries and limited the training of Indian engineers, to spare India the social upheavals that had accompanied the Industrial Revolution in Europe while protecting British industry from Indian competition.

At the turn of the century most Indians—especially peasants, landowners, and princes—accepted British rule. But the Europeans' racist attitude toward dark-skinned people increasingly offended Indians who had learned English and absorbed English ideas of freedom and representative government, only to discover that racial quotas excluded them from the Indian Civil Service, the officer corps, and prestigious sporting clubs.

In 1885 a small group of English-speaking Hindu professionals founded a political organization called the **Indian National Congress**. For twenty years its members respectfully petitioned the government for access to higher administrative positions and for a voice in official decisions, but they had little influence. Then, in 1905, Viceroy Lord Curzon divided the province of **Bengal** in two to improve the efficiency of its administration. This decision, made without consulting anyone, angered not only educated Indians, who saw it as a way to lessen their influence, but also millions of uneducated Hindu Bengalis, who found themselves outnumbered by Muslims in East Bengal. Soon Bengal was the scene of demonstrations, boycotts of British goods, and even incidents of violence against the British.

In 1906, while the Hindus of Bengal were protesting the partition of their province, Muslims, fearful of Hindu dominance elsewhere in India, founded the **All-India Muslim League**. (Note the English names of these political groups.) The government responded by granting Indians a limited franchise based on wealth. Muslims, however, were on average poorer than Hindus,

Indian National Congress A movement and political party founded in 1885 to demand greater Indian participation in government. Its membership was middle class, and its demands were modest until World War I. Led after 1920 by Mohandas K. Gandhi, it appealed increasingly to the poor, and it organized mass protests demanding self-government and independence.

Bengal Region of northeastern India. It was the first part of India to be conquered by the British in the eighteenth century and remained the political and economic center of British India throughout the nineteenth century. The 1905 split of the province into predominantly Hindu West Bengal and predominantly Muslim East Bengal (now Bangladesh) sparked anti-British riots.

All-India Muslim League Political organization founded in India in 1906 to defend the interests of India's Muslim minority. Led by Muhammad Ali Jinnah, it attempted to negotiate with the Indian National Congress. In 1940, the League began demanding a separate state for Muslims, to be called Pakistan.

World Commercial Map, 1920 The primacy of Great Britain in the world of commerce shows up in the table detailing the distribution of the world's wealth and in the steamship lines linking Britain to the United States and to India by way of the Mediterranean. Railroads in South America and Africa were designed to facilitate exports rather than unify the continents.

The Peoples Atlas, London Geographical Institute, 1920

possibly because many poor and low-caste Hindus had converted to Islam to escape caste discrimination. Taking advantage of these religious divisions, the British instituted separate representation and different voting qualifications for Hindus and Muslims. Then, in 1911, the British transferred the capital of India from Calcutta (Kolkata) to Delhi **(DEL-ee)**, the former capital of the Mughal **(MOO-guhl)** emperors. These changes disturbed Indians of all classes and religions and raised their political consciousness. Politics, once primarily the concern of westernized intellectuals, turned into two mass movements: one by Hindus and one by Muslims.

British geologists looked for minerals like coal and manganese that British industry required. However, when the only Indian member of the Indian Geological Service, Pramatha Nath Bose, wanted to prospect for iron ore, he had to resign because the government wanted no part of an Indian steel industry that might compete with that of Britain. Bose joined forces with Jamsetji Tata, a Bombay textile magnate who decided to produce steel in spite of British opposition. With the help of German and American engineers and equipment, Tata's son Dorabji opened the first steel mill in India in 1911, in a town called Jamshedpur in honor of his father. Although it produced only a fraction of the steel that India required, Jamshedpur became a powerful symbol of Indian national pride. It also prompted Indian nationalists to ask why a country that could produce its own steel needed foreigners to run its government.

During World War I Indians supported Britain enthusiastically; 1.2 million men volunteered for the army, and millions more voluntarily contributed money to the government. Many expected the British to reward their loyalty with political concessions. Others organized to demand a voice in the government. In 1917, in response to the agitation, the British government announced "the gradual development of self-governing institutions with a view to the progressive realization of responsible government in India as an integral part of the British Empire." This sounded like a promise of self-government, but the timetable was so vague that nationalists denounced it as a devious maneuver to postpone India's independence.

On April 13, 1919, in the city of Amritsar, General Reginald Dyer ordered his troops to fire into a peaceful crowd of some 10,000 demonstrators, killing at least 379 and wounding 1,200. While waves of angry demonstrations swept over India, the British House of Lords voted to approve Dyer's actions, and a fund was raised in appreciation of his services. Indians interpreted these gestures as showing British contempt for their colonial subjects. In the charged atmosphere of the time, the period of gradual accommodation between the British and the Indians came to a close.

Mahatma Gandhi and Militant Nonviolence

Mohandas K. Gandhi Leader of the Indian independence movement and advocate of nonviolent resistance. After being educated as a lawyer in England, he returned to India and became leader of the Indian National Congress in 1920. He appealed to the poor, led nonviolent demonstrations against British colonial rule, and was jailed many times. Soon after independence he was assassinated for attempting to stop Hindu-Muslim rioting.

For the next twenty years India teetered on the edge of violent uprisings and harsh repression. That it did not succumb was due to **Mohandas K. Gandhi (GAHN-dee)** (1869–1948), a man known to his followers as "Mahatma," the "great soul."

Gandhi began life with every advantage. His family was wealthy enough to send him to England for his education. After his studies he lived in South Africa and practiced law for the small Indian community there. During World War I he returned to India and was one of many Western-educated Hindu intellectuals who joined the Indian National Congress.

Unlike many radical political thinkers of his time, Gandhi denounced the popular ideals of power, struggle, and combat. Instead, inspired by both Hindu and Christian ideals, he preached the saintly virtues of *ahimsa* **(uh-HIM-sah)** (nonviolence) and *satyagraha* **(suh-TYAH-gruh-huh)** (the search for truth). He refused to countenance violence among his followers and called off several demonstrations when they turned violent.

In 1921 Gandhi gave up the Western-style suits worn by lawyers and the fine raiment of wealthy Indians and henceforth wore simple peasant garb: a length of homespun cloth below his waist (*dhoti*) and a shawl to cover his torso. He spoke for the farmers and the outcasts, whom he called *harijan* **(HAH-ree-jahn)**, "children of God." He attracted ever-larger numbers of followers among the poor and the illiterate, who soon began to revere him; and he transformed the cause of Indian independence from an elite movement of the educated into a mass movement with a quasi-religious aura.

Gandhi was a brilliant political tactician and a master of public relations gestures. In 1929, for instance, he led a few followers on an 80-mile (129-kilometer) walk, camped on a beach, and gathered salt from the sea in a blatant and well-publicized act of civil disregard for the government's monopoly on salt. But he discovered that unleashing the power of popular participation was one thing and controlling its direction was quite another. Within days of his "Walk to the Sea," demonstrations of support broke out all over India, in which the police killed a hundred demonstrators and arrested over sixty thousand.

Many times during the 1930s Gandhi threatened to fast "unto death," and several times he came close to death, to protest the violence of both the police and his followers and to demand independence. He was repeatedly arrested and spent a total of six years in jail. But every arrest made him more popular. He became a figure of adulation not only in his own country but also in the Western media. In the words of historian Percival Spear, he made the British "uncomfortable in their cherished field of moral rectitude," and he gave Indians the feeling that theirs was the ethically superior cause.

Gandhi's Salt March to the Sea Mohandas Gandhi, bareheaded and more simply dressed than his followers, led a march of 80 miles to collect sea salt in an act of civil disobedience. News photographs like this played a key role in popularizing his cause and displaying his saintly habits. To his left one man carries a sitar and another has a drum hanging from his shoulder.

Dinodia Photos/Alamy

Gandhi and the Media

Political figures in many countries made use of radio, newspaper, and newsreel coverage to spread their messages. The Fascists in Italy and the Nazis in Germany used photographs of their uniformed leaders as symbols, filmed their mass rallies, and broadcast their bombastic speeches. But no one showed as much skill in using the new media to publicize his movement as Mahatma Gandhi. To identify with the common people of India, he appeared in a plain white loincloth (dhoti) and shawl instead of a uniform. To show the power of civil disobedience, he led his followers in much-photographed marches and demonstrations. Some of his most important speeches were delivered in trial court or to urge people to break the law and then reported in the press.

In 1922, after two thousand followers of Gandhi's nonviolent movement responded to police gunfire by burning down the police station at Chauri Chaura and killing twenty-two policemen, he was charged with "bringing or attempting to excite disaffection towards His Majesty's Government established by law in British India." Before reading a written statement in which he detailed governmental acts that he considered to be tyrannical, Gandhi said the following.

I would like to state that I entirely endorse the learned Advocate-General's remarks in connection with my humble self. . . . I have no desire whatsoever to conceal from this court the fact that to preach disaffection towards the existing system of Government has become almost a passion with me. . . . I wish to endorse all the blame that the learned Advocate-General has thrown on my shoulders in connection with the Bombay occurrences, Madras occurrences and the Chauri Chaura occurrences. Thinking over these things deeply and sleeping over them night after night, it is impossible for me to dissociate myself from the diabolical crimes of Chauri Chaura or the mad outrages of Bombay. He is quite right when he says, that as a man of responsibility, a man having received a fair share of education, having had a fair share of experience of this world, I should have known the consequences of every one of my acts. I know them. I knew that I was playing with fire. I ran the risk and if I was set free I would still do the same.

I have felt it this morning that I would have failed in my duty, if I did not say what I said here just now.

I wanted to avoid violence. Non-violence is the first article of my faith. It is also the last article of my creed. But I had to make my choice. I had either to submit to a system which I considered had done an irreparable harm to my country, or incur the risk of the mad fury of my people bursting forth when they understood the truth from my lips. I know that my people have sometimes gone mad. I am deeply sorry for it and I am, therefore, here to submit not to a light penalty but to the highest penalty. I do not ask for mercy. I do not plead any extenuating act. I am here, therefore, to invite and cheerfully submit to the highest penalty that can be inflicted upon me for what in law is a deliberate crime, and what appears to me to be the highest duty of a citizen.

In 1930, before embarking on the Salt March, a demonstration of civil disobedience that was heavily covered by newspaper and newsreel reporters, Gandhi delivered the following speech.

In all probability this will be my last speech to you. Even if the Government allow me to march tomorrow morning, this will be my last speech on the sacred banks of the Sabarmati. Possibly these may be the last words of my life here. . . .

From what I have seen and heard during the last fortnight, I am inclined to believe that the stream of civil resisters will flow unbroken. But let there be not a semblance of breach of peace even after all of us have been arrested. We have resolved to utilize all our resources in the pursuit of an exclusively nonviolent struggle. Let no one commit a wrong in anger. This is my hope and prayer. I wish these words of mine reached every nook and corner of the land. My task shall be done if I perish and so do my comrades. . . . Wherever possible, civil disobedience of salt should be started. These laws can be violated in three ways. It is an offence to manufacture salt wherever there are facilities for doing so. The possession and sale of contraband salt, which includes natural salt or salt earth, is also an offence. The purchasers of such salt will be equally guilty. To carry away the natural salt deposits on the seashore is likewise violation

India Moves Toward Independence

In the 1920s, slowly and reluctantly, the British handed over control of "national" areas such as education, the economy, and public works to Indians. They also gradually admitted more Indians into the Civil Service and the officer corps.

In the years before the Second World War, Indian politicians obtained the right to erect high tariff barriers against imports to protect India's infant industries from foreign competition. Behind these barriers, Indian entrepreneurs built plants to manufacture iron and steel, cement, paper, textiles, sugar, and other products. This early industrialization did not provide enough jobs to improve the lives of the Indian peasants or urban poor, but it created a class of wealthy Indian businessmen who supported the Indian National Congress and its demands for independence. Though paying homage to Gandhi, they preferred his designated successor as leader of of law. So is the hawking of such salt. In short, you may choose any one or all of these devices to break the salt monopoly.

We are, however, not to be content with this alone. . . . I stress only one condition, namely, let our pledge of truth and nonviolence as the only means for the attainment of Swaraj [self-rule] be faithfully kept. For the rest, every one has a free hand. But, that does not give a license to all and sundry to carry on their own responsibility. Wherever there are local leaders, their orders should be obeyed by the people. Where there are no leaders and only a handful of men have faith in the programme, they may do what they can, if they have enough self-confidence. . . .

Much can be done in many other ways besides these. The Liquor and foreign cloth shops can be picketed. We can refuse to pay taxes if we have the requisite strength. The lawyers can give up practice. The public can boycott the law courts by refraining from litigation. Government servants can resign their posts. . . . Let all who are co-operating with the Government in one way or another, be it by paying taxes, keeping titles, or sending children to official schools, etc. withdraw their co-operation in all or as many ways as possible. Then there are women who can stand shoulder to shoulder with men in this struggle.

Gandhi's successor, Jawaharlal Nehru, enjoyed remarkable success as India's first elected prime minister. But his public image was much more conventional. His most famous speech celebrated the granting of India's independence on August 14, 1947.

Long years ago we made a tryst with destiny, and now the time comes when we shall redeem our pledge, not wholly or in full measure, but very substantially. At the stroke of the midnight hour, when the world sleeps, India will awake to life and freedom. A moment comes, which comes but rarely in history, when we step out from the old to the new, when an age ends, and when the soul of a nation, long suppressed, finds utterance. It is fitting that at this solemn moment we take the pledge of dedication to the service of India and her people and to the still larger cause of humanity.

At the dawn of history India started on her unending quest, and trackless centuries are filled with her striving and the grandeur of her success and her failures. Through good and ill fortune alike she has never lost sight of that quest or forgotten the ideals which gave her strength. We end today a period of ill fortune and India discovers herself again. The achievement we celebrate today is but a step, an opening of opportunity, to the greater triumphs and achievements that await us. Are we brave enough and wise enough to grasp this opportunity and accept the challenge of the future? . . .

That future is not one of ease or resting but of incessant striving so that we may fulfill the pledges we have so often taken and the one we shall take today. The service of India means the service of the millions who suffer. It means the ending of poverty and ignorance and disease and inequality of opportunity. The ambition of the greatest man of our generation [i.e., Gandhi] has been to wipe every tear from every eye. That may be beyond us, but as long as there are tears and suffering, so long our work will not be over.

And so we have to labour and to work, and work hard, to give reality to our dreams. Those dreams are for India, but they are also for the world, for all the nations and peoples are too closely knit together today for any one of them to imagine that it can live apart. Peace has been said to be indivisible; so is freedom, so is prosperity now, and so also is disaster in this one world that can no longer be split into isolated fragments. . . .

QUESTIONS FOR ANALYSIS

1. How does the rhetoric of Gandhi compare with that of Nehru?

2. To what degree does nonviolence as a means of governmental and social change depend on news media?

3. Why did Gandhi's type of movement have so few antecedents?

4. How did Gandhi's example change later world politics?

Sources: *Selected Works of Mahatma Gandhi, Vol. VI: The Voice of Truth*, Part I, "Some Famous Speeches," ed. Shriman Narayan Gandhi (1952); Brian McArthur, *Penguin Book of Twentieth Century Speeches* (London: Penguin Viking, 1992), pp. 234–237.

Jawaharlal Nehru Indian statesman who succeeded Mohandas K. Gandhi as leader of the Indian National Congress. He negotiated the end of British colonial rule in India and became India's first prime minister (1947–1964).

the Indian National Congress, **Jawaharlal Nehru (NAY-roo)** (1889–1964). Unlike Gandhi, Nehru looked forward to creating a modern industrial India.

Congress politicians won regional elections but continued to be excluded from the viceroy's cabinet, the true center of power. When World War II began (see Chapter 30), Viceroy Lord Linlithgow declared war without consulting a single Indian. The Congress-dominated provincial governments resigned in protest and found that boycotting government office increased their popular support. When the British offered to give India its independence once the war ended, Gandhi demanded full independence immediately. His "Quit India" campaign aroused popular demonstrations against the British and provoked a wave of arrests, including his own. The Second World War divided the Indian people. Most Indian soldiers felt they were fighting to defend their country rather than to support the British Empire. As in World War I, Indians contributed heavily to the Allied war effort, supplying 2 million soldiers and enormous amounts of resources, especially the timber needed for emergency construction. A small number of Indians were so anti-British that they joined the Japanese side.

Muhammad Ali Jinnah Indian Muslim politician who founded the state of Pakistan. A lawyer by training, he joined the All-India Muslim League in 1913. As leader of the League from the 1920s on, he negotiated with the British and the Indian National Congress for Muslim participation in Indian politics. From 1940 on, he led the movement for the independence of India's Muslims in a separate state of Pakistan, founded in 1947.

Partition and Independence

When the war ended, Britain's new Labour Party government prepared for Indian independence, but deep suspicions between Hindus and Muslims complicated the process. The break between the two communities had started in 1937, when the Indian National Congress won provincial elections and refused to share power with the Muslim League. In 1940 the leader of the League, **Muhammad Ali Jinnah (JIH-nah)** (1876–1948), demanded what many Muslims had been dreaming of for years: a country of their own, to be called Pakistan.

As independence approached, talks between Jinnah and Nehru broke down and battle lines were drawn. Violent rioting between Hindus and Muslims broke out. Gandhi's appeals for tolerance and cooperation fell on deaf ears. The British made frantic proposals to keep India united, but their authority was waning fast.

In early 1947 the Indian National Congress accepted the partition of India into two states, one secular but dominated by Hindus, the other Muslim. On August 15 British India gave way to a new India and Pakistan. The Indian National Congress, led by Nehru, formed the first government of India; Jinnah and the Muslim League established a government for the provinces that made up Pakistan.

The rejoicing over independence was marred by violent outbreaks between Muslims and Hindus. In protest against the mounting chaos, Gandhi refused to attend the independence day celebration. Throughout the land, Muslim and Hindu neighbors turned on one another, and armed members of one faith hunted down people of the other faith. Leaving most of their possessions behind, Hindus fled from predominantly Muslim areas, and Muslims fled from Hindu areas. Trainloads of desperate refugees of one faith were attacked and massacred by members of the other or were left stranded in the middle of deserts. Within a few months some 12 million people had abandoned their ancestral homes and a half-million lay dead. In January 1948 Gandhi died too, gunned down by an angry Hindu refugee.

After the sectarian massacres and flights of refugees, Muslims were a minority in all but one state of India. That state was Kashmir, a strategically important region in the foothills of the Himalayas. India annexed Kashmir because the local maharajah was Hindu and because the state held the headwaters of the rivers that irrigated millions of acres of farmland. Most inhabitants would have joined Pakistan if they had been allowed to vote on the matter. The annexation of Kashmir turned India and Pakistan into bitter enemies that fought several wars over the next half century.

SECTION REVIEW

- Under British rule, India's population grew but remained divided by religion and caste.

- The British introduced certain modern technologies but discouraged Indian industry that might compete with British industry.

- British racial policies, brutality, and arrogance awakened a sense of nationhood among educated Indians.

- The Indian National Congress and the All-India Muslim League demanded independence.

- Mahatma Gandhi led the independence movement using nonviolent tactics and turned an upper-class rebellion into one involving all of India.

- Nehru, Gandhi's successor, wanted to modernize India, and the Indian National Congress resisted British rule during World War II.

- When the British left India in 1947, it split into two nations amidst widespread riots and massacres between Hindus and Muslims.

MEXICO, ARGENTINA, AND BRAZIL, 1917–1949

Though some parts of the world, notably Latin America, were untouched by the Great War, they still experienced the disruptions and new ways of life of the postwar period. In the early 1920s, after a decade of violence that exhausted all classes (see Chapter 26), the Mexican Revolution lost momentum. President Obregón and his closest associates made all the important decisions, and his successor, Plutarco Elías Calles **(KAH-yace)**, founded the National Revolutionary Party, or PNR (the abbreviation of its name in Spanish). The PNR was a forum where all the pressure groups and vested interests—labor, peasants, businessmen, landowners, the military, and others—worked out compromises. The establishment of the PNR gave the Mexican Revolution a second wind.

The Cárdenas Reforms

Lázaro Cárdenas President of Mexico (1934–1940). He brought major changes to Mexican life by distributing millions of acres of land to the peasants, bringing representatives of workers and farmers into the inner circles of politics, and nationalizing the oil industry.

Lázaro Cárdenas (LAH-sah-roe KAHR-dih-nahs), chosen by Calles to be president in 1934, brought peasants' and workers' organizations into the party, removed generals from government positions, and implemented the reforms promised in the Constitution of 1917.

In 1938 Cárdenas seized the foreign-owned oil industry, which had gained importance with the wartime recognition that modern navies needed petroleum. The American and British oil companies expected their governments to come to their rescue, perhaps with military force. But Mexico and the United States chose to resolve the issue through negotiation, and Mexico retained control of its oil.

The Transformation of Argentina

Most of Argentina consists of *pampas* **(POM-pus)**, flat, fertile land that is easy to till, much like the prairies of the midwestern United States and Canada. At the end of the nineteenth century railroads and refrigerator ships changed Argentina's exports and land use. In the 1920s, European consumers, freed from wartime rationing, savored fresh meat. To safeguard valuable herds, the pampas were divided, cultivated, and fenced with barbed wire. Wheat- and grain-fed beef and mutton replaced the lean free-range cattle of earlier generations. Soon the pampas became one of the world's great centers of wheat and meat production.

Argentina's government represented the interests of the *oligarquía* **(oh-lee-gar-KEE-ah)**, a small group of wealthy landowners and exporters. They owned fine homes in Buenos Aires **(BWAY-nos EYE-res)**, a city that was built to resemble Paris, traveled frequently to Europe, and spent lavishly. However, they were content to let British companies build Argentina's railroads, processing plants, and public utilities. Argentina imported almost all its manufactured goods from Europe and the United States. So important were British interests in the Argentinean economy that English, not Spanish, was used on the railroads.

Brazil and Argentina, to 1929

Before the First World War, Brazil produced most of the world's coffee and cacao, grown on vast estates. Natural rubber came from rubber trees growing wild in the Amazon rain forest but had not yet been recognized as a key strategic commodity. Like their Argentinean counterparts, Brazil's elite built palaces in Rio de Janeiro **(REE-oh day zhuh-NAIR-oh)** and even an opera house deep in the Amazon. British companies build railroads, harbors, and other infrastructure and imported most manufactured goods.

Both Argentina and Brazil had small but outspoken middle classes that demanded a share in government and looked to European models. The poor, at the bottom of the social pyramid, were mainly Spanish and Italian immigrants turned landless laborers and meat processors in Argentina or sharecroppers and plantation workers, many descended from slaves, in Brazil.

Hipólito Irigoyen Argentine politician, president of Argentina from 1916 to 1922 and 1928 to 1930. The first president elected by universal male suffrage, he began his presidency as a reformer but later became conservative.

Rubber exports collapsed after 1912, replaced by cheaper plantation rubber from Southeast Asia. Two years later the outbreak of war put an end to imports from Europe as Britain and France focused all their industries on war production and Germany was cut off entirely. The disruption of the old trade patterns weakened the landowning class. In Argentina the urban middle class obtained the secret ballot and universal male suffrage in 1916 and elected a liberal politician, **Hipólito Irigoyen (ee-POH-lee-toe ee-ree-GO-yen)**, as president. To a certain extent, the United States replaced the European countries as suppliers of machinery and consumers of coffee. European immigrants built factories to manufacture textiles and household goods.

The postwar years were a period of prosperity in South America. Trade with Europe resumed; prices for agricultural exports remained high; and both Argentina and Brazil used profits accumulated during the war to industrialize and improve their transportation systems and public utilities. Yet it was also a time of social turmoil, as workers and middle-class professionals demanded the same social reforms and enhanced voice in politics as their European counterparts. In Argentina students' and workers' demonstrations were brutally crushed. In Brazil junior officers faced off several times against the government. Though they accomplished little, these demonstrations laid the groundwork for later reformist movements.

Yet as Argentina and Brazil prospered, new technologies again left them dependent on the advanced industrial countries. Aviation reached Latin America after World War I, when

European and American companies such as Aéropostale and Pan American Airways introduced airmail service between cities and linked Latin America with the United States and Europe.

Before and during World War I, radio was used only for point-to-point communications. Transmitters powerful enough to send messages across oceans or continents were complex and expensive, with antennas covering many acres. They used as much electricity as a small town. Right after the war, no Latin American country possessed the knowledge or funds to build its own transmitters. Four powerful radio companies—one British, one French, one German, and one American—formed a cartel to control all radio communications in Latin America. Thus, even as Brazil and Argentina were asserting state control over their railroads and older industries, as Mexico had done with its oil industry, the major industrial countries controlled the diffusion of the newer aviation and radio technologies.

The Depression and the Vargas Regime in Brazil

Getulio Vargas Dictator of Brazil from 1930 to 1945 and from 1951 to 1954. Defeated in the presidential election of 1930, he overthrew the government and created Estado Novo ("New State"), a dictatorship that emphasized industrialization and helped the urban poor but did little to alleviate the problems of the peasants.

The Great Depression (see Chapter 30) hit Latin America as hard as it hit Europe and the United States and proved a more important turning point for the region than either world war. As long-term customers cut back orders, the value of agricultural and mineral exports fell by two-thirds between 1929 and 1932. Argentina and Brazil could no longer afford imported manufactured goods. An imploding economy also undermined their shaky political systems. Like European countries, Argentina and Brazil veered toward authoritarian regimes that promised to solve their economic problems.

In 1930 **Getulio Vargas** (jay-TOO-lee-oh VAR-gus) (1883–1954), a state governor, staged a coup and proclaimed himself president of Brazil. He proved to be a masterful politician. He wrote a new constitution that broadened the franchise and limited the president to one term. He also raised import duties and promoted national firms and state-owned enterprises. By 1936 industrial production had doubled, especially in textiles and small manufactures. Under his guidance, Brazil was on its way to becoming an industrial country, as well as a model for other Latin American countries attempting to break away from neocolonial dependency.

The industrialization of Brazil brought the familiar environmental consequences. Powerful new machines allowed the reopening of old mines and the digging of new ones. Cities grew as poor peasants looking for work arrived from the countryside. In Rio de Janeiro and São Paulo (sow PAL-oh), the poor turned steep hillsides and vacant lands into immense *favelas* (feh-VEL-luhs) (slums) of makeshift shacks.

The countryside also was transformed. Scrubland was turned into pasture or planted in wheat, corn, and sugar cane. Even the Amazon rain forest—half of the land area of Brazil—was affected. In 1930 American industrialist Henry Ford invested $8 million to clear land along the Tapajós River and prepare it to become the site of the world's largest rubber plantation. Ford encountered opposition from Brazilian workers and politicians; the rubber trees proved vulnerable to diseases; and he had to abandon the project—but not before leaving 3 million acres (1.2 million hectares) denuded of trees.

Bettmann/Corbis

Juan and Eva Perón Juan Perón's presidency of Argentina (1946–1955) relied on his, and especially on his wife Eva's, popularity with the working class. To sustain their popularity, they often organized parades and demonstrations in imitation of the fascist dictators of Europe. This picture shows them riding in a procession in Buenos Aires in 1952.

Juan Perón President of Argentina (1946–1955, 1973–1974). As a military officer, he championed the rights of labor. Aided by his wife Eva Duarte Perón, he was elected president in 1946. He built up Argentinean industry, became very popular among the urban poor, but harmed the economy.

Eva Duarte Perón Wife of Juan Perón and champion of the poor in Argentina. She was a gifted speaker and popular political leader who campaigned to improve the life of the urban poor by founding schools and hospitals and providing other social benefits.

Although Vargas instituted many reforms favorable to urban workers, he refused to help the millions of landless peasants or challenge the great landowners. In 1938, prohibited by his own constitution from being reelected, Vargas staged another coup, abolished the constitution, and instituted the Estado Novo (esh-TAH-doe NO-vo), or "New State," with himself as supreme leader. He abolished political parties, jailed opposition leaders, and turned Brazil into a fascist state, though one that contributed troops and ships to the Allied war effort once the Second World War broke out.

Argentina After 1930

Economically, the depression hurt Argentina almost as badly as it hurt Brazil. Politically, however, the consequences were delayed. In 1930 General José Uriburu (hoe-SAY oo-ree-BOO-roo) overthrew the popularly elected President Irigoyen. For thirteen years the generals and the oligarchy ruled, doing nothing to lessen the poverty of the workers or the frustrations of the middle class. When World War II broke out, Argentina remained officially neutral.

In 1943 another military revolt flared, this one among junior officers led by Colonel **Juan Perón (hoo-AHN pair-OWN)** (1895–1974). The intentions of the rebels were clear:

Civilians will never understand the greatness of our ideal; we shall therefore have to eliminate them from the government and give them the only mission which corresponds to them: work and obedience.[4]

SECTION REVIEW

- Lázaro Cárdenas fulfilled some of the promises of the Mexican Revolution and nationalized the oil industry.

- Under its landowning oligarchy, Argentina became a major exporter of beef and wheat and depended on Europeans for its industrial products.

- After World War I, Argentina and Brazil prospered but were still dependent on the United States and Europe for advanced technology.

- Brazil and Argentina suffered greatly from the depression; in the 1930s Vargas's dictatorship modernized Brazil but left the majority in poverty.

- Argentina, under Juan Perón, also industrialized, but his unstable government came to an end in the 1950s.

Once in power the officers took over the highest positions in government and business and began to lavish money on military equipment and their own salaries. Their goal, inspired by Nazi victories (see Chapter 30), was nothing less than the conquest of South America.

As the war turned against the Nazis, the officers saw their popularity collapse. Perón, however, had other plans. Inspired by his charismatic wife **Eva Duarte Perón (AY-vuy doo-AR-tay pair-OWN)** (1919–1952), he appealed to the urban workers. Eva Perón became the champion of the descamisados (des-cah-mee-SAH-dohs), or "shirtless ones," and campaigned tirelessly for social benefits and for the cause of women and children. With his wife's help, Perón won the presidency in 1946 and created a populist dictatorship in imitation of the Vargas regime in Brazil. When Eva died in 1952, however, he lost his political skills (or perhaps they were hers), and soon thereafter was overthrown in yet another military coup.

SUB-SAHARAN AFRICA, 1900–1945

In contrast with India and Latin America, sub-Saharan Africa experienced very few of the transformations that marked the first half of the twentieth century. Africa was the last continent to come under European rule (see Chapter 26), and it was still being subjected to the economic and political organizational forces of imperialism when territories that had been colonized longer were already in the beginning stages of political awakening. After World War I Britain, France, Belgium, and South Africa divided Germany's African colonies among themselves. Then in the 1930s Italy invaded Ethiopia. The colonial empires reached their peak shortly before World War II.

Yet it would be a mistake to conclude that developments in Africa would have resembled those elsewhere if imperialism had started sooner. European attitudes toward sub-Saharan African peoples were affected by a long history of racism. One economic theory, for example, "the backward bending supply curve of labor," maintained that people who were accustomed to living at a bare subsistence level would work fewer hours if their pay was raised above what little was needed

[4] George Blankstein, *Perón's Argentina* (Chicago: University of Chicago Press, 1953), 37.

to maintain that level. They would prefer to idle their lives away sitting around the village rather than striving to better their standard of living the way European workers theoretically would. This theory was used to stigmatize African workers and justify paying them very low wages.

Colonial Africa: Economic and Social Changes

Outside of Algeria, Kenya, and South Africa, few Europeans lived in Africa, and they variously spoke Portuguese, Spanish, German, French, English, or Afrikaans. In 1930 Nigeria, with a population of 20 million, was ruled by 386 British officials and by 8,000 policemen and military personnel, of whom 150 were European. Yet even such a small presence stimulated deep social and economic changes.

The colonial powers had built railroads from coastal cities to mines and plantations in the interior to transport raw materials to the industrial world, but few Africans benefited from these changes. Colonial governments took lands from Africans and sold or leased them to European companies or to white settlers. Large European companies dominated wholesale commerce, while Indians, Greeks, and Syrians handled much of the retail trade.

Where land was divided into small farms, some Africans benefited from the boom. Farmers in the Gold Coast (now Ghana [GAH-nuh]) profited from the high price of cacao, as did palm oil producers in Nigeria and coffee growers in East Africa. In most of Africa women played a major role in the retail trades, selling cloth, food, pots and pans, and other items in the markets. Many maintained their economic independence and kept their household finances separate from those of their husbands, following a custom that predated the colonial period.

For many Africans, however, economic development meant working in European-owned mines and plantations, often under compulsion. Colonial governments were eager to develop the resources of the territories under their control but would not pay wages high enough to attract workers. Instead, they used their police powers to force Africans to work under harsh conditions for little or no pay. In the 1920s, when the government of French Equatorial Africa decided to build a railroad from Brazzaville to the Atlantic coast, a distance of 312 miles (502 kilometers), it drafted 127,000 men to carve a roadbed across mountains and through rain forests. For lack of food, clothing, and medical care, 20,000 of them died, an average of 64 deaths per mile of track.

Europeans prided themselves on bringing modern health care to Africa; yet before the 1930s other aspects of colonialism actually worsened public health. Migrants and soldiers spread syphilis, gonorrhea, tuberculosis, and malaria. Sleeping sickness and smallpox epidemics raged throughout Central Africa. In recruiting men to work, colonial governments also depleted rural areas of farmers needed to plant and harvest crops. Forced requisitions of food to feed the workers left the remaining populations undernourished and vulnerable to diseases. Not until the 1930s did colonial governments realize the negative consequences of their labor policies and begin to invest in agricultural development and health care for Africans.

Making Palm Oil Oil palms produce two products, a red palm oil squeezed from the pulpy fruit and a yellow palm kernel oil extracted from the fruit's seeds with a simple press. Because it stands up well to heat, it is widely used as a cooking oil and is a major export crop in West Africa and other tropical regions.

Eye Ubiquitous/SuperStock

In 1900 Ibadan **(ee-BAH-dahn)** in Nigeria was the only city in sub-Saharan Africa with more than 100,000 inhabitants; fifty years later, dozens of cities had reached that size. Africans migrated to cities because they offered hope of jobs and excitement and, for a few, the chance to become wealthy.

However, migrations damaged the family life of those involved, for almost all the migrants were men leaving women in the countryside to farm and raise children. Reflecting the colonialists' attitudes, cities built during the colonial period had racially segregated housing, clubs, restaurants, hospitals, and other institutions. Patterns of racial discrimination were most rigid in the white-settler colonies of eastern and southern Africa.

Religious and Political Changes

Traditional religious belief could not explain the dislocations that foreign rule, migrations, and sudden economic changes brought to the lives of Africans. Many therefore turned to Christianity or Islam.

Christianity was introduced into Africa by Western missionaries, except in Ethiopia, where it was indigenous. It was most successful in West and South Africa, where the European influence was strongest. A major attraction of the Christian denominations was their mission schools, which taught both craft skills and basic literacy, providing access to employment as minor functionaries, teachers, and shopkeepers. These schools educated a new elite, many of whom learned not only skills and literacy but Western political ideas as well. Yet very few students continued their education to the university level. Many Africans accepted Christianity enthusiastically, reading the suffering of their own peoples into the biblical stories of Moses and the parables of Jesus. The churches trained some pupils to become catechists, teachers, and clergymen. Independent Christian churches associated Christian beliefs with radical ideas of racial equality and participation in politics.

Islam spread inland from the East African coast and southward from the Sahel **(SAH-hel)** through the influence and example of Arab and African merchants. Islam also emphasized literacy—in Arabic rather than a European language—and was less disruptive of traditional African customs such as polygamy. In some areas, such as Somalia, Sudan, and Mali, certain Muslim Sufi brotherhoods became associated with resistance to European imperialism.

In Dakar in Senegal and Cape Town in South Africa, small numbers of Africans could obtain secondary education. Even smaller numbers went on to college in Europe or America. Though few in number, they became the leaders of political movements. The contrast between the liberal ideas imparted by Western education and the realities of racial discrimination under colonial rule contributed to the rise of nationalism among educated Africans. In Senegal **Blaise Diagne (dee-AHN-yuh)** agitated for African participation in politics and fair treatment in the French

Blaise Diagne Senegalese political leader. He was the first African elected to the French National Assembly. During World War I, in exchange for promises to give French citizenship to Senegalese, he helped recruit Africans to serve in the French army. After the war, he led a movement to abolish forced labor in Africa.

A Quranic School In Muslim countries, religious education is centered on learning to read, write, and recite the Quran, the sacred book of the Islamic religion, in the original Arabic. This picture shows boys in a Libyan madrasa (Quranic school) studying writing and religion.

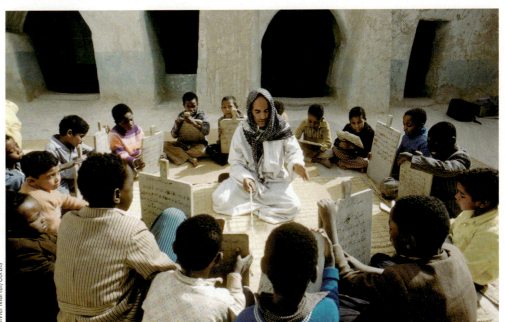

Olivier Martel/Corbis

African National Congress An organization dedicated to obtaining equal voting and civil rights for black inhabitants of South Africa. Founded in 1912 as the South African Native National Congress, it changed its name in 1923. Though it was banned and its leaders were jailed for many years, it eventually helped bring majority rule to South Africa.

Haile Selassie Emperor of Ethiopia (r. 1930–1974) and symbol of African independence. He fought the Italian invasion of his country in 1935 and regained his throne during World War II, when British forces expelled the Italians. He ruled Ethiopia as a traditional autocracy until he was overthrown in 1974.

army during World War I, and in the 1920s J. E. Casely Hayford began organizing a movement for greater autonomy in British West Africa. These nationalist movements were inspired by the ideas of Pan-Africanists from America such as W. E. B. Du Bois and Marcus Garvey, who advocated the unity of African peoples around the world, as well as by European ideas of liberty and nationhood. To defend the interests of Africans, Western-educated lawyers and journalists in South Africa founded the **African National Congress** in 1912. Before World War II, however, these nationalist movements were small and had little influence.

The Second World War had a profound effect on the peoples of Africa, even those far removed from the theaters of war. The war brought hardships, such as increased forced labor, inflation, and requisitions of raw materials. Yet it also brought hope. During the campaign to oust the Italians from Ethiopia, Emperor **Haile Selassie (HI-lee seh-LASS-ee)** (r. 1930–1974) led his own troops into Addis Ababa, his capital, and reclaimed his title. A million Africans served as soldiers and carriers in Burma, North Africa, and Europe, where many became aware of Africa's role in helping the Allied war effort. They listened to Allied propaganda in favor of European liberation movements and against Nazi racism and returned to their countries with new and radical ideas.

Africa and the New Media

South Africa saw the first tries at radio broadcasting in 1924, but these enjoyed very little success until the South African Broadcasting Corporation was established with monopolistic control over the medium in 1936. Down to World War II it broadcast only in English and Afrikaans. Most efforts in other colonies, such as Mozambique and Kenya, likewise targeted European listeners. The exception was British West Africa—Sierra Leone, Ghana, and Nigeria—where African languages were used. Rather than wireless service, subscribers had loudspeakers in their homes that were connected by wire to the radio station. After 1936 the British authorities generally began to see radio as a medium for reaching Africans who did not understand English.

Africa had almost no cinematic presence prior to World War II, apart from fourteen stereotype-filled Tarzan films made in Hollywood between 1918 and 1949. A few films were made for British and Afrikaner audiences in South Africa, but the French issued a decree in 1934 prohibiting the shooting of movies.

SECTION REVIEW

- Colonial rule developed Africa's economies at the expense of its peoples' livelihoods and health.

- Many Africans turned to Christianity or Islam; some, especially those who participated in World War II, began to demand independence.

- The new media were not widely used in Africa.

CONCLUSION

The First and Second World Wars and the intervening period of economic depression, fascism, and militarism constituted the great dramas of the first half of the twentieth century. But not all parts of the world experienced these convulsions to the same degree. Moreover, these narratives of world war, global depression, and varying regional development do not incorporate the profound changes in ways of living that affected most parts of the world between 1900 and 1950.

While participating in many of these changes, the nonindustrialized nations also had their own technological breakthroughs, such as the rickshaw, and did not use some inventions, such as electricity, in the same way as the West. New media such as cinema and radio were used in different ways as well and sometimes perpetuated themes and images from local cultural sources. At the same time, traditional patterns of village life began to erode as cities grew and urban life, at least for the privileged classes, took on the demeanor and attitudes of Europe. But becoming like Europe did not mean coming to like Europe.

To a much greater degree, the industrialized world experienced a flood of new inventions—automobiles, electric lights, radios, movies, airplanes—that stimulated not only a broader respect for science, but also an expectation that science would continue indefinitely to improve human lives. This was the cult of the modern. Technology even affected the arts, providing new materials for architecture and furniture design, new electronic means of amplifying and distributing music, and an ever-expanding array of tools for making and reproducing images, both still and moving. Yet the devastating human tragedies of war and depression also encouraged currents of nihilism, despair, and questioning of faith.

Imperialism being focused, as always, on benefits for the home country and disdain for native peoples with darker skins, colonial administrators in different parts of the world tried to control the flow of global technological and ideological changes. Having a larger and better-educated middle class than many other non-European lands, India entered more fully into the new ways of living than did sub-Saharan Africa. Latin America, with many European immigrants, was closer economically and ideologically to Europe. Political and cultural independence became a realizable goal in India, where Mahatma Gandhi's nonviolent movement pioneered an entirely new form of political activism. In sub-Saharan Africa, however, European racism and the unwavering favoritism shown to European settlers stifled almost all attempts at change.

KEY TERMS

Auguste and Louis Lumière p. 741
Margaret Sanger p. 743
Max Planck p. 744
Albert Einstein p. 744
Sigmund Freud p. 744
Pablo Picasso p. 744
Igor Stravinsky p. 744
Dada p. 744

Wilbur and Orville Wright p. 744
KLM Royal Dutch Airlines p. 745
Marie Curie p. 745
Baron Pierre de Coubertin p. 745
Le Corbusier p. 746
Indian National Congress p. 749

Bengal p. 749
All-India Muslim League p. 749
Mohandas K. Gandhi p. 751
Jawaharlal Nehru p. 753
Muhammad Ali Jinnah p. 754
Lázaro Cárdenas p. 755
Hipólito Irigoyen p. 755

Getulio Vargas p. 756
Juan Perón p. 757
Eva Duarte Perón p. 757
Blaise Diagne p. 759
African National Congress p. 760
Haile Selassie p. 760

SUGGESTED READING

Achebe, Chinua. *Arrow of God.* 1964. A classic novel about the conflict between traditional beliefs and Christianity in a Nigerian village.

Boahen, Adfu. *African Perspectives on Colonialism.* 1987. A work recounting the African reactions to colonial rule.

Bose, Sugata, and Ayesha Jalal. *Modern South Asia: History, Culture, and Political Economy,* 3d ed. 2011. An up-to-date general account.

Brown, Judith M. *Gandhi: Prisoner of Hope.* 1989. The classic biography of the Indian leader.

Collins, Larry, and Dominique Lapierre. *Freedom at Midnight.* 1975. A popular account of the coming of independence and the partition of India.

Davis, Darrell William. *Picturing Japaneseness: Monumental Style, National Identity, Japanese Film.* 1996. Details how Japanese cinema helped shape the country's identity, especially in the 1930s.

Dikötter, Frank. *Exotic Commodities: Modern Objects and Everyday Life in China.* 2006. Excellent study of changes in transportation, urban life, and personal styles between 1850 and 1949.

DuBois, Ellen. *Woman Suffrage and Women's Rights.* 1998. The best description of the women's movement at the beginning of the twentieth century.

Finnane, Antonia. *Changing Clothes in China: Fashion, History, Nation.* 2008. History of the relationship between changing clothing styles, mass media, and political ideology.

Gadgil, M., and R. Guha. *This Fissured Land: An Ecological History of India.* 1993. The classic work on the history of the Indian environment.

Nye, David E. *Electrifying America: Social Meanings of a New Technology.* 1990. The cultural history of American electrification and modernization.

Sarkar, Sumit. *Modern India, 1885–1947.* 1983. The classic history of the independence movement.

Strand, David. *Rickshaw Beijing: City People and Politics in the 1920s.* 1989. Describes how the rickshaw transformed China's capital city.

Torpey, John. *The Invention of the Passport: Surveillance, Citizenship and the State.* 1999. Discusses increasing government controls of identity in the nineteenth and twentieth centuries.

Warren, James Francis. *Rickshaw Coolie: A People's History of Singapore, 1880–1940.* 2003. Focuses on the relationship between Chinese immigration and the rickshaw industry.

CourseMate Go to the History CourseMate website for primary source links, study tools, and review materials for this chapter. www.cengagebrain.com

Chapter Outline

German Dive-Bomber over Eastern Europe   A German Messerschmidt Bf-110 fighter plane attacks a Soviet troop convoy on the Eastern Front.

The Collapse of the Old Order, 1929–1949

Before the First World War the Italian poet Filippo Marinetti exalted violence as noble and manly: "We want to glorify war, the world's only hygiene—militarism, deed, destroyer of anarchisms, the beautiful ideas that are death-bringing, and the subordination of women."[1] His friend Gabriele d'Annunzio added: "If it is a crime to incite citizens to violence, I shall boast of this crime."[2] Poets are sometimes more prescient than they imagine.

In the nineteenth century the governments of the great powers were manipulated by politicians through appeals to popular nationalism. Internationally, the world order relied on the maintenance of empires by military or economic means. And the global economy was based on free-market capitalism in which the industrial countries exchanged manufactured goods for the agricultural and mineral products of the nonindustrial world.

After the trauma of World War I the world seemed to return to what U.S. president Warren Harding called "normalcy": prosperity in Europe and America, European colonialism in Asia and Africa, American domination of Latin America, and peace almost everywhere. But in 1929 normalcy vanished. As the Great Depression spread around the world, governments turned against one another in desperate attempts to protect their people's livelihood.

Most survivors of the war had learned to abhor violence. For a few, however, war and domination became a creed, a goal, and a solution to their problems. The Japanese military tried to save their country from the depression by conquering China, which erupted in revolution. In Germany many blamed their troubles on communists and Jews and turned to the Nazis, who promised to save German society by crushing others. In the Soviet Union, Stalin used energetic and murderous means to force his country into a communist version of the Industrial Revolution.

As the old order collapsed, the world was engulfed by a second Great War, one far more global and destructive than the first. Unlike World War I, this was a war of movement in which entire countries were conquered in a matter of weeks. It was also a war of machines: fighter planes and bombers that targeted civilians, tanks, aircraft carriers, and, finally, atomic bombs that obliterated entire cities.

At the end of World War II much of Europe and East Asia lay in ruins, and millions of destitute refugees sought safety in other lands. The colonial powers were either defeated or so weakened that they could no longer prevent their Asian and African subjects from demanding independence.

---

[1] Apollonio Umbro, ed., *Documents of Twentieth Century Art: Futurist Manifestos* (New York: Viking Press, 1973), 23.

[2] Richard F. Hamilton and Holger H. Herwig, *Decisions for War, 1914–1917* (Cambridge: Cambridge University Press, 2004), 199.

THE STALIN REVOLUTION

During the 1920s the Soviet Union recovered from the Revolutions of 1917 and the civil war that followed (see Chapter 28). After Stalin achieved total mastery over this huge nation in 1929, he led it through an economic and social transformation that turned it into a great industrial and military power and intensified both admiration for and fear of communism throughout the world.

Five-Year Plans

Joseph Stalin Bolshevik revolutionary, head of the Soviet Communist Party after 1924, and dictator of the Soviet Union from 1928 to 1953. He led the Soviet Union with an iron fist, using Five-Year Plans to increase industrial production and terror to crush all opposition.

Five-Year Plans Plans that Joseph Stalin introduced to industrialize the Soviet Union rapidly, beginning in 1928. They set goals for the output of steel, electricity, machinery, and most other products and were enforced by the police powers of the state. They succeeded in making the Soviet Union a major industrial power before World War II.

Joseph Stalin (1879–1953) was the son of a poor shoemaker. Before becoming a revolutionary, he studied for the priesthood. Under the name *Stalin* (Russian for "man of steel"), he played a small part in the Revolutions of 1917. He was a hard-working and skillful administrator who rose within the party bureaucracy and filled its upper ranks with men loyal to himself. He then proceeded to make himself absolute dictator and transform Soviet society.

Stalin's ambition was to turn the USSR into an industrial nation. However, industrialization was to serve a different purpose than in other countries. It was not expected to produce consumer goods for a mass market or to enrich individuals. Instead, its aim was to increase the power of the Communist Party domestically and that of the Soviet Union in relation to other countries.

Stalin was determined to prevent a repetition of the humiliating defeat Russia had suffered at the hands of Germany in 1917. His goal was to quintuple the output of electricity and double that of heavy industry—iron, steel, coal, and machinery—in five years. To do so, he devised the first of a series of **Five-Year Plans**. Beginning in October 1928, the Communist Party and government created whole industries and cities from scratch, then trained millions of peasants to work in the new factories, mines, and offices. In every way except actual fighting, Stalin's Russia resembled a nation at war.

Rapid industrialization hastened environmental changes. Hydroelectric dams turned rivers into strings of reservoirs. Roads, canals, and railroad tracks cut the landscape. Forests and grassland were turned into farmland. From an environmental perspective, the Five-Year Plans resembled the transformation that had occurred in the United States and Canada a few decades earlier.

Poster concerning the 1st 5 Year Plan with a photograph of Joseph Stalin 1879-1953), 'At the end of the Plan, the basis of collectivisation must be completed', 1932 (colour litho), Klutchis (fl.1932/Deutsches Plakat Museum, Essen, Germany/Archives Charmet/The Bridgeman Art Library

Collectivization of Agriculture

Since the Soviet Union was still a predominantly agrarian country, the only way to pay for these massive investments, provide the labor, and feed the millions of new industrial workers was to squeeze the peasantry. Stalin therefore proceeded with the most radical social experiment conceived up to that time: the collectivization of agriculture.

Collectivization meant consolidating small private farms into vast collectives and making the farmers work together in commonly owned fields. Each collective was expected to supply the government with a fixed amount of food and distribute what was left among its members. Collectives were to become outdoor factories where food was manufactured through the techniques of mass production and the application of machinery. The purpose of this collectivization was to bring the peasants under government control so they never again could withhold food supplies, as they had done during the Russian civil war of 1918–1921.

The Collectivization of Soviet Agriculture   One of the goals of collectivization was to introduce modern farm machinery. This poster highlights Josef Stalin's personal connection with mechanization. The tractors and operators were assigned to tractor stations, which then supplied them to individual collective farms.

CHRONOLOGY

	United States, Europe, and North Africa	Asia and the Pacific
1920	1928 Stalin introduces Five-Year Plans and the collectivization of agriculture 1929 Great Depression begins in United States	
1930	1931 Great Depression reaches Europe 1933 Hitler comes to power in Germany	1931 Japanese forces occupy Manchuria 1934–1935 Mao leads Communists on Long March
1935	1936 Hitler invades the Rhineland 1939 (Sept. 1) German forces invade Poland	1937 Japanese troops invade China, conquer coastal provinces; Chiang Kai-shek flees to Sichuan 1937–1938 Japanese troops take Nanjing
1940	1940 (March–April) German forces conquer Denmark, Norway, the Netherlands, and Belgium 1940 (May–June) German forces conquer France 1940 (June–Sept.) Battle of Britain 1941 (June 21) German forces invade USSR 1942–1943 Allies and Germany battle for control of North Africa 1943 Soviet victory in Battle of Stalingrad 1943–1944 Red Army slowly pushes Wehrmacht back to Germany 1944 (June 6) D-day: U.S., British, and Canadian troops land in Normandy	1941 (Dec. 7) Japanese aircraft bomb Pearl Harbor 1942 (Jan.–March) Japanese conquer Thailand, Philippines, Malaya 1942 (June) United States Navy defeats Japan at Battle of Midway
1945	1945 (May 7) Germany surrenders	1945 (Aug. 6) United States drops atomic bomb on Hiroshima 1945 (Aug. 14) Japan surrenders 1945–1949 Civil war in China 1949 (Oct. 1) Communists defeat Guomindang; Mao proclaims People's Republic of China

When collectivization was announced, the government mounted a massive propaganda campaign and sent party members into the countryside to enlist the farmers' support. At first all seemed to go well, but soon *kulaks* (COO-lock) ("fists"), the better-off peasants, began to resist giving up all their property. When soldiers came to force them into collectives at gunpoint, they burned their crops, smashed their equipment, and slaughtered their livestock. Within a few months they slaughtered half of the Soviet Union's horses and cattle and two-thirds of the sheep and goats. In retaliation, Stalin ruthlessly ordered the "liquidation of kulaks as a class" and incited the poor peasants to attack their wealthier neighbors. Over 8 million kulaks were arrested. Many were executed, and the rest were sent to slave labor camps, where most starved to death.

The peasants who were left had been the least successful before collectivization and proved to be the least competent after. Many were sent to work in factories. The rest were forbidden to leave their farms. With half of their draft animals gone, they could not plant or harvest enough to meet the swelling demands of the cities. Yet government agents took whatever they could find, leaving little or nothing for the farmers themselves. After bad harvests in 1933 and 1934, a famine swept through the countryside, killing some 5 million people, about one in every twenty farmers.

Stalin's second Five-Year Plan, designed to run from 1933 to 1937, was originally intended to produce consumer goods. But when the Nazis took over Germany in 1933 (see below), Stalin changed the plan to emphasize heavy industries that could produce armaments. Between 1927 and 1937 the Soviet output of metals and machines increased fourteen-fold while consumer goods became scarce and food was rationed. After a decade of Stalinism, the Soviet people were more poorly clothed, fed, and housed than they had been before the war.

Terror and Opportunities

The 1930s brought both terror and opportunities to the Soviet people. The forced pace of industrialization, the collectivization of agriculture, and the uprooting of millions of people could be accomplished only under duress. To prevent any possible resistance or rebellion, the NKVD, Stalin's secret police force, created a climate of suspicion and fear.

As early as 1930 Stalin had hundreds of engineers and technicians arrested on trumped-up charges of counterrevolutionary ideas and sabotage. Three years later, he expelled a million members of the Communist Party—one-third of the membership—on similar charges. He then turned on his most trusted associates.

In December 1934 Sergei Kirov, the party boss of Leningrad (now St. Petersburg), was assassinated, perhaps on Stalin's orders. Stalin made a public display of mourning Kirov while blaming others for the crime. He then ordered a series of spectacular purge trials in which he accused most of Lenin's associates of treason. In 1937 he had his eight top generals and many lower officers executed, leaving the Red Army dangerously weakened. Under torture or psychological pressure, almost all the accused confessed to the "crimes" they were charged with.

While "Old Bolsheviks" and high officials were being put on trial, terror spread steadily downward. The government regularly made demands that people could not meet, so everyone was guilty of breaking some regulation or other. People from all walks of life were arrested, some on mere suspicion or because of a false accusation by a jealous coworker or neighbor, some for expressing a doubt or working too hard or not hard enough, some for being related to someone previously arrested, some for no reason at all. Millions of people were sentenced without trials. At the height of the terror, some 8 million were sent to *gulags* **(GOO-log)** (labor camps), where perhaps a million died each year of exposure or malnutrition. To its victims the terror seemed capricious and random. Yet it turned a sullen and resentful people into docile hard-working subjects of the party.

In spite of the fear and hardships, many Soviet citizens supported Stalin's regime. Suddenly, with so many people gone and new industries and cities being built everywhere, there were opportunities for those who remained, especially the poor and the young. Women entered careers and jobs previously closed to them, becoming steelworkers, physicians, and office managers; but they retained their household and child-rearing duties, receiving little help from men (see Diversity and Dominance: Women, Family Values, and the Russian Revolution). People who moved to the cities, worked enthusiastically, and asked no questions could hope to rise into the upper ranks of the Communist Party, the military, the government, or the professions—where the privileges and rewards were many.

Stalin's brutal methods helped the Soviet Union industrialize faster than any country had ever done. By the late 1930s the USSR was the world's third largest industrial power, after the United States and Germany. To foreign observers it seemed to be booming with construction projects and labor shortages. Even anti-Communist observers admitted that government planning worked. To millions of Soviet citizens who took pride in the new strength of their country and to many foreigners who contrasted conditions in the Soviet Union with the unemployment and despair in the West, Stalin's achievement seemed worth any price.

SECTION REVIEW

- Once in power, Stalin issued Five-Year Plans to accelerate Soviet industrialization.

- When farms were merged into collectives, millions of farmers who resisted were deported and killed; those who were left suffered famine.

- Under the terror, Stalin executed many generals and government officials and sent millions of people to slave labor camps.

- Stalin's measures subjugated the Russian people but made the Soviet Union the world's third largest industrial power.

THE DEPRESSION

On October 24, 1929—"Black Thursday"—the New York stock market went into a dive. Within days stocks had lost half their value. The fall continued for three years, ruining millions of investors. People with bank accounts rushed to make withdrawals, causing thousands of banks to collapse.

Economic Crisis

What began as a stock market crash soon turned into the deepest depression in history. As consumers reduced their purchases, businesses cut production, laying off thousands of workers. Female employees were the first laid off on the grounds that men had to support families while women worked only for "pin money." Jobless men deserted their families. Small farmers went bankrupt and lost their land. By mid-1932 the American economy had shrunk by half, and unemployment had risen to an unprecedented 25 percent of the workforce. Many observers thought that free-enterprise capitalism was doomed.

In 1930 the U.S. government, hoping to protect American industries from foreign competition, imposed the Smoot-Hawley tariff, the highest in American history. In retaliation, other countries raised their tariffs in a wave of "beggar thy neighbor" protectionism. The result was crippled export industries and shrinking world trade. While global industrial production declined by 36 percent between 1929 and 1932, world trade dropped by a breathtaking 62 percent.

Depression in Industrial Nations

By 1931 the depression had spread to Europe. Governments canceled reparations payments and war loans, but it was too late to save the world economy. Though their economies stagnated, France and Britain weathered the depression by making their colonial empires purchase their products rather than the products of other countries. Nations that relied on exports to pay for imported food and fuel suffered much more. In Germany unemployment reached 6 million by 1932, twice as high as in Britain. Half the German population lived in poverty, while those who kept their jobs saw their salaries cut and their living standards fall. In Japan the burden of the depression fell hardest on the farmers and fishermen.

This massive economic upheaval had profound political repercussions. Nationalists everywhere called for autarchy, or independence from the world economy. In the United States Franklin D. Roosevelt was elected president in 1932 on a "New Deal" platform of government programs to stimulate and revitalize the economy. Although the American, British, and French

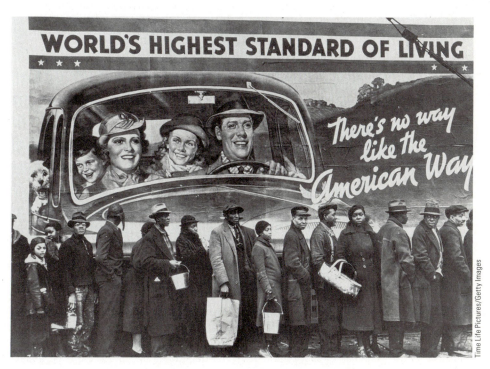

Two Views of the American Way   In this classic photograph, *Life* magazine photographer Margaret Bourke-White captured the contrast between advertisers' view of the ideal American family and the reality of bread lines for the poor.

Women, Family Values, and the Russian Revolution

The Bolsheviks were of two minds on the subject of women. They were opposed to bourgeois morality and to the oppression of women, especially working-class women, under capitalism. But what to put in its place?

Alexandra Kollontai was the most outspoken of the Bolsheviks on the subject of women's rights. She advocated the liberation of women, the replacement of housework by communal kitchens and laundries, and divorce on demand. Under socialism, love, sex, and marriage would be entirely equal, reciprocal, and free of economic obligations. Childbearing would be encouraged, but children would be raised communally: "The worker mother . . . must remember that there are henceforth only our children, those of the communist state, the common possession of all workers."

In a lecture she gave at Sverdlov University in 1921, Kollontai declared:

. . . it is important to preserve not only the interests of the woman but also the life of the child, and this is to be done by giving the woman the opportunity to combine labour and maternity. Soviet power tries to create a situation where a woman does not have to cling to a man she has learned to loathe only because she has nowhere else to go with her children, and where a woman alone does not have to fear for her life and the life of her child. In the labour republic it is not the philanthropists with their humiliating charity but the workers and peasants, fellow-creators of the new society, who hasten to help the working woman and strive to lighten the burden of motherhood. . . . I would like to say a few words about . . . the question of abortion, and Soviet Russia's attitude toward it. On 20 November 1920 the labour republic issued a law abolishing the penalties that had been attached to abortion. What is the reason behind this new attitude? Russia after all suffers not from an overproduction of living labour but rather from a lack of it. Russia is thinly, not densely populated. Every unit of labour power is precious. Why then have we declared abortion to be no longer a criminal offence? . . .

Abortion exists and flourishes everywhere, and no laws or punitive measures have succeeded in rooting it out. A way round the law is always found. But "secret help" only cripples women; they become a burden on the labour government, and the size of the labour force is reduced. Abortion, when carried out under proper medical conditions, is less harmful and dangerous, and the woman can get back to work quicker. Soviet power realizes that the need for abortion will only disappear on the one hand when Russia has a broad and developed network of institutions protecting motherhood and providing social education, and on the other hand when women understand that *childbirth is a social obligation*; Soviet power has therefore allowed abortion to be performed openly and in clinical conditions.

Besides the large-scale development of motherhood protection, the task of labour Russia is to strengthen in women the healthy instinct of motherhood, to make motherhood and labour for the collective compatible and thus do away with the need for abortion. This is the approach of the labour republic to the question of abortion, which still faces women in the bourgeois countries in all its magnitude. In these countries women are exhausted by the dual burden of hired labour for capital and motherhood. In Soviet Russia the working woman and peasant woman are helping the Communist Party to build a new society and to undermine the old way of life that has enslaved women. As soon as woman is viewed as being essentially a labour unit, the key to the solution of the complex question of maternity can be found.

---

governments intervened in their economies, they remained democratic. In Germany and Japan, as economic grievances worsened long-festering political resentments, radical leaders came to power and turned their nations into military machines, hoping to acquire, by war if necessary, empires large enough to support self-sufficient economies and at the same time provide employment in arms factories.

Depression in Nonindustrial Regions

The depression also spread to Asia, Africa, and Latin America, but very unevenly. In 1930 India erected a wall of import duties to protect its infant industries from foreign competition; its living standards stagnated but did not drop. China was little affected by trade with other countries; its problems were more political than economic.

Countries that depended on exports were hard hit by the depression. Malaya, Indochina, and the Dutch East Indies produced most of the world's natural rubber; when automobile production in the United States and Europe dropped by half, so did imports of rubber, devastating their economies. Egypt, dependent on cotton exports, was also affected, and in the resulting political strife, the government became autocratic and unpopular.

Fifteen years later Joseph Stalin reversed the Soviet policy on abortion.

The published draft of the law prohibiting abortion and providing material assistance to mothers has provoked a lively reaction throughout the country. It is being heatedly discussed by tens of millions of people and there is no doubt that it will serve as a further strengthening of the Soviet family. . . .

When we speak of strengthening the Soviet family, we are speaking precisely of the struggle against the survivals of a bourgeois attitude towards marriage, women, and children. So-called "free love" and all disorderly sex life are bourgeois through and through, and have nothing to do with either socialist principles or the ethics and standards of conduct of the Soviet citizens. Socialist doctrine shows this, and it is proved by life itself.

The elite of our country, the best of the Soviet youth, are as a rule also excellent family men who dearly love their children. And vice versa: the man who does not take marriage seriously, and abandons his children to the whims of fate, is usually also a bad worker and a poor member of society. . . .

It is impossible even to compare the present state of the family with that which obtained before the Soviet regime—so great has been the improvement towards greater stability and, above all, greater humanity and goodness. The single fact that millions of women have become economically independent and are no longer at the mercy of men's whims, speaks volumes. Compare, for instance, the modern woman collective farmer who sometimes earns more than her husband, with the pre-revolutionary peasant woman who completely depended on her husband and was a slave in the household. Has not this fundamentally changed family relations, has it not rationalized and strengthened the family? The very motives for setting up a family, for getting married, have changed for the better, have been cleansed of atavistic and barbaric elements.

Marriage has ceased to be a matter of sell-and-buy. Nowadays a girl from a collective farm is not given away (or should we say "sold away"?) by her father, for now she is her own mistress, and no one can give her away. She will marry the man she loves. . . .

We alone have all the conditions under which a working woman can fulfill her duties as a citizen and as a mother responsible for the birth and early upbringing of her children.

A woman without children merits our pity, for she does not know the full joy of life. Our Soviet women, full-blooded citizens of the freest country in the world, have been given the bliss of motherhood. We must safeguard the family and raise and rear healthy Soviet heroes!

QUESTIONS FOR ANALYSIS

1. How does Kollontai expect women to be both workers and mothers without depending on a man? How would Soviet society make this possible?

2. Why does Alexandra Kollontai advocate the legalization of abortion in Soviet Russia? Does she view abortion as a permanent right or as a temporary necessity?

3. Why does Stalin characterize a "lighthearted, negligent attitude toward marriage" and "all disorderly sex life" as "bourgeois through and through"?

4. How does Stalin's image of the Soviet family differ from Kollontai's? Are his views a variation of her views, or the opposite?

Sources: First selection from Alexandra Kollontai, "The Labour of Women in the Revolution of the Economy," in *Selected Writings of Alexandra Kollontai*, translated by Alix Holt (Lawrence Hill & Company, 1978), pp. 148–149. Second selection from Discussion of the Law on Abolition of Legal Abortion, Pravda, Editorials of May 28 and June 9, 1936 (English translation in Rudolf Schlesinger, ed., Changing Attitudes in Soviet Russia: The Family in the USSR, London, Routledge & Kegan Paul, 1949, pp. 251–54, 268–69.

Throughout Latin America unemployment and homelessness increased markedly. The industrialization of Argentina and Brazil was set back a decade or more. Disenchanted with liberal politics, military officers seized power in several Latin American countries (see Chapter 29). Consciously imitating dictatorships emerging in Europe, they imposed authoritarian control over their economies, hoping to stimulate local industries and curb imports.

Other than the USSR, only southern Africa boomed during the 1930s. As other prices dropped, gold became relatively more valuable. Copper deposits, found in Northern Rhodesia (now Zambia) and the Belgian Congo (now Democratic Republic of the Congo), proved to be cheaper to mine than Chilean copper. But this mining boom benefited only a small number of European and white South African mine owners. For Africans it was a mixed blessing; mining provided jobs and cash wages to men while women stayed behind in the villages, farming, herding, and raising children without their husbands' help.

SECTION REVIEW

- The New York stock market crash of 1929 caused business and bank failures and massive unemployment.

- The depression soon spread to all industrial nations hitting Germany particularly hard.

- Nonindustrial countries, especially those that depended on exports to industrial countries, were also hard hit; only southern Africa was spared.

- In the face of this threat, some countries turned to dictatorship to save their economies.

THE RISE OF FASCISM

The Russian Revolution and its Stalinist aftermath frightened property owners in Europe and North America. In western Europe and North America, middle- and upper-income voters took refuge in conservative politics. In southern and central Europe, the war had turned people's hopes of victory to bitter disappointment. Many blamed ethnic minorities, especially Jews, for their troubles. In their yearning for a mythical past of family farms and small shops, increasing numbers rejected representative government and sought more dramatic solutions.

Radical politicians applied wartime propaganda techniques to appeal to a confused citizenry. They promised to use any means necessary to bring back full employment, stop the spread of communism, and achieve the territorial conquests that World War I had denied them. While defending private property from communism, they borrowed the communist model of politics: a single party and a secret police that ruled by terror and intimidation.

Mussolini's Italy

The first country to seek radical answers was Italy. World War I, which had never been popular, left thousands of veterans who found neither pride in their victory nor jobs in the postwar economy. Unemployed veterans and violent youths banded together into *fasci di combattimento* (fighting units) to demand action and intimidate politicians. When workers threatened to strike, factory and property owners hired gangs of these *fascisti* to defend them.

Benito Mussolini (1883–1945) had supported Italy's entry into the war. A spellbinding orator, he quickly became the leader of the **Fascist Party**, which glorified warfare and the Italian nation. By 1921 the party had 300,000 members, many of whom used violent methods to repress strikes, intimidate voters, and seize municipal governments. A year later Mussolini threatened to march on Rome if he was not appointed prime minister. The government, composed of timid parliamentarians, gave in.

Mussolini proceeded to install Fascist Party members in all government jobs, crush all opposition parties, and jail anyone who criticized him. The party took over the press, public education, and youth activities and gave employers control over their workers. The Fascists lowered living standards but reduced unemployment and provided social security and public services. They proved to be neither ruthless radicals nor competent administrators.

What Mussolini and the Fascist movement really excelled at was bombastic speeches, spectacular parades, and signs everywhere proclaiming "Il Duce **(eel DOO-chay)** [the Leader] is always right!" Mussolini's genius was to apply the techniques of modern mass communications and advertisement to political life. Movie footage and radio news bulletins galvanized the masses in ways never before done in peacetime. His techniques of whipping up public enthusiasm were not lost on other radicals. By the 1930s fascist movements had appeared in most European countries, as well as in Latin America, China, and Japan. Fascism appealed to many people who were frightened by rapid changes and placed their hopes in charismatic leaders. Of all of Mussolini's imitators, none was as sinister as Adolf Hitler.

Hitler's Germany

Germany had lost the First World War after coming very close to winning. The hyperinflation of 1923 wiped out the savings of middle-class families. Less than ten years later the depression caused more unemployment and misery than in any other country. Millions of Germans blamed Socialists, Jews, and foreigners for their troubles.

Adolf Hitler (1889–1945) joined the German army in 1914 and was wounded at the front. He later looked back fondly on the clear lines of authority and the camaraderie he had experienced in battle. After the war he used his gifts as an orator to lead a political splinter group called the National Socialist German Workers' Party—**Nazis** for short. While serving a brief jail sentence he wrote *Mein Kampf* **(mine compf)** (*My Struggle*), in which he outlined his goals and beliefs.

When it was published in 1925, *Mein Kampf* attracted little notice. Its ideas seemed so insane that almost no one took it, or its author, seriously. Hitler's ideas went far beyond ordinary nationalism. He believed that Germany should incorporate all German-speaking areas, even those in neighboring countries. He distinguished among a "master race" of Aryans (he meant Germans, Scandinavians, and Britons), a degenerate "Alpine" race of French and Italians, and an inferior

Benito Mussolini Fascist dictator of Italy (1922–1943). He led Italy to conquer Ethiopia (1935), joined Germany in the Axis pact (1936), and allied Italy with Germany in World War II. He was overthrown in 1943 when the Allies invaded Italy.

Fascist Party Italian political party created by Benito Mussolini during World War I. It emphasized aggressive nationalism and was Mussolini's instrument for the creation of a dictatorship in Italy from 1922 to 1943.

Adolf Hitler Born in Austria, Hitler became a radical German nationalist during World War I. He led the National Socialist German Workers' Party—the Nazis—in the 1920s and became dictator of Germany in 1933. He led Europe into World War II.

Nazis German political party led by Adolf Hitler, emphasizing nationalism, racism, and war. When Hitler became chancellor of Germany in 1933, the Nazis became the only legal party and an instrument of Hitler's absolute rule. The party's formal name was National Socialist German Workers' Party.

race of Russian and eastern European Slavs, fit only to be slaves of the master race. He reserved his most intense hatred for Jews, on whom he blamed every disaster that had befallen Germany, especially the defeat of 1918. He glorified violence and looked forward to a future war in which the "master race" would defeat and subjugate all others.

Hitler's first goal was to reverse the humiliation and repeal the military restrictions of the Treaty of Versailles. Next he planned to annex all German-speaking territories to a greater Germany, then gain *Lebensraum* **(LAY-bens-rowm)** (room to live) at the expense of Poland and the USSR. Finally, he planned to eliminate all Jews from Europe.

From 1924 to 1930 Hitler's followers remained a tiny minority, for most Germans found his ideas too extreme. But when the depression hit, the Nazis gained supporters among the unemployed, who believed their promises of jobs for all, and among property owners frightened by the growing popularity of communists.

In March 1933 Hitler became chancellor of Germany. Once in office, he quickly assumed dictatorial powers. He put Nazis in charge of all government agencies, educational institutions, and professional organizations; banned all other political parties; and threw their leaders into concentration camps. The Nazis deprived Jews of their citizenship and civil rights, prohibited them from marrying "Aryans," ousted them from the professions, and confiscated their property. In August 1934 Hitler proclaimed himself *Führer* **(FEW-rer)** ("leader") and called Germany the "Third Reich," the third German empire after the Holy Roman Empire of medieval times and the German Empire of 1871 to 1918.

The Nazis' economic and social policies were spectacularly effective. The government undertook massive public works projects. Businesses got contracts to manufacture weapons. Women who had entered the workforce were urged to release their jobs to men. By 1936 business was booming; unemployment was at its lowest level since the 1920s; and living standards were rising. Most Germans believed that their economic well-being outweighed the loss of liberty.

The Road to War, 1933–1939

However, Hitler's goal was not prosperity or popularity, but conquest. As soon as he came to office, he began to build up the armed forces. Meanwhile, he tested the reactions of the other powers through a series of surprise moves followed by protestations of peace.

A Nazi Rally Hitler organized mass rallies at Nuremberg to whip up popular support for his regime and to indoctrinate young Germans with a martial spirit. Thousands of men in uniform marched in torch-lit parades before Hitler and his top officials.

AP Images

In 1933 Hitler withdrew Germany from the League of Nations. Two years later he announced that Germany was going to introduce conscription, build up its army, and create an air force—in violation of the Versailles treaty. Neither Britain nor France was willing to risk war by standing up to Germany.

In 1935, emboldened by the weakness of the democracies, Italy invaded Ethiopia, the last independent state in Africa and a member of the League of Nations. The League and the democracies protested but refused to close the Suez Canal to Italian ships or impose an oil embargo. The following year, when Hitler sent troops into the Rhineland on the borders of France and Belgium, the other powers merely protested.

By 1938 Hitler decided that his rearmament plans were far enough advanced that he could afford to escalate his demands. In March Germany invaded Austria. Most Austrians were German-speakers and accepted the annexation of their country without protest. Then came Czechoslovakia, where a German-speaking minority lived along the German border. Hitler first demanded their autonomy from Czech rule, then their annexation to Germany. Throughout the summer he threatened to go to war. At the Munich Conference of September 1938, the leaders of France, Britain, and Italy gave him everything he wanted without consulting Czechoslovakia. Once again, Hitler learned that aggression paid off.

The weakness of the democracies—now called "appeasement"—had three causes. The first was the deep-seated fear of war among people who had lived through World War I. Unlike the dictators, politicians in the democracies could not ignore their constituents' yearnings for peace. Most people believed that the threat of war might go away if they wished for peace fervently enough. The second cause of appeasement was fear of communism among conservatives, who feared Stalin more than Hitler because Hitler claimed to respect Christianity and private property. The third cause was the very novelty of fascist tactics. Britain's prime minister Neville Chamberlain assumed that political leaders (other than the Bolsheviks) were honorable men and that an agreement was as valid as a business contract. Thus, when Hitler promised to incorporate only German-speaking people into Germany and said he had "no further territorial demands," Chamberlain believed him.

After Munich it was too late to stop Hitler, short of war. Germany and Italy signed an alliance called the Axis, and in March 1939 Germany invaded what was left of Czechoslovakia. Belatedly realizing that Hitler could not be trusted, France and Britain sought Soviet help. Stalin, however, distrusted the "capitalists" as much as they distrusted him. When Hitler offered to divide Poland between Germany and the Soviet Union, Stalin accepted. The Nazi-Soviet Pact of August 23, 1939, freed Hitler from the fear of a two-front war and gave Stalin time to build up his armies. One week later, on September 1, German forces swept into Poland, and the war was on.

SECTION REVIEW

- The depression gave opportunities to ultranationalist politicians who promised prosperity and order.

- Mussolini, head of the Fascist Party, became dictator of Italy in 1922 and proceeded to quell all opposition.

- After gaining power in 1933, Hitler began to transform the German economy and society and to build up the German armed forces.

- Germany and Italy made aggressive moves that the democracies, fearing another war, did not oppose, but when Germany invaded Poland, Hitler's aggressive objectives were clear.

EAST ASIA, 1931–1945

When the depression hit, the collapse of demand for silk and rice ruined thousands of Japanese farmers; to survive, some even sold their daughters into prostitution, while many poor young men flocked to the military. Ultranationalists resented their country's dependence on foreign trade and what they believed was unnecessary party politics that sullied the righteousness of the divine imperial will. If only Japan had a colonial empire, they thought, it would not be beholden to the rest of the world. But Europeans and Americans had already taken most potential colonies in Asia. Japanese nationalists saw the conquest of China, with its vast population and resources, as the solution to their country's problems.

The Manchurian Incident of 1931

Meanwhile, in China the Guomindang (gwo-min-dong) (see Chapter 28) was becoming stronger and preparing to challenge the Japanese presence in Manchuria, a province rich in coal and iron ore. Junior officers in the Japanese army, frustrated by the caution of their superiors, took action. In September 1931 they blew up part of a railroad track as a pretext for invading the entire province. This invasion was promoted as achieving the "independence" of Manchuria under the name *Manchukuo* (man-CHEW-coo-oh), but in reality, Manchukuo remained under Japanese control. Many civilian officials and military leaders back in Tokyo had not approved of the attack, but they soon joined the overwhelming positive reaction to the incident expressed by the public, press, and even leftist critics.

The U.S. government condemned the Japanese conquest, and the League of Nations refused to recognize Manchukuo and urged the Japanese to remove their troops from China. Persuaded that the Western powers would not fight, Japan resigned from the League.

During the next few years the Japanese built railways and heavy industries in Manchuria and northeastern China and sped up their rearmament. At home, production was diverted to the military, especially to building warships. The government grew more authoritarian, jailing thousands of dissidents. On several occasions, ultranationalists, many of them junior officers, mutinied or assassinated leading political figures. The mutineers received mild punishments, and generals and admirals sympathetic to their views replaced more moderate civilian politicians.

The Long March

Until the Japanese seized Manchuria, the Chinese government seemed to be creating conditions for a national recovery. The main challenge to the government of **Chiang Kai-shek** (chang kie-shek) came from the Communists. The Chinese Communist Party had been founded in 1921 by a handful of intellectuals, and for several years it lived in the shadow of the Guomindang. Its efforts to recruit members among industrial workers came to naught in 1927, when Chiang Kai-shek arrested and executed Communists and labor leaders alike. The few Communists who escaped the mass arrests fled to the remote mountains of Jiangxi (jang-she), in southeastern China.

Among them was **Mao Zedong** (ma-oh zay-dong) (1893–1976), a farmer's son who had left home to study philosophy. Mao was a man of action whose first impulse was to call for violent effort: "To be able to leap on horseback and to shoot at the same time; to go from battle to battle; to shake the mountains by one's cries, and the colors of the sky by one's roars of anger." In the early 1920s Mao discovered the works of Karl Marx, joined the Communist Party, and soon became one of its leaders.

In Jiangxi Mao began studying conditions among the peasants, in whom Communists had previously shown no interest. He planned to redistribute land from the wealthier to the poorer peasants, thereby gaining adherents for the coming struggle with the Guomindang army. His goal was a complete social revolution from the bottom up. Mao's reliance on the peasantry was a radical departure from Marxist-Leninist ideology, which stressed the backwardness of the peasants and pinned its hopes on industrial workers. Mao therefore had to be careful to cloak his pragmatic tactics in communist rhetoric to allay the suspicions of Stalin and his agents.

Mao was an advocate of women's equality. Before 1927 the Communists had organized the women who worked in Shanghai's textile mills, the most exploited of all Chinese workers. Later, in their mountain stronghold in Jiangxi, they organized women farmers, allowed divorce, and banned arranged marriages and footbinding. But the party was still run by men whose primary task was warfare.

The Guomindang army pursued the Communists into the mountains, building small forts throughout the countryside. Rather than risk direct confrontations, Mao responded with guerrilla warfare. He harassed the army at its weak points with hit-and-run tactics, relying on the terrain and the support of the peasantry. Whereas government troops often mistreated civilians, Mao insisted that his soldiers help the peasants, pay a fair price for food and supplies, and treat women with respect.

In spite of their good relations with the peasants of Jiangxi, the Communists gradually found themselves encircled by government forces. In 1934 Mao and his followers decided to break out of the southern mountains and trek to Shaanxi (SHAWN-she), an even more remote province in northwestern China. The so-called **Long March** took them 6,000 miles (nearly 9,700 kilometers) in one year over desolate mountains and through swamps and deserts, pursued by the army and bombed by Chiang's aircraft. Of the 100,000 Communists who left Jiangxi in October 1934, only 4,000 reached Shaanxi a year later (see Map 30.1). Chiang's government thought it was finally rid of the Communists.

Chiang Kai-shek Chinese military and political leader. Succeeded Sun Yat-sen as head of the Guomindang in 1925; headed the Chinese government from 1928 to 1948; fought against the Chinese Communists and Japanese invaders. After 1949 he headed the Chinese Nationalist government in Taiwan.

Mao Zedong Leader of the Chinese Communist Party (1927–1976). He led the Communists on the Long March (1934–1935) and rebuilt the Communist Party and Red Army during the Japanese occupation of China (1937–1945). After World War II, he led the Communists to victory over the Guomindang. He ordered the Cultural Revolution in 1966.

Long March The 6,000-mile flight of Chinese Communists from southeastern to northwestern China. The Communists, led by Mao Zedong, were pursued by the Chinese army under orders from Chiang Kai-shek. The four thousand survivors of the march formed the nucleus of a revived Communist movement that defeated the Guomindang after World War II.

MAP 30.1 **Chinese Communist Movement and the Sino-Japanese War, to 1938** During the 1930s, China was the scene of a three-way war. The Nationalist government attacked and pursued the Communists, who escaped into the mountains of Shaanxi. Meanwhile, Japanese forces, having seized Manchuria in 1931, attacked China in 1937 and quickly conquered its eastern provinces. © Cengage Learning

The Sino-Japanese War, 1937–1945

In Japan politicians, senior officers, and business leaders disagreed on how to solve their country's economic problems. Some proposed a quick conquest of China; others advocated war with the Soviet Union. While their superiors hesitated, junior officers decided to take matters into their own hands.

On July 7, 1937, Japanese troops attacked Chinese forces near Beijing. The junior officers who ordered the attack quickly obtained the support of their commanders and then, reluctantly, of the government. Within weeks Japanese troops seized Beijing, Tianjin, Shanghai, and other coastal cities, and the Japanese navy blockaded the entire coast of China.

Once again, the United States and the League of Nations denounced the Japanese aggression. Yet the Western powers were too preoccupied with events in Europe and with their own economic problems to risk a military confrontation in Asia. When the Japanese sank a U.S. gunboat and shelled a British ship on the Yangzi River, the U.S. and British governments responded only with righteous indignation and pious resolutions.

The Chinese armies were large and fought bravely, but they were poorly led and armed and lost every battle. Japanese planes bombed cities while soldiers broke dikes and burned villages, killing thousands of civilians. Within a year Japan controlled the coastal provinces of China and the lower Yangzi and Yellow River Valleys, China's richest and most populated regions (see Map 30.1).

In spite of Japanese organizational and fighting skills, the attack on China did not bring the victory Japan had hoped for. The Chinese people continued to resist, either in the army or with the Communist guerrilla forces. As Japan sank deeper into the Chinese quagmire, life became harsher and more repressive for the Japanese people, as taxes rose, food and fuel became scarce, and more and more young men were drafted.

Warfare between the Chinese and Japanese was incredibly violent. In the winter of 1937–1938 Japanese troops took Nanjing, raped 20,000 women, killed roughly 200,000 prisoners and civilians, and looted and burned the city. To slow them down, Chiang ordered the Yellow River dikes blasted open, causing a flood that destroyed four thousand villages, killed 890,000 people, and made millions homeless. Two years later, when the Communists ordered a massive offensive, the Japanese retaliated with a "kill all, burn all, loot all" campaign, destroying hundreds of villages down to the last person, building, and farm animal.

The Chinese government, led by Chiang Kai-shek, escaped to the mountains of Sichuan in the center of the country. There Chiang built up a huge army, not to fight Japan but to prepare for a future confrontation with the Communists. The army drafted over 3 million men, even though it had only a million rifles and could not provide food or clothing for all its soldiers. The Guomindang raised farmers' taxes, even when famine forced farmers to eat the bark of trees.

Such taxes were not enough to support both a large army and the thousands of government officials and hangers-on who had fled to Sichuan. To avoid taxing its wealthy supporters the government printed money, causing inflation, hoarding, and corruption.

From his capital of Yan'an in Shaanxi province, Mao also built up his army and formed a government. Unlike the Guomindang, the Communists listened to the grievances of the peasants, especially the poor, to whom they distributed land confiscated from wealthy landowners. They imposed rigid discipline on their officials and soldiers and tolerated no dissent or criticism from intellectuals. Though they had few weapons, the Communists obtained support and intelligence from farmers in Japanese-occupied territory. They turned military reversals into propaganda victories, presenting themselves as the only group in China that was serious about fighting the Japanese.

SECTION REVIEW

- Seeing conquest as a solution to its economic problems, in 1931 Japan conquered Manchuria.

- The Chinese government under Chiang Kai-shek fought both the Japanese and the Communists led by Mao Zedong, who fled into the mountains of northern China.

- In 1937, Japanese forces conquered the coastal provinces of China; in the ensuing violent war, however, Japan gained few real advantages.

- Chiang Kai-shek fled to the interior and prepared to fight the Communists.

THE SECOND WORLD WAR

Many people feared that the Second World War would be a repetition of the First. Instead, it was much bigger in every way. It was fought around the world, from Norway to New Guinea and from Hawaii to Egypt, and on every ocean. It killed far more people than World War I, involved all civilians and productive forces, and showed how effectively industry, science, and nationalism could be channeled into mass destruction.

The War of Movement

In World War II motorized weapons gave back the advantage to the offensive. Opposing forces moved fast, their victories hinging as much on the aggressive spirit of their commanders and the military intelligence they obtained as on numbers of troops and firepower.

The Wehrmacht **(VAIR-mokt)**, or German army, was the first to learn this lesson. It not only had tanks, trucks, and fighter planes but had also perfected their combined use in a tactic called *Blitzkrieg* **(BLITS-creeg)** (lightning war): fighter planes scattered enemy troops and disrupted communications, tanks punctured the enemy's defenses, and then, with the help of the infantry, they encircled and captured enemy troops. At sea, both Japan and the United States had developed aircraft carriers that could launch planes against targets hundreds of miles away.

Armies ranged over vast theaters of operation, and countries were conquered in days or weeks. The belligerents mobilized the economies of entire continents, squeezing them for every possible resource. They tried not only to defeat their enemies' armed forces but—by blockades, submarine attacks, and bombing raids—to damage the economies that supported those armed forces. They thought of civilians as legitimate targets and, later, as vermin to be exterminated.

War in Europe and North Africa

It took less than a month for the Wehrmacht to conquer Poland (see Map 30.2). Britain and France declared war on Germany but took no military action. Meanwhile, the Soviet Union invaded eastern Poland and the Baltic republics. Although the Poles fought bravely, their infantry and cavalry were no match for German and Russian tanks. During the winter of 1939–1940 Germany and the Western democracies faced each other in what soldiers called a "phony war."

In March 1940 Hitler went on the offensive again, conquering Denmark, Norway, the Netherlands, and Belgium in less than two months. In May he attacked France. Although the French army had as many soldiers, tanks, and aircraft as the Wehrmacht, its morale was low and it quickly collapsed. By the end of June Hitler was master of all of Europe between Russia and Spain.

Germany still had to face Britain. The British had no army to speak of, but they had other assets: the English Channel, the Royal Navy and Air Force, and a tough new prime minister, Winston Churchill. The Germans knew they could invade Britain only by gaining control of the airspace over the Channel, so they launched a massive air attack—the Battle of Britain—lasting from June through September. The attack failed because the Royal Air Force used radar and code-breaking to detect approaching German planes.

Frustrated in the west, Hitler turned his attention eastward, even though it meant fighting a two-front war. So far he had gotten the utmost cooperation from Stalin, who supplied Germany with grain, oil, and strategic raw materials. Yet he had always wanted to conquer Lebensraum in the east and enslave the Slavic peoples who lived there, and he feared that if he waited, Stalin would build a dangerously strong army. In June 1941 Hitler launched the largest attack in history, with 3 million soldiers and thousands of planes and tanks. Within five months the Wehrmacht conquered the Baltic states, Ukraine, and half of European Russia, captured a million prisoners of war, and reached the very gates of Moscow and Leningrad. The USSR seemed on the

Soviet Tanks at Stalingrad In the winter of 1942–1943, the Red Army encircled a German army at Stalingrad, a strategic city in southern Russia that marked the furthest eastward advance of the Wehrmacht. The Soviets deployed their new T-34s, the best tanks in the world at the time. Unlike the Germans, Soviet soldiers were equipped with warm winter uniforms with a white outer layer for camouflage in the snow.

TASS-Sovfoto

Stalingrad City in Russia, site of a Red Army victory over the German army in 1942–1943. The Battle of Stalingrad was the turning point in the war between Germany and the Soviet Union. Today Volgograd.

verge of collapse. Then the weather turned cold, machines froze, and the fighting came to a halt. Like Napoleon, Hitler had ignored the environment of Russia to his peril.

The next spring the Wehrmacht renewed its offensive. It surrounded Leningrad in a siege that was to cost a million lives. Leaving Moscow aside, it turned toward the Caucasus and its oil wells. In August the Germans attacked **Stalingrad** (now Volgograd), the key to the Volga River and the supply of oil. For months German and Soviet soldiers fought over every street and every house. When winter came, the Red Army counterattacked and encircled the city. In February 1943 the remnants of the German army in Stalingrad surrendered. Hitler had lost an army of 200,000 men and his last chance of defeating the Soviet Union and of winning the war (see Map 30.2).

MAP 30.2 **World War II in Europe and North Africa** In a series of quick and decisive campaigns from September 1939 to December 1941, German forces overran much of Europe and North Africa. There followed three years of bitter fighting as the Allies slowly pushed the Germans back. © Cengage Learning

From Europe the war spread to Africa. When France fell in 1940, Mussolini decided that the time had come to realize his imperial ambitions. Italian forces quickly overran British Somaliland, then invaded Egypt. Their victories were ephemeral, however, for when the British counterattacked, Italian resistance crumbled. During 1941 British forces conquered Italian East Africa and invaded Libya as well. The Italian rout in North Africa brought the Germans to their rescue, and during 1942 the German army and the forces of the British Commonwealth seesawed back and forth across the deserts of Libya and Egypt. At **El Alamein** in northern Egypt the British prevailed because they had more weapons and supplies and were better informed about their enemies' plans. The Germans were finally expelled from Africa in May 1943.

El Alamein Town in Egypt, site of the victory by Britain's Field Marshal Bernard Montgomery over German forces led by General Erwin Rommel (the "Desert Fox") in 1942–1943.

War in Asia and the Pacific

The fall of France and the involvement of Britain and the USSR against Germany presented Japan with the opportunity it had been looking for. Suddenly the European colonies in Southeast Asia, with their abundant oil, rubber, and other strategic materials, seemed ripe for the taking. In July 1941, when the French government, then under German control, allowed Japanese forces to occupy Indochina, the United States stopped shipments of steel, scrap iron, oil, and other products that Japan desperately needed. This left Japan with three alternatives: giving up its conquests, as the Americans insisted; facing economic ruin; or widening the war. Japan chose war.

Admiral Isoroku Yamamoto, commander of the Japanese fleet, told Prime Minister Fumimaro Konoye: "If I am told to fight regardless of the consequences, I shall run wild for the first six months or a year, but I have utterly no confidence for the second or third year. . . . I hope that you will endeavor to avoid a Japanese-American war." Ignoring his advice, the war cabinet made plans for a surprise attack on the United States Navy, followed by an invasion of Southeast Asia. They knew they could not hope to defeat the United States, but they calculated that the shock of the attack would be so great that isolationist Americans would accept the Japanese conquest of Southeast Asia as readily as they had acquiesced to Hitler's conquests in Europe.

On December 7, 1941, Japanese planes bombed the U.S. naval base at **Pearl Harbor**, sinking or damaging scores of warships but missing the aircraft carriers, which were at sea. Then, in early 1942, the Japanese conquered all of Southeast Asia and the Dutch East Indies. They soon began to confiscate food and raw materials and demand heavy labor from the inhabitants.

Japan's dream of an East Asian empire seemed within reach, for its victories surpassed even Hitler's in Europe. The United States, however, quickly began preparing for war. In April 1942 American planes bombed Tokyo. In May the United States Navy defeated a Japanese fleet in the Coral Sea, ending Japanese plans to conquer Australia. A month later, at the **Battle of Midway**, Japan lost four of its six largest aircraft carriers. Without them, Japan faced a long and hopeless war (see Map 30.3).

Pearl Harbor Naval base in Hawaii attacked by Japanese aircraft on December 7, 1941. The sinking of much of the U.S. Pacific Fleet brought the United States into World War II.

Battle of Midway U.S. naval victory over the Japanese fleet in June 1942, in which the Japanese lost four of their best aircraft carriers. It marked a turning point in World War II.

The End of War

After the Battle of Stalingrad the advantage on the Eastern Front shifted to the Soviet Union. By 1943 the Red Army was receiving a growing stream of supplies from factories in Russia and the United States. Slowly at first and then with increasing vigor, it pushed the Wehrmacht back toward Germany.

The Western powers, meanwhile, staged two invasions of Europe. Beginning in July 1943 they captured Sicily and invaded Italy. Italy signed an armistice, but German troops held off the Allied advance for two years. On June 6, 1944—forever after known as D-day—156,000 British, American, and Canadian troops landed on the coast of Normandy in western France—the largest shipborne assault ever staged. Within a week the Allies had more troops in France than Germany did, and by September Germany faced an Allied army of over 2 million men and half a million vehicles.

Although the Red Army was on the eastern border of Germany, ready for the final push, Hitler transferred part of the Wehrmacht westward. Despite overwhelming odds, Germany held out for almost a year, a result of the fighting qualities of its soldiers and the terror inspired by the Nazi regime, which commanded obedience to the end. On May 7, 1945, a week after Hitler committed suicide, German military leaders surrendered.

Japan fought on a while longer because the United States had aimed most of its war effort at Germany. Pacific islands had to be captured by amphibious landings, with high casualty rates on both sides. In June 1944 U.S. bombers began attacking Japan and American submarines sank many Japanese merchant ships, cutting Japan off from its sources of oil and other raw materials. After May 1945, with Japanese fighters grounded for lack of fuel, U.S. planes began destroying Japanese shipping, industries, and cities at will.

Even as their homeland was being pounded, the Japanese still held strong positions in Asia. Despite its name, "Greater East Asian Co-Prosperity Sphere," the Japanese occupation was harsh and brutal. By 1945 Asians were eager to see the Japanese leave, but not to welcome back the Europeans. Instead, they looked forward to independence (see Chapters 29 and 32).

On August 6, 1945, the United States dropped an atomic bomb on **Hiroshima**, killing some 80,000 people in a flash and leaving about 120,000 more to die in agony from burns and radiation. Three days later another atomic bomb destroyed Nagasaki. On August 14 Emperor Hirohito gave the order to lay down arms. Two weeks later Japanese leaders signed the terms of surrender. The war was officially over.

Hiroshima City in Japan, the first to be destroyed by an atomic bomb, on August 6, 1945. The bombing hastened the end of World War II.

MAP 30.3 **World War II in Asia and the Pacific** Having conquered much of China between 1937 and 1941, Japanese forces launched a sudden attack on Southeast Asia and the Pacific in late 1941 and early 1942. American forces slowly reconquered the Pacific islands and the Philippines. In August 1945, the atomic bombing of Hiroshima and Nagasaki forced Japan's surrender. © Cengage Learning

Hiroshima After the Atomic Bomb   On August 6, 1945, an atomic bomb destroyed the city, killing some eighty thousand people. This fire truck, stationed at the Hiroshima Fire Department, is one of the few identifiable objects in the photo. It was located 4,000 feet from ground zero.

Bettmann/CORBIS

SECTION REVIEW

- World War II was a war of machines and movement covering entire continents and oceans.

- Hitler's armies quickly overran western Europe, but Hitler failed to defeat Britain by air.

- In 1941 Germany attacked the USSR, but its defeat at Stalingrad in the winter of 1942–1943 sealed its fate.

- After the United States stopped shipments of vital supplies to Japan, in December 1941 Japanese planes bombed Pearl Harbor; a few months later Japan conquered Southeast Asia and Indonesia.

- After mid-1942, however, American forces pushed the Japanese back across the Pacific and began bombing Japan.

- In 1944, on D-day, the Allies landed troops on Normandy beaches and then fought their way into Germany; meanwhile, two atomic bombs forced Japan to surrender.

- After Japan's defeat, Chiang Kai-shek's army failed from its own ineptness and Mao's Communists took over China.

Were these atomic weapons necessary? At the time, Americans believed that the conquest of the Japanese homeland would take more than a year and cost the lives of hundreds of thousands of American soldiers. Although some believed the Japanese were determined to fight to the bitter end, others thought they would surrender if they could retain their emperor. Winston Churchill wrote: "It would be a mistake to suppose that the fate of Japan was settled by the atomic bomb. Her defeat was certain before the first bomb fell."[3]

Collapse of the Guomindang and Communist Victory

The formal Japanese surrender in September 1945 surprised the Guomindang. The United States gave millions of dollars of aid and weapons to the Guomindang, all the while urging "national unity" and a "coalition government" with the Communists. But Chiang used all means available to prepare for a civil war. By late 1945 he had U.S. support, control of China's cities, and an army of 2.7 million, more than twice the size of the Communist forces. But the Guomindang's behavior eroded whatever popular support they had. As they moved into formerly

---

[3]Gar Alperowitz, *Atomic Diplomacy: Hiroshima and Potsdam* (New York: Simon & Schuster, 1965), 176–181 and 236–242.

Sale of Gold in the Last Days of the Guomindang   This picture was taken by famed French photojournalist Henri Cartier-Bresson in Shanghai just before the arrival of the Communist-led People's Liberation Army in 1949. It shows people desperate to buy gold before their Guomindang currency becomes worthless.

Henri Cartier-Bresson/Magnum Photos

Japanese-held territory, they acted like an occupation force. They taxed the people they "liberated" more heavily than the Japanese had, confiscated supplies, and enriched themselves at the expense of the population. Chiang's government printed money so fast that it soon lost all its value. In the countryside the Guomindang's brutality alienated the peasants.

Meanwhile, the Communists obtained Japanese equipment seized by the Soviets in the last weeks of the war and American weapons brought over by deserting Guomindang soldiers. In Manchuria, where they were strongest, they pushed through a radical land reform program, distributing the properties of wealthy landowners among the poorest peasants. In battles against government forces, the higher morale and popular support they enjoyed outweighed the heavy equipment of the Guomindang, whose soldiers began deserting by the thousands.

By 1949 the Guomindang armies were collapsing everywhere, defeated more by their own greed and ineptness than by the Communists. As the Communists advanced, high-ranking members of the Guomindang fled to Taiwan, protected from the mainland by the U.S. Navy. On October 1, 1949, Mao Zedong announced the founding of the People's Republic of China.

THE CHARACTER OF WARFARE

The war left an enormous death toll. Recent estimates place the figure at close to 60 million deaths, six to eight times more than in World War I. Over half of the dead were civilian victims of massacres, famines, and bombs. The Soviet Union lost between 20 million and 25 million people, more than any other country. China suffered 15 million deaths; Poland lost some 6 million, of whom half were Jewish; the Jewish people lost another 3 million outside Poland. Over 4 million Germans and over 2 million Japanese died. Great Britain lost 400,000 people, and the United States 300,000. In much of the world, families mourned one or more of their members.

Many parts of the world were flooded with refugees. Some 90 million Chinese fled the Japanese advance. In Europe millions fled from the Nazis or the Red Army or were herded back and forth on government orders. Many refugees never returned to their homes.

Belligerents identified not just soldiers but entire peoples as enemies. Some even labeled their own ethnic minorities as "enemies." Another reason for the devastation was the appearance of new technologies that carried destruction deep into enemy territory, far beyond the traditional battlefields. New technologies of warfare and changes in morality formed a lethal combination.

The Science and Technology of War

As fighting spread around the world, the mobilization of manpower and economies and the mobility of the armed forces grew increasingly crucial, while new aspects of war took on a growing importance. Chemists found ways to make synthetic rubber from coal or oil. Physicists perfected radar, which warned of approaching enemy aircraft and submarines. Cryptanalysts broke enemy codes and were able to penetrate secret military communications. Pharmacologists developed antibiotics that saved the lives of wounded soldiers, who in any earlier war would have died of infections. The war also brought new inventions in media technology (see Environment and Technology: The Magnetophon).

Aircraft development was especially striking. As war approached, German, British, and Japanese aircraft manufacturers developed fast, maneuverable fighter planes. U.S. industry was especially noted for heavy bombers designed to fly in huge formations and drop tons of bombs on enemy cities. Germany responded with radically new designs, including the first jet fighters, low-flying unmanned buzz bombs, and, finally, V-2 missiles against which there was no warning or defense.

Military planners expected scientists to furnish secret weapons that could doom the enemy. In October 1939 President Roosevelt received a letter from physicist Albert Einstein, a Jewish refugee from Nazism, warning of the dangers of nuclear power: "There is no doubt that sub-atomic energy is available all around us, and that one day man will release and control its almost infinite power. We cannot prevent him from doing so and can only hope that he will not use it exclusively in blowing up his next door neighbor." Roosevelt placed the vast resources of the U.S. government at the disposal of physicists and engineers. By 1945 they had built two atomic bombs, each one powerful enough to annihilate an entire city.

Bombing Raids

Since it was very hard to pinpoint individual buildings, especially at night, British air chief marshal Arthur "Bomber" Harris decided that "operations should now be focused on the morale of the enemy civilian population and in particular the industrial workers."

In May 1942, 1,000 British planes dropped incendiary bombs on Cologne, setting fire to the old city. Between July 24 and August 2, 1943, 3,330 British and American planes fire-bombed Hamburg, killing 50,000 people, mostly women and children. Later raids destroyed Berlin, Dresden, and other German cities. The bombing raids against Germany killed 600,000 people—more than half of them women and children—and injured 800,000, but they failed to break the morale of the German people. German armament production continued to increase until late 1944, and the population remained obedient and hard-working. However, bombing raids against oil depots and synthetic fuel plants almost brought the German war effort to a standstill by early 1945.

Japanese cities were also the targets of American bombing raids. As early as April 1942 sixteen planes launched from an aircraft carrier bombed Tokyo. Later, as American forces captured islands close to Japan, the raids intensified. Their effect was even more devastating than the fire-bombing of German cities, for Japanese cities were made mostly of wood. In March 1945 bombs set Tokyo ablaze, killing 80,000 people and leaving a million homeless.

U.S. Army Medics and Holocaust Victims   When Allied troops entered the Nazi concentration camps, they found the bodies of thousands of victims of the Holocaust. In Dachau in southern Germany, two U.S. Army medics are overseeing a truckload of corpses to be taken to a burial site.

Hulton Deutsch Collection/Corbis

The Holocaust

In World War II, for the first time, more civilians than soldiers were deliberately put to death. The champions in

The Magnetophon

American intelligence officers monitoring German radio broadcasts during World War II were puzzled to hear Nazi leaders giving public speeches at all hours of the day and the Berlin Philharmonic performing Wagner in the middle of the night. The quality of the broadcasts was so much better than what was available on the phonograph records and wire recorders they were familiar with that they concluded that German scientists had perfected a new way of preserving and reproducing sound.

In fact, two German radio engineers had discovered in 1940 a way to remove hissing background sounds from recordings made on magnetized plastic tape, and the German chemical giant I. G. Farben had developed a consistently reliable tape for the purpose. Knowing that their new recording device, the Magnetophon, was much advanced over anything the Allies had, the German military command ordered retreating radio operators to destroy their equipment to keep it out of enemy hands. In April 1944, however, two Magnetophons were captured inside Germany. A Signal Corps technician named John T. Mullin was one of the specialists sent to examine it. When the war ended, Mullin brought the two Magnetophons and 500 reels of I. G. Farben tape back to the United States with him.

Radio was then at its peak of popularity, but some of the biggest stars resented network demands that they perform live at the same time in the evening on the same day every week of the year. The ABC network was thus able to hire the phenomenally popular crooner Bing Crosby away from NBC by promising him that he could record his show in advance.

At first his producers used wax disks, but listeners complained that the sound was tinny and fuzzy. Then Crosby's technical director attended a demonstration by Mullin of a Magnetophon on which he had made his own improvements. Mullin repeated the demonstration for Crosby, and on October 1, 1947 the *Bing Crosby Show* aired on tape. Crosby hired Mullin as his chief engineer and invested $50,000 in a fledgling company named Ampex that was looking for a civilian product to replace its wartime production of airborne radar motors.

The recorders developed by Ampex used tape developed by the 3M Company.

Soon tape recording became a radio standard, and later it became a new basis for recording music on multiple tracks, which allowed a singer to sing harmony with or accompany herself. A decade later, in 1956, a neck-and-neck competition between three design teams resulted in Ampex bringing out the first video recorder.

German Magnetophon Wartime technical advances often played an important role in civilian life once the fighting ended. INTERFOTO/Alamy

Auschwitz Nazi extermination camp in Poland, the largest center of mass murder during the Holocaust. Close to a million Jews, Gypsies, Communists, and others were killed there.

Holocaust Nazis' program during World War II to kill people they considered undesirable. Some 6 million Jews perished during the Holocaust, along with millions of Poles, Gypsies, Communists, Socialists, and others.

the art of killing defenseless civilians were the Nazis. Their murders were not the accidental byproducts of some military goal but a calculated policy of exterminating whole races of people.

Their first targets were Jews. Soon after Hitler came to power, he deprived German Jews of their citizenship and legal rights. When eastern Europe fell under Nazi rule, the Nazis herded its large Jewish population into ghettos in the major cities, where many died of starvation and disease. Then, in early 1942, the Nazis decided to carry out Hitler's "final solution to the Jewish problem" by applying modern industrial methods to the slaughter of human beings. Thousands of ordinary German citizens supported and aided the genocide. Every day trainloads of cattle cars arrived at the extermination camps in eastern Europe and disgorged thousands of captives and the corpses of those who had died along the way. The strongest survivors were put to work and fed almost nothing until they died. Women, children, the elderly, and the sick were shoved into gas chambers and asphyxiated with poison gas. **Auschwitz**, the biggest camp, was a giant industrial complex designed to kill up to twelve thousand people a day. This mass extermination, now called the **Holocaust** ("burning"), claimed some 6 million Jewish lives.

Besides the Jews, the Nazis also killed 3 million Polish Catholics—especially professionals, army officers, and the educated—in an effort to reduce the Polish people to slavery. They also exterminated homosexuals, Jehovah's Witnesses, Gypsies, the disabled, and the mentally ill—all in the interests of "racial purity." Whenever a German was killed in an occupied country, the Nazis retaliated by burning a village and all its inhabitants. After the invasion of Russia the Wehrmacht was given orders to execute all captured communists, government employees, and officers. They also worked millions of prisoners of war to death or let them die of starvation.

The Home Front in Europe and Asia

In the First World War there had been a clear distinction between the "front" and the "home front." Not so in World War II, where rapid military movements and air power carried the war into people's homes. For the civilian populations of China, Japan, Southeast Asia, and Europe, the war was far more terrifying than their worst nightmares. Armies swept through the land, confiscating food, fuel, and anything else of value. Bombers and heavy artillery pounded cities into rubble, leaving only the skeletons of buildings, while survivors cowered in cellars. Even when a city was not targeted, air-raid sirens awakened people throughout the night. In countries occupied by the Germans, the police arrested civilians, deporting many to die in concentration camps or to work as slave laborers in armaments factories. Millions fled their homes in terror, losing their families and friends. Even in Britain, children and the elderly were sent to live in the countryside.

The war demanded an enormous and sustained effort from all civilians, but more so in some countries than in others. In 1941, the Soviets dismantled over fifteen hundred factories and rebuilt them in the Ural Mountains and Siberia, where they soon turned out more tanks and artillery than the Axis.

Half of the ships afloat in 1939 were sunk during the war, but the Allied losses were more than made up for by American shipyards, while Axis shipping was reduced to nothing by 1945. The production of aircraft, trucks, tanks, and other materiel showed a similar imbalance. Although the Axis powers made strenuous efforts to increase their production, they could not compete with the vast outpouring of Soviet tanks and American materiel.

The Red Army eventually mobilized 22 million men; Soviet women took over half of all industrial and three-quarters of all agricultural jobs. In the other Allied countries, women also played major roles in the war effort, replacing men in fields, factories, and offices. The Nazis, in contrast, believed that German women should stay home and bear children, and they imported 7 million "guest workers"—a euphemism for captured foreigners.

The Home Front in the United States

The United States flourished during the war. Safe behind their oceans, Americans felt no bombs, saw no enemy soldiers, had almost no civilian casualties, and suffered fewer military casualties than other countries. The economy went into a prolonged boom after 1940. By 1944 the United States was producing twice as much as all the Axis powers combined. Thanks to huge military orders, jobs were plentiful, bread lines disappeared, and nutrition and health improved. Most Americans saved part of their paychecks, laying the basis for a phenomenal postwar consumer boom. Many Americans later looked back on the conflict as the "good war."

World War II also did much to weaken the hold of traditional ideas, as employers recruited women and members of racial minorities to work in jobs once reserved for white men. Six million women entered the labor force during the war, 2.5 million of them in manufacturing jobs previously considered "men's work." In a book entitled *Shipyard Diary of a Woman Welder* (1944), Augusta Clawson recalled her experiences in a shipyard in Oregon:

> *The job confirmed my strong conviction—I have stated it before—what exhausts the woman welder is not the work, not the heat, nor the demands upon physical strength. It is the apprehension that arises from inadequate skill and consequent lack of confidence; and this can be overcome by the right kind of training. . . . And so, in spite of the discomforts of climbing, heavy equipment, and heat, I enjoyed the work today because I could do it.*[4]

---

[4]Rosalyn Fraad Baxandall, Linda Gordon, and Susan Reverby, eds., *America's Working Women* (New York: Random House, 1976), 253.

Many men opposed women doing work that would take them away from their families. As the labor shortage got worse, however, employers and politicians grudgingly admitted that the government ought to help provide day care for the children of working mothers. The entry of women into the labor force proved to be one of the most significant consequences of the war.

The war loosened racial bonds as well. Seeking work in war industries, 1.2 million African Americans migrated to the north and west. In the southwest Mexican immigrants took jobs in agriculture and war industries. But no new housing was built to accommodate the influx of migrants to the industrial cities, and many suffered from overcrowding and discrimination. In addition, 112,000 Japanese Americans living on the west coast of the United States were arrested and herded into remote interior internment camps until the war was over, ostensibly for fear of spying and sabotage, but actually because of their race.

War and the Environment

During the depression, construction and industry had slowed to a crawl, reducing environmental stress. The war reversed this trend, sharply accelerating pressures on the environment.

One reason for the change was the fighting itself. Battles scarred the landscape, leaving behind spent ammunition and damaged equipment. Retreating armies flooded large areas of China and the Netherlands. The bombing of cities left ruins that remained visible for a generation or more.

The main cause of environmental stress, however, was not the fighting but the economic development that sustained it. The war's half-million aircraft required thousands of air bases, many of them in the Pacific, China, Africa, and other parts of the world that had seldom seen an airplane before. Barracks, shipyards, docks, warehouses, and other military construction sprouted on every continent.

As war industries boomed, so did the demand for raw materials. Mining companies opened new mines and towns in Africa to supply strategic minerals. Latin American countries deprived of manufactured imports began building their own steel mills, factories, and shipyards. In India, China, and Europe, timber felling accelerated far beyond the reproduction rate of trees, replacing forests with denuded land. In a few instances, however, the war was good for the environment. For example, submarine warfare made fishing and whaling so dangerous that fish and whale populations had a few years in which to increase.

SECTION REVIEW

- World War II caused 60 million deaths, most of them civilians, as well as many refugees.

- Scientific technology, especially aircraft design, contributed to the mobility and violence of warfare.

- Allied bombing raids set fire to entire cities in both Europe and Japan.

- In the Holocaust, the Nazis murdered millions of Jews, Poles, Gypsies, and other minorities.

- Industrial economies, especially in the United States and Russia, mobilized civilians to manufacture war materiel.

- A booming American economy provided jobs for women and African Americans.

- Environments in war zones were badly damaged, and construction for the war transformed the environments of many countries.

CONCLUSION

After the Great War ended, the world seemed to return to its prewar state, but it was an illusion. In the Soviet Union, Joseph Stalin was determined to turn his country into a modern industrial state at breakneck speed, regardless of the human cost. Several million people—most of them peasants—died, and millions more were enslaved during the Five-Year Plans and the collectivization of agriculture. By 1941 the USSR was much better prepared for a war with Germany than Russia had been in 1914–1917.

In 1929, after a few years of prosperity, the New York stock market collapsed. Within a few months, the world economy fell into the Great Depression, throwing millions out of work throughout the world. France and Britain survived the depression by making their colonial empires purchase their products. Countries that were dependent on exports, such as Germany and Japan, suffered more until they turned their economies toward arms production. Only the USSR and southern Africa boomed during the 1930s.

In Italy, Mussolini installed Fascist Party members in all government jobs and jailed anyone who criticized him. In Germany, economic collapse led people to entrust their government to Adolf Hitler and his Nazi followers, who quickly set to work establishing a totalitarian government. Nazi Germany's rebuilding of its military and its invasion of Austria and Czechoslovakia were greeted with a policy of appeasement by Western democracies, until finally they could no longer overlook Germany's intentions.

Hard hit by the depression, Japan saw China as a potential colony with resources to help solve its economic problems. In 1931, Japan conquered Manchuria. The United States and the League of Nations protested but did little else. Starting in 1937, a long and brutal war with China became a drain on the Japanese economy and resources. Meanwhile, the Communists, led by Mao Zedong, were slowly gaining support in the Chinese countryside.

The war spread to Europe in 1939 when Germany conquered Poland, then Denmark, Norway, the low countries, and France in 1940. The war turned global in 1941 when Germany invaded the Soviet Union and Japan attacked the United States. In 1943, the Red Army began to push the Germans back. Beginning in June 1944, Anglo-American forces, backed by the overwhelming industrial resources of the United States, drove German forces back from the west. U.S. naval victories in the Pacific and atomic weapons defeated Japan and ended the war in 1945.

The Second World War was by far the deadliest in history. Modern mechanized forces swept across entire nations and oceans. Their targets were not only each other's armed forces, but their civilian populations as well. Though Germany had considerable scientific and technical talent, the war favored the nations with the most heavy industries, namely, the United States and the Soviet Union. The Allies destroyed German and Japanese cities with fire-bombs, and the United States dropped atomic bombs on Hiroshima and Nagasaki. Of the roughly 60 million people who died in the war, most were civilians.

KEY TERMS

Joseph Stalin p. 764	**Adolf Hitler** p. 770	**Long March** p. 773	**Battle of Midway** p. 778
Five-Year Plans p. 764	**Nazis** p. 770	**Stalingrad** p. 777	**Hiroshima** p. 779
Benito Mussolini p. 770	**Chiang Kai-shek** p. 773	**El Alamein** p. 778	**Auschwitz** p. 783
Fascist Party p. 770	**Mao Zedong** p. 773	**Pearl Harbor** p. 778	**Holocaust** p. 783

SUGGESTED READING

Burleigh, Michael. *Third Reich: A New History.* 2000. A thorough and up-to-date analysis of the history of Nazi Germany.

Chang, Jung. *Wild Swans: Three Daughters of China.* 1991. A biography of three generations of Chinese women who lived through the wars and revolutions of twentieth-century China.

Conquest, Robert. *The Great Terror: A Reassessment.* 1990. The definitive account of Stalin's purges and terror during the 1930s.

Dower, John. *War Without Mercy: Race and Power in the Pacific War.* 1987. An analysis of the role of racism—on both sides—that made the Pacific War especially brutal.

Frank, Anne. *The Diary of a Young Girl.* 1952. A classic account of the life of a Jewish family in hiding during the Nazi occupation of the Netherlands.

Hsiung, James, and Steven Levine, eds. *China's Bitter Victory: The War with Japan, 1937–1945.* 1992. Documents and accounts of the war in China.

Keegan, John. *The Second World War.* 1990. The best short history of the war by an eminent military historian.

McElvaine, Robert. *The Great Depression: America, 1929–1941.* 1993. A brief but well written account of the hardships of the 1930s.

Rabe, John. *The Good Man of Nanking: The Diaries of John Rabe.* 1998. Firsthand account of the Nanking massacre by a German who helped secure a safety zone for residents in Nanjing.

Rhodes, Richard. *The Making of the Atomic Bomb.* 1986. A fascinating account of the Manhattan Project and its consequences.

Solzhenitsyn, Alexander. *One Day in the Life of Ivan Denisovich.* 1978. The novel that first revealed the existence of Stalin's concentration camps.

Spector, Ronald. *Eagle Against the Sun.* 1988. A popular history of the Pacific War.

Terkel, Studs. *"The Good War": An Oral History of World War Two.* 1984. Interviews with Americans about their experiences during World War II.

Volkogonov, Dmitrii. *Stalin: Triumph and Tragedy.* 1991. A classic biography of the great tyrant.

Wiesel, Eli. *Night.* 1960. The classic work recounting the horrors of the Holocaust.

CourseMate Go to the History CourseMate website for primary source links, study tools, and review materials for this chapter. www.cengagebrain.com

Famines and Politics

Human history is filled with tales of famines—times when crops failed, food supplies ran out, and people starved.

Natural Famines

India, dependent on the monsoon rains, has been particularly prone to such calamities, with famines striking two to four times a century, whenever the rains fail for several years in succession. Three times in the eighteenth century famines killed several million people. The nineteenth century was worse, with famines in 1803–1804, 1837–1838, 1868–1870, and 1876–1878. The famine of 1876–1878 also afflicted northern China, causing between 9 and 13 million deaths from hunger and from the diseases of malnutrition. There were even incidents of cannibalism, as starving adults ate starving children.

When drought hit a region, it decimated not only the human population but also the animals they relied on to transport crops or plow the land. When water levels dropped in rivers and canals, food could not be transported by boat to areas where people were starving.

Commercial Famines

That all changed in the nineteenth century. Railroads and steamships could transport foodstuffs quickly across great distances, regardless of the weather. Great Britain, for example, became dependent on imports of wheat and beef. Yet the global death toll from starvation has been far higher since the mid-nineteenth century than ever before. Why?

Consider Ireland. By the early nineteenth century the potato had become the main source of nutrition for the Irish people. Potatoes grew abundantly and produced more calories per acre than any other crop, allowing the population to increase dramatically.

In 1845 a blight turned the potatoes in the fields black, mushy, and inedible. The harvest was ruined the following year as well. It recovered slightly in 1847 but was bad again in 1848. Tens of thousands died of starvation, while hundreds of thousands died from dysentery, typhus, or cholera. Travelers saw corpses rotting in their hovels or on the sides of roads. Altogether, a million or more people died, while another million emigrated, reducing the population of Ireland by half.

Throughout those years, Ireland exported wheat to England, where people had money to pay for it. Food cost money, and the Irish, poor even before the famines, were destitute and could not afford to buy wheat or bread. The British government was convinced that interfering with the free market would only make things worse. Relief efforts were half-hearted at best; the official responsible for Irish affairs preferred to leave the situation to "the operation of natural causes."

The same held true in India, like Ireland a colony of Great Britain. The drought of 1876–1878 killed over 5 million Indians in the Deccan region, while British officials stood by helpless or indifferent. Part of the problem was transportation. In the 1870s most goods were still transported in bullock carts, but the bullocks starved during the drought. Another obstacle was political. The idea that a government should be responsible for feeding the population was unthinkable at the time. And so, while millions were starving in the Deccan, the Punjab was exporting wheat to Britain.

Over the next twenty years, so-called famine railways were built in the regions historically most affected by the failures of the monsoon. When drought struck again at the end of the century, the railways were ready to transport food to areas that had previously been accessible only by bullock carts. However, the inhabitants of the affected regions had no money with which to buy what little food there was, and the government was still reluctant to interfere with free enterprise. Grain merchants bought all the stocks, hoarded them until the price rose, then used the railways to transport them out of the famine regions to regions where the harvests were better and people had more money.

In the twentieth century, commercial famines became rare as governments realized that they had a responsibility to provide food not only for their own people but also for people in other countries. Yet commercial famines have not entirely disappeared. In 1974, when a catastrophic flood covered half of Bangladesh, the government was too disorganized to distribute its stocks of rice, while merchants bought what they could and exported it to India. Thousands died, and thousands more survived only because of belated shipments of food from donor countries.

Political Famines

To say that governments are responsible for food supplies does not mean that they exercise that responsibility for the good of the people. Some do, but in many instances food is used as a weapon. In the twentieth century global food supplies were always adequate for the population of the world, and transportation was seldom a problem. Yet the century witnessed the most murderous famines ever recorded.

As commercial famines declined, war famines became common. The destruction or requisitioning of crops caused famines in the Russian civil war of 1921–1922, the Japanese occupation of Indochina in 1942–1945, and the Biafran war in Nigeria in 1967–1969.

In 1942 the Japanese army had conquered Burma, a rich rice-producing colony. Food supplies in Bengal, which imported rice from Burma, dropped by 5 percent. As prices began to rise, merchants bought stocks of rice and held them in the hope that prices would continue to increase. Sharecroppers sold their stocks to pay off their debts to landlords and village moneylenders. Meanwhile, the railroads that in peacetime would have carried food from other parts of India were fully occupied with military traffic. By the time Viceroy Lord Wavell ordered the army to transport food to Bengal in October 1943, between 1.5 and 2 million Bengalis had died.

Worst of all were the famines caused by deliberate government policies. The most famous was the famine of 1932–1933 caused by Stalin's collectivization of agriculture. The Communists tried to force the peasants to give up their land and livestock and join collectives, where they could be made to work harder and provide food for the growing cities and industries. When the peasants resisted, their crops were seized. Millions were sent to prison camps, and millions of others died of starvation.

An even worse famine took place in China from 1958 to 1961 during the "Great Leap Forward" (see Chapter 32). Communist Party Chairman Mao Zedong decided to hasten the transformation of China into a communist state by relying not on the expertise of economists and technocrats but on the enthusiasm of the masses. Farms were consolidated into huge communes. Peasants were told to make steel out of household utensils in backyard furnaces. The harvest of 1959 was poor, and later ones were even worse. The amount of grain per person declined from 452 pounds (205 kilograms) in 1957 to 340 pounds (154 kilograms) in 1961. Since the Central Statistical Bureau had been shut down, the central government was unaware of the shortages and demanded ever higher requisitions of food to feed the army and urban and industrial workers and to export to the Soviet Union to pay off China's debts. The amount of food left to the farmers was between one-fifth and one-half of their usual subsistence diet. From 1958 to 1961 between 20 and 30 million Chinese are estimated to have starved or died of the diseases of malnutrition. It was the worst famine in the history of the world. Mao denied its existence.

Nothing quite as horrible has happened since the Great Leap Forward. During the droughts in Africa in the 1970s and 1980s, most people in the affected regions received international food aid. However, to crush rebellions, the governments of Ethiopia and Sudan denied that their people were hungry and prevented food shipments from reaching drought victims.

In the world today, natural disasters are as frequent as ever, and many countries are vulnerable to food shortages. No one now claims that governments have no business providing food to the starving. Though food is not equitably distributed, there is enough for all human beings now, and there will be enough for the foreseeable future. However, humanitarian feelings compete with other political agendas, and the specter of politically motivated famines still stalks the world.

Earth Imaging/Stone/Getty Images

Satellite Photograph of the Globe Photography from space revolutionized mapping, making physical features more important than political boundaries and clearly displaying transient features, such as cloud coverage and storm patterns. In this photograph the distinctive whorl of a tropical storm is visible off the east coast of Japan. More specialized photographic techniques are used to appraise natural resources and environmental problems.

Perils and Promises of a Global Community, 1945 to the Present

After World War II an increasingly interconnected world faced new hopes and fears. The United Nations promoted peace, international cooperation, and human rights. Colonized peoples gained independence, and global trade expanded. At the same time the United States and the Soviet Union, victorious former Allies in the war against the Axis, mobilized every resource in a global contest for economic and political influence. This "Cold War" led to nuclear stalemate as well as a new round of warfare, dispelling dreams of world peace. Wars in Korea and Vietnam, as well as proxy conflicts from Nicaragua to Afghanistan, pitted the United States against communist regimes. Following the Cold War, nuclear proliferation and terrorism became top concerns. The 9/11 attacks by Muslim extremists on the World Trade Center and the Pentagon triggered an American-led "global war on terrorism." The ensuing invasions of Afghanistan and Iraq made the Middle East a top danger spot.

The industrialized nations, including Germany and Japan, recovered quickly from World War II. Elsewhere economic development came slowly, except in a handful of countries: South Korea, Taiwan, Brazil, Argentina, and, after 2000, China and India. In Africa and other poor regions, population growth usually offset economic gains.

Although the Green Revolution of the 1960s and the fruits of genetic engineering thirty years later alleviated much world hunger, industrial growth and automobile use increased pollution and competition for petroleum supplies. Global warming became an international concern, along with overfishing, deforestation, and endangerment of wild species.

Globalization affected culture as well. Transnational corporations selling uniform products threatened localized economic enterprises, and Western popular culture aroused fears of cultural imperialism, fear offset in part by the rise of Asian economic powers. The Internet and the emergence of English as the global language improved international communication but also stimulated fears that cultural diversity could be lost.

Chapter Outline

The Cold War
➤ *What were the major threats to world peace during the Cold War?*

Decolonization and Nation Building
➤ *How were the experiences of Asia, Africa, and Latin America similar in this period?*

Beyond a Bipolar World
➤ *How did the rivalry between the Cold War superpowers affect the rest of the world?*

Conclusion

● **ENVIRONMENT + TECHNOLOGY**   The Green Revolution
● **DIVERSITY + DOMINANCE**   Race and the Struggle for Justice in South Africa

Fidel Castro Arrives in Havana   Castro and his supporters overthrew a brutal dictatorship and began the revolutionary transformation of Cuba that led to a confrontation with the United States.

Bettmann/Corbis

The Cold War and Decolonization, 1945–1975

On January 1, 1959, the thirty-two-year-old Fidel Castro entered Havana, Cuba, after having successfully defeated the dictatorship of Fulgencio Batista (ful-HEHN-see-oh bah-TEES-tah). Castro had initiated his revolution in 1953 with an attack on a military barracks, but the attack failed. At his trial, Castro put on a spirited defense that he later published as *History Will Absolve Me*. He proclaimed his objectives as the restoration of Cuban democracy and an ambitious program of social and economic reforms designed to ameliorate the effects of underdevelopment.

On September 26, 1960, Castro addressed the United Nations General Assembly. Relations between the Castro government and the United States were already heading toward confrontation as a result of Castro's policies. In his speech, Castro offered a broad internationalist and anti-imperialist criticism of the world's developed nations and of the United Nations. He criticized the role of the United Nations in the Congo, suggesting that it had supported Colonel Mobutu Sese Seko, a client of imperialism, rather than Patrice Lumumba, identified by the United States as a dangerous radical. He also strongly supported the independence struggle of the Algerians against the French.

In this speech, Castro outlined an ambitious program of new revolutionary reforms in Cuba, claiming that the United States had supported the Batista dictatorship to protect American investors. Once back in Cuba, Castro pressed ahead with economic reforms that included concentrating power in the hands of his closest allies and nationalizing most American investments. Cuba became a flash point in the Cold War when the United States tried and failed to overthrow Castro in 1961. Castro declared himself to be a socialist and forged an economic and military alliance with the Soviet Union that led in 1962 to the Cuban missile crisis.

The intensity of the Cold War, with its accompanying threat of nuclear destruction, obscured a postwar phenomenon of more enduring importance. The colonial empires were overthrown, and Western power and influence declined in Asia, Africa, and Latin America. The leaders who headed these new nations were sometimes able to use Cold War antagonisms to their own advantage when they sought economic or military assistance. Some, like Castro, became frontline participants in this struggle, but most focused on nation building.

Each former colony had its own history and followed its own route to independence. Thus these new nations had difficulty finding a collective voice in a world increasingly oriented toward two superpowers, the United States and the Soviet Union. Some former colonies sided openly with one or the other, while others banded together in a posture of neutrality. All spoke with one voice about their need for economic and technical assistance and the obligation of the wealthy nations to satisfy those needs.

The Cold War military rivalry led to extraordinary advances in weaponry and associated technologies, but many new nations faced basic problems of educating their citizens, nurturing industry, and escaping the economic constraints imposed by their former imperialist masters. The environment suffered severe pressures from oil exploration and transport to support the growing economies of the wealthy nations and from deforestation and urbanization in poor regions. Neither rich nor poor nations fully anticipated the ultimate costs that would be associated with these environmental changes.

THE COLD WAR

iron curtain Winston Churchill's term for the Cold War division between the Soviet-dominated East and the U.S.-dominated West.

Cold War The ideological struggle between communism (Soviet Union) and capitalism (United States) for world influence. The Cold War came to an end when the Soviet Union dissolved in 1991.

North Atlantic Treaty Organization (NATO) Organization formed in 1949 as a military alliance of western European and North American states against the Soviet Union and its east European allies.

Warsaw Pact The 1955 treaty binding the Soviet Union and countries of eastern Europe in an alliance against the North Atlantic Treaty Organization.

United Nations International organization founded in 1945 to promote world peace and cooperation. It replaced the League of Nations.

For more than a century, political and economic leaders in the industrialized West had viewed socialism as a threat to free markets and private property. The Russian Revolution as well as the destabilizing economic effects of the Great Depression heightened these fears. The wartime alliance between the United States, Great Britain, and the Soviet Union had therefore succeeded despite these antagonisms and fears. With the defeat of Germany, however, growing Soviet assertiveness in Europe and communist insurgencies in China and elsewhere confirmed to Western leaders the threat of worldwide revolution.

Western leaders identified the Soviet Union as the sponsor of world revolution and as a military power capable of launching a war as destructive and terrible as the one recently ended. As early as 1946 Great Britain's wartime leader, Winston Churchill, said in a speech in Missouri, "From Stettin in the Baltic to Trieste in the Adriatic, an iron curtain has descended across the Continent. . . . I am convinced there is nothing they [the communists] so much admire as strength, and there is nothing for which they have less respect than weakness, especially military weakness." The phrase "**iron curtain**" became a watchword of the **Cold War**, the state of political tension and military rivalry then beginning between the United States and its allies and the Soviet Union and its allies.

Each side viewed every action by its rival a direct threat. Fearful of growing Soviet power, the United States and the nations of western Europe established a military alliance in 1949, the **North Atlantic Treaty Organization (NATO)**. Soviet leaders, struggling to recover from the terrible losses sustained in the war against the Axis, responded by creating their own military alliance, the **Warsaw Pact**, in 1955. The distrust and suspicion of the two alliances would now play out on a worldwide stage.

The United Nations

In 1944 representatives from the United States, Great Britain, the Soviet Union, and China drafted proposals that led to a treaty called the United Nations Charter, ratified on October 24, 1945. Like the earlier League of Nations, the **United Nations** had two main bodies: the General Assembly, with representatives from all member states; and the Security Council, with five permanent members—China (the anticommunist Chinese government based in Taiwan until 1971), France, Great Britain, the United States, and the Soviet Union—and seven rotating members. A full-time bureaucracy headed by a Secretary General carried out the organization's day-to-day business and directed agencies focused on specialized international problems—for example, UNICEF (United Nations Children's Emergency Fund), FAO (Food and Agriculture Organization), and UNESCO (United Nations Educational, Scientific and Cultural Organization) (see Environment and Technology: The Green Revolution). Unlike the League of Nations, which required unanimous agreement in both deliberative bodies, the United Nations operated by majority vote, except that the five permanent members of the Security Council had veto power in that chamber.

All signatories to the United Nations Charter renounced war and territorial conquest. Nevertheless, peacekeeping, the sole preserve of the Security Council, became a vexing problem as permanent members exercised their vetoes to protect their allies and interests. Throughout the Cold War the United Nations was seldom able to forestall or quell international conflicts, though from time to time it sent observers or peacekeeping forces to monitor truces or other international agreements.

MAP 31.1 **Cold War Confrontation** A polar projection is shown on this map because Soviet and U.S. strategists planned to attack one another by missile in the polar region; hence the Canadian-American radar lines. © Cengage Learning

Legend

NATO nations
Warsaw Pact nations
Soviet military base
U.S. military base
U.S. Strategic Air Command base
U.S. Intercontinental Ballistic Missile base

U.S. naval fleet
Cold War point of conflict

Map labels

PACIFIC OCEAN
INDIAN OCEAN
ARCTIC OCEAN
ATLANTIC OCEAN

7th fleet
Okinawa (U.S.)
FORMOSA (TAIWAN) 1958
PHILIPPINES
SOUTH VIETNAM 1945–1954 1957–1975
CAMBODIA 1969–1975
INDONESIA 1965
LAOS 1960–1975
THAILAND
JAPAN
SOUTH KOREA 1950–1953
CHINA
MONGOLIA
SOVIET UNION

AFGHANISTAN 1979
PAKISTAN
IRAN 1945–1946 1951–1953
SOMALIA 1970s–1980s
ETHIOPIA 1975–1991
TURKEY 1945–1947
IRAQ 1958
SAUDI ARABIA
LEBANON 1958
EGYPT 1956 1967 1973
6th fleet
GREECE 1946–1949
LIBYA
DEMOCRATIC REPUBLIC OF THE CONGO 1961–1965
ANGOLA 1976–1992

E. GER.
W. GER.
POLAND
CZECH.
HUNG.
ROMANIA
BULG.
YUGO.
ITALY
ALB.
DEN.
NETH.
BELG.
FRANCE
PORT.
SPAIN
MOROCCO
NORWAY
ICELAND
GREAT BRITAIN
GREENLAND (DEN.)
Azores (Port.)

Distant Early Warning (DEW) Radar Line
Mid-Canada Radar Line
Pinetree Radar Line
ALASKA (U.S.)
CANADA
UNITED STATES

2nd fleet
1st fleet
CUBA 1961–1962
DOMINICAN REPUBLIC 1965–1966
Puerto Rico (U.S.)
GRENADA 1983
NICARAGUA 1981–1990
PANAMA
GUATEMALA 1954
EL SALVADOR 1979–1992

PACIFIC OCEAN
HAWAI'I (U.S.)

CZECHOSLOVAKIA 1948,1968
EAST GERMANY 1948–1949, 1953,
POLAND 1956
YUGOSLAVIA 1958–1962
HUNGARY 1948–1953
1956

Scale

1000 Mi.
1000 Km.
500
500
0
0

120°E
150°E
30°N
60°N
90°E
60°E
30°E
0°
0°
30°W
60°W
90°W
120°W
150°W
Equator

sides agreed to a truce but could not agree to a formal peace treaty. As a result, fear of renewed warfare between the two Koreas has lingered until the present.

The United States and Vietnam

The most important postwar communist movement arose in French Indochina in Southeast Asia. The Vietnamese leader Ho Chi Minh **(hoe chee min)** (1890–1969) had spent several years in France during World War I and helped form the French Communist Party. In 1930, after training in Moscow, he returned to Vietnam to found the Indochina Communist Party. Forced to take refuge in China during World War II, Ho cooperated with the United States while Japan controlled Vietnam.

At war's end the French government was determined to keep its colonial possessions. Ho Chi Minh's nationalist coalition, called the Viet Minh, fought the French with help from the People's Republic of China. After a brutal struggle, the French stronghold of Dienbienphu **(dee-yen-bee-yen-FOO)** fell in 1954, marking the end of France's colonial enterprise. Ho's Viet Minh government took over in the north, and a noncommunist nationalist government ruled in the south.

Under President Dwight D. Eisenhower (1953–1961), the United States provided limited support to the French but ultimately decided not to prop up French colonial rule in Vietnam, perceiving that the European colonial empires were doomed (see Chapter 32). After winning independence, communist North Vietnam supported a communist guerrilla movement—the Viet Cong—against the noncommunist government of South Vietnam. At issue was the ideological and economic orientation of an independent Vietnam.

As President John F. Kennedy (served 1961–1963) changed American policy to support the South Vietnamese government of President Ngo Dinh Diem **(dee-YEM)**, North Vietnam committed its military forces more directly to the war with support from the Soviet Union and the Republic of China. Although he knew that the Diem government was corrupt and unpopular, Kennedy feared that a communist victory would encourage communist movements throughout Southeast Asia and alter the Cold War balance of power. He therefore significantly increased the number of American military advisers and also encouraged South Vietnamese military officers to overthrow their government. After Diem was overthrown and assassinated in early November 1963, American military involvement grew. On November 22, 1963 the unrelated assassination of President Kennedy in Dallas, Texas elevated Lyndon B. Johnson (served 1963–1969) to the American presidency. He gained congressional support for an unlimited U.S. military deployment that eventually reached 500,000 troops. Because South Vietnam's new rulers proved to be as corrupt and unpopular as the earlier Diem government, many South Vietnamese supported the Viet Cong and Hanoi's drive for national reunification. Despite battlefield success in the **Vietnam War**, the United States failed to achieve a comprehensive victory. In the massive 1968 Tet Offensive, the Viet Cong guerrillas and their North Vietnamese allies gained significant military credibility while suffering significant losses. With a clear victory now unlikely, the antiwar movement in the United States grew in strength (see below).

In 1973 a treaty between North Vietnam and the United States ended U.S. involvement in the war and promised future elections. Two years later, in violation of the treaty, Viet Cong and North Vietnamese troops overran the South Vietnamese army and captured the southern capital of

Vietnam War Conflict pitting North Vietnam and South Vietnamese communist guerrillas against the South Vietnamese government, aided after 1961 by the United States.

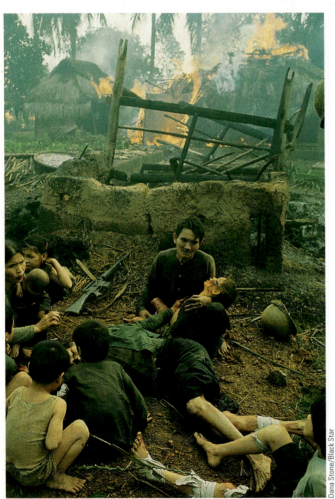

Dana Stone/Black Star

The Vietnamese People at War American and South Vietnamese troops burned many villages to deprive the enemy of refuges among civilian populations. This policy undermined support for the South Vietnamese government in the countryside.

Saigon, renaming it Ho Chi Minh City. They then united the two Vietnams in a single state ruled from the north. Over a million Vietnamese and 58,000 Americans had died during the war. As the victors imposed a new economic and political order, hundreds of thousands of refugees from South Vietnam left for the United States and other Western nations.

While the United States had rationalized its military involvement in South Vietnam as part of its global confrontation with communism, the communist-led government of a newly reunited Vietnam soon found itself at war with its communist neighbors, rather than with U.S. allies in the region. In 1975 communist revolutionaries (the Khmer Rouge) gained power in Cambodia, Vietnam's western neighbor. Not only did this brutal regime led by Pol Pot execute more than 1 million of their fellow citizens, but they also provoked a war with the communist government of Vietnam in 1978. A Vietnamese force of more than 150,000 defeated the Khmer Rouge and set up an occupation government that lasted a decade. During this occupation, the Vietnamese found themselves facing a resilient guerrilla force that eventually compelled them to withdraw. The Vietnamese invasion of Cambodia also led the Vietnamese into a two-month-long war with the Republic of China, which favored the Cambodians.

President Johnson began his administration committed to a broad program of social reforms and civil rights initiatives, called the Great Society, and was instrumental in passing major civil rights legislation that responded to the heroic campaign for voting rights and integration led by Martin Luther King, Jr. As the commitment of U.S. troops in Vietnam grew, a massive antiwar movement applied the tactics of the civil rights movement to end the war. Growing economic problems and a rising tide of antiwar rallies, soon international in character, undermined support for Johnson, who declined to seek reelection.

The Race for Nuclear Supremacy

The terrible devastation of Hiroshima and Nagasaki by atomic weapons (see Chapter 30) framed the strategic decisions in the Korean and Vietnamese Wars. The Soviet Union had exploded its first nuclear device in 1949. The United States claimed a new advantage when it exploded a more powerful hydrogen bomb in 1952, but the Soviet Union followed suit less than a year later. As a result, the United States took care not to directly challenge the Soviet Union or China (a nuclear power from 1964) during the Korean or Vietnamese conflicts. But while the Cold War rivals avoided a direct confrontation, the use of threats and the proliferation of small conflicts frightened a world deeply scarred by two world wars.

Cuban missile crisis Brink-of-war confrontation between the United States and the Soviet Union over the latter's placement of nuclear-armed missiles in Cuba.

In 1954 President Eisenhower warned Soviet leaders against attacking western Europe. In response to such an attack, he said, the United States would reduce the Soviet Union to "a smoking, radiating ruin at the end of two hours." A few years later the Soviet leader Nikita Khrushchev (**KROOSH-chef**) made an equally stark promise: "We will bury you." He was referring to economic competition, but Americans interpreted the statement to mean literal burial. Rhetoric aside, both men—and their successors—had the capacity to deliver on their threats, and everyone in the world knew that all-out war with nuclear weapons would produce the greatest global devastation in human history.

The Soviet Union's deployment of nuclear missiles to Cuba in 1962 pushed the two sides to the brink of war. Reacting to U.S. efforts to overthrow the Cuban government, Khrushchev and Fidel Castro decided that the deployment of nuclear weapons in Cuba would force the United States to accept the island's status quo. When the missiles were discovered, the United States declared a naval blockade and prepared to invade Cuba, forcing Khrushchev to remove the missiles. As frightening as the **Cuban missile crisis** was, the fact that the superpowers chose diplomacy over war gave reason to hope that nuclear weapons might be contained.

Fear of a nuclear holocaust produced an international effort to limit proliferation. In 1963 Great Britain, the United States, and the Soviet Union agreed to ban the testing of nuclear weapons in the atmosphere, in space, and under water, thus reducing the danger of radioactive fallout. In 1968 the United States and the Soviet Union

SECTION REVIEW

- The United Nations was created to manage international disputes and facilitate decolonization and development.

- The United States developed the Marshall Plan to aid European recovery from the devastation of World War II.

- The Cold War was a confrontation between two military alliances, NATO and the Warsaw Pact, and two distinct economic systems, capitalism and communism.

- The United States and the Soviet Union avoided a direct conflict, but the Cold War led to wars in Korea and Vietnam.

- The development of nuclear weapons made the Cold War a threat to the survival of the human race and led to nonproliferation treaties.

together proposed a world treaty against further proliferation, leading ultimately to the Nuclear Non-Proliferation Treaty (NPT) signed by 137 countries. Not until 1972, however, did the two superpowers begin the arduous and extremely slow process of negotiating weapons limits.

The atomic powers France and Britain were economically unable to keep up with the Soviet-American arms race. Instead, they led the European states in an effort to relax tensions. Between 1972 and 1975 the Conference on Security and Cooperation in Europe (CSCE) brought delegates from thirty-seven European states, the United States, and Canada to Helsinki. The Soviet Union's chief objective was European acceptance of the political boundaries of the Warsaw Pact nations as a condition for broad cooperation. In the end, the **Helsinki Accords** affirmed these boundaries and also called for economic, social, and governmental contacts and for cooperation in humanitarian fields between the rival alliances.

Helsinki Accords Political and human rights agreement signed in Helsinki, Finland, by the Soviet Union and western European countries.

Space exploration was another offshoot of the nuclear arms race. The contest to build larger and more accurate missiles prompted the superpowers to prove their skills in rocketry by launching space satellites. The Soviet Union placed a small *Sputnik* satellite into orbit around the earth in October 1957, and the United States responded with its own satellite three months later. The space race was on, a contest in which accomplishments in space were understood to signify equivalent achievements in the military sphere. In 1969, when Neil A. Armstrong and Edwin E. ("Buzz") Aldrin became the first humans to walk on the moon, America had demonstrated its technological superiority.

DECOLONIZATION AND NATION BUILDING

After World War I Germany, Austria-Hungary, and the Ottoman Empire lost their empires, and many colonies and dependencies were transferred to the victors, especially to Great Britain and France. In the two decades following World War II, nearly all remaining colonies gained independence (see Map 31.2). Circumstances differed profoundly from place to place. In some Asian countries, where colonial rule was of long standing, new states possessed viable industries, communications networks, and education systems. In other countries, notably in Africa, decolonized nations faced dire economic problems and disunity resulting from language and ethnic differences.

Most Latin American nations had achieved political independence in the nineteenth century (see Chapter 25). Following World War II, mass political movements in this region focused on the related issue of economic sovereignty—freedom from growing American economic domination. Great Britain and other European nations still retained colonies in the Caribbean after World War II. In the 1960s Barbados, Guyana, Jamaica, and Trinidad Tobago gained independence from Britain, and the smaller British colonies followed in the 1970s and 1980s, as did Surinam, which gained independence from the Netherlands.

Despite their differences, a sense of kinship arose among the nations of Latin America, Africa, and Asia. All shared feelings of excitement and rebirth. As North Americans, Europeans, and the Chinese settled into the exhausting deadlock of the Cold War, visions of independence and national development captivated the rest of the world.

New Nations in South and Southeast Asia

After partition in 1947 the independent states of India and Pakistan were strikingly dissimilar. Muslim Pakistan defined itself according to religion and quickly fell under the control of military leaders. India, a secular republic led by Prime Minister Jawaharlal Nehru, was much larger and inherited the considerable industrial and educational resources developed by the British, along with a large share of trained civil servants and military officers. Ninety percent of its population was Hindu and most of the rest Muslim.

Adding to the tensions of independence (see Chapter 29) was the decision by the Hindu ruler of the northwestern state Jammu and Kashmir, now commonly called Kashmir, to join India without consulting his overwhelmingly Muslim subjects. As a result, war between India and Pakistan over Kashmir broke out in 1947 and ended with an uneasy truce. In 1965 war broke out again, this time involving large military forces and the use of air power by both sides. Kashmir has remained a flash point, with new clashes in 1999 and 2000.

Despite early predictions that multilingual India might break up into a number of linguistically homogeneous states, most Indians recognized that unity benefited everyone; and the

MAP 31.2 Decolonization, 1947–1990 Independence was achieved a decade or so earlier in South and Southeast Asia than in Africa. © Cengage Learning

Former ruler

1960 Year independence achieved

- Belgium
- Portugal
- United States
- Other
- Great Britain
- France
- Netherlands
- Italy

ATLANTIC OCEAN

PACIFIC OCEAN

INDIAN OCEAN

Arabian Sea

Bay of Bengal

Caspian Sea

Black Sea

Mediterranean Sea

Equator 0°

Tropic of Cancer

Tropic of Capricorn

GREAT BRITAIN

FRANCE

SPAIN

PORTUGAL

ITALY

NETHERLANDS

BELGIUM

JAPAN

NORTH KOREA 1948

SOUTH KOREA 1948 (From Japan)

PHILIPPINES 1946

BRUNEI 1984 (From Gr. Br.)

MALAYSIA 1963

SINGAPORE 1965 (From Malaysia)

INDONESIA 1949

TIMOR-LESTE 1999 (From Indonesia)

PAPUA NEW GUINEA 1975 (From Australia)

NORTH VIETNAM 1954 (Unified 1975)

SOUTH VIETNAM 1954

CAMBODIA 1953

LAOS 1949

MYANMAR (BURMA) 1947

PAKISTAN 1947; BANGLADESH 1973

INDIA 1947

SRI LANKA (CEYLON) 1948

MALDIVES 1975 (From Gr. Br.)

PAKISTAN 1947

OMAN 1971

P.D.R. OF YEMEN 1967 (Unified 1990) YEMEN

UNITED ARAB EMIRATES 1971

QATAR 1971

BAHRAIN 1971

KUWAIT 1961

IRAQ 1932

JORDAN 1946

SYRIA 1944

LEBANON 1944

ISRAEL 1948

CYPRUS 1960

MALTA 1964 (From Gr. Br.)

EGYPT 1922

LIBYA 1951

TUNISIA 1957

MOROCCO 1956

WESTERN SAHARA 1975 (Morocco) (From Spain)

MAURITANIA 1960

MALI 1960

NIGER 1960

CHAD 1960

SUDAN 1956

ERITREA 1993 (From Ethiopia)

DJIBOUTI 1977

ETHIOPIA

SOMALIA 1960

CENTRAL AFRICAN REPUBLIC 1960

CAMEROON 1960

NIGERIA 1960

BENIN 1960

BURKINA FASO 1960

GHANA 1957

TOGO 1960

CÔTE D'IVOIRE 1960

GUINEA 1958

GUINEA-BISSAU 1974

GAMBIA 1965

SENEGAL 1960

CAPE VERDE 1975 (From Port.)

SIERRA LEONE 1961

LIBERIA 1820s

EQUATORIAL GUINEA 1968 (From Spain)

SÃO TOMÉ AND PRÍNCIPE 1975 (From Port.)

GABON 1960

REPUBLIC OF CONGO 1960

DEM. REP. OF CONGO 1960

UGANDA 1962

KENYA 1963

RWANDA 1962

BURUNDI 1962

TANZANIA 1964

ANGOLA 1975

ZAMBIA 1964

MALAWI 1964

MOZAMBIQUE 1974

ZIMBABWE 1980

NAMIBIA 1990 (From South Africa)

BOTSWANA 1966

SOUTH AFRICA (Republic 1961)

SWAZILAND 1968

LESOTHO 1966

MADAGASCAR 1960

COMOROS 1975 (From France)

SEYCHELLES 1976 (From Gr. Br.)

MAURITIUS 1968 (From Gr. Br.)

2,000 Mi.

2,000 Km.

N

country pursued a generally democratic and socialist line of development. Pakistan, in contrast, did break up. In 1971 the Bengali-speaking eastern section seceded to become the independent country of Bangladesh. During the fighting Indian military forces again struck against Pakistan. Despite their shared political heritage, India, Pakistan, and Bangladesh have found cooperation difficult and have pursued markedly different economic, political, religious, and social paths.

During the war the Japanese supported anti-British Indian nationalists as a way to weaken their enemy; they also encouraged the aspirations of nationalists in the countries they occupied in Southeast Asia. Many Asian nationalists saw Japanese victories over British, French, and Dutch colonial armies as a demonstration of the political and military capacities of Asian peoples. In the Dutch East Indies, Achmad Sukarno (1901–1970) cooperated with the Japanese in the hope that the Dutch, who had dominated the region economically since the seventeenth century, could be expelled. The Dutch finally negotiated withdrawal in 1949, and Sukarno became dictator of the resource-rich but underdeveloped nation of Indonesia. He ruled until 1965, when a military coup ousted him and brutally eliminated the nation's once-powerful Communist Party. The nation's large Chinese ethnic community was the target of violence during this period, and the new Indonesian government attempted to compel its assimilation, leading to decades of ethnic tension and discrimination.

In 1946 the United States kept its promise of postwar independence for the Philippine Islands but retained close economic ties and leases on military bases, later renegotiated. Britain granted independence to Burma (now Myanmar [my-ahn-MAR]) in 1948 and established the Malay Federation the same year. Singapore, once a member of the federation, became an independent city-state in 1965.

The Struggle for Independence in Africa

Between 1952 and 1956 France granted independence to Tunisia and Morocco, but it sought to retain Algeria. France had controlled this colony for nearly 150 years and had encouraged settlement; in 1950, 10 percent of the Algerian population was of French or other European origin. France also granted political rights to the settler population and asserted the fiction of Algeria's political and economic integration in the French nation. In reality few Algerians benefited from this arrangement, and most resented their continued colonial status.

The Vietnamese military victory over France in 1954 helped provoke a nationalist uprising in Algeria, during which both sides acted brutally. The Algerian revolutionary organization, the Front de Libération National (FLN), was supported by Egypt and other Arab countries who sought the emancipation of all Arab peoples. French colonists considered the country theirs and fought to the bitter end. When Algeria finally won independence in 1962, a flood of angry colonists returned to France. Since few Arabs had received technical training, this departure undermined the economy. Despite harsh feelings left by the war, Algeria retained close and seemingly indissoluble economic ties to France, and Algerians in large numbers emigrated to France in the decades that followed.

Independence was achieved in most of sub-Saharan Africa through negotiation, not revolution. In colonies with significant white settler minorities, however, the path to independence followed the violent experience of Algeria. African nationalists were forced to overcome many obstacles, but they were also able to take advantage of many consequential changes put in place during colonial rule. In the 1950s and 1960s world economic expansion and growing popular support for liberation overcame African worries about potential economic and political problems that might follow independence. Moreover, improvements in medical care and public health had led to rapid population growth in Africa, and the continent's young population embraced the idea of independence.

Western nationalist and egalitarian ideals also helped fuel resistance to colonialism. Most of the leaders of African independence movements were among the most westernized members of these societies. African veterans of Allied armies during World War II had exposure to Allied propaganda that emphasized ideas of popular sovereignty and self-determination. In addition, many leaders were recent graduates of educational institutions created by colonial governments, and a minority had obtained advanced education in Europe and the United States.

African nationalists were able to take advantage of other legacies of colonial rule as well. Schools, labor associations, and the colonial bureaucracy itself proved to be fertile nationalist recruiting centers. Languages introduced by colonial governments were useful in building

Jomo Kenyatta Kenya's newly elected premier, Jomo Kenyatta, cheered by crowds in Nairobi in 1963. Kenyatta (waving ceremonial "wisk") had led the struggle to end British colonial rule in Kenya.

Bettmann/CORBIS

multiethnic coalitions, while networks of roads and railroads built to promote colonial exports forged new national identities and a new political consciousness.

The young politicians who led the nationalist movements devoted their lives to ridding their homelands of foreign occupation. An example is Kwame Nkrumah **(KWAH-mee nn-KROO-muh)** (1909–1972), who in 1957 became prime minister of Ghana (formerly the Gold Coast), the first British colony in West Africa to achieve independence. After graduating from a Catholic mission school and a government teacher-training college, Nkrumah spent a decade studying philosophy and theology in the United States, where he absorbed ideas about black pride and independence propounded by W. E. B. Du Bois and Marcus Garvey.

During a brief stay in Britain, Nkrumah joined Kenyan nationalist Jomo Kenyatta, a Ph.D. in anthropology, to found an organization devoted to African freedom. In 1947 Nkrumah returned to the Gold Coast to work for independence. The time was right. There was no longer strong public support in Britain for colonialism, and Britain's political leadership was not enthusiastic about investing resources to hold restive colonies. When Nkrumah's party won a decisive election victory in 1951, the British Gold Coast governor appointed him prime minister. Full independence came in 1957. Although Nkrumah remained an effective international spokesman for colonized peoples, he was overthrown in 1966 by a disaffected group of army officers.

Britain soon granted independence to its other West African colonies, including large, populous, and resource-rich Nigeria in 1960. In some British colonies in eastern and southern Africa, however, long-established white settler populations resisted independence. In Kenya a small but influential group of wealthy coffee planters claimed that a protest movement among the Kikuyu **(kih-KOO-you)** people was proof that Africans were not ready for self-government. The settlers called the movement "Mau Mau," a made-up name meant to evoke an image of primitive savagery. When violence between settlers and anticolonial fighters escalated after 1952, British troops hunted down movement leaders and resettled the Kikuyu in fortified villages. They also declared a state of emergency, banned all African political protest, and imprisoned Kenyatta and other nationalists. Released in 1961, Kenyatta negotiated with the British to write a constitution for an independent Kenya, and in 1964 he was elected the nation's first president. Kenyatta proved to be an effective, though autocratic, ruler, and Kenya benefited from greater stability and prosperity than Ghana and many other former colonies.

African leaders in the sub-Saharan French colonies were more reluctant than their counterparts in British colonies to call for full independence. Promises made during World War II by the Free French movement of General Charles de Gaulle at a conference in Brazzaville, in French Equatorial Africa, seemed to offer dramatic changes without independence. Dependent on the troops and supplies of French African colonies, de Gaulle had promised Africans a more democratic government, broader suffrage, and greater access to employment in the colonial government. He had also promised better education and health services and an end to many abuses in the colonial system. He had not promised independence, but the politics of postwar colonial self-government ultimately proved irresistible.

Most Africans elected to office following the reforms were trained civil servants. Because of the French policy of job rotation, they had typically served in a number of different colonies and thus had a broad regional outlook. They realized that some colonies—such as Ivory Coast, with coffee and cacao exports, fishing, and hardwood forests—had good economic prospects, while others, such as landlocked, desert Niger, did not. Furthermore, they recognized the importance of French public investment in the region—a billion dollars between 1947 and 1956—and their own dependence on colonial civil service salaries. As a result, they generally looked to achieve greater self-government incrementally.

When Charles de Gaulle returned to power in France in 1958, at the height of the Algerian war, he warned that a rush to independence would have costs, saying: "One cannot conceive of both an independent territory and a France which continues to aid it." Ultimately, however, African patriotism prevailed in all of France's West African and Equatorial African colonies. Guinea, under the dynamic leadership of Sékou Touré (SAY-koo too-RAY), gained full independence in 1958 and the others in 1960.

Independence in the Belgian Congo was chaotic and violent. Contending political and ethnic groups found external allies; some were supported by Cuba and the Soviet Union, while others were supported by the West or by business groups tied to the rich mines. Civil war, the introduction of foreign mercenaries, and the rhetoric of Cold War confrontation roiled the waters and led to a heavy loss of life and great property destruction. In 1965 Mobuto Sese Seko seized power in a military coup that included the assassination of Patrice Lumumba, the nation's first prime minister. Once in power, Mobuto maintained one of the region's most corrupt governments until driven from power in 1997.

The opposition of European settler communities delayed decolonization in southern Africa. While the settler minority tried to defend white supremacy, African-led liberation movements were committed to the creation of nonracial societies and majority rule. In the 1960s African guerrilla movements successfully fought to end Portuguese rule in Angola and Mozambique. Their efforts led to both the overthrow of the antidemocratic government of Portugal in 1974 and independence the following year. After a ten-year fight, European settlers in the British colony of Southern Rhodesia accepted African majority rule in 1980. The new government changed the country's name to Zimbabwe, the name of a great stone city built by Africans long before the arrival of European settlers.

South Africa and neighboring Namibia remained in the hands of European minorities much longer. The large white settler population of South Africa achieved effective independence from Britain in 1961 but kept the black and mixed-race majority in colonial-era subjection, separating the races in a system they called *apartheid* (a-PART-hite). Descendents of Dutch and English settlers made up 13 percent of the population but controlled the productive land, the industrial, mining, and commercial enterprises, and the government. Meanwhile, discrimination and segregation in housing, education, and employment confined the lives of people of mixed parentage (10 percent of the population) and South Asians (less than 3 percent).

Indigenous Africans, 74 percent of the population, were subjected to even stricter limitations on housing, freedom of movement, and access to jobs and public facilities. The government created fictional African "homelands" as a way of denying the African majority citizenship and political rights. Not unlike Amerindian reservations, these "homelands" were located in poor regions far from the more dynamic and prosperous urban and industrial areas. Overcrowded and lacking investment, they were impoverished and lacking in services and opportunities.

The African National Congress (ANC), formed in 1912, led opposition to apartheid (see Diversity and Dominance: Race and the Struggle for Justice in South Africa). After police fired on demonstrators in the African town of Sharpeville in 1960 and banned all peaceful political protest by Africans, a lawyer named Nelson Mandela (b. 1918) organized guerrilla resistance by the ANC. The government sentenced Mandela to life in prison in 1964 and persecuted the ANC, but it was unable to defeat the movement. Facing growing opposition internationally, South Africa freed Mandela from prison in 1990 and began the transition to majority rule (see Chapters 32 and 33).

The Quest for Economic Freedom in Latin America

Although Latin America had achieved independence from colonial rule more than a hundred years earlier, European and American economic domination of the region created a semicolonial order (see Chapters 26 and 29). Foreigners controlled Chile's copper, Cuba's sugar, Colombia's coffee, and Guatemala's bananas, leading by the 1930s to growing support for economic nationalism. During the 1930s and 1940s populist political leaders experimented with programs that would constrain foreign investors or, alternatively, promote local efforts to industrialize (see discussion of Getulio Vargas and Juan Perón in Chapter 29).

In Mexico the revolutionary constitution of 1917 began an era of economic nationalism that culminated in the expropriation of foreign oil interests, mostly American, in 1938. The Institutional Revolutionary Party, or PRI (the abbreviation of its name in Spanish), controlled Mexico until the 1990s and had overseen a period of economic expansion during World War II. But a yawning gulf between rich and poor persisted. Although the government dominated important industries like petroleum and restricted foreign investment, rapid population growth, uncontrolled migration to Mexico City and other urban areas, and political corruption undermined efforts to lift the nation's poor. Economic power was concentrated at the top of society, with two thousand elite families controlling much of the nation's wealth. At the other end of the economic scale were the millions of poor Mexicans struggling to survive. Thwarted by limited opportunities at home, millions of Mexicans migrated to the United States.

Guatemala's situation was more representative of Latin America in 1950. An American corporation, the United Fruit Company, was Guatemala's largest landowner; it also controlled much of the nation's infrastructure, including port facilities and railroads. To limit banana production and keep international prices high, United Fruit kept much of its Guatemalan lands fallow. Jacobo Arbenz Guzmán, elected in 1951, advocated positions broadly similar to those of leaders like Perón of Argentina and Vargas of Brazil (see Chapter 29), who confronted powerful foreign interests. He advocated land reform, which would have transferred these fallow lands to the nation's rural poor. The threatened expropriation angered the United Fruit Company. Simultaneously, Arbenz tried to reduce U.S. political influence, raising fears in Washington that he sought closer ties to the Soviet Union. Reacting to the land reform efforts and to reports that Arbenz was becoming friendly to communism, the U.S. Central Intelligence Agency (CIA), in one of its first major overseas operations, sponsored a takeover by the Guatemalan military in 1954. CIA intervention removed Arbenz, but it also condemned Guatemala to decades of governmental instability and violence.

By the 1950s American companies dominated the Cuban economy. They controlled sugar production, the nation's most important industry, as well as banking, transportation, tourism, and public utilities. The United States was also the most important market for Cuba's exports and the most important source of Cuba's imports. Thus the performance of the U.S. economy largely determined the ebb and flow of Cuban foreign trade. By 1956 sugar accounted for 80 percent of Cuba's exports and 25 percent of Cuba's national income. But demand in the United States dictated keeping only 39 percent of the land owned by the sugar companies in production, while Cuba experienced chronic underemployment. Similarly, immense deposits of nickel in Cuba went untapped because the U.S. government, which owned them, considered them to be a strategic reserve.

While high unemployment and slow growth afflicted the nation, profits went north to the United States or to a small class of

Cuban Poster of Ernesto ("Che") Guevara   Che became a leading theorist of communist revolution in Latin America. He died in 1967 while leading an insurgency in Bolivia.

Barry Lewis/Alamy

Race and the Struggle for Justice in South Africa

One of South Africa's martyrs in the struggle against apartheid was the thinker and activist Steve Biko (1946–1977). Biko was one of the founders of the Black Consciousness Movement, which focused on the ways in which white settlers had stripped Africans of their freedom. Between 1975 and 1977 police arrested and interrogated him four times. After his arrest in August 1977, the police severely beat him and denied him medical care. His death in police custody caused worldwide outrage. The excerpt below is from his I Write What I Like.

[T]hese are not the people we are concerned with [those who support apartheid]. We are concerned with that curious bunch of nonconformists . . . that [go] under all sorts of names—liberals, leftists etc. These are the people who argue that they are not responsible for white racism and the country's "inhumanity to the black man." These are the people who claim that they too feel the oppression just as acutely as the blacks and therefore should be jointly involved in the black man's struggle for a place under the sun. In short, these are the people who say that they have black souls wrapped up in white skins.

Nowhere is the arrogance of the liberal ideology demonstrated so well as in their insistence that the problems of the country can only be solved by a bilateral approach involving both black and white. This has, by and large, come to be taken in all seriousness as the modus operandi in South Africa by all those who claim they would like a change in the status quo. . . . The integration they talk about is . . . a one-way course, with the whites doing all the talking and the blacks the listening. . . .

Once the various groups within a given community have asserted themselves to the point that mutual respect has to be shown then you have the ingredients for a true and meaningful integration. From this it becomes clear that as long as blacks are suffering from [an] inferiority complex—a result of

300 years of deliberate oppression, denigration and derision—they will be useless as co-architects of a normal society where man is nothing else but man for his own sake. Hence what is necessary as a prelude to anything else that may come is a very strong grassroots build-up of black consciousness such that blacks can learn to assert themselves and stake their rightful claim.

Thus in adopting the line of a nonracial approach, the liberals are playing their old game. They are claiming a "monopoly on intelligence and moral judgement" and setting the pattern and pace for the realisation of the black man's aspirations. They want to remain in good books with both the black and white worlds. They want to shy away from all forms of "extremisms," condemning "white supremacy" as being just as bad as "Black Power!" They vacillate between the two worlds, verbalising all the complaints of the blacks beautifully while skillfully extracting what suits them from the exclusive pool of white privileges. But ask them for a moment to give a concrete meaningful programme that they intend adopting, then you will see on whose side they really are. Their protests are directed at and appeal to white conscience, everything they do is directed at finally convincing the white electorate that the black man is also a man and that at some future date he should be given a place at the white man's table.

In the following selection Anglican bishop Desmond Tutu (b. 1931) expressed his personal anguish at the death of Steve Biko, summarizing Biko's contributions to the struggle for justice in South Africa. Tutu won the Noble Peace Prize in 1984 and was named archbishop in 1988. From 1995 to 1998 he chaired the Truth and Reconciliation Commission, which investigated atrocities in South Africa during the years of apartheid. He stated that his objective was to create "a democratic and just society without racial divisions."

wealthy Cubans. Cuba's government was also notoriously corrupt and subservient to the wishes of American interests. As reform-minded young Cubans organized for a national election, Fulgencio Batista, a former military leader and president, illegally seized power in a coup in 1953. Hostility to Batista and anger with the corruption, repression, and foreign economic domination of his government gave rise to the revolution led by Fidel Castro.

Fidel Castro (b. 1927), a young lawyer who had played a prominent role in left-wing politics while at university, led a failed uprising in 1953. Convicted, jailed, and then sent into exile, Castro returned to Cuba in 1956 to establish a successful revolutionary movement in the countryside. His supporters included student groups, labor unions, and adherents of Cuba's traditional parties. When he and his youthful followers took power in 1959, they vowed not to suffer the fate of Arbenz and the Guatemalan reformers. Ernesto ("Che") Guevara (CHAY-guh-VAHR-uh), Castro's Argentine-born chief lieutenant who became the main theorist of communist revolution in Latin America, had witnessed the CIA coup in Guatemala firsthand. He and Castro believed that confrontation with the United States was inevitable and moved quickly to remove the existing military leadership and begin revolutionary changes in the economy.

When we heard the news "Steve Biko is dead" we were struck numb with disbelief. No, it can't be true! No, it must be a horrible nightmare, and we will awake and find that really it is different—that Steve is alive even if it be in detention. But no, dear friends, he is dead and we are still numb with grief, and groan with anguish "Oh God, where are you? Oh God, do you really care—how can you let this happen to us?"

It all seems such a senseless waste of a wonderfully gifted person, struck down in the bloom of youth, a youthful bloom that some wanted to see blighted. What can be the purpose of such wanton destruction? God, do you really love us? What must we do which we have not done, what must we say which we have not said a thousand times over, oh, for so many years— that all we want is what belongs to all God's children, what belongs as an inalienable right—a place in the sun in our own beloved mother country. Oh God, how long can we go on? How long can we go on appealing for a more just ordering of society where we all, black and white together, count not because of some accident of birth or a biological irrelevance—where all of us black and white count because we are human persons, human persons created in your own image.

God called Steve Biko to be his servant in South Africa—to speak up on behalf of God, declaring what the will of this God must be in a situation such as ours, a situation of evil, injustice, oppression and exploitation. God called him to be the founder father of the Black Consciousness Movement against which we have had tirades and fulminations. It is a movement by which God, through Steve, sought to awaken in the Black person a sense of his intrinsic value and worth as a child of God, not needing to apologise for his existential condition as a black person, calling on blacks to glorify and praise God that he had created them black. Steve, with his brilliant mind that always saw to the heart of things, realised that until blacks asserted their humanity and their personhood, there was not the remotest chance for reconciliation in South Africa. For true reconciliation is a deeply personal matter. It can happen only between persons who assert their own personhood, and who acknowledge and respect that of others. You don't get reconciled to your dog, do you? Steve knew and believed fervently that being pro-black was not the same thing as being anti-white. The Black Consciousness Movement is not a "hate white movement," despite all you may have heard to the contrary. He had a far too profound respect for persons as persons, to want to deal with them under readymade, shopsoiled [sic] categories.

All who met him had this tremendous sense of a warm-hearted man, and as a notable acquaintance of his told me, a man who was utterly indestructible, of massive intellect and yet reticent; quite unshakeable in his commitment to principle and to radical change in south africa by peaceful means; a man of real reconciliation, truly an instrument of god's peace, unshakeable in his commitment to the liberation of all South Africans, black and white, striving for a more just and more open South Africa.

QUESTIONS FOR ANALYSIS

1. What are Steve Biko's charges against white liberals in South Africa?

2. What was the proper role for whites in the anti-apartheid movement according to Biko?

3. How does Bishop Tutu's eulogy differ from the political spirit and point of view expressed in Biko's 1970 essay?

4. According to Bishop Tutu, what were Biko's strongest characteristics? Were these characteristics demonstrated in Biko's essay?

Sources: First selection from Steve Biko, *I Write What I Like*, ed. by Aelred Stubbs C.R. Bowerdean Publishing Co., Ltd.; second selection from Bishop Desmond Tutu, *Crying in the Wilderness: The Struggle for Justice in South Africa*, ed. John Webster (William B. Eerdmans Publishing Co., 1982), pp. 61–63.

Within a year Castro's government seized and redistributed land, lowered urban rents, and raised wages, effectively transferring 15 percent of the national income from the rich to the poor. Within two years the Castro government had nationalized the property of almost all U.S. corporations in Cuba as well as the wealth of Cuba's elite. To achieve his revolutionary objectives, Castro sought economic support from the Soviet Union. He also consolidated his personal political power, putting aside promises of democratic reform made when fighting Batista.

The United States responded by seeking to destabilize the Cuban economy and undermine the Castro government. These punitive measures by the United States, the nationalization of so much of the economy, and the punishment of Batista supporters caused tens of thousands of Cubans to leave, including some who had opposed Batista. Initially, most emigrants were from wealthy families and the middle class, but when the economic failures of the regime became clear, many poor Cubans fled to the United States or to other Latin American nations.

There is little evidence that Castro was committed to communism before the revolution, but his commitment to break the economic and political power of the United States in Cuba and undertake dramatic social reforms led inevitably to conflict with the United States and to reliance

SECTION REVIEW

- Independence in India and Pakistan led to war over Kashmir, which has continued to cause conflict.

- Algeria gained independence from France after a long and violent revolution.

- West African colonies eventually gained independence from Great Britain and France through negotiation, but the Belgian Congo fell under the power of a dictator.

- In southern African colonies, large white settler populations resisted independence, and whites in South Africa instituted the system of segregation called apartheid.

- In Latin American nations economic nationalists sought to reduce or eliminate the economic influence of the United States.

- The CIA interfered forcefully in Guatemala, and its attempt to do the same in Cuba helped lead to the Cuban missile crisis; meanwhile, Castro created a socialist economy.

on the Soviet Union. In April 1961, in an attempt to apply the strategy that had removed Arbenz from power in Guatemala, an army of Cuban exiles trained and armed by the CIA landed at the Bay of Pigs in an effort to overthrow Castro. The Cuban army defeated the attempted invasion in a matter of days. The Eisenhower administration had planned the invasion, but the newly elected U.S. president, John F. Kennedy, agreed to carry it out and lived with the embarrassment. This failure helped precipitate the Cuban missile crisis. Fearful of a new invasion, Castro and Khrushchev placed nuclear weapons as well as missiles and bombers in Cuba to forestall an anticipated second attack.

The failure of the Bay of Pigs tarnished the reputation of the United States and the CIA and gave heart to revolutionaries all over Latin America. But the armed revolutionary movements that imitated the tactics and objectives of Cuba's bearded revolutionaries experienced little success. Among the thousands to lose their lives was Che Guevara, captured and executed in 1967 by Bolivian troops trained by the United States. Nevertheless, Castro had demonstrated that revolutionaries could successfully challenge American power and put in place a radical program of economic and social reform in the Western Hemisphere.

BEYOND A BIPOLAR WORLD

Although no one doubted the dominating role of the East-West superpower rivalry in world affairs, newly independent nations had concerns that were primarily domestic and regional. Their challenge was to pursue their ends within the bipolar structure of the Cold War—and when possible to take advantage of the East-West rivalry. Where nationalist forces sought to assert political or economic independence, Cold War antagonists provided arms and political support even when the nationalist goals were quite different from those of the supporting superpower. For other nations, the ruinously expensive superpower arms race opened opportunities to expand industries and exports. In short, the superpowers dominated the world but did not control it.

The Third World

As a leader of the decolonization movement, Indonesia's President Sukarno was an appropriate figure to host a 1955 meeting of twenty-nine African and Asian countries at Bandung, Indonesia, that proclaimed solidarity among those fighting against colonial rule. This conference marked the beginning of an effort by the many new, poor, mostly non-European nations emerging from colonialism to gain more influence in world affairs. The terms **nonaligned nations** and **Third World**, which became commonplace in the following years, signaled these countries' collective stance toward the rival sides in the Cold War. If the West, led by the United States, and the East, led by the Soviet Union, represented two worlds locked in mortal struggle, the Third World consisted of everyone else.

Leaders of so-called Third World countries preferred the label *nonaligned*, which signaled their independence from Soviet or U.S. control. Leaders in the West noted that the Soviet Union supported many national liberation movements and that the nonaligned movement included communist countries such as China and Yugoslavia. As a result, they refused to take the term *nonaligned* seriously. In a polarized world, they saw Sukarno, Nehru, Nkrumah, and Egypt's Gamal Abd al-Nasir (gah-MAHL AHB-d al–NAH-suhr) as stalking horses for an ambitious campaign to extend Soviet influence globally. This may have been the view of some Soviet leaders as well, since they were quick to offer military and financial aid to many nonaligned countries.

For the movement's leaders, however, nonalignment was primarily a way to extract money and support from one or both superpowers. By flirting with the Soviet Union or its ally, the

nonaligned nations Developing countries that announced their neutrality in the Cold War.

Third World Term applied to a group of developing countries who professed nonalignment during the Cold War.

Bandung Conference, 1955 India's Jawaharlal Nehru (in white hat) was a central figure at the conference held in Indonesia to promote solidarity among non-aligned developing nations.

AP Photo/George Sweers

People's Republic of China, a country could get weapons, training, and barter agreements that offered an alternative to selling agricultural or mineral products on Western-dominated world markets. The same flirtation might also prompt the United States and its allies to proffer grants and loans, cheap or free surplus grain, and investments in new industries or in infrastructure development.

Nonaligned countries could sometimes play the Cold War rivals against each other. Nasir, who had led a military coup against the Egyptian monarchy in 1952, and his successor Anwar al-Sadat **(al-seh-DAT)** played this game skillfully. The United States offered to build a dam at Aswan **(AS-wahn)**, on the Nile River, to increase Egypt's electrical generating and irrigation capacity, but it withdrew the offer when Egypt turned to the Warsaw Pact for armaments in 1956. Worsened relations with the West then led Nasir to nationalize the Suez Canal and the Soviet Union to commit to building the dam. Later that same year Israel, Great Britain, and France allied to invade Egypt, aiming to overthrow Nasir, regain the Suez Canal, and secure Israel from any Egyptian threat. The invasion succeeded militarily, but the United States and the Soviet Union both pressured the invaders to withdraw, thus saving Nasir's government. In 1972 Sadat evicted Soviet military advisers, but a year later he used his Soviet weapons to attack Israel. After he lost that war, he disengaged from the Soviets; he then improved relations with, and sought increased aid from, the United States.

Other nations adopted similar balancing strategies. In each case, local leaders sought to develop their nations' economies and assert or preserve their nations' interests. Manipulating the superpowers was a means toward those ends and implied very little about true ideological orientation.

Japan and China

No countries took more effective advantage of opportunities presented by the superpowers' preoccupations than Japan and China. Japan signed a peace treaty with most of its former enemies in 1951 and regained independence from American occupation the following year. Renouncing militarism and its imperialist past (see Chapter 30), Japan remained on the sidelines throughout the Korean War. Its new constitution, written under American supervision in 1946, allowed only a limited self-defense force, banned the deployment of Japanese troops abroad, and gave the vote to women.

Like the Europeans, the Japanese had suffered high levels of population loss and property destruction in the war. With peace restored, they focused their resources on rebuilding industries and expanding trade. Peace treaties with countries in Southeast Asia specified reparations payable in the form of goods and services, thus reintroducing Japan to that region as a force for economic development rather than as a military occupier. Beginning during the U.S. occupation, Japan had become closely tied to the West by trade and soon benefited from the postwar recovery. At the same time, controls placed on Japan by peace conditions kept its military expenditures low during the Cold War, providing an exceptional environment to invest in economic development and infrastructure.

Three industries that took advantage of government aid and new technologies were key to Japan's emergence as an economic superpower after 1975. Electricity was in short supply in 1950, and Tokyo suffered from chronic power outages. Japan responded by constructing a power grid between 1951 and 1970 that produced 60 million kilowatts of electricity. Most of this new capacity came from hydroelectric sources. At the same time steel production and shipbuilding developed rapidly, placing Japan among world leaders in both industries.

While Japan benefited from avoiding the heavy defense costs associated with the Cold War, China was at the center of Cold War politics. When Mao Zedong (maow dzuh-dong) and the communists defeated the nationalists in 1949 and established the People's Republic of China (PRC), their main ally and source of arms was the Soviet Union. By 1956, however, the PRC and the Soviet Union were beginning to diverge politically, partly in reaction to the Soviet rejection of Stalinism and partly because of China's reluctance to accept the role of subordinate. Mao had his own notions of communism that focused strongly on the peasantry, which the Soviets had ignored in favor of the industrial working class.

Mao's Great Leap Forward in 1958 was intended to propel China into the ranks of world industrial powers by maximizing the output of small-scale, village-level industries and by instituting mass collectivization in agriculture. These untested policies demonstrated Mao's willingness to carry out massive economic and social experiments of his own devising in the face of

Chinese Red Guards   During the Cultural Revolution, the Red Guards, young Chinese militants, sought to identify enemies of the Communist Party and Chairman Mao, sometimes labeling their own teachers, parents, and neighbors as enemies of the people. In this photo a victim wears a dunce cap on which his crimes are written.

AP Images

criticism by the Soviets as well as by traditional economists. By 1962 the revolutionary reforms had failed comprehensively, leading to an estimated 20 to 30 million deaths.

Cultural Revolution (China)
Campaign in China ordered by Mao Zedong to purge the Communist Party of his opponents and instill revolutionary values in the younger generation.

In 1966 Mao instituted another radical program, the **Cultural Revolution**, that ordered the mass mobilization of Chinese youth into Red Guard units. His goal was to kindle revolutionary fervor in a new generation to ward off the stagnation and bureaucratization he saw in the Soviet Union, as well as to increase his own power within the Communist Party. Red Guard units criticized and purged teachers, party officials, and intellectuals for "bourgeois values." Executions, beatings, and incarcerations were widespread, leading to a half-million deaths and 3 million purged by 1971. Finally, Mao admitted that attacks on individuals had gotten out of hand and intervened to reestablish order. Mao's wife Jiang Qing (jyahn ching) and radical allies dominated the last years of the Cultural Revolution, harshly restricting artistic and intellectual activity.

The rift between the PRC and the Soviet Union allowed U.S. president Richard Nixon (served 1969–1974) to revive relations with China. In 1971 the United States agreed to allow the PRC to join the United Nations and occupy China's permanent seat on the Security Council. This decision necessitated the expulsion of the Chinese nationalist government based on the island of Taiwan, which had previously claimed to be the only legal Chinese authority. The following year, Nixon visited Beijing, initiating a new era of enhanced cooperation between the People's Republic of China and the United States.

The Middle East

Independence came gradually to the Arab countries of the Middle East. Britain granted Syria and Lebanon independence after World War II. Iraq, Egypt, and Jordan enjoyed nominal independence between the two world wars but remained under indirect British control until the 1950s. Military coups overthrew King Faruq (fuh-ROOK) of Egypt in 1952 and King Faisal (FIE-suhl) II of Iraq in 1958. King Husayn (hoo-SANE) of Jordan dismissed his British military commander in 1956 in response to the Suez crisis, but his poor desert country remained dependent on British and later American financial aid.

Overshadowing all Arab politics, however, was the struggle with Israel, a clear illustration that the superpowers could not control all dangerous international disputes. British policy on Palestine between the wars oscillated between favoring Zionist Jews—who emigrated to Palestine, encouraged by the Balfour Declaration—and support for the indigenous Palestinian Arabs, who suspected that the Zionists were aiming at an independent state. As more and more Jews sought a safe haven from persecution by the Nazis, Arabs felt more and more threatened. The Arabs unleashed a guerrilla uprising against the British in 1936, and Jewish groups turned to militant tactics a few years later. Occasionally, Arabs and Jews confronted each other in riots or killings, making it clear that peaceful coexistence in Palestine would be difficult or impossible to achieve.

After the war, under intense pressure to resettle European Jewish refugees, Britain turned the Palestine problem over to the United Nations. In November 1947 the General Assembly voted in favor of partitioning Palestine into two states, one Jewish and one Arab. The Jewish community made plans to declare independence, while the Palestinians, who felt that the proposed land division was unfair, took up arms. When Israel declared its independence in May 1948, neighboring Arab countries sent armies to help the Palestinians crush the newborn state.

Israel prevailed and some 700,000 Palestinians became refugees, finding shelter in United Nations refugee camps in Jordan, Syria, Lebanon, and the Gaza Strip (a bit of coastal land on the Egyptian-Israeli border). The right of these refugees to return home remains a focal point of Arab politics today. In 1967 Israel responded to threatening military moves by Egypt's Nasir by preemptively attacking Egyptian and Syrian air bases. In six days Israel won a smashing victory. When Jordan entered the war, Israel took control of Jerusalem, which it had previously split with Jordan, and the West Bank. Acquiring all of Jerusalem satisfied Jews' deep longing to return to their holiest city, but Palestinians continued to regard Jerusalem as their destined capital, and Muslims in many countries protested Israeli control of the Dome of the Rock, a revered Islamic shrine located in the city. Israel also occupied the Gaza Strip, the strategic Golan Heights in southern Syria, and the entire Sinai Peninsula (see Map 31.3). These acquisitions resulted in a new wave of Palestinian refugees.

MAP 31.3 Middle East Oil and the Arab-Israeli Conflict, 1947–1973 Private European and American companies had long controlled oil resources. In the 1960s OPEC negotiated agreements for sharing control and eventually establishing national ownership. This set the stage for the use of oil as a weapon in the 1973 Arab-Israeli war as well as for subsequent price increases. © Cengage Learning

Shortage at the Pumps   As prices rose in the late 1970s, consumers tried to hoard supplies by filling gas cans at neighborhood stations. For the first time gas prices exceeded $1 a gallon.

James Pozarik/Getty Images

The rival claims to Palestine continued to plague Middle Eastern politics. The Palestine Liberation Organization (PLO), headed by Yasir Arafat **(AR-uh-fat)**, waged guerrilla war against Israel, frequently engaging in acts of terrorism. The Israelis were able to blunt or absorb these attacks and launch counterstrikes that likewise involved assassinations and bombings. Though the United States was a firm friend to Israel and the Soviet Union armed the Arab states, neither superpower saw the struggle between Zionism and Palestinian nationalism as a vital concern—until oil became a political issue.

The phenomenal concentration of oil wealth in the Middle East—Saudi Arabia, Iran, Iraq, Kuwait, Libya, Qatar, Bahrain, and the United Arab Emirates—was not fully realized until after World War II, when demand for oil rose sharply as civilian economies recovered. In 1960, as world demand rose, oil-producing states formed the **Organization of Petroleum Exporting Countries (OPEC)** to promote their collective interest in higher revenues.

Organization of Petroleum Exporting Countries (OPEC) Organization formed in 1960 by oil-producing states to promote their collective interest in generating revenue from oil.

Oil politics and the Arab-Israeli conflict intersected in October 1973 during the Yom Kippur War. Surprise attacks by Syria and Egypt threw the Israelis into temporary disarray, but Israel won a clear military victory in the end. Supported by military supplies from the United States, it drove back Syrian forces and trapped an Egyptian army at the Suez Canal's southern end. The United States then arranged a ceasefire and the disengagement of forces. But before that could happen, the Arab oil-producing countries voted to embargo oil shipments to the United States and the Netherlands as punishment for their support of Israel.

The implications of using oil as an economic weapon profoundly disturbed the worldwide oil industry. Prices rose—along with feelings of insecurity. In 1974 OPEC responded to the turmoil in the oil market by quadrupling prices, setting the stage for massive transfers of wealth to the producing countries and provoking a feeling of crisis throughout the consuming countries.

The Emergence of Environmental Concerns

The Cold War and the massive investments made in postwar economic recovery focused public and governmental attention on technological innovations and enormous projects such as hydroelectric dams and nuclear power stations. Only a few people warned that untested technologies and industrial expansion were degrading the environment. The superpowers were

SECTION REVIEW

● After decolonization new nations organized the "nonaligned movement" to assert a middle ground between the Cold War rivals.

● After World War II Japan followed the capitalist industrial model while China under Mao tried and failed to industrialize using mass mobilizations and central planning.

● Israel's military victories over its Arab neighbors in 1967 and 1973, while expanding the nation's borders, initiated an enduring cycle of regional tensions and violence between Israelis and Palestinians.

● OPEC's 1973 embargo of oil shipments to nations that supported Israel soon led to steep price increases and a massive redistribution of wealth to oil-producing nations.

● During the 1970s young people provided crucial leadership to a worldwide movement to conserve natural resources and protect the environment.

particularly negligent of the environmental impact of pesticide and herbicide use, automobile exhaust, industrial waste disposal, and radiation.

The wave of student unrest that swept many parts of the world in 1968 and the early 1970s created a new awareness of environmental issues and a new constituency for environmental action. As youth activism grew, governments in the West began to pass new environmental regulations. Among them was the Clean Air Act of 1970. Earth Day, a benchmark of the new awareness, was also first celebrated in 1970, the year in which the United States also established its Environmental Protection Agency.

When oil prices skyrocketed, the problem of finite natural resources became more broadly recognized. Making gasoline engines and home heating systems more efficient and lowering highway speed limits to conserve fuel became matters of national debate in the United States, while poorer countries struggled to find the money to import oil. A widely read 1972 study called *The Limits of Growth* forecast a need to cut back on consumption of natural resources in the twenty-first century. Ecological and environmental problems now vied for public attention with superpower rivalry and Third World nation building.

CONCLUSION

The alliance between the Soviet Union and the Western democracies led by the United States did not survive into the post–World War II era. Shortly after the war, both sides began to prepare for a new round of hostilities, establishing competing military alliances and attempting to influence the new governments of nations formerly occupied by the Axis. In the end this confrontation was projected into space, as each side sought to advertise its technological capacity through satellite launches and finally a moon landing.

Each side portrayed this tension as a struggle between irreconcilably different social and economic systems, and each side emphasized the corruption, injustice, and unfairness of its opponent. When Winston Churchill spoke in 1946 of Soviet control in eastern Europe as an iron curtain, he suggested that the Soviet system was, in effect, a prison.

Massive armies armed with increasingly sophisticated weapons, including nuclear weapons far more destructive than those dropped on Japan, defended the boundary that separated the United States and its allies and the Soviet Union and its allies. This Cold War quickly became global in character as distant civil wars, regional conflicts, and nationalist revolutions were transformed by support provided by these rivals for global ascendancy.

The desire of colonized peoples to throw off imperial controls and establish independent nations provided many of the era's flash points. The Western nations had defined World War II as a war for freedom and self-determination. The Free French had promised greater autonomy to African colonies, the United States had used nationalist forces to fight against the Japanese in the Philippines and in Vietnam, and Britain also had used forces recruited throughout its empire to fight the war. Once organized and set in motion, these nationalist energies eventually overwhelmed colonial rule. The most powerful force in the postwar era was nationalism, the desire of peoples to control their own destinies.

In Africa, the Middle East, South Asia, and Latin America, this desire to throw off foreign controls led to the creation of scores of new nations by the 1970s. Each nation's struggle had its own character. While in India these passions led to independence, similar sentiments led in China to the overthrow of a government seen as weak and subordinate to foreign powers and to the creation of a communist dictatorship. In much of Africa, the Middle East, and the Caribbean, nationalism overturned colonial rule. In the Middle East the desire for self-government was complicated by the creation of the state of Israel. In Latin America, where most nations had been independent for well over a century, nationalist passions focused on a desire for economic independence and an end to foreign military interventions.

The end of Japanese control in Korea and Vietnam led to territorial partitions that separated Soviet-leaning and Western-allied polities. Civil war and foreign interventions soon followed. In both cases the Soviet Union and China supported communist forces. The United States committed large military forces to protect the anticommunist governments, gaining a stalemate in Korea and eventually failing in Vietnam. While these outcomes were mixed for the superpowers, the wars were contained and managed so as to prevent direct engagement and nuclear conflict.

This period also witnessed the beginning of the international environmental movement. Public attention increasingly focused on resource management, pollution, and the preservation of endangered species. In response, the United States and governments in western Europe put in place the first generation of environmental laws. The Clean Air Act in the United States and other measures had an immediate impact, but both policymakers and the public grew aware of ever more serious challenges. The gas crisis of the 1970s gave these efforts a sense of urgency.

KEY TERMS

iron curtain p. 794
Cold War p. 794
North Atlantic Treaty Organization (NATO) p. 794
Warsaw Pact p. 794

United Nations p. 794
World Bank p. 795
Marshall Plan p. 797
European Economic Community (Common Market) p. 797

Korean War p. 798
Vietnam War p. 800
Cuban missile crisis p. 801
Helsinki Accords p. 802
nonaligned nations p. 810

Third World p. 810
Cultural Revolution (China) p. 813
Organization of Petroleum Exporting Countries (OPEC) p. 815

SUGGESTED READING

Barrass, Gordon. *The Great Cold War: A Journey Through the Hall of Mirrors.* 2007. A broad overview of the period and a focused examination of objectives of the competing alliances.

Becker, Jasper. *Hungry Ghosts.* 1998. Explores the Great Leap Forward in China.

Chamberlain, M. E. *Decolonization: The Fall of the European Empires,* 2d ed. 1999. A comprehensive overview.

Citing, Nathan. *From Arab Nationalism to OPEC: Eisenhower, King Sa'ud, and the Making of U.S.-Saudi Relations.* 2010. Useful background to development of OPEC.

De Witte, Ludo, trans. Ann Wright. *The Assassination of Lumumba.* 2003. A concise summary of this violent era.

Dower, John. *Embracing Defeat: Japan in the Wake of World War II.* 1999. An excellent history of the American occupation of Japan.

Gaddis, John Lewis. *The Cold War.* 2007. One of the most reliable and readable examinations of this topic.

Gelvin, James. *The Modern Middle East: A History.* 2007. A reliable introduction to the region.

Hitchcock, William. *The Struggle for Europe: The Turbulent History of a Divided Continent 1945–2002.* 2003. An excellent recent study of Cold War–era Europe.

Jian, Chen. *Mao's China and the Cold War.* 2000. A comprehensive discussion of China's place in the Cold War.

Karnow, Stanley. *Vietnam: A History,* 2d ed. 1997. A detailed and balanced history.

Lawrence, Mark Atwood. *The Vietnam War: A Concise International History.* 2010. An accessible, short history of the war.

Low, D. A. *The Egalitarian Moment: Asia and Africa, 1950–1980.* 1996. Explores the end of the colonial period.

Mazower, Mark. *Dark Continent.* 1999. An outstanding reappraisal of Europe's twentieth-century history.

Meisner, Maurice. *Mao's China and After: A History of the People's Republic,* 3d ed. 1999. A highly regarded survey.

Nakamura, Takafusa. *A History of Showa Japan, 1926–1989.* 1998. A solid Japanese study of the reign of Emperor Hirohito.

Nguyen, Lien-Hang T. *Hanoi's War: An International History of the War for Peace in Vietnam.* 2012. One of the most important studies of war in Southeast Asia.

Rabe, Stephen. *The Most Dangerous Area in the World: John F. Kennedy Confronts Communist Revolution in Latin America.* 1999. A useful exploration of the era.

Reynolds, David. *One World Divisible: A Global History Since 1945.* 2000. A very useful discussion of recent events.

Smith, Charles D. *Palestine and the Arab-Israeli Conflict,* 6th rev. ed. 2007. Comprehensive coverage of an ongoing crisis.

Spence, Jonathon. *Mao Zedong: A Life.* 2006. A good introduction to this important historical actor.

Zubok, Vladislav, and Constantine Pleshakov. *Inside the Kremlin's Cold War: From Stalin to Khrushchev.* 1997. Among the best treatments of the Cold War Soviet Union.

Go to the History CourseMate website for primary source links, study tools, and review materials for this chapter.
CourseMate www.cengagebrain.com

Chapter Outline

Postcolonial Crises and Asian Economic Expansion
➤ *How did the Cold War affect economic policies and politics in Latin America, the Middle East, and Asia in the 1970s and 1980s?*

The End of the Bipolar World
➤ *What forces led to the collapse of the Soviet Union?*

The Challenge of Population Growth
➤ *What explains differences in the rate of population growth among the world's cultural regions?*

Unequal Development and the Movement of Peoples
➤ *How does wealth inequality among nations impact international migration patterns?*

Technological and Environmental Change
➤ *How has technological change affected the global environment in the recent past?*

Conclusion

● **DIVERSITY + DOMINANCE** The Struggle for Women's Rights in an Era of Global Political and Economic Change

● **ENVIRONMENT + TECHNOLOGY** Connected

● **MATERIAL CULTURE** Fast Food

Shanghai—Old Meets New The city of Shanghai is one of the great success stories in a rapidly growing Chinese economy, but its prosperity has left many behind. In this photo a poor man crosses a street in Shanghai's rich, modern commercial district carrying goods in hand-woven baskets balanced on a neck yoke, a technology thousands of years old.

Robert Van Der Hilst/Getty Images

The End of the Cold War and the Challenge of Economic Development and Immigration, 1975–2000

At the end of the 1970s China began an ambitious program of economic reforms. Until then China, with the world's largest population, was a very poor nation with a gross domestic product (GDP) per capita of approximately $110.00 per year (total goods and services produced divided by population). It lagged far behind the mature industrialized nations of Europe and North America in economic performance, as well as behind more dynamic neighboring nations like Japan and South Korea. Since the reforms, China has experienced rapid economic growth and has become one of the few socialist nations to successfully make the transition to a market economy, reaching a GDP per capita of $5,413.57 in 2010. Despite this remarkable expansion, millions of Chinese still live in poverty. As is indicated in the opening illustration, ancient technology and poverty can exist in close proximity with modernity and affluence in China. These same problems of poverty and inequality exist across the globe. In an era of astounding technological change and, until the recession of 2008, spreading prosperity, more than a billion of the world's population still live on less than $1.25 a day.

At the end of the twentieth century, population growth continued to outstrip economic resources in many of the nations of the developing world. Since the deep recession that began in 2008, politicians as well as social reformers in the wealthy industrialized nations have criticized the effects of high levels of unemployment, family breakdown, substance abuse, and homelessness. At the start of the twenty-first century, as in the Industrial Revolution (see Chapter 22), an era of relative affluence, increased global economic integration, and rapid technological progress coincided with problems of social dislocation and inequality. Among the most important events of the period were the emergence of new industrial powers in Asia, the precipitous demise of the Soviet Union and its socialist allies, and the migration of tens of millions of people from poor to rich nations.

POSTCOLONIAL CRISES AND ASIAN ECONOMIC EXPANSION

proxy wars During the Cold War, local or regional wars in which the superpowers armed, trained, and financed the combatants.

Between 1975 and the end of the century, wars and revolutions spread death and destruction through many of the world's least-developed regions. In most cases the origins of conflict were found in the experience of colonialism and foreign intervention, but each conflict also had a unique historical character. Throughout these decades of conflict the two superpowers sought to avoid direct military confrontation while working to gain strategic advantages. The United States and the Soviet Union each supplied arms and financial assistance to nations or insurgent forces hostile to the other. Once linked to superpower rivalries, local conflicts became deadlier. Conflicts where the rival superpowers financed and armed competing factions or parties are called **proxy wars**.

In Latin America superpower rivalry transformed limited conflicts over political rights, social justice, and economic policies into a violent cycle of revolution, military dictatorship, and foreign meddling. In Iran and Afghanistan resentment against foreign intrusion and a growing religious hostility to secular culture led to revolutionary transformations. Here again, superpower ambitions and regional political instability helped provoke war and economic decline. These experiences were not universal, however. During this period some Asian nations experienced rapid economic transformation. Japan emerged as one of the world's leading industrial powers, and a small number of other Asian economies entered the ranks of industrial and commercial powers. Socialist China joined this group of fast-developing Asian nations after initiating market-based economic reforms.

At the end of the 1980s the Cold War ended with the collapse of the Soviet system in eastern Europe, but the transition to democracy and market economy proved difficult. As both developing and former socialist nations opened their markets to foreign investment and competition, they experienced wrenching social change. Increased globalization coincided with increased inequality in many nations, but some developing nations also attained substantial benefits from rapid technological change and world economic integration.

This period also witnessed a great increase in world population and international immigration. Population growth and increased levels of industrialization had a dramatic impact on the global environment, with every continent feeling the destructive effects of forest depletion, soil erosion, and pollution. Wealthy nations with slow population growth found it easier to respond to these environmental challenges than did poor nations experiencing rapid population growth.

Revolutions, Repression, and Democratic Reform in Latin America

In the 1970s Latin America entered a dark era of political violence. When revolutionary movements challenged the established order, militaries in many countries overturned constitutional governments and instituted repressive measures. A region of weak democracies in 1960 became a region dominated by military dictatorships with little patience for civil liberties and human rights fifteen years later.

The ongoing confrontation between Fidel Castro and the government of the United States (see Chapter 31) helped propel the region toward crisis. The fact that the Cuban communist government survived efforts by the United States to overthrow it energized the revolutionary left throughout Latin America. Fearful that revolution would spread across Latin America, the United States increased support for its political and military allies in that region, training many of the military leaders who led coups during this period.

Brazil was the first nation to experience the region-wide conservative reaction to the Cuban Revolution. Claiming that Brazil's civilian political leaders could not protect the nation from communist subversion, the army overthrew the constitutional government of President João Goulart (ju-wow go-LARHT) in 1964. Once in power, the military suspended the constitution, outlawed all existing political parties, and exiled former presidents and opposition leaders. Death squads—illegal paramilitary organizations sanctioned by the government—detained, tortured, and executed thousands of citizens. The dictatorship also undertook an ambitious economic program that promoted industrialization through import substitution, using tax and

CHRONOLOGY

	The Americas	Middle East/Africa	Asia	Eastern Europe
1970	1970 Salvador Allende elected president of Chile 1973 Allende overthrown 1976 Military takeover in Argentina 1979 Sandinistas overthrow Anastasio Somoza in Nicaragua	1979 Shah of Iran overthrown in Islamic Revolution	1975 Vietnam War ends 1979 China begins economic reforms	1978 USSR sends troops to Afghanistan
1980	1983–1990 Democracy returns in Argentina, Brazil, and Chile 1989 United States invades Panama	1980–1988 Iran-Iraq War 1989 USSR withdraws from Afghanistan	1986 Average Japanese income overtakes income in United States 1989 Tiananmen Square confrontation	1985 Mikhail Gorbachev becomes Soviet head of state 1989 Berlin Wall falls 1989–1991 Communism ends in eastern Europe
1990	1990 Sandinistas defeated in elections in Nicaragua 1998 Election of Hugo Chávez in Venezuela	1990 Iraq invades Kuwait 1991 Persian Gulf War 1994 Nelson Mandela elected president of South Africa; Tutsi massacred in Rwanda	1990s Japanese recession 1997 Asian financial crisis begins	1990 Reunification of Germany 1992 Yugoslavia disintegrates; Croatia and Slovenia become independent nations 1992–1995 Bosnia crisis

tariff policies to successfully compel foreign-owned companies to increase investment in manufacturing, especially the auto industry.

This combination of dictatorship, violent repression, and government promotion of industrialization came to be called the "Brazilian Solution." Elements of this "solution" were later imposed across much of the region. In 1970 Chile's newly elected president, **Salvador Allende (sal-VAH-dor ah-YEHN-day)**, undertook an ambitious program of socialist reforms and nationalized Chile's heavy industry and mines, including the American-owned copper companies that dominated the economy. From the beginning of Allende's presidency the administration of President Richard Nixon (served 1969–1973) sought to undermine the Chilean government. Afflicted by inflation, mass consumer protests, and declining foreign trade, a military uprising led by General Augusto Pinochet **(ah-GOOS-toh pin-oh-CHET)** and supported by the United States overthrew Allende in 1973. President Allende and thousands of Chileans died in the uprising, and thousands more were jailed, tortured, and imprisoned without trial. Once in power Pinochet rolled back Allende's socialist innovations, dramatically reducing state participation in the economy and encouraging foreign investment.

In 1976 Argentina followed Brazil and Chile into dictatorship. Juan Perón had been exiled in 1955 after a military uprising, but with Argentina torn by rising levels of political violence he was allowed to return and was then elected president in 1973 (see Chapter 29). Perón had insisted that his third wife, Isabel Martínez de Perón **(EES-ah-bell mar-TEEN-ehz deh pair-OWN)**, be elected vice president, and she inherited the presidency after his death in 1974. Her weak administration faced a potent guerrilla insurgency, a wave of kidnappings, high inflation, and labor protests. Impatient with the policies of the president, the military seized power and suspended the constitution in 1976. During the next seven years it fought what it called the **Dirty War** against terrorism. More than nine thousand Argentines lost their lives, and thousands of others endured arrest and torture before democracy was restored.

Salvador Allende Socialist politician elected president of Chile in 1970 and overthrown by the military in 1973. He died during the military attack.

Dirty War War waged by the Argentine military (1976–1983) against leftist groups. Characterized by the use of illegal imprisonment, torture, and executions by the military.

Susan Meiselas/Magnum Photos, Inc.

The Nicaraguan Revolution Overturns Somoza   A revolutionary coalition that included Marxists drove the dictator Anasta-sio Somoza from power in 1979. The Somoza family had ruled Nicaragua since the 1930s and maintained a close relation-ship with the United States.

Sandinistas Members of a leftist coalition that overthrew the Nicaraguan dictatorship of Anastasia Somoza in 1979 and attempted to install a socialist economy. The United States financed armed opposition by the Contras. The Sandinistas lost national elections in 1990.

While the left suffered these reverses in South America, a revolutionary movement came to power in Nicaragua in 1979, overthrowing the corrupt dictatorship of Anastasio Somoza. This broad alliance of revolutionaries and reformers called themselves **Sandinistas** (sahn-din-EES-tahs). They took their name from Augusto César Sandino, who had led Nicaraguan opposition to U.S. military intervention between 1927 and 1932. Once in power, the Sandinistas moved left-ward, seeking to imitate the command economies of Cuba and the Soviet Union and national-izing properties owned by members of the Nicaraguan elite and U.S. companies.

U.S. president Jimmy Carter (served 1977–1980) championed human rights in the hemi-sphere and stopped the flow of U.S. arms to military regimes with the worst records, like Argen-tina. Carter also agreed to the reestablishment of Panamanian sovereignty in the Canal Zone at the end of 1999, but his effort to find common ground with the Sandinistas failed due to their intransigence.

Carter was defeated in the next election by Ronald Reagan, who was committed to over-turning the Nicaraguan Revolution and defeating a revolutionary movement in neighboring El Salvador. With the memory of the Vietnam War still strong (see Chapter 31), the U.S. Congress resisted any use of U.S. combat forces in Nicaragua and El Salvador and put strict limits on mil-itary aid. As a result, the Reagan administration tried to roll back the Nicaraguan Revolution through punitive economic measures and the recruitment and arming of a proxy force of anti-Sandinista Nicaraguans, called Contras (counter-revolutionaries).

Confident that they were supported by the majority of Nicaraguans and assured that the U.S. Congress was close to cutting off aid to the Contras, the Sandinistas called for free elections in 1990. But they had miscalculated politically. Exhausted by more than a decade of violence, a majority of Nicaraguan voters rejected the Sandinistas and elected a middle-of-the-road coali-tion led by Violeta Chamorro (vee-oh-LET-ah cha-MOR-roe).

In neighboring El Salvador another guerrilla movement, the Farabundo Martí (fah-rah-BOON-doh mar-TEE) National Liberation Front, or FMLN (acronym for Spanish name) seemed on the verge of taking power. The Reagan administration responded by providing hundreds of millions of dollars in military assistance and by training units of the El Salvadoran army. The assassination of Archbishop Oscar Romero and other members of the Catholic clergy by death squads tied to the Salvadoran government as well as the murder of thousands of noncombatants by military units trained by the United States undermined this effort. However, the electoral defeat of the Sandinistas in Nicaragua and the collapse of the Soviet Union (see below) finally forced the FMLN rebels to negotiate peace, transforming themselves into a civilian political party.

During this same period, the violent political confrontation of right and left abated in South America as well. The right-wing military dictatorships established in Brazil, Chile, and Argentina all came to an end between 1983 and 1990, brought down by their own excesses and by popular desires for a return to constitutional government. By 2000, with the Cold War ended, 95 percent of Latin America's population lived again under civilian rule.

At the same time, the influence of the United States grew substantially. The United States had thwarted the left in Nicaragua and El Salvador by funding military proxies. It used its own military in a 1983 invasion of the tiny Caribbean nation of Grenada and again in 1989 to overthrow and arrest dictator General Manuel Noriega (MAN-wel no-ree-EGG-ah) of Panama. These actions were powerful reminders to Latin Americans of prior interventions (see Chapter 26), but they also served as reminders of American power at a time when socialism was discredited by the collapse of the Soviet bloc.

From this position of strength the United States pushed Latin American nations to reform their economies by removing limitations on foreign investment, eliminating many social welfare programs, and reducing public-sector employment. Latin American governments responded by selling public-sector industries, like national airlines, manufacturing facilities, and public utilities, to foreign corporations. But popular support for these policies, what Latin Americans called neo-liberalism, eroded quickly due to political scandals and a slowing world economy. A catastrophic economic and political meltdown in Argentina between 2001 and 2002 contributed to the appearance of a reinvigorated nationalist left in Latin America that sought to roll back neo-liberal reforms (see Diversity and Dominance: The Struggle for Women's Rights in an Era of Global Political and Economic Change). Among the most vocal critic of neo-liberalism and American influence was Hugo Chávez (HUGH-go SHAH-vez), elected president of Venezuela in 1998 and serving as the region's chief critic of U.S. policy until his death in 2013. Left-of-center presidents were later elected in Brazil (Luiz Inácio Lula da Silva, 2002), Argentina (Néstor Kirchner, 2003), Bolivia (Evo Morales, 2005), and Ecuador (Rafael Correa, 2007).

Islamic Revolutions in Iran and Afghanistan

Although the Arab-Israel conflict and the oil crisis (see Chapter 31) concerned both superpowers, the prospect of direct military involvement remained remote. When unexpected crises developed in Iran and Afghanistan, however, significant strategic issues for the superpowers came to the foreground. Both countries adjoined Soviet territory, making Soviet military intervention more likely. Exercising post–Vietnam War caution, the United States reacted with restraint in Iran. The Soviet Union chose a bolder and ultimately disastrous course in Afghanistan.

Muhammad Reza Pahlavi (REH-zah PAH-lah-vee) succeeded his father as shah of Iran in 1941. In 1953 covert intervention by the U.S. Central Intelligence Agency (CIA) helped the shah retain his throne in the face of a movement to overturn royal power. Even when he finally nationalized the foreign-owned oil industry, the shah continued to enjoy American support. As oil revenues increased following the price increases of the 1970s, the United States encouraged the shah to spend his nation's growing wealth on equipping the Iranian army with American weaponry. By the 1970s popular resentment against the ballooning wealth of the elite families that supported the shah and the brutality, inefficiency, malfeasance, and corruption of his government led to mass opposition.

Ayatollah Ruhollah Khomeini (A-yat-ol-LAH ROOH-ol-LAH ko-MAY-nee), a Shi'ite (SHE-ite) philosopher-cleric who had spent most of his eighty-plus years in religious and academic pursuits, became the leader of the opposition. Massive protests forced the shah to flee Iran and ended the monarchy in 1979. In the Islamic Republic of Iran, which replaced the monarchy, Ayatollah Khomeini was supreme arbiter of disputes and guarantor of the government's religious

Ayatollah Ruhollah Khomeini Shi'ite philosopher and cleric who led the overthrow of the shah of Iran in 1979 and created an Islamic republic.

Muslim Women Mourning the Death of Ayatollah Khomeini in 1989   An Islamic revolution overthrew the shah of Iran in 1979. Ayatollah Khomeini sought to lead Iran away from the influences of Western culture and challenged the power of the United States in the Persian Gulf.

Mohsen Shandiz/Sygma/Corbis

legitimacy. He oversaw a parliamentary regime based on European models but imposed religious control over legislation and public behavior. The electoral process was not open to monarchists, communists, and other opposition groups. Shi'ite clerics with little training for government service held many of the highest posts, and stringent measures were taken to combat Western styles and culture. Universities were temporarily closed, and their faculties were purged of secularists and monarchists. Women were compelled to wear modest Islamic garments outside the house, and semiofficial vigilante committees policed public morals and cast a pall over entertainment and social life. Many sectors of the Iranian economy were also placed under the direction of clerically controlled foundations, leading to massive capital flight. Clerical mismanagement and inflation have contributed to decades of economic stagnation in Iran.

President Carter had criticized the shah's repressive regime, but the overthrow of a long-standing ally and the creation of the Islamic Republic were blows to American prestige. The new Iranian regime was anti-Israeli and anti-American. Seeing the United States as a "Great Satan" opposed to Islam, Khomeini fostered Islamic revolutionary movements that threatened the United States and Israel. In November 1979 Iranian radicals seized the U.S. embassy in Tehran and held fifty-two diplomats hostage for 444 days. Americans felt humiliated by their inability to rescue the hostages or negotiate their release.

Saddam Husain   President of Iraq from 1979 until overthrown by an American-led invasion in 2003. Waged war on Iran from 1980 to 1988. His invasion of Kuwait in 1990 was repulsed in the Persian Gulf War in 1991.

In the fall of 1980, shortly after negotiations for the release of the hostages began, **Saddam Husain (sah-DAHM hoo-SANE)**, the ruler of neighboring Iraq, invaded Iran to topple the Islamic Republic. His own dictatorial rule rested on a secular, Arab-nationalist philosophy and long-standing friendship with the Soviet Union, which had provided him with advanced weaponry. He feared that the fervor of Iran's revolutionary Shi'ite leaders would infect his own country's Shi'ite majority and threaten his power. The war pitted American weapons in the hands of the Iranians against Soviet weapons in the hands of the Iraqis, but the superpowers avoided overt involvement during eight years of bloodshed. Covertly, however, the United States used Israel to transfer arms to Iran, hoping to gain the release of other American hostages held by radical Islamic groups in Lebanon and to help finance the Contra war against the Sandinista government of Nicaragua. When this deal came to light in 1986, the resulting political scandal intensified American hostility to Iran. Openly tilting toward Iraq, President Reagan sent the United States Navy to the Persian Gulf, ostensibly to protect nonbelligerent shipping. The move helped force Iran to accept a cease-fire in 1988.

While the United States dealt with Iran, the Soviet Union faced even more serious problems in neighboring Afghanistan. In 1978 a Marxist party with a secular agenda seized power.

Offended by the new regime's efforts to reform education and grant rights to women, traditional Afghan ethnic and religious leaders led a successful rebellion. The Soviet Union responded by sending its army into Afghanistan to install a communist regime. With the United States, Saudi Arabia, and Pakistan paying, equipping, and training Afghan rebels, the Soviet Union found itself in an unwinnable war like the one the United States had stumbled into in Vietnam. Facing growing economic problems and widespread domestic discontent over the war, Soviet leaders withdrew their troops in 1989. Three years later rebel groups took control of the entire country and then began to fight among themselves over who should rule. In this chaotic situation a radical Islamic party with close ties to Pakistan, the Taliban, took power in 1996. They installed a harsh religious regime and soon faced armed opposition. The Taliban had received financial support from the Saudi Arabian Osama bin Laden during their rise to power and later provided him with protection as he organized the militant organization al-Qaeda that later attacked the United States (see Chapter 33).

Asian Transformation

Although Japan has few mineral resources and is dependent on oil imports, the Japanese economy weathered the oil price shocks of the 1970s much better than did the economies of Europe and the United States. In fact, Japan experienced a faster rate of economic growth in the 1970s and 1980s than did any other major developed economy, growing at about 10 percent a year and becoming the world's second largest economy. Average income also increased rapidly, overtaking that of the United States in 1986.

There were major differences between the Japanese and U.S. industrial models. During the American occupation, Japanese industrial conglomerates known as *zaibatsu* (see Chapter 27) were broken up. Although ownership of major industries became less concentrated, business leaders created new industrial alliances to control competition and facilitate the allocation of

keiretsu Alliances of corporations and banks that dominate the Japanese economy.

resources. During the period of dramatic growth there were six major **keiretsu (kay-REHT-soo)**, each of which included a major bank as well as firms in industry, commerce, and construction tied together in an interlocking ownership structure. There were also minor keiretsu dominated by major industrial corporations, like Toyota.

Tariffs and import regulations inhibiting foreign competition were crucial to the early stages of development of Japan's major industries. These restrictions and Japanese success at exporting manufactured goods through the 1970s and 1980s produced huge trade surpluses with other nations. Although the United States and the European Community engaged in tough negotiations to try to force open the Japanese market, these efforts had only limited success, and by 1990 Japan's trade surplus with the rest of the world was double that of 1985.

Many experts assumed that Japan's competitive advantages would propel it past the United States as the world's preeminent industrial economy, but during the 1990s Japan entered what would become a two-decade-long crisis that dramatically slowed the growth of both GDP (gross domestic product) and average income. In the thirty months between January 1990 and July 1992, Japanese stocks and real estate markets lost $2.5 trillion in market value, while the national growth rate fell from 3.1 percent a year to 0.2 percent.

Before the crisis, Japanese real estate and stock markets had become highly overvalued as the nation's huge trade imbalances with the United States and other trading partners flooded the economy with cash and fueled speculation. As the crisis deepened and prices collapsed, the close relationships between industry, government, and banks proved to be a liability, as these powerful institutions acted to prop up inefficient companies and support unsustainable market values. By the end of the 1990s Japan's GDP had suffered a loss greater than that suffered by the United States in the Great Depression, leaving the nation with a crushing debt burden. Despite government efforts to promote recovery with public works projects and low interest rates, Japan's economy has grown very slowly to the present.

Other Asian states imitated the Japanese model of development in the 1970s and 1980s. These nations protected new industries from foreign competition while encouraging close alliances among industries and banks. The largest and most successful of them, the Republic of Korea, commonly called South Korea, used a combination of inexpensive labor, strong technical education, and substantial domestic capital reserves to support a massive industrialization effort. Success in heavy industries such as steel and shipbuilding as well as in consumer industries such as automobiles and consumer electronics soon made it a global economic power.

DIVERSITY + DOMINANCE

The Struggle for Women's Rights in an Era of Global Political and Economic Change

The struggle for women's rights has been one of the most important social movements of the twentieth and twenty-first centuries. Although we can identify fundamental similarities in objectives across cultural and political boundaries, women in less developed nations are forced to recognize that their objectives and strategies must take into account international inequalities in power and wealth.

In this section Gladys Acosta, a militant Peruvian feminist, discusses the appropriate agenda for this struggle in the era after the fall of the Soviet Union and the rise of **neo-liberalism**, *the term used in Latin America to identify the free-market economic policies advocated by the United States. Among its chief characteristics are an end to the protection of local industries, a reduction in government social welfare policies, a reduction in public-sector employment, a commitment to paying debts to international creditors, and the removal of impediments to foreign investment. Many Latin Americans believe that neo-liberalism is a new form of imperialism. While written in the 1990s, this political manifesto deals directly with issues of great relevance today: international indebtedness, the social costs of austerity, and gender inequality.*

Neo-Liberalism in Action

When I talk of neo-liberalism, I mean austerity measures, foreign debts, and increased liberties for all those who have the power of money at their disposal and the power of repression over those who make demands. We have now reached a new form of capitalist accumulation. The world's economic system is in a state of change and capital has become more concentrated and centralised. I would not go as far as to say countries don't exist anymore but national identities do certainly play a different role now. . . . If we look at the bare face of neo-liberalism from a woman's point of view, we cannot fail to notice its murderous consequences. . . . At the moment we're experiencing capitalism's greatest ideological offensive. It's all business: everything is bought and sold and everything has its price.

The Consequences of Neo-Liberal Politics

[W]omen play an important role in this ever-more internationalized economy because we represent, as ever, a particularly exploitable workforce. A number of studies have revealed the

neo-liberalism The term used in Latin America and other developing regions to describe free-market policies that include reducing tariff protection for local industries; the sale of public-sector industries, like national airlines and public utilities, to private investors or foreign corporations; and the reduction of social welfare policies and public-sector employment.

Asian Tigers Collective name for South Korea, Taiwan, Hong Kong, and Singapore—nations that became economic powers in the 1970s and 1980s.

newly industrialized economies (NIEs) Rapidly growing, new industrial nations of the late twentieth century, including the Asian Tigers.

The small nations of Taiwan and Singapore, along with Hong Kong, a British colony until 1997, also became industrial powerhouses. As a result of their rapid development, these three economies along with South Korea were called the **Asian Tigers**. While Taiwan suffered a number of political reverses, including the loss of its United Nations seat to the People's Republic of China in 1971 and the withdrawal of diplomatic recognition by the United States, it achieved remarkable economic progress, based in large part on investment in the economy of the People's Republic of China. Hong Kong and Singapore—long British colonies with extremely limited natural resources—also enjoyed rapid economic development. Both were historically important Asian ports and commercial centers that later developed successful manufacturing, banking, and commercial sectors.

These **newly industrialized economies (NIEs)** shared many characteristics that help explain their rapid industrialization. All had disciplined and hard-working labor forces, and all invested heavily in education. For example, as early as 1980 South Korea had as many engineering graduates as Germany, Britain, and Sweden combined. All had very high rates of personal saving, about 35 percent of GDP, that funded new technologies, and all emphasized outward-looking export strategies. And, like Japan, all benefited from government sponsorship and protection. Despite this momentum, the region was deeply shaken by a financial crisis that began in 1997. Like the recession that afflicted Japan in 1990, a combination of bad loans, weak banks, and the international effects of currency speculation led to a deep regional crisis that was stabilized only by the efforts of the United States, Japan, and international institutions like the International Monetary Fund.

China Rejoins the World Economy

After Mao Zedong's death in 1976, the Chinese communist leadership began economic reforms that relaxed state control, allowing more initiative and permitting individuals to accumulate existence of subcontractor chains who work for transnational companies "informally" and mainly employ women. Basically we are dealing with a kind of integration into the world market which often uses our own homes as its outlet. Obviously, this work is badly paid and completely unprotected and has to be done without any of those social rights which were formerly achieved by trade union struggles. . . . As it advances worldwide, this capitalism also encourages the expansion of certain kinds of tourism. A visible increase in prostitution is part of this, whereby women from poor countries are smuggled into large, internationally operated rings which exploit them. The reports of Filipina women traded on the West German market send shivers down our spines. . . .

How the Adoption of Austerity Measures Affects Women's Lives

It is obvious that foreign debt is one of the most inhuman forms of exploitation in our countries when one considers the ratio between work necessary for workers' needs and work producing profit for employers. The experts have already explained how the prevailing exchange and investment structures have created international finance systems which keep whole populations in inhuman conditions. . . . Women in every household are suffering every day as a result of impoverished economies and those who are most exposed to the effects of foreign debt are women.

When it comes to shopping, caring for sick children or the impossibility of meeting their schooling costs, the illusion of "leaving poverty behind" evaporates. Yet the problem is not only of an economic nature because under such circumstances the constant tension leads to grave, often lasting exhaustion. The psychosocial damage is alarming. The adoption of austerity measures means a curtailment of the state's commitment to social services with a direct effect on women. Daily life becomes hell for them. The lack of even minimal state welfare presents women (and obviously children too) with crushing working days.

QUESTIONS FOR ANALYSIS

1. What is neo-liberalism?

2. According to Acosta, how does global economic integration fostered by neo-liberalism affect the lives of women as workers?

3. Acosta claims that indebtedness to foreign lenders leads to austerity measures. How do these measures impact families in poor countries?

Source: From Gladys Acosta, "The View of a Peruvian Militant," in *Compañeras. Voices from the Latin American Women's Movement*, edited by Gaby Küppers (London: Latin American Bureau, 1994). Reprinted with permission of the publisher.

Deng Xiaoping Communist Party leader who forced Chinese economic reforms after the death of Mao Zedong.

wealth. The results were remarkable. Under China's leader **Deng Xiaoping** (dung shee-yao-ping) China permitted foreign investment for the first time since the communists came to power in 1949. Between 1979 and 2005 foreign direct investment in China grew to more than $600 billion as McDonald's, General Motors, Coca-Cola, Airbus, Toyota, and many other foreign companies began doing business. As a result, by 2010 China had become a major industrial power and the world's most important exporting nation. Despite these changes, state-owned enterprises still employed more than 100 million workers, and most foreign-owned companies were limited to special economic zones. The result was a dual industrial sector—one modern, efficient, and connected to international markets, the other directed by political decisions. While the Chinese have not yet privatized land, by 1990 over 90 percent of China's agricultural land was in the hands of farmers permitted to sell what they produced.

In 2010 China became the world's second largest economy, surpassing Japan. The scale of this achievement can be represented by the remarkable growth of China's GDP, the total value of all goods and services produced by the nation. In 1970 China, with a population of nearly 1 billion, had a GDP of $56 billion, smaller than the GDP of Italy ($111 billion), which had a population of 55 million people. By 2010 China's GDP had increased eighty-one times, surpassing $4,520 billion. Other developing countries grew substantially in this period as well. India's economy, for example, was larger than China's in 1970 ($66 billion) and increased nineteen times by 2010, to $1,251 billion.

Despite its enormous achievement, China, with a per capita GDP of $5,413.57, has remained substantially poorer than mature industrial economies, which have an average per capita GDP of $42,063. However, China is now richer than much of the developing world. Latin America has a per capita GDP of $4,299, the Middle East $2,329, and sub-Saharan Africa $940. While poverty levels in China have fallen swiftly during this period of rapid development, inequality, especially between rural and urban dwellers, has increased.

Tiananmen Square Site in Beijing where Chinese students and workers gathered to demand greater political openness in 1989. The demonstration was crushed by Chinese military with great loss of life.

The combination of economic reforms, high levels of foreign investment, and technology transfers from developed industrial nations has helped make China one of the world's major

SECTION REVIEW

- During the 1970s and 1980s, political violence grew in Latin America, sponsored in part by U.S. fears of communist subversion.

- The United States opposed revolutionary movements in Nicaragua and El Salvador.

- In the 1990s the United States pushed Latin American nations to introduce neo-liberal reforms that opened economies to greater foreign investment.

- A radical anti-American Islamic revolution led by Ayatollah Khomeini triumphed in Iran in 1979 and led to a ten-year war with Iraq.

- The Soviets intervened in Afghanistan in 1979 but failed to defeat local opponents backed by the United States and Pakistan.

- After three decades of rapid economic growth, Japan entered a deep recession in the 1990s.

- The four Asian Tigers experienced rapid economic growth.

- After Deng Xiaoping reformed and modernized China's economy in 1979, China has experienced three decades of rapid growth.

industrial powers. As was true earlier with Japan and the Asian Tigers, China's expansion has depended heavily on exports, which accounted for over 40 percent of GPD in 2008. Success in foreign markets produced a large foreign trade surplus. As was the case with Japan three decades ago, these cash surpluses paid for the government's massive investments in infrastructure, promoted speculation in real estate and stocks, and propped up a weak banking sector. While the Chinese economy continued to grow at a healthy rate during the worldwide recession that began in 2008, some economists wonder if the speculative excesses can be overcome without a deep contraction similar to that experienced by Japan in the 1990s.

Deng Xiaoping's strategy of balancing change and continuity avoided some of the social and political costs experienced by Russia and other socialist countries that abruptly embraced capitalism and democracy (see next section), but he faced a major challenge in 1989. Responding to inflation and to worldwide mass movements in favor of democracy, Chinese students and intellectuals led a series of protests demanding more democracy and an end to corruption. This movement culminated in **Tiananmen (tee-yehn-ahn-men) Square**, in the heart of Beijing, where hundreds of thousands of protesters gathered and refused to leave. After weeks of standoff, tanks pushed into the square, killing hundreds and arresting thousands. The Communist Party has not faced another direct challenge to its power since then, but growing levels of labor unrest, protests in favor of political rights, corruption scandals, and ethnic confrontations continue to challenge this one-party dictatorship.

THE END OF THE BIPOLAR WORLD

After the end of World War II, competition between the alliances led by the United States and the Soviet Union created a bipolar world (see Chapter 31). Every conflict, no matter how local its origins, had the potential of engaging the attention of one or both of the superpowers. The Korean War, decolonization in Africa, the Vietnam War, the Cuban Revolution, and hostilities between Israel and its neighbors increased tension between the nuclear-armed superpowers. Given this succession of provocations, politics everywhere was dominated by arguments over the relative merits of the competing systems.

Few in 1980 predicted the startling collapse of the Soviet Union. Western observers tended to see communist nations as both more uniform in character and more subservient to the Soviet Union than was true. Long before the 1980s, deep divisions had appeared among communist states. Similarly, nationalism had reappeared as a powerful force among the once-independent nations and ethnic groups brought together within the Soviet Union. By the late 1980s these forces threatened the survival of this communist world power.

Crisis in the Soviet Union

Under U.S. president Ronald Reagan and the Soviet Union's general secretary Leonid Brezhnev **(leh-oh-NEED BREZ-nef)**, Cold War rhetoric remained intense. Massive new U.S. investments in armaments placed heavy competitive burdens on a Soviet economy already suffering from shortages and mismanagement. Obsolete industrial plants and centralized planning stifled initiative in the Soviet Union and led to a declining standard of living relative to the West, while the arbitrariness of the bureaucracy, the manipulation of information, and material deprivations created a crisis in morale.

Despite the unpopularity of the war in Afghanistan and growing discontent, Brezhnev refused to modify his unsuccessful policies, but he could not escape criticism. Self-published

Mikhail Gorbachev Head of the Soviet Union from 1985 to 1991. His liberalization effort improved relations with the West, but he lost power after his reforms led to the collapse of communist governments in eastern Europe.

perestroika Policy of "restructuring" that was the centerpiece of Mikhail Gorbachev's efforts to liberalize communism in the Soviet Union.

Solidarity Polish trade union created in 1980 to protest working conditions and political repression. It began the nationalist opposition to communist rule that led in 1989 to the fall of communism in eastern Europe.

underground writings (*samizdat* [sah-meez-DAHT]) by critics of the regime circulated widely despite government efforts to suppress them. In a series of powerful books, the writer Alexander Solzhenitzyn **(sol-zhuh-NEET-sin)** castigated the Soviet system. Although he won a Nobel Prize in literature, authorities charged him with treason and expelled him in 1974.

By the time **Mikhail Gorbachev (GORE-beh-CHOF)** came to power in 1985, weariness with war in Afghanistan, economic decay, and vocal protest had reached critical levels. Casting aside Brezhnev's hard line, Gorbachev authorized major reforms in an attempt to stave off total collapse. His policy of political openness (*glasnost*) permitted criticism of the government and the Communist Party. His policy of **perestroika (per-ih-STROY-kuh)** ("restructuring") was an attempt to address long-suppressed economic problems by moving away from central state planning. In 1989 he ended the unpopular war in Afghanistan.

The Collapse of the Socialist Bloc

In 1980 protests by Polish shipyard workers in the city of Gdansk led to the formation of **Solidarity**, a labor union that grew to 9 million members. The Roman Catholic Church in Poland, strengthened by the elevation of a Pole, Karol Wojtyla **(KAH-rol voy-TIL-ah)**, to the papacy as John Paul II in 1978, gave strong moral support to the protest movement.

The Polish government imposed martial law in 1981 in response to the growing power of Solidarity and its allies, giving the army effective political control. Seeing Solidarity under tight controls and many of its leaders in prison, the Soviet Union decided not to intervene. But Solidarity remained a potent force with a strong institutional structure and nationally recognized leaders. As Gorbachev loosened political controls in the Soviet Union after 1985, communist leaders elsewhere lost confidence in Soviet resolve, and critics and reformers in Poland and throughout eastern Europe were emboldened.

Beleaguered Warsaw Pact governments vacillated between relaxation of control and suppression of dissent. Just as the Catholic clergy in Poland had supported Solidarity, Protestant and Orthodox religious leaders aided the rise of opposition groups elsewhere. This combination of nationalism and religion provided a powerful base for opponents of the communist regimes. Communist governments sought to quiet the opposition by turning to the West for trade and financial assistance. They also opened their nations to travelers, ideas, styles, and money from Western countries, all of which accelerated the demand for change.

By the end of 1989 communist governments across eastern Europe had fallen. The dismantling of the Berlin Wall vividly represented this transformation. While communist leaders in Poland, Hungary, Czechoslovakia, and Bulgaria decided that change was inevitable, the dictator Nicolae Ceausescu **(nehk-oh-LIE chow-SHES-koo)** of Romania refused to surrender power and was overthrown and executed. The comprehensiveness of these changes became clear in 1990, when the Polish people elected Solidarity leader Lech Walesa **(leck wah-LEN-sah)** as president and the people of Czechoslovakia elected dissident playwright Vaclav Havel **(vah-SLAV hah-VEL)** as president.

Following the fall of the Berlin Wall, a tidal wave of patriotic enthusiasm swept aside the once-formidable communist government of East Germany. In the chaotic months that followed, East Germans crossed to West Germany in large numbers, and government services in the eastern

Bossu Regis/Corbis Sygma

The Fall of the Berlin Wall The Berlin Wall was the most important symbol of the Cold War. Constructed to keep residents of East Germany from fleeing to the West and defended by armed guards and barbed wire, it was the public face of communism. As the Soviet system fell apart, the residents of East and West Berlin broke down sections of the wall.

sector nearly disappeared. The collapse of the East German government led quickly in 1990 to reunification.

Soviet leaders knew that similarly powerful nationalist sentiments existed within the Soviet Union as well. The year 1990 brought declarations of independence by Lithuania, Estonia, and Latvia, three small states on the Baltic Sea that the Soviet Union had annexed in 1939. The end of the Soviet Union then came suddenly in 1991 (see Map 32.1). After communist hardliners botched a coup against Gorbachev, disgust with communism boiled over. Boris Yeltsin, the president of the Russian Republic, emerged as the most powerful leader in the country. Russia, the largest republic in the Soviet Union, was effectively taking the place of the disintegrating USSR. In September 1991 the Congress of People's Deputies—the central legislature of the USSR—voted to dissolve the union. Then in December a weak successor state with little central control, the Commonwealth of Independent States (CIS), was created and Gorbachev resigned.

The ethnic and religious passions that fueled the breakup of the Soviet Union also overwhelmed the Balkan nation of Yugoslavia. In 1991 it dissolved into a morass of separatism and warring ethnic and religious groups. Slovenia and Croatia, the most westerly provinces, both heavily Roman Catholic, became independent states in 1992. The population of Bosnia and Herzegovina was more mixed: 40 percent were Muslims, 30 percent Serbian Orthodox, and 18 percent Catholics. Following the declaration of Bosnian national independence in 1992, the nation's Orthodox Serbs attempted to rid the state of Muslims in a violent process called **ethnic cleansing**. After extensive television coverage of atrocities and wanton destruction, the United States intervened and eventually brokered a settlement in 1995 that effectively created two ethnically separate political entities.

In 1999 new fighting and a new round of ethnic cleansing occurred in the southernmost Yugoslavian province of Kosovo. Seen by Serbs as their homeland, Kosovo had a predominantly Muslim and Albanian population. When Serbia refused to stop military action, the United States, Britain, and France acted on behalf of NATO by launching an aerial war on Serbian targets in Kosovo and in Serbia itself that forced the withdrawal of Serbian forces from Kosovo. Serbia's president during this violent period, Slobodan Milosevic, was forced from power and turned over to a war crimes tribunal in The Hague, where he died in prison.

ethnic cleansing Effort to eradicate a people and its culture by means of mass killing and the destruction of historical buildings and cultural materials. Ethnic cleansing was used by both sides in the conflicts that accompanied the disintegration of Yugoslavia in the 1990s.

Africa in the Era of Global Political Change

Sub-Saharan Africa has experienced political instability, military coups, civil wars, and conflicts over resources since independence. It has also remained among the poorest regions in the world. Southern Africa, however, has seen democratic progress and a steady decline in armed conflicts since 1991. A key change came in South Africa in 1994, when long-time political prisoner Nelson Mandela and his African National Congress (ANC) won the first national elections in which the African majority could participate equally. Also hopeful has been the return to democracy of Nigeria, Africa's most populous state, after decades of military rulers. In 1999, after a succession of military governments, Nigerians elected President Olusegun Obasanjo (oh-LOO-she-gun oh-BAH-san-jo) (a former coup leader), and a 2003 vote gave him a second term, despite serious voting irregularities. Similarly, in 2002 Kenyans voted out the Kenya African National Union Party that had held power for thirty-nine years.

Africa was also a scene of ethnic cleansing. In 1994 the political leaders of the Central African nation of Rwanda incited the Hutu people to massacre their Tutsi neighbors. Although the major powers had earlier promised to intervene in genocides, they sought to avoid military involvement in Rwanda by not using the word *genocide* to describe the slaughter. Without foreign intervention, the carnage claimed 750,000 lives, with millions more becoming refugees. Finally, the United States and other powers intervened and the United Nations set up a tribunal to try those responsible for the genocide. In 1998 violence spread from Rwanda to neighboring Congo, where growing opposition and ill health had forced President Joseph Mobutu from office after over three decades of dictatorial misrule. Various peacemaking attempts failed to restore order, and by mid-2003 more than 3 million Congolese had died from disease, malnutrition, and injuries related to the fighting.

The Persian Gulf War

The Persian Gulf War was the first significant military conflict to occur after the breakup of the Soviet Union and the end of the Cold War. Iraq's ruler, Saddam Husain, had borrowed a great

MAP 32.1 **The End of the Soviet Union** When communist hardliners failed to overthrow Gorbachev in 1991, popular anti-communist sentiment swept the Soviet Union. Following Boris Yeltsin's lead in Russia, the republics that constituted the Soviet Union declared their independence. © Cengage Learning

SECTION REVIEW

- The Cold War ended when growing unrest and criticism led to the collapse of the Soviet Union and allied socialist nations. Mikhail Gorbachev's reform policies accelerated this process.

- The rise of ethnic nationalism led to war and genocide in Yugoslavia.

- South Africa, Nigeria, and Kenya escaped from oppressive conditions, but hundreds of thousands lost their lives in ethnic violence in Rwanda and Congo.

- After Saddam Husain invaded Kuwait, the United States and its allies defeated Iraq in the first Gulf War of 1990.

deal of money from neighboring Kuwait and failed to get Kuwait's royal family to reduce this debt. He was also eager to control Kuwait's oil fields. Husain believed that the smaller and militarily weaker nation could be quickly defeated, and he suspected that the United States would not react. The invasion occurred in August 1990.

The United States decided to react. Saudi Arabia, an important ally of the United States and a major oil producer, also supported intervention. With his intention to use force endorsed by the United Nations and with many Islamic nations supporting military action, President George H. W. Bush ordered an attack in early 1991. Iraq's military defeat was comprehensive, but Husain remained in power, crushing an uprising just months following his defeat. The United States imposed various conditions on Iraq that kept tensions high, helping create the conditions for a new, larger, war in 2003 (see Chapter 33).

THE CHALLENGE OF POPULATION GROWTH

For most of human history, governments viewed population growth as beneficial, a source of national wealth and power. Since the late eighteenth century, however, many intellectuals and politicians have viewed population increases with alarm, fearing that the production of food and other essential resources could not keep up with population growth. Late in the nineteenth century some social critics expressed concern that growing populations would lead to class and ethnic struggle. By the second half of the twentieth century, fears of population growth were primarily attached to environmental concerns. Are urban sprawl, pollution, and soil erosion the inevitable results of population growth? The questions and debates continue today, but clearly population growth is both a cause and a result of increased global interdependency.

Demographic Transition

The population of Europe almost doubled between 1850 and 1914, putting enormous pressure on rural land and urban housing and overwhelming fragile public institutions that provided crisis assistance (see Chapter 27). This dramatic growth forced a large wave of immigration across the Atlantic, helping to develop the Western Hemisphere and invigorating the Atlantic economy (see Chapter 25). Population growth also contributed to Europe's Industrial Revolution by lowering labor costs and increasing consumer demand.

Thomas Malthus Eighteenth-century English intellectual who warned that population growth threatened future generations because, in his view, population growth would always outstrip increases in agricultural production.

While some Europeans saw the rapid increase in human population as a blessing, others warned of disaster. The best-known pessimist was the English cleric **Thomas Malthus**, who in 1798 argued that unchecked population growth would outstrip food production. When Malthus looked at Europe's future, he used a prejudiced image of China to terrify his readers. A visitor to China, he claimed, "will not be surprised that mothers destroy or expose many of their children; that parents sell their daughters for a trifle; . . . and that there should be such a number of robbers. The surprise is that nothing still more dreadful should happen."[1]

The generation that came of age in the years after World War II lived in a world where Malthus seemed to have little relevance. Industrial and agricultural productivity had multiplied supplies of food and other necessities. At the same time, cultural changes associated with expanded female employment, older age at marriage, and more effective family planning had slowed the rate of population increase. By the 1960s Europe and other industrial societies had made the **demographic transition** to lower fertility rates (average number of births per woman) and reduced mortality. This meant that populations would age quickly. In the world's most developed nations, for example, median age rose from twenty-nine years in 1950 and to thirty-seven years by 2000.

demographic transition A change in the rates of population growth. Before the transition, both birthrates and death rates are high, resulting in a slowly growing population; then the death rate drops but the birthrate remains high, causing a population explosion; finally the birthrate drops and the population growth slows down.

By the late 1970s, the developing world had still not experienced the demographic transition and the global discussion of population growth became politicized. Leaders in some developing nations actively promoted large families, arguing that larger populations increased national power. When industrialized nations, mostly white, raised concerns about rapid population growth in Asia, Africa, and Latin America, populist political leaders in these regions responded by asking whether these concerns were racist.

This question exposed the influence of racism in the population debate and temporarily disarmed Western advocates of birth control. However, once the economic shocks of the 1970s and 1980s had revealed the vulnerability of poor nations, governments in the developing world jettisoned policies that promoted population growth. Mexico is a good example. In the 1970s the government had encouraged high fertility, and population grew an average of 3 percent per year. In the 1980s Mexico rejected these policies and began to promote birth control, leading by the 1990s to an annual population growth of 1.7 percent.

World population exploded in the twentieth century, more than doubling between 1950 and 2000 (see Table 32.1). Although the rate of growth has slowed since the 1980s, world population still increases by a number equal to the total population of the United States roughly every three years. If fertility were to remain constant from today, with a world average of 2.5 children per woman, population would reach nearly 27 billion in 2100. This will not happen, however, because fertility is declining in most developing nations and is at less than replacement levels in most industrialized countries. As a result, most experts estimate a world population in 2100 of around 10 billion.

At the same time mortality rates have increased in some areas as immigration, commercial expansion, and improved transportation have facilitated the transmission of disease. The rapid spread of HIV/AIDS is an example of this phenomenon. Less developed regions with poorly funded public health institutions and with few resources to invest in prevention and treatment experience the highest rates of infection and the greatest mortality. Of the countries with the highest HIV/AIDS rates in 2010, thirty-seven are in Africa, three in Asia, and six in Latin

---

[1]Quoted in Antony Flew, "Introduction," in Thomas Robert Malthus, *An Essay on the Principle of Population and a Summary View of the Principle of Population* (New York: Penguin Books, 1970), 30.

Chinese Family-Planning Campaign To slow population growth, the Chinese government has sought to limit parents to a single child. Billboards and other forms of mass advertising have been an essential part of the campaign.

TABLE 32.1	Population for World and Major Areas, 1750–2050						
	Population Size (Millions)						
Major Area	**1750**	**1800**	**1850**	**1900**	**1950**	**1995**	**2050***
World	791	978	1,262	1,650	2,521	5,666	8,909
Africa	106	107	111	133	221	697	1,766
Asia	502	635	809	947	1,402	3,437	5,268
Europe	163	203	276	408	547	728	628
Latin America and the Caribbean	16	24	38	74	167	480	809
North America	2	7	26	82	172	297	398
Oceania	2	2	2	6	13	28	46
	Percentage Distribution						
Major Area	**1750**	**1800**	**1850**	**1900**	**1950**	**1995**	**2050***
World	100	100	100	100	100	100	100
Africa	13.4	10.9	8.8	8.1	8.8	12	23.7
Asia	63.5	64.9	64.1	57.4	55.6	61	57.1
Europe	20.6	20.8	21.9	24.7	21.7	13	5.3
Latin America and the Caribbean	2.0	2.5	3.0	4.5	6.6	8	9.4
North America	0.3	0.7	2.1	5.0	6.8	5	4.1
Oceania	0.3	0.2	0.2	0.4	0.5	1	0.5

* Estimated

Source: J. D. Durand, "Historical Estimates of World Population: An Evaluation" (Philadelphia: University of Pennsylvania, Population Studies Center, 1974, mimeographed); United Nations, *The Determinants and Consequences of Population Trends*, vol. 1 (New York: United Nations, 1973); United Nations, *World Population Prospects as Assessed in 1963* (New York: United Nations, 1966); United Nations, *World Population Prospects: The 1998 Revision* (New York: United Nations, forthcoming); United Nations Population Division, Department of Economic and Social Affairs, World Population to 2300. (2004.), http://www.un.org/esa/population/publications/longrange2/WorldPop2300final.pdf.

America and the Caribbean. These countries are home to 87 percent of all HIV/AIDS infections. By 2007 approximately 25 million people had died of AIDS and another 33 million were infected worldwide. In recent years prevention programs and improved drug therapies have slowed both mortality and infection rates, with the greatest successes registered in rich countries with the greatest medical resources.

The Industrialized Nations

In the developed industrial nations of western Europe and in Japan, fertility levels are so low that population would fall without immigration. Japanese women have an average of 1.4 children, while Italian women have 1.2. Although Sweden tries to promote fertility with cash payments, tax incentives, and job leaves to families with children, the average number of births per woman is 1.4. By comparison, the average African woman now has 4.6 children. Higher levels of female education and employment, the material values of consumer culture, and access to contraception and abortion explain the low fertility of mature industrial nations. An Italian woman in Bologna, the city with the lowest fertility in the world, put it this way: "I'm an only child and if I could, I'd have more than one child. But most couples I know wait until their 30's to have children. People want to have their own life, they want to have a successful career. When you see life in these terms, children are an impediment."[2]

In industrialized nations life expectancy improved as fertility declined. The combination of abundant food, improved hygiene, and more effective medicines and medical care has lengthened human lives. In 2000 about 20 percent of the population in Europe was sixty-five or over. By 2050 this proportion will rise to over one-third. Italy soon will have more than twenty adults fifty years old or over for each five-year-old child. Because of higher fertility and greater levels of immigration, the United States is moving in this direction more slowly than western Europe; by 2050 the median age in Europe will be fifty-two, while it will be thirty-nine in the United States.

The combination of falling fertility and rising life expectancy in the industrialized nations presents a challenge very different from the one foreseen by Malthus. These nations generally offer a broad array of social services, including retirement income, medical services, and housing supplements for the elderly. As the number of retirees increases relative to the number of employed people, the cost of these programs may become unsustainable. Economists track this problem by using the PSR (potential support ratio): the ratio of persons fifteen to sixty-four years old (likely workers) to persons sixty-five or older (likely retirees). Between 1950 and 2000 the world's PSR fell from 12 to 9. In mature industrial countries the PSR fell from 8 to 5. By 2050 it will fall to 4 for the world's population and to an unsustainable 2 in mature industrial countries.

The Developing Nations

At current rates, 95 percent of all future population growth will be in developing nations (see Map 32.2 and Table 32.1). A comparison between Europe and Africa illustrates these changes. In 1950 Europe had more than twice the population of Africa. By 1985 Africa's population had drawn even with Europe, and, according to United Nations projections, its population will be three times larger than Europe's by 2050.

Rapid population growth continued after 2000 in the developing world even as birthrates fell. Among all developing nations, average birthrates fell from 44 births per thousand inhabitants in 1950 to 22 today. Birthrates fell most steeply in countries experiencing the most rapid economic development. In China the birthrate fell from 42 births per thousand in 1950 to a First World level of 13 today. In this same period birthrates declined from 43 per thousand to 23 in India, another fast-growing economy. Change occurred much more slowly in sub-Saharan Africa, where the birthrates fell from 47 per thousand to 38, and in Muslim countries like Pakistan and Afghanistan, where birthrates declined from 42 to 28 and 53 to 45 per thousand, respectively. The populations of Latin America were also expanding, but at rates much slower than in sub-Saharan Africa and the Muslim nations. In this same period, Latin America's birthrate declined from 43 per thousand in 1950 to 19 in 2010. Regardless of these changes, birthrates remain more than twice as high in the developing world as in the mature industrial nations, with the highest levels in the poorest countries.

---

[2]"Population Implosion Worries a Graying Europe," *New York Times*, July 10, 1998.

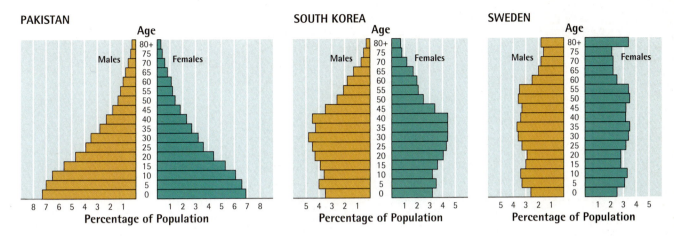

FIGURE 32.1 **Age Structure Comparison** Islamic Nation (Pakistan), Non-Islamic Developing Nation (South Korea), and Developed Nation (Sweden), 2001.   *Source:* U.S. Bureau of the Census, International Database, 2001.

Old and Young Populations

Population pyramids generated by demographers clearly illustrate the profound transformation in human reproductive patterns and life expectancy since World War II. Figure 32.1 shows the 2001 age distributions in Pakistan, South Korea, and Sweden—nations at three different stages of economic development. Sweden is a mature industrial nation. South Korea is rapidly industrializing and has surpassed many European nations in both industrial output and per capita wealth. Pakistan is a poor, traditional Muslim nation with rudimentary industrialization, low educational levels, and little effective family planning.

In 2001 nearly 50 percent of Pakistan's population was under age sixteen. The resulting pressures on the economy have been extraordinary. Every year approximately 150,000 men reach age sixty-five—and another 1.2 million turn sixteen. Pakistan, therefore, has to create more than a million new jobs a year or face growing unemployment and declining wages. Sweden confronts a different problem. Sweden's aging population, growing demand for social welfare benefits, and declining labor pool means that its industries may become less competitive and living standards may decline. In South Korea, a decline in fertility dramatically altered the ratio of children to adults, creating an age distribution similar to that of western Europe.

SECTION REVIEW

- In the twentieth century the developed nations made the demographic transition to low birthrates, while the developing nations began by stressing higher birthrates.

- World population more than doubled between 1950 and 2000.

- In developed nations birthrates fell but longer life expectancy led to slow population growth; in most of the former Soviet Union the combination of low birthrates and limited improvements to life expectancy led to gradually declining populations.

- Developing nations will contribute most of the world's future population growth, despite changing economies and population planning efforts.

- With declining fertility and increasing life expectancy the populations in industrialized nations are growing older rapidly. Developing nations have much younger populations due to declining mortality and high fertility.

UNEQUAL DEVELOPMENT AND THE MOVEMENT OF PEOPLES

Two characteristics of the postwar world should now be clear. First, despite decades of experimentation with state-directed economic development, most nations that were poor in 1960 are still poor today. There are notable exceptions. In Asia, first Japan, then the Asian Tigers (Taiwan, Singapore, South Korea, and Hong Kong), and more recently China have generated high rates of growth and are now among the world's most competitive industrial powers. In recent years

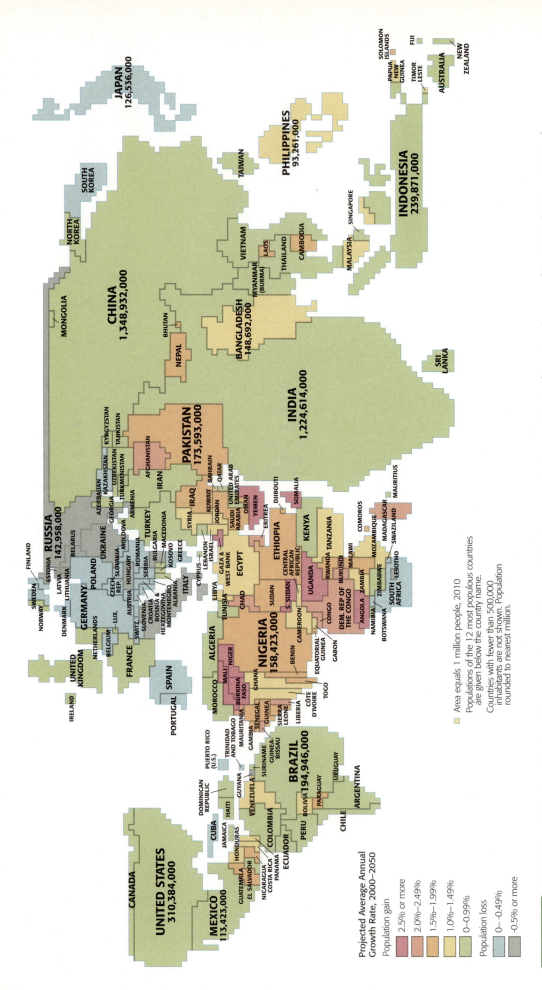

MAP 32.2 **World Population Growth** Every three years the world's population increases by the equivalent of a nation the size of the United States. Most of this population increase will be in some of the world's poorest nations. By 2050, for example, Pakistan, a nation of only 40 million in 1950, will have the world's third largest population. Source: Data from www.worldbank.org. © Cengage Learning

Projected Average Annual
Growth Rate, 2000–2050

Population gain

- 2.5% or more
- 2.0%–2.49%
- 1.5%–1.99%
- 1.0%–1.49%
- 0–0.99%

Population loss

- 0–-0.49%
- -0.5% or more

▪ Area equals 1 million people, 2010

Populations of the 12 most populous countries
are given below the country name.

Countries with fewer than 500,000
inhabitants are not shown. Population
rounded to nearest million.

© Cengage Learning

CANADA

UNITED STATES
310,384,000

MEXICO
113,423,000

BRAZIL
194,946,000

NIGERIA
158,423,000

RUSSIA
142,958,000

CHINA
1,348,932,000

JAPAN
126,536,000

INDIA
1,224,614,000

PAKISTAN
173,593,000

BANGLADESH
148,692,000

PHILIPPINES
93,261,000

INDONESIA
239,871,000

Brazil, Mexico, and India have also experienced significant growth. This industrial transformation has increased world demand for raw materials, which in turn has elevated the wealth of an equally small number of oil-exporting nations. Second, world population has increased to startlingly high levels, and much of the increase was, and will continue to be, in the poorest nations.

The combination of intractable poverty and growing population has generated a surge in international immigration. Few issues have stirred more controversy. Even moderate voices have sometimes framed this discussion of immigration as a competition among peoples. Large numbers of legal and illegal immigrants from poor nations with growing populations are entering the developed industrial nations, with the exception of Japan. Large-scale migrations within developing countries are a related phenomenon. The movement of impoverished rural residents to the cities of Asia, Africa, and Latin America (see Map 32.2 and Table 32.2) has increased steadily since the 1970s. This internal migration often serves as the first step toward migration abroad.

The Problem of Inequality

Since 1945 the global economy has expanded more rapidly than at any time in the past. Faster, cheaper communications and transportation have combined with improvements in industrial and agricultural technologies to create material abundance that would have amazed those who experienced the first Industrial Revolution (see Chapter 22). Despite this remarkable economic expansion, the differences between rich and poor nations remain stark.

The gap between rich and poor nations has grown wider since 1945, although the 2008 recession has had a powerful negative effect on many advanced industrial economies. China's spectacular rise as an industrial power since 1980 is a strong indicator that some once-poor countries can modernize and become competitive industrial nations. Nevertheless, the vast majority of the world's population continues to live in poverty. There are many measures of the

TABLE 32.2 The World's Largest Cities (Urban Agglomerations of 13 Million or More)

City	1970	City	1990	City	2011	City	2025
1 Tokyo	23.3	1 Tokyo	32.5	1 Tokyo	37.2	1 Tokyo	38.7
2 New York	16.2	2 New York	16.1	2 Delhi	22.7	2 Delhi	32.9
		3 Mexico City	15.3	3 Mexico City	20.4	3 Shanghai	28.4
		4 São Paulo	14.8	4 New York	20.4	4 Mumbai	26.6
		5 Mumbai	12.4	5 Shanghai	20.2	5 Mexico City	24.6
		6 Osaka-Kobe	11.0	6 São Paulo	19.9	6 New York	23.6
		7 Calcutta	10.9	7 Mumbai	19.7	7 São Paulo	23.2
		8 Los Angeles	10.9	8 Beijing	15.6	8 Dhaka	22.9
		9 Seoul	10.5	9 Dhaka	15.4	9 Beijing	22.6
		10 Buenos Aires	10.5	10 Calcutta	14.4	10 Karachi	20.2
				11 Karachi	13.9	11 Lagos	18.9
				12 Buenos Aires	13.5	12 Calcutta	18.7
				13 Los Angeles	13.4	13 Manila	16.3
						14 Los Angeles	15.7
						15 Shenzhen	15.5
						16 Buenos Aires	15.5
						17 Guangzhou	15.5
						18 Istanbul	14.9
						19 Cairo	14.7
						20 Kinshasa	14.5
						21 Chongqing	13.6
						22 Rio de Janeiro	13.6
						23 Bangalore	13.2

Source: United Nations, Economic and Social Affairs, World Urbanization Prospects: The 2011 Revision Highlights, 6-7.

relative wealth of nations; GDP (gross domestic product) per capita measured in U.S. dollars is among the most common.

In 2010 the per capita GDP of Luxembourg was the highest in the world, $104,512; the U.S. figure was $46,702, and the Japanese figure was $43,063. The countries of the European Union were generally rich, but some of the former Soviet satellites recently admitted to the European Union have the GDP per capita of developing nations. France and Germany have per capita GDPs of $39,170 and $39,852, respectively. The poorest countries in the European Union, Bulgaria and Romania, have per capita GDPs similar to Russia's ($6,335)—$7,539, and $10,481, respectively.

Many countries in the developing world now approach the poorest tier of European countries in per capita GDP. Per capita GDP for Mexico is $9,133, Brazil $10,993, Chile $12,640, South Africa $7,272, and Gabon $8,768. But many more countries, especially in Asia and Africa, remain very poor: the Philippines, $2,140; India, $1,375; Pakistan, $1,019; Nigeria, $1,242; and Sudan, $1,538. The poorest, like Haiti, Kenya, and Bangladesh, have per capita GDP levels under $1,000.

Internal Migration: The Growth of Cities

In developing nations migration from rural areas to urban centers increased threefold between 1925 and 1950; the pace of migration then accelerated (see Table 32.2). While slums around the major cities of developing nations are seen as signs of social breakdown and economic failure, life in these urban slums was generally better than life in the countryside. A World Bank study estimated that three out of four rural-to-urban migrants made economic gains. Residents of cities in sub-Saharan Africa, for example, were six times more likely than rural residents to have safe water. An unskilled migrant from the depressed northeast of Brazil could triple his or her income by moving to Rio de Janeiro.

Garbage Dump in Manila, Philippines   In Third World nations thousands of poor families live by sorting and selling bottles, aluminum cans, plastic, and newspapers in urban landfills.

Eco Images/Universal Images Group/Getty Images

As the scale of rural-to-urban migration grew, these benefits became more elusive. In the cities of the developing world basic services have been crumbling under the pressure of rapid population growth. In cities like Mexico City and Manila, which are among the world's largest cities, tens of thousands live in garbage dumps, scavenging for food. In Rio de Janeiro alone an estimated 350,000 abandoned children live in the streets and parks, begging, selling drugs, stealing, and engaging in prostitution to survive. Some nations have tried to relocate migrants back to the countryside. Indonesia, for example, has relocated more than a half-million urban residents since 1969.

Global Migration

Each year hundreds of thousands of men and women leave developing nations to go to industrialized nations. Dramatically rising numbers after 1960 have led to increased ethnic and racial tensions. Political refugees and immigrants have faced murderous violence in Germany; growing anti-immigrant sentiment has strengthened right-wing political movements and led to riots in cities with large immigrant populations in France and Greece; and in the United States the government has dramatically expanded its effort to control its southern border.

Immigrants from developing nations have brought host nations many of the same benefits that the great migration of Europeans to the Americas provided a century earlier (see Chapter 25). The United States actively recruited Mexican workers during World War II, and many European nations promoted guest worker programs and other inducements to immigration in the 1960s, when an expanding European economy experienced labor shortages. However, attitudes toward immigrants have changed as the size of immigrant populations has grown, particularly during periods of economic contraction like the recession that began in 2008. Under intense pressure, native-born workers demanded an end to immigration, seeing immigrants as competitors willing to work for lower wages and less likely to support labor unions.

High fertility among immigrants contributes to these tensions. Most immigrants are young adults who retain the positive attitudes toward early marriage and large families of their native cultures in Latin America, Africa, and the Middle East and have higher fertility rates than do host populations. Spain provides a useful example. In 2000 Spain had one of the world's lowest fertility rates, 1.2 births per woman. A member of the European Union, its economy was growing and employment opportunities were available to immigrants from Latin America, North Africa, and elsewhere. As a result, Spain briefly became the major immigrant-receiving nation in the European Union, and the immigrant component of Spain's population rose from 2.1 to 14.1 percent between 1990 and 2010. Because the birthrate of the immigrant population is twice as high as that of the native-born population, the effect of this trend has been multiplied, with foreign-born mothers accounting for 20 percent of all births. Since the beginning of the recession in 2008, immigration to Spain has slowed and birthrates of both native-born and foreign-born have fallen. But even in this altered context, immigrant groups continue to grow much faster than the native-born population. Similarly, as immigrant populations have increased across Europe and in the United States in the twenty-first century, the resulting cultural conflicts have tested definitions of citizenship and nationality.

SECTION REVIEW

- As the world economy expanded after World War II, the gap between rich and poor nations grew.

- In the fast-growing nations of the developing world, urban populations have grown as a result of rural-to-urban migration.

- Most of the world's migration is the movement of young men and women from poor nations to rich nations with low birthrates and aging populations.

TECHNOLOGICAL AND ENVIRONMENTAL CHANGE

Technological innovation powered the economic expansion that began after World War II. New technologies increased productivity and disseminated human creativity. They also altered the way people lived, worked, and played. Because most of the economic benefits were initially concentrated in the advanced industrialized nations, technology increased the power of those nations relative to the developing world. This has changed in the last decade with globalization and the rising industrial role of China. Even within developed nations, postwar technological innovations did not benefit all classes, industries, and regions equally. There were losers as well as winners.

Population growth and increased levels of migration and urbanization multiplied the numbers of acres farmed and factories, intensifying environmental threats. In the early twenty-first century, loss of rain forest, soil erosion, global warming, air and water pollution, and extinction of species threatened the quality of life and the survival of human societies. Environmental protection, like the acquisition of new technology, had progressed most in societies with the greatest economic resources.

New Technologies and the World Economy

Nuclear energy, jet engines, radar, and tape recording were among the many World War II developments that later had an impact on consumers' lives. New technology increased industrial productivity, reduced labor requirements, and improved the flow of information that made markets more efficient. The consumer electronics industry rapidly developed new products, changes seen in the music industry's movement from vinyl records to 8-track tapes, CDs, and then MP3 technologies. Computers became faster and less expensive, cell phones were transformed into smartphones, and the speed of news and data accelerated at an unanticipated rate, transforming business, education, and politics globally.

Improvements in existing technologies accounted for much of the developed world's productivity increases during the 1950s and 1960s, as faster, more efficient transportation and communication cut costs and expanded markets. But new technologies were important as well. Governments bore much of the cost of developing and constructing nuclear power plants and sponsored research into new technologies. None has proved more influential in the last four decades than the computer, which transformed both work and leisure (see Environment and Technology: Connected). The first computers were expensive, large, and slow, and only corporations, governments, and universities could afford them. Each new generation of computer has been smaller, faster, and less expensive. As a result, the serial utilization of desktops, laptops, tablets, and smartphones transformed commerce, education, and government. Today the computational capacity of a 1970s university mainframe computer can be found in the affordable and portable laptops of individual university students. The modern smartphone continues this pattern, serving as a platform for basic computing, search functions, and gaming as well as a sophisticated means of communication.

Computers also altered manufacturing. Small dedicated computers now control and monitor machinery in most modern industries. In the developed world, as well as in China and other fast-growing developing economies, factories forced by global competition to improve efficiency and product quality increasingly depend on robots. Japan's early lead in robotics in the 1990s has been reduced as Europe, the United States, and China have all raced to introduce robotics across their economies.

The transnational corporation became the primary agent for these technological changes. By the twentieth century the growing economic power of corporations in industrialized nations allowed them to invest directly in the mines, plantations, and public utilities of less developed regions. In the post–World War II years many of these companies became truly transnational, having multinational ownership and management. International trade agreements and open markets furthered the process. Ford, Nissan, BMW, and other car companies not only produced and sold cars internationally, but their shareholders, workers, and managers also came from numerous nations.

The location of manufacturing plants overseas and the acquisition of corporate operations by foreign buyers rendered such global firms as transnational as the products they sold. In the 1970s and 1980s American brand names like Levi's, Coca-Cola, Marlboro, Gillette, McDonald's, and Kentucky Fried Chicken were global phenomena (see Material Culture: Fast Food). But in time Asian names—Honda, Hitachi, Sony, Sanyo, and Mitsubishi—were blazoned in neon and on giant video screens on the sides of skyscrapers, along with European brands such as Nestlé, Mercedes, Pirelli, and Benetton. Since 1979, China's emergence as a global industrial power has accelerated this process of integration and diffusion.

As transnational manufacturers, agricultural conglomerates, and financial giants became wealthier and more powerful, they increasingly escaped the controls imposed by national governments. If labor costs were too high in Japan, antipollution measures too intrusive in the United States, or taxes too high in Great Britain, transnational companies relocated—or

Connected

The period since World War II witnessed wave after wave of technological innovations. None has had greater impact on the way people work, learn, and live than the computer. Until the 1970s most computing was done on large and expensive mainframe computers. These massive computers were primarily used for data storage and analysis, and the government agencies, universities, and large corporations that owned them controlled access.

Today most computers are in private hands, and most are devoted to communication and information searches, a transformation symbolized when the market value of the search engine Google surpassed that of IBM, developer of mainframe and PC computing. Few had anticipated the technological innovations that revolutionized the computer industry through miniaturization during the last three decades. The key development leading to smaller and cheaper computers was the microprocessor, a silicon chip that contained the computer's brains.

Initially developed to facilitate American defense research in the 1960s, the Internet was the second key to the communication revolution. It allowed smaller, faster computers and now tablets and smartphones to become research portals that could access a vast international database of research, opinion, entertainment, and commerce. Small personal computers and related devices and the Web have had a revolutionary impact on modern culture, allowing individuals and groups—without the support of governments, corporations, or other powerful institutions—to collect and disseminate information more freely than at any time in the past (see Chapter 33). The disruptive potential of this new forum was indicated in February 2010 when WikiLeaks published more than 250,000 classified U.S. government cables on the Web. Many of the most embarrassing documents were then published by traditional print media.

In the last decade new technologies have permitted the integration of previously distinct devices. As a result, software and hardware providers now routinely blend the functions and uses of small laptop computers, cellular phones, and MP3 players to provide new business and professional applications and entertainment. Hand-held "convergence devices" evolving from the cellular telephone allow users to make phone calls, send e-mail, search the Internet, read books, play music and videos, and store electronic texts. No corporation has played a more central role in this stage of the computer revolution than Apple, a computer company that has become a major innovator in the smartphone and tablet market. It is now one of the five most valuable companies ever.

One result of these technological revolutions is the appearance of plugged-in, self-identifying communities in venues like blogs, social media, and chat rooms that transcend or supplement older forms of community based on ethnic, regional, or economic identities. At the same time these innovations have undermined traditional expectations of privacy as corporations and governments routinely follow online activity.

Lawren Lu/Photodisc/Getty Images

Always Connected   Two students simultaneously apply the power of smartphone, tablet, and laptop to a project.

threatened to do so. In 1945, for example, the U.S. textile industry was located in low-wage southern states, dominating the American market and exporting to the world. As wages in the American South rose and global competition increased, producers began relocating plants to Puerto Rico in the 1980s and to Mexico after NAFTA went into effect in 1994 (see Chapter 33). Now China is the primary manufacturer of textiles.

Conserving and Sharing Resources

In the 1960s environmental activists and political leaders began warning about the devastating environmental consequences of population growth, industrialization, and the expansion of agriculture onto marginal lands. Assaults on rain forests, the disappearance of species, and the poisoning of streams and rivers raised public consciousness, as did the depletion and pollution of the world's oceans. Environmental damage occurred both in the advanced industrial economies and in developing nations. The former Soviet Union, where industrial and nuclear wastes were routinely dumped with little concern for environmental consequences, had the worst environmental record.

Fast Food

Since early times empires and commercial enterprises have moved foods and beverages across national borders and cultural boundaries. The list of examples is very long. Sugar, coffee, tea, chocolate, corn, manioc, potatoes, wheat, wine, beer, distilled alcohols, tomatoes, and bananas are a small number of the foods and beverages carried from their origins to new continents and new peoples. In each case, host cultures accepted these additions to their cuisines while at the same time changing their preparation and altering their cultural meanings. Europeans sweetened chocolate, a bitter beverage consumed ritually by the Aztec elite, with sugar and it quickly became a beverage of mass consumption.

In modern industrialized nations fast food has come to cater to changing needs. Women and men in modern industrial societies marry later or not at all, and families have fewer meals together because of intense school and work schedules. As a result, fast food outlets have appeared everywhere to meet the needs of this busy, mobile population. In 2006 alone the world market for fast food grew by just under 7 percent, reaching sales of $155 billion.

Increased immigration and travel, as well as greater cultural connectivity promoted by films, television, and the Web, have combined to globalize ideas about food preparation and delivery. McDonald's now operates more than 31,000 restaurants in 119 countries. When a new franchise opened in Kuwait City, the drive-through line was over 10 kilometers (6.2 miles) long. Generally fast food meals cost the same in every cultural setting. In the United States, one of the richest countries in the world, McDonald's provides low-cost food to the masses, while in Pakistan, one of the poorest, these meals are luxuries. For many in the developing world, the fast food cuisines, restaurant designs, and styles of preparation represent the world of modernity and sophistication, not unlike the enthusiasm in the developed world for Mexican, Thai, or Ethiopian restaurants and cuisines.

Indeed, McDonald's is merely one of numerous examples of fast food globalization. KFC had 3,200 outlets in China by the end of 2010, surpassing the McDonald's presence in this dynamic economy. Papa John's opened its fortieth outlet in Seoul and its twentieth outlet in Shanghai. Wendy's, Dominos, Cinnabon, and Subway have followed.

Many condemn this process as Yankee imperialism or as the unwanted homogenization of global culture. Tens of thousands have demonstrated, and some have gone to jail as a result of attacks on these symbols of foreign cultural penetration. Yet, as in earlier examples of unequal cultural exchange, local cultures have found ways to impose their tastes and values on these powerful international businesses. In Singapore McDonald's serves its signature hamburger on rice cakes instead of buns, and in Israel McDonald's established Kosher outlets. KFC, the most successful American chain in China, serves a Beijing Duck Wrap with spring onions and rice gruel for breakfast. In India, with its large vegetarian population, McDonald's, Pizza Hut, and other successful franchises devote as much as 75 percent of their menu to vegetarian foods. In 2012 McDonald's opened its first completely vegetarian outlets in India, where it planned to increase its total number of outlets to 500.

Every society produces a range of products that serve as class and culture markers and as forms of self-expression. In the modern world food helps mark consumers as "traditional" or "sophisticated" and as "rich" or "poor." Both the global success of fast food companies and the popular protests against them suggest the complexity of this form of cultural transmission.

McDonald's in India
McDonald's has adapted its menu in India to reflect the religious mandates of Hinduism. In this restaurant in New Delhi the chain announces that no beef products are prepared or sold.

Stephanie Maze/CORBIS

Loss of Brazilian Rain Forest   The destruction of large portions of Brazil's virgin rain forest has come to symbolize the growing threat to the environment caused by population growth and economic development. In this photograph we see the scale of environmental destruction.

In the developed world, industrial activity increased much more rapidly than the population grew, and the consumption of energy (coal, electricity, and petroleum) rose proportionally. This pattern is now clear in India, China, and other industrializing nations as well. Indeed, the consumer-driven economic expansion of the post–World War II years became an obstacle to addressing environmental problems, since modern economies depend on a profligate consumption of goods and resources (see Map 32.3). When consumption slows, industrial nations enter a recession, as recently demonstrated in 2008. How could the United States, Germany, Japan, or China change consumption patterns to protect the environment without endangering corporate profits, wages, and employment levels?

Since 1945 population growth has been most dramatic in the developing countries, where environmental pressures have also been extreme. In Brazil, India, and China, for example, the need to expand food production led to rapid deforestation and the extension of farming and grazing onto marginal lands. The results were predictable: erosion and water pollution. These and many other poor nations sought to stimulate industrialization because they believed that the transition from agriculture to manufacturing was the only way to provide for their rapidly growing populations. The argument was compelling: Why should Indians or Brazilians remain poor while Americans, Europeans, and Japanese grew rich?

Responding to Environmental Threats

Despite the gravity of environmental threats, there were many successful efforts to preserve and protect the environment. The Clean Air Act, the Clean Water Act, and the Endangered

Population Density and Water Stress

Water stress

Low–
medium High

Population density

High
Medium
Low
Extremely low
No data

MAP 32.3 **Fresh Water Resources** This map links population density and the availability of water. Red areas are highly stressed environments where populations use at least 40 percent or more of available water. Less stressed environments are blue. The deeper the shade of red or blue the greater the environmental stress. Source: From "Global Water Stress," *National Geographic*, September 2002, pp. 14–16. Reprinted by permission of the National Geographic Society. © Cengage Learning

Species Act were passed in the United States in the 1970s as part of an environmental effort that included the nations of the European Community and Japan. Grassroots political movements and the media encouraged environmental awareness, and most nations in the developed world enforced strict antipollution laws and sponsored massive recycling efforts. Many also encouraged resource conservation by rewarding energy-efficient factories and manufacturers of fuel-efficient cars and by promoting the use of alternative energy sources such as solar and wind power.

Environmental efforts produced significant results. In western Europe and the United States, air quality improved dramatically. Smog levels in the United States fell nearly a third from 1970 to 2000, even though the number of automobiles increased more than 80 percent. Emissions of lead and sulfur dioxide were down as well. The Great Lakes, Long Island Sound, and Chesapeake Bay were all much cleaner at the beginning of the new century than they had been in 1970.

New technologies made much of the improvement possible; for example, pollution controls on automobiles, planes, and factory smokestacks reduced harmful emissions. At the same time, the desire to preserve the natural environment was growing around the world. In developed nations continued political organization and enhanced awareness of environmental issues seemed likely to lead to step-by-step improvements in environmental policy. In the developing world and most of the former Soviet bloc, however, population pressures and weak governments were major obstacles to effective environmental policies. Since the 1990s the rapid expansion of China's industrial sector as well as industrial growth in other developing nations like India and Brazil has put additional pressure on the environment.

It now seems likely that industrialized nations will have to fund global improvements and that the cost will be high. Slow growth and fiscal crises in the mature industrial economies after the 2008 recession have politicized and slowed the progress of environmental reform. Nevertheless, growing evidence of environmental degradation and global warming have continued to propel popular reform efforts, as when the media drew attention to the precipitous shrinkage of Peru's Andean glaciers and to loss of rain forest in Brazil. Yet, without broad agreement among the rich nations, the economic and political power necessary for environmental protections on a global scale will be very difficult to institute. When representatives from around the world negotiated a far-reaching treaty to reduce greenhouse gases in Kyoto, Japan, in 1997, President George W. Bush refused American participation even though the treaty was affirmed by nearly all other industrial nations. Canada subsequently withdrew from the agreement, and China and other rapidly industrializing nations were largely exempted from the treaty's limits. This agreement, as a result, has had a limited effect on greenhouse gas emissions.

SECTION REVIEW

- Improvements in existing technology and new technologies such as the computer have improved manufacturing efficiency and transformed leisure.

- Globalization created a more integrated world economy, connecting producers and consumers from different regions and nations and reducing the ability of a single nation to escape the effects of distant events.

- The environmental movement achieved some successes in developed nations, reducing pollution and improving resource management, but global progress was hindered by a lack of cooperation between developed and developing nations.

CONCLUSION

The world was profoundly altered between 1975 and the first decade of the twenty-first century. Both the United States and the Soviet Union feared that every conflict and every regime change represented a potential threat to their strategic interests, and every conflict threatened to provoke confrontation between them. As a result, the superpowers inserted themselves into a succession of civil wars and revolutions. The costs in lives and property were terrible, the gains small. As defense costs escalated, the Soviet system crumbled. By 1991 the Soviet Union and the socialist Warsaw Pact had disappeared, transforming the international stage.

The world was also altered by economic growth and globalization, by population growth and movement, and by technological and environmental change. Led by the postwar recovery of the industrial powers and the remarkable economic expansion of Japan, the Asian Tigers, and more recently China, the world economy grew dramatically until the global recession of 2008. The development and application of new technology contributed significantly to this process. International markets were more open and integrated than at any other time. However, not all the nations of the world benefited from the new wealth and exciting technologies of the postwar era. The capitalist West and a handful of Asian nations grew richer and more powerful, while most of the world's nations remained poor.

Population growth in the developing world was one reason for this divided experience. Despite falling birthrates in many poor countries, most of the world's population growth in recent decades is in developing nations with limited economic growth. Unable to find adequate employment or, in many cases, bare subsistence, people in developing nations have migrated across international borders, hoping to improve their lives. These movements have often provided valuable labor in the factories and farms of the developed world, but they have also provoked cultural, racial, and ethnic tension. Problems of inequality, population growth, and international migration will continue to challenge the global community in the coming decades.

Growing population and the development process have forced marginal lands into production and stimulated the exploitation of new resources. The need to feed a rapidly growing world population has also pressured ocean resources. As the world's population surpassed 6 billion and the largest cities reached 20 million, the need to produce and deliver raw materials and finished goods has put tremendous stress on the environment. In the 1990s the rapid development of the Chinese and Indian economies compounded these pressures.

At the same time, new technologies and the wealth produced by economic expansion have allowed the world's richest nations to implement ambitious programs of environmental protection. As a result, pollution produced by automobiles and factories has actually declined in the richest nations. The question that remains is whether rapidly developing nations, such as Brazil, China, and India, will move more quickly than the mature industrial nations did to introduce these new technologies.

KEY TERMS

proxy wars p. 820
Salvador Allende p. 821
Dirty War p. 821
Sandinistas p. 822
Ayatollah Ruhollah Khomeini p. 823

Saddam Husain p. 824
keiretsu p. 825
neo-liberalism p. 826
Asian Tigers p. 826
newly industrialized economies (NIEs) p. 826

Deng Xiaoping p. 827
Tiananmen Square p. 827
Mikhail Gorbachev p. 829
perestroika p. 829
Solidarity p. 829
ethnic cleansing p. 830

Thomas Malthus p. 832
demographic transition p. 832

SUGGESTED READING

Bakhash, Shaul. *The Reign of the Ayatollahs: Iran and the Iranian Revolution.* 1990. An account of the Iranian Revolution and the early days of the Islamic Republic of Iran.

Berry, John A., and Carol Pott Berry, eds. *Genocide in Rwanda: A Collective Memory.* 1999. Covers a major calamity too readily forgotten.

Birch, Eugenie L., and Susan M. Wachter, eds. *Global Urbanization: The City in the Twenty-first Century.* 2011. Collection of essays covering most of the key issues.

Christakis, Nicolas A., and James H. Fowler. *Connected: The Surprising Power of Our Social Networks and How They Shape Our Lives.* 2011. Although focused on the developed world, especially the United States, this is an important work for understanding the modern social environment.

Dyson, Tim, et al., eds. *Twenty-first Century India: Population, Economy, Human Development, and the Environment.* 2005. The culmination of a large research project.

Edgerton, Robert. *The Troubled Heart of Africa: A History of the Congo.* 2002. A convincing examination of this nation's history.

Foster, John Bellamy. *Economic History of the Environment.* 1994. An important synthesis.

Gaddis, John Lewis. *The Cold War: A New History.* 2005. A solid overview.

Helpman, Elhanan. *Understanding Global Trade.* 2011. A clear and convincing discussion of recent developments in world trade relationships.

Kenez, Peter. *A History of the Soviet Union from the Beginning to the End*. 2006. Explains the demise of the USSR.

Lardy, Nicholas R. *Sustaining China's Economic Growth After the Global Financial Crisis*. 2012. A well-researched study of recent economic events and the likely direction of future change.

Livi-Bacci, Massimo. *A Concise History of World Population*, 5th ed. 2012. Full coverage of this complex story from the beginning but with strong engagement with recent trends.

Maier, Charles. *Dissolution: The Crisis of Communism and the End of East Germany*. 1997. Covers the collapse of the Soviet empire in Europe.

McNeill, John R. *Something New Under the Sun: An Environmental History of the Twentieth Century World*. 2000. A survey coverage of a rising field of historical study.

Meredith, Martin. *The Fate of Africa: From the Hopes of Freedom to the Heart of Despair*. 2005. An overview of recent African history.

Osterhammel, Jürgen, Niels P. Peterson, and Dona Gever. *Globalization: A Short History*. 2009. Places the modern phenomenon in historical perspective.

Rostow, W. W. *The Great Population Spike and After: Reflections on the 21st Century*. 1998. A challenging work that examines consequences of falling fertility in developed nations.

Rubin, Barnett. *The Fragmentation of Afghanistan*. 1995. Provides excellent coverage of the struggle between Soviet forces and the Muslim resistance.

Sachs, Jeffrey. *The End of Poverty: Economic Possibilities for Our Time*. 2006. A combination of human anecdotes drawn from many national settings and a broad discussion of progress and obstacles to underdevelopment.

Sampson, Anthony. *Mandela: The Authorized Biography*. 2000. A valuable introduction to the life and politics of the man.

Shenkar, Oded. *The Chinese Century: The Rising Chinese Economy and Its Impact on the Global Economy, the Balance of Power, and Your Job*. 2004. A business-oriented appraisal of the surging Chinese economy.

Skidmore, Thomas E., Peter H. Smith, and James Green. *Modern Latin America*, 7th ed. 2009. Provides an excellent general introduction to the period 1975 to the present.

Stiglitz, Joseph E. *Globalization and Its Discontents*. 2003. An overview by a major economic thinker.

Thompson, Leonard. *A History of South Africa*, 3d ed. 2005. Looks at a key African country.

Westad, Odd Arne. *The Global Cold War: Third World Interventions and the Making of Our Times*. 2005. A very useful discussion of the effects of Cold War rivalry on the developing world.

Wolf, M. *Revolution Postponed: Women in Contemporary China*. 1985. An informative survey based on over 300 interviews with Chinese women.

CourseMate Go to the History CourseMate website for primary source links, study tools, and review materials for this chapter. www.cengagebrain.com

Chapter Outline

Globalization and Economic Crisis
➤ *What are the main benefits and dangers of growing political, economic, and cultural integration?*

The Question of Values
➤ *What roles do religious beliefs and secular ideologies play in the contemporary world?*

Global Culture
➤ *How has technology contributed to the process of global interaction?*

● **DIVERSITY + DOMINANCE**   Conflict and Civilization

● **ENVIRONMENT + TECHNOLOGY**   Global Warming

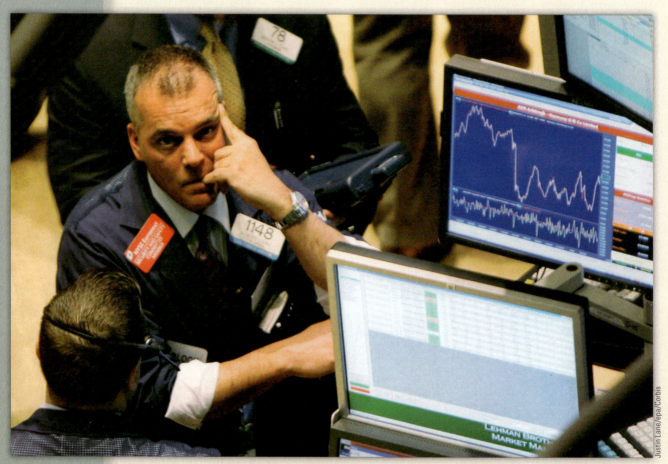

Watching Financial Markets Fall   After years of economic boom, much of it fueled by inflated housing prices in the United States and ingenious new financial instruments that concealed risk, the world's stock markets fell drastically in 2008–2009. American stocks lost approximately one-third of their value. The banking crisis and resulting unemployment reminded economists of the Great Depression of the 1930s. People in all walks of life, from heads of state, to retirees, to ordinary workers, were forced to reappraise their financial situations.

New Challenges in a New Millennium

The workday began normally at the World Trade Center in lower Manhattan on the morning of September 11, 2001. The 50,000 people who worked there were making their way to the two 110-story towers. Suddenly, at 8:46 A.M., an American Airlines Boeing 767 with 92 people on board, traveling at a speed of 470 miles per hour (756 kilometers per hour), crashed into floors 94 to 98 of the north tower, igniting the 10,000 gallons (38,000 liters) of fuel in its tanks. Just before 9:03 A.M. a United Airlines flight with 65 people on board and a similar fuel load hit floors 78 to 84 of the south tower.

As the burning jet fuel engulfed the collision areas, the buildings' occupants struggled through smoke-filled corridors and down dozens of flights of stairs. Many of those trapped above the crash sites used cell phones to say good-bye to loved ones. Rather than endure the flames and fumes, a few jumped to their deaths.

Just before 10 o'clock, temperatures that had risen to 2,300° Fahrenheit (1,260° Celsius) caused the steel girders in the impacted area of the south tower to give way. The collapsing upper floors crushed the floors underneath one by one, engulfing lower Manhattan in a dense cloud of dust. Twenty-eight minutes later the north tower pancaked in a similar manner. Miraculously, most of the buildings' occupants had escaped before the towers collapsed. Besides the people on the planes, nearly 2,600 lost their lives, including some 400 police officers and firefighters helping in the evacuation.

That same morning another American Airlines jet crashed into the Pentagon, killing all 64 people on board and 125 others inside the military complex near Washington, D.C. Passengers on a fourth plane managed to overpower their hijackers, and the plane crashed in rural Pennsylvania, killing all 45 on board.

The four planes had been hijacked by teams of Middle Eastern men who slit the throats of service and flight personnel and seized control. Of the nineteen hijackers, fifteen were from Saudi Arabia. All had links to an extremist Islamic organization, al-Qaeda (ahl–KAW-eh-duh) (the base or foundation), commanded by a rich Saudi named Usama bin Laden (oo-SAH-mah bin LAH-din), who was incensed with American political, military, and cultural influence in the Middle East. The men were educated and well traveled, had lived in the United States, and spoke English. Some had trained as pilots so that they could fly the hijacked aircraft.

The hijackers left few records of their motives, but the acts spoke for themselves. The World Trade Center was a focal point of international business, the Pentagon the headquarters of the American military. The fourth plane was probably meant to hit the Capitol or the White House, the legislative and executive centers of the world's only superpower.

The events of September 11, which became commonly referred to as 9/11, can be understood on many levels. The hijackers and those who sympathized with them saw themselves as engaged in a holy struggle against economic, political, and military institutions they believed to be evil. People directly affected, political leaders around the world, and most television watchers described the attacks as evil deeds against innocent victims.

To understand why the nineteen attackers were heroes to some and terrorists to others, one needs to explore the historical context of global changes at the turn of the millennium and the ideological tensions they have generated. The unique prominence of the United States in every major aspect of global integration, as well as its support for pro-American governments overseas, also elicits sharply divergent views.

GLOBALIZATION AND ECONOMIC CRISIS

globalization The economic, political, and cultural integration and interaction of all parts of the world brought about by increasing trade, travel, and technology.

The turn of the millennium saw the intensification of **globalization** trends that had been building since the 1970s. Growing trade and travel and new technologies were bringing all parts of the world into closer economic, political, and cultural integration and interaction (see Maps 33.1 and 33.2). The collapse of the Soviet Union had completed the dissolution of territorial empires that had been under way throughout the twentieth century. Autonomous national states (numbering about two hundred) became an almost universal norm, and a growing number of them had embraced democratic institutions. However, increasing interdependency would also facilitate a global economic crisis that exploded in 2008 when the massive accumulation of debt in American financial institutions became unsustainable.

An Interconnected Economy

The expansion of trade, global interconnections, and privatization of government enterprises that gained momentum with the dismantling of Soviet-style socialist economies in the 1990s cooled abruptly in the wake of 9/11. The rate of growth in world trade fell from 13 percent in 2000 to only 1 percent in 2001.

Growth in China and India resumed quickly, however, and the large populations of these two countries marked them as future world economic powers. Their growth increased pressure on world energy supplies, though the United States continued to consume a quarter of the world's petroleum production and by 2013 had resumed its position of world's largest producer through the production of oil derived from shale deposits. OPEC's manipulation of world oil prices, combined with political instability in the Middle East, had caused crude oil prices to soar between 1973 and 1985. But aside from those years, the average price of oil remained consistently below $20 per barrel (adjusted for inflation) throughout the second half of the twentieth century. In the year 2000, however, oil prices began a new period of increase caused not by OPEC but by rising demand and confidence in the fevered pace of world economic expansion. By the middle of 2006, the price of a barrel of crude had crept past $70, and in 2008 it spiked to $145 a barrel. This increase fueled ambitious economic programs in producing countries like Russia, Venezuela, Iran, Saudi Arabia, and the small sheikhdoms of the Persian Gulf, as well as in the newer OPEC states Ecuador, Nigeria, and Angola. With the economic crisis of 2008, prices fell abruptly, but by 2013 the price per barrel was back in the $90–$100 range.

Regional trade associations came into being to promote growth, reduce the economic vulnerability of member states, and, less explicitly, balance American economic dominance. The twenty-seven-member European Union (EU) was the most successful (see Map 33.2). The euro, a common currency inaugurated in 2002 and used in twelve member states, competed with the U.S. dollar for investment and banking. However, unequal levels of development among members became a source of crisis in 2009 as the world economic downturn devastated stock markets and increased rates of unemployment. Countries like Greece that had taken on more debt than the revenues produced by their shrunken economies could cover sought assistance from the rest of the EU, but the wealthier countries, led by Germany, proved reluctant to rescue them. Instead

CHRONOLOGY

Politics	Economics and Society
2000 2000 Al-Qaeda attacks American destroyer USS *Cole* in Yemen	1947 Partition of India 1949 Dutch withdraw from Indonesia
2001 2001 George W. Bush becomes president of the United States 2001 Terrorists destroy the World Trade Center and damage the Pentagon on September 11 2001 United States armed forces overthrow Taliban regime in Afghanistan	2001–2003 Terrorist attacks trigger global recession 2001 Shanghai Cooperation Organization formed
2002	2002 Euro currency adopted in twelve European countries
2003 2003 Unfounded fears of weapons of mass destruction lead United States and allies to invade and occupy Iraq	
2004 2004 Terrorists bomb Spanish trains 2004–2009 Genocidal conflict ongoing in Darfur region of Sudan	2004 Facebook popularizes Internet social media
2005 2005 Terrorists bomb London transit system 2005 Mahmoud Ahmedinejad elected president of Iran	
2006 2006 Iraqis elect a government under a new constitution 2006 Hamas movement defeats PLO in Palestinian election 2006 Israel attacks Hezbollah in Lebanon in response to its seizure of Israeli soldiers	
2007 2007 Assassination of Benazir Bhutto deepens political crisis in Pakistan	
2008 2008 Barack Obama elected president of the United States	2008 Collapse of mortgage debt bubble in United States triggers global recession
2010 2010 American forces withdraw from Iraq	
2011 2011 Arab Spring demonstrations topple authoritarian governments 2011 American raiders kill Usama bin Laden in Pakistan	2011 Muslim Brotherhood emerges as powerful force in Egypt
2012 2012 Barack Obama reelected president of the United States 2012 Vladimir Putin returns to the presidency in Russia	

they urged an austerity program of radical cutbacks in public expenditures, which increased unemployment and popular discontent. The idea of the euro, a common currency that symbolized Europe's progress toward unity, also came into question because countries belonging to the euro zone were not at liberty to devalue their currency and thereby reduce their debt burdens. In an increasingly globalized network of financial markets and institutions, Europe's recurrent debt crises generated economic anxiety from Japan to New York City.

Despite the EU's expansion, the North American Free Trade Agreement (NAFTA), which eliminated tariffs among the United States, Canada, and Mexico in 1994, governed the world's largest free-trade zone. Yet heated debate in the United States over illegal immigration across the Mexican border, as well anti-Hispanic prejudice, limited popular enthusiasm for the agreement. The third largest free-trade zone, Mercosur, created by Argentina, Brazil, Paraguay (now suspended), and Uruguay in 1991 and subsequently expanded to include Venezuela and Bolivia,, visualized a parliament consisting of eighteen representatives from each member state. Other free-trade associations operated in West Africa, southern Africa, Southeast Asia, Central America, the Pacific Basin, and the Caribbean.

Palm Island, Dubai
The seemingly unlimited wealth of the oil-producing states of the Persian Gulf spurred ambitious development plans like this one in Dubai, one of the United Arab Emirates. Its publicists proclaimed that "Palm Island" would include 2,000 villas, up to 40 luxury hotels, shopping complexes, cinemas, and the Middle East's "first marine park" and would be "visible from the moon."

Jorge Ferrari/epa/Corbis Sygma

The Shanghai Cooperation Organization (SCO), formed in 2001 with China, Russia, and four former Soviet Central Asian republics as members, originally pursued common security interests, such as combating separatist movements and terrorism. But the organization's five observer members—Iran, India, Pakistan, Afghanistan, and Mongolia—the first a major oil exporter and the last two possessing huge unexploited mineral deposits, also lent credence to its twenty-year-plan for reducing barriers to trade and population movement. Iran's application for membership, formally made in 2008, has been held up by international pressure. U.S.-led international sanctions designed to curb Iran's nuclear program have encountered resistance from both Russia and China, but the SCO has a rule barring countries subjected to sanctions from membership.

World Trade Organization (WTO) An international body established in 1995 to foster and bring order to international trade.

In 1995 the world's major traders established the **World Trade Organization (WTO)**, dedicated to reducing barriers and enforcing international agreements. With the accession of Russia as its 157th member in 2012, the largest economy not to be included was Iran. The WTO had many critics and regularly encountered street protests during its ministerial meetings. Some protesters claimed that the organization's idea of free trade enabled low-cost foreign manufacturers to attract business and shrink the job opportunities in richer states; others demanded continuing tariff protection for local farmers.

Global Financial Crisis

The global financial crisis that began in 2008 had complicated roots. During an Asian financial crisis a decade earlier, vast amounts of European and American investment in Thailand, Indonesia, South Korea, and other East Asian countries had created an illusion of great economic dynamism. However, in 1997 the investment boom burst, leading to a severe economic downturn in the region. When economic stability returned, greater investor caution reversed the flow of money. The United States in particular became a favorite place to invest, helping spur a rapid increase in stock market and housing prices and massive growth in the purchase of imported goods. Seeing the value their houses increase at an unprecedented rate, Americans became wedded to borrowing money with their homes as collateral. Money from overseas invested in the U.S. treasury also made it possible for the United States to fight wars in Afghanistan and Iraq (see below) while lowering taxes. The American national debt climbed dramatically.

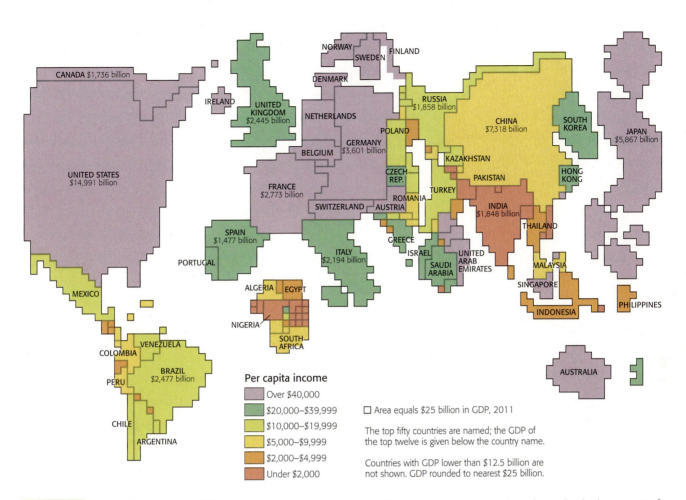

MAP 33.1 **Global Distribution of Wealth** Early industrialization and efficient investment contributed to individual prosperity for the citizens of Japan and Western countries by the 1990s. However, economic dynamism in late-industrializing countries like China and India began to change the world balance of economic power in the early twenty-first century. In nearly all countries the distribution of wealth among individuals varies tremendously, with the gap between rich and poor generally increasing. © Cengage Learning

In 2008 the fevered boom in housing prices collapsed, leaving many homeowners so deeply in debt on their mortgages that they lost their homes. Their mortgage debts, however, were no longer being held by a local bank in the traditional fashion. New and risky lending techniques based on homeowners' assumptions that home prices would continue to rise indefinitely had caused the bad debts to be distributed throughout the banking system, not just in the United States but around the world. Similar housing speculation occurred in Spain and other countries. When Lehman Brothers, one of the country's foremost financial firms, declared bankruptcy in September, a recession turned into a catastrophic economic downturn. Stock prices fell, banks teetered on the brink of collapse, and unemployment climbed as employers laid off workers they could no longer afford or did not need as consumer demand plummeted. The effects spread worldwide. Knowledgeable political leaders and economists proclaimed it the worst economic crisis since the Great Depression of the 1930s.

The sense that Barack Obama had a firm understanding of the crisis and the ability to lead the country out of it contributed to his election as president. During the first weeks after he took office in January 2009, he proposed a series of steps, including massive increases in government spending, to jolt the economy back to health. Some of the plans yielded fruit, such as a rescue of the American automobile industry. Others were stymied after 2010, however, when Republicans who felt national debt and government budget deficits were more important than unemployment took over the House of Representatives. The legislative deadlock that ensued curbed administration plans to address unemployment through increased government spending, but Republican sponsorship of tax and governmental budget cuts failed to attract enough voters to

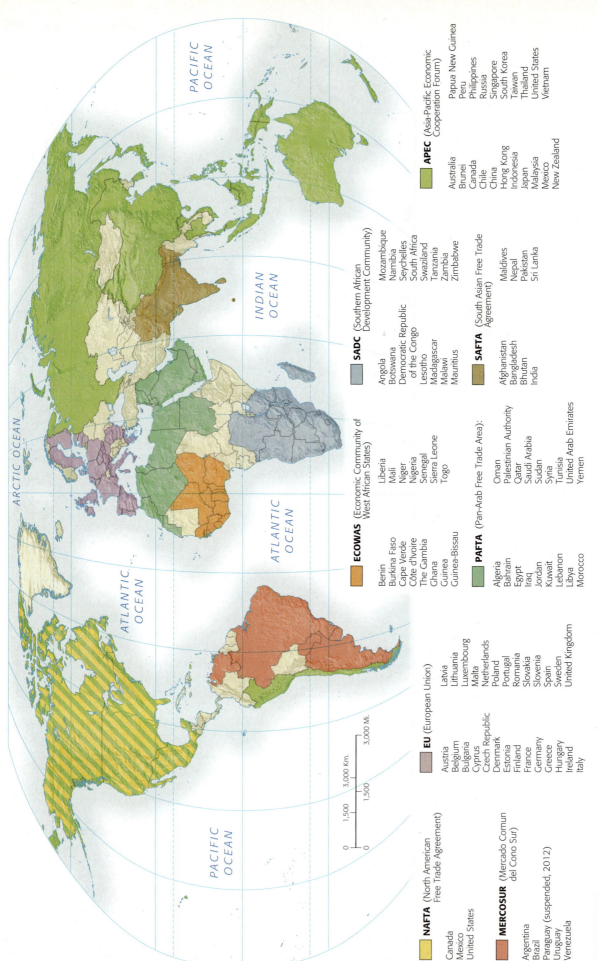

MAP 33.2 **Regional Trade Associations, 2004** International trade and development are major concerns of governments in developed and developing countries. NAFTA, Mercosur, and the EU are free-trade areas. The other associations promote trade and development. © Cengage Learning

PACIFIC OCEAN

INDIAN OCEAN

ARCTIC OCEAN

ATLANTIC OCEAN

ATLANTIC OCEAN

PACIFIC OCEAN

NAFTA (North American Free Trade Agreement)

Canada
Mexico
United States

MERCOSUR (Mercado Comun del Cono Sur)

Argentina
Brazil
Paraguay (suspended, 2012)
Uruguay
Venezuela

EU (European Union)

Austria
Belgium
Bulgaria
Cyprus
Czech Republic
Denmark
Estonia
Finland
France
Germany
Greece
Hungary
Ireland
Italy

Latvia
Lithuania
Luxembourg
Malta
Netherlands
Poland
Portugal
Romania
Slovakia
Slovenia
Spain
Sweden
United Kingdom

ECOWAS (Economic Community of West African States)

Benin
Burkina Faso
Cape Verde
Côte d'Ivoire
The Gambia
Ghana
Guinea-Bissau

Liberia
Mali
Niger
Nigeria
Senegal
Sierra Leone
Togo

PAFTA (Pan-Arab Free Trade Area):

Algeria
Bahrain
Egypt
Iraq
Jordan
Kuwait
Lebanon
Libya
Morocco

Oman
Palestinian Authority
Qatar
Saudi Arabia
Sudan
Syria
Tunisia
United Arab Emirates
Yemen

SADC (Southern African Development Community)

Angola
Botswana
Democratic Republic of the Congo
Lesotho
Madagascar
Malawi
Mauritius

Mozambique
Namibia
Seychelles
South Africa
Swaziland
Tanzania
Zambia
Zimbabwe

SAFTA (South Asian Free Trade Agreement)

Afghanistan
Bangladesh
Bhutan
India

Maldives
Nepal
Pakistan
Sri Lanka

APEC (Asia-Pacific Economic Cooperation Forum)

Australia
Brunei
Canada
Chile
China
Hong Kong
Indonesia
Japan
Malaysia
Mexico
New Zealand

Papua New Guinea
Peru
Philippines
Russia
Singapore
South Korea
Taiwan
Thailand
United States
Vietnam

0   1,500   3,000 Km.

0   1,500   3,000 Mi.

Unemployment Protest
Recovery from the job losses of the economic recession of 2008 proved particularly slow. In the United States, banks and businesses returned to profitability but found they did not need so many workers. In Spain, Greece, and other parts of Europe, the unemployment rate was triple that of the United States in 2013, sometimes fueling the growth of radical and anti-immigrant political movements.

prevent Barack Obama from being reelected in 2012. Economic recovery remained slow and fragile. In both the United States and the European Union, the trade expansion that had signaled the promise of globalization at the beginning of the century faded from memory, and the interdependence that had bound the world's economies in a cycle of growth became a dead weight that dragged many countries down.

Globalization and Democracy

The last decades of the twentieth century saw expansions of democratic institutions and personal freedom. People in many countries recognized that elections offered a peaceful way to settle differences among a country's social classes, cultural groups, and regions. Although majority votes could swing from one part of the political spectrum to another, democracies tended to encourage political moderation. Moreover, wars between fully democratic states were extremely rare.

The nations of eastern Europe embraced democracy after the fall of the Soviet Union, though some newly democratic states became subject to great mood swings among the electorate. The shift to private ownership of businesses after decades of rigid state control brought riches to a select few, and the removal of trade barriers characteristic of Cold War rivalry opened up new markets and fostered investment from the West.

By 2008, however, rising unemployment and falling export levels and stock prices threatened these experiments in free elections and free markets. In Russia, the popular but somewhat authoritarian leader Vladimir Putin followed his country's constitution by stepping down in 2008 after two terms as president. However, he engineered the election of his protégé Dimitri Medvedev as his successor, took the office of prime minister for himself, and then was elected to a new presidential term in 2012. These moves led some political thinkers to fear a possible return to Soviet-era Russian domination.

Asian democracies proved somewhat more stable. Beginning with free parliamentary elections in 1999, the populous state of Indonesia moved from years of authoritarian and corrupt rule toward more open political institutions. The following years saw a violent independence movement of the Acheh (ah-CHEH) district of northern Sumatra, the secession in 2002 of East Timor after years of brutal Indonesian military occupation, terrorist bombings on the island of Bali in 2004, and a devastating earthquake and tsunami in the same year. But democratic elections were regularly held. The losing candidates left office peacefully, and the populace at large accepted the results.

Myanmar (formerly Burma), where stifling military governments had held sway since 1962, experienced a rapid move toward democracy after free elections were held in 2010. The following year the military junta was dissolved, and the formerly banned opposition party led by the female Nobel Peace Prize winner Aung San Suu Kyi **(owng SAHN soo chi)** gained a significant role in parliament.

In India a major political shift seemed to be at hand in 1998 when the Bharatiya Janata Party (BJP) secured an electoral victory that interrupted four decades of Congress Party rule. The BJP success came through blatant appeals to Hindu nationalism, the condoning of violence against India's Muslims, and opposition to the social and economic progress of the Untouchables (those traditionally confined to the dirtiest jobs). In 2004, however, the Congress Party returned to power and governmental stability proved strong even in the face of sensational terrorist attacks in Mumbai by Pakistani gunmen in 2008.

Democracy in Pakistan itself proved more uncertain. President and former military commander Pervez Musharraf's **(pair-VEZ moo-SHAH-ref)** abrupt firing of the country's chief justice, combined with his unpopular support of the Bush administration's war policies, sparked protests and calls for impeachment. He resigned the presidency in 2008. Asif Ali Zardari **(AH-sef AH-lee zar-DAH-ree)**, who succeeded him, had inherited the leadership of the majority Pakistan People's Party after the assassination the year before of his charismatic wife Benazir Bhutto, the daughter of a popular earlier prime minister. Zardari faced difficulties forming a strong government because of the growing movement of the Pakistani Taliban to impose their own governance and a rigid Muslim behavioral code in outlying districts, as well as popular opposition to American antiterrorist attacks launched from Afghanistan. In 2013 he was succeeded by his long-time rival Nawaz Sharif.

In sub-Saharan Africa, democracy had mixed results. Nelson Mandela, the leader of the African National Congress (ANC) who had become the first post-apartheid president of South Africa in 1994 (see Chapters 31 and 32), left office in 1999 and was succeeded by the deputy president and ANC leader Thabo Mbeki **(TAA-boh um-BEH-kee)**. Mbeki stepped down in 2008 amidst turmoil in the leadership of the ANC. But the democratic system did not seem threatened. Elsewhere some elected leaders, such as Robert Mugabe **(moo-GAH-bay)** in Zimbabwe, used violence and intimidation to hold on to power, and other states, such as Congo, were plagued with internal revolts and civil wars. Liberians emerged from fourteen years of civil war in 2003 and two years later chose Ellen Johnson-Sirleaf **(SUHR-leef)** to be Africa's first elected female head of state. In Sudan, the general who had led a military coup in 1989, Omar al-Bashir, became the first sitting head of state to be charged with genocide and crimes against humanity by the International Criminal Court in 2009. A festering conflict in Darfur in western Sudan, which had then cost hundreds of thousands of lives and displaced over 2 million people, was at the heart of the charges. However, a long rebellion in the south finally came to an end in 2011 with the creation of a new country with a democratic constitution, the Republic of South Sudan.

In the Arab world, a rash of popular demonstrations starting at the end of 2010 led to the "Arab Spring," an anti-authoritarian political current that toppled the rulers of Tunisia, Libya, Egypt, and Yemen and plunged Syria into a grinding civil war. Though not the instigators of the demonstrations, previously suppressed Muslim political parties like Egypt's Muslim Brotherhood emerged as the best-organized contenders as shaky democratic regimes struggled into being.

Regime Change in Iraq and Afghanistan

The most closely watched experiments in democratization took place in Iraq and Afghanistan, countries that the United States invaded after the terrorist attacks of 9/11. Afghanistan's provision of a safe haven for Usama bin Laden and his al-Qaeda organization gave clear justification for the overthrow in December 2001 of the militantly religious Taliban regime. However, the rationale for invading Iraq was less persuasive. Leading up to the war the American government contended that Iraq was a clear and present danger to the United States because it possessed **weapons of mass destruction** (WMDs): nuclear, chemical, and biological weapons that it might supply to terrorists like bin Laden.

When United Nations inspectors failed to find any banned weapons, a split widened between those nations wanting to continue inspections and those, led by the United States, wanting to intervene militarily. Deciding to go it alone, an American-led "coalition of the willing" opened

weapons of mass destruction Nuclear, chemical, and biological devices that are capable of injuring and killing large numbers of people.

Arab Spring Demonstrators
Part of the enormous crowds that unseated the rulers of Egypt, Tunisia, Libya, and Yemen, these women in Cairo's Tahrir Square wear the colorful head scarves that are commonplace in Egypt, sometimes to demonstrate allegiance to Islam and sometimes because they are stylish.

AP Photos/Khalil Hamra

the invasion of Iraq with a spectacular aerial bombardment of Baghdad on March 20, 2003. Twenty-five days later the United States declared that "major fighting" had ended, little realizing that guerrilla insurgency, sectarian violence, and economic devastation would continue for years.

Though Iraq fell into a state of turmoil because the coalition army was too small or otherwise unprepared to prevent the looting and destruction of government facilities and other lawlessness, a thorough search was launched for WMDs. The search came up empty, and intelligence analyses failed to uncover any evidence that Saddam Husain, Iraq's fallen dictator, had played a role in the 9/11 attacks. American troops finally withdrew from the country in 2010, leaving behind a government elected under a new constitution adopted in 2006 but nevertheless divided by strong animosity between a Shi'ite majority and separate Arab and Kurdish Sunni minorities.

American concern for WMDs was not confined to Iraq. North Korea had an open program to build nuclear weapons, and Iran was suspected of having a covert plan based in part on technological aid secretly given by the head of Pakistan's successful nuclear program. Iran's outspokenly anti-American and anti-Israeli president, Mahmoud Ahmedinejad, who served from 2005 to 2013, and North Korea's dictator Kim Jong-il **(kim jong-ill)** presented the United States with difficult challenges. But the military invasion option chosen for Iraq, though favored by some Bush advisers, was held in abeyance in favor of diplomatic initiatives that continued into Obama's second term in office.

Iran's challenge to America's hopes for a democratic reshaping of the Middle East took a step forward in 2005 when the Lebanese Shi'ite movement Hezbollah captured 23 out of 128 seats in the Lebanese parliament; then in 2006 the militantly anti-Israeli Hamas movement won an absolute majority of the vote in elections for the Palestine Governing Authority. Both groups were firmly allied with Iran. Attacks launched by Israel against both Hamas and Hezbollah in response to kidnappings of Israeli soldiers in 2006 suggested that Israeli fear of Islamic movements, and of Iran, might someday become more consequential than Arab world democratization, particularly if Iran should acquire a nuclear weapon.

In 2007 the elected Hamas government succeeded in driving its Palestinian rivals out of the Gaza Strip. During the following months, largely inaccurate rocket barrages launched from there against Israel became a major factor in Israeli politics. A security barrier built on the West Bank had almost eliminated attacks by Palestinian suicide bombers, but the rockets provoked public outrage even though the number of casualties was very small. During the final month of the manifestly pro-Israeli Bush administration, the Israel Defense Force undertook to deal once and for all with Hamas in the Gaza Strip. Aerial bombardments and ground force incursions left well over a thousand Palestinians dead, while Israeli casualties were negligible. However,

SECTION REVIEW

- Since the Cold War, global political relations have been defined largely by economic interconnections.

- To manage economic change, many nations have joined a variety of trade organizations, and free-trade policies have caused widespread controversy.

- Global interdependence and rapid economic expansion and speculation led to a global financial crisis in 2008 that plunged the world into the worst economic slowdown since the Great Depression of the 1930s.

- There has been a general worldwide trend toward democracy, especially in Asian countries.

- However, U.S. intervention in Iraq and Afghanistan has shown that the promotion of democracy by military force is very difficult, and in the Middle East the Israeli-Palestinian deadlock and the challenge of Iran stand in the way of fundamental political change.

there was no sign that Hamas had been seriously harmed as a political organization. Indeed, in 2012 a renewed exchange of Hamas rockets and Israeli air strikes showed the persistence of the stalemate in Gaza. Worldwide reactions to these events engendered sufficient criticism of Israel that a resolution in the United Nations General Assembly to grant the Palestinian Governing Authority enhanced observer status saw only one major nation, Canada, vote no along with the United States and Israel.

American hopes for democratization also were disappointed in Afghanistan. The Afghan government elected with enthusiastic American support in 2004 proved corrupt and uncooperative and did not extend over the entire country. By 2008 the Taliban were again a serious threat, and opium production, the key to the country's unrest, was higher than ever. Though the United States was able to enlist the participation of NATO forces in helping to police Afghanistan, the prospects for the country were so dim that President Barack Obama made intensification of efforts to bring peace and stability and suppress terrorism a key part of his foreign policy while at the same time promising to withdraw American troops by the end of 2014.

THE QUESTION OF VALUES

As people around the world first faced the opportunities of globalization and then the fear of global recession, they tried to make sense of these changes in terms of their own value systems. With 7 billion people, the world was big enough to include many different approaches, whether religious or secular, local or international, traditional or visionary. In some cases, however, conflicting visions fed violence.

Faith and Politics

Religious beliefs increasingly inspired political actions during the second half of the twentieth century, and the trend intensified in the new century (see Map 33.3). Though for Americans this change reversed two centuries of growing secularism, Western analysts did not agree on the cause of the religious revival.

Evangelical Protestants became a powerful conservative political force in the United States, particularly during the Bush presidency. Around the world, Catholic conservatives led by Pope John Paul II, Pope Benedict XVI, and Pope Francis who succeeded to the post in 2013 after Benedict's retirement, forcefully reiterated politically sensitive teachings: opposition to abortion, homosexuality, marriage of priests, and admission of women to the priesthood. In Israel, hyperorthodox Jews known as *haredim* played a leading role in settling the Palestinian territories captured by Israel in 1967 and vehemently resisted both Israel's unilateral withdrawal from Gaza in 2005 and subsequent plans for withdrawal from the West Bank. And in India, Hindu zealots made the BJP party a powerful political force (see above).

Yet most discussions of faith and politics focused on Islam (see Diversity and Dominance: Conflict and Civilization). The birth of the Islamic Republic of Iran in the revolution of 1979 made visible a current of Muslim political assertiveness that had been building there for twenty-five years. By the year 2000, however, non-Iranian Muslim groups claiming to be acting for religious reasons were capturing the headlines with acts of **terrorism**.

Terrorism is a political tactic by which comparatively weak militants use grotesquely inhumane and lethal acts to convince a frightened public that danger is everywhere and their government is incapable of protecting them. Although terrorism has a long history, the instantaneous media links made possible by satellite communications, and the tradition in the news business of publicizing violence, increased its effectiveness from the 1980s onward.

terrorism Political belief that extreme and seemingly random violence will destabilize a government and permit the terrorists to gain political advantage. Though an old technique, terrorism gained prominence in the late twentieth century with the growth of worldwide mass media that, through their news coverage, amplified public fears of terrorist acts.

Bombings, kidnappings, and assassinations made political sense to all sorts of political groups: secular Palestinians confronting Israel; national separatists like the Tamils in Sri Lanka, Basques in Spain, and Chechens in Russia; and Catholic and Protestant extremists in Northern Ireland, to name a few. But Muslim groups gained the lion's share of attention when they targeted the United States and Europe, recruited from Muslim populations all over the world, and made effective use of news coverage and audiovisual communications.

Their media star and ideological spokesman was **Usama bin Laden**. Born into a wealthy Saudi family and educated as an engineer, bin Laden fought against the Soviet Union in Afghanistan and there recruited and trained a core group of fighters called al-Qaeda. Though his family disowned him and Saudi Arabia stripped him of his citizenship, his calls for holy war (*jihad*) and his portrayal of the United States as a puppet-master manipulating both non-Muslim (e.g., Israel, India, Russia) and Muslim (e.g., Egypt, Algeria, Saudi Arabia) governments to murder and oppress innocent Muslims made sense to millions of Muslims, even if only a very few committed themselves to follow him into battle.

Al-Qaeda blew up American embassies in Kenya and Tanzania in 1998, crippled the U.S. Navy destroyer *Cole* during a port call in Yemen in 2000, and then capped everything by attacking the World Trade Center and the Pentagon on 9/11. When the "global war on terrorism" declared by President Bush failed to eliminate bin Laden, his mystique grew. Further terrorist attacks—by Indonesians on tourists on the island of Bali in 2002, by North Africans on commuter trains servicing Madrid in 2004, by English-born Muslims on the London transit system in 2005, and by Pakistanis on luxury hotels in Mumbai, India, in 2008—made it clear that the current of violence unleashed by al-Qaeda had become decentralized and that recruits and cells might no longer be taking orders from bin Laden. Even after an American commando operation killed bin Laden in his hideout in Pakistan in 2011, groups affiliated with al-Qaeda continued to operate in Yemen, Libya, and Mali. In response, the United States expanded its use of pilotless drone aircraft to kill suspected terrorists from afar.

In trying to explain a current of violence that could strike anywhere in the world but seemed to be centered on Muslims, some analysts argued that Islam itself encouraged violence against non-Muslims. The counterargument pointed out that terrorists came from many backgrounds and that the vast majority of Muslims saw their religion as one of peace. Others maintained that rigidly conservative Muslims were blindly opposed to freedom and modernity. The counterargument pointed out that al-Qaeda used modern military and propaganda techniques and that many of its operatives, like bin Laden himself, graduated from modern technical programs. A third school of thought felt that the United States instigated al-Qaeda's wrath by supporting Israel and stationing troops in Saudi Arabia. The counterargument pointed out that the United States had also championed the Muslim cause in Bosnia, driven the secular dictator Saddam Husain out of Kuwait, and supported the popular uprisings of the Arab Spring.

Usama bin Laden Saudi-born Muslim extremist who funded the al-Qaeda organization that was responsible for several terrorist attacks, including those on the World Trade Center and the Pentagon in 2001.

Universal Rights and Values

Alongside the growing influence of religion on politics, efforts to promote adherence to universal human rights also expanded. The modern human rights movement grew out of secular statements like the French Declaration of the Rights of Man (1789) and the U.S. Constitution (1788) and Bill of Rights (1791). The **Universal Declaration of Human Rights**, passed by the United Nations General Assembly in 1948, culminated this movement by proclaiming itself "a common standard of achievement for all peoples and nations." Its thirty articles condemned slavery, torture, cruel and inhuman punishment, and arbitrary arrest, detention, and exile. The Declaration called for freedom of movement, assembly, and thought. It asserted rights to life, liberty, and security of person; to impartial public trials; and to education, employment, and leisure. The principle of equality was most fully articulated in Article 2:

Universal Declaration of Human Rights A 1948 United Nations covenant binding signatory nations to the observance of specified rights.

> *Everyone is entitled to all the rights and freedoms set forth in this Declaration, without distinction of any kind, such as race, color, sex, language, religion, or political or other opinion, national or social origin, property, birth or other status.[1]*

This passage reflected an international consensus against racism and imperialism and a growing acceptance of the importance of social and economic equality. Most newly independent

---

[1]"Universal Declaration of Human Rights," in *Twenty-five Human Rights Documents* (New York: Center for the Study of Human Rights, Columbia University, 1994), 6.

Conflict and Civilization

In 1993 Samuel P. Huntington, a professor of government at Harvard University, published "The Clash of Civilizations?" in the journal Foreign Affairs. *This article provoked extraordinary debate, particularly after the 9/11 attacks on the World Trade Center and the Pentagon. Some readers deemed it an accurate description of a post–Cold War world in which Islamic countries were destined to conflict violently with the countries of Europe and North America. Others saw it as imprecise in its failure to clarify what a "civilization" is, imperialistic in its unquestioning assumption of Western superiority, and encouraging of anti-Muslim prejudice.*

The interactions between civilizations vary greatly in the extent to which they are likely to be characterized by violence. Economic competition clearly predominates between the American and European subcivilizations of the West and between both of them and Japan. On the Eurasian continent, however, the proliferation of ethnic conflict, epitomized at the extreme in "ethnic cleansing," has not been totally random. It has been most frequent and most violent between groups belonging to different civilizations. In Eurasia the great historic fault lines between civilizations are once more aflame. This is particularly true along the boundaries of the crescent-shaped Islamic bloc of nations from the bulge of Africa to central Asia. Violence also occurs between Muslims, on the one hand, and Orthodox Serbs in the Balkans, Jews in Israel, Hindus in India, Buddhists in Burma and Catholics in the Philippines. Islam has bloody borders.

Rejoinders to Huntington's thesis saw it as a cornerstone of the aggressive policies adopted by the Bush administration after 9/11. As an alternative, they stressed the common values held by peaceful societies and the need for intercultural understanding. Mohammed Khatami, the president of the Islamic Republic of Iran, found support for a more positive framing of the matter when the United Nations, following his proposal, declared 2001 the year of "Dialogue Among Civilizations." Almost simultaneously, the Organization of the Islamic Conference (now called the Organization of Islamic Cooperation), a 57-member international body headquartered in Saudi Arabia and composed of states with large Muslim populations, elaborated upon this concept in the "Tehran Declaration on Dialogue Among Civilizations."

Tehran Declaration on Dialogue Among Civilizations

Praise be to Allah and peace and blessing be upon His prophet and kin and companion.

The representatives of Heads of State and Government of OIC member states . . . [recognizing] the United Nations General Assembly resolution 53/22, designating the year 2001 as the United Nations year of Dialogue among Civilizations;

Guided by the noble Islamic teachings and values [*each of the following principles is accompanied by reference to a verse in the Quran*] on human dignity and equality, tolerance, peace and justice for humankind, and promotion of virtues and proscription of vice and evil;

Drawing upon the Islamic principles of celebration of human diversity, recognition of diversified sources of knowledge, promotion of dialogue and mutual understanding, genuine mutual respect in human interchanges, and encouragement of courteous and civilized discourse based on reason and logic;

Reaffirming the commitment of their Governments to promote dialogue and understanding among various cultures and civilizations, aimed at reaching a global consensus to build a new order for the next millennium founded in faith as well as common moral and ethical values of contemporary civilizations;

Requests the Secretary-General of the OIC to submit this declaration for endorsement to the Chairman of the Eighth Islamic Summit and the 26th Islamic Conference of Foreign Ministers for appropriate action:

A) General principles of dialogue among civilizations

1. Respect for the dignity and equality of all human beings without distinctions of any kind and of nations large and small;
2. Genuine acceptance of cultural diversity as a permanent [quality] of human society and a cherished asset for the advancement and welfare of humanity at large;
3. Mutual respect and tolerance for the views and values of various cultures and civilizations, as well as the right of members of all civilizations to preserve their cultural heritage and values, and rejection of desecration of moral, religious or cultural values, sanctities and sanctuaries;
4. Recognition of diversified sources of knowledge throughout time and space, and the imperative of drawing upon the areas of strengths, richness and wisdom of each civilization in a genuine process of mutual enrichment;
5. Rejection of attempts for cultural domination and imposition as well as doctrines and practices promoting confrontation and clash between civilizations;
6. Search for common grounds between and within various civilizations in order to face common global challenges;

Acceptance of cooperation and search for understanding as the appropriate mechanism for the promotion of common universal values as well as for the suppression of global threats;

7. Commitment to participation of all peoples and nations, without any discrimination, in their own domestic as well as global decision-making and value distribution processes;

8. Compliance with principles of justice, equity, peace and solidarity as well as fundamental principles of international law and the United Nations Charter. . . .

A few years later, a joint proposal by the governments of Spain and Turkey received a similar endorsement by the United Nations. This led to the creation of the Alliance of Civilizations. The underlying principles of this organization were expressed in the 2006 report of its "High-Level Group," a body of eminent political, intellectual, and spiritual figures from around the world.

Alliance of Civilizations Report of the High-Level Group

I. Bridging the World's Divides

1.1 Our world is alarmingly out of balance. For many, the last century brought unprecedented progress, prosperity, and freedom. For others, it marked an era of subjugation, humiliation and dispossession. Ours is a world of great inequalities and paradoxes: a world where the income of the planet's three richest people is greater than the combined income of the world's least developed countries; where modern medicine performs daily miracles and yet 3 million people die every year of preventable diseases; where we know more about distant universes than ever before, yet 130 million children have no access to education; where despite the existence of multilateral covenants and institutions, the international community often seems helpless in the face of conflict and genocide. For most of humanity, freedom from want and freedom from fear appear as elusive as ever.

1.2 We also live in an increasingly complex world, where polarized perceptions, fueled by injustice and inequality, often lead to violence and conflict, threatening international stability. Over the past few years, wars, occupation and acts of terror have exacerbated mutual suspicion and fear within and among societies. Some political leaders and sectors of the media, as well as radical groups have exploited this environment, painting mirror images of a world made up of mutually exclusive cultures, religions, or civilizations, historically distinct and destined for confrontation.

1.3 The anxiety and confusion caused by the "clash of civilizations" theory regrettably has distorted the terms of the discourse on the real nature of the predicament the world is facing. The history of relations between cultures is not only one of wars and confrontation. It is also based on centuries of constructive exchanges, cross-fertilization, and peaceful coexistence. Moreover, classifying internally fluid and diverse societies along hard-and-fast lines of civilizations interferes with more illuminating ways of understanding questions of identity, motivation and behavior. Rifts between the powerful and the powerless or the rich and the poor or between different political groups, classes, occupations and nationalities have greater explanatory power than such cultural categories. Indeed, the latter stereotypes only serve to entrench already polarized opinions. Worse, by promoting the misguided view that cultures are set on an unavoidable collision course, they help turn negotiable disputes into seemingly intractable identity-based conflicts that take hold of the popular imagination. It is essential, therefore, to counter the stereotypes and misconceptions that deepen patterns of hostility and mistrust among societies.

QUESTIONS FOR ANALYSIS

1. How important are culture and religion, as opposed to governing ideology or economic inequality, in explaining current world conflicts?

2. Can idealistic statements by governments be effective in curbing acts of violence carried out by individual zealots or terrorist groups?

3. Should general statements about culture play a role at the level of personal relations in the neighborhood, the workplace, or the classroom?

Sources: Samuel P. Huntington, "The Clash of Civilizations?," *Foreign Affairs* 72, no. 3 (Summer 1993). "The Tehran Declaration on Dialogue Among Civilizations," Organization of the Islamic Conference, *www.isesco.org.ma/english/publications/dig/CH11.php*; "High-Level Group Report," Alliance of Civilizations, available online at *www.unaoc.org/content/view/64/94/lang,english/*.

Majority religion
- Christian
- Muslim
- Unaffiliated
- Hindu
- Buddhist
- Folk religions
- Judaism
- No majority

Minority religion (20% or more)

0 1,000 2,000 Km.
0 1,000 2,000 Mi.

MAP 33.3 **World Religions** The distribution of Buddhism, Christianity, and Islam reflects centuries of missionary efforts. Hinduism and Judaism have expanded primarily through trade and migration. Chinese governments have actively curtailed religious practice. As religion revives as a source of social identity or a rationale for political assertion or mass mobilization, the possibility of religious activism across broad geographic regions becomes greater, as does the likelihood of domestic discord in multireligious states. (Data from Pew Research Center, "The Global Religious Landscape." © 2012, http://www.pewforum.org/global-religious-landscape.aspx) © Cengage Learning

Notes:
1. Israel: the majority of the population is Jewish
2. Tibet: the majority of the population is Buddhist
3. Chinese province of Xinjiang: the majority of the population is Muslim
4. Indonesian island of Bali: the majority of the population is Hindu
5. Europe: 18% of the population is Unaffiliated
6. India: has the second-largest Muslim population in the world, at 176,190,000

Number of Adherents, 2010 (in millions)

Religion	Adherents
Christians	2,173,180,000
Muslims	1,598,510,000
Unaffiliated	1,126,500,000
Hindus	1,033,080,000
Buddhists	487,540,000
Folk religionists	405,120,000
Jews	13,850,000
Other religions	58,110,000

Captured Somali Pirates   The anarchic conditions and intermittent civil war that have plagued the East African state of Somalia since 1991 gave rise to a wave of piracy in the western Indian Ocean. Pirates in small boats seized merchant ships and held them and their crews to ransom. Naval actions by various governments lessened the threat, but political instability and poverty frustrated efforts to eradicate it.

nongovernmental organizations (NGOs) Nonprofit international organizations devoted to investigating human rights abuses and providing humanitarian relief. Two NGOs won the Nobel Peace Prize in the 1990s: International Campaign to Ban Landmines (1997) and Doctors Without Borders (1999).

countries joining the United Nations willingly signed the Declaration because it implicitly condemned European colonial regimes.

Besides the official actions of the United Nations and various national governments, individual human rights activists, often working through philanthropic bodies known as **nongovernmental organizations (NGOs)**, have been important forces promoting human rights. Amnesty International, founded in 1961, concentrates on gaining the freedom of people who have been tortured or imprisoned without trial and campaigns against summary execution by government death squads or other gross violations of rights. Arguing that no right is more fundamental than the right to life, other NGOs have devoted themselves to famine relief, refugee assistance, and health care around the world. Médecins Sans Frontières (Doctors Without Borders), founded in 1971, was awarded the Nobel Peace Prize in 1999 for offering medical assistance in scores of crises.

While NGOs often worked in specific countries, other universal goals became enshrined in international agreements. Such agreements made genocide a crime and promoted environmental protection of the seas, of Antarctica, and of the atmosphere (see Environment and Technology: Global Warming). The United States and a few other nations were greatly concerned that such treaties would limit their sovereignty or threaten their national interests. For this reason the U.S. Congress delayed ratifying the 1949 convention on genocide until 1986. More recently the United States drew widespread criticism for demanding exemption for Americans from the

Global Warming

Until the 1980s environmental alarms focused mainly on localized episodes of air and water pollution, exposure to toxic substances, waste management, and the disappearance of wilderness. The development of increasingly powerful computers and complex models of ecological interactions in the 1990s, however, made people aware of the global scope of certain environmental problems.

Many scientists and policymakers came to perceive global warming, the slow increase of the temperature of the earth's lower atmosphere, as an environmental threat requiring preventive action on an international scale. The warming is caused by a layer of atmospheric gases (carbon dioxide, methane, nitrous oxide, and ozone) that allow solar radiation to reach earth and warm it but that keep infrared energy (heat) from radiating from earth's surface back into space. Called the *greenhouse effect*, this process normally keeps the earth's temperature at a level suitable for life. However, increases in greenhouse-gas emissions—particularly from the burning of fossil fuels in industry and transportation—have added to this insulating atmospheric layer.

Recent events have confirmed predictions of global temperature increases and melting glaciers and icecaps. Greenland glaciers and Arctic Ocean sea ice are melting at record rates, and huge sections of the Antarctic ice shelf are breaking off and floating away. Andean glaciers are shrinking so fast they could disappear in a decade, imperiling water supplies for drinking, irrigation, and hydroelectric production. Drought has affected much of the United States in recent years, and Australia has experienced the "Big Dry," its worst drought in a century.

Despite this evidence, governments of the industrialized countries that produce the most greenhouse gasses have been slow to adopt measures stringent enough to reduce emissions. They cite the negative effects they believe this could have on their economies. Because of these fears, many nations hesitated to sign the 1997 Kyoto Protocol, the first international agreement to impose penalties on countries that failed to cut greenhouse-gas emissions. It was a major environmental victory when Japan added its signature in March 2001, but to the consternation of many world leaders President George W. Bush rejected the agreement.

Shortly after being elected in 2008, Barack Obama announced to an audience of scientists and citizens concerned with climate matters: "You can be sure that the United States will once again engage vigorously in these negotiations, and help lead the world toward a new era of global cooperation on climate change." Yet when he ran for reelection in 2012, the issue of global warming, which his Republican opponents denied was a real phenomenon, played no role in his campaign. Ironically, a tropical superstorm named Sandy that dealt a devastating blow to New York and New Jersey just before the election seemed to vindicate the prediction that the increased energy in the atmosphere caused by global warming would produce severe weather anomalies around the world.

Flooding in Bangladesh Typhoon-driven floods submerge the low-lying farmlands of Bangladesh with tragic regularity. Any significant rise in the sea level will make parts of the country nearly uninhabitable.

David Greedy/Getty Images

jurisdiction of the International Criminal Court, created in 2002 to try international criminals, and for declaring that "enemy combatants" taken prisoner during the "global war on terrorism" should not be treated in accordance with the Third Geneva Convention (1950) on humane treatment of prisoners of war.

AP Photo/Anat Givon

Beijing Women's Conference in 1995   This gathering of women from every part of the world, under United Nations auspices, illustrated the challenges posed by women's search for equality. The Chinese government, consistent with its policies of suppressing dissent and closely regulating social life, tried to limit press access to the conference. As in many other instances, these efforts to silence or control women's voices on issues like abortion and family planning proved ineffective. The "peace torch" had been carried to Beijing from Africa.

Women's Rights

The women's rights movement, which began on both sides of the North Atlantic in the nineteenth century, became an important human rights issue in the twentieth century. Rights for women became accepted in Western countries and were enshrined in the constitutions of many nations newly freed from colonial rule. In 1979 the United Nations General Assembly adopted the Convention on the Elimination of All Forms of Discrimination Against Women, and in 1985 the first international conference on the status of women, sponsored by the United Nations Division for the Advancement of Women, was held in Nairobi, Kenya. A second conference in Beijing ten years later added momentum to the movement. By 2012, all but seven UN member countries—Iran, Palau, Somalia, Sudan, South Sudan, Tonga, and the United States—had ratified the convention, though the United States and Palau had signed it without ratification.

Besides highlighting the problems women face around the world, international conferences have also revealed great variety in the views and concerns of women. Feminists from the West, who had been accustomed to dictating the agenda and who had pushed for the liberation of women in other parts of the world, sometimes found themselves accused of having narrow concerns and condescending attitudes. Some non-Western women complained about Western feminists' endorsement of sexual liberation and about the deterioration of family life in the West. They found Western feminists' concern with matters such as comfortable clothing misplaced and trivial compared to the issues of poverty and disease.

SECTION REVIEW

- The second half of the twentieth century has seen an increase in political action inspired by religious belief.

- Militant Islam has risen in response to authoritarian oppression in many Muslim countries and to the claim that the United States supports such authoritarianism.

- Universal standards of human rights have gained wider acceptance and underlie the work of the United Nations, individual states, and NGOs.

- Concepts of human rights have expanded to address genocide and environmental protection.

- Global debates on women's rights have addressed a variety of economic, political, and social problems but have also involved clashes over cultural values.

Other cultures came in for their share of criticism. Western women and many secular leaders in Muslim countries protested Islam's requirement that a woman cover her head and wear loose-fitting garments to conceal the shape of her body, practices enforced by law in countries such as Iran and Saudi Arabia. Nevertheless, many outspoken Muslim women voluntarily donned concealing garments as expressions of personal belief, statements of resistance to secular dictatorship, or defense against coarse male behavior.

The conferences were more important for the attention they focused on women's issues than for the solutions they generated. Such efforts raised the prominence of human rights as a global concern and put pressure on governments to consider human rights when making foreign policy decisions. Skeptics observed, however, that a Western country might successfully prod a non-Western country to improve its human rights performance—for example, by granting women better access to education and careers—but that reverse criticism of a Western country often fell on deaf ears—for example, condemnation of the death penalty in the United States. For such critics the human rights movement was seen not as an effort to make the world more humane but as another form of Western cultural imperialism.

GLOBAL CULTURE

Because of changes in electronic technology, today political and economic events have almost instantaneous impact in all parts of the world. A global language, a global educational system, and global forms of artistic expression have all come into being. Trade, travel, and migration have made a common popular culture unavoidable. These changes have delighted and enriched some but angered others.

The Media and the Message

cultural imperialism Domination of one culture over another by a deliberate policy or by economic or technological superiority.

The fact that the most pervasive elements of global culture have their origins in the West raised concerns in many quarters about **cultural imperialism**. Critics complained that entertainment conglomerates were flooding the world's movie theaters and television screens with Western images and that goods catering to Western tastes but manufactured in countries with low labor costs, like China and Indonesia, were flooding world markets. In this view, global marketing was especially insidious in trying to shape a world with a single Western outlook based on capitalist ideology, and at the same time suppressing or devaluing traditional cultures and alternative ideologies. As the leader of the capitalist world, the United States was seen as the primary culprit.

The pace of cultural globalization began to quicken during the economic recovery after World War II. The Hollywood films and American jazz recordings that had become popular in Europe and parts of Asia before the war (see Chapter 29) continued to spread. But the birth of electronic technology opened contacts with large numbers of people who could never have afforded to go to a movie or buy a record.

The first step was the development of cheap transistor radios that could run on a couple of small batteries. Perfected by American scientists at Bell Telephone Laboratories in 1948, solid-state electronic transistors replaced power-hungry and less reliable glass tubes in radios and other devices. Tube radios, which in some countries required a license to own, had spread worldwide in the decades before the war, but small portable transistor radios reached parts of the world where homes lacked electricity.

Television, made possible by the electron-scanning gun invented in 1928, became widely available to Western consumers in the 1950s. In poorer parts of the world TVs were not common until the 1980s and 1990s, after mass production and cheap transistors made sets more affordable. Outside the United States, television broadcasting was usually a government monopoly at first, following the pattern of telegraph and postal service and radio broadcasting. Governments expected news reports and other programming to disseminate a unified national viewpoint.

However, government monopolies eroded as the high cost of television production opened up global markets for rebroadcasts of American, Indian, and Mexican soap operas and dramas. By the 1990s a global network of satellites brought privately owned television broadcasting to even remote areas of the world, and the VCR (videocassette recorder) provided an even greater variety of programs. In the following decade DVD players continued the trend. As a result of wider circulation of programming, people often became familiar with different dialects of English and other languages. People in Portugal who in the 1960s had found it difficult to understand Brazilian Portuguese became avid fans of Brazilian soap operas. And immigrants from Albania and North Africa often arrived in Italy with a command of Italian learned from Italian stations whose signals they could pick up at home.

CNN (Cable News Network) expanded its international market after becoming the most-viewed and informative news source during the 1991 Persian Gulf War, when it broadcast live from Baghdad. Other 24-hour news broadcasters followed this lead. Some, like CNN and the British Broadcasting Corporation (BBC), reflected the outlook of their home audiences. In response, Al-Jazeera, based in the Persian Gulf emirate of Qatar, broadcast statements by Usama bin Laden from 2001 onward and offered video footage and interpretation that differed greatly from American coverage of the war in Iraq in 2003. It gradually gained a reputation for vivid and generally reliable coverage of news events in the Muslim world.

The Internet, a linkage of academic, government, and business computers developed by the American Department of Defense in the 1960s, began to transform world culture in the early years of the twenty-first century. Personal computers proliferated in the 1980s, and with the establishment of the easy-to-use graphic interface of the World Wide Web in 1994, the number of Internet users skyrocketed. Myriad new companies formed to exploit "e-commerce," the commercial dimension of the Internet, and students were soon spending less time studying conventional books and more exploring the Web for information and entertainment. Blogs, or weblogs, offered a vehicle for anyone in the world to place his or her opinions, experiences, and creative efforts before anyone with access to a computer. Easy access to the Internet took a step forward with the establishment of "social media" sites like Facebook (2004) and Twitter (2006). Initially these were mainly means of keeping in touch with friends, but the Arab Spring of 2011 saw them develop as tools for communication among antiregime protesters.

As had happened so often throughout history, technological developments had unanticipated consequences. Although the new telecommunications and entertainment technologies derived disproportionately from American invention, industry, and cultural creativity, Japan and other East Asian nations took the lead in manufacturing and refining electronic devices. Cellular mobile phones became increasingly used for taking and transmitting pictures and connecting to the Internet. Non-Western countries that had adopted telephones late and had limited networks of copper wire benefited most from the improved communication. In 2012 the United States ranked 114th in per capita cellular phone use, sandwiched between the Congo Republic and the Dominican Republic. Qatar topped the list as the country with the highest per capita use.

The Spread of Pop Culture

For most of history, popular culture consisted of folk tales and highly localized styles of dress, cooking, music, and visual expression. Only the literate few had full access to the riches of a broader "great tradition," such as Confucianism, Islam, or Buddhism. In modern times, government school systems increased literacy rates but also promoted specifically national values and cultural tastes. Prescribed languages of instruction eroded the use and memory of local languages and traditions. In their place there arose **global pop culture**.

global pop culture Popular cultural practices and institutions that have been adopted internationally, such as music, the Internet, television, food, and fashion.

Initially, the content was heavily American. Singer Michael Jackson was almost as well known to the youth of Dar-es-Salaam (Tanzania) and Bangkok (Thailand) as to American fans. Businesses sought out worldwide celebrities like basketball star Michael Jordan and championship golfer Tiger Woods to endorse their products. American television programs, following in the path of American movies, acquired immense followings and inspired local imitations.

But the United States had no monopoly on global pop culture. Rap music showed up in almost every language. Latin American soap operas, *telenovelas*, had a vast following in the Americas, eastern Europe, and elsewhere. Mumbai, India, long the world's largest producer of

Japanese Comic Books After World War II comic magazines emerged as a major form of publication and a distinctive product of culture in Japan. Different series are directed to different age and gender groups. Issued weekly and running to some three hundred pages in black and white, the most popular magazines sell as many copies as do major newsmagazines in the United States.

Eye Ubiquitous/Photoshot

films, made or inspired more films for international audiences, like the 2009 Academy Award–winning *Slumdog Millionaire*. And the martial arts film makers of Hong Kong saw their style flourish in high-budget international spectaculars like director Ang Lee's *Crouching Tiger, Hidden Dragon* (2000) and the *Matrix* trilogy (1999–2003), which relied heavily on Hong Kong fight choreographers.

Emerging Global Elite Culture

While the globalization of popular culture has been criticized, cultural links across national and ethnic boundaries at a more elite level have generated little controversy. The end of the Cold War reopened intellectual and cultural contacts between former adversaries, making possible such things as Russian-American collaboration on space missions and extensive business contacts among former rivals. The English language, modern science, and higher education became the key elements of this **global elite culture**.

global elite culture At the beginning of the twenty-first century, the attitudes and outlook of well-educated, prosperous, Western-oriented people around the world, largely expressed in European languages, especially English.

The emergence of English as the first global language began with the British Empire's introduction of the language to its far-flung colonies. After achieving independence in the wake of World War II, most former colonies chose to continue using English as an official language because it provided national unity and a link to the outside world that local languages could not. Countries that chose instead to make a local language official often found the decision counterproductive. Indian nationalists had pushed for Hindi to be India's official language, but they found that students taught in Hindi were unable to compete internationally because of poor knowledge of English. Sri Lanka, which had made Sinhala its official language in 1956, reversed itself after local reporters revealed in 1989 that prominent officials were sending their children to English-medium private schools.

While similar postcolonial language developments extended the reach of French, Spanish, and other European tongues, the use of English as a second language was greatly stimulated by the importance of the United States in postwar world affairs. After the collapse of Soviet domination, students in eastern Europe flocked to study English instead of Russian. Ninety percent of students in Cambodia (a former French colony) chose to study English, even though a Canadian agency offered a sizable cash bonus if they would study French. In the 1990s China made the study of English as a second language nearly universal from junior high school onwards.

English has become the language of choice for most international academic conferences, business meetings, and diplomatic gatherings. International organizations that provide equal status to many languages, such as the United Nations and the European Union, often conduct

Three Gorges Dam on China's Yangzi River   The world's largest hydroelectric facility, completed in 2012, the dam is also designed to improve river shipping and reduce the danger of flooding. However, 1.3 million people were displaced in its construction and many archaeological sites inundated.   DBA Images/Alamy

informal committee meetings in English. In cities throughout the world, signs and notices are commonly posted in the local language and in English. Writers from Africa and India have received high honors for novels written in English, as have Arab and Caribbean authors for works written in French. Nevertheless, world literature remains highly diverse in form and language.

By contrast, science and technology have become standardized components of global culture. Though imperialism helped spread the Western disciplines of biology, chemistry, and physics around the world, their importance expanded even further after decolonization as students from newly independent nations sought to compete at an international level. Standardization of scientific terms, weights and measures, and computer codes underlay the worldwide expansion of commerce.

The third pillar of global elite culture, along with science and globalized languages, is the university. The structure and curricula of modern universities are nearly indistinguishable around the world, making student experiences similar across national boundaries. Instruction in the pure sciences varies little from place to place. Some doctoral science programs in American universities now enroll mostly students from non-Western countries. Standardization is nearly as common in applied sciences such as engineering and medicine and only slightly less so in the social sciences. Although the humanities preserve greater diversity in subject matter and approach, professors and students around the world pay attention to the latest literary theories and topics of historical interest.

New universities, many of them privately funded, have mushroomed in many parts of the world as young people increasingly strive for learning that will improve their employment opportunities. Some American universities have contributed to this educational expansion by opening branches or research centers in foreign countries.

While university subjects are taught in many languages, instruction in English is spreading rapidly. Because discoveries are often first published in English, advanced students in science, business, and international relations need to know that language to keep up with the latest developments. Many courses in northern European countries have long been offered in English, and elsewhere in Europe courses taught in English have facilitated the EU's efforts to encourage students to study outside their home countries.

Enduring Cultural Diversity

Although protesters regularly denounce the "Americanization" of the world, a closer look suggests that cultural globalization is more complex. Just as English has spread widely as a second language, so global culture is primarily a second culture that dominates some contexts but does not displace other traditions. From this perspective, American music, fast food, and fashions are more likely to add to a society's options than to displace local culture.

Japan might appear to be the most "westernized" country in Asia. Japan was one of the first countries in Asia to adopt and adapt political, educational, military, and even corporate institutions from western Europe and the United States during the late nineteenth and early twentieth centuries. Those institutions promoted what many believed to be traditional Japanese cultural characteristics, such as respect for hierarchy, the importance of the group over the individual, and solid work ethic. Such traits, observers argued, contributed to Japan's rapid economic recovery and global eminence since the end of World War II. While culture may have played some role in Japan's economic success story, structural problems led to the bursting of the economic bubble during the 1990s. Those so-called traditional values were rejected by young people who could no longer find secure employment. Instead of touting business culture, then, the Japanese government promoted Japan's popular culture—graphic novels (manga), anime, and J-pop music—as its unique cultural contribution to the world.

As awareness of the economic impact of Japanese culture and society began to spread, it became apparent that Taiwan and South Korea, along with Singapore and Hong Kong (a British colony before being reunited with China in 1997), were developing dynamic industrial economies of their own. Today India, Brazil, Turkey, and the People's Republic of China are following the same path without forsaking their national tastes and heritages.

This does not mean that the world's cultural diversity is secure. Every decade a number of minority languages cease to be spoken. Televised national ceremonies or performances for tourists may prevent folk customs and costumes from dying out, but they also tend to devitalize rituals that once had many local variations. While a century ago it was possible to recognize the nationality of people from their clothing and grooming, today most urban men dress the same the world over, although women's clothing shows greater variety. As much as one may regret the disappearance or commercialization of some folkways, most anthropologists would agree that change is characteristic of all healthy cultures. What doesn't change risks extinction.

SECTION REVIEW

- The global pervasiveness of Western culture has provoked charges of U.S. cultural imperialism.

- Technology such as radio, television, and the Internet has played a major role in the spread of Western culture since World War II.

- Technology has also contributed to the emergence of a global pop culture that blends a variety of cultural elements from different countries.

- A global elite culture has developed combining the English language, science, and higher education.

- Despite globalizing forces, cultural diversity remains strong, if not completely secure.

KEY TERMS

globalization p. 850
World Trade Organization
  (WTO) p. 852
weapons of mass
  destruction p. 856

terrorism p. 858
Usama bin Laden
  p. 859
Universal Declaration of
  Human Rights p. 859

nongovernmental
  organizations
  (NGOs) p. 863
cultural imperialism
  p. 866

global pop culture p. 867
global elite culture p. 868

SUGGESTED READING

Appadurai, Arjun. *Modernity at Large: Cultural Dimensions of Globalization.* 1996. Treats the interrelationships between high culture and popular culture.

Barber, Benjamin R. *Jihad vs. McWorld: How Globalism and Tribalism Are Reshaping the World.* 1995. A widely read attempt to describe the world at the turn of the millennium.

Bulliet, Richard W. *The Case for Islamo-Christian Civilization.* 2004. Takes issue with Samuel Huntington's "clash of civilizations" theory.

Chua, Amy. *World on Fire: How Exporting Free Market Democracy Breeds Ethnic Hatred and Global Instability.* 2003. A pessimistic perspective on globalization and world trade.

Devine, Carol, and Carol Rae Hansen. *Human Rights: The Essential Reference.* 1999. A standard work on the subject.

Friedman, Thomas L. *The Lexus and the Olive Tree.* 1999. A readable and influential analysis of alternative pathways to the future.

Hoffman, Bruce. *Inside Terrorism,* 2d ed. 2006. A well-regarded work on a complex topic.

Huntington, Samuel P. *The Clash of Civilizations and the Remaking of the World Order.* 1996. A controversial thesis that Islam and the West are destined for irresolvable conflict.

Kaplan, Robert. *Of Paradise and Power: America and Europe in the New World Order.* 2002. Examines the growing gulf between the United States and Europe.

Kupchan, Charles A. *The End of the American Era: U.S. Foreign Policy and the Geopolitics of the Twenty-first Century.* 2002. A realist perspective on the world balance of power.

Mamdani, Mahmood. *Good Muslim, Bad Muslim: America, the Cold War, and the Roots of Terror.* 2004. Explores the origins of Muslim militancy in opposition to the West.

Moore, Mike. *A World Without Walls: Freedom, Development, Free Trade and Global Governance.* 2003. A view of the global economy from a former director-general of the World Trade Organization.

Norris, Pippa. *Rising Tide: Gender Equality and Cultural Change Around the World.* 2003. Surveys the condition of women.

Pennycock, Alistaire. *The Cultural Politics of English as an International Language.* 1994. The rise of English as a global means of communication.

Priest, Dana. *Mission: Waging War and Keeping Peace with America's Military.* 2003. A critique of American military policies in the twenty-first century.

CourseMate   **Go to the History CourseMate website for primary source links, study tools, and review materials for this chapter.**
www.cengagebrain.com

Index